OPERATIONS MANAGEMENT

COMPETING IN A CHANGING ENVIRONMENT

OPERATIONS MANAGEMENT

COMPETING IN A CHANGING ENVIRONMENT

BYRON J. FINCH

MIAMI UNIVERSITY

RICHARD L. LUEBBE

MIAMI UNIVERSITY

THE DRYDEN PRESS
HARCOURT BRACE COLLEGE PUBLISHERS

FORT WORTH   PHILADELPHIA   SAN DIEGO   NEW YORK   ORLANDO   AUSTIN   SAN ANTONIO
TORONTO   MONTREAL   LONDON   SYDNEY   TOKYO

Acquisitions Editor	SCOTT ISENBERG
Developmental Editor	VAN STRENGTH
Project Editor	EMILY THOMPSON
Art Director	MELINDA WELCH
Production Manager	MANDY MANZANO
Permissions Editor	SHIRLEY WEBSTER; DORIS MILLIGAN
Product Manager	SCOTT TIMIAN
Marketing Assistant	KATHLEEN SHARP
Photo Editor	NANCY MOUDRY
Copy Editor	JANET WILLEN
Indexer	SYLVIA COATES
Compositor	GTS GRAPHICS
Text Type	10/12 TIMES ROMAN

ADDRESS FOR ORDERS
THE DRYDEN PRESS
6277 SEA HARBOR DRIVE
ORLANDO, FL 32887-6777
1-800-782-4479 OR 1-800-433-0001 (IN FLORIDA)

ADDRESS FOR EDITORIAL CORRESPONDENCE
THE DRYDEN PRESS
301 COMMERCE STREET, SUITE 3700
FORT WORTH, TX 76102

ISBN: 0-03-096876-3

LIBRARY OF CONGRESS CATALOG CARD NUMBER: 94-72111

PRINTED IN THE UNITED STATES OF AMERICA

4 5 6 7 8 9 0 1 2 3   0 4 8   9 8 7 6 5 4 3 2 1

THE DRYDEN PRESS
HARCOURT BRACE COLLEGE PUBLISHERS

With love to our wives, Kim and Karen,
and to our children, Matthew and Meredith,
and Jenny, Beth, and Jim

THE DRYDEN PRESS
SERIES IN MANAGEMENT

Holley and Jennings
THE LABOR RELATIONS PROCESS
Fifth Edition

Jauch and Coltrin
THE MANAGERIAL EXPERIENCE:
CASES AND EXERCISES
Sixth Edition

Kemper
EXPERIENCING STRATEGIC
MANAGEMENT

Kindler and Ginsburg
TRANSFORMATIONAL CHANGE IN
ORGANIZATIONS

Kirkpatrick and Lewis
EFFECTIVE SUPERVISION: PREPARING FOR
THE 21ST CENTURY

Kuehl and Lambing
SMALL BUSINESS:
PLANNING AND MANAGEMENT
Third Edition

Kuratko and Hodgetts
ENTREPRENEURSHIP:
A CONTEMPORARY APPROACH
Third Edition

Kuratko and Welsch
ENTREPRENEURIAL STRATEGY:
TEXT AND CASES

Lee
INTRODUCTION TO MANAGEMENT
SCIENCE
Second Edition

Lengnick-Hall, Cynthia, and Hartman
EXPERIENCING QUALITY

Lewis
IO ENTERPRISES SIMULATION

Long and Arnold
THE POWER OF ENVIRONMENTAL
PARTNERSHIPS

McMullen and Long
DEVELOPING NEW VENTURES:
THE ENTREPRENEURIAL OPTION

Matsuura
INTERNATIONAL BUSINESS: A NEW ERA

Montanari, Morgan, and Bracker
STRATEGIC MANAGEMENT:
A CHOICE APPROACH

Morgan
MANAGING FOR SUCCESS

Northcraft and Neale
ORGANIZATIONAL BEHAVIOR:
A MANAGEMENT CHALLENGE
Second Edition

Penderghast
ENTREPRENEURIAL SIMULATION
PROGRAM

Sandburg
CAREER DESIGN SOFTWARE

Shipley and Ruthstrom
CASES IN OPERATIONS MANAGEMENT

Sower, Motwani, and Savoie
CLASSIC READINGS IN OPERATIONS
MANAGEMENT

Van Matre
FOUNDATIONS OF TQM: A READINGS
BOOK

Vecchio
ORGANIZATIONAL BEHAVIOR
Third Edition

Walton
CORPORATE ENCOUNTERS: LAW, ETHICS,
AND THE BUSINESS ENVIRONMENT

Zikmund
BUSINESS RESEARCH METHODS
Fourth Edition

**THE HARCOURT BRACE COLLEGE
OUTLINE SERIES**

Pentico
MANAGEMENT SCIENCE

Pierson
INTRODUCTION TO BUSINESS
INFORMATION SYSTEMS

Sigband
BUSINESS COMMUNICATION

PREFACE

A NEW PERSPECTIVE FOR A NEW ENVIRONMENT

In the short span of a decade, U.S. businesses have seen and been affected by tremendous change. After a decade of losing business to foreign competitors, many U.S. industries now are regaining market share and their former patterns of growth. The productivity of manufacturers and service industries has increased, but frequently at the expense of tens of thousands of experienced midlevel managers who have lost their jobs.

Many jobs have been eliminated as companies have become leaner and meaner. Combined with an overriding emphasis on product and service quality and a globalization of business in general, the movement toward leaner businesses has resulted in a new perspective from which they must be managed. Leanness means that companies must do more with less. Less inventory, a smaller work force, lower costs, fewer managers, and fewer mistakes must be combined to yield highly productive, highly responsive, and, as a result, highly competitive companies. Many manufacturers and service industries have begun an extensive effort to identify goods and services that customers value, to enhance these goods and services, and to eliminate the rest.

Change is occurring at a rapid rate. It is being driven, to a great extent, by dynamic trends in technologies, approaches, and philosophies, many of which originate from the operations function and are designed to enhance the firms' abilities to meet new business needs.

A NEW PERSPECTIVE ON OPERATIONS

Since the phrase "business as usual" has become synonymous with the phrase "a direct route to bankruptcy," business educators have recognized the need to respond to changing conditions. Just as business schools have embraced a different perspective, so must the field of operations management.

Operations Management: Competing in a Changing Environment is designed to provide the foundation for a course devoted to operations management, a traditional part of the business curricula. Students enrolled in introductory operations courses are about to journey down a great variety of career paths; they may be majoring in accounting, marketing, finance, decision sciences, economics, human resource management, organizational behavior, or even operations management. However, because most of the students taking such a course will ultimately assume managerial positions, but not necessarily in the operations function, this book is intended for managers in all fields. It is designed to do what operations managers are trying to do in their firms: continuously improve the level of customer satisfaction by increasing flexibility and eliminating waste and costs that do not contribute to the value of the final product.

In today's business environment, it is crucial for everyone in business education to obtain and retain a fundamental understanding of all aspects of the business. Businesses cannot afford managers who operate in an informational vacuum or from a narrow perspective. Managers must make decisions that are the best for the entire firm, not merely best for a single department. Managers, whether financial, marketing, operations, purchasing, human resources, information system, or accounting, will be held responsible not only for their actions but also for the effects of those actions. The ability to predict all of these effects stems from a knowledge of the connections among the various business functions.

Managers must not only be experts in their own specialties, but possess a global understanding of their businesses, and, in particular, how they operate. The motivation to develop a thorough, holistic understanding of operations management and its role can only be attained once students recognize its importance, whatever their majors, as they envision themselves in their future careers.

In order to facilitate a holistic understanding of operations, *Operations Management: Competing in a Changing Environment* is structured around themes of competitiveness and cross-functional integration. We organized the book in this way not only because of the role operations plays in a firm's ability to compete, but because competitiveness is the common basis of all business enterprises. To provide a book that will assist students in obtaining a competitive edge, we have paid close attention to the appropriate coverage of the topics presented in each chapter and the sequences in which they are presented.

THE TEXT

The text of *Operations Management: Competing in a Changing Environment* consists of four parts. Part I, Foundations of Operations Management, lays the groundwork by describing the operations function, the service and manufacturing environments in which it exists, and its importance to strategic objectives. Part II, New Directions in Operations Management, provides an overview of three emerging forces in modern operations: total quality management (TQM), just-in-time (JIT), and constraint management. The discussion of these three topics prior to the remaining topics allows for the complete integration of these new approaches with the more traditional subjects that follow. Part III, Planning for Operations, consists of five chapters related to the specific planning responsibilities of operations: demand forecasting, aggregate planning, planning facility locations, planning facility layouts, and project planning. These chapters provide integrated coverage of the planning systems and techniques applicable to service and manufacturing environments. Part IV, Managing the Physical System, includes chapters on short- and medium-term resource decisions, including those needed for managing inventory, managing capacity, and work-center scheduling. Improving the use of resources through productivity management is addressed in the final chapter of the part.

FACILITATING FEATURES

Providing students a new business management perspective requires new methods of communicating information. A number of new pedagogical devices are incorporated into the book to better prepare students for business environments that have lowered or even eliminated barriers between departments.

In Chapter 5, the first chapter in Part II, you are introduced to the first of thirteen Cross-Links video cases. Cross-Links present problems as they exist in businesses. Problems do not respect departmental boundaries and organizational charts but, rather, wreak havoc in the organization's distant corners. Cross-Links outlines problems that may be rooted in operations management but that affect accountants, human resource managers, marketing managers, and many other unsuspecting employees and departments within an organization.

For the chapters beginning with Cross-Links video cases, the end-of-chapter discussions begin with a "Cross-Links Revisit," which goes back to the "scene of the crime" and presents an opportunity to apply the concepts of the chapter to the problem encountered via class or small-group discussions or through short case analyses. The accompanying video series may be used with the Cross-Links cases, or they can be used alone strictly by implementing the information found within the text itself.

In order to demonstrate the wide variety of operations management practices employed from company to company and to point out business trends related to these issues, two types of examples are used throughout the book. The first, titled Cutting-Edge Companies, describes the practices of companies on the forefront of management practices and decision making. The second, titled Operations Outlook, examines industry trends or changes that have implications for, or are the result of, operations management practices. The companies and industries used in both types of examples represent a broad cross-section of service and manufacturing firms and are drawn from an equally diverse set of publications.

As new terms are introduced within each chapter, a running glossary in the page margins emphasizes new concepts by providing precise definitions to be used as a study guide. The format of the book's end-of-chapter questions is also novel to better reflect the cutting-edge perspectives of the text. In addition to Questions for Review and Questions for Thought and Discussion, a third group of questions has been included to encourage thought and discussion on a more holistic level. This set of questions, titled Integrative Questions, links the chapter's issues and concepts to those of previous chapters in order to facilitate the student's ability to make the important cognitive connections. Each chapter concludes with a Suggested Readings section designed to provide the student who wishes to learn more about a particular topic with current publication sources.

SUPPORT MATERIALS

Just as operations departments cannot efficiently produce products and services without the support of other business units, a textbook cannot deliver its product efficiently without the help of support materials. The support materials developed to enhance the study of operations include the previously mentioned *Introductory and Cross-Links Videos.* Also included is the student study guide designed to provide students with a structured approach to studying and reviewing the text. The study guide is complemented by a software package that offers self-testing in a Windows-driven format. The instructor's/solutions manual provides chapter outlines, pedagogical suggestions, and suggestions for additional examples to supplement Cutting-Edge Companies and Operations Outlook. The instructor's manual also provides the solutions to the end-of-chapter questions and problems. The book's test bank is available in bound form as well as in a computerized format to assist the instructor in the development of meaningful and challenging examinations. Additionally, a set of transparency masters is included. Color transparencies for all figures in the book are available to enhance the in-class presentation of material.

ACKNOWLEDGMENTS

As is the case with any large project, the first edition of a textbook is the combined result of the work of many people. We would like to express our special thanks to our families for their eager support, enthusiasm, and help. We are also indebted to our supportive colleagues of the Richard T. Farmer School of Business Administration of Miami University and specifically to those in the Management Department.

Many reviewers have made significant suggestions and contributions to this text through their insightful critiques of early drafts. We thank the following individuals for their contributions: John Adamitis, Saint Bonaventure University; Joseph Biggs, California Polytechnic State University; Ray Boykin, California State University at Chico; Cecil Bozarth, North Carolina State University; Karlene Crawford, Georgia State University; Susan Engelmeyer, Babson College; Barbara Flynn, Iowa State University; Lawrence Fredendall, Clemson University; Jim Gilbert, University of Georgia; Robert Handfield, Michigan State University; Mark Hanna, Miami University; Ray M. Haynes, California Polytechnic State University; G. G. Hedge, University of Pittsburgh; Farzod Mahmoodi, Clarkson University; Ann Marucheck, University of North Carolina; Jerry Murphy, Portland State University; William Newman, Miami University; Ernest Nichols, Memphis State University; Joseph Ormsby, Stephen F. Austin State University; Gerhard Plenert, Brigham Young University; Stephen Repolge, University of Arkansas; Edward Rosenthal, Temple University; Chwen Sheu, Kansas State University; Victor Sower, Sam Houston State University; Caron St. John, Clemson University; Chang Wang, California State University—Sacramento; Charles Watts, Bowling Green State University; and Craig Wood, University of New Hampshire.

The following individuals attended a focus group discussing this book and its ancillary package. Their comments gave our editors numerous insights into classroom presentation techniques, thereby creating a professor- and student-responsive package: Timothy Bergquist, University of Oregon; Veejay Cannon, James Madison University; Kathy Fitzpatrick, Appalachian State University; Robert Handfield, Michigan State University; and Tracy Rischel, Susquehanna University.

Finally, we would like to thank the editorial staff at The Dryden Press. We thank our acquisitions editor, Scott Isenberg, for convincing us to do this project and obtaining the best support for the project. We are especially grateful to Van Strength, developmental editor, and Emily Thompson, project editor, for their efforts. Without them, this book would still be a stack of manuscript and disks. We express our sincere thanks to other members of the book team, including Mandy Manzano, our production manager, who kept this project on schedule; Melinda Welch, Shirley Webster, Sarah Jones, and the photo research team, Doris Milligan and Nancy Moudry; Nancy's work added a new dimension to the material. Also, we would like to thank Clyde Brant of Miami University for his work in checking text and test bank problems. The ancillary authors, especially Alice Fugate, Sean Lanham, and Walter Wheatley made invaluable contributions to the test bank and study guide.

A SPECIAL NOTE TO THE INSTRUCTOR

As authors of *Operations Management: Competing in a Changing Environment,* we hope we have created a product that meets your needs. Having created this product not just for ourselves, but for others, we are committed to an ongoing evolution of improvement. Not only are we open to your comments or suggestions, we strongly encourage them. We encourage you to contact us by phone or by e-mail to answer questions that you or your students may have or to assist you in any way we can.

A SPECIAL NOTE TO THE STUDENT

As firms continue to adapt to changes in operations management approaches, they also continue to use many traditional, time-tested methods. In our coverage of operations management, we have discussed the new approaches and those that are old. You will notice that there are often contradictions inherent in the traditional and the new methods as well as inherent strengths and weaknesses of each. As a result, managers throughout the United States and the world are currently facing the dilemmas you will face on a daily basis. One cannot make informed choices, however, without a thorough understanding of the alternatives.

Whether you choose to embark upon a career in systems management, human resource management, marketing, accounting, finance, economics, or whether you assume all functions of a small, family business, this book is designed to provide you with the operations management knowledge you need to move upward in a company and move the company forward in the marketplace. If you find the topic of operations management of special interest and you pursue advanced courses in operations management, this book will provide a firm foundation for those advanced courses.

Your predictions about your career ultimately may be quite accurate, or you may find that your future in business is quite different from that which you foresee. Time will tell. Whatever adventures your career holds for you, we wish you success.

BYRON J. FINCH
Department of Management
Richard T. Farmer School of
    Business Administration
Miami University
Oxford, Ohio 45056
Phone: 513/529-4215
FAX: 513/529-6992
Internet: BFINCH
    @ sba-laws.sba.muohio.edu

RICHARD L. LUEBBE
Department of Management
Richard T. Farmer School of
    Business Administration
Miami University
Oxford, Ohio 45056
Phone: 513/529-4215
FAX: 513/529-6992
Internet: RLUEBBE
    @ sba-laws.sba.muohio.edu

BRIEF CONTENTS

CONTENTS

ABOUT THE AUTHORS

BYRON J. FINCH, PH.D., CPIM Dr. Finch received his
B.S. and M.S. degrees from Iowa State University. After
three years in facility management at The University of
Georgia, he entered the graduate program at the William
Terry College of Business Administration at the University
of Georgia and received his Ph.D. in Production/Operations
Management in 1986. Following a year as an Assistant Professor at Auburn University, he began his work at Miami
University in Oxford, Ohio, where he is currently an Associate Professor. From 1986 to 1988, Dr. Finch's research was
focused primarily on production planning and control systems for process-oriented manufacturers. His case study of
several systems was published by APICS under the title
*Planning and Control System Design: Principles and Cases
for Process Manufacturers.* He has served on the executive
committee of the Process Industry Specific Industry Group
(SIG) of APICS, where he headed the SIG's research effort
and has consulted in the food processing and paper industries.

In addition to process-oriented production planning and
control, Dr. Finch's current research interests include quality
improvement and spreadsheet applications in production/op-
erations management. He has been involved in the development of several spreadsheet applications, specifically in the
areas of learning curve application, quality control, and using spreadsheets in simulations. These have been published
in such journals as *LOTUS, International Journal of Quality*

and Reliability Management, and *Production and Inventory Management Journal,* as well as a textbook titled *Spreadsheet Applications for Production and Operations Management,* published by Richard D. Irwin, Inc. He has published on other topics in the *International Journal of Production Research, The Academy of Management Journal,* and the *Journal of Operations Management.*

Dr. Finch's teaching innovations have been published in the *Journal of Management Education* and the *Journal of Education for Business.* He received the 1987 Southern Business Administration Innovative Teaching Award and the 1990 NCR Computer Innovation Award for his efforts in integrating the use of personal computers into the Operations Management curriculum at Miami University.

 **RICHARD L. LUEBBE, PH.D.** Richard L. Luebbe is professor of Management at Miami University in Oxford, Ohio, where he has taught operations management courses since 1984. He has also taught in the Mathematics departments at Concordia College (Nebraska) and Triton College (Illinois). He holds a masters degree in Mathematics from the University of Texas at Austin, and Ph.D. in Management from the University of Nebraska at Lincoln. Professor Luebbe has taught courses as part of Miami University's honors and international programs, including two summers in Austria.

Dr. Luebbe's research interests have included topics such as integer programming, continuous improvement, and the use of spreadsheets in solving operations problems. His publications have appeared in a number of different journals including *Decision Sciences, Computers and Operations, Research, Computers and Industrial Engineering, International Journal of Production Research, Production and Inventory Management Journal,* and the *International Journal of Quality and Reliability Management.* In addition, he also has coauthored a textbook titled *Spreadsheet Applications for Production and Operations Management.*

Dr. Luebbe has been active in several professional organizations. He served as Secretary and President of the Midwest Decision Sciences Institute and has served on numerous other professional committees.

OPERATIONS MANAGEMENT

COMPETING IN A CHANGING ENVIRONMENT

PART I

FOUNDATIONS OF
OPERATIONS MANAGEMENT

"**W**hat's the matter with you!" screams the marketing manager of a sporting goods manufacturer at the production manager. "Don't you ever meet your completion dates? You told me those hightops would be ready by July 15, and it's already the first week in August! We're losing our back-to-school customers!" ■ "Do we really need additional scanners?" asks the comptroller of a large insurance company at a capital budget meeting. "How come? The ones we have aren't fully utilized!" ■ "Why do we do this every year?" mutters a human resources specialist in an accounting firm. "Every December, we go into this hiring frenzy, and I have to scramble like mad to train new employees for the tax season. Isn't there a better way?" ■ We hear so much about so many aspects of operating a business that it's often difficult to separate the symptoms of problems from their causes. Although businesses exist to sell products or services for a profit, a deluge of information often causes managers to lose sight of their real purpose. Moreover, the high expectations of today's customers and the intense competition for their patronage mean that a product or service must be exactly *what* customers want *when* they want it. The operations function is responsible for the success of a business as a whole, making sure that all the other business functions work together to evaluate information and solve problems to meet customer demands. ■ During the 1980s and early1990s, most successful businesses recognized the important role that operations plays in capturing and retaining the market share necessary to ensure growth. They also recognized that nothing done in other functions could compensate for poor performance in operations. Great advertising can't make up for a lousy product, and state-of-the-art financial management doesn't offset the effects of poor customer service. Firms that haven't acknowledged this truth—and operations' potential for effecting a successful integration of all business functions—risk going out of business. ■ In Part I we explore the fundamental material necessary for understanding operations, its span of control, its environment, and how it fits into strategic planning. Operations management resources and decisions are examined in light of their linkage with marketing, accounting and finance, human resources, and information systems. ■

LEARNING OBJECTIVES

Upon completing this chapter, you should be able to explain

- what the responsibilities of the operations function are
- how the operations function contributes to competitive advantage
- what role value plays in achieving the goals of a business
- what categories of resources are managed by operations
- which differentiating capabilities originate in operations
- how value, resources, and capabilities collectively relate to operations
- what organizing, planning, controlling, and improving mean with respect to operations
- how operations management is defined from the perspective of resources, management tasks, and differentiating capabilities
- how the operations function is linked to the other business functions
- why cross-functional integration is important and how it relates to competitive advantage

CHAPTER 1

INTRODUCTION TO OPERATIONS MANAGEMENT

CROSS-LINKS **Out of the Doldrums**

As we approach the year 2000, it has become clear that U.S. businesses can no longer expect to sell just any product or service they produce. They must offer something customers want and something their competitors don't have. The U.S. auto industry learned this painful lesson during the 1980s, as did the U.S. consumer electronics industry. It can be difficult to determine what will persuade customers to buy a product or service, but a look at how some businesses did so can provide some enlightening insights. ■ After the U.S. auto industry lost market share in the '80s it became determined to regain it, and it has begun an unprecedented comeback. The industry has recaptured the U.S. customer's interest by offering high-quality products at a good price. Suppliers to the Big Three automakers—General Motors, Ford, and Chrysler—have also had to endure tough economic times, but they, too, are seeing an increase in demand. Some suppliers, unfortunately, have fallen by the wayside because they could not offer their customers what they needed to compete against the Japanese auto manufacturers. The Big Three needed high-quality components at a good price as well as dependable delivery of the components, quick response time, and suppliers who could rapidly adapt to a changing environment. ■ Competition in all service and manufacturing industries is so tough, both from U.S. and foreign competitors, that mere survival depends on being able to offer customers what they need. Being truly successful requires being able to offer customers what they need before they even know they need it. And U.S. businesses that are flourishing are doing so not only by producing what customers want but also by delivering each product or service when, where, and how customers want it. ■ Recently, the Big Three automakers have begun to act on an understanding that customer satisfaction is determined as much by the quality of the service offered as by the quality of the product manufactured. Responding to numerous surveys indicating that, for most people, buying a car is an agonizing experience, these U.S. firms have begun to insist that their dealerships change their approaches toward customers. The traditional hard-sell, high-pressure tactics of floor sales people are giving way to innovative sales strategies designed to make the process of buying a car as satisfying as owning it. General Motors, Ford, and Chrysler have all taken steps—in the form of sales incentives, training programs, and staffing guidelines—to ensure that customers find their purchasing experience a pleasant one. This is not simply a matter of professionalism: The Big Three are banking on the belief that implementing such measures will increase sales, deepen customer loyalty, and result in greater long-term customer satisfaction. ■ These companies have also realized that the important product characteristics—those characteristics that customers demand—must be designed *and* built into a product or service, and that they must be exactly the way the customer wants them, time after time after time. They cannot simply be planned at the design stage. They cannot simply by created by hiring good people. And they cannot simply be added by a service representative after the fact. The creation of a genuinely desirable product, therefore, is the result of the combined efforts of the entire organization, working as a team. And at the heart of this team is operations. ■

Source Paul Grey, "Nice Guys Finish First?" *Time Magazine,* July 25, 1994, 48.

WHAT IS OPERATIONS MANAGEMENT?

OPERATIONS FUNCTION
The business function that manages the resources required to produce a product or service. These resources include people, facilities, inventories, processes, and systems.

Like engineering, accounting, marketing, human resource management, and purchasing, operations is a business function. In a business, the **operations function** is charged with the management of the resources required to produce a product or service, including people, facilities, inventory, processes, and systems.

To understand the operations function, it is useful to examine what it contributes to the accomplishment of a business's goals. But first, those goals must be defined. For many businesses, the stockholders have defined the goal. It seems quite straightforward: to maximize shareholders' wealth. This objective is not specific enough to guide a manager's actions, however, so there must be more to it than that. The goals of privately held businesses, not-for-profit organizations, and public corporations, may differ, but the dictionary of the American Production and Inventory Control Society (APICS) provides a statement of the goals of an organization that can be applied to all of them:

> *The goals of an organization are to make short- and long-term profits and to increase market share. The goals of nonprofit and government organizations are similar—to provide maximum customer service without exceeding budgets and to increase market share.*[1]

Thus, the primary goal of a business is not to employ people, sell a product, provide a service, minimize costs, lead the industry in research and development (R&D), or have a positive public image. These may, however, be the objectives of a functional area within a business or the means by which it can better meet its goals. They may also be necessary conditions to meeting the goals of short- and long-term profit and market share.

The sale of a product or service creates the revenue that (owners and employees hope) exceeds total costs, and results in a profit. Because the revenue generated by that sale is the lifeblood of a business, the production of the product or service can be described as the heart of any business. Without the production of the product or service, the business dies—no revenues, no money to manage or invest, no accounts and records to keep, no products or services to advertise and sell, no need for management information systems, no need for laborers, no need for managers.

In defining the goals of a business, it is necessary to establish the role of its customers in the success of the firm. Revenue, unquestionably necessary for the firm's survival and success in the short and long term, is dependent on customers' willingness to buy the product or service. As will be examined in detail often in this text, customers are interested in a company's product or service and will compare the characteristics of what is offered to the desired characteristics. Many customers will go beyond this simple comparison, however. Some will examine not only the product or service but also the company before patronizing it. Customers may demand that a company demonstrate good citizenship, responsible environmental actions, community support, and other qualities before they purchase its product or service. As they become more conscious of the environmental and sociological impacts of business practices, some customers may regard companies' social actions as of equal importance to their product and service characteristics.

These characteristics of business citizenship may or may not be goals of a firm's owners, but the desire to maintain a revenue stream through satisfied customers makes them priorities, even for companies that lack internal motivation for such good citizenship.

---

[1]J.F. Cox, J. H. Blackstone, and M. S. Spencer, eds., *APICS Dictionary* 7th ed. (Falls Church, Va.: American Production and Inventory Control Society, 1992).

THE IMPORTANCE OF OPERATIONS: ADDING VALUE

Production of a good or service is often thought of as a conversion process. Inputs are converted into outputs, which are then sold. This conversion process is controlled by the operations function. The **purchasing (or procurement) function** supplies the conversion process with the necessary material inputs. The **logistics function** is responsible for transporting the outputs of the conversion process to the customer. The outputs might be manufactured goods, such as clothing, cars, appliances, computers, compact discs, or furniture, or they might be services, such as meals, broadcast music, advertising, banking, legal assistance, house cleaning, consulting, transportation, health care, or education. Both for-profit and not-for-profit firms must create *value* to be of interest to potential customers. Value must be added during the conversion process, just as it is added by other activities, such as by purchasing when quality of inputs is increased, by logistics when transporting the finished good, or by marketing by educating the public about its attributes. Whatever the outputs are, they establish the most important contact the business has with its customers. More than anything else, a customer's perceived value of the outputs will determine whether or not that customer returns to the business. The degree to which customers return establishes the company's future.

The amount of value manifested in the product or service is determined, quite simply, by what the customer is willing to pay. From this perspective, the primary task of the operations function is the management of the resources in order to bring about the value-adding conversion of inputs to outputs. Figure 1.1 provides a traditional view of the value-adding conversion process, its inputs, and its outputs.

As Figure 1.1 shows, profit is contingent on several events. The revenue-generating sale can only be expected to occur if value (from the buyer's point of view) is added during the conversion process. The revenue-generating sale will result in profit only if the value added is greater than the costs incurred.

PURCHASING FUNCTION
The business function that supplies the conversion process with necessary material inputs.

LOGISTICS FUNCTION
The business function responsible for bringing inputs to the location of the product or service delivery (*inbound logistics*) and transporting outputs to the customer (*outbound logistics*).

OPERATIONS, VALUE, AND COMPETITIVENESS

Michael Porter identifies the strategically relevant activities of a firm as its *value chain.*[2] The value chain includes all activities performed to design, produce, market, deliver, and support the company's product or service. There are three components to Porter's value chain: primary value adding activities, support activities, and margin. Porter identifies the following five categories of primary value-adding activities: inbound logistics, operations, outbound logistics, marketing and sales, and service.

Inbound logistics adds value to the product or service by bringing inputs to the location of the product or service delivery. Operations adds value through the actual conversion process. Outbound logistics adds value by bringing the finished product or service to the customer. Marketing and sales add value by educating the customer about the products or service. After-the-sale service adds value by extending the life and usefulness of the product. Although many products look identical, consumers may value them differently because of their perceptions about the products' quality, dependability, service, and other characteristics. (See Box 1.1.)

[2]Michael E. Porter, *Competitive Advantage* (New York: Free Press, 1985), 38–41.

| FIGURE 1.1 | **Traditional View of Value-Adding Conversion Process** |

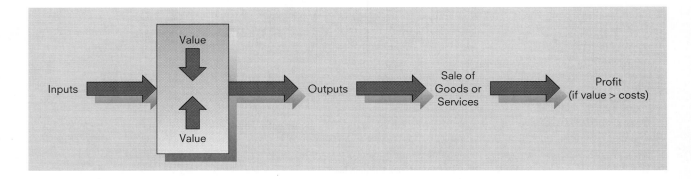

Support activities provide the backing primary activities need to function. Examples include firm infrastructure, human resource management, technology development, and procurement. In addition to primary activities and support activities, the value chain includes *margin.* Margin is the difference between the cost of the primary and support activities and the total value. Margin presents the opportunity for profit.

While adding value during the conversion process is necessary for the generation of short-term profit, it is not sufficient to guarantee that all three goals will be met. In order to ensure that the goals of short-term and long-term profits as well as increased market share are reached, the firm must successfully and continuously compete in the marketplace.

COMPETITIVE ADVANTAGE
Superior value to that of the competition, which results in consumer preference.

To compete in the marketplace in the long term, a firm must have something that customers want and competitors lack. It must do something differently or it must do something better. The business must offer superior value to differentiate itself from the competition in order to maintain a **competitive advantage.** In his discussion of value chains, Porter main-

Southwest Airlines differentiates itself from its competitors on the basis of high-quality customer service combined with low operating costs and simple, low fares. Because these capabilities demand high employee productivity, Southwest regards its employees as its most valuable resource. Here, Southwest Airlines salutes its ground operations coordinators as Heroes of the Heart for going beyond the call of duty to ensure the best customer service.

Source   The Dallas Morning News/David Woo.

OPERATIONS OUTLOOK

BOX 1.1

Computers May Look Alike—But Customers Don't Think They're Alike

An objective observer might conclude that all personal computers are essentially the same, particularly those that are IBM-compatible and run on the same microprocessor. The results of a recent study show otherwise. McKinsey & Company and Intelliquest Inc. asked 300 computer buyers how much more they would be willing to pay for a number of different computers than they would pay for an average brand. The results showed that the brand name of a computer was second only to overall performance as the most important purchasing criterion. Among the nondiscount computer brands that were based on Intel microprocessing technology (IBM-compatible), IBM came out on top. Consumers were willing to pay $295 more for the IBM computer than for the average computer. Hewlett-Packard was lowest with a $76 dollar advantage over the average computer. Among those perceived to be "discount" brands, ZEOS was valued highest at $15 below the average, while Packard Bell was valued lowest at $69 below average.

Source "Computers: They're No Commodity," *The Wall Street Journal,* October 15, 1993, sec. B, 1.

---

tains that **value activities** form the building blocks of competitive advantage.[3] Every value activity utilizes resources (purchased inputs, human resources, equipment, technology, and the like) to accomplish its purpose of adding value. The manner in which resources are used to execute a value activity, combined with the costs of the resources and supporting activities, establishes a firm's costs relative to its competitors' costs. The way each value activity is accomplished may either persuade customers to find or dissuade customers from finding sufficient value in the product or service to buy it. Value activities provide the means by which a company can differentiate itself from its competitors.

The importance of resources in establishing competitiveness is reinforced by the resource theory of firm competitiveness. Robert M. Grant describes the linkage between the use of resources and a firm's competitiveness in an overview of this theory.[4] The resource theory of the firm recognizes two separate entities within a firm: resources and capabilities. **Resources** are direct inputs to the production process and include such things as equipment, inventory, facilities, skills of employees, patents, and copyrights. Grant describes a **capability** as the ability of a team of resources to perform some task or activity. He describes how resources and capabilities relate to one another in this way: "While resources are the source of a firm's capabilities, capabilities are the main source of its competitive advantage" (pp. 118–119). Customers and potential customers differentiate one firm from another by their capabilities. Capabilities, brought about by grouping resources together, enable a firm to perform specific value activities that differentiate it from its competition. Procter & Gamble, for instance, maintains state-of-the-art research and development facilities; but these facilities would be of little benefit without the R&D staff, market research, process engineering, and production capabilities. By combining these resources, Procter & Gamble is often able to provide "new and improved" products that meet market needs at low prices before its competitors can. The capabilities that result in differentiation and competitive advantage are referred to as **differentiating capabilities.** Some examples of

VALUE ACTIVITIES
The means by which a company can differentiate itself from its competitors.

RESOURCES
Direct inputs to the production process for services and manufacturers.

CAPABILITY
The ability of a group of resources to perform a task or activity.

DIFFERENTIATING CAPABILITY
A capability that results in a firm's differentiation and competitive advantage.

---

[3]Michael E. Porter, *Competitive Advantage* (New York: Free Press, 1985), 48.
[4]Robert M. Grant, "The Resource-Based Theory of Competitive Advantage: Implications for Strategy Formulation," *California Management Review* 33 (Third Quarter, 1991): 114–135.

resources that are grouped together to form differentiating capabilities are presented in Table 1.1.

Some value activities are essential to doing business but do not lead to differentiation and competitive advantage. For example, a manufacturer must be able to purchase raw materials. The purchase of raw materials adds value to the product, but it doesn't differentiate the firm from its competitors unless the firm can purchase the materials at a lower price or higher quality or unless the materials have special characteristics. As another example, an amusement park must hire ride operators, but hiring operators doesn't differentiate the amusement park from its competitors.

Combining the resources of business size and skilled purchasing agents, however, may give the manufacturer the capability to purchase raw materials at a lower cost, which may be a differentiating capability that results in a competitive advantage. Combining the capability to hire ride operators through the resources of good interviewers and a skilled training staff may give the amusement park the capability to provide a better service to visitors, which may differentiate it from its competitors.

In the U.S. domestic market it is not difficult to identify ways to add value. As U.S. markets become more open to outside competitors and as U.S. businesses seek customers from other cultures, however, the concept of adding value becomes more complex. The customer's concept of value is, to a great extent, culturally based. What is seen as valuable in the U.S. is not necessarily seen in the same light in other cultures. Cultural biases are also evident within different regions of the United States. As U.S. businesses globalize, they will encounter a more diverse base of customers, and they will need to define value from many different perspectives and develop competitive capabilities that mesh with various cultural value systems.

THE IMPORTANCE OF CROSS-FUNCTIONAL INTEGRATION

Differentiating capabilities do not come about from just one resource, as we saw in Table 1.1. Rather, they result from combinations or groups. We must recognize additionally that, in many cases, the resources needed to establish a capability are controlled by different business functions. For example, a short product development cycle in the auto industry requires resources from many functional areas, including engineering, manufacturing, and marketing. (See Box 1.2.) To achieve a short pizza delivery time, the combined talents of those involved in pizza preparation, cooking, and delivery must be involved.

Differentiating capabilities do not often spring from a single business function. Because differentiating capabilities usually result from cooperative efforts among several business functions, some businesses find it difficult to develop these capabilities. The more successful firms employ managers who are more aware of the potential that lies in resources outside of their functional area. Managers who are aware of the resources (such as expertise, knowledge, skills, equipment, and personnel) in their own and other business functions have the ability to imagine the capabilities that may result from bringing these resources together. Managers who are limited in perspective to one business function, however, cannot easily contribute to the improvement of their firm's competitive position because they cannot creatively envision new differentiating capabilities.

CROSS-FUNCTIONAL INTEGRATION
The ability to pull together resources from different business functions to create differentiating capabilities.

The need for cooperation and communication among business functions, to provide a means by which differentiating capabilities can be conceived, is crucial to a firm's competitive future. The ability of a firm's functional managers to see through functional boundaries and pull together resources that provide new and different capabilities is known as **cross-functional integration.** In many firms the holistic or big picture view necessary for

TABLE 1.1	Examples of Resources Combined to Bring about Differentiating Capabilities

Resources Combined	Differentiating Capabilities
Concurrent engineering Excellent supplier cooperation Creative engineers Line workers' input High team morale	Development of the Chrysler Neon in only 42 months at a cost less than that of any other subcompact car
High-temperature ovens Special dough recipe Standardized pizza assembly Large number of deliverers One or two deliveries per trip Small delivery area for each store	Fast delivery of Domino's pizza

cross-functional integration is present only at the organizational level above each of the functional managers. This kind of vision limits the development of differentiating capabilities to those that come from the top down. Companies whose managers have a broad perspective and whose reward systems encourage more than a local perspective are able to obtain new differentiating capabilities from the bottom up as well.

Cross-functional integration is one of the most important differentiating capabilities of all because it is often a prerequisite for the development of others. The resources necessary

OPERATIONS OUTLOOK

BOX 1.2

Cross-Functional Management

It may appear impossible, but Chrysler is betting on being able to sell 300,000 units a year to turn a profit on its new Neon. The Chrysler Neon is an example of how cross-functional teams can speed up the product-development process. A core group of 150 engineers, marketers, and purchasing and financial staff, plus 600 additional engineers and more than 4,000 blue-collar workers planned to deliver the car in 42 months, from conception to production. The 42-month turnaround was expected to cut about 40 percent off the total engineering cost of the car and about 20 percent off the total development costs.

Ford Motor Company has also increased the use of work teams, at even lower levels of the organization. Because of the team-based management approach at its Batavia, Ohio, transmission plant, Ford selected it as the site to receive a $530 million overhaul to manufacture the new CD4E automatic transmission. Each department is organized around teams with 6 to 12 hourly employees, and each team member is cross-trained to handle any job in the department. Ford used teams in the equipment design and layout of the facility.

Outside of the auto industry, Thermos recognized a need to develop a new product, increase its level of innovation, and offer value to customers. The company created product-development teams to build and organize around markets, not business functions. The first contained six middle managers from different disciplines. The interdisciplinary nature of the team avoided costly mistakes. The resultant product was a new design for an electric grill that maintains the higher temperatures necessary to barbeque foods and not bake them as most electric grills do.

Source "Chrysler's Neon—Is This the Small Car Detroit Couldn't Build?" *Business Week,* May 3, 1993, 116–126. "Geared-up Team," *The Cincinnati Enquirer,* June 7, 1993, sec. D,1,3. "Payoff from the New Management," *Fortune,* December 13, 1993, 103–110.

for cross-functional integration to exist are quite simple: functional managers who are both experts in their own area and well-versed in all other business functions as well as top-level managers who value and reward this type of behavior. As many owners of successful businesses will attest to, however, these resources are in short supply.

Not only is cross-functional integration necessary for the development of many differentiating capabilities, but it is also necessary for effective day-to-day decision making. Many decisions that are made solely within one business function are not optimal for the firm as a whole. Consider, for example, the decision of how much finished goods inventory a manufacturer should carry. If this decision were to be made by operations alone, the result might be to carry high levels of inventory. Carrying high levels of finished goods inventory would allow operations to produce large batches of products, reducing the need and frequency of changing equipment over from producing one product to another. These changeovers take a great deal of time and effort. Finance would desire low levels of inventory to minimize investment. Marketing would desire high levels of inventory to minimize the chance of running out. Human resources would desire a build-up of finished goods inventory during low-demand periods so that layoffs would not be necessary and employment could be stabilized. Yet none of these positions would necessarily be the best for the firm.

Another issue that prompts different desires from different business functions is that of product variety. How many options should exist? Marketing wants as many products as possible to satisfy the needs of as many customers as possible. Operations and engineering want as few as possible because the greater the variety, the more difficult the process design and the greater the number of changeovers. Finance, because of a desire to minimize inventory investment, would favor low product variety. Purchasing would also favor low product variety to minimize the variety of purchased parts and the number of suppliers.

Different business functions have different objectives when analyzing these decisions because of the measures used to evaluate their performance. Many measures are not global in nature, and, therefore, high performance on a particular measure does not necessarily mean that what is being done is best for the firm as a whole. The need for cross-functional integration is increased by the existence of these measures and the conflicting functional objectives that frequently result.

THE EFFECTIVELY MANAGED CONVERSION PROCESS

When the premise that effective management and grouping of resources can provide differentiating capabilities is accepted, a different view of the conversion process emerges. The results are an awareness of the importance of the interfunctional linkages and a better understanding of the role of the operations function. The effectively managed conversion process must not merely convert resources to saleable outputs by adding value, but it must also engender differentiating capabilities. Figure 1.2 presents an overview of the effectively managed conversion process, which not only adds value but also provides the firm with differentiating capabilities that move it toward its goals of short- and long-term profit and increased market share.

OPERATIONS RESOURCES AND CAPABILITIES

Although there are many specific resources managed by operations, they fall into the four basic categories: *processes, inventory, work force, and facilities and equipment.* These four categories form fundamental inputs to the conversion process, provide numerous opportu-

FIGURE 1.2	The Effectively Managed Conversion Process

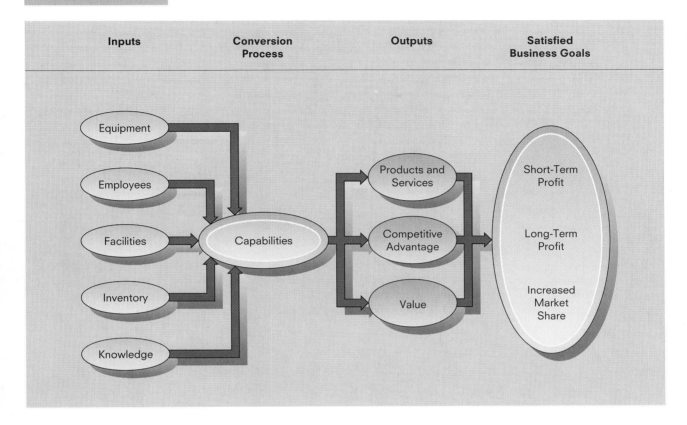

nities for creating differentiating capabilities, and for many firms, can make up more than 70 percent of their assets. They are described more precisely below.

Processes refers to the actions that are taken to convert inputs to outputs. Processes are generally composed of specific procedures, which are approved methods of accomplishing tasks.[5] A process might be as simple as hand carrying material from one work center to another or cooking a hamburger patty. Or it might be extremely complex, like extracting agar (an ingredient in toothpaste and a fat substitute in nonmeat hamburgers) from kelp or computing the federal income tax obligation for a large corporation. Processes might be generic and universal to an industry, or they might be patented and owned by one company.

PROCESSES
Specific procedures comprising actions taken to convert inputs into outputs.

Inventory consists of stocked items used to support the production of the product or service. For a manufacturing firm, inventory consists of raw materials (inputs to the production process), work-in-process (inventory within the production process), and finished goods (outputs that have not yet been sold). Services may also utilize raw materials, work-in-process, and finished goods inventories. A restaurant, for example, would possess all three types of inventories. For other service organizations, work-in-process might take on a different meaning. For a

INVENTORY
Stocked material used to support the production of a good or service.

---

[5]J.F. Cox, J. H. Blackstone, and M. S. Spencer, eds., *APICS Dictionary* 7th ed. (Falls Church, Va.: American Production and Inventory Control Society, 1992), 37.

bank, it might refer to loan applications currently being evaluated. Many services have unusual inventories. A radio station, for example, sells time on the air. Its inventory could be viewed as minutes. A theater sells seats for a given period of time. A common characteristic of work-in-process and finished goods inventories is that both are forms of stored capacity. For many services and manufacturers, a substantial investment is required in maintenance, repair, and operating (MRO) inventories. MRO inventory items consist of goods that are tangential to the conversion processes but are required to support it. An example of an MRO inventory item for a manufacturer would be a repair part for a machine used in production. For a bank, pencils, memo pads, computer diskettes, and various printed forms would be included as MRO inventory.

WORK FORCE
Human resources required to produce a good or service.

Work force consists of the human resources required to produce the good or service. Obviously, all members of the firm's work force do not fall within the management responsibilities of the operations function. Those that do, however, will usually include employees contributing direct labor to the production of the good or service as well as employees responsible for managing the human and nonhuman resources within operations.

FACILITIES AND EQUIPMENT
Machinery and tools (and the buildings in which they are housed) used in various processes to produce a product or service.

Facilities and equipment refers to the machinery and tools used in the various processes as well as the buildings in which they are housed. The capability to produce the desired product or service, by pulling together specific resources from all four categories is frequently referred to as a company's **capacity.**

CAPACITY
The capability to produce a desired good or service by combining the four basic resources of the firm: processes, inventory, work force, and facilities and equipment.

THE COMPETITIVE PRIORITIES IN OPERATIONS

Before resources can be teamed to allow the company to reap the benefits of differentiating capabilities, the types of capabilities that should originate in the operations function must be identified. Five **competitive priorities** provide specific direction to the operations function for the development of differentiating capabilities that can give the firm competitive advantage. These can be summarized as: *price, quality, dependability, flexibility,* and *time.* Traditionally, many strategists felt that because of trade-offs involved, a firm could not place priority on all five and, therefore, could not compete on the basis of high performance in all five areas. As new management approaches have evolved, particularly those involving continuous improvement techniques, computer integration, and better cross-functional integration in decision making, many firms have striven to compete on the basis of performance in the five areas. In fact, failure to meet customer expectations on only one of the priorities could be sufficient to cause a customer to go elsewhere. Firms must still set priorities, however, because if resources are limited or if there are direct trade-offs, they must have identified which of the five is the most important to them in order to make decisions consistent with competitive objectives.

COMPETITIVE PRIORITIES
Price, quality, dependability, flexibility, and time.

PRICE
The amount a customer pays for a product or service.

Price has a strong influence on competitive advantage because of its direct impact on the value received by the customer. Everything else remaining equal, offering a reduced price to a customer increases the value per unit received by that customer. Cost is sometimes mentioned, instead of price, as a competitive priority. The ability to produce a product at a lower cost is a competitive advantage because it enables a firm to better compete on the basis of price. In this text, price will be used because it has a direct effect on value from the customer's perspective. Despite the emphases on quality in recent years, price is still a formidable competitive weapon that will be used to increase customers' perceptions of value. (See Box 1.3.)

Quality is the degree to which a good or service conforms to requirements, as defined by the consumer. Quality is a differentiating capability because increased levels of quality result in increased value, as perceived by the customer. Given two products priced equally, the one with higher quality will yield more value to the customer.

Dependability refers to how reliably the product or service functions and how reliably the firm delivers what it promises and when it promises it. Does the product or service accomplish what is promised? If it doesn't, the customer will likely not return to the firm. If the firm agrees to deliver a service by a certain date, does it fulfill that promise?

Flexibility refers to the adaptability of the product or service and the adaptability of the company to respond to needed volume changes. Changes may take place in the market, in the external environment, or in customer expectations. Can the company react to unexpected events, or even calamities, and still come through with what it promised? Is the company able and willing to adapt the order to fit the specific needs of a customer? Can the company gear up for an unusually short delivery time required because of a customer's emergency situation? Does it have the ability to "go the extra mile" to personalize a service?

Time has taken on a new level of importance in the business world. Not only do customers want reliable deliveries, but they also prefer short response times. For customers of services, response time often defines one aspect of quality. Waiting for a service is so common that the amount of time one must wait is often almost synonymous with service quality.

QUALITY
The degree to which a product or service conforms to requirements, as defined by the consumer.

DEPENDABILITY
The reliability of a product or service in terms of function and the reliability of the producer in meeting promises.

FLEXIBILITY
The ability of a business to adapt to change.

TIME
The speed at which a business can respond to customers.

OPERATIONS OUTLOOK

BOX 1.3

Everyday Low Prices

Not only has the U.S. buying public come to demand value, but it has also begun to resist paying full price . . . for anything. Consumers often do not compliantly accept price increases, so producers are forced to cut costs. Cost-cutting results in slow salary growth, which further reinforces the resistance to accept price increases. General economic uncertainty has also contributed to this trend.

In response, virtually everyone is getting into the discount business. In 1985 there were only 96 "no-frills" discount, warehouse clubs such as Price Club. By 1995, there are expected to be more than 1,000. Demand for private-label food and generic health-care products is also cutting into sales of name-brand products that cost 15 to 30 percent more.

In addition to the expectation of lower price and higher value, consumers are expecting products to last longer and are forcing manufacturers to comply. The average age of a car before trade-in, for example, has increased to over seven years.

Source J. Cox, "Frugal Public Forces Firms to Hold Line," *USA Today,* November 22, 1993, sec. B, 1–2. J. Cox, "Savvy Buying More Than a Passing Fad," *USA Today,* November 23, 1993, sec. B, 1–2.

At Giddings & Lewis, a Michigan-based manufacturer of automation and machine tools, customer-focused employees give the firm its competitive edge. When the loss of a key part caused his entire line to shut down at 3:00 PM one Friday, a New York customer called Giddings & Lewis project manager Bill Denny to explain the emergency. Two hours later, the part was ready. Then, because the commercial overnight delivery time had already passed, Chris Domzalski-Roy, a company engineer and weekend pilot, volunteered to fly the part to New York. She and Bill delivered the new part at 7:00 PM—just four hours after the call for help.

Source   Courtesy of Giddings & Lewis, Inc.

MANAGEMENT TASKS IN OPERATIONS

ORGANIZING
Designing and implementing systems to provide structure and consistency.

DECISION SUPPORT SYSTEMS
Systems that assemble and make available valuable information to be used in decision making.

INFORMATION SYSTEMS
Systems that provide consistent information used in decision making and aid in the processes of planning and control.

PHYSICAL SYSTEMS
Systems composed of the equipment, facilities, inventory, and work force used to produce a product or service.

Traditionally, managers have been described as performing the tasks of planning, organizing, leading, and controlling. These tasks, however, tend to be biased toward the management of people only and may not reflect the management of physical resources. The terminology must reflect both types of tasks because operations managers must, in fact, manage both types of resources. It is not enough for operations managers—or any manager, for that matter—to organize, plan, and control: They must also continuously improve if they are to keep ahead of their competitors. The fundamental tasks for operations managers, then, are *organizing, planning, controlling,* and *improving.* These tasks provide the means by which resources are grouped to form capabilities.

ORGANIZING THE OPERATIONS FUNCTION

For operations, **organizing** often takes the form of designing and implementing systems, which bring consistency and pattern to management action. Many operations decisions depend on the accuracy and availability of information, and systems often support these decisions. Several types of systems exist in operations. **Decision support systems** (DSS) exist to give decision makers consistency and a pattern of decision making that is consistent with competitive priorities. **Information systems** exist to promote consistency of information used in decision making and aid the processes of planning and controlling by assembling information that managers need.

Physical systems, composed of the equipment, facilities, inventory, and work force, must be designed and installed to organize the actual conversion process, be it for a service or manufacturer. The conversion of inputs to outputs can be a complex process that requires sophisticated preparation and high levels of consistency. Events that take place in a service, and processing steps for a product, must often be accomplished in a particular sequence to use resources productively. These steps can be managed only through effectively designed and constructed physical systems.

Although not often considered a physical system in the same way that an assembly line of machines is, the work force is also a system that must be organized. Organizational structures that facilitate human decision making and problem solving and organize the work force in a way that is most supportive of business goals are significant contributors to a firm's ability to compete.

Along with decision support, information, and physical systems, more general types of systems are often adopted to provide focus and direction for all of management. The three management philosophies, *total quality management, just-in-time,* and *constraint management,* which are described in Part II, provide a way to organize decision making and ensure that all aspects of a business are managed consistently.

PLANNING THE OPERATIONS FUNCTION

Most people plan in their daily lives. But why is **planning** necessary? What happens if plans are not developed? What happens if plans are unsuccessful? These are serious questions that must be answered if goals are to be successfully reached. Poor planning is used as an excuse for almost any failure. Plans are the means by which goals are accomplished. If goals do not exist, plans have no reason for existing. If plans do not exist, goals will go unreached. Having no plan is like taking a long trip without a map. It is possible to identify the current location and the destination, but it will be difficult to get from here to there. Good plans define how goals can be accomplished even if undesired contingencies arise; they anticipate them and include ways to succeed in spite of them.

PLANNING
Arranging in advance for all prerequisites for accomplishing an objective.

CONTROLLING THE OPERATIONS FUNCTION

Controlling is the act of comparing what is actually happening to what was planned and if the two don't match, taking action to get things back on track. It provides the connection between what ought to happen and what does happen. Without control, there is no link between plans and execution.

When, for example, large projects take longer than anticipated, there is a discrepancy between plan and execution. These breakdowns between plans and actions can result from three different phenomena. First, the plans may have been overly optimistic—too difficult or impossible to accomplish. If this is the case, no matter how tight the controls are, the plans cannot be accomplished within the desired time. Second, the control mechanisms may not have been implemented. In this case, even though the plans are feasible, they cannot be achieved within the anticipated time because actual progress cannot be monitored and compared to desired progress. That is, without an appropriate feedback loop it is impossible to make the adjustments necessary to keep activities on schedule. Third, even though the plans were feasible, the control mechanisms in place, and the comparison between actual and required progress made, the actions needed to correct the variance may not have been taken.

Several questions present themselves. Why are controls needed? If the plans are good, why must progress be constantly checked to see if adjustments are needed? If something is happening that makes adjustments necessary, isn't that just an admission that the plans were faulty? To understand what can happen between the planning of a project and its completion, it is necessary to remember that most plans are based, at least in part, on a forecast.

CONTROLLING
Comparing what is actually happening to what was planned and taking appropriate actions to correct the variance.

It might be a forecast of demand, or a forecast of economic conditions, or even a forecast of the weather. It might just be an assumption that environmental conditions will be the same as they are now. Whatever forecast is used, it will be wrong to some degree. (This is cavalierly known as the First Universal Law of Forecasting!)

After the execution of plans has begun, the time remaining until plan completion gets shorter and shorter. As time passes, forecast accuracy improves because the forecast does not extend as far into the future. This change in timing is one reason for making adjustments: New and more accurate information results in more accurate forecasting. The second reason for making adjustments has to do with the myriad things that can occur unexpectedly. Equipment can break down. Materials can be late. People can be absent from work. Murphy's law always applies: What can go wrong *will* go wrong. Murphy is alive and well and is a powerful force in the world of business. Although Murphy cannot be predicted accurately, businesses can develop plans that acknowledge his existence and provide protection.

IMPROVING THE OPERATIONS FUNCTION

As U.S. businesses have acknowledged that their competitors are no longer just U.S. firms but increasingly include firms from all over the world, they have also realized that they must constantly improve in order to remain competitive. For many firms, a process of continuous improvement has become standard. Although the continuous improvement effort extends to all functions of the business, the operations function is responsible for many aspects of the improvement thrust. Improvement cannot occur without change. Therefore, continuous improvement requires continuous change. Because continuous change is often threatening and goes against the desire of many individuals for stability and security, the improvement process can be complex and difficult. Thus a number of systematic approaches to improvement have been developed.

To sum up, planning is the means by which goals are accomplished. Controls help managers recognize when reality differs from plans and what steps to take to correct the situation. Planning and control activities are easier and more likely to be successful when the operations function is organized around effective decision, support, information, and physical systems. If a company is improving on all aspects of managing, it is getting better at each activity and is enhancing those attributes that give it competitive advantage. Thus, competitive advantage increases as do market share and profit.

OPERATIONS MANAGEMENT DEFINED

The operations function has been described as it relates to the goals of a business, the types of resources it utilizes, and the tasks of management. The following definition incorporates all of these descriptions:

> **Operations management** organizes, plans, controls, and improves the use of process, inventory, work force, and facilities and equipment in order to appropriately determine the ranking of the competitive priorities—price, quality, dependability, flexibility, and time—thereby providing short-term profit, long-term profit, and improved market share.

This definition provides a systematic way to view operations, as presented in Figure 1.3. The management activities within each cell of the matrix represent the means by which business goals are achieved. A firm that is committed to its goals must act appropriately in

FIGURE 1.3   **The Task/Resource Model of Operations Management**

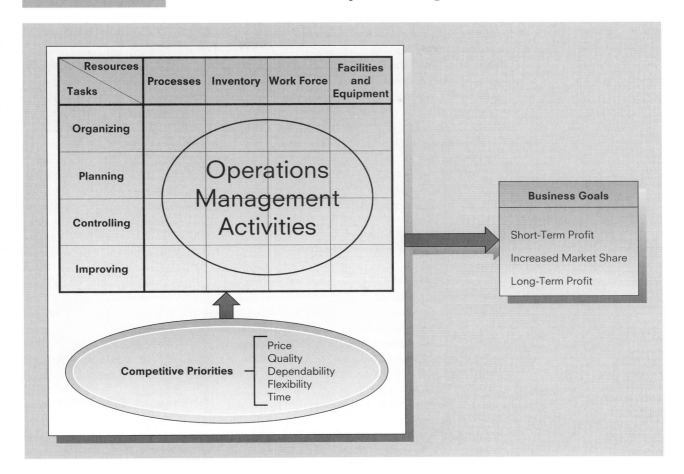

all cells of the matrix. This is not to imply, however, that there are precise boundaries between management tasks or resource areas. For example, it is often impossible to separate organizing efforts from those of planning, controlling, or improving. Similarly, it may be impossible to completely isolate efforts to manage processes from inventory, work force, or facilities and equipment. Many management activities will have a focus of one management task or the management of one resource category, but most will have implications far beyond these boundaries. This model is critical to gaining an understanding of operations management. It will reappear frequently in this text to provide a basis for understanding the focus of the chapter and its importance to business goals.

OPERATIONS DECISIONS

Embedded within the tasks of organizing, planning, controlling, and improving are myriad short- and long-term decisions. The decisions made in operations are complicated not only because they are interrelated, but also because the operations function does not exist in a vacuum. It is affected by events that are not always within the control of management and often are even outside of the control of the organization. These influences might be government regulations, weather, international politics, employee illness, quality fluctuations of raw materials, lead time variability of a purchased component, labor problems at a supplier of components, or any number of other external influences.

There is even a degree of uncertainty about events that are under the control of operations managers. The amount of time it takes for workers to perform certain tasks, for example, varies because people are not like robots. In reality, there are subtle fluctuations which, when accumulated, can result in significant variability. For this reason, much of the information used in planning is based on *averages*. Although the averages provide a good basis for planning, predicting how long it would take a particular worker to accomplish a particular task would likely result in error. The average performance over time, however, is easier to predict.

An example of this fluctuation phenomenon will help clarify it. Suppose a particular supplier of food for a restaurant provides extremely high-quality vegetables. On the average, the restaurant might be able to use more than 90 percent of the vegetables delivered. Even though deliveries average 90 percent that is useable, there might be an occasional delivery that is only 70 percent useable. This decrease would affect the success of the restaurant's plan for that day. It might run out of lettuce, for instance, even though the correct amount, based on 90 percent quality, had been ordered. The existence of variability in much of what goes on in operations makes it a **probabilistic environment.** Many plans and decisions are based on the probabilities of certain events or outcomes, but there is always a chance for error. Although quantitative data provide excellent support for decision making, some information cannot be described quantitatively. Operations decisions must combine the use of objective, quantitative data and qualitative data. Decisions made solely on the basis of objective data often lack an important ingredient—judgment. On the other hand, decisions made in the absence of objective data often lack the detail necessary to provide specific direction.

The operations functions, like other functional areas of business, makes use of models—representations of reality—to facilitate decision making. In operations, models often reflect mathematical relationships between several aspects of the business. They answer this question: What happens (or what *should* happen) to one aspect of the business when changes are made to other aspects? For example, what should happen to the price of a product or service if labor cost increases? What would happen to the ability to satisfy customer demands if finished goods inventory levels are reduced? How frequently should raw materials be ordered if the rate of obsolescence changes?

There are two general approaches to modeling in operations management. The first type, known as deterministic modeling, is used when representing **deterministic environments**—situations that can be described with certainty. Because there is no variability in a deterministic environment, there is no variability in a deterministic model. The second type is known as probabilistic, or stochastic, modeling. It is used in environments of uncertainty, in which an event is described in terms of the probability of its occurrence. In this text we'll use both types to describe specific topics within the operations function.

PROBABILISTIC ENVIRONMENT

An uncertain environment in which events can be determined as probabilities.

DETERMINISTIC ENVIRONMENT

An environment in which events can be described with certainty.

OPERATIONS AND OTHER BUSINESS FUNCTIONS: WHAT'S THE CONNECTION?

We now have a general concept of the operations function, its importance to business goals, and its responsibilities. But why should we care? A prospective accountant, purchasing manager, investment banker, or marketing manager may be thinking, "Sure, the operations function has a great deal of impact on competitiveness. But why can't the operations man-

Information exchange among business functions helped Hewlett-Packard Company meet the explosive growth in customer demand for DeskJet Printers. Manufacturing teams from plant sites in Oregon, Washington, and Singapore worked with research, design, and development teams, as well as outside suppliers, to expand the company's output and to design cartridges that would hold more ink. To facilitate this effort, information technology employees devised a database system that allowed the teams from different functions at all three sites to access real-time manufacturing data.

Source Courtesy of Hewlett-Packard Company.

agers do their part and let me do mine? If each functional area works efficiently and well, won't the company do fine?" This is a valid question.

Business decisions must be made with the whole company—not just a single function—in mind. The linkages between the operation and other functions are so numerous that every other functional area of business depends on inputs from operations, and every other functional area provides operations with inputs. Many of these inputs are pieces of information needed to make critical decisions. So, in addition to the effect of operations on competitiveness (which should concern all managers) and on the cross-functional integration needed to create differentiating capabilities, operations affects and is affected by **information exchange.**

All aspects of a business depend on the customer because the customer is the source of revenues: The customer is the firm's reason for being. Various business functions add value to the product or service the customer receives, but no business function, acting alone, can completely satisfy the customer. Nor will the customer be satisfied if all functions fail to act together, even though each acts to the best of its ability independently. Imagine a band in which the members are simultaneously playing and singing different songs—songs at which each is most skilled—certainly not Top 40 material. Just like a group of musicians, a collection of business functions must act in concert to achieve the maximum value added, thereby ensuring short- and long-term profit together with increased market share.

All business functions, then, are linked to each other, and operations plays a major role in many of these linkages. Consider the following general examples of linkages between operations and other business functions.

INFORMATION EXCHANGE
The passage of information from one business function to another.

MARKETING AND OPERATIONS

Marketing professionals often provide the only link between those who make the product and those who use it. This link forms a crucial control loop. The marketing manager, then, must understand the capabilities of the operations function with respect to quality and dependability. Customer contacts with sales representatives often involve discussions of the quality of past purchases as well as service requests and specifications of future purchases. Sales representatives cannot provide customers the expertise needed to make purchase decisions without up-to-date knowledge of the operations function and its abilities to keep promises. Sales representatives, for example, must be aware of the negative effect on the timing of other orders when promises of quicker-than-normal response times are made to favorite customers. Similarly, the brand manager must understand the way a product or service is produced in order to exploit its strengths and minimize its weaknesses. Thus, from a strategic perspective, the marketing function must understand the differentiating capabilities of the operations function in order to take advantage of them.

The relationship between marketing and operations is, in effect, an interpretive one. That is, unless marketing managers understand the operations function, they cannot translate customer needs into a product that can actually be produced and they cannot translate operations capabilities into products that customers actually want. The concurrent activities that drive new product development must include marketing's input related to customer needs. It would be a waste of valuable resources if the operations function were to produce a product for which there were no market. Similarly, it would be a waste of marketing resources if marketing were to create a demand for a product that could not be produced by that company. Neither activity would result in profit or increased market share. Progressive companies have found that a more successful approach is to focus their marketing efforts on selling the company's capabilities, rather than just its current line of products or services.

In some firms the logistics function is a part of marketing. Because all aspects of getting products to the customer affect the timing decisions and plans made within operations, marketing must consider logistics when determining customer promise dates.

ACCOUNTING AND OPERATIONS

The relationship between operations and managerial accounting has received a tremendous amount of attention in recent years. Managerial accounting's charge is to provide managers with information to aid in decision making, primarily focusing on the resources of inventory and direct labor. As technology has changed in operations, businesses have recognized a growing need to adapt cost accounting approaches to the present environment, including new operations management approaches. The accounting profession has responded admirably to this need with new cost accounting systems, such as activity-based costing (ABC), which closely tracks the costs of producing goods and services as well as performance measures that fit today's business environment.

From a financial accounting perspective, the operations function must acknowledge the importance of and contribute to the reliability and timeliness of financial reports. Accountants must recognize the impact that the timing and source of reports have on managerial action. Monthly financial reports, for example, result in what is frequently a massive push to get orders out of inventory and sold at the end of each month. This pressure has significant impact on quality levels and productivity. Inventory valuation, in turn, is greatly affected by inventory management approaches, especially as most firms are reducing total inventories. Because inventory is valuable, its impact on the total company asset value can be significant.

FINANCE AND OPERATIONS

The operations function of a business can control more than 70 percent of a business's assets, including the facilities, equipment, inventory, and work force. The decisions that identify resources in which to invest are crucial to the future of a firm because these resources form the basis for differentiating capabilities. The skills and knowledge of financial managers are of key importance in making these investment decisions. Financial managers must also depend heavily on subjective information from operations managers to ensure that the money invested will be for the kind of facilities or equipment that accomplishes what is necessary.

One example of an asset controlled by the operations function is inventory. The impact of inventory decisions on financial statements and on the liquidity of the firm's assets is substantial. Financial managers must recognize the relationships between costs and profits. All the resources used by the operations function involve investments and must show benefits that outweigh costs. However, many of these benefits and costs cannot be quantified. The financial manager must understand the operations function in order to include these costs and benefits in the decision-making process. Equipment and facility decisions are also of an investment nature but are often more long term than inventory decisions. The knowledge of financial managers is crucial to making these decisions correctly. Investments in inventory, facilities, and equipment may involve foreign currency, adding the complexity of foreign exchange rates and increasing the importance of the financial manager's skills.

From an investment perspective, the investment manager who understands the operations function, its approaches and trends, can add to the information on a firm, thereby increasing the ability of the investor to make a more informed judgment on the quality of a firm's investment potential. The ability to recognize whether a company is utilizing its resources competitively and is managing its operations appropriately can supplement an investor's ability to evaluate potential returns.

PURCHASING AND OPERATIONS

For many services and manufacturers, the costs of raw materials are significant. For some firms they are substantially greater than labor costs. Dollars spent by purchasing have a direct impact on profit. A dollar saved by this function goes directly to the bottom line. Purchasing decisions, however, also have a potential impact on quality levels, process design, inventory levels, reliability of delivery, and other issues crucial to operations and to competitive advantage. Operations decisions, such as "make versus buy" for components, and vertical integration decisions have significant ramifications for purchasing.

HUMAN RESOURCE MANAGEMENT AND OPERATIONS

Like every other business function, the operations function has become increasingly aware of its most important resource—people. As technological advances create more and more change, the skills of workers become increasingly important. Human resource management's role in selecting appropriate workers, providing training, and using compensation systems that are effective in keeping the work force enthusiastic and motivated contributes to the level of quality and cost management necessary to be competitive.

This has been especially true in recent years as firms have become more committed to an aggressive approach to quality management and have shifted the responsibility of maintaining quality from the quality control department to every employee. There is no question that absenteeism, turnover, worker safety, and training all have a direct impact on quality levels in service and manufacturing firms. Along with increasing worker responsibility comes the need for additional skills and commitment. The human resource management function also offers a key service in identifying labor capacity problems and planning for adjustments to the labor force that will be consistent with anticipated changes in capacity.

INFORMATION SYSTEMS AND OPERATIONS

The information systems (IS) function provides much of the organization that allows operations to utilize information from other functions, including purchasing, human resources, accounting, finance, marketing, and engineering. The interaction between operations and IS takes place on a daily basis as standard reports are generated or as special analyses are completed for operations. Operations and IS depend on each other in the long term as well. Most management information systems are in a constant state of improvement. As IS staff work to increase the capabilities of operations-related systems, operations managers provide information requirements to the project team.

SUMMARY

The changes that have taken place in businesses in recent years have greatly reinforced the need for all managers to have a fundamental understanding of the entire business rather than narrowly defined areas. The decisions made in operations affect every other area of the business, just as the decisions made in other areas of the business affect operations. Making the "best" decisions means that managers must be able to make the right decisions for the company and not just the best ones for operations, marketing, accounting, finance, engineering, information systems, or human resources. To do this consistently, managers must have a broad perspective.

Manufacturers and services in the United States are changing to keep up with global competition. Many of the changes that are taking place originate in the operations function. These changes in the operations function are engendering changes in the other functional areas as well. As the rate of these changes escalates, and as businesses continue to recognize the need for all managers to understand that their decisions have impacts far beyond their immediate areas, the need for managers to understand all business functions will increase.

QUESTIONS FOR REVIEW

1. What are the goals of a business?
2. Describe the traditional view of the value-adding conversion process.
3. How does the traditional value-added conversion process change when the importance of competitive advantage is recognized?
4. What is the resource theory of firm competitiveness?
5. What are the resource categories managed by operations?
6. What are the competitive priorities of operations?
7. Why is cross-functional integration important?
8. What roles do decision, information, and physical systems play in the management of operations?
9. What are the roles of management tasks in operations?
10. Describe operations management from the standpoint of resource categories, management tasks, and business goals.
11. Why are the boundaries between cells in the task/resource model indistinct in reality?
12. Why are both quantitative and qualitative data important in decision making?
13. What is the difference between a deterministic model and a probabilistic model?

QUESTIONS FOR THOUGHT AND DISCUSSION

1. How do you feel about the contributions manufacturing and services make to the U.S. economy and standard of living?
2. Identify the value activities of a local business you are familiar with. How do these activities influence the competitiveness of this business?
3. How do you utilize planning and control practices in your day-to-day life?
4. When making your own plans, how do you protect yourself from unexpected events?
5. Identify a business you are familiar with that is not competing well. Why is it not succeeding in accomplishing its goals?
6. Describe the value added by marketing, purchasing, finance, engineering, and accounting.
7. For your major, develop a model linking its activities and objectives to the business goals presented in this chapter.

SUGGESTED READINGS

Chew, W. B., Leonard-Barton, D., and Bohn, R. E. "Beating Murphy's Law." *Sloan Management Review 32* (July 1991): 5–16.

Coccari, R. L. "How Quantitative Business Techniques Are Being Used." *Business Horizons* (July-August 1989): 70–74.

Porter, Michael E. *Competitive Advantage.* New York: Free Press, 1985.

Whyte, G. "Decision Failures: Why They Occur and How to Prevent Them." *Academy of Management Executive* 5 (August 1991): 23–31.

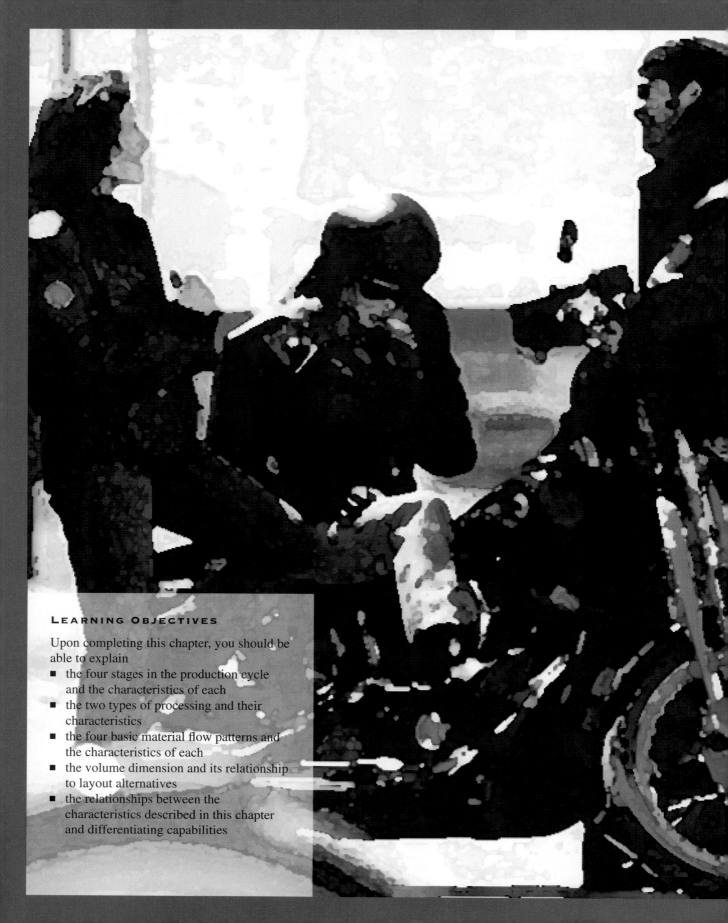

LEARNING OBJECTIVES

Upon completing this chapter, you should be
able to explain
■ the four stages in the production cycle
and the characteristics of each
■ the two types of processing and their
characteristics
■ the four basic material flow patterns and
the characteristics of each
■ the volume dimension and its relationship
to layout alternatives
■ the relationships between the
characteristics described in this chapter
and differentiating capabilities

CHAPTER 2

INTRODUCTION TO MANUFACTURING ENVIRONMENTS

CROSS-LINKS **Hog Heaven**

Few U.S. comeback stories are as exciting as that of Harley-Davidson, manufacturer of the famous motorcycle known as the "Harley," or "Hog." It is a classic example of a company on the verge of disaster that took control of its own destiny and continues to thrive. The company's history is fascinating not only because of the firm's incredible improvement but also because of the various ways in which its departments came together to overcome adversity. ■ Anyone who has driven through the Black Hills of South Dakota or Cherokee, North Carolina, during a HOG rally can attest to the mystique and rabid support engendered by these machines. The Harley has truly become an American institution. In the mid-1970s, under the ownership of AMF, Harley-Davidson had tripled production, but it was becoming notorious for quality problems. More than 50 percent of the bikes came off the production line missing parts. In many instances, dealers had to repair the bikes before they could sell them. Oil leaks were almost universal. Dealers often placed cardboard or cat litter under the bikes in showrooms to absorb leaking oil. Fortunately for the company, repeat sales were not affected because most Harley enthusiasts had the skills and commitment to modify and upgrade their own bikes. Harley-Davidson was aware that the problem with quality was prohibiting them from capturing new entrants to the market. Sales of Harleys were limited to those already sold on the fun and challenge of owning a Harley, while new business went primarily to Japanese manufacturers. ■ In 1975, personnel changes brought quality to the forefront. Attitudes began to change at Harley-Davidson, but change didn't happen overnight.

Along with an overall improvement in quality, which was needed to help the company keep up with Japanese competitors, the most important change was the development of new engines to provide better performance. ■ Initially, management knew that there would be a long lead time for new engines and that Harley needed to do something quickly to carry the company until the engines could be developed. Several executives credit William G. ("Willie G.") Davidson, the styling vice president, with creating a series of new designs that became extremely popular and enabled the company to survive. Willie G. understood what customers did and didn't want, and he translated that knowledge into such new products as the Super Glide, the Low Rider, and the Wide Glide. ■ By 1981, Harley-Davidson had new products, new engines, and quality improvements, but it was still losing market share. So long-term improvements continued, such as efforts to eliminate quality problems and increase flexibility. Most important, Harley capitalized on its understanding of customers' desires. Knowledge of the customer—the direct link between the product and the customer—is critical in any industry; but in an industry as tied to fashion as motorcycle manufacturing it means everything. As Willie G. says: "They rank the Harley look right up there with motherhood and God, and they don't want us to screw around with it." ■ By the 1990s Harley-Davidson was transformed. Despite the fact that Harley-Davidson cannot come close to meeting its demand and customers have long waits for delivery, in 1993 the company owned 63 percent of the U.S. market share in heavyweight motorcycles—triple what it was in 1983. With sales of more than $1 billion (up 60 percent from 1987), the value of Harley stock rose from $3 to over $35. Moreover, Harley-Davidson's sales abroad accounted for nearly a quarter of its total sales. Ironically, Harley-Davidson even defied the recession in Japan with a 15 percent growth in sales to a 20 percent share of that country's large bike market in 1993. This performance is even more impressive given that Harley-Davidson bikes cost two to four times as much as those of their Japanese competitors. The company's phenomenal sales record may be due to the fact that customers are buying more than a motorcycle. According to CEO Richard Teerlink, Harley-Davidson sells "excitement." ■

Sources "How Harley Beat Back the Japanese," *Fortune,* September 25, 1989, 155–164. Peter Reid, *Well-Made in America* (New York: McGraw-Hill, 1989). M. Boyd, "Harley Davidson Motor Company," *Incentive,* September, 1993, 26–31. "The Rumble Heard Around the World," *Business Week,* May 24, 1993, 58–60. "Harley-Davidson Riding High on the Hog," *Japan Times Weekly International Edition,* November 29–December 5, 1993, 13.

MANUFACTURERS
Businesses that produce a tangible or material product.

Businesses that produce a tangible or material product are frequently known as **manufacturers.** In today's service economy it is difficult to escape the often negative publicity about the U.S. manufacturing sector. From the mid-1970s to the late 1980s particularly, it seemed that U.S. manufacturing was in a tailspin. In recent years, as U.S. manufacturers have increased quality to levels comparable with those of overseas competitors, many manufacturers have also increased market share. (See Box 2.1.) Employment in the manu-

OPERATIONS OUTLOOK

BOX 2.1

Time for a Turnaround

In 1991, the Japanese auto manufacturers' share of the U.S. market peaked at 25.7 percent. By mid-1993, it had slipped to 22.4 percent. This decline is significant because every percentage point is equal to approximately $3 billion in annual sales. Observers credit two phenomena. First, because the value of the Japanese yen rose 19 percent in the first seven months of 1993, prices for Japanese-built cars were forced up. Second, U.S. cars were perceived as safer and comparable with Japanese models in quality and reliability. Chrysler's sales, for example, jumped nearly 27 percent by mid-1993 from the year before, while its market share climbed to 10 percent from 7.7 percent. Meanwhile, during the same one-year period, Honda's sales fell 27.3 percent.

While U.S. automakers are taking overall market share from their Japanese competitors, they are also improving sales of smaller cars. Chrysler and Ford for example, are each projected to take significant market share from Japanese automakers in the compact-car segment, long dominated by Japanese cars. By 1996, it is expected that the Ford Contour/Mercury Mistique and the Chrysler JA series will each possess close to 10 percent of the market. The new models will have quality levels comparable with those of Japanese products, but their prices will be $2,000 to $5,000 less. An entry-level JA, for example, will have a sticker price of $13,000, compared with more than $16,000 for a similarly equipped Honda Accord. Detroit expects to reduce the Accord's share from 13 percent to 11 percent.

The U.S. auto industry is not the only success story in the manufacturing sector. U.S. manufacturers of semiconductors doubled their share of the Japanese market between 1990 and 1993. Japanese manufacturers have been forced to slash prices in response to U.S manufacturers' high levels of quality, performance, and value. Apple, for example, has set a goal of doubling its sales in Japan to $1 billion by 1995.

Sources "Detroit Begins Tailgating Japan's Small Sedans," *Business Week,* December 27, 1993, 38. "Dog Days at Honda Are the Cat's Meow for Chrysler's Dealers," *The Wall Street Journal,* August 19, 1993, sec. A, 1, 6. "Japanese Auto Market Share Skids," *USA Today,* August 19, 1993, sec. B, 1. "U.S. PC's Invade Japan," *Fortune,* July 12, 1993, 68–73.

Magma Copper Co., a vertically integrated firm, performs two functions in the production cycle. Because it owns copper mines and maintains its own mining operations, Magma is a basic producer of raw material. And since it smelts and refines that raw ore, Magma is also a converter, producing cathode copper, shown here, which is sold to fabricators that make assembled products such as computers, TVs, and telephones.

Source ©1994 Arthur Meyerson. Courtesy of Magma Copper Co.

facturing sector does not necessarily follow the market share trend. In the 500 largest U.S. industrial companies employment dropped 1.3 million between 1987 and 1992. In small manufacturing firms, those with fewer than 100 employees, employment increased by 483,000 jobs. This 13.4 percent increase in employment exceeded the 11.3 percent job growth of the service sector during that five-year period.[1] The future for manufacturing growth as a portion of the U.S. economy lies with small manufacturers.

THE PRODUCTION CYCLE

A full understanding of the manufacturing environment requires an understanding of the possible roles a manufacturer can take in the production cycle. The beginning of the production cycle for any product is a natural resource. Natural resources are raw materials, animal, vegetable, or mineral, that have been grown or caught, harvested, or mined. A manufacturer that uses natural resources to produce materials for other manufacturers is known as a **basic producer.**[2] These basic producers, like steel and paper mills, complete the first stage of the production cycle and provide the primary inputs for the **converter,** the next stage in the production cycle. The converter "changes the products of the basic producer

BASIC PRODUCERS
Manufacturers that transform natural resources into inputs for converters.

CONVERTERS
Manufacturers that receive inputs from basic producers and provide inputs for fabricators.

[1]M. Selz, "Small Manufacturers Display the Nimbleness the Times Require," *The Wall Street Journal,* December 29, 1993, sec. A,1, 4.

[2]J. F. Cox, J. H. Blackstone, and M. S. Spencer, Eds., *APICS Dictionary* 7th ed. (Falls Church, Va.: American Production and Inventory Control Society, 1992).

FIGURE 2.1   **General Material Flows for Four Stages of Steel Production**

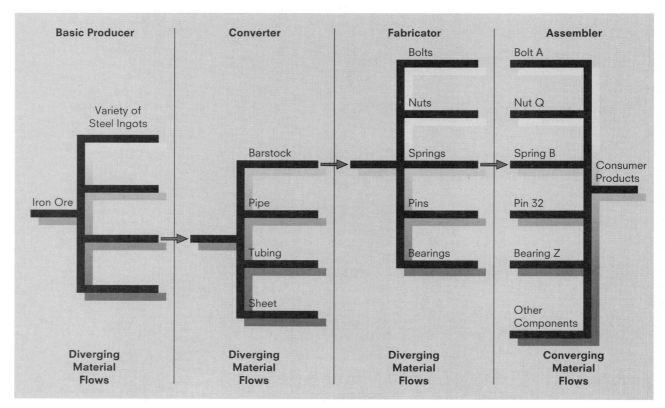

Source   Adapted from B. J. Finch and J. F. Cox, "WIP Inventory: An Asset or a Liability." Proceedings of the 1987 Academy of Management National Meeting (abstract only), August 1988, Anaheim, California.

into a variety of industrial and consumer products."[3] An example of converting is changing the steel ingots produced by the basic producer into bar stock or sheet steel. A converter would also change paper roll stock, produced by a basic producer, into cut paper. The third stage of the production cycle is undertaken by the fabricator.[4] The **fabricator** transforms the products of the converter into a variety of products that have more specific applications. For example, fabricators transform steel bar stock into nuts and bolts, stamp out washers from sheet steel, and make bags and boxes from paper. The fourth and final stage in the production cycle is accomplished by the **assembler.** The assembler combines the outputs of different fabricators into component parts and finished products. The four stages in the production cycle of iron ore are shown in Figure 2.1

Some products do not go through all four stages of the production cycle. For example, flour is processed by a basic producer, then packaged and sold. Also, a different manufacturer does not have to accomplish each of the four stages. It is quite common for manufacturers to be vertically integrated, that is, to perform more than one of the production stages.

FABRICATORS
Manufacturers that receive inputs from converters and provide inputs to assemblers.

ASSEMBLERS
Manufacturers that receive inputs from fabricators and provide finished products for consumers.

---

[3]Cox, Blackstone, and Spencer.
[4]Cox, Blackstone, and Spencer.

FIGURE 2.2	**Material Flows for Denim Manufacturing**

Packing ↑	Rolls are wrapped in plastic, labeled, and stored or shipped	Linear	
Cutting ↑	Denim rolls are cut to customer size	Divergent	
Mapping ↑	Defects or flaws are identified and marked	Linear	
Sanforizing ↑	Preshrinking process	Linear	
Finishing ↑	Cloth is given any needed chemical treatments	Divergent	
Weaving ↑	Yarn is woven into cloth on looms	Linear	
Slashing ↑	Yarn is placed on beams so that there are 3,720 separate strands	Linear	
Section Beams ↑	Yarn is placed on beams so that there are 372 separate strands	Linear	
Dyeing ↑	Yarn is dyed	Divergent	
Warping ↑	Yarn is wrapped in large balls	Linear	
Spinning ↑	Sliver is spun into yarn	Divergent	
Finisher Drawing ↑	Sliver is drawn tighter into a longer, thinner rope	Linear	
Breaker Drawing ↑	Cotton is blended into a thick rope called a sliver	Linear	
Carding ↑	Fibers are cleaned and made parallel to each other	Linear	
Opening	Cotton is fluffed, blended, and blown to carding	Linear	

A textile mill that produces the denim for jeans, for example, accomplishes the basic producer stage processing bales of raw cotton into yarn (thread, in nontechnical terms) through a series of steps, which are shown in Figure 2.2.[5] At the converter stage the manufacturer dyes and weaves the yarn into fabric. The apparel manufacturer then cuts the fabric into the required shapes (for the fabrication stage) and sews them together to make articles of clothing (the assembly stage). This kind of upward and downward integration—that is, **vertical integration**—is often a natural evolution of firms; as they grow, they strive to gain economies of scale and better control of the inputs to their processes.

It is important to recognize the different stages in the production cycle because the differences between cycles have implications for operations management. Differences in material flow (converging, diverging, linear), kinds of physical inputs (raw materials, types of equipment, labor requirements), and types of customers (industrial or consumer, requiring

VERTICAL INTEGRATION
A form of business operation in which one firm performs more than one of the stages in the production cycle.

---

[5] Adapted from B. J. Finch and J. F. Cox, *Planning and Control System Design* (Falls Church, Va.: American Production and Inventory Control Society, 1987), 77.

different marketing strategies) compel manufacturers to adopt operations management techniques that accommodate the requirements of each cycle.

The inputs a manufacturer uses in the manufacturing process depend on the manufacturer's role in the production cycle. The characteristics of the inputs have many implications for the management tasks of organizing, planning, controlling, and improving. For example, basic producers, who utilize natural resources as inputs in the manufacturing process, often find that the quality of the raw material is quite variable. It should not be a surprise that Nature doesn't always produce at a consistent level of purity, concentration, or quality. Different sources of ore, for example, might yield different amounts of metal. Different bales of cotton might contain fibers of different lengths and quality. Different crates of grapes might contain different concentrations of sugar solids.

PROCESS YIELD VARIABILITY
Fluctuation of the output of a process caused by inconsistent quality or concentration of inputs.

Variability of raw materials almost always translates into variability of outputs, usually in terms of quality or volume. This variability is known as **process yield variability.** When it exists, basic producers may have difficulty planning for raw material needs. (See Box 2.2.) In addition, when natural resources are primary inputs, the basic producer must cope with the problems of unpredictability of availability (and therefore cost) of raw material, limited flexibility in facility location, dependence on weather conditions, and potential for direct environmental impact. Converters, fabricators, and assemblers also have distinguishing characteristics that affect managerial decision making.

PROCESSING METHODS

DISCRETE MANUFACTURING
The manufacture of products that can be produced and sold in identifiable units.

NONDISCRETE MANUFACTURING
The manufacture of products that are in a liquid or powder form for much of the manufacturing process and which are not in discrete units until packaged.

The processing of inputs into outputs can be broken down into two major methods. The first, **discrete manufacturing,** is the type of processing most people know as manufacturing. It is the production of goods that are sold in separate, identifiable units. Examples of discrete manufacturing include the manufacture of automobiles, furniture, and computers.

The second method is **nondiscrete manufacturing.** Nondiscrete manufacturing produces products that are not distinct units and typically involves liquids, powders, or gases. Examples include such products as gasoline, pharmaceuticals, flour, and paint and such nondiscrete processes as the manufacture of textiles and the production of electricity. Ultimately, almost all nondiscrete manufactured products become discrete, but this change

---

CUTTING-EDGE COMPANIES

BOX 2.2
Fruit Processing

At its Marysville facility Mariani Packaging Company, of San Jose, California, receives raw or dried fruit directly from growers. As fruit is needed to fill finished goods inventory in the San Jose facility, it is shipped from Marysville, where it is washed, sorted, and rehydrated and where a preservative is added. Depending on the type of fruit, three or four other operations are performed as well. Some fruit is graded, some is pitted, and some is refrigerated. Yield variability is of concern throughout the operation. Weather conditions, for example, cause changes in inventory poundage. As moisture is lost in the processes through evaporation, inventory reports would indicate that less came out than went in unless this yield loss is carefully tracked. Moisture content must be measured and recorded at each production phase so that Mariani is able to predict the percentage of finished goods for each pound of raw inventory.

Source "The Inherent Complexity of Fruit Processing," *Manufacturing Systems,* September 1993, 18, 20.

might not take place until the packaging stage or the point of sale, as is the case for electrical power. Because of the nature of their natural resource inputs, many basic producers are nondiscrete processors. Nondiscrete manufacturers are sometimes referred to as process manufacturers.

A particular manufacturing plant may contain both nondiscrete and discrete processing. For example, the manufacture of audio and video tape consists of a wet process in which a liquid coating is prepared and applied to a clear synthetic tape. The formulation, mixing, and application of the coating is a form of nondiscrete manufacturing. It becomes part of a discrete product, however, when it is applied to the tape. Such dual functions are especially common in those operations that accomplish more than one stage of the production cycle, such as those completing basic production and converting. It is, however, important to recognize the difference between discrete processing and nondiscrete processing because the characteristics of each have implications for operations management, particularly for capacity and inventory decisions.

PROCESS DESIGN AND SELECTION

MATERIAL FLOW

Basic producers, converters, and fabricators generally take a small number of inputs and create a larger number of outputs. Assemblers typically do the reverse: they combine many inputs to form a relatively smaller number of outputs. These differences result from the dominant material flows in the manufacturing process. Material flows can be divergent, convergent, or linear.

Divergent flows refine or separate one input into several outputs.

Convergent flows bring several inputs together.

Sun Company refines one input—crude oil—into several outputs, including gasoline, heating oil, and lubricants as well as petrochemicals. Shown here is one of the five refineries that Sun Company owns and operates in the United States.

Source Courtesy of Sun Company, Inc.

Linear flows are the result of sequential steps in the production process that maintain a stable input/output ratio.

In many cases, managers must determine the dominant material flow characteristic. This decision is one aspect of process design. For example, the manufacturer of three models of computer shells must decide if each model will be produced on one dedicated production line, resulting in three separate linear flows, or if all models will be produced on the same line until the differences in the models require branching into three distinct lines. The second option would require divergent flows. The different process designs would have implications for inventory management, scheduling, personnel training, and costs.

Figure 2.1, for example, shows the dominant material flows for the four stages of steel production. Iron ore is one of a few primary inputs that the basic producer processes through several linear steps until it is used to produce steel ingots of different types. The dominant flow is divergent because one input is separated into several outputs. The dominant material flow of the converter is also divergent, as is that of the fabricator. The assembler, however, brings a variety of components together into major assemblies, or actual finished goods. It is dominated by converging material flow. Each stage in the production cycle may have linear processing steps as well as either converging or diverging flows. The manufacture of denim (Figure 2.2), for example, requires both linear and divergent material flows. The dominant flow is divergent, however.

Material flow patterns have many implications for the management of inventories and processes. For example, by allowing work-in-process inventory to accumulate just prior to diverging points, producers can postpone, for as long as possible, the commitment of inventory and processing time to a particular finished good. The commitment can then be made when an order is received. In this way, a customer has to wait only as long as it takes to process the item from the point of divergence to the final step in the process, and the producer doesn't have to maintain high levels of finished goods inventory in order to provide a reasonable response time to the customer.

The general material flows have been given simple, easy-to-remember names based on their shapes. The manufacturing plant with a dominant material flow that is divergent is known as a **V-plant,** and one whose dominant flow is converging is known as an **A-plant.**[6] A plant that has a linear dominant flow of materials and no divergent or convergent processing points is an **I-plant.** A **T-plant** is one in which there is a very large divergence of flow at or near the last processing step.

Most material flows in a T-plant have V, A, or I characteristics, but the number of end items is increased because of the divergence.[7] This increase can be the result of one of two causes. First, it might be due to the variety of packaging for one or a few basic contents. In a large brewery for example, four different beers are made for four states, but because of the various types of packaging, the company produces 192 different items, as Figure 2.3 shows. These items include pony kegs, half-barrel kegs, 12-ounce cans, 12-ounce short-neck bottles, 12-ounce long-neck bottles, quart bottles, 6 packs, 12 packs, cases for 12-ounce cans, and short- and long-neck bottles. For each state supplied by the brewery, every container must have the correct state seal. With special holiday packaging and any other state-to-state differences, the brewery would have more end products. Second, a T-plant may result from the assembly possibilities that options create. Consider the manufacture of furniture. A chair, for example, might have four frame styles, four wood finishes, and eight

V-PLANT
A manufacturing process dominated by diverging material flows.

A-PLANT
A manufacturing process dominated by converging material flows.

I-PLANT
A manufacturing process dominated by linear material flows.

T-PLANT
A manufacturing process that has a V-, A-, or I-type of material flow but expands in the last few stages to provide a large number of end products.

---

[6]M. M. Umble and M. L. Srikanth, *Synchronous Manufacturing* (Cincinnati: South-Western Publishing, 1990), 226.
[7]Umble and Srikanth, 239.

FIGURE 2.3	**T-Plant Resulting from Packaging in a Brewery**

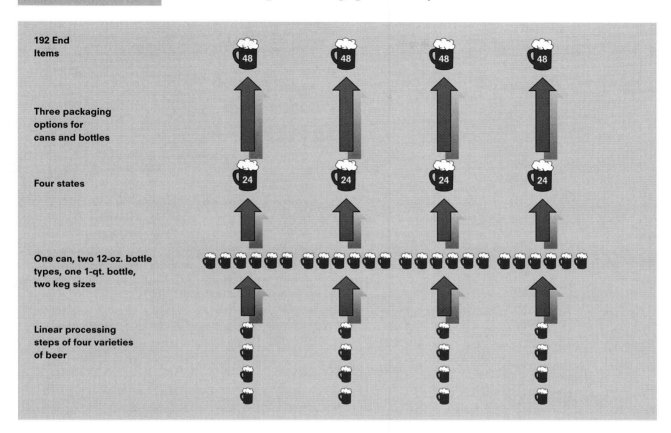

192 End Items

Three packaging options for cans and bottles

Four states

One can, two 12-oz. bottle types, one 1-qt. bottle, two keg sizes

Linear processing steps of four varieties of beer

types of upholstery. These options give customers 128 (4 × 4 × 8) choices. This approach to product variety is commonplace in the automotive industry as well.

ROUTINGS

When examining manufacturers from the standpoint of material flow, it would be a mistake to ignore another critical aspect of process design: fixed versus variable routings. A **routing** is a description of the steps required to process a particular item. It is sometimes referred to as an operations list or bill of operations. A routing includes a description of the processing steps, the work center responsible for each one, and the sequence in which the steps must be accomplished. For some manufacturers the product routings are fixed. In other words, the steps and sequences are always the same. For other manufacturers, the product routings may differ considerably from item to item, depending on a customer's needs. These are known as variable routings. It is conceivable that some manufacturers could have a different routing for every item produced. A manufacturer that makes a highly standardized product will have predominantly fixed routings and can use specialized equipment. Usually each piece of equipment is dedicated to a few tasks and is arranged so that the machines are in the same sequence as the steps in the routing. The choice between

ROUTING
A description of the steps required to produce a product or part.

fixed and variable routings is a means of organizing processes, equipment, and facilities in a way that will best accomplish business goals.

LAYOUT

LAYOUT
The physical arrangement of equipment or departments required in producing a product or service.

PRODUCT-ORIENTED LAYOUT (FLOW SHOP)
An arrangement of equipment or departments to follow the sequence of steps needed to produce a specific product.

A third aspect of process design is that of the **layout,** or the arrangement of the equipment involved in the process. Arranging the machines to follow the steps in producing the product is known as a **product-oriented layout.** A factory with this approach to manufacturing is often called a flow shop because the material has a consistent, steady flow through the transformation processes. Even though products moving through the process may have slightly different material specifications, the same sequence of resources may be used to accomplish processing steps. Items produced in this manner are typically standardized and are produced in large quantities. This approach to manufacturing is often referred to as mass production or repetitive manufacturing. Manufacturers that use this approach are able to produce items at high volumes and low cost consistently, but are unable to accommodate much customization because of their specialized and dedicated equipment. This environment makes use of the product-oriented layout to organize processes, equipment, and facilities in a way that results in low price and high dependability of delivery, but low flexibility.

PROCESS-ORIENTED LAYOUT (JOB SHOP)
An arrangement in which equipment or departments that perform similar functions are grouped together.

When product customization is desired, variable routings are required. To facilitate the use of routings that may deviate from one order to another, a **process-oriented layout** is typically used. In a process-oriented layout, equipment that performs similar functions is grouped together. This is also frequently called a functional layout or job shop. Because routings vary from order to order to accommodate customization requirements, equipment can't be arranged to match the sequence of the routings. Material flows are variable and appear chaotic when compared to the consistent, structured flow of the flow shop. The process-oriented layout is often arranged to minimize material movement from one department to another. For example, if most items are painted immediately after assembly, the painting department would be located close to the assembly department. Because different orders require different processing, general purpose equipment tends to be used rather than the dedicated, special-purpose equipment used when routings are fixed. Because the equipment is general purpose, more decision making is required by the operator. This typically means that highly skilled operators are needed. Because of the less efficient flow through the job shop, production of high volumes is more costly than it would be in a flow shop. Customization, however, is more easily accommodated in the job shop than in the flow shop. This organization of processes, facility, and equipment sacrifices a price advantage for added flexibility. The material flows in these two settings are compared in Figure 2.4.

CELLULAR MANUFACTURING
A compromise between product- and process-oriented layouts, in which small groups of equipment are laid out together to produce a family of products requiring similar processes.

Recently, **cellular manufacturing** has become a popular approach to gaining many of the advantages of both the job shop and flow shop. The cellular approach identifies families of products that require similar processing resources. Cells are constructed that contain all the resources necessary to manufacture a family of products, and all steps necessary in the manufacture of a product are accomplished in that cell. But because the resources common to a number of products are grouped together, a cell has greater flexibility than a typical product-oriented line. Thus instead of one large welding department, for example, a cellular layout may consist of several cells that have the resources necessary to do welding. The routings through the resources within a cell might not be the same for all products, but the great bulk of material movement from one functional department to another is eliminated. Because the resources are more flexible than in a flow shop, the amount of customization possible is increased. The resources have been designed for lower volume and,

| FIGURE 2.4 | Comparison of Material Flows in a Flow Shop to Material Flows in a Job Shop |

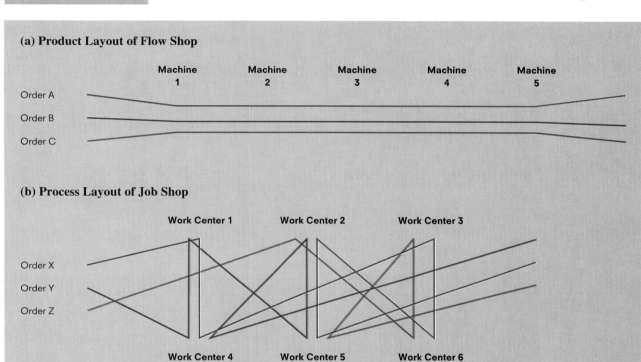

(a) Product Layout of Flow Shop

(b) Process Layout of Job Shop

therefore, are smaller in scale than they would be in a flow shop, but some of the advantages of the flow shop—primarily consistency and predictable, organized flow—are maintained.

As an example of layout possibilities, consider automobile floor mats, which come in several varieties. Some mats are merely molded synthetic rubber. Others have a molded backing with a color-coordinated carpet insert. Still others are rubber-backed with a carpet insert and embroidered insignia that match the model of the car. Some mats are small, for just one side of the floor. Others, used in back seats, vans, and pickup trucks, are wide enough to cover the full width of the floor. A flow shop would probably establish a production line for each type and size of mat, maintaining six dedicated, but inflexible lines. A process-oriented layout would utilize three departments, a molding department, carpet attachment department, and an embroidery department, and transfer batches of mats from one department to the next as required by the routing. A cellular layout could utilize three cells: one for all mats that are just rubber, one for all mats with a carpet insert, and one for all mats requiring embroidery. Each cell would contain equipment flexible enough to produce any size mat in the product family.

VOLUME

The volume of products has implications that affect several aspects of manufacturing operations. Volume, for example, has an impact on material flows and on the product or process orientation of the layout. Figure 2.5 outlines how production volume may relate to

---

| FIGURE 2.5 | **Relationships among Manufacturing Characteristics** |

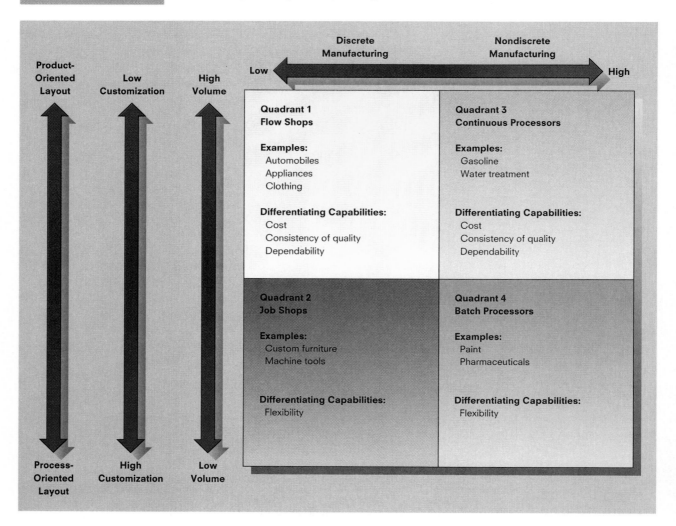

various aspects of manufacturing. Keep in mind, however, that these relationships are general tendencies. With respect to material flow, for example, high-volume producers are often considered to be repetitive manufacturers or flow shops if the products are discrete, and continuous processors if the products are not discrete. Breweries, for example, which actually produce in large batches rather than continuously, are often called continuous processors because of the continuous nature of the bottling/canning step. Medium-volume discrete-product manufacturers, which typically produce in batches, are considered to be flow shops if routings are fairly standard, but job shops if a functional layout is needed to accommodate differences in routings. Medium- or low-volume producers of nondiscrete products are often called batch processors. Manufacturers that produce in low volumes are typically job shops. But in industries such as construction, where each item produced is a one-of-a-kind product, they have a project orientation.

Figure 2.5 is only a guide. A discrete product firm does not have to fall into quadrant 1 or quadrant 2. Several factors affect where firms belong because the quadrants offer different opportunities for differentiating capabilities. Often, for new products, a manufacturer starts out in quadrant 2 because demand is low and volumes are small. If the product is successful, however, and volume picks up, job-shop costs become prohibitive and production must follow a flow-shop approach to gain economies of scale. Manufacturers also choose between flow shops and job shops and continuous processing and batch processing to gain differentiation from competitors. Quadrants 1 and 3, because of their standardized, high-volume output, offer price advantages that cannot be matched by job shops and batch processors. Job shops and batch processors, however, can compete well on the basis of flexibility, but because of the nonstandardized routing, they may be less able to predict a completion date. The customer defines quality, so the producer chooses the approach that will best ensure customer satisfaction.

Although the role a firm plays in the production cycle doesn't necessitate that the manufacturer produce at a certain volume, there are some generalizations that can be made about volume and the production cycle. Basic producers are often high-volume producers because many of them produce high volumes of commonly used items known as commodities. Converters, fabricators, and assemblers can each produce to any volume level. Because of the nature of many conversion processes, converters are often flow shops with several points of divergence. Fabricators may be flow shops, but they are often job shops because of the customization required in the fabrication process. Assemblers may be high-volume, batch, or even extremely low-volume (project) manufacturers, depending again on the needed level of customization. They are characterized by converging material flows.

DEMAND INFORMATION SOURCE

Manufacturers also differ significantly on how they interact with customers. The degree of interaction varies with the **demand information source,** which is the point of origin of demand information. For operations, the source of demand information may be a customer or a warehouse. The source has a significant impact on the information system that supports production planning and control. Manufacturers may take different approaches in linking with customers. One approach is known as **make-to-order (MTO),** in which the source of the demand information is the customer. The MTO producer schedules what product to make, what quantity to make, and when to make it on the basis of actual customer orders. Usually a manufacturer decides to be an MTO producer to allow for some level of product customization. Some MTO manufacturers, however, take that approach to eliminate having to manage an inventory of finished goods. Examples of MTO firms range from custom-furniture shops and cabinetmaking firms to manufacturers of industrial products, such as computer software, robots, automated welders, or even customized institutional carpet.

Some manufacturers take customization to an even higher level by having **engineer-to-order (ETO)** capabilities, by which products may be designed to order. Thus, instead of manufacturing or assembling previously designed products to meet various option specifications, the ETO manufacturer must translate customer requirements into an original design and then manufacture it.

At the other extreme is the **make-to-stock (MTS)** approach, which requires that the manufacturer produce goods to be stored as finished goods inventory in a warehouse or storage facility. The MTS manufacturer must then schedule what product to make, what quantity to make, and when to make it, based on what the warehouse needs to maintain its desired level of customer service. Typically the customer of an MTS firm orders from a catalog or product list, and the order is filled from the finished goods inventory. From a customer's perspective, turnaround time is generally shorter when ordering from an MTS

DEMAND INFORMATION SOURCE
The point from which demand information is provided to production. The demand source can be the customer or a warehouse.

MAKE-TO-ORDER (MTO)
A manufacturer that produces specifically what a customer requests.

ENGINEER-TO-ORDER (ETO)
A manufacturer that designs a product specifically to meet customer requests.

MAKE-TO-STOCK (MTS)
A manufacturer that produces goods to replenish a finished goods stock.

FIGURE 2.6	**Demand Information Source and Customization**

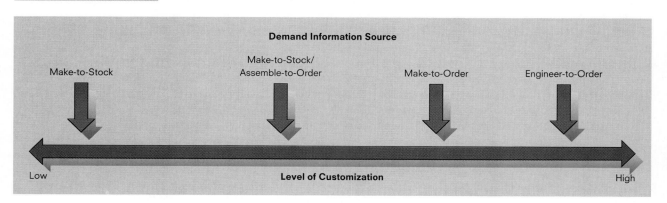

manufacturer, but, the amount of customization an MTS manufacturer can accommodate is less also. Most consumer goods are made to stock.

These differences have a significant impact on the management of processes, inventory, work force, and facilities and equipment. For example, the pure MTO producer has no finished goods inventory. This manufacturer would not be able to even out capacity requirements by building up stocks of finished goods during low-demand periods and drawing down inventory levels during peak-demand periods. Even though differentiation on the basis of flexibility would be enhanced in such a case, response time would be lengthened. Investment in capital equipment would be increased because capacity would have to be sufficient to meet demand during peak periods, but that equipment would lie idle during low-demand periods.

Many manufacturers use a combination of the MTO and MTS approaches but are typically dominated by one or the other. They produce some standard high-demand products that are warehoused and also produce some products to customer order, depending on the nature and volume of their products and the types of customers they have.

Manufacturers who must have the ability to customize products but must also provide customers with a short turnaround time have developed a hybrid of the MTO and MTS approaches known as **make-to-stock/assemble-to-order (MTS/ATO)** approach. This type of manufacturer produces the major components of each product, which are stored for future use. When a customer's order is received, the corresponding components and modules are pulled from inventory and assembled. This approach allows for customization but reduces the turnaround time for the customer. It has the added benefit of reducing the total amount of inventory required by the manufacturer. Recall the discussion of T-plants from earlier in this chapter. One type of T-plant, like the chair manufacturer, resulted from the large number of combinations of a few basic options. Most T-plants of this type are MTS/ATO. The modules are manufactured to stock, and upon receipt of an order, they are assembled in the correct combination to meet customer demands. Figure 2.6 compares the various demand information sources according to customization.

MAKE-TO-STOCK/ ASSEMBLE-TO-ORDER (MTS/ATO)
A manufacturer that produces product components that are stored for later use; the components are pulled from stock and assembled as orders are received.

TRENDS IN MANUFACTURING

Technological and philosophical changes are having a broad impact on manufacturing. Two trends dominate the technological changes that are occurring in manufacturing firms. The first trend involves the increased use of various types of automation, and the second

MascoTech, Inc., which produces subassemblies for Big Three and Japanese automakers, uses computerized numerically controlled (NC) machines equipped with automatic tool changers in its high-speed manufacturing operations.

Source Courtesy of MascoTech, Inc. Dana Duke, photographer.

consists of an increased level of integration and communication among various aspects of manufacturing systems. The changes in management philosophy are driven primarily by approaches used by competitors from other countries.

AUTOMATION

Since the early 1900s, manufacturers have striven to use machines rather than people to do repetitive or dangerous tasks. After machines were developed to eliminate the need for people to do work, better machines were developed that didn't need people to operate them. Automatic machines evolved into robots, which could be programmed to do a variety of tasks, particularly tasks like painting or welding, which are both repetitive and relatively complex.

As machines became more automated, movement of material from one work center to the next became automated as well. Early in the development of automated manufacturing systems, during the 1950s and 1960s, systems that incorporated advanced levels of automation were attractive because of their speed and consistency. They were inflexible, however, and forced the manufacturer to choose between low unit cost and the flexibility necessary to customize products. It was impossible to do both. But computer technology is changing all that. It has caught up with the mechanical technologies of many automated machines and robots and has increased flexibility. **Numerically controlled (NC) machines** use computer programs that can be changed to do a variety of tasks or produce several variations of a product.

NUMERICALLY CONTROLLED (NC) MACHINE
A machine that can be programmed (via mathematical processing instructions) to perform a variety of tasks or produce several variations of a product.

INFORMATION FLOW

The increase in the technology of individual machines and material handling systems would not have resulted in the productivity increases evident in manufacturing without a concomitant increase in communication among machines, both between machines and materials-handling systems and between machines and computerized designing systems.

The technological capability to link automated machines and materials-handling systems together has resulted in **flexible manufacturing systems (FMSs)** that can automatically adjust to meet the specifications of various products and move products from one machine to the next. FMSs have been used predominantly in machining metal components.

Product design engineers have greatly improved productivity through the use of **computer-aided design (CAD),** which allows engineers to automatically make changes to drawings, incorporating aspects from one drawing into another. CAD systems are also capable of providing different views of a product without requiring different drawings to be entered. A comparison of design using CAD to mechanical drawing is similar to the comparison of word processing to writing by hand. CAD has significantly decreased the time required for one of the most time-consuming aspects of product development, enabling producers to reduce their time to market. *Computer-aided manufacturing* (CAM) is a term frequently applied to the use of highly automated flexible machines, such as NC machines. **Computer-aided design/computer-aided manufacturing (CAD/CAM)** is an integrated system that links the manufacturing process directly with an engineer's design. The machine that produces the product gets its instructions directly from the design through a computer linkage. While computer technology offers significant competitive advantages, primarily in reducing time to market and increasing flexibility, it is very expensive and requires highly trained specialists to operate and maintain. Both of these drawbacks have proven to be barriers for many firms, particularly smaller ones.

FLEXIBLE MANUFACTURING SYSTEM (FMS) Automated machines and materials-handling systems that can adjust to meet the specifications of a variety of products.

COMPUTER-AIDED DESIGN (CAD) Computer programs that speed up the engineering tasks that used to require drawing.

COMPUTER-AIDED DESIGN/ COMPUTER-AIDED MANUFACTURING (CAD/CAM) The linkage of computer-aided design and numerically controlled machines so that engineering designs are communicated directly to manufacturing.

CONTINUOUS IMPROVEMENT

Manufacturing has been the proving ground for a number of new management approaches that have crossed over to affect the service sector as well. These philosophies include just-in-time management (JIT) approaches, total quality management (TQM), and constraint management. Although these philosophies have their roots in manufacturing, they have become major forces in the service sector as well. All three, discussed in detail in Part II, will have significant implications for manufacturing and service management for the next decade.

SUMMARY

Although manufacturers are similar in many ways, they have many differences that grow out of the strategic decisions they make. These differences dictate specific requirements for the management of operations resources, make certain differentiating capabilities possible, and contribute directly to accomplishing business goals. Because the differences between manufacturers affect resource management and because effective resource management yields competitive capabilities, an understanding of these differences helps manufacturers gain competitive advantage. Organizing resources involves a significant financial commitment and changes in resource organization are expensive. Therefore, decisions made regarding layout, demand information source, volume, material flow, and routings are critical to manufacturing success and must be made with great care and consideration.

QUESTIONS FOR REVIEW

1. Describe and provide examples of the four stages of the production cycle.
2. What is the difference between nondiscrete and discrete manufacturing? Give some examples of each.
3. Describe the four basic material-flow patterns.
4. Give two reasons for the great amounts of divergence that can exist in a T-plant.

5. What is a routing?
6. Compare the characteristics of a flow shop to those of a job shop.
7. How does volume relate to material flow patterns?

QUESTIONS FOR THOUGHT AND DISCUSSION

1. Compare the characteristics of inputs at the four stages of the production cycle.
2. Identify the four stages in the production cycle of several products you commonly use.
3. What are some distinguishing characteristics of basic producers, converters, fabricators, and assemblers?
4. What are the "costs" of the economies of scale gained by high-volume manufacturing?

5. Identify converging, diverging, and linear product flows at your favorite fast-food restaurant.
6. How would planning in an environment of fixed routings compare with planning in an environment of variable routings?

INTEGRATIVE QUESTIONS

1. Compare and contrast the most important competitive priorities that are likely to exist among basic producers, converters, fabricators, and assemblers.
2. From a customer's perspective, compare the values being added by product-oriented, process-oriented, and cellular layouts.

3. How might volume decisions result in differentiation on price, quality, dependability, flexibility, and time?
4. How might a production stage influence differentiation on price, quality, dependability, flexibility, and time?

SUGGESTED READINGS

Chandler, A. D. "The Enduring Logic of Industrial Success." *Harvard Business Review* (March–April 1990): 130–140.

Drucker, P. F. "The Emerging Theory of Manufacturing." *Harvard Business Review* 68 (May–June 1990): 94–102.

Edmondson, H. E., and Wheelwright, S. C. "Outstanding Manufacturing in the Coming Decade." *California Management Review* (Summer 1989): 70–90.

Ettlie, J. E. "What Makes a Manufacturing Firm Innovative?" *Academy of Management Executive* 4 (November 1990): 7–20.

Gunn, T. G. *Twentieth Century Manufacturing.* New York: Harper Business, 1992.

Hayes, R. H., and Wheelwright, S. C. *Restoring Our Competitive Edge: Competing Through Manufacturing.* New York: John Wiley, 1984.

Hayes, R. H., Wheelwright, S. C., and Clark, K. B. *Dynamic Manufacturing.* New York: Free Press, 1988.

Venkatesan, R. "Cummins Engine Flexes Its Factory." *Harvard Business Review* 68 (March-April 1990): 120–127.

Zinn, W. "Should You Assemble Products Before an Order Is Received?" *Business Horizons,* March-April 1990, 70–73.

CHAPTER 3

INTRODUCTION TO SERVICE ENVIRONMENTS

CROSS-LINKS | **Speed the Day**

After years of saying "You just can't get good service!" U.S. consumers are finally witnessing an emphasis on quality in the service sector. Plagued by high levels of employee turnover resulting from low-wage jobs, many services have been short-staffed, causing customers to turn to competitors. As competition has heated up across the service sector, many industries have finally begun to utilize technology in ways that improve customer service instead of merely reducing administrative costs. ■ The travel and hospitality industries, for example, have applied technology to eliminate, or at least minimize, the bane of many services—the waiting line. Although this technology often reduces the face-to-face interaction of employees and customers, it can speed transactions, which is particularly desirable for business travelers. Typical applications of this so-called information technology let travelers book their own airline tickets and hotel rooms through online services, such as CompuServe. Check-in and checkout have also been made nearly painless. With hotels' express check-in, customers simply present their credit cards to receive an envelope containing the contract and room key. Many hotels allow guests to review their bills, approve them, and check out electronically through the room television set. A 1991 survey of 5,000 hotel managers found that 88 percent had computerized at least a portion of their establishments. Seventy percent stated that faster check-in and checkout were their most important improvements. ■ Interactive TV is also being used to provide guests with information on such items as restaurants, cab fares, and museums. Some hotels are experimenting with interactive TV systems that allow guests to purchase tickets to cultural events and even to shop. There is no additional charge to the customer for the convenience because participating restaurants and shops pay to be included. Some hotels have also begun to offer access to airline schedules, electronic mail, and stock quotes. ■ Car rentals, a chronic time waster for busy travelers, have also increased their use of technology to speed customers on their way. Alamo Rent-A-Car, for example, has initiated a service that allows customers to sweep their credit cards through a machine to receive their car rental contracts and learn the locations of their cars without dealing with an agent. ■ It may be difficult to imagine faster service, but there may come a day when hotel guests check in by passing a credit card through a machine in the hotel lobby, describe their room preferences via interactive TV, and get room assignments without having had any face-to-face contact with employees. Customers' credit cards would be the keys that would unlock the room doors. ■ The travel and hospitality industries are prime examples of how technology can be used in the service sector. Many other service industries lag behind because they or their customers are unwilling to accept technological change. ■

Sources "Hotel TVs Dispense Local Knowledge," *The Wall Street Journal,* August 2, 1993, sec. B, 1. "Travel Industry Speeds Up Check-ins and Check-outs," *The Wall Street Journal,* September 20, 1993, sec. B, 1, 4. "The Power of Lodging Technology," *Hotel and Motel Management,* November 1, 1993, 74.

WHAT ARE SERVICES?

SERVICES
Businesses whose primary
objectives are met through
the sale of services.

The term **service** has several meanings, depending on the context, the type of firm, and the environment. Some gasoline service stations, for example, provide both full-service and self-service alternatives. For most fill-ups it may cost a dollar or two more for the full-service option. The additional charge purchases *services,* meaning that an employee will pump the gas and maybe even clean the windows and check the oil. Most people who purchase gas choose not to purchase full service, but it is available for those customers who expect it.

Another perspective on service can be found in the following statement about "service after the sale," which appeared in a 1912 L. L. Bean Catalog:

> *I do not consider a sale complete until the goods are worn out and the customer still satisfied. We will thank anyone to return goods that are not satisfactory. Should the person reading this notice know of anyone who is not satisfied with our goods, I will consider it a favor to be notified. Above all things we wish to avoid having a dissatisfied customer.[1]*

Both the gas stations and the L. L. Bean Catalog offer a product and a service. Those businesses whose primary objectives are achieved through the production of products are manufacturers, and they belong to the manufacturing sector. Those organizations whose objectives are met through the production of services are known as **services** and belong to the service sector.

It is relatively easy to classify a firm as a manufacturer or a service based on its dominant products, but it is not easy to find firms that are 100 percent service or 100 percent manufacturing. Manufacturing organizations have front-office activities that involve interaction with suppliers and customers. Often performed by purchasing, logistics, and marketing functions, these are service-oriented activities that provide the means by which manufacturers can differentiate themselves from the competition. One manufacturer's product may be no different from another's, but improved dependability, flexibility, or response time adds value. Dependability, flexibility, and time are service components of what the manufacturer does because they are characteristics of the delivery process and not of the product itself. As manufacturers find that it is no longer possible to differentiate just on the basis of price or quality because their competitors all sell low-price and high-quality products, service-related attributes of delivery become the obvious competitive characteristics to emphasize.

By contrast, businesses, like gas stations, catalog companies, and restaurants, may belong to the service sector even though products are the primary component of the sale. Various businesses provide the same product with different forms of service. In restaurants, for example, a hamburger may be served at a fast-food facility or with dinner music and fine wine in an elegantly designed and tastefully furnished dining room. Similarly, automobile dealers definitely sell a product produced in the manufacturing sector, but service is a very important part of the sale and remains important after the sale.

PURE SERVICE
A service business whose
services do not accompany
and are not linked to a
tangible product.

Some services do not involve and are not linked to a tangible product. These industries are known as **pure services** and include such businesses as education, health care, transportation, banking, investments, insurance, entertainment, and hospitality.

---

[1]Reprinted from J. L. Heskett, W. E. Sasser, Jr., and C. W. L. Hart, *Service Breakthroughs* (New York: Free Press, 1990), 88.

OPERATIONS OUTLOOK

BOX 3.1

Belt-Tightening in the Service Sector

Economists attribute the belt-tightening that has taken place in the service sector to such basic forces as overexpansion, runaway costs, new technology, and increased competition.

In the 1980s many services expanded, adding 19 million new jobs and $800 billion worth of new technology. With that growth, construction has boomed, totaling 16,000 new shopping malls and 3 billion square feet of new office space. For many retailers, fast-food restaurants, and financial services, excess capacity was added, and for banks, too many branches. Wages and other service costs, which had grown no faster than manufacturing costs in the 1960s and 1970s, sky-rocketed in the 1980s. Services found that they could not absorb the increasing costs through higher productivity levels and could not increase prices.

New technologies have made it possible for services to increase sales without adding labor, but services have only exploited technology when they have been under tremendous pressure, for example, from increased competition. Much of the increases in competition have come from the effects of deregulation. Numerous hungry, low-cost, customer-friendly, powerful businesses like American Airlines, Wal-Mart, CNN, and Taco Bell were anxiously awaiting opportunities to expand. Foreign competition has increased as well. New global competitors have arisen in construction, shipping, travel, and other services.

Source "How the Service Industry Got into a Mess," *The Cincinnati Enquirer,* January 2, 1992, 8. "Bank Branches May Go the Way of Dime Stores and Dinosaurs," *The Wall Street Journal,* December 16, 1993, sec. B, 1, 6.

Services contribute a greater portion of the gross domestic product (GDP) and employ a greater portion of the work force than do manufacturers. During the 1980s about 19 million service jobs were created. Moreover, while concern has focused on the U.S. manufacturing trade deficit, the fact that there is a large service trade surplus is often overlooked. In fact, the service trade surplus increased fivefold after 1986 to a $59 billion level in 1992.[2] But this rapid rate of growth has slowed dramatically. (See Box 3.1.) Growth in the service sector in the 1990s is expected to be the slowest that it has been since the 1950s.[3] Economists and executives can only speculate as to why this has happened. While the service economy has grown, some of the manufacturing sector has shrunk. Many economists say that the service and manufacturing sectors are not independent of each other, and that each manufacturing job supports eight jobs in the service sector. Thus, with a decline in manufacturing, some aspects of the service sector must also decline.

Managers of services are faced with many of the same challenges as manufacturing managers, but there are also many differences, particularly in a pure service. The service provided to each customer must be designed to meet the specific needs of each customer.

Although pure services do not deliver a tangible product and may not concern themselves with manufacturing issues, manufacturers must consider the service component of their businesses. All manufactured products are sold with implied and expected services, which include activities of the sales force, which takes orders and promises delivery, and activities of the customer service department, which deals with customers after the sale. Manufacturers must also be aware of some business functions that operate as service functions within the manufacturing enterprise, such as equipment maintenance.

---

[2]"U.S. Service Exports Are Growing Rapidly, but Almost Unnoticed," *Wall Street Journal,* April 22, 1993, sec. B, 1, 6.

[3]S. Nasar, "Job Boom Ends in Painful Crash," *The Cincinnati Enquirer,* January 2, 1992, 1.

It has become increasingly clear in recent years that there is no distinct line between the service and manufacturing sectors. When the word *service* is used in this text to describe the primary output of a business, it refers to an activity that has value in its own right. Service may take place for a customer who pays for it directly, such as at a car wash, or a customer may expect to receive it with a purchased manufactured product. In any event, the activities associated with the service must be managed as such. The differences between the production of a manufactured good and the production of a service have implications for effective management. To manage effectively and gain competitive advantage, whether in the manufacturing or service sector, the production of the service must be clearly understood. In the service sector, as in manufacturing, the capabilities that differentiate a service from that of the competition are derived from the effective performance of management tasks on resources. The management tasks and resource categories are the same in services as they are in manufacturing.

For manufacturers, the "what," or the final product, has traditionally mattered most to customers. The manufacturing process was of little concern to customers as long as the quality of the product met their expectations. In services, however, "how" the service is accomplished may be at least as important as the final result. This difference between manufacturing and services exists because service customers often take part in the actual production process and, as a result, a much closer link is necessary to connect marketing and everyday operations management practices than in the manufacturing sector.

THE SERVICE ENCOUNTER

SERVICE ENCOUNTER
The point at which the customer comes into contact with the component of the organization that provides a service.

At the center of a service exchange is the **service encounter**[4]—the point at which the customer comes into contact with some component of the organization providing the service. The encounter may be with another person, or it may be provided through some form of technology. It is therefore in the service encounter that the organization's resources are brought to bear to meet the customer's needs.

THE MOMENT OF TRUTH

MOMENT OF TRUTH
The point in a service encounter in which the customer can judge the quality of the service provided.

Jan Carlzon, the CEO for Scandinavian Airlines, coined the phrase *moments of truth,* when he used it as the title of a book.[5] The moment of truth is at the heart of the service encounter. A **moment of truth**[6] is defined as a point in the service encounter at which a customer can judge the quality of the service that the organization is providing. The need to respond to customers is important in manufacturing, but in services, listening and responding to customers are vital. The opportunity for service may be available for less than a moment, after which time the customer may be no longer interested.

The moment of truth is also that time when the collective wisdom of marketing, operations and human resource management must respond by providing a service that meets a customer's needs and expectations. For each moment of truth, a customer has expectations. The service that is delivered may *match* expectations, in which case it is viewed in a neutral sense; it may *exceed* expectations, in which case the customer perceives that he or she has received quality service; or it may *fail to meet* expectations, in which case the customer doesn't get what he or she expects. This experience causes customers to view the service

---

[4]J. L. Heskett, W. E. Sasser, Jr., and C. W. L. Hart, *Service Breakthroughs* (New York: Free Press, 1990), 2.
[5]Jan Carlzon, *Moments of Truth* (Cambridge, Mass.: Ballinger Press, 1987).
[6]R. Zemke and D. Schaaf, *The Service Edge* (New York: Penguin, 1989), 19.

McDonald's Corporation experiences 28 million service encounters each day—across more than 14,000 counters in more than 70 countries. In food-quality specifications, equipment technology, marketing and training programs, and operational and supply systems, McDonald's resources are considered the standards of the industry throughout the world. These resources contribute to McDonald's global growth and successful service exchanges by satisfying customers with good-tasting food, time-saving convenience, and friendly, personal service.

Source Reprinted with permission of McDonald's Corporation.

negatively and may possibly force them to go elsewhere in the future. In general, service received exemplifies, enhances, or distracts from what the customer wants.

Some businesses perform moment-of-truth impact analyses to provide managers insights into their services. Table 3.1 shows an analysis that GTE North's repair answering service completes when a customer contacts it. The lists of experience enhancers,

TABLE 3.1	**Selections from a Moment-of-Truth Analysis for GTE North**	
Experience Enhancers	**Standard Expectations**	**Experience Detractors**
The operator had a melodious, well-modulated voice.	I will only have to call one number.	I can't understand the operator's words.
The operator apologized sincerely.	The operator will speak clearly.	I had to listen to a recording that made me feel unwelcome.
The operator communicated a sense of urgency.	I will be treated fairly.	I felt the operator rushed me.
The operator offered to have work done at my convenience.	The operator will seem competent, helpful, and understanding.	I was not able to walk into an office and talk to someone personally.
The operator told me how I could prevent the problem in the future.	The operator will explain what needs to happen next.	The operator sounded bored.

Source From *The Service Edge* by Ron Zemke and Dick Schaaf. Copyright © 1989 by Ron Zemke and Dick Schaaf. Used by permission of Dutton Signet, a division of Penguin Books USA Inc.

detractors, and standard expectations help to identify the critical points from a customer's perspective. This type of analysis provides insights into acceptable service and how the service can be improved. The company uses these analyses to identify behaviors that are not enhancers and then through training works to change behaviors.

DEFECTIONS

DEFECTION
A dissatisfied customer who, rather than return, does business with competitors.

In the service sector, poor quality cannot be fixed before it gets to the customer. Unlike manufacturing, where poor quality results in scrap, rework, or returned goods, poor quality in the service sector results in customer **defections,** that is, customers who do not return. Reducing the number of customer defections is important because the longer customers remain, the more profitable they become to the organization. According to Reichheld and Sasser,[7] companies have increased profits by almost 100 percent by retaining just 5 percent more of their customers. People are generally willing to pay more to receive a service from someone they trust and feel comfortable with, and this level of trust is built on repeated positive experiences. Loyal, longtime customers also provide a significant amount of free advertising that generates new business. Defections can, however, offer a business a service in the form of negative feedback. That is, firms can gain valuable insight into what is wrong with their service by gathering information from defectors. Feedback that can reduce the number of defections is essential to providing specific direction for a firm's efforts to improve. The feedback must be used to drive change, however, or it serves no purpose.

SERVICE CHARACTERISTICS

A thorough examination of the differences between manufacturers and services is crucial to understanding the significance they hold for effective management and competitive advantage. These differences are summarized in Table 3.2.

TABLE 3.2	**Differences between Manufacturing and Services**
Manufacturing Characteristics	**Service Characteristics**
Tangible product	Intangible product
Product can be resold	Difficult to resell service
Product can be inventoried	Production and consumption take place simultaneously
Quality is directly measured	Quality is perceived and difficult to measure
Sale is distinct from production	The sale is often a part of the service
There is little customer interaction	Customer interaction may be high
The product is transportable	Often difficult to transport
Longer response time is often acceptable	A short response time is usually necessary
Site of facility is moderately important	Site of facility is extremely important
Human element not important	Human element may be very important

---

[7]F. F. Reichheld and W. E. Sasser, Jr., "Zero Defections: Quality Comes to Services," *Harvard Business Review* 68 (September–October 1990): 105–11.

The principal difference between pure services and manufacturers is that the latter makes a tangible product, while a service does not. A manufacturer's product exists. It can be put on a shelf, inventoried, moved, reworked, packaged, shipped, thrown away, or depreciated. A service is an intangible product that does not exist until it is requested by the customer. A service cannot be stored, inventoried, or viewed as a finished good. It has zero shelf life; if it is not consumed immediately upon production, it disappears. Services that cannot be performed when demanded are usually lost business. Thus, if a theater or restaurant does not have enough seats or if an auto-repair shop does not have enough mechanics to accommodate every customer, each business simply loses sales. And if empty tables (excess capacity) exist at a restaurant between 6:00 and 8:00 PM, they cannot be stored to help meet heavy demand after 8:00. The intangibility of service products has many implications, as we see in Box 3.2.

Because services do not have an inventory of finished goods that they can use to absorb fluctuations in demand, they have to use other methods to control fluctuations in demand. Typical methods include reservations and appointments. Some services, like airlines, use *off-loading demand,* in which they give incentives for using off-peak hours. Airlines provide a significantly reduced rate if travelers fly over the weekend and include a Saturday-night stay. This incentive helps airlines control demand by moving some of the demand from the workweek to the weekend. Another method is to use a multifunctional work force that can create more capacity for specific jobs at peak periods. By putting a bank vice president or loan officer to work as a cashier on Friday evenings when demand is high, for example, a bank is using the multifunctional worker concept.

For some services, expansion into new markets often requires innovative pricing strategies that segment markets. One technique used to segment markets is **yield management.** Airlines and hotels frequently use yield management to maximize revenues by segmenting the market in such a way as to sell the service for different prices to different market segments.

YIELD MANAGEMENT
Increasing revenues to the greatest amount possible by segmenting the market in such a way as to sell a service for different prices to different segments.

Because services are intangible, they are difficult to transport and must be located where the customer wants to be served. Thus, site selection can be much more important in services than in manufacturing. It is, in fact, a truism that for a retail store or a restaurant location is everything. Because location is so important, the size of the facility is also important. For example, it might provide economies of scale to have only one McDonald's, one Domino's Pizza, one dry cleaners, or one car wash in a city of 50,000 people, but convenience demands that services be where customers want them. If a facility is designed to serve a specific geographic area, the advantages of economies of scale may cease to exist. Some economies of scale, like centralized purchasing, may be obtained for franchises, but that is often the extent to which economies of scale can occur in services.

Quality measurement for a manufactured good involves measuring, weighing, and comparing an item to a well-defined standard. For a service, quality is measured by observing the service as it is performed and comparing it to what the customer wants. A customer's level of satisfaction provides the only valid measure of quality. Service quality is linked to a perception, which is more difficult to measure, and, therefore, more difficult to control than the quality of a tangible product.

Another important characteristic of services is that customers often participate in and influence the service process. For example, a customer may direct a hair stylist to cut "more off the top" or "leave the sides longer." Similarly, a fast-food customer may say, "I want only pickle and ketchup on my hamburger." The service process must have the capability to add complexity and variety to the design process in order to meet the customer's needs. The direct involvement of the customer in the production process has two important ramifications. First, it increases the need for flexibility. Second, it increases the importance of the *human element* in the service. Whether it is the bedside manner of a physician or the

CUTTING-EDGE COMPANIES

BOX 3.2

BAM . . . The Future of Rock and Roll

The broadcasting business is unlike other businesses in many ways. The inventory is time on the air, and it has no shelf life. A minute available at 9:40 has absolutely no value at 9:41. The inventory automatically replenishes itself, however, and to a great extent, selling additional inventory does not increase expenses. WOXY FM, serving the Cincinnati-Oxford-Dayton area, may very well have been heard by more people than any other radio station in the world. Its slogan, "97X—the future of rock and roll," may sound familiar to those who heard it repeated by Dustin Hoffman's character in the movie *Rainman*. WOXY has been ranked by *Rolling Stone* magazine as one of the top 15 radio stations for three consecutive years. Doug and Linda Balogh, owners of WOXY, purchased the then little known radio station in 1980 and have been successful in an industry full of failures. The station's so-called adult alternative format was modeled after that of KROQ in Los Angeles, but in ten years it has evolved into its own eclectic mix of music. In that time, the station has grown from a staff of 6 to 22 employees and has developed a national reputation as a model for the alternative rock format.

Measuring quality in the service sector is always difficult, but with a product as intangible as broadcasting, it is even more troublesome. Doug and Linda, however, have no norm for comparison because only 36 out of the 11,000 radio stations in the country have similar formats. They have worked hard to develop a station and a reputation that is different. They must provide a quality product to two constituencies, the listener and the advertising client, often by following their own intuition and gut feelings.

Quality programming is their key to success. WOXY is a listener-focused station. Doug describes the station's relationship with the listeners as most important of all. "They listen for our music, not for cheap humor, innuendo, or hype," he says. "We turn down many remote advertising events, like carpet warehouses and car dealerships, because we know our listeners would be offended by them. We get numerous calls and letters from listeners. We follow up on all of them with phone calls and letters to maintain this close relationship with our listeners. Accessibility to our listeners is very important." Doug describes how, at the same time, a careful balance must be maintained. Fewer than 10 percent of the listeners will ever call a radio station. The other 90 percent are known as passive listeners. Passive listeners are extremely important to the program director, but they are very difficult to read. The program director sets the direction for the product from the listeners' perspective and must be able to put aside personal biases and the influences of the more vocal call-ins and concertgoers to remain in touch with the passive listeners. This total focus on the customer is a priority for WOXY.

Like any business, WOXY depends on revenues, and advertisers provide those revenues. Because WOXY is not a typical radio station, it has difficulty when dealing with advertising clients or agencies with no experience outside of the standard formats. For this reason, WOXY prefers to deal with advertising clients directly, rather than through agencies. Doug and Linda seek long-term clients and develop close, intense relationships with them, just as they do with their listeners.

Despite the existence of two constituencies, they cannot be treated as unrelated. Programming greatly influences who listens, and the listener base attracts advertisers. In an industry where a 33 percent annual turnover in advertising clients is the norm, quality service to clients is critical. Advertisers must market to the desired age groups. WOXY must program to meet the radio needs of the age group it is targeting. Currently, 90 percent of WOXY's listeners are in the 18–34-year-old group. Nearly twice as many listeners are between 25 and 34 years old than are between 18 and 24. Good new music may meet the needs of the 18–24 year olds, but the 25–34 year olds are much more difficult to attract as listeners and take more work to keep. They require what they consider to be more sophisticated music. "Superserving" the core of vocal 18–24-year-old listeners may turn off the more passive 25–34-year-old majority. From an advertising perspective, that would mean a loss of revenues.

Sources   Personal interview; and J. Greer, "A Year in the Life of Rock 'n' Roll," *SPIN*, July 1994, 60.

---

attentive treatment offered by a car salesperson, the human element affects the perception of the service received. (See Box 3.3.) Most people have never met the individuals who manufactured their cars or home appliances, but they have met the sales force that sold them their Fords and Maytags—and it is often the quality of the service that determines whether they will return to do business again.

CUTTING-EDGE COMPANIES

BOX 3.3

Four Minutes Translates into Success

Parisian, a chain of 26 department stores, has been a solid southern retailer since its 1887 founding in Birmingham, Alabama. The company has recently expanded into Ohio and is planning to open an additional eight stores, in Michigan, Tennessee, Georgia, and Florida, by 1995.

President and CEO Ronald Hess states that Parisian's commitment to customer service sets it apart from its competitors. The stated recruitment goal of Parisian is to hire "aggressively nice" people. The emphasis on good customer service, without hovering over a customer, has resulted in strong customer loyalty. Market analysts say that the average department store will attract shoppers within a 16-minute radius of the store. Parisian draws customers from a 20-minute radius. The extra 4 minutes may seem small, but it translates into a customer base that is 36 percent larger than that of the average department store.

Source "Parisian Perspective," *The Cincinnati Enquirer,* September 5, 1993, sec. F, 1–2.

PROCESS DESIGN AND SELECTION

Because of the different degrees of customer involvement and labor intensity, services may vary with respect to both inputs and outputs. A haircut, a brake job, and a gourmet meal at a restaurant, are familiar services, but the outputs of each must clearly reflect what the customer perceives as necessary. It is generally true that services have more customer interaction and are more labor intensive than manufacturing.

Four aspects of process design and selection illustrate how different services require different management tasks and the development of differentiating capabilities—level of customer interaction, level of labor intensity, level of customization, and patterns of customer flow.

CUSTOMER INTERACTION

Customer interaction is the extent to which a customer actively intervenes in the service process. Customer interaction may be low, as it is when customers receive mail from an insurance company about a claim, or it may be high, as it is in a patient–doctor relationship. Consider a continuum from low to high customer interaction. The service requirements vary considerably along that continuum. The kinds of people-related skills required of the work force in a low interaction environment, for example, vary significantly from those in a high-interaction environment. In a low-interaction environment, the work force has less need for people-oriented skills and more need for task-oriented skills. In a high contact environment, the work force must be able to interact with the customer more successfully. People skills are a resource that, when grouped with others, creates a differentiating capability that attracts customers.

In general, high-interaction environments are more difficult to manage than low-interaction environments. High-interaction environments must be located closer to the customer, they must provide the service promptly when the customer appears, and they must allow for more customer involvement in defining and providing the service. High-interaction environments have much more variability in terms of when a service will be performed, what the actual service will be, and the length of time required to perform it. These uncertainties make the service more difficult to organize, plan, and control.

| TABLE 3.3 | Effects of Differences in Customer Interaction on Management Activities |

Activity Most Affected	High Customer Interaction	Low Customer Interaction	Other Management Tasks
Facility location	Must be near customer	May be placed near supplier, transportation, or labor	Organizing, planning
Facility layout	Must accommodate customer needs	Can enhance production	Organizing, planning
Product design	Environment as well as the physical product defines the service	Product can be defined by fewer attributes because the customer is excluded	Organizing, planning
Process design	Process has a direct effect on the customer	Customer not involved in most of the process	Organizing, planning
Scheduling	Customer must be accommodated	Customer is primarily concerned with completion dates	Planning, controlling
Production management	Orders cannot be stored, loss of sales results from smoothing production	Backlogging and production smoothing are possible	Planning, controlling
Worker skills	Work force must be able to interact well with public	Direct work force needs only technical skills	Controlling, improving
Quality management	Quality levels perceived	Quality standards measurable	Controlling, improving
Time standards	Service time depends on cusomer requirements	Time standards can be tight	Controlling, improving
Wage payment	Variability requires time-based wage system	Output-based wage system possible	Planning, controlling
Capacity management	Capacity must match demand to avoid lost sales	Storable outputs permit leveling output rates	Planning, controlling
Forecasting	Short term, time-oriented	Long-term, more output-oriented	Organizing, planning

Source   Adapted from R. B. Chase and N. J. Aquilano, *Production and Operations Management,* 6th ed. (Homewood, Ill.: Irwin, 1992), 117.

Table 3.3 provides an overview of the activities and management tasks that are affected by the differences between high and low customer interaction. Each management activity must conform to the presence of the customer and the amount of customer interaction: as the amount of customer interaction decreases, managers have greater freedom to design more efficient production systems. We can see these differences in terms of the distinction between front-office and back-office activities. Front-office activities require high customer interaction and are people-oriented. Back-office activities require less variability and judgment because customer interaction is low, but they must produce high levels of standardization and efficiency. Because of the different levels of customer interaction, standardization, and efficiency, the two groups are organized, trained, and rewarded in different ways.

The differences summarized in Table 3.3 can be generalized to many environments. In high-interaction environments, activities such as the design and planning of the actual ser-

Beverly Enterprises, a provider of nursing facilities and health-care programs, is a labor-intensive service that requires considerable customer interaction and a high degree of customization. Beverly's 3,300 licensed therapists, who provide uniquely tailored rehabilitation services, shown here, must be patient, caring, and compassionate. These people skills are a resource for this firm, creating a differentiating capability that attracts customers.

Source   © 1994 Robb Kendrick.

vice processes, day-to-day scheduling of workers, and planning for sufficient capacity must take account of the customer's presence. For low-interaction environments, the tasks need not be adjusted to accommodate customer involvement and may be more like those of a manufacturing environment.

LABOR INTENSITY AND CAPITAL INTENSITY

Another classification scheme focuses on the capital intensity versus the labor intensity of the environment. Some services, such as teaching, nursing, and counseling are highly labor intensive, whereas other services tend to be more capital intensive. Each type requires a different approach to accomplishing management tasks. Typically, services with a high level of customer interaction and high degree of customization, like specialty retailing and fine-dining restaurants, lack opportunities for automation and therefore remain fairly labor intensive. Firms with reduced levels of customer interaction and greater levels of standardization are able to exchange employee labor for technology and automation. Examples of industries that have been able to increase levels of technology and reduce labor intensity successfully include travel services, brokerage firms, fast-food restaurants, and information services.

The more automated the process, the less variability it can handle, and, consequently, the easier the process is to manage. Price tends to be lower and consistency of quality higher, but flexibility to meet unique needs of a particular customer is not available.

LEVEL OF CUSTOMIZATION

A service that is highly customized is designed to satisfy customers' needs by tailoring its services specifically to each one of them. Although the degree of customization correlates highly with the amount of labor intensity and level of customer interaction, some services incorporate automation and high levels of customization. The more an organization is able to provide tailor-made service for its customers, the greater is its customization. A fast-food facility such as McDonald's provides little customization: but Burger King claims that it encourages customization. It has backed up its claims with slogans like "Have it *your* way," from the early 1970s, and "*Your* way, right away," from the early 1990s. High levels of customization occur in areas such as personal financial services, interior decorating, and medical and legal services.

According to Schmenner,[8] the degree of labor intensity should form one dimension, and the combination of customer interaction and customization should form the second dimension upon which to analyze services. The combination of these two dimensions provides the labor/interaction matrix, as shown in Figure 3.1. The cells of the matrix form four distinct service environments.

SERVICE FACTORY
A service having low levels of customer interaction and low levels of labor intensity.

Low customer interaction and customization combine with low labor intensity to make up the types of service in quadrant 1. These kinds of services are often called the **service factory.** The company's tools and equipment provide the capability of delivering a standardized product requiring little customer interaction. Many of the businesses in quadrant 1 provide high-volume and standardized services that utilize automation to a great extent. Efficiency of the operation is high and of crucial importance. Check processing and other automated operations and most of the one- or two-day priority mail alternatives fit in this cell, as do the services provided by airlines, hotels, and trucking companies.

MASS SERVICES
Services having low levels of customer interaction and high levels of labor intensity.

The combination of low customer interaction and levels of customization with high labor intensity in quadrant 2 characterizes **mass services.** These services are provided to large groups of people at one time with very little interaction with the customer. They include sporting events, concerts, live entertainment, and retailing. The output is typically standardized, but because of the nature of the service, automation cannot be incorporated to any significant degree.

SERVICE SHOPS
Services having high levels of customer interaction and low levels of labor intensity.

The combination of high customer interaction and customization with low labor intensity (quadrant 3) characterizes **service shops.** They incorporate substantial amounts of customization and take advantage of various types of automation to reduce labor intensity. Examples of service shops include hospitals, travel agencies, auto repair services, repair services for high-technology goods such as computers or cameras, and highly specialized medical treatment services.

PROFESSIONAL SERVICES
Services having high levels of customer interaction and high levels of labor intensity.

The last cell, quadrant 4, encompasses services with high levels of customer interaction and customization in a very labor intensive environment. These services are often referred to as **professional services.** Examples of professional services include medical diagnoses, legal services, tutoring, tax services, financial consulting, and interior decorating. These services are all characterized by significant interaction between the customer and the professional to provide individualized service. Services falling in this quadrant are perhaps the most inefficient because of high labor costs and high interaction with the customer.

Professional services (quadrant 4) are typically the most expensive, primarily because they provide a lot of customization, which tends to cost a lot. Service factories and mass services (quadrants 1 and 2) are typically least expensive. Service shops (quadrant 2) tend to be less expensive than professional services.

Like manufacturers, service organizations must emphasize particular competitive priorities in order to successfully develop differentiating capabilities. The labor/interaction

---

[8]R. W. Schmenner, "How Can Service Businesses Survive and Prosper?" *Sloan Management Review* 27 (Spring 1986): 21–32.

FIGURE 3.1   **Labor/Interaction Matrix**

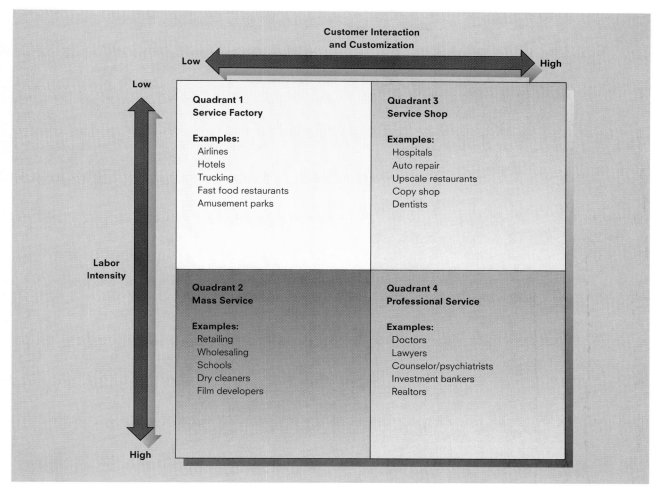

Source   R. W. Schmenner, "How Can Service Business Survive and Prosper?" *Sloan Management Review* 27 (Spring 1986): 21–32.

matrix provides a means to group and compare services not only on the basis of customization and labor intensity, but also on the basis of competitive priorities. It also helps to identify differences between particular services that have managerial and competitive implications. For example, one of the challenges of service factories and mass services is to make these low customer interaction environments feel warm and friendly to the customer. Service shops and professional services, however, with high levels of customization and customer interaction must provide high levels of variability to the service process, making the service more costly, less efficient, and more difficult to manage.

There are many examples of services that try by operating in quadrants different from the environments typical for their type. For example, most legal firms fit into the professional services quadrant. Some, however, have limited the degree of customization they provide and offer more standardized services, such as real estate or workers' compensation litigation; these firms could be categorized as a mass service. In a similar way, most auto repair shops are service shops, but some have become more standardized and perform just brake work, lubrication, or transmission repair. They have clearly become service factories. These differences have evolved as firms have identified ways to differentiate themselves from their competitors. Because of the differences among the four quadrants, services have opportunities to place different levels of emphasis on the competitive priorities of price, quality, dependability, flexibility, and time.

Figure 3.2 presents a summary of the characteristic competitive priorities of each of the four quadrants of the labor/interaction matrix in Figure 3.1. Service factories (quadrant 1), which have high levels of standardization and automation, provide opportunities for low price, consistency of quality, and dependability, but they do not differentiate well on issues related to flexibility and time because of their standardized and rather rigid physical systems. Mass services (quadrant 2) also compete well with respect to price and depend-

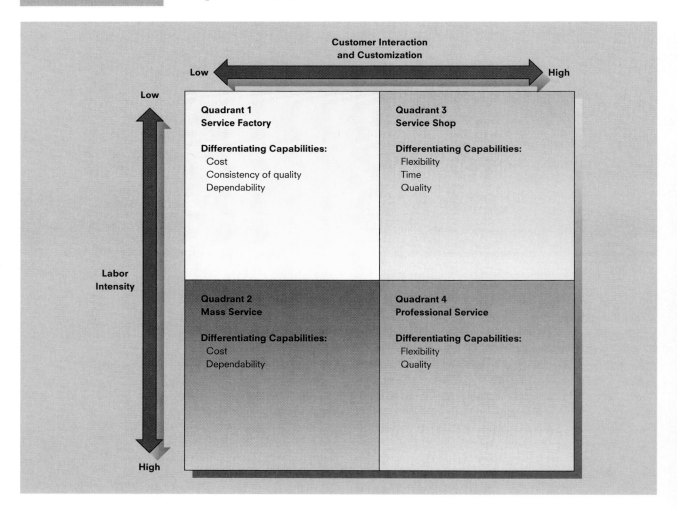

FIGURE 3.2   **Competitive Priorities Associated with the Labor/Interaction Matrix**

ability, but because of the lack of automation, quality consistency may be less than that in a service factory. Mass services do not compete well on the basis of flexibility. Service shops (quadrant 3) emphasize flexibility and are competitive in this area. Because of their flexibility, service shops can often provide exceptional response time; but because of the variability involved in each service, service shops may not be as dependable as service factories. Professional services (quadrant 4) emphasize quality and to some extent, flexibility, depending on the level of specialization. Price, dependability, and time are of less importance and not typically competitive advantages of professional services.

Regardless of the quadrant selected and the differentiating capabilities developed, meeting customer expectations is the most important issue for services. Managers must ask themselves, for example, is it more important to be open long hours so the customer can shop at almost any hour, or is the customer more interested in having quick service at a relatively restricted schedule? Trade-offs among competitive priorities are common in services, just as they are in manufacturing. Knowing what the customer wants determines what a service may choose to emphasize. Recent changes in services, for example, reflect the fact that time is becoming an important competitive priority. One-day mail, one-hour eyeglasses, and 15-minute lube jobs all attest to customers' desires to be served quickly. Care must be taken to set priorities appropriately, however, because they may be difficult and expensive to change.

CUSTOMER FLOW PATTERNS

Services utilize many of the same approaches to managing flows as manufacturing. In manufacturing, as discussed in chapter 2, differences in material flow provide a useful way to categorize businesses and better understand them. Because the customer rather than a product is involved in the production process in services, customer flow provides a means to analyze group businesses. In services, just as in manufacturing, product-oriented layouts and process-oriented layouts are commonly used to accomplish different objectives. For example, a hospital is organized by functional departments—a process-oriented layout. One patient may go to X ray, to a laboratory for a blood test, and then to the operating room, but the next patient may have an entirely different routing. The routing of each patient reflects the individual patient's needs. Therefore, the process-oriented layout is the most logical and economical means of accomplishing a hospital's goals.

A product-oriented layout, or flow shop, would be used in a fast-food operation, for example, to produce a standard product with little or no customization. Flow shops are also used in cafeterias where every customer picks up a tray and makes a selection, in many state agency offices that the public must enter in some organized process of registration or fee payment, and in some health-care facilities. In all cases, the routing is the same for all customers. Cafeteria customers follow the same path on the food line, for example, and at a state motor vehicle agency all applicants for a driver's license move from the eye exam to testing to fee payment and finally have their pictures taken. In a dental facility patients move from a location where cleaning occurs, to X ray, and then to another area where other dental work is performed. Routings are standardized.

TRENDS IN SERVICES

Changes in the competitive environment of services have resulted in two common trends: service guarantees and automation. These trends are evident in pure services as well as in service aspects of manufacturing firms.

Southwestern Bell is pilot-testing automated, easy-order centers called "Connections by Southwestern Bell" in Oklahoma City department stores like Dillard and Sears. These centers make it easy for customers to order such services as Caller ID and Call Return.

At the Land's End and L. L. Bean catalog companies and at Nordstrom department stores, the guarantees are, to paraphrase, "We accept any return for any reason at any time." Federal Express's familiar slogan is "Absolutely, positively, overnight," and the once familiar, "If we fail to deliver in 30 minutes, you will receive $3 off the price of your pizza," was Domino's. All of these service guarantees provide a clear marketing message to the customer—and at the same time, a clear message to the operations function to deliver what has been promised. The service guarantee is viewed as a way to remove risk and give peace of mind to the customer.

The use of automation in the service area ranges from automatic teller machines (ATM) for routine banking operations to the "pain pump," which allows patients to administer their own medication for controlling pain. (See Box 3.4.) Service firms, like manufacturers, often seek ways to eliminate labor from the process and to substitute technology for people.

The use of technology to replace the role of a human being in a service is not always successful, however. Customers must believe that they gain some benefit from using the technology or they will resist and, possibly, reject it. Customers may need to be educated to see the value. Even services now as routine as direct dialing of long distance calls were not readily accepted until customers understood that direct dialing was faster and more convenient than operator-assisted calls.

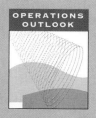

OPERATIONS OUTLOOK

BOX 3.4

High-Tech Invades Services

Chevron has installed credit card readers at nearly 800 service stations so that drivers can get quicker service and completely avoid time-consuming human contact. Motorists can pay and get a receipt right at the pump, reducing their purchase time to three minutes. Satellite dishes on top of the stations provide a response time of five seconds for credit card approval. Shell, Exxon, Mobil, and BP America have also installed card readers. Texaco is in the process of producing a $100,000 robot gas pump that "reads" a car, unscrews the gas cap, fills the car with gas, and takes payment from the driver.

Hotels are also increasing the use of technology. Guests at the Tropicana Resorts and Casino Hotel in Las Vegas can be checked in by employees using hand-held computers. Other hotels use hand-held computers to check guests into hotels while they travel on van shuttles from nearby airports. In many hotels guests can review their bills and check out through their room television set. The Milford Plaza Hotel has implemented machines similar to ATMs in the lobby to allow guests to check out and receive printed copies of their bill.

Sources "Self-Service at Gas Stations Includes Paying," *The Wall Street Journal,* May 21, 1992, sec. B, 1, 2. "Computers Add Zip to Hotel Check-ins," *The Wall Street Journal,* May 28, 1992, sec. B, 1.

Automation has had a major impact on financial services, communications, health care, education, hotel/motel services, telemarketing, and leisure services. As automation continues and more services become automated, a change in the type of employee skills required will also occur.

SUMMARY

Every organization, be it a pure service or a manufacturing firm, must be involved in service operations management. The key to effective management of services, like the key to managing a manufacturing business, is to know the customer, understand what the customer expects, and provide it. How this is accomplished, however, is different and much more apparent to the service customer than to the manufacturing customer.

Services are impossible to store and difficult to measure, and they are consumed upon delivery. Despite the characteristics that make them difficult to manage, they make up a greater part of the GNP than do manufacturing firms.

Services can be classified in a number of ways, including the degree of customer interaction, customization, and labor intensity. Service firms with low customer interaction environments where a highly standardized service is produced are similar to manufacturing operations; services differ significantly from manufacturers in environments with high customer interaction.

In determining how best to compete in the service sector, managers must consider such issues as degree of customization, customer interaction, labor intensity, and competitive priorities that can be supported through available resources and capabilities.

U.S. manufacturers and services are changing their methods as they strive to compete globally. Manufacturers are increasing their emphases on aspects of quality beyond the specifications of the products. They are emphasizing before- and after-the-sale services related to dependability, flexibility, and time and in many ways are becoming more like services. Services, on the other hand, are increasing their level of automation and becoming more like manufacturers. The distinction between manufacturing and services is getting smaller. As boundaries between service and manufacturing disappear, the need for managers attuned to both environments will increase, as will the need, in both environments, to link management activity directly to enhancing competitive advantage.

QUESTIONS FOR REVIEW

1. Identify the differences between manufacturing and services.
2. What is a moment of truth? Is it unique to services?
3. How is quality determined for a service?
4. What are the dimensions used in classifying services?
5. What is the major difference between a service factory and a mass service?

6. What are the potential advantages and disadvantages of automation of services?
7. Classify each of the following using the service design matrix: a gynecologist, a muffler shop, an elementary school, UPS, an insurance firm.

QUESTIONS FOR THOUGHT AND DISCUSSION

1. From a customer's perspective, which procedures would need to be changed to improve the class scheduling process at your university?
2. Service operations need to be near the customer, often implying the need for multiple sites for an organization. On the other hand, too many locations for an organization may not be financially feasible. How would you resolve this problem?

3. As organizations automate activities, direct contact with another human being is sometimes eliminated. What are the implications of minimizing customer contact?
4. For a service with which you are familiar, identify how quality can be measured.
5. For a service with which you are familiar, identify its quadrant on the labor/interaction matrix. How could it be moved to a different quadrant?

INTEGRATIVE QUESTIONS

1. Compare the strengths and weaknesses of product- and process-oriented manufacturing layouts to the strengths and weaknesses of product- and process-oriented service layouts.
2. Determine from a customer's perspective how several restaurants you are familiar with rank in importance price, quality, dependability, flexibility, and time.

3. Which cross-functional linkages within services would you expect to be most important? Which cross-functional linkages within manufacturing would you expect to be most important?

SUGGESTED READINGS

Carlzon, Jan. *Moments of Truth.* Cambridge, Mass.: Ballinger Press, 1987.

Enderwick, P. "The International Competitiveness of Japanese Service Industries: A Cause for Concern?" *California Management Review* 32 (Summer 1990): 22–37.

Harris R. L. *The Customer Is King.* Milwaukee: ASQC Quality Press, 1991.

Heskett, J. L., Sasser, W. E., Jr., and Hart, C. W. L. *Service Breakthroughs: Changing the Rules of the Game.* New York: Free Press, 1990.

Hestand, R. "Measuring the Level of Service Quality." *Quality Progress* 24 (September, 1991): 55–59.

Lawton, R. L. "Creating a Customer-Centered Culture in Service Industries." *Quality Progress* 24 (September 1991): 69–72.

Onkvisit, S., and Shaw, J. J. "Service Marketing: Image, Branding, and Competition." *Business Horizons* 32 (January-February 1989): 13–18.

Quinlan, R. M. "How Does Service Drive the Service Company?" *Harvard Business Review* 69 (November-December 1991): 146–158.

Schlesinger, L. A., and Hesket, J. L. "Breaking the Cycle of Failure in Services." *Sloan Management Review* 32 (Spring 1991): 17–27.

Showalter, M. J., and Mulholland, J. A. "Continuous Improvement Strategies for Service Organizations." *Business Horizons* 35 (July-August 1992): 82–87.

Zeithaml, V. A., Parasuraman, A., and Berry, L. L. *Delivering Quality Service: Balancing Customer Perceptions and Expectations.* New York: Free Press, 1990.

Zemke, R., and Schaaf, D. *The Service Edge.* New York: Penguin, 1989.

LEARNING OBJECTIVES

Upon completing this chapter, you should be able to explain

- operations strategy and the strategy formulation process
- strategic decision categories of operations: the competitive priorities most significantly affected by each decision category and the role each plays in maintaining or increasing competitiveness
- the trade-offs involved in translating operations strategies into day-to-day decisions
- the relationship between positioning and the product life cycle
- the changes that may be required in order to compete in a global environment
- the relationship between continuous improvement and operations strategy

CHAPTER **4**

OPERATIONS AS A STRATEGIC WEAPON

Jockeying for Jeans

Few products are as popular with different age groups, cultures, and lifestyles as denim jeans. Their appeal crosses so many boundaries that in 1992 38 percent of Levi Strauss's sales and 58 percent of its profits came from outside the United States. ■ Levi Strauss has gained a reputation for producing a high-quality product that has mass appeal, and at the same time the company is a model for corporate citizenship. As the largest apparel manufacturer in the world, with 24,500 employees in the United States and 9,500 abroad, it is a major competitive force in the market. As market demographics change, however, so must business strategies; and as business strategies change, patterns of decision making in all business functions must change also. Recent developments in the jeans and pants industry provide an example of the domino effect of these types of changes. ■ Shrinking populations of 18–34-year olds and growing populations of middle-aged men presented a challenge to Levi and competitor Lee in the jeans industry. Men older than 34 wanted casual pants that were a little dressier than jeans. Levi responded with its Dockers line of all-cotton slacks. Introduced in 1986, it took just seven years for Dockers to reach the $1 billion mark in wholesale sales. Lee countered with its Casuals line. And while Levi and Lee were establishing products that were a little more formal than denim jeans, Haggar—another competitor—saw a new opportunity to fill the niche between dress slacks and denim jeans. Despite Levi's immediate capture of the market, it didn't take long for Haggar to create a product designed to compete. In 1993 it introduced Haggar

Wrinkle-Free Cotton Slacks, supported by a well planned marketing campaign. Television advertising tied to NFL and NBA games targeted sports-minded men. In addition, realizing that women purchase 70 percent of the casual slacks for men, Haggar also targeted women in advertising. Within one year, Haggar had captured 73 percent of the market for wrinkle-resistant slacks. ■ With new product characteristics, such as wrinkle resistance, came new processes, techniques, and procedures. Accompanying these were new resources as well as additional planning requirements. ■ Attempting to remain successful in an environment as competitive as this one has resulted in many changes for Levi Strauss. The company has linked its business strategies more directly to day-to-day activities and has implemented a new program, called Partners in Performance, which ties individual performance to the company's global strategies. In this program, each employee forms a partnership with the company by aligning individual objectives with strategic business goals. Employees and managers together define responsibilities, performance objectives, special projects, and ways to improve. Pay is determined by the successful completion of the objectives that have been agreed upon. ■ Levi Strauss has also continued to improve quality and productivity. For example, recent implementations of new manufacturing approaches, primarily in the cutting function, have increased cutting quality, fostered teamwork, enhanced worker health and safety, and improved customer service. As a result of these and other improvements, expenses have been cut and a cost per unit decrease of 14 percent has been effected. ■ As the so-called jeans war continues, the competitors will continue to adapt corporate strategies to the work environment and develop mechanisms in all business functions to make sure the strategies are successful.   ■

Sources   "Fine-Tuning Strategies for Fall: Casual Pants Category Begins to Slack Off," *Stores* 74 (July 1992): 66–68. "Joe Three Fights Back," *Forbes,* November 22, 1993, 46–47. "Levi's Net Strategy Pays Big Dividends," *Network World,* September 4, 1989, 19–20. "Levi Strauss & Company Implements New Pay and Performance System," *Employee Benefit Plan Review* 48 (January 1994): 46–48. "Marketing Magic," *Stores* 76 (January 1994): 44–46; "Modular Makes a Hit in Cutting," *Bobbin* 34 (July 1993); "HR's Vital Role at Levi Strauss," *Personnel Journal* 71 (December 1992): 34–46.

During the decades of the seventies and eighties, many U.S. industries found that they could not meet the challenge provided by international competition. In the mid-1980s the U.S. semiconductor industry, which had invented the integrated circuit and random access memory had lost almost 25 percent of the U.S. market to foreign competition. During the same period, American auto manufacturers found that they were at a serious disadvantage in producing cars. Toyota, for example, took less than an hour to produce an engine that took five and one-half hours to build in the United States.[1] By the mid-1980s, imports had taken about 25 percent of the U.S. auto, steel, and textile markets.

A once mighty, seemingly invincible, manufacturing nation was being outproduced by its competitors around the world. What had gone wrong? There are many opinions as to the cause of the decline of U.S. manufacturing, but one fact cannot be overlooked: In almost every industry where the United States had lost market share, competing foreign products were perceived to be higher in quality than the American-made items. And this perception had a basis in reality. For example, a 1980 study done by Hewlett Packard's Data Systems Division found that the failure rate of American-produced memory chips was at least 20 times greater than those produced by Japanese firms.[2] Moreover, in the late 1980s, financial and banking services and other industries within the service sector were also losing market share to foreign-owned competitors. What had happened in manufacturing was beginning to threaten the service sector.

U.S. COMPETITIVENESS

THE DECLINE IN U.S. COMPETITIVENESS: WHERE WE'VE BEEN

In 1989, the Massachusetts Institute of Technology (MIT) Commission on Industrial Productivity reported on findings from a two-year study of U.S. productivity.[3] The commission found that the inability of U.S. manufacturers to compete did not appear to be highly

---

[1]Robert W. Hall, *Attaining Manufacturing Excellence* (Homewood, Ill.: Dow Jones-Irwin, 1987), 31–34.

[2]"The Anderson Bombshell," *The Rosen Electronics Letter,* March 31, 1980, 3–5.

[3]Suzanne Berger, Michael L. Dertouzos, Richard K. Lester, Robert M. Solow, and Lester C. Thurow, "Toward a New Industrial America," *Scientific American,* June 1989, 39–47.

correlated to current economic conditions, U.S. interest rates, or tax policies. The study reported five fundamental reasons why U.S. corporations were no longer competitive.

1. *U.S. industries overemphasized mass production.* Producing high volumes of standardized products at low costs, American firms neglected such other bases on which they could compete as quality, dependability, flexibility, and time—features that were of interest to their customers. Foreign competitors were, however, paying attention to these competitive features. In addition, U.S. industries tended to be parochial. That is, they paid attention to technological advances from U.S. factories and laboratories but ignored scientific and technical innovations from other countries. This narrow focus caused U.S. industries to lag behind the rest of the world in developing new products and processes.

2. *U.S. firms neglected human resources.* Firms achieved flexibility by hiring and firing workers rather than by developing workers. The limited training U.S. workers received usually consisted of on-the-job training from other workers. The study attributed some aspects of the problem to U.S. elementary and secondary schools because American students' reading, writing, and problem-solving skills were significantly below those of students from other countries. These skills are fundamental to activities employees must perform in the workplace.

3. *U.S. industries displayed widespread lack of cooperation between and within organizations.* The report described undeveloped relations among organized labor, management, suppliers, and customers. The goals of labor unions and management, for example, were in conflict, and significant resources were required to resolve the differences. Also, the level of coordination and communication among departments such as engineering, operations, and marketing was unacceptable.

4. *U.S. firms exhibited technological weakness in development and production.* Although the United States was the world leader in basic research, Japanese manufacturers led in translating research into products, making those products higher in quality, and making them faster, than their U.S. counterparts could. For instance, competitors in the auto industry had the ability to go from the concept stage of a new model to its introduction into the market in three and a half years, while U.S. automakers needed at least five.

   The commission attributed part of this problem to the American system of engineering education, which places little emphasis on product design and testing or on manufacturing and process improvements. It also said many U.S. firms had not devoted enough effort to improving the manufacturing process. More U.S. research and development (R&D) money went to product improvement and development than to process improvement and process technology development. The converse was true for Japanese companies, which concentrated on enhancement of three of the key competitive priorities—quality, flexibility, and response time—which are rooted in process technology and not in product development.

5. *U.S. industries were more concerned about short-term profits than long-term competitive advantages, such as market share and process improvement.* Many decision makers were evaluated only on how well they performed in the short run. Faced with a trade-off between short-term and long-term

benefits (and such trade-offs are numerous), U.S. managers tended to prefer the short-term advantage. Expenditures for research and development and process improvement were postponed, sometimes indefinitely, because the financial payback was considered too slow, even though such investments might have resulted in a positive impact on competitive capabilities.

IMPROVEMENTS: WHERE WE'RE GOING

Although U.S. businesses have yet to fully regain many of the markets lost to foreign competition, substantial progress has been made. Many U.S. products are now comparable in quality to those from Japan, and productivity levels are improving as well, as Table 4.1 shows.

Not only have some U.S. manufacturers faltered and recovered, but also many businesses have dominated their industry worldwide, as Tom Peters describes.[4] Services, such as leisure and hospitality industries, continue to attract customers from all over the world. For example, in terms of tourist dollars, Disney World (U.S.) and Las Vegas are in a league all their own. Several companies devoted to information services, ranging from the news coverage of Cable News Network (CNN) to the computer information systems of Electronic Data Systems (EDS), are clearly models of success. Health care is also an area of U.S. leadership. Hospitals like Johns Hopkins and medical equipment and supply companies like Baxter Healthcare are examples of world-class competitors.

DEVELOPING AN OPERATIONS STRATEGY: HOW WE'LL GET THERE

The United States entered the decade of the sixties as the world industrial leader. American industry had a substantial capital base, an experienced work force, and unparalleled dominance in product and process technologies. Analysts argue, however, that managers at that time tended to view facilities and work force as liabilities on a balance sheet—an attitude that led them to manage "around" rather than "through" these resources and to fail to keep them current.[5] Performance, therefore, was thwarted by obsolete equipment and poor employee morale. In many cases, plants were forced to close down or move somewhere else to start over.

As we can see, U.S. managers of the 1960s had not yet learned to use the operations function to develop a competitive advantage and enhance the overall performance of the organization. That is, they had not developed or implemented an operations strategy. In 1969, however, operations strategy began to develop as a theory, much of which can be traced to the work of Wickham Skinner in the area of manufacturing strategy.[6] This theory offered progressive U.S. firms a new understanding of the strategic implications that operations has for competitiveness, as well as for social responsibility. Such firms have acknowledged that long-term, holistic planning must extend beyond the traditional boundaries of the corporation to the society and environment of the present and future.

---

[4]Tom Peters, "10 Ways We Do It Right," *USA Weekend,* July 3–5, 1992, 4–6.

[5]R. H. Hayes, S. C. Wheelwright, and K. B. Clark, *Dynamic Manufacturing* (New York: Free Press, 1988), 16.

[6]Wickham Skinner, "Manufacturing—Missing Link in Corporate Strategy," *Harvard Business Review* 47 (May-June 1969): 136–145.

TABLE 4.1	Gross Value Added in Manufacturing				
	Value per Hour Worked				
Year	**United States**	**The Netherlands**	**Japan**	**Germany**	**France**
1950	100[1]	40.2	18	39	32
1975	195.9	154.8	123.4	162.6	129.3
1989	289.2	244.6	235.1	229.5	218.2
1975–1989 (increase per year)	3.4%	4.2%	6.5%	2.9%	4.9%

[1]100 = USA, 1950.

Source   Adapted from "U. S. First, Dutch Second," *Manufacturing Engineering* (June 1993): 18.

OPERATIONS STRATEGY

As we learned in Chapter 1, resources contribute to the creation of differentiating capabilities, and competitive capabilities make it possible to accomplish the organizational goals of short- and long-term profit and increased market share. A **strategy** is the pattern or direction an organization can adopt to link resources, through decisions about their use, to goals. Strategies usually differ by organizational levels and structure. Wheelwright defines three levels of strategies.[7]

> A **corporate strategy** focuses on what business the firm should be in and how resources will be committed to those activities.
>
> A **business strategy** specifies the boundaries of a business in a way that links it to the corporate strategy and specifies the basis on which the business will compete.
>
> A **functional strategy** is designed to carry out the business strategy in each of its functional areas. It specifies how that function will support the desired competitive advantage and how it will complement other functional strategies.

All three levels of strategies need to be consistent with and supportive of one another. Corporate strategy provides direction for business strategy, business strategy provides direction for functional strategies, and functional strategies provide direction for such day-to-day management activities as organizing, planning, controlling, and improving. Not only must top-down consistency be present, but corporate strategies should also reflect capabilities at business and functional levels.

A well designed strategy must be integrated at each level of the organization and should seek a match between the organization's capabilities and the opportunities that

STRATEGY
The pattern of decision making an organization chooses in order to link resources to goals.

CORPORATE STRATEGY
Strategy that focuses on what businesses a corporation should be in and how resources should be committed to those businesses.

BUSINESS STRATEGY
Strategy that specifies the boundaries of a business and the basis on which it will compete.

FUNCTIONAL STRATEGY
Strategy that specifies how each functional area of a business carries out the business strategy.

[7]S. C. Wheelwright, "Manufacturing Strategy: Defining the Missing Link," *Strategic Management Journal* 5 (January-March 1984): 77–91.

Caterpillar's long-term strategy for global growth includes expanding sales opportunities in the Commonwealth of Independent States (CIS), China, and other regions of the world with strong growth potential. In the CIS, Caterpillar is implementing this strategy by forming joint ventures to manufacture, market, and service Caterpillar equipment. Shown here is part of an order for Cat-type tractors, which are being shipped to Russia from the Port of Milwaukee.

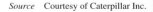

Source Courtesy of Caterpillar Inc.

exist in the external environment. The impact that the operations function may have on an organization's ability to compete has not always been well understood. Only recently, after observing the tremendous advantage Japanese firms have gained by competing through quality, have U.S. managers recognized that distinctive strategic competencies can be gained through the operations function.

As described in chapter 1, it isn't the amount of resources controlled that determines competitiveness but the ability to develop capabilities by effectively grouping these resources. The resources controlled by the operations function have great potential for creating differentiating capabilities that lead to competitive advantage.

The strategic planning process has two major components: strategy formulation and strategy implementation. During the strategy formulation process, the content of the strategy is developed, and during the strategy implementation process, the methodology is determined. In other words, strategy formulation answers the question, "What are we going to do?" and strategy implementation responds to "How are we going to do it?"

Strategy formulation is based upon an analysis of both the internal and external environments. External factors that need to be considered include economic and political conditions, legal and social issues, and technological and customer/market-driven issues. Internal factors include the organization's financial and human resources, facilities, expertise, customers, and suppliers. These two streams of information come together to provide the basis for formulating corporate strategy, as shown in Figure 4.1. Strategy implementation is the process of translating the strategy into decision-making processes.

| FIGURE 4.1 | **Internal and External Factors in Strategy Formulation** |

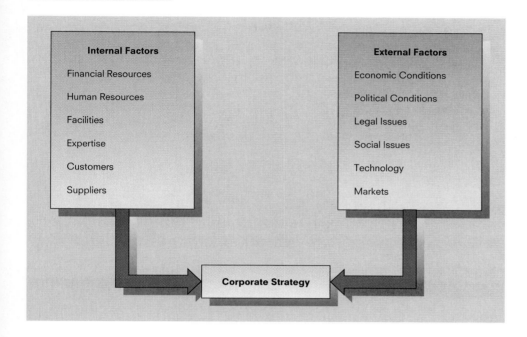

THE LINK BETWEEN OPERATIONS STRATEGY AND PRODUCT DESIGN

We see the evidence of effective corporate and business strategies both in what is offered and how it is offered. Companies may determine what to offer and the means by which they offer it in any number of ways. First, they establish parameters, or limits, for operations through *positioning* decisions. Once they set these limits, firms can establish their *competitive priorities,* which have a direct impact on operations decisions, often on a day-to-day basis.

POSITIONING

Positioning is one of the ways in which corporate and business strategy is linked to the operations function. An organization may assume one of two positioning strategies: a process focus or a product/market focus.[8]

A **process focus** means that the business concentrates on its process as a means of competing. Thus plants are dedicated not to particular products but to specific types of processes, such as mining or refining ore. Typically treated as cost centers rather than profit centers because they do not complete a finished product,

POSITIONING STRATEGY
A strategy that links the corporate and business strategy to the operations function.

PROCESS FOCUS
A positioning strategy that concentrates on processes as a means of competing.

---

[8]R. H. Hayes, and S. C. Wheelwright, "Link Manufacturing Process and Product Life Cycles," *Harvard Business Review* 57 (January-February 1979): 133–140.

process-focused plants tend to produce goods that are inputs for other manufacturing processes. Basic producers and converters, for example, are usually process focused. Plants of this type are characterized by high overhead costs which are offset by high production volumes.

A **product/market focus** means that the resources of a business are organized around the product or service it produces. Typically entailing the use of plants or service centers that are decentralized and self-contained, the product/market focus is most likely to be successful when flexibility and quick response to change are important means of competing. The product/market focus results in lower overhead costs, lower inventory, lower logistics costs, and quicker delivery times.

Positioning plays an important role in ensuring that the operations strategy is consistent with corporate and business strategies. To a great extent, positioning decisions determine the characteristics of the resources that will be used because they dictate how production resources will be selected and organized. And these characteristics, in turn, lend themselves to the development of desired competitive priorities.

One criterion used in determining appropriate positioning strategies is the **product life cycle,** shown in Figure 4.2. Most successful products and services go through this five-stage cycle, from their introduction into the marketplace to their obsolescence.

- In the first stage, the **introduction,** the demand for a new, unknown product is low, so production volumes are low. A process focus is likely to be appropriate at this point because of the low volume and because the demand pattern is not well enough defined to risk standardization.
- During the second stage, **growth,** demand increases as consumers become more aware of the product or service. Growing demand may generate increased production volumes if it is appropriate to standardize products. That

PRODUCT/MARKET FOCUS
A positioning strategy in which the resources of the business are organized around the products or services produced.

PRODUCT LIFE CYCLE
A series of stages characterized by demand levels for the product. The stages include introduction, growth, maturation, saturation, and decline.

INTRODUCTION
The first stage of the product life cycle, characterized by low volume and low demand.

GROWTH
The second stage in the product life cycle, characterized by increased demand as consumers become aware of the product.

FIGURE 4.2   **The Product Life Cycle**

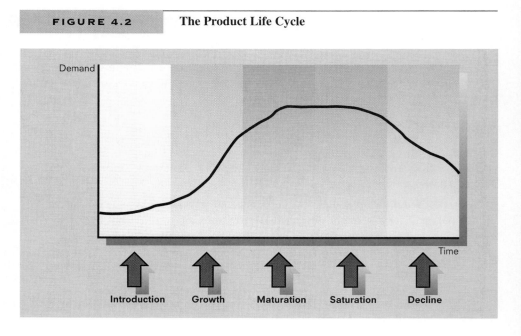

is, the investment in expensive specialized equipment may be justified if the demand patterns indicate a reduction in the need for customization and product variety. Few products or services maintain growth for extended periods of time.

- At **maturation,** the third stage, growth begins to level off as consumer demands are being satisfied. During this stage, product standardization tends to reduce production costs, so that product prices may be lower.
- **Saturation,** the fourth stage, follows as the demand for the product subsides. During this stage, the market may be saturated and/or alternatives begin to replace the original product or service.
- The final stage, **decline,** occurs as the product is replaced by more technologically advanced or reliable alternatives. Often, firms drop prices substantially at this stage in order to stimulate demand and prolong the life of the product or service.

The length of time from introduction to decline varies tremendously from product to product. Producers of high-fidelity phonographs, for example, enjoyed many years of increasing or level demand before the compact disc (CD) digital technology finally replaced vinyl as a recording medium. Computer manufacturers, on the other hand, are finding that because of the incredible rate of technological advances, product life cycles for some products are only one or two years long. When life cycles are this short, the ability to get a product to the market quickly can mean the difference between a success or failure. Businesses often try to control their products' life cycles in an effort to effect changes in demand and the ability of other products to compete with theirs. (See Box 4.1.)

The need to get products to market quickly to get the most profit possible is supported by a McKinsey & Company study which showed that bringing a product to market six months late results in a 33 percent reduction in the potential profit of the product over its

MATURATION
The third stage of the product life cycle, characterized by stable demand and a leveling of growth.

SATURATION
The fourth stage of the product life cycle, characterized by subsiding demand.

DECLINE
The final stage of the product life cycle, characterized by low demand.

CUTTING-EDGE COMPANIES

BOX 4.1

Coke Seeks to Shorten Cycles

In an attempt to capitalize on the speedy shifts in consumers' taste, Coca-Cola announced that it will reduce both the time it takes to launch new products and product life cycles. Rather than introduce new products and try to market them for as long as possible, as the company has been doing, Coca-Cola plans to bring trendier products into the market, make money from them, and then pull them.

The new strategy reflects the increased popularity of a large number of noncola drinks, including teas and clear, so-called new age beverages. Coke spokespersons said the market is becoming increasingly fragmented and requires a shift in strategy.

This announcement comes at a time when both Tab Clear and Crystal Pepsi are about to die. Crystal Pepsi had sales of approximately $102.4 million, less than 10 percent of that of regular Pepsi. Tab Clear had supermarket sales of less than $4 million. The shift in strategy is an acknowledgement of the market trend toward shorter life products.

Industry experts recognize that Coke is undertaking a risky strategy. Because of the strength of the name that Coke has built through its brand equity, there is a danger that short-life products may erode the association many customers feel with the company.

Source L. M. Grossman, "Coca-Cola Plans to Shorten Time of Soda Launches," *The Wall Street Journal,* November 18, 1993, sec. C, 10.

lifetime.[9] Regardless of the length of the life cycle, capabilities necessary for the accomplishment of organization goals change as a product progresses through its cycle.

When products are introduced, production usually focuses on flexibility and not on cost efficiencies because the wants and needs of customers aren't fully developed or known. Increasing demand permits patterns to be identified. Then, as the product moves through the product life cycle, production tends to move in the direction of increasing standardization, mechanization, and automation. In the early stages of the product life cycle, then, systems are designed to provide flexibility in both product and volume changes. But as the processes move toward more standardization, the emphasis shifts to reliability, predictability, and cost.[10] As emphasis shifts from the customization and product variety of the introduction and growth stages to the high volume and standardization of the maturity stage, the positioning strategy may need to shift from a product/market focus to a process focus in order to achieve cost reduction.

COMPETITIVE PRIORITIES

Once corporate and business strategies are formulated, they are translated into priorities that provide focus for the operations function. Price, quality, dependability, flexibility, and time—the competitive priorities—are ranked according to their importance.[11] The competitive priorities provide a framework for deciding what is offered to the customers and how it is offered. The priorities also provide direction for the development of differentiating capabilities.

Price is, to a great extent, limited by the cost to produce the product. Production costs that are higher than a competitor's make it more difficult for the firm to compete on the basis of price. Higher prices, given no other change, mean less value for the customer and typically result in a decrease in demand. Increased costs can be absorbed by reducing the profit margin per unit, but this typically results in reducing the firm's net profit. Decreases in profit margin resulting from higher costs may sometimes be offset by increases in volume sold, however.

Quality can be difficult for a producer to define, because the level of quality is ultimately determined by the consumer. From a consumer's point of view, quality refers to characteristics such as performance, reliability, durability, features, and aesthetics. From a producer's point of view, quality must be more measurable and is defined as conformance to the specifications customers demand.

Organizations can compete on quality in at least two distinct ways. First, the product or service may be viewed as having a high level of quality because of its consistency. A second approach to viewing quality is to offer the "best" product that is possible. The product or service must have features that are more advanced or technologically superior to those of others and it must be consistent. In the service sector, where there is no tangible product, quality is more difficult to measure, making customer feedback even more important.

Dependability refers to the reliability of the product or service, the firm's ability to deliver it as specified in the amount of time requested as well as the company's pattern of doing what it promises. Dependability and timeliness of delivery are becoming increasingly

---

[9]J. T. Vesey, "The New Competitors: They Think in Terms of 'Speed-to-Market,'" *Academy of Management Executive* 5 (May 1991): 23–33.

[10]Hayes and Wheelwright, 133–140.

[11]R. H. Hayes and S. C. Wheelwright, *Restoring our Competitive Edge—Competing through Manufacturing* (New York: John Wiley, 1984), 40.

Airborne Express achieves a competitive advantage by being the low-cost producer in express delivery of small packages and documents. This firm's philosophy is to perform high-quality work while delivering the best customer service in the most efficient and economical way. Airborne accomplishes this by using computer technology and cross-functional teams to boost productivity in all stages of delivery, from handling paperwork to sorting shipments and transporting packages in the air and on the ground.

Source   Jeff Zaruba/Courtesy of Airborne Express.

important both for manufacturers and services. If a company is to remain flexible and dependable, the companies that supply it with raw materials and other inputs must also be dependable. This puts pressure on the dependability of all organizations, from basic producers to the purchaser.

Flexibility refers to an organization's ability to respond to change, whether to the needs of a specific customer or to different customers and/or conditions. It may require that companies alter their product mix—that is, adjust the proportions of its products—to meet changing conditions. A flexible company might, for instance, find ways to produce its products profitably in small lots to adapt to significant changes in demand. Or flexibility may require that companies modify the products themselves as a means of satisfying a particular customer's requirements. For an example of flexibility, consider the Kao Corporation of Japan, whose success is described in Box 4.2.

Time has become an increasingly important dimension by which companies may differentiate themselves as levels of quality improve. If all companies are providing top-quality products or services, no company can be differentiated on that basis. Thus differentiation must come from some other competitive capability. In many industries, time is viewed as a valuable competitive capability because quick response to a customer's orders improves that customer's response time to its own customers. Also, with the shortening of product life cycles, particularly in high-tech industries, time becomes critical. The quicker the product development, the quicker the product gets to the market and the more likely it is that competitors will be outstripped. (See Box 4.3.)

OPERATIONS OUTLOOK

BOX 4.2

Japan Becomes More Flexible

While U.S. manufacturers now stress quality and have virtually caught up with Japanese manufacturers by that measure, the Japanese have moved on to another priority—flexibility. The Japanese take as givens such quality issues as conformance to specification, durability, and dependability of delivery. But Japanese and U.S. firms differ on the priority of flexibility. In fact, the difference between Japanese and U.S. flexibility objectives is that Japanese manufacturers are about a third more likely to say that increased flexibility is important in their plans. In a study by Deloitte & Touche consultants, 900 U.S. and Japanese companies were asked to describe their manufacturing strategies. The results showed marked differences in the focus of the two countries' manufacturers. Japanese manufacturers placed significant emphasis on issues related to flexibility, while U.S. manufacturers placed more stress on aspects of quality, such as customer service and reliability. Japanese manufacturers were more likely than U.S. manufacturers to rate the following strategies as above average in importance for the future:

- Enhanced product features
- Introduction of many new products
- Rapid change in product mix
- State-of-the-art manufacturing processes
- Products with a high R&D component
- Lower priced products
- Rapid change in production volumes

U.S. manufacturers were more likely than Japanese manufacturers to rate the following strategies as above average in importance for the future:

- Rapid handling of customer orders
- Reliable delivery

- Durable products
- Strong supplier relationships
- Broad distribution channels
- Flexible work force

Despite the up-front costs associated with flexibility, it can save money. Japan spent $3 trillion in domestic plant and equipment from 1986 to 1991. This trend has slowed, but even in 1991 Japan's private industries bought the equivalent of $5,320 U.S. in plant and equipment per person, compared with $2,177 in the United States. These figures reflect the fact that Japan's capital-equipment market is so competitive that its costs are 30 percent lower than those of the United States.

Kao Corporation is an excellent example of the results obtained from improved flexibility. Kao is Japan's largest soap and cosmetics company and is the sixth largest in the world. Its information system supports a distribution effort that allows the company and its wholesalers to deliver products within 24 hours to 280,000 shops, whose average order is just seven items. Kao claims that its information system is so complete that accountants can produce year-end closing statements by noon of the first day of the new year. The information system also includes a test-marketing function that virtually eliminates the time lag between purchase of an item and Kao's knowing about it. This speed allows Kao to assess the success or failure of a new product within two weeks of its launch, thereby greatly reducing the company's reliance on forecasts. Thus Kao's inventories of finished goods, usually needed to buffer against forecast error, tend to be exact.

Source "Brace for Japan's Hot New Strategy," *Fortune*, September 21, 1992, 62–74.

Moreover, the need to shorten the product development cycle in order to get new products to the market faster has increased the use of cross-functional teams. Cross-functional teams allow complex processes, such as the design of a new product, to be done with parallel rather than sequential tasks. The ability to accomplish multiple tasks at the same time, rather than one after another, provides great savings in time.

Time-based competition requires the effective management of three cycles:

The make/market loop: The time necessary to take an order, manufacture it, and deliver the product to the customer

CUTTING-EDGE COMPANIES

BOX 4.3

Intel Beats the Clock

Few industries provide as elegant an example of the importance of time in business strategy as the computer chip industry. Intel dominates the market for microprocessors used in personal computers made by every manufacturer except Apple. Intel controls this market so tightly that its customers must wait for the latest chips before they can produce new models of PCs. The Pentium chip, also known as the 586, is the successor to the 486. Even though the Pentium was released in March 1993, Intel customers were told not to release Pentium-based machines until May. A customer that didn't agree to this policy would not be one of the first to receive the chips and would not be one of the first producers into the market with a Pentium-based PC.

Intel's successful strategy is dependent on its ability to bring out a new chip every three or four years and on the fact that it takes its competitors about three years to develop chips that duplicate Intel's. Intel develops a new chip that supersedes its previous one quickly, then sells it at a premium price. By the time the competition enters the market with a duplicate, thereby driving the price of the chip down, Intel is ready with the next generation. The rival chips, because they are based on "old" technology, must then sell very cheaply.

Source "Newest Chip Computes More Success," *USA Today,* March 10, 1993, sec. B, 1, 2.

The design/development loop: The time between a product's conception and when it begins to make a profit

The strategic-thrust loop: The time between the start of a new business or identification of a new strategy and the new business or strategy's actually showing effect.[12]

For the customer of a manufactured product, the response times for purchased components or raw materials define how far into the future demand for finished goods or services must be forecast. If suppliers can reduce response times, their customers do not need to order far in advance, and hence do not need to forecast far into the future. This is advantageous because short-term forecasts are much more accurate than long-term forecasts. Thus better plans and schedules become possible.

The competitive priorities reviewed here provide opportunities for a firm to differentiate itself from its competitors. They translate directly into the ability to attract customers and win orders. A company's managers' hope is that enhancements to price, quality, dependability, flexibility, and time will put the company in a better competitive position, bring an increase in demand, and result in increased revenues. There are often necessary trade-offs among the competitive priorities, however. That is, improvements in one criterion may come at the expense of another. For example, increased levels of flexibility may require increased investment in equipment, which may increase costs and drive up prices.

By establishing its priorities, an organization achieves focus, thus ensuring that the corporate, business, and functional strategies are consistent and mutually supportive. Without the linkage brought about by priority setting, decisions made in the operations function would probably be inconsistent with the desired pattern of decision making prescribed by the business and corporate strategies.

---

[12]G. E. Spanner, J. P. Nuno, and C. Chandra, "Time-Based Strategies—Theory and Practice," *Long Range Planning* 26 (August 1993): 90–101.

Some decisions related to trade-offs are easy to make. For example, a company would be unlikely to double the cost of an item in order to reduce the customer response time from ten days to nine. Other trade-offs are much more difficult. It is hard to quantify the impact of improved quality, dependability, flexibility, or response time in order to compare it to the required costs of making the improvement. For this reason, improvements that reduce the price are often given priority over other improvements, simply because they are easier to quantify and therefore easier to justify.

Even though managers often recognize the potential benefits of an investment, they often leave nonfinancial data out of the analysis of a proposal because its presence might trigger the biases of a corporation's financial staff.[13] The decisions made in the capital budgeting process require management to compare the costs and revenues of a proposal to a base case.[14] Many managers assume that the base case is a continuation of the status quo, from internal and external perspectives. The true costs of an action, however, must be developed from assuming that competitors will take action. For example, a comparison of the costs and revenues of increasing flexibility to a base case of not increasing flexibility would not be adequate if it included an assumption that competitors' flexibility will continue unchanged. The base case must include the scenario of competitors' increasing their flexibility as well. Revenue projections must therefore include changes in market share resulting from increased competitiveness of competitors. This point, examined in detail by Hayes, Wheelwright, and Clark, is crucial when evaluating investment decisions that directly affect those resources that provide certain competitive capabilities.

Unquestionably, one of the weakest links in the strategy implementation process is the inability to know whether each decision made at the functional level supports the corporate- and business-level strategies. This difficulty is a direct result of the complexity of organizations and the inadequacies of many performance measurement systems. Some of the new management philosophies described in the next four chapters address this problem.

As organizations have grown in size and complexity, it has become clear that what is best for one department is not necessarily best for the firm. Not only is it difficult to know if a specific decision is consistent with strategic objectives, but it is also often difficult to know if a specific decision will positively affect profit, even in the short term.

STRUCTURAL DECISIONS
Decisions that include determinations of capacity, facilities, technology, and vertical integration.

INFRASTRUCTURAL DECISIONS
Decisions that include determinations of work force, quality, production and inventory control, and organizational structure.

STRATEGIC DECISION CATEGORIES

After a firm has identified the competitive priorities it will emphasize, it must translate these priorities into patterns of decisions. The strategic operations decision categories are of two types, structural and infrastructural.[15] The categories of **structural decisions** include capacity, facilities, technology, and vertical integration. The categories of **infrastructural decisions** consist of management systems used to determine structural issues. They include work force, quality, production and inventory control, and organization. Decisions are made within these categories, consistent with the limits established by the competitive priorities. Both structural and infrastructural decisions can be related to the management tasks of organizing, planning, controlling, and improving. Infrastructural

---

[13]Hayes, Wheelwright, and Clark, 77–79.
[14]Hayes, Wheelwright, and Clark, 74–75.
[15]Hayes, Wheelwright, and Clark, 21.

TABLE 4.2	Operations Strategic Decision Categories

	Categories	Examples
Structural Decisions	Capacity	High- or low-volume equipment, timing, flexibility
	Facilities	Location, size, function, design
	Process technology	Type of equipment, degree of automation, layout
	Vertical integration/vendors	Linkages to other businesses, direction of integration, balance
Infrastructural Decisions	Human resources	Skill level, salary, security
	Quality	Prevention versus detection, control mechanisms, specifications
	Production planning/ materials control	Make versus buy, inventory planning and control, vendor and outsourcing policies
	New product development	Sequential versus parallel activities, use of teams
	Performance measurement and reward	Focus on individual versus group performance, types of meaures
	Organization/systems	Organization structure, line and staff relationships

Source Adapted from Hayes and Wheelwright, *Restoring Our Competitive Edge: Competing through Manufacturing,* p. 31 and Hayes, Wheelwright, and Clark, *Dynamic Manufacturing,* p. 351.

decisions tend to be of an organizing nature so that systems are developed to facilitate planning, controlling, and improving structural decisions. These categories and examples of applicable decisions are presented in Table 4.2.

STRUCTURAL DECISIONS

Capacity decisions deal with how much is produced and in what time period. A company can obtain capacity before it is needed, as it is needed, or after it is needed. The appropriate time for increasing capacity depends on factors such as the incremental cost of increasing capacity, the importance of capturing market share, and the capacity of competitors in the same industry. Increasing capacity after the need has been established entails the least risk and allows for full utilization of existing facilities. Basing capacity on predicted growth involves significant risk if the expected demand does not materialize but can provide significant gains in market share early in the product life cycle.

The most significant impacts of capacity decisions are on the competitive priorities of price, dependability, flexibility, and time. Price is affected because of the large investment required to obtain capacity. Dependability, flexibility, and time are linked to capacity because levels of excess and protective capacity contribute to a firm's ability to respond quickly to change.

Facilities decisions concern the number, size, location, and the specific nature of facilities. Location, for example, is important for service organizations which do not produce a tangible product. Banks, motels, and fast-food restaurants cannot operate unless they are near customers. Manufacturers whose products are very bulky or heavy must also consider location, as such products and their inputs are costly to transport.

A larger number of widely dispersed, smaller facilities can provide better customer service in both the service and manufacturing sectors by reducing customer lead times. They can also reduce production costs by allowing for lower levels of finished goods inventories and decreased distribution costs. Economies of scale may, however, enter into the decision. Facilities need to be large enough to justify their operating costs, but enlarging a facility does not necessarily guarantee a lower cost per unit. Facility decisions are key determinants of a firm's ability to compete on the basis of price and time. Price is influenced not only because of the facility investment but also because location dictates transportation costs. Time is linked to facility decisions because transportation time is a major component of the customer response time.

Process technology decisions involve how items and services will be produced in order to meet demand. The decision makers consider the appropriate way to produce the product or service, given the price, quality, delivery patterns, degree of flexibility, and response time necessary to accomplish strategic objectives. They evaluate the use of technologies in manufacturing, such as robotics, computer-assisted design/computer-assisted manufacturing (CAD/CAM), and flexible manufacturing systems, and in services, the use of automation and reduced customer contact models. Variables such as volume, lot size requirements, the degree of interaction with the customer, and the amount of customization/standardization are influenced by the choice of process technology and must be considered as well. Process technology decisions seek to bring about improvements in the competitive capabilities of price, quality, and flexibility. Process technology choices result in significant influence on costs because different technologies have different costs. Different technology choices also result in different levels of quality and flexibility.

VERTICAL INTEGRATION DECISIONS
Choices an organization makes about the portion of a product or service it will produce itself as opposed to what it will purchase.

Vertical integration decisions deal with the portion of the product or service an organization will produce itself versus the portion it will purchase and the extent to which it will market, distribute, and sell the product. Vertical integration of suppliers is referred to as upstream or backward integration and has significant impact on the firm's supply base. The selection of the total number of suppliers, the number of suppliers for a specific purchased item, and the types of relationships developed with suppliers are all key decisions within this category. The primary impact of vertical integration on competitive capabilities is the effect that it has on price and quality. Price is influenced by vertical integration decisions because of the impact that suppliers' prices have on material costs. Most organizations seek to increase their control of raw material or purchased item quality through backward integration. This is typically done to increase quality levels. However, outsourcing is occasionally adopted as a means of maintaining or increasing levels of quality without taking on the costs that would be incurred by producing in-house. (See Box 4.4.)

INFRASTRUCTURAL DECISIONS

Human resources decisions entail employee selection, training, compensation, and issues of work force welfare. Specific decisions relate to the required employee skill level, employee benefits, the required levels of employee responsibility, and the commitment of the organization to the individual. The importance of the role that human resources plays in

CUTTING-EDGE COMPANIES

BOX 4.4

A Make–Buy Decision

Kevin Voecks is chief loudspeaker designer for Snell Acoustics, a high-end producer of audio speakers. In an interview with *Stereophile* magazine, he described how quality requirements and cost considerations led to the company's decision to purchase speaker drivers rather than manufacture them. (Speaker drivers convert electronic signals to magnetic energy, which moves the speaker and produces sonic vibration.) Voecks described how Snell decided to outsource. First, Snell considered that companies that specialize in manufacturing drivers can probably do it better than a company that doesn't have that specialty. Snell's expertise is in designing and building speakers not speaker drivers. Second, in building electronic devices of this type, some will be less than perfect. The manufacturer must be able to do something with the rejects.

Snell's requirements are stringent and result in some drivers not being up to its high standards. Some companies use the same drivers in all speaker models and put those of lower quality in the less expensive speakers. Others sell the reject drivers to hobbyists who are not as particular about driver quality. Neither of these alternatives was acceptable to Snell Acoustics. The company wanted only perfect drivers and did not want to be burdened with finding an outlet for those that didn't meet that standard. Outsourcing results in the manufacturer's supplying Snell with perfect drivers and selling the defective ones to people with lower standards.

Source "Loudspeakers, Crossovers, and Rooms," *Stereophile,* March 1990, 100–112.

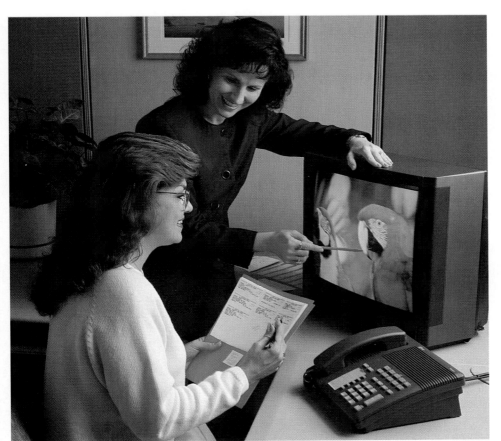

An empowered work force gives AT&T a competitive edge in the global marketplace. AT&T's Workplace of the Future, a model of labor/management cooperation, involves employees and unions in planning and decision making. Such cooperation benefits customers with improved quality goods and services, increases employees' sense of job fulfillment, and improves the company's flexibility. Shown here is a production associate and coach, examining the graphics of a Still-Image Phone produced at AT&T's Shreveport Works plant.

Source © Frank Moscati.

any organization is finally being recognized. Human resources decisions significantly affect the competitive priorities of price and quality, and employee characteristics affect direct and indirect labor costs. Increased levels of skills and responsibility increase costs, but they also improve levels of quality, creating one of many trade-offs.

Quality decisions relate to how well the quality of the product or service meets customers' expectations. Product and service quality is determined by a variety of issues including the process design, engineering specifications, quality of the materials used, and the execution and control of the production processes. Because quality is directly related to meeting customers' needs, the ability of a firm to incorporate changes into the production processes to meet customers' needs must also be considered. Quality decisions not only affect a firm's ability to compete on the basis of quality, but they also influence costs.

Production planning and materials control decisions must be able to support a delivery system that can provide the customer with the right product or service in the right quantities at the right time. They determine how scheduling and other short-term planning and control tasks are accomplished and contribute to the success or failure of these efforts. These decisions include such issues as inventory management and production scheduling and control. A firm's ability to compete on the basis of dependability, flexibility, and time are affected by planning and control decisions.

New product development consists of decisions related to new products, such as quantity, sequencing, and timing. Organizations can choose to become innovative, or they can imitate existing products. These decisions relate closely to flexibility and time because they dictate the processes involved in getting a product or service from its idea phase to the marketplace.

Performance measurement and reward systems refer to the process of assessing performance so that control mechanisms can be incorporated to ensure that plans are achieved. Performance measures that are not in line with desired outcomes result in frustrated employees and poor morale as well as difficulty in reaching objectives. Measures within functional departments must be consistent with actions required to support business- and corporate-level strategies. Performance measures affect all of the competitive priorities because they are the means by which improvement is demonstrated and encouraged.

Decisions related to the organization/systems used to manage operations consist of the number of levels of management, the number of divisions within the operations function, and the extent to which responsibility and authority are provided to all levels of the work force. Organization structure decisions affect price because of their impact on human resources decisions. Dependability, flexibility, and time are affected because the organization's structure shapes its ability to respond to customers and to environmental change.

Notice how the strategic operations decision categories compare to the short-term operations decision categories of process, inventory, work force, and facilities and equipment presented in chapter 1. Because of the different nature of strategic decision making and the focus on structure and infrastructure, they are somewhat different, but strategic operation decisions and short-term operations decisions overlap substantially. This overlap should not be surprising because the day-to-day decision-making patterns relevant to process, inventory, work force, and facilities and equipment are the means by which a company carries out its strategies.

Figure 4.3 presents a flow diagram of the strategy formulation process. It shows the corporate strategy, business strategy, and operations strategy and how the hierarchy of strategies provides necessary input through the ranking of competitive priorities to structural and infrastructural decisions. Control mechanisms must exist to evaluate and compare actual decisions to strategic plans to ensure that the strategy is being implemented effectively. These controls are represented in the Figure as feedback and control loops.

FIGURE 4.3   **Operations Strategy and Development Hierarchy**

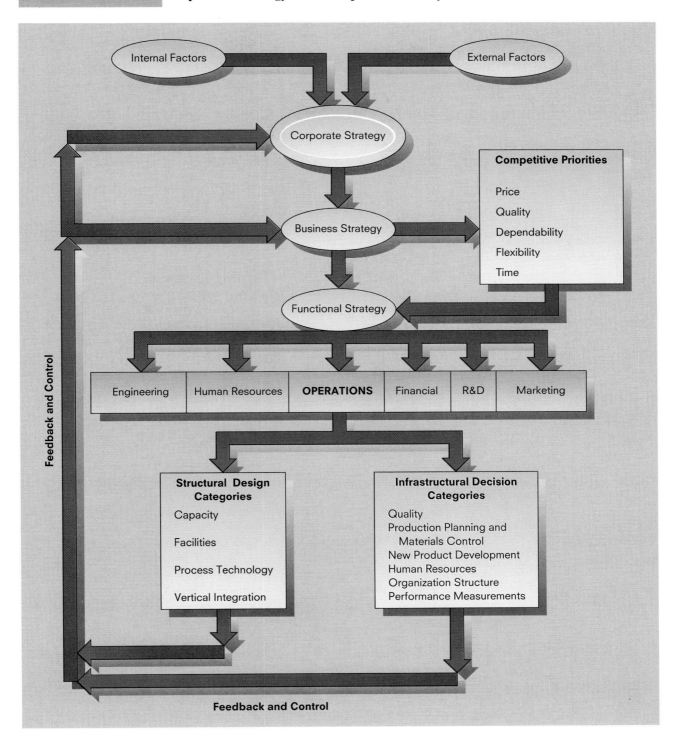

FIGURE 4.4   **Strategic Management Process**

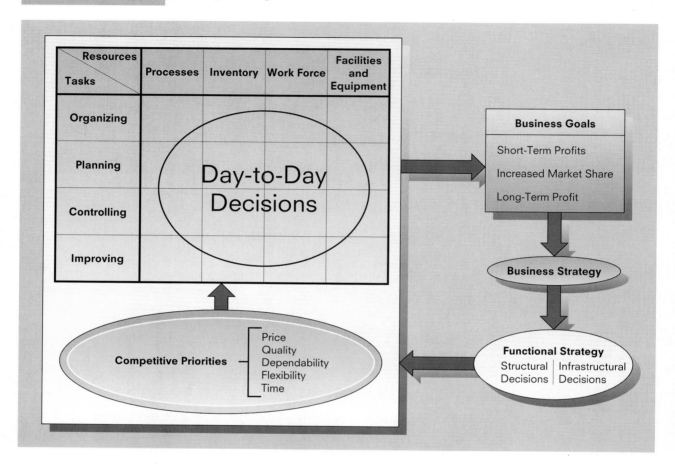

The strategic management process is a continuous loop of examining internal and external factors, incorporating needed changes into the strategic plan, and through functional strategies, ensuring that it is implemented and drives day-to-day decision-making patterns. The results of these day-to-day decisions are examined and provide further input to the process. In operations, the strategic plan drives day-to-day decision making through the five competitive priorities. Figure 4.4 presents this process as it relates to the task/resource model of operations.

PRODUCT AND SERVICE DESIGN

Once the strategy formulation process has extended to the point of establishing competitive priorities, these priorities not only guide day-to-day decisions but they also provide an input to the actual product or service design process.

One of the outcomes of the last decade of regaining U.S. competitiveness has been a recognition that the sources of product and service quality are in all functions of the business. This recognition has spawned an increased emphasis in team approaches to product and service design because they allow quality, as it relates to all functions, to be designed into the product or service. The ability to design quality into a product or service, rather than trying to identify defects after the fact, requires a merging of both product and process technologies.

Traditional approaches to product and service development have included a series of sequential steps, each performed by different business functions. For today's firms to remain competitive by quickly providing the quality products that the market wants requires that team members within the firms communicate intensely so they can perform parallel tasks.

GLOBAL ISSUES

As organizations seek to compete in the global marketplace, they need a change in perspective. For some, the changes will come because they will work with organizations in different countries. For many global organizations, the role that information technology plays will change how business is conducted. Technology will allow sales representatives, distributors, retailers, and suppliers to communicate directly to a factory regardless of its location. Product design teams around the world will communicate via fax and satellite transmission, and computer-aided design workstations and information networks will link designers, engineers, and suppliers to one another so they can design, produce, and sell new products in much less time than is now required.[16] Information technology will serve as one method of overcoming large distances that global competition creates.

Some organizations, including 3M, Heinz, IBM, Hewlett-Packard, and General Electric, suggest that a new kind of management structure is required to manage organizations that compete globally. These organizations use the team approach that links designers, engineers, and marketers to one another to speed communications and information flow. The right mix of global, regional, and local components must be assembled to satisfy the needs of the marketplace. Traditional hierarchical organization structures cannot accomplish the necessary tasks quickly enough to be competitive, and they are being replaced by decentralized team-based structures. The team approach not only reduces communication problems but also allows different sets of activities to be completed simultaneously.

Competing globally has also created the existence of joint ventures and other forms of strategic alliances that provide access to markets, technology, or key parts and materials. A joint venture is an alliance in which both partners share equally in the responsibility. Alliances vary significantly in terms of time frame and commitment. These forms of global sourcing have typically resulted in lower costs, greater availability and in some cases, improved quality.[17]

The joint ventures and strategic alliances may be an early form of what is called the virtual corporation. The virtual corporation is a temporary network of independent compa-

[16]J. D. Goldhar and D. Lei, "The Shape of the Twenty-first Century Global Manufacturing," *The Journal of Business Strategy* 12 (March-April 1991): 37–41.

[17]M. L. Fagan, "A Guide to Global Sourcing," *The Journal of Business Strategy* (March/April 1991): 21–25.

CUTTING-EDGE COMPANIES

BOX 4.5

Global Implications for L. L. Bean

For L. L. Bean, renowned as the benchmark for mail-order distribution systems, the impact of the new globalization of business is here. L. L. Bean projects that approximately 10 percent to 13 percent of its 1994 revenues will come from international sales. That's twice as much as in 1992. There are currently two stores in Japan, and a third is projected to open there. The company employs 200 sales representatives in its international department. (During the holiday season, L. L. Bean has a total of 3,000.) Most of its international business is from Japan—70 percent, and nearly a third of that business is conducted by fax machine. The international sales reps speak a total of 14 languages, and 11 of them speak Japanese.

Source "Firm Takes Season Rush in Stride," *USA Today,* December 17–19, 1993, sec. A, 1, 2.

nies linked by information technology to share skills, costs, and access to one another's markets. For example, a product design firm would decide what to make, a manufacturing firm would make the product, and a marketing firm would sell the product. Thus, what an organization does best can be linked with the strengths of other organizations, producing superior products and getting them to the market more quickly.[18]

Some businesses choose to adapt to the global marketplace because their customers are from a different country, not their suppliers. (See Box 4.5.) The concept of value is customer focused. Different cultures have different value systems. A product that does extremely well in the United States may have no demand in another culture, and service that is defined as high quality in the United States may not meet another country's standards.

For the first ten years of what has been a global marketplace, U.S. businesses have struggled with ways to compete with foreign companies on U.S. soil. Finally, U.S. businesses are reaching the point where they are looking for ways to compete with foreign companies on *their* soil.

OPERATIONS STRATEGY AND NEW DIRECTIONS

One of the most important strategic developments in operations management during the past decade has been the concept of continuous improvement. The continuous improvement theme influences strategic decisions and places organizations in a dynamic position in which they instigate change and don't merely respond to it.

Structural and infrastructural decisions are dramatically affected by continuous improvement efforts. Improvements are made in the use of capacity, facilities, and technology. Improvements in supply requirements may have implications for vertical integration. Improvements in quality are obtained by improvements in all other categories, particularly in production planning/materials control. Work force improvements are predominantly obtained through the organization.

---

[18] J. A. Byrne, R. Brandt, and O. Port, "The Virtual Corporation," *Business Week,* February 8, 1993, 98–102.

An organization's structure, reward systems, and line and staff relationships are perhaps most affected by a philosophy of continuous improvement. The role of a worker changes from being primarily physical in nature to include mental activities as well. The key mental activities include identifying and solving problems. Because the role of the work force includes problem-solving skills, process improvement becomes more of an integral part of the system. The work force becomes an active participant in problem-solving activities and is given support by supervisors and other staff personnel. Decision making is pushed to the lowest level possible, creating a management structure with fewer layers.

Significant competitive advantages emerge when decision making takes place at low levels in the organization because the knowledge base improves. Because there are fewer managerial layers, decisions can be made more quickly, creating a quicker response time. As workers acquire a broader range of skills, an organization becomes more flexible. Quality is also enhanced because processes and products continue to improve. This improvement of processes and products also results in cost reduction.

The traditional emphasis of U.S. managers on product improvement, rather than process improvement, shifts to a much more balanced approach under a continuous improvement ideology. This change results in a much more integrated approach to new product development and a stronger link between product and process design. This is evidenced in progressive manufacturing firms by the increased significance of designing for manufacturability. Many firms, however, have had problems implementing continuous improvement programs. In their discussion of the relationships between continuous improvement programs and strategic objectives, Robert H. Hayes and Gary P. Pisano point out that firms encountering difficulties of implementation may be focusing on the mechanics of the process instead of the capabilities and skills that can result.[19] This analysis is consistent with the resource theory of the firm, which credits capabilities derived from grouping resources—not the resources themselves—with the development of competitive advantage. Thus, firms should base their strategies on selling capabilities, rather than products or services; and continuous improvement programs should be veiwed as guides to movement in a direction consistent with competitive objectives, rather than as solutions in themselves.

SUMMARY

The inability of many American manufacturing firms to compete effectively at the international level has had a major impact on the U.S. economy and is sending a warning to service industries that have yet to face significant competition from abroad. A new and dedicated effort is under way to reestablish American businesses as competitive forces. One approach is to use the operations function as a competitive weapon, through the development of an operations strategy and the implementation of new management philosophies that enable a firm to improve competitive performance. This process cannot be merely a top-down approach. The corporate and business strategies must be designed to take advantage of the competencies available throughout the organization, and specifically those available in the operations function. This means that not only must business and functional strategies be consistent with the corporate strategy, but corporate and business strategies must also consider functional capabilities during their conception.

---

[19]R. H. Hayes and G. P. Pisano, "Beyond World-Class: The New Manufacturing Strategy," *Harvard Business Review* 72 (January-February 1994): 77–86.

QUESTIONS FOR REVIEW

1. What reasons did the MIT commission report give to explain why the United States has been unable to compete internationally?
2. What are the five components that provide focus to an organization's strategy?
3. What is the difference between strategy formulation and strategy implementation?
4. Describe the product life cycle.
5. In what ways should a functional level strategy relate to the corporate level strategy?
6. What is continuous improvement?
7. What role do continuous improvement programs play in the development of competitive advantage?

QUESTIONS FOR THOUGHT AND DISCUSSION

1. Compare strategy planning for services with that for manufacturing.
2. Suppose an organization has adopted a continuous improvement philosophy. Which of the strategy decision categories are affected? How are these categories affected?
3. Discuss whether you believe the United States will be able to be competitive at the international level during the decade of the nineties. Justify your response.
4. Suppose you are the head of strategic planning for Taco Taco, a national chain of Mexican fast-food restaurants. Identify and discuss the internal and external factors relevant to your strategy.
5. Suppose a manufacturer of home appliances produced the total demand for the year for dishwashers in one long production run, then produced the total demand for the year for refrigerators, and produced all other appliances in the same fashion. You start a company that can produce in, one week, the approximate demand for the entire line of products for the next week. You have this capability from the entire year. Discuss the advantages and disadvantages of your system compared to that of the other manufacturer. Upon which competitive priority are you focusing?
6. What are some examples of products that made it only to the introductory stage of the life cycle? What are some products that never seem to decline?
7. Why is the time it takes to get a product from its initial conception to the market more critical when product life cycles are short?

INTEGRATIVE QUESTIONS

1. What are the strategic implications of volume and layout decisions for services and manufacturers?
2. What is the link between manufacturing process design decisions and the firm's product development capabilities?
3. How do process design decisions affect service design and development?

SUGGESTED READINGS

Agarwal, R. "The Strategic Challenge of the Evolving Global Economy." *Business Horizons* 30 (July-August 1987): 38–44.

Bower, J. L., and Hout, T. M. "Fast-Cycle Capability for Competitive Power." *Harvard Business Review* 66 (November-December 1988): 110–118.

Davidow, W. H., and Uttal, B. "Service Companies: Focus or Falter." *Harvard Business Review* 67 (July-August 1989): 77–85.

Haas, E. A. "Breakthrough Manufacturing." *Harvard Business Review* 65 (March-April 1987): 75–81.

Hayes, R. H. "Strategic Planning—Forward in Reverse." *Harvard Business Review* 63 (November–December 1985): 111–119.

Hayes, R. H., and Pisano, G. P. "Beyond World-Class: The New Manufacturing Strategy." *Harvard Business Review* 72 (January-February 1994): 77–86.

Heskett, J. L. "Lessons in the Service Sector." *Harvard Business Review* 65 (March-April 1987): 118–126.

Hill, T., and Chambers, Stuart. "Flexibility—A Manufacturing Conundrum." *International Journal of Operations and Production Management* 11 (1991): 5–13.

Kumpe, T., and Bolwijn, P. T. "Manufacturing: The New Case for Vertical Integration." *Harvard Business Review* 66 (March-April 1988): 75–81.

Potts, G. W. "Exploit Your Product's Service Life Cycle." *Harvard Business Review* 66 (September-October 1988): 33–36.

Quinn, J. B., Doorley, T. L., and Paquette, P. C. "Beyond Products: Services-Based Strategy." *Harvard Business Review* 68 (March-April 1990): 58–67.

Safizadeh, M. H. "The Case of Workgroups in Manufacturing Operations." *California Management Review* 33 (Summer 1991): 61–82.

Shetty, Y. K. "Product Quality and Competitive Strategy." *Business Horizons* 30 (May-June 1987): 46–52.

Stalk, G., Jr. "Time—The Next Source of Competitive Advantage." *Harvard Business Review* 66 (July-August 1988): 41–51.

Vesey, J. T. "The New Competitors: They Think in Terms of 'Speed-to-Market'." *Academy of Management Review* 5 (April 1991): 23–33.

Walton, R. E., and Susman, G. I. "People Policies for the New Machines." *Harvard Business Review* 65 (March-April 1987): 98–106.

Wheelwright, S. C., and Hayes, R. H. "Competing Through Manufacturing." *Harvard Business Review* 63 (January-February 1985): 99–109.

Whitney, D. E. "Manufacturing by Design." *Harvard Business Review* 66 (July-August 1988): 83–91.

PART II

NEW DIRECTIONS IN
OPERATIONS MANAGEMENT

"**W**hy're inventory levels so low?" a product manager argues. "You're the warehouse manager. How come you can't keep enough high-speed drills on hand to meet WeeBee Hardware's last-minute order? They're our biggest customer! You think they're gonna hang around just waiting on us to get our act together?" ■ "What do you mean you can't ship those bits until you get final approval for quality assurance?" a sales rep shouts. "That order's gotta go out today, or I won't make my weekly quota! And there goes my bonus . . . right out the window!" ■ "What's with this new accounting system?" the cost accountant mutters as he sits through a week-long training seminar. "There's no point in all this change. Cost is cost. A dollar's a dollar." ■ It's difficult to pick up any business publication, or even a newspaper, without encountering stories of dramatic changes in U.S. businesses. Although some changes have come about through advances in technology, like robotics or computer imaging, many are the result of changes in management philosophy brought about by increased levels of competition in the global marketplace. "Business as usual" isn't usual anymore. ■ In Part II we take an in-depth look at the three dominant management philosophies in today's business: just-in-time, total quality management, and constraint management. While each of these prescribes somewhat different tactics, they are all striving to gain similar objectives. All three acknowledge the fact that it's impossible to evaluate day-to-day decisions on the basis of such broad measures as profit or return on investment. Instead, these philosophies offer more immediate, precise guidelines for decision making and provide techniques that can help firms enhance performance, improve quality, and lower costs. ■

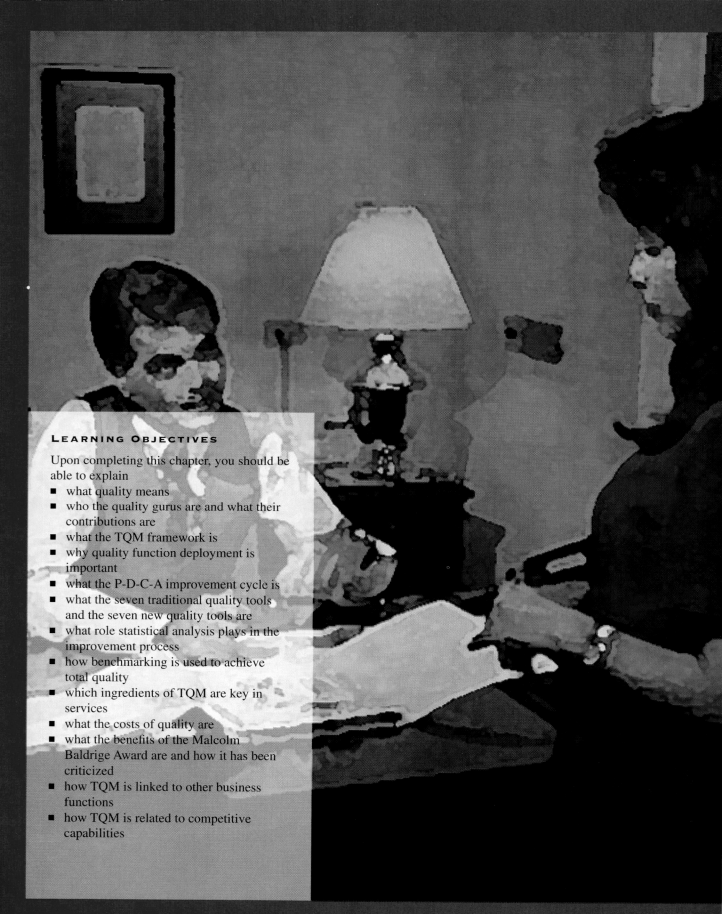

LEARNING OBJECTIVES

Upon completing this chapter, you should be able to explain
- what quality means
- who the quality gurus are and what their contributions are
- what the TQM framework is
- why quality function deployment is important
- what the P-D-C-A improvement cycle is
- what the seven traditional quality tools and the seven new quality tools are
- what role statistical analysis plays in the improvement process
- how benchmarking is used to achieve total quality
- which ingredients of TQM are key in services
- what the costs of quality are
- what the benefits of the Malcolm Baldrige Award are and how it has been criticized
- how TQM is linked to other business functions
- how TQM is related to competitive capabilities

CHAPTER 5

TOTAL QUALITY MANAGEMENT

CROSS-LINKS **Hospital Trades Accuracy for Better Bedside Manner**

Smith-Taylor Memorial is a regional hospital in a small midwestern town just 60 miles from a large metropolitan center. Like other small hospitals, it has been hit hard by rising costs and declining occupancy. Under a new chief administrator, Smith-Taylor has done a number of things to increase its popularity and regain market share lost to the larger metropolitan hospitals.
■ Victoria Sanchez, accounts manager for Smith-Taylor Memorial, enjoyed her job despite the fact that much of the contact she had with customers was, in her words, "of a less-than-positive nature." It was her responsibility to contact patients who had not settled account balances, and she was usually the person that patients chastised when there were errors in billing statements. She enjoyed the challenge, however, and prided herself on attention to detail and accuracy. Her relationship with the hospital staff was good, but she always felt like a bit of an outsider. Doctors and nurses always seemed so busy with one crisis after another that they had little time to talk. ■ After several years of declining revenues, it appeared that Smith-Taylor had finally turned things around. Thousands of dollars spent on staff training, process improvement, computers, and new diagnostic equipment seemed to be having a payoff. The complete renovation of the birthing center and the new focus on family involvement were probably the best move Smith-Taylor had ever made. Young adults starting new families seemed to be content with the small and intimate center, which was so different from the chaotic and impersonal metropolitan centers. As an outsider, Victoria could also observe that the patient interaction training provided to nursing staff had also had an effect. Nurses had become more sensitive to patients' needs, and their at-

tention was having a direct effect on patient attitudes. Victoria even noticed an improvement in patients' disposition after they left the hospital and were paying their bills. Although she was skeptical at first, it appeared that the quality emphasis initiated by the new chief administrator was working. She was surprised at the changes that could take place in just one year. ■ As new approaches and training requirements began to require fewer hours, Allen Hoyt, the chief administrator, began to focus on routine practices. One of the tasks that had been put off was an audit of all patient charts. This was typically done yearly, but it was seven months late. There were thousands of charts from the past 19 months to check for accuracy, and it would take at least two months to complete the audit. ■ In late August the phone calls began. The audit of patient charts was progressing and had already identified hundreds of missed charges. Since the audit started with the oldest charts, these claims were nearly two years old. Claims were sent to patients' insurance companies and were being paid as fast as they could be processed. The insurance companies understood the process and were quite cooperative. Patients were another matter, however. Most patients were on insurance plans that required them to pay 20 percent of the charge. The bills began to go out to patients the third week in August. ■ Patients were more upset than Victoria had ever seen. They didn't understand why, after almost two years, they were being billed for parts of their hospital stays. As the audit team progressed chronologically through the charts, they found that the accuracy of the charts diminished. It appeared that paperwork mistakes increased as the quality of patient/staff interaction improved. ■ The patients Victoria called had become so heated that Victoria made an appointment with Allen Hoyt. Because he didn't interact directly with patients, he was somewhat isolated from their responses. She wanted him to be aware of the anger many of these people were expressing. Allen then contacted the audit team, which reinforced what Victoria had told him. The chart audit was exposing a tremendous amount of errors, averaging more than one charge omission per bed-night. ■   Allen faced a quandary. This process could destroy all of the gains the hospital had made in the past year, but writing off 20 percent of the charges exposed in the audit could make the difference between success or failure for the year. His instincts told him that he had to write off the charges or lose the loyalty of the offended patients. He also knew that the decision to write off these charges would have to be made by the board of trustees. He didn't doubt that they would agree with him, but they would also want to know what he had done to prevent such a fiasco from happening again. Allen needed a plan. ■

Over the past two decades the concept of quality has changed dramatically in the United States. As late as the 1970s, quality-related activities for most organizations were centered in a quality control department that had complete charge of all quality functions. Today, in many successful organizations, quality suggests a companywide effort focused on satisfying the customer. This approach, which has become a management philosophy, involves all aspects of the organization and leads to a process of continuous improvement. Continuous improvement is one of the dominant themes in this chapter as well as in chapters 6, 7 and 8. Both continuous improvement and quality are now approached from a global perspective.

For most organizations, quality plays a major role in defining how well organizations will compete. The loss of market share by many U.S. industries has been linked to a perception that U.S. products lack quality. Labovitz, Chang, and Rosansky make a strong case for having customers perceive a product as being a quality product.[1] Their analysis is based on the Profit Impact of Market Strategy (PIMS) project that studied 3,000 business units. The results indicated that those businesses that ranked in the top fifth in terms of customer-perceived quality had a pretax return on investment of more than 30 percent, but those in the bottom two-fifths had a pretax return on investment of 16 percent. Labovitz, Chang, and Rosansky also summarized a 1991 report from the U.S. General Accounting Office, which indicated that companies that used total quality management practices had better employee relations, greater customer satisfaction, increased market share and improved profitability.[2]

WHAT IS QUALITY?

Expressions such as *quality, quality assurance, quality control, total quality, total quality management,* and *total quality control* have all been used to reflect our understanding of the changing concept of quality. Philip B. Crosby[3] defines quality as "conformance to re-

---

[1]G. Labovitz, Y. S. Chang, and V. Rosansky, *Making Quality Work* (New York: HarperCollins, 1993), 48–50.
[2]Labovitz, Chang, and Rosansky, 49.
[3]Philip B. Crosby, *Quality Is Free* (New York: McGraw Hill, 1979), 2.

quirements," while J. M. Juran defines it as "fitness for use."[4] These definitions demonstrate two of the many perspectives on quality.

There are five different approaches to defining quality.[5] **User-based quality** refers to a product's or service's fitness for use. This approach is based upon the concept that quality lies in the eyes of the beholder. **Manufacturer-based quality** refers to the product or service's conformance to specifications. This perspective focuses primarily on engineering or manufacturing practices. **Transcendent quality** is an ideal or a condition of excellence. This perspective suggests that quality cannot easily be defined, but it can be understood only after exposure to a number of objects that display quality characteristics. **Value-based quality** is the degree of excellence at an acceptable price. Quality is defined in terms of costs and or prices, and a quality product is one that provides performance at an acceptable price. **Product-based quality** is based upon a product characteristic or attribute. A higher quality item would have more of a desirable characteristic, like a greater density of fiber content in a carpet or a larger percentage of real orange juice in a citrus punch.

It has also been suggested that the different approaches to defining quality are related to the different views held by different functional departments. Marketing, for example, often takes a user-based approach, while operations and engineering focus more on conformance to specifications.

Garvin identified eight dimensions of product quality.[6] Pisek extended and modified these to include services as well.[7] The dimensions are described below.

Performance deals with specific characteristics of the product or service. It may refer to something like the life expectancy in miles of an automobile tire or the time required to successfully respond to a customer's needs.

Features relate to additional capabilities or characteristics that can accompany a product or service. A calculator, for example, may have features that give it the capability to store dates, phone numbers, or messages as well as the normal mathematical functions. A car dealership's feature may be an additional service; it may offer to drive customers to work when they leave their car for repair and to pick them up when their car is ready.

Reliability measures the consistency of performance of the item. For products, this means the item always works. In services, for example, the overnight mail delivery is *always* made on time.

Durability describes how long the item will last. It is interesting to note that some service organizations, L. L. Bean for instance, allow the customer to determine how durable the product should be by permitting customers to return an item at any time if they are not satisfied with it.

Serviceability refers to the level of difficulty, expense, and time required to repair an item. In services, serviceability refers to how quickly and accurately an organization responds to errors, such as when a restaurant customer says, "My steak is well done, and I asked for it to be medium rare."

Asthetics deals with the senses and may be difficult to measure. How a fabric

---

USER-BASED QUALITY
Quality as defined by a product's or service's fitness for use.

MANUFACTURER-BASED QUALITY
Quality as defined by a product's or service's conformance to specifications.

TRANSCENDENT QUALITY
Quality as defined by an ideal or condition of excellence.

VALUE-BASED QUALITY
Quality as defined by the degree of excellence at an acceptable price.

PRODUCT-BASED QUALITY
Quality as defined by a characteristic or attribute of a product or service.

---

[4]J. M. Juran, *Juran on Planning For Quality* (New York: Free Press, 1988), 11.

[5]David A. Garvin, "What Does Product Quality Really Mean?" *Sloan Management Review* 26 (Fall 1984): 25–34.

[6]Garvin, "What Does Product Quality Really Mean?" 29–30.

[7]Paul E. Pisek, "Defining Quality at the Marketing/Development Interface," *Quality Progress* 20 (June 1987): 28–36.

Stone Container Corporation, a producer of containerboard and corrugated containers, uses advertisements like this one to promote the performance dimension of product quality.

Source Courtesy of Stone Container Corporation.

feels, the sound of a stereo, the smell of fresh brewed coffee, or the taste of a gourmet dessert are all examples of aesthetic experiences.

Response refers to interaction the customer has with the service provider. The interaction may be defined in a variety of ways including courteous, friendly, helpful, or rude.

Reputation describes the past performance of the organization. This may be measured by word of mouth, advice from friends, or reviews in such publications as *Consumer Reports*. It is the perception of the level of quality received and relates to both the reputation of the firm and the customers' experiences with the item.

The total quality management (TQM) philosophy has added the concept of continuous improvement to quality. This concept is reflected in Proctor and Gamble's definition of quality: "The unyielding and continually improving effort by everyone in an organization to understand, meet, and exceed the expectations of the customers."[8] Despite the fact that there may seem to be as many definitions of quality as there are managers, the TQM philosophy brings the concepts together under a focused process of improvement.

THE QUALITY GURUS

Several champions of quality, called quality gurus, have played tremendous roles in elevating the importance of quality to its current position. Three of these individuals are Philip B. Crosby, W. Edwards Deming, and Joseph M. Juran.

CROSBY

Philip B. Crosby has been referred to as the quality evangelist,[9] probably because his approach causes people to change their attitudes. Crosby began in industry as a quality inspector and rose through the industrial ranks to become vice president of quality at ITT. His

[8]Corporate Quality Improvement brochure, Procter & Gamble, January 6, 1989.
[9]J. Macdonald and J. Piggott, *Global Quality: The New Management Culture* (London: Gold Arrow, 1990), 97.

| **TABLE 5.1** | **Crosby's 14 Points** |

1. **Management commitment** to make it clear where management stands on quality.
2. **Quality improvement team** to run the quality improvement program.
3. **Quality measurement** to provide a display of current and potential non-conformance problems in a manner that permits objective evaluation and action.
4. **Cost of quality** to define the ingredients of the cost of quality and explain its use as a management tool.
5. **Quality awareness** to raise the personal concern felt by all personnel.
6. **Corrective action** to provide a systematic method of resolving forever the problems that are identified.
7. **Zero defects planning** to examine the activities that must be conducted in preparation for the zero defects program.
8. **Supervisor training** to define the type of training that supervisors need in order to carry out their part of the program.
9. **ZD day** to create an event that will let all employees realize that there has been a change.
10. **Goal setting** to turn pledges and commitments into action.
11. **Error-cause removal** to give the individual employee a method of communicating to management the situations that make it difficult to improve.
12. **Recognition** to appreciate those who participate.
13. **Quality councils** to bring together the professional quality people for communication on a regualr basis.
14. **Do it over again** to emphasize that the quality improvement program never ends.

Source   Adapted from Philip B. Crosby, *Quality Is Free* (New York: McGraw-Hill, 1979). Used with permission.

main focus has been on top management, and he has attempted to change its attitudes about quality. He believes that as quality improves, overall costs go down, and, he says, quality is free.[10]

According to Crosby, the key ingredients required for quality are a definition that everyone can understand, a system to manage quality, a clear and specific performance standard, and a method for measurement that provides focus on the improvement process.[11] Crosby defines quality as conformance to requirements. His system is prevention, his performance standard is zero defects, and his measurement process is the cost of quality (described later in this chapter). These four ingredients, along with Crosby's 14 points (see Table 5.1), form the basis of his contribution.

DEMING

Dr. W. Edwards Deming has been given much of the credit for revolutionizing quality in Japan. His influence in the United States was insignificant until the 1980s. Deming identifies management and the management systems in place as the primary reasons for poor quality. He recognized that organizations need to change in order to realize significant quality gains and that the responsibility for change rests with management. Although

---

[10]Crosby, *Quality Is Free.*
[11]Macdonald and Piggott, *Global Quality: The New Management Culture,* 99.

TABLE 5.2	Dr. Deming's 14 Points (revised January 1990)

1. **Create and publish to all employees a statement of the aims and purposes of the company or other organization.** The management must demonstrate constantly their commitment to this statement.
2. **Learn the new philosophy,** top management and everybody.
3. **Understand the purpose of inspection,** for improvement of processes and reduction of cost.
4. **End the practice of awarding business on the basis of price tag alone.**
5. **Improve constantly** and forever the system of production and service.
6. **Institute training.**
7. **Teach and institute leadership.**
8. **Drive out fear.** Create trust. Create a climate for innovation.
9. **Optimize toward the aims and purposes of the company** the efforts of teams, groups, staff areas.
10. **Eliminate exhortations** for the work force.
11a. **Eliminate numerical quotas** for production. Instead, learn and institute methods for improvement.
11b. **Eliminate management by objective.** Instead, learn the capabilities of processes, and how to improve them.
12. **Remove barriers** that rob people of pride of workmanship.
13. **Encourage education** and self-improvement for everyone.
14. **Take action** to accomplish the transformation.

Source Reprinted from *Out of the Crisis* by W. Edwards Deming by permission of MIT and The W. Edwards Deming Institute. Published by MIT, Center for Advanced Engineering Study, Cambridge, MA 02139. Copyright 1986 by W. Edwards Deming.

Deming's methods are grounded in the use of statistics, his 14 points cover far more than the use of statistical techniques.

Deming strongly supported systems leading to continuous improvement and, although management must lead the way, insisted that the work force receive the necessary training so they know what they must do and how to do it. His 14 points, presented in Table 5.2, apply to manufacturing and service organizations. His influence in forming and shaping total quality management has been significant. Dr. Deming died in 1993.

JURAN

Joseph M. Juran has had a major impact on quality, both in Japan and in the United States. As early as the 1940s, Juran, a statistician, argued that quality was achieved through people rather than techniques. He, like Deming, believed that management is the cause of the majority of quality problems. Juran's approach to improvement revolved around three basic activities: structured annual improvement plans, massive training programs, and top management leadership. He said that all managers need to have an understanding of quality, and that top management particularly needs a knowledge of quality because quality issues are interdepartmental.

For Juran, the management of quality incorporates three elements—quality planning, quality control, and quality improvement. Quality planning involves providing the operating focus required to produce products that meet customers' needs. Quality control is the process of evaluating performance, comparing actual performance with stated goals, and taking action on the difference. Quality improvement involves analyzing the symptoms of problems, theorizing about the causes, and then testing the theories to confirm the cause. Once the cause has been identified and confirmed, the system can be improved.

THE TQM FRAMEWORK

For many organizations, the quality concept has become an all-encompassing, all-out effort to produce products and provide services that will generate satisfied customers. The commitment to continually focus the organization's efforts on understanding and satisfying the needs of the customer is a major undertaking. The key components required to carry out the TQM process are shown in Figure 5.1 and are based on the work of Deming, Juran, and Crosby.

All three gurus agree that top management is responsible for quality problems and must be involved in and committed to quality. And each has a program that is demanding and difficult to implement. While Deming and Juran emphasize statistical tools and Crosby is more interested in motivation, both Deming and Crosby agree on the need for ongoing efforts to achieve zero defects. Juran's cost of quality concept, however, suggests that zero is not necessarily the optimum number of defects. Deming's popularity is strongest in Japan, where Juran also enjoys many adherents owing to his appeal to scientific and high-technology companies. Crosby's approach has been most effective in changing attitudes and is frequently used in conjunction with other programs.

SATISFYING THE CUSTOMER

The TQM philosophy argues that an organization can best achieve financial results for its investors by ensuring that everyone in the entire organization undertake a relentless and unending pursuit to meet or exceed customers' expectations. Organizations that focus on

---

FIGURE 5.1   **The TQM Framework**

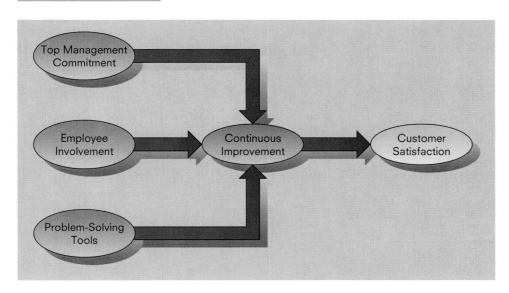

Microsoft has achieved financial success in the marketplace by finding out customer needs. As part of the product definition stage for a new software program, Microsoft developers interview potential customers and follow them around their homes. The information they collect is displayed in this room for review and analysis.

All Microsoft senior executives—including CEO Bill Gates—spend time in the field listening to customers.

Source © 1993 Davis Freeman for Microsoft Corporation.

HOSHIN KANRI
A form of strategic planning that focuses on a few clearly defined customer breakthroughs to be accomplished in the next three to five years.

financial measures will often be faced with conflicts between making short-term profits and satisfying the customer. In that environment, the desire to gain short-term profits—which Deming called one of the seven "deadly diseases"—often wins at the expense of quality. But the long-term bottom line, which requires a commitment to customer satisfaction, is what counts.

The focus on the customer must begin with the strategic plan of the organization. The organization chooses which customers it will satisfy as part of its strategic plan. A form of strategic planning called **hoshin kanri,** which means "policy management" in Japanese, is a type of strategic planning done in Japan. This form of planning focuses on establishing a set of three to five clearly defined customer breakthroughs to be accomplished over a few years. This customer-focused approach identifies those work processes most vital to achieving the breakthrough objectives and focuses on quality improvement activities in these important processes.[12]

Knowing and understanding the customer are absolutely essential. There are two distinct types of customers: internal customers and external customers. Internal customers may be viewed as the next step in a production process or an internal receiver of service or materials. External customers are usually viewed as the final recipients of the product or service. Organizations must know who their customers are, and determine which customers are most important to their organization.

---

[12]Labovitz, Chang, and Rosansky, *Making Quality Work,* 111–120.

One approach used to better understand the customer in services as well as in manufacturing is to focus on the defectors—those customers who no longer patronize the business. Through the study of defectors, one can determine, for example, if the prices are too high, the lines are too long, or the phone system inadequate. And by eliminating such causes for dissatisfaction, an organization can reduce the number of defections.[13]

QUALITY FUNCTION DEPLOYMENT

In 1984 Ford Motor Company implemented **quality function deployment (QFD),** another approach to incorporate customers' needs in the final product both for services and manufacturing. Customers' wants and needs for a specific product have usually been disregarded while a product is being designed. If a customer's needs are taken into account during the design stage, they would likely be lost at a later stage in the manufacturing process. Also, because a number of different departments are involved in design, there are likely many different interpretations of a customer's specifications.[14] Many products fell short of customers' expectations because of these problems, which can be summarized as a lack of a linkage connecting the product or service to what the customer wants.

To solve these problems, in the mid-1980s, American manufacturers borrowed quality function deployment from the Japanese. QFD translates customers' needs into a set of design and manufacturing requirements. It provides the all-important linkage from the product or service to the customers' desires. A key concept related to QFD is the house of quality, depicted in Figure 5.2. The **house of quality** aids in transforming the customers' requirements into engineering and design decisions that will satisfy the customer.

Several variations of the house of quality are used. They all have the following common parts. The WHATs describe the qualities or attributes that the customer says the product or service must contain. The WHATs are compared with those of competitors and are usually ranked according to their importance. The HOWs provide the means of satisfying the WHATs. The HOWs are normally technical in nature and specify the precise requirements.

The correlation matrix, or roof, analyzes the positive or negative relationships among the HOWs and seeks to find the best way of using resources. The relationship matrix evaluates the relationship between the WHATs and the HOWs and identifies the best way to satisfy the customer.

QFD is a four-phase process, consisting of product planning, part deployment, process planning, and production planning, as shown in Figure 5.3.[15] In each phase, a separate house of quality is developed:

- Phase I, **product planning,** focuses on translating customer desires into technical design parameters.
- Phase II, **part deployment,** focuses on product engineering. In this phase, the technical design parameters are transformed into target component characteristics and target values for fit, function, and performance are established.
- Phase III, **process planning,** transforms target values from phase II into process requirements for manufacturing and assembly. In this phase, process

Sidebar definitions

QUALITY FUNCTION DEPLOYMENT (QFD)
A four-phase process that links customer needs and desires to product or service characteristics in the design phase.

HOUSE OF QUALITY
A system of related matrices used in quality function deployment that aids in transforming customer requirements into engineering and design decisions.

PRODUCT PLANNING
Phase I of QFD, which translates customer desires into technical design parameters.

PART DEPLOYMENT
Phase II of QFD, which transforms technical design parameters into parts characteristics and target values.

PROCESS PLANNING
Phase III of QFD, which transforms target values into process requirements for manufacturing.

[13]F. F. Reichheld and W. E. Sasser, Jr., "Zero Defections: Quality Comes to Services," *Harvard Business Review* 68 (September-October 1990): 105–111.

[14]W. E. Euraka and N. Ryan, *The Customer-Driven Company: Managerial Perspectives on QFD* (Dearborn, Mich.: ASI Press, 1988), 16–17.

[15]A. R. Shores, *A TQM Approach to Achieving Manufacturing Excellence* (Milwaukee: ASQ Press, 1990), 266–268.

FIGURE 5.2   **Generic House of Quality**

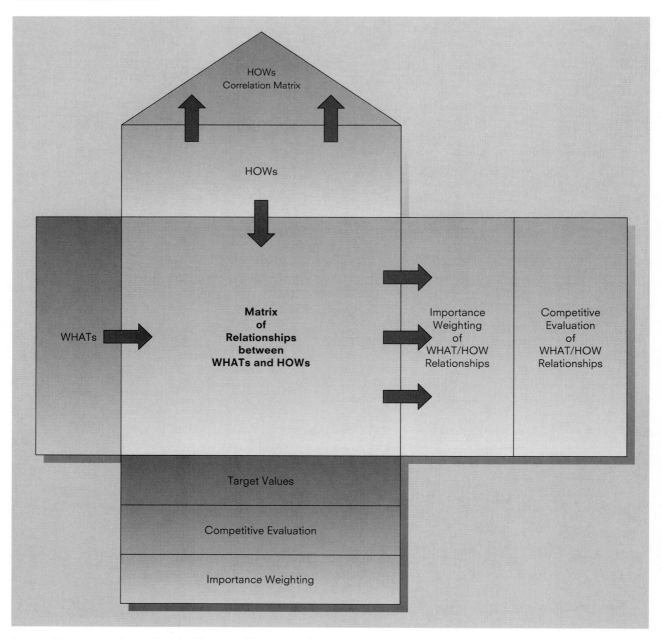

HOWs
Correlation Matrix

HOWs

**Matrix
of
Relationships
between
WHATs and HOWs**

WHATs

Importance
Weighting
of
WHAT/HOW
Relationships

Competitive
Evaluation
of
WHAT/HOW
Relationships

Target Values

Competitive Evaluation

Importance Weighting

Source   Adapted from Thomas Pyzdek, *What Every Manager Should Know About Quality* (New York: Marcel Dekker, 1991), 160.

PRODUCTION PLANNING
Phase IV of QFD, which
links all previous phases to
online quality control.

capability levels are developed, and procedures for continuous process improvement are established.

■ Phase IV, **production planning,** links the demands of the customer from phase I, through engineering in phase II and process planning in phase III, to online quality control.

| FIGURE 5.3 | The Quality Function Deployment Process |

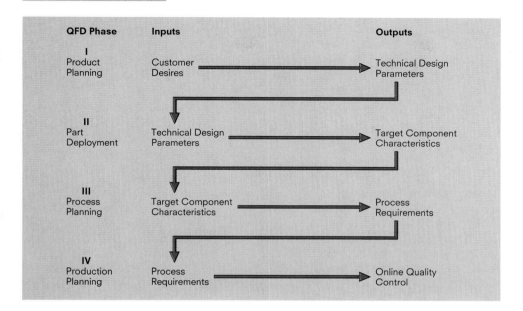

Through this four-phase process, customers' requirements are translated into all aspects of producing the product or service to ensure that the outcome is precisely what the customer wants. Figure 5.3 shows how the four phases of QFD relate to one another.

To illustrate the four-phase process, consider the following example.[16] A manufacturer of power tools discovers that its industrial customers want a more powerful drill. More power becomes a WHAT. The organization determines that there are three ways, or HOWs, to develop the drill: *(a)* with a larger motor, *(b)* with a new motor technology, or *(c)* with a different motor winding technology. Suppose that after creating and evaluating a correlation matrix, the team discovers the best way to satisfy more power is by making a larger motor.

Thus, in phase II, "larger motor" becomes the WHAT. The HOW required to satisfy the requirement turns out to be changes to the shaft of the motor. Suppose that the shaft characteristics are determined to be the most critical component to handle the additional torque required for the larger motor. Thus, for phase III the WHAT is the shaft, and phase III investigates the HOWs required to handle the shaft's higher torque requirements. The choices for HOWs that will best accomplish needed shaft characteristics are *(a)* new materials for the shaft and *(b)* a different heat-treating process.

The fourth phase identifies how to make the new shaft and assemble the motor. Suppose two HOWs are presented as alternatives. The first HOW suggests a modification of several existing machines, and the second suggests the purchase of a new machine. The alternative that best meets the customer's needs is selected.

QFD uses cross-functional teams from a number of areas including marketing, engineering, and operations. By focusing on the customer early in the design stage, fewer engineering changes are required during product and process development or after the product has been introduced. In Japanese companies, QFD has reduced the design cycle time by

---

[16]Adapted from L. R. Guinta and N. C. Praizler, *The QFD Book* (New York: Amacom, 1993), 28–29.

30 percent to 50 percent, reduced the engineering changes by 30 percent to 50 percent, and reduced startup costs by 20 percent to 60 percent.[17] Although many U.S. companies have used QFD through phases I and II, very few have applied it through phases III and IV. These phases are where the most substantial improvements can be made, however, and hold the greatest potential for cost reduction and quality improvement. Toyota, for example, realized a 61 percent reduction in production launching costs by involving floor workers in phases III and IV of the QFD process.[18] QFD has been used successfully by both manufacturing and service organizations and has also been used to deal more effectively with internal customers and suppliers.[19]

TOP MANAGEMENT'S ROLE: AGENT OF CHANGE

The role that top management plays in the success or failure of quality efforts has been highlighted by many of the quality gurus, including Deming, Crosby, and Juran. Deming advocates the 85–15 rule, which says that when something goes wrong, 85 percent of the quality problems can be attributed to the system and 15 percent can be attributed to the individual person or thing.[20] Juran's position is similar. He suggests that less than 20 percent of the quality problems can be attributed to the work force. Crosby believes that it would be possible to have zero defects if management established and expected higher levels of quality and communicated its views throughout the organization.[21]

For the TQM process to begin, changes must occur. The responsibility for these changes rests with management. Deming has suggested that the organization must first develop goals that match or exceed customers' expectations. Next, a process of ongoing improvement must be established to guarantee that the ever-changing customers' needs are met. An orientation toward process improvement rather than inspection must be developed. The total participation of the entire organization must exist and the work force must be trained and empowered to carry out its tasks. An environment without fear and finger pointing must be created, and a global, rather than a local, perspective must be developed.

Table 5.3 illustrates the types of changes that occur in an organization that adopts Deming's philosophy. It shows a conventional company's activities on the left, and those of a Deming company on the right. Massive changes such as these can only be accomplished with the support and leadership of top management.

EMPLOYEE INVOLVEMENT

In a TQM environment, top management must provide the direction for improvement to occur, including the training in problem-solving and decision-making techniques. Teams focusing on improvement activities are the heart of most quality programs. The work force must be encouraged to become involved and convinced that its contribution will be recognized and rewarded. (See Boxes 5.1 and 5.2.) Managers must be facilitators willing to share responsibility and accountability with a work force that is trained to function in a team-oriented environment.

---

[17]Guinta and Praizler, 100.

[18]Guinta and Praizler, 277.

[19]K. N. Gopalakrishnan, B. E. McIntyre, and J. C. Spragure, "Implementing Internal Quality Improvement with the House of Quality," *Quality Progress* (September 1992): 57–60.

[20]Mary Walton, *Deming Management at Work* (New York: Putnam, 1990), 20.

[21]Crosby, *Quality Is Free*.

TABLE 5.3	Comparison of Deming's Suggested Changes to Traditional Activities

Standard Company	Deming Company
Quality is expensive.	Quality leads to lower costs.
Inspection is the key to quality.	Inspection is too late. If workers can produce defect-free goods, eliminate inspections.
Quality control experts and inspectors can assure quality.	Quality is made in the boardroom.
Defects are caused by workers.	Most defects are caused by the system.
The manufacturing process can be optimized by outside experts. No change in system afterward. No input from workers.	Process is never optimized; it can always be improved.
Work standards, quotas, and goals can help productivity.	Work standards and quotas must be eliminated.
Fear and reward are proper ways to motivate.	Fear leads to disaster.
People can be treated like commodities—buying more when needed, laying off when needing less.	People should be made to feel secure in their jobs.
Rewarding the best performers and punishing the worst can lead to productivity and creativity.	Most variation is caused by the system. Review systems that judge, punish, and reward above- and below-average performance destroy teamwork and the company.
Buy on lowest cost.	Buy from vendors committed to quality.
Play one supplier off against another.	Work with suppliers.
Switch suppliers frequently based on cost.	Invest time and knowledge to help suppliers improve quality and costs. Develop long-term relationships with suppliers.
Profits are made by keeping revenue high and costs down.	Profits are generated by loyal customers.
Profit is the most important indicator.	Running the company by profit alone is like driving a car by looking in the rearview mirror. It tells you where you've been, not where you are going.

Source From *Dr. Deming: The American Who Taught the Japanese about Quality* by Rafael Aguayo. Published by arrangement with Carol Publishing Group.

CONTINUOUS IMPROVEMENT

From an organizational perspective, TQM must establish and maintain procedures that lead to systematic and continuous improvement in the capability, reliability, and efficiency of business processes. Business processes have inputs, value-added activities, and outputs, each of which can be measured, compared to performance objectives, and improved. Many

BOX 5.1

Motivating Employees at Zytec

Zytec Corporation, a 1991 winner of the Malcolm Baldrige Quality Award, manufactures power supplies for original equipment manufactureres of computers and for electronic office, medical, and testing equipment. "We have been on a quality journey since 1984," says CEO Ronald D. Schmidt. A significant part of the company's success is related to employees' involvement and motivation to keep the quality plans on track. This success has been achieved through the following techniques:

- *Assigning interdepartmental teams to design and develop new products:* Self-managed teams work directly with customers to design and develop new products.
- *Empowering employees through training:* Employees are all trained in analytical and problem-solving methods. Additional training is provided as employees advance in their skill levels.
- *Developing skills with a multifunctional employee program:* Employees are given the opportunity to improve their jobs skills and gain flexibility and are rewarded by the number of job skills they acquire.
- *Instituting employee recognition/suggestion programs:* Employees need only get the approval of their supervisor to change something. With the approval of the supervisor, employees are totally responsible for implementing their ideas.

Source Adapted from *Profiles of Malcolm Baldrige Award Winners* (Needham Heights, Mass.: Allyn & Bacon, 1992), 90–92.

differentiating capabilities come about from interdepartmental groupings of resources. Even though many decisions must be interdepartmental in nature, traditional lines of responsibility are within, not between, departments. To make the decisions necessary to provide customers with the quality outputs that will satisfy them, managers' view of business processes must span functional boundaries and focus on continual improvement of the processes. Departmental allegiances must be broken down, and a more global view must be assumed.

Continuous improvement must focus on the customers to be served and the competitive priorities established by the organization. It should be directed toward serving a particular set of customers better, providing more timely service, or producing a product that

BOX 5.2

Criteria for Problem-Solving Teams at Ford

According to John Durstine, assistant general manager of Ford Motor Company's Body and Assembly Operations, there are a number of criteria that should be met in order for problem-solving teams to be effective. These criteria include

Size: Teams must be small enough to be effective.

Training: The team members must have the necessary skills to complete their tasks.

Time: The team must be given the necessary amount of time to accomplish the assigned tasks.

Authority: The team must be able to resolve problems and implement corrective action.

Champion: The champion must have the capability of getting around obstacles and roadblocks as they occur.

Source Adapted from *Profiles in Quality* (Needham Heights, Mass.: Allyn & Bacon, 1991), 71.

| **FIGURE 5.4** | **The P-D-C-A Cycle** |

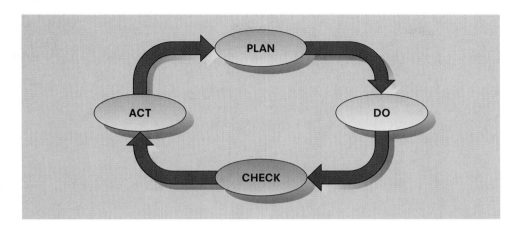

customers want. Through this process, continuous improvement can be used to enhance the competitive priorities established by the organization.

A systematic method often used to accomplish continuous improvement is the She-whart's PLAN, DO, CHECK, ACT (P-D-C-A) cycle developed by Walter A. Shewhart, an early pioneer in the study of statistical process control (and W. Edwards Deming's teacher). This circular approach (see Figure 5.4) to continuous improvement focuses on processes rather than on specific tasks or problems. *Processes* can never be solved, only improved. When improving processes, however, problems are often solved.

The four steps in the **P-D-C-A cycle** can be difficult to implement. The PLAN stage is the first, the most time consuming, and the source of most difficulties. It is here that a thorough analysis of the existing process is performed. This analysis typically involves gathering data that can help in understanding the processes and products of the company and the competitors and in identifying what the customer desires. A plan is developed to specify the resources required and assign responsibilities and any necessary training before the start of the next phase.

The DO stage introduces into the system the changes that were identified in the PLAN stage to provide the actual improvement. Sometimes the DO stage is implemented on a small scale with a test market to evaluate the results.

The CHECK stage involves the analysis of the data obtained from the DO stage. This analysis compares the results of the DO stage with expected results so that the differences are noted and clearly understood. The results of the CHECK stage must be validated because they often form the basis for the next improvement activity in the cycle. The CHECK stage also involves identifying what worked, what didn't, and what can be used in the future.

The ACT stage establishes the results of the CHECK stage throughout the organization, making the current best way of doing things standard operating procedure. Potential additional improvements are identified, perhaps from those areas that did not work well in the current model (as identified in the CHECK stage). These activities then form the basis for the new PLAN stage. The cycle then repeats. Closely related to the cycle is the quality improvement story that provides a mechanism to carry out the continuous improvement process of the Shewhart P-D-C-A cycle.

P-D-C-A CYCLE
The circular "plan, do, check, act" improvement cycle that is at the core of many TQM efforts.

QUALITY IMPROVEMENT STORIES

In Japan, quality improvement (QI) teams are often used to carry out the improvement process. Quality improvement teams are groups of employees who work together to improve quality, usually on company time. Employees in U.S. and Japanese firms often use the **QI story** as a format for analyzing quality problems throughout the firm and presenting improvement studies to management. Typically, the causes of a problem are investigated, and cause and effect relationships are analyzed. These analyses lead to the development of appropriate countermeasures or actions. There are a variety of QI stories, but their differences are slight. Most of them have seven steps and convey the same meaning. The process resembles a quality drama and, therefore, is referred to as a story.

QI STORY
A seven-step process for continuous improvement in which the causes of problems are investigated and cause-and-effect relationships are analyzed.

The seven steps in the QI story are

1. Problem definition and validation
2. Observation of features of the problem from a wide range of viewpoints so the current circumstances can be understood
3. Analysis of causes
4. Corrective action to eliminate causes and propose solutions
5. Check of the effectiveness of the action to prevent backslides
6. Standardization—permanently eliminate causes
7. Conclusion—review activities and plan for the next step[22]

The emphasis of the QI story is clearly on the problem-solving process. Figure 5.5 shows how the QI story and the P-D-C-A cycle are linked. Steps 1, 2, and 3 are part of the PLAN stage. Step 4 is the DO stage. Step 5 is the CHECK stage, and steps 6 and 7 are the ACT stage. (A specific example of how the QI story is used is presented in chapter 6.)

SEVEN TRADITIONAL QUALITY TOOLS

To perform basic analysis and decision-making tasks, seven traditional tools are used for information collection, display, and analysis prior to taking action. These tools are shown in Figure 5.6.

1. The **flow chart,** or **process flow diagram,** provides an overview of how a system or process works. It shows the inputs, operations, and outputs of the process. This visual representation of the steps in the process is particularly useful in services.
2. The **run chart** represents the results of a process over time or in the sequence the items were produced. Plotting the data points provides an effective way of finding out about a process and should be performed before other statistical measures, such as the mean and standard deviation, are determined. Without a run chart, other analysis tools can lead to the wrong conclusions.
3. The **cause-and-effect chart,** often called a fishbone diagram because of its shape, identifies all of the factors thought to affect a problem or a desired outcome. Causes of a specific problem are grouped into categories.
4. The **Pareto chart,** is a simple bar chart that is used after data have been collected to identify and rank problems. Vilfredo Pareto (1848–1923), an Italian

---

[22]GOAL/QPC, *Total Quality Control in Japan,* Research Report No. 89–10–01, Methuen, Mass., 1989.

| **FIGURE 5.5** | **Relationship between the QI Story and the P-D-C-A Cycle** |

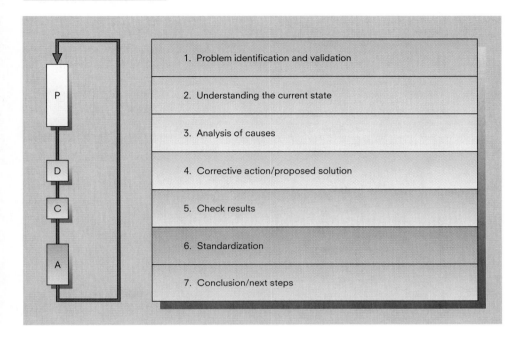

economist, focused attention on the idea of the critical few versus the trivial many. His analyses have led to the 80–20 rule, which suggests that 80 percent of the problems stem from 20 percent of the causes.

5. The **histogram** is a bar chart of various measures of a process. It is used to measure the distribution of data from a process. A histogram can help determine if a process is capable of performing acceptably, that is, according to established goals.

6. **Control charts,** the most statistically sophisticated of the traditional tools, are designed to monitor and control the variation of a process. Control charts are actually run charts with statistically determined upper and lower control limits. Control charts make it possible to distinguish between common causes (random fluctuation) and special causes (fluctuation that has an assignable cause). If a process generates data that fall within the control limits, the process is said to be in control. Data points that fall outside of the control limits are caused by something other than a common cause or random fluctuation and, therefore, must have a special or assignable cause. Their presence indicates that the process is out of control. (Control charts are described in more detail in chapter 6.)

7. The **scatter diagram** represents the correlation between two variables and may be used to help identify the cause of a problem. The identification of relationships between the number of defects and such variables as temperature, raw materials, and machine settings are all examples of likely uses of scatter diagrams.

Applications of all seven of these tools are provided in chapter 6.

FIGURE 5.6   The Seven Traditional Quality Tools

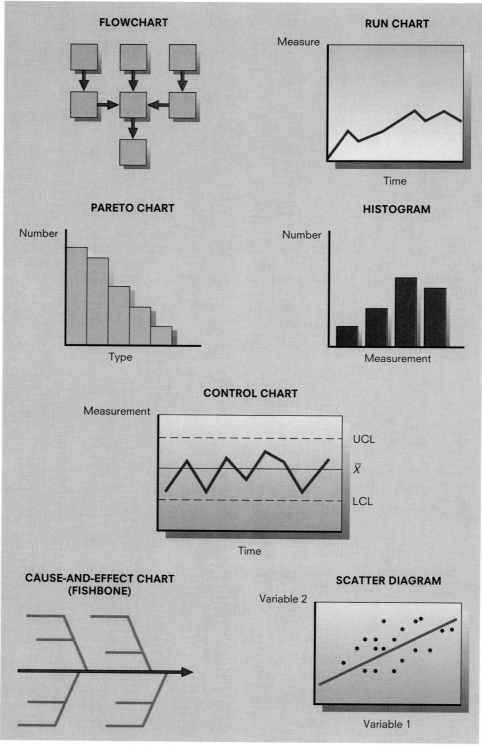

Source   Seven Tools of Quality Control. ©1985 GOAL/QPC. Used with permission from GOAL/QPC, 13 Branch Street, Methuen, MA 01844-1953. Tel. 508-685-3900.

SEVEN NEW QUALITY TOOLS

Seven new tools, which have been designed to organize nonnumeric data, can be applied in all business functions:

1. The **affinity diagram** provides a means of organizing, grouping, and condensing large amounts of verbal data into manageable categories based upon natural relationships. The process is more creative than logical and helps groups extract important information from massive amounts of disorganized data. Groups using affinity diagrams often work in silence to encourage the right side of the brain to function.

2. The **interrelationship digraph** is designed to clarify complex causal relationships. It is a logical technique typically used in a group problem-solving environment. Interrelationship digraphs attempt to define the way ideas influence each other. Typically, the process begins by writing down causes or effects on small pieces of paper, such as Post-it Notes. These are displayed on a larger piece of paper, such as a flip chart, with arrows drawn to identify relationships between items. If an item has arrows that leave but none that enter, the item is identified as a root cause. The root causes are keys to improving the system.

3. **Tree diagrams** create, in progressively greater detail, the complete set of paths and tasks that must be accomplished in order to achieve every goal and subgoal. This technique simplifies and clarifies the process so it is easier to understand precedence relationships and solve problems.

4. **Matrix diagrams** utilize a two-dimensional matrix to represent data. The matrix diagram is designed to expedite the problem-solving process by indicating the existence and correlation of two sets of factors. Its focus on the two related points makes further analysis from both points of view easy to conduct.

5. **Arrow diagrams** are scheduling tools. They provide a basis for detailed planning and can easily be adjusted to take into account work delays or activities not completed on time.

6. The **process decision program chart** (PDPC) is designed to provide contingency plans to obtain the desired results. The PDPC is used to anticipate problems and provide countermeasures that will lead to the best possible outcome under a given set of conditions. The emphasis is on anticipation of potential problems that may occur.

7. The **matrix data analysis chart** is the only quantitative tool of the seven new tools. It is sometimes referred to as the principal component analysis method. This approach arranges data in a matrix format and quantifies the relationships at the intersection of each row and column. The matrix analysis approach is related to factor analysis. In both techniques the goal is to reduce a complex problem to a relatively small number of important relationships.

The major emphasis of these seven new tools is to help small groups make optimal decisions with nonnumeric and/or poorly structured data. Using these tools, it is possible to identify patterns that are useful in decision making, as in determining root causes for problems. The seven new quality tools are also used to assist in the P-D-C-A cycle. Combined with the seven traditional quality tools and the P-D-C-A cycle, they are often linked together in problem-solving activities. In Figure 5.7, the P-D-C-A cycle has been broken down into 15 specific steps, and the tools that may be helpful with each are identified.

FIGURE 5.7	Problem-Solving Steps, Quality Tools, and the P-D-C-A Cycle

	Problem-Solving Steps	Cause-and-Effect Diagrams	Pareto Charts	Flowcharts	Histograms	Scatter Diagrams	Control Charts	Run Charts	Affinity Diagrams	Interrelationship Digraphs	Tree Diagrams	Matrix Diagram Method	Arrow Diagrams	PDPC Method	Matrix Analysis Chart
PLAN	Understanding problem areas	X	X	X	X		X	X	X	X	X				
	Selecting the theme		X				X		X	X					
	Forming the support group						X					X			
	Creating the activity plan						X					X	X	X	
	Understanding current circumstances	X	X	X	X	X	X	X	X	X	X	X			X
	Establishing objectives		X	X	X		X					X			
	Analyzing causes	X	X	X	X	X	X	X		X		X			X
	Researching improvement plans	X							X	X	X	X			
DO	Planning execution of improvement plans												X	X	
	Executing improvement plans						X						X	X	
CHECK	Verifying improvement results		X	X	X	X	X	X							X
	Reviewing activities														
ACT	Standardization		X								X				
	Establishing full control		X					X							
	Topics for the future	X	X					X						X	

Source Adapted from JUSE Problem-Solving Research Group, *TOC Solutions,* Vol. I (Cambridge, Mass.: Productivity Press, 1991), 112.

BENCHMARKING

COMPETITIVE BENCHMARKING
The process of judging a company's processes or products by comparing them to the world's best, including those in other industries.

When developing a process of ongoing improvement, it is helpful for organizations to identify goals as standards of performance, or benchmarks. Organizations use benchmarks to validate their level of attainment through a process known as **competitive benchmarking.** Benchmarking is frequently included as a part of developing target values for the HOWs, when building a QFD house of quality. Competitive benchmarking is the process of judging a company's processes, products, or practices against the world's best, including those

| | TABLE 5.4 | | **Benchmarks for General Motors** | |

Issue	GM Level of Performance	Best-in-Class Level	Best-in-Class Company
Labor hours per vehicle	30	19	Ford
Defects per vehicle	3.1	1.0	Toyota
Warranty cost per vehicle	$250	$170	Toyota
First-time paint OK	75%	90%	Suzuki
Product development time (months)	60	30	Honda
Order response time (days)	10	2	Toyota
Die change time (minutes)	60	10	Honda
External JIT parts	5%	70%	NUMMI
Internal JIT parts	5%	100%	NUMMI
Fastener part numbers	700	330	NUMMI
Fasteners per car	2,000	1,400	Toyota

Source Adapted from E. E. Sprow, "Benchmarking: A Tool for Our Time," *Manufacturing Engineering* (September 1993): 56–69.

in other industries. General Motors, for instance, compares its performance to that of the best-in-class company, as Table 5.4 shows. Organizations using this approach claim that it provides clear indications of where they are trailing the leader and clear evidence that higher quality is attainable within their organization.

Customer satisfaction is the most important of all benchmarks. It also receives the most weight in evaluating the official quality award of the United States, the Malcolm Baldrige National Quality Award. Customer service receives 300 out of a total possible 1,000 points in the scoring process. In a 1992 study, 79 percent of companies surveyed felt that they needed to benchmark to survive.[23]

Xerox, the 1989 winner of the Malcolm Baldrige award, has successfully used benchmarking to improve quality. It has used AT&T and Hewlett-Packard for research and product development benchmarks, L. L. Bean as its distribution benchmark, American Express as its collection benchmark, and American Hospital Supply as its automated inventory control benchmark.[24]

Benchmarking makes it easy to identify the gap between where an organization is and where it would like to be because it contrasts where that organization is compared to others with respect to a particular process. This gap provides a measure of the improvement an organization would like to make. Many organizations set their benchmarks on past performance or other internally generated data. This type of contrast may result in conservative and noncompetitive benchmarks that will not provide an appropriate rate of improvement. Competitive benchmarking also provides the opportunity to determine which areas need improvement, in which order to make improvements, and where to focus resources to accomplish the improvement required to be competitive. The P-D-C-A cycle or QI story can be used to put improvements into effect. Some of the nation's leading organizations that companies use as benchmarks are listed in Table 5.5.

[23]E. E. Sprow, "Benchmarking: A Tool for Our Time," *Manufacturing Engineering* (September 1993): 55–69.
[24]R. L. Harris, *The Customer Is King* (Milwaukee: ASQC Quality Press, 1991), 78.

TABLE 5.5	Where American Companies Go to Benchmark

Category	America's Best
Benchmarking methods	AT&T, Digital Equipment, Ford, IBM, Motorola, Texas Instruments, Xerox
Billing and collection	American Express, MCI, Fidelity Investments
Customer satisfaction	L. L. Bean, Federal Express, GE Plastics, Xerox
Distribution and logistics	L. L. Bean, Wal-Mart,
Employee empowerment	Corning, Dow, Milliken, Toledo Scale
Equipment maintenance	Disney
Flexible manufacturing	Allen-Bradley, Baldor, Motorola, Health-Care Programs, Allied Signal, Coors
Marketing	Procter & Gamble
Product development	Beckman Instruments, Calcamp, Cincinnati Milacron, DEC, Hewlett-Packard, 3M, Motorola, NCR
Quality methods	AT&T, IBM, Motorola, Westinghouse, Xerox
Quick shop-floor changes	Dana, GM Lansing, Johnson Controls
Supplier management	Bose, Ford, Levi Strauss, 3M, Motorola, Xerox
Worker training	Disney, General Electric, Ford, Square D

Source   "Beg, Borrow—and Benchmark," *Business Week,* November 30, 1992, 74–75.

TQM IN SERVICES

The general concepts of TQM apply to services as well as manufactured products, but there are some differences. Because of the intangible nature of the product in the service sector, the focus of quality measurement is more on customers' assessment after the service has been provided. Feedback processes must be developed to allow for improvement linked to customer assessment. Analysis of defectors is helpful. Quality in a service is the difference between the service provided and what the customer expected. Superior service is present only when the customer says it is. The most difficult task associated with measurement is to determine what the customer expects. Setting standards can be difficult. Once customers' expectations are known or can be estimated, it is possible to carry out the analysis necessary to determine the causes of deficient service. Standards that do not include customers' expectations are inadequate. For example, the type of service at McDonald's is different from that at a restaurant with table service because customer expectations differ, resulting in different standards.

SETTING STANDARDS AND MEASURING SERVICE QUALITY

There is no acceptable rate of error for many services. (See Box 5.3.) It is not acceptable for example, to have a 98 percent success rate for landing airplanes or a 99 percent rate for having prescriptions filled properly. High-quality service is as 3M defines it, "Conformance to customer requirements."[25]

---

[25]R. Zemke and D. Schaaf, 408.

OPERATIONS OUTLOOK

BOX 5.3

Cleaning Up a Quality Problem

If doctors and nurses would only wash their hands, as much as $10 billion could be eliminated from the nation's annual health-care costs. Nosocomial infections, those infections that a patient acquires as a result of a hospital stay, are a serious problem in U.S. hospitals. The responsible bacteria are transported to patients on the hands of health-care workers. Many nosocomial infections occur in intensive care units (ICUs).

One of the easiest and most efficient ways to prevent nosocomial infections is frequent handwashing. A University of Iowa study reported that washing with a disinfectant called chlorhexidine reduced ICU infections 25 percent compared to isopropyl alcohol and soap. Even with the disinfectant, however, inconsistency in how nurses and doctors used the product diminished confidence in the results.

Researchers used an intensive education program, including video demonstrations, written instructions, and mailings to educate doctors and nurses about the study results. An editorial accompanying the report of the study in the *New England Journal of Medicine* reported, "A more aggressive program can hardly be imagined." Despite the aggressive effort to educate personnel, compliance ranged from only 30 percent to 48 percent—no better than routine practice. Preventing ICU infections requires up to 40 handwashings per eight-hour shift. The researchers estimate that if the compliance percentages were doubled, the infections would be reduced between 25 percent and 50 percent.

Source Adapted from "Medical Personnel Could Wash Hands of Infection," *The Wall Street Journal*, September 14, 1992, sec. B, 1.

The perspective used by customers to view service quality has been researched extensively.[26] Service quality has the following components:

Reliability: The ability to provide the desired service dependably, accurately, and consistently

Assurance: Courtesy and knowledge of employees and their ability to convey trust and confidence

Responsiveness: Willingness to respond quickly and in a helpful manner

Empathy: The amount of caring and individual attention provided to customers

Tangibles: The physical facilities, equipment, and appearance of the personnel

Although these five points provide insight and a general representation of a customer's perspective, most organizations need a specific understanding of how their customers view service quality in order to correct problems. Most organizations find that the more general the feedback, the less effective it is for corrective purposes.

Zemke and Schaaf[27] provide some guidelines for developing a service performance measurement system. Most organizations should begin with a service strategy. If a goal is same-day service, or 30-minute delivery, or clean rooms, or zero defects, performance toward the goal is measurable. Second, organizations should measure performance frequently. Measurements should be taken at least monthly and preferably more often. It is important to ask customer-based questions. These questions should deal with the specifics

---

[26]V. Zeithaml, A. Parasuraman, and L. L. Berry, *Delivering Service Quality: Balancing Customer Perceptions and Expectations* (New York: Free Press, 1990), 26.

[27]R. Zemke and D. Schaaf, 55–57.

Satisfying customers by delivering quality medical care is a priority of FHP, Inc., a health maintenance organization (HMO). At FHP, a formal feedback process that allows patients to measure service quality ensures that customers' concerns are heard and acted on promptly. An independent survey confirms the fact that FHP's focus on customer assessment has resulted in a high level of customer satisfaction. On a scale of 1 to 5, where 1 is "not satisfied" and 5 is "extremely satisfied," FHP earned a ranking of 4.54. Shown here is a well-baby class in which FHP members are practicing parenting skills.

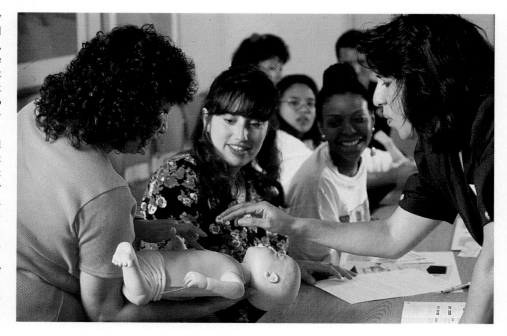

Source Courtesy of FHP International Corp.

of what happened to the customer and how he or she felt about it. Companies should benchmark. For instance, if a company is a department store in a mall, management should ask customers of stores that are the best in class the same questions they ask their own customers. They must find out how their competitors are doing and what must be done to provide the highest quality service in the mall. After data have been gathered, the search for causes of poor quality should begin. At Federal Express, for example, the concept of a service quality indicator (SQI) was used to track work process failures that led to customer dissatisfaction. The SQIs tracked a total of 12 events that led to customer dissatisfaction.

The tools for analysis are the same for services as for manufacturing. The QI story process has been used successfully by a number of service companies, including Florida Power and Light, Hospital Corporation of America, and the U.S. Navy.[28]

THE COST OF QUALITY

COST OF QUALITY (COQ)
All costs associated with maintaining the quality of goods and services.

How expensive is quality? How expensive is poor quality? It is generally agreed that the costs of poor quality, that is, the costs of scrap, rework, inspections, warranties, and so on, make up between 15 percent and 20 percent of the cost of goods sold. All costs associated with maintaining the quality of goods and services are referred to as the **cost of quality (COQ).** Quality costs are divided into four areas: internal failure costs, external failure costs, appraisal costs, and prevention costs.

---

[28]Walton, *Deming Management at Work*, 25–179.

Internal failure costs are associated with correcting a defect before the customer receives the item. In a manufacturing environment, these costs include scrap, rework, inspecting raw materials, selling an item to an alternative distributor as a second, and administrative costs associated with a defect. In the services sector, the costs are linked to the inability to provide the service because of such errors as scheduling two clients for the same time, or failing to keep an appointment. Secondary costs due to these errors may also occur. These costs are linked to poor employee morale, lack of productivity, and high employee turnover.

External failure costs are linked to the failure of a product or service in the field. In the service sector, external failures include incorrect bank statements or receipt of the wrong mail-order item. Costs associated with external failure are difficult to measure, but they include loss of customer goodwill, warranty costs, replacement costs, and the loss of future sales. From a customer's perspective, external failures often result in loss of time and money and significant aggravation in having the item replaced or repaired.

Appraisal costs are associated with item inspection and testing and with system auditing. These activities are designed to make sure the product or service is acceptable. Inspection can occur in a manufacturing environment at any time from the raw material stage through the end-product stage. In a service environment, inspection is of little value after the customer becomes involved. Testing is also difficult in a service environment because production and consumption occur simultaneously. It is impossible, for example, to test a baseball game before spectators see it. System auditing, like a pilot's preflight check, in a service environment can be valuable in that it can diagnose and prevent problems.

Prevention costs are related to preventing errors or defects from occurring. These costs include quality planning activities, design, training, and process improvement and control activities. In services, error prevention focuses on the hiring, training, and retention activities because such a large part of the service involves customer interaction. Investing money in the prevention of defects is clearly the most important activity and will have the greatest impact on reducing the other costs.

The COQ concept was developed for manufacturing organizations. Organizations vary somewhat with respect to the costs on which they focus and how the COQ data are used. (See Box 5.4.)

AWARDS AND STANDARDS

GOVERNMENT AWARDS

In 1987, President Ronald Reagan signed into law the Malcolm Baldrige Improvement Act, which established the Malcolm Baldrige National Quality Award, named after a former Secretary of Commerce. (See Box 5.5.) The objectives of the award are *(a)* to increase awareness of quality as an important element in competitiveness, *(b)* to share the information about the successful quality strategies and the benefits resulting from the implementation of these strategies, and *(c)* to promote understanding of the requirements for quality excellence.

INTERNAL FAILURE COSTS
The costs associated with correcting a defect before the customer receives the product or service.

EXTERNAL FAILURE COSTS
The costs associated with failure of a product or service in the field.

APPRAISAL COSTS
Costs associated with item inspection, testing, and system auditing.

PREVENTION COSTS
Costs related to preventing errors or defects from occurring.

BOX 5.4

Costs of Quality in a Service Business

The U.S. Marketing Group (USMG), a division of Xerox, describes its cost of quality program by defining three separate costs: the cost of conformance, the cost of nonconformance, and the cost of lost opportunities. Conformance costs are expenses associated with meeting customer expectations and include inspection, prevention, and training costs. Nonconformance costs are the costs associated with not meeting the customers' requirements before and after delivery. These costs include rework costs, waste, or the cost required to interact with the customer. Lost opportunities costs include the missed opportunities because resources are used for rework in the event of a product failure or a customer cancellation.

The total COQ for USMG was $1.05 billion per year or 25 percent of sales. USMG used the COQ as a source to identify problems that needed solutions. The company believed that dealing with the problems that caused the COQ would result in improved customer satisfaction, which was the ultimate goal. Eleven major problems associated with the COQ were identified, and teams were formed to identify root causes and solve the problems wherever possible. The COQ associated with the 11 projects was $250 million. Through the efforts of the 11 teams, the COQ was reduced by $53 million the first year.

Source   L. P. Carr," Applying Cost of Quality to a Service Business," *Sloan Management Review* 33 (Summer 1992), 72–77.

BOX 5.5

The Malcolm Baldrige National Quality Award

Award Criteria Purposes

- To help raise quality performance standards and expectations
- To facilitate communication and sharing among and understanding of key quality and performance requirements
- To serve as a working tool for planning, training, assessment, and other uses

Award Criteria Goals

- Delivery of ever-improving value to customers
- Improvement of overall company operational performance

Core Values and Concepts

- Customer-driven quality
- Leadership
- Continuous improvement

- Employee participation and development
- Fast response
- Design quality and prevention
- Long-range outlook
- Management by fact
- Partnership development
- Corporate responsibility and citizenship

Criteria Framework

- Leadership
- Information and analysis
- Strategic quality planning
- Human resource development and management
- Management of process quality
- Quality and operational results
- Customer focus and satisfaction

Source   1993 Award Criteria Malcolm Baldrige National Quality Award, United States Department of Commerce Technology Administration, National Institute of Standards and Technology.

Up to two awards may be given each year in each of three categories. The categories are manufacturing companies or subsidiaries; service companies or subsidiaries; and small businesses. The award is managed by the U.S. Department of Commerce.

Scoring for the award is based on the seven categories, as listed under Criteria Framework in Box 5.5. A total of 1,000 points are possible for all categories. Each company that applies is reviewed by three examiners. Those companies that score high are selected as finalists and must undergo an on-site visit by at least one judge.

Most of the awards have been given to manufacturing, rather than service firms, as Table 5.6 shows. Collier attributes manufacturers' success to the intensive international pressure they have felt and the fact that it is often more difficult to design, manage, and measure service processes than goods-producing processes.[29]

There has been a significant amount of criticism directed toward the Baldrige award. Criticisms include issues related to the time and cost required to compete for the award, the emphasis on results that suggest a short-term mentality (despite the continuous improvement mechanism built into the award), and the numbers of winners (some critics suggest there be a total of two not six winners, but others say awards should go to all who meet the criteria).[30] Still others fault the award because winners have not necessarily performed well

TABLE 5.6	Malcolm Baldrige Award Winners
Year	**Award Winners**
1988	Globe Metallurgical
	Motorola
	Westinghouse, Commercial Nuclear Fuel Division
1989	Milliken
	Zerox, Business Products
1990	Cadillac
	IBM Rochester
	Federal Express
	Wallace
1991	Marlow Industries
	Solectron
	Zytec
1992	AT&T Network Systems Group/ Transmission Systems Business Unit
	AT&T Universal Card Services
	Granite Rock
	Ritz-Carlton Hotel
	Texas Instruments Defense Systems and Electronics Group
1993	Eastman Chemical Company
	Ames Rubber Corporation
1994	AT&T Consumer Communications Services
	GTE Directories
	Wainwright Industries

[29]D. A. Collier, "Service, Please: The Malcolm Baldrige National Quality Award," *Business Horizons* (July-August 1992): 88–95.

[30]David A. Garvin et al., "Does the Baldrige Award Really Work?" *Harvard Business Review* (January-February 1992): 126–147.

in the marketplace. Garvin believes that the award is positioned appropriately and that it will serve as an agent for transforming and improving the quality of U.S. business.[31]

THE DEMING PRIZE AND THE BALDRIGE AWARD

The Deming Prize, named after Dr. W. Edwards Deming, was established in Japan in 1951 and is given annually. It inspired the Malcolm Baldrige Quality Award in this country. Organizations and individuals throughout the world are eligible for the Deming Prize. Florida Power and Light, which received the award in 1989, was the first U.S. company to be so honored. Both the Deming and Baldrige awards are designed to raise the quality levels of businesses in their respective countries, but they reward different achievements. Unlike the Baldrige Award, which does not deal with improvement methods, the Deming Prize has specific criteria that relate to describing quality improvement methods. The Baldrige Award emphasizes results, whereas the Deming Prize stresses the process that produces the results. Baldrige candidates compete against one another, but the Deming candidates compete against a standard. The Baldrige Award has a continuous improvement mechanism that provides for changes and updates.

INTERNATIONAL STANDARDS

ISO 9000 is a series of standards developed by the International Organization for Standardization (ISO). It was first published in 1987. The ISO standards have been adopted without change by at least 51 countries including the United States, Japan, the European Community (EC) (12 countries including Germany), and the European Free Trade Association (currently 8 countries). ISO 9000 serves as the benchmark for acceptance of goods and services traded among these countries. The ISO standards focus on systems for managing quality and not on specifications for individual products. In the United States the American National Standards Institute (ANSI) is the official member of ISO.

The EC has divided all products into two categories, regulated and nonregulated. Products that are regulated are linked to health, safety, or the environment. Between 10 percent and 15 percent of all products sold in the EC and half the dollar volume are regulated by ISO 9000. The United States exports more than $100 billion per year to the EC, about half of which are regulated by ISO 9000. Any firm wishing to sell regulated products in the countries that have adopted the ISO 9000 series must comply with it.

The ISO 9000 series is a set of five standards, or criteria, numbered sequentially from 9000. ISO 9000 explains how to select and use the other four standards. ISO 9001 establishes requirements for quality systems in design/development, production, installation, and servicing of products or services. It is typically used by organizations that design and build their own products.

ISO 9002 provides requirements for quality assurance systems when conformance to specified production and installation requirements are necessary. ISO 9003 is the least detailed and deals with conformance in final inspection and testing. It is used by such organizations as testing laboratories and calibration houses. ISO 9004 is an internal standard to help managers build and develop their own quality systems. The system includes responsibilities for management, marketing, human resources, purchasing, product safety, and

---

[31]David A. Garvin, "How the Baldrige Award Really Works," *Harvard Business Review* (November-December 1991): 80–93.

statistical methods.[32] The ISO standards are subject to review every five years to reflect marketplace changes.

TQM CROSS-LINKS

Central to TQM is the belief that satisfying the customer is the most important aspect of anyone's job. This belief requires a commitment to cross-functional integration because poor quality of any value-adding activity in any business function will ultimately affect the quality of the product or service the company provides. All functions must be constantly aware of the effect each one has on customer satisfaction and the motivations of other business functions. Specific phases of QFD, for example, require involvement of process and product engineering, marketing, and operations. Similarly, if accounting measures are allowed to emphasize short-term financial aspects, quality and customer satisfaction could be ignored.

TQM AND OPERATIONS STRATEGY

Total quality management, because it uses the word *total,* means that the highest level of quality possible is necessary everywhere in the organization. Poor quality in any function will ultimately affect customer satisfaction. As organizations have gotten larger and more complex, managers have found it increasingly difficult to evaluate day-to-day decisions about how to suppport business and corporate strategies. Management philosophies have helped them to make decisions that support higher level strategies. Because TQM is consistent with corporate goals, management decisions that are consistent with TQM are almost certain to support corporate goals as well.

Because TQM focuses on the highest level of performance in all areas of the business, it does more than merely enhance product or service quality. Price, dependability, flexibility, and response time are improved as well because of the overall focus on quality performance.

Through the task/resource model, Figure 5.8 shows how TQM provides an intermediate set of objectives, consistent with business goals, to help guide local management action and decisions.

TQM AND JUST-IN-TIME

Any discussion of TQM would be incomplete without also mentioning the just-in-time (JIT) philosophy. JIT emphasizes elimination of waste and doing work correctly the first time. Wherever possible, JIT systems are designed so that errors cannot occur. The term used to describe these fail-safe or mistake-proof systems is **poka-yoke.** The poka-yoke approach prevents the worker from making an error that would lead to a defect. For example, if there were only one correct way to put an electrical cord into an outlet, the poka-yoke would be to design the plug in such a way—perhaps by making the prongs slightly different sizes—that no one could plug it in incorrectly.

POKA-YOKE
Characterization of a system whose design prevents mistakes or defects.

---

[32]G. Spizizen,"The ISO 9000 Standards: Creating a Level Playing Field for International Quality," *National Productivity Review* 11 (Summer 1992): 331–346.

FIGURE 5.8 **TQM's Contribution to Meeting Business Goals**

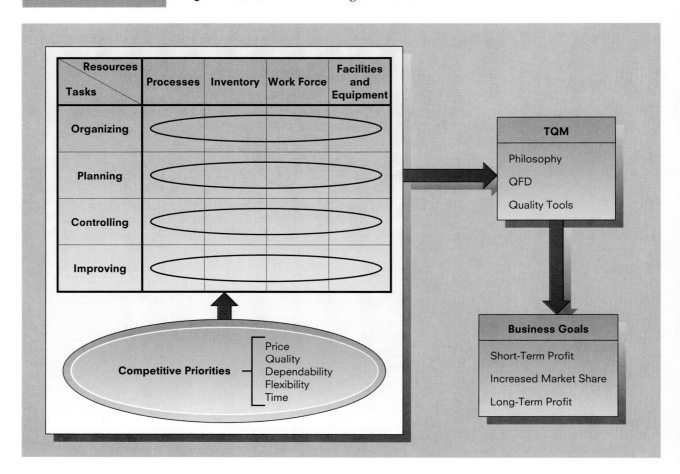

JIT also embraces the concept of continuous improvement through the ongoing reduction of waste. The reduction of waste has a strong relationship to quality improvement. JIT is discussed in depth in the next chapter.

SUMMARY

Quality has become an extremely important factor in determining a firm's competitiveness, and it will remain important as long as some organizations have not achieved it. For most organizations, total quality consists of an unending effort to meet or exceed customers' expectations. Total quality management should not be viewed, however, as a quick means to an end. Numerous companies have tried and failed to embrace the TQM philosophy. (See Box 5.6.)

In a recent study of Fortune 500 firms, only 36 percent of the firms felt that TQM was having a significant impact on competitiveness. Part of the problem is that U.S. managers expect instant success. Many do not have the patience that is required to make TQM a success. Another key ingredient to successful implementation is the labor/management relationship. If economic conditions dictate significant layoffs, TQM efforts are often discon-

OPERATIONS OUTLOOK

BOX 5.6

Are Quality Programs Effective?

"A lot of companies read lots of books, did lots of training, formed teams and tried to implement 9,000 new practices simultaneously," says Terrence R. Ozan, a partner with Ernst & Young, which ran the study with the American Quality Foundation. "But you don't get results that way. It's just too much."

The study represents one of the most comprehensive and critical reviews to date of quality-management programs. In recent years, thousands of organizations have embraced such efforts in a quest for improved performance. Based on a survey of 584 companies in the United States, Canada, Germany, and Japan, the study details failings across a range of quality-improvement activities in the auto, computer, banking and health-care industries. Among its United States findings:

Computer companies involve only 12% of their employees in idea-suggestion programs. Automakers, which rate highest in this area, involve just 28% of their workers. 78% of the surveyed Japanese car makers' employees are involved.

Customer complaints are of "major or primary" importance in identifying new products and services among only 19% of banks and 26% of hospitals. 26% of U.S computer makers use customer complaints to help identify new products, compared to 73% in Japan and 60% in Germany.

Quality performance measures, such as defect rates and customer-satisfaction levels, play a key role in determining pay for senior managers among fewer than one in five companies across all four industries surveyed. Profitability still matters most.

Bright spots

More than half of all workers in the surveyed U.S. companies participate in at least occasional meetings about quality.

There have been increases in quality-related activities during the past 3 years.

Tom Vanderpool, a quality consultant with Gemini Consulting, in Morristown, N.J., says many companies aren't seeing results—and may tire of trying—because they mistakenly isolate quality programs from day-to-day activities. "They tend to put it off as something special, as an objective with 10,000 activities unto itself," he says. "It's not. It is a way to meet business objectives."

Joshua Hammond, of the American Quality Foundation blames "the proliferation of consultants, each of whom preaches his own pet strategy." Indeed, the new study found that the surveyed companies used a total of 945 different quality-management tactics. He suggests that the most successful programs typically include strong personal involvement by senior executives, companywide awareness of strategic plans and goals, and an emphasis on simplifying processes.

Johnson & Johnson has recently moved from a program based on doing it right the first time because it wasn't specific enough, according to Jeffery M. Nugent, vice president of Worldwide Quality Management. The company recently established three more explicit quality goals: boosting customer satisfaction, reducing product introduction time, and cutting costs.

tinued.[33] Failure of a TQM effort can often be attributed to management responsibilities, as Box 5.7 shows.

The TQM paradigm requires a strong commitment by management to change the organization so that the focus is on the customer. Successful TQM companies have total involvement by a trained work force that is empowered to continually improve processes and products. Decision making is based on logical thought and action supported by a number of decision-making tools that benefit services and manufacturing organizations. In the final analysis, an organization may not have a choice about TQM. At a time of strong competition, TQM may be required if an organization is to be able to compete.

---

[33]J. Mathews and P. Katel, "The Cost of Quality," *Newsweek,* September 7, 1992.

BOX 5.7

Common Reasons for TQM Failures

Inappropriate Motivation: Companies often take a "fix-it" approach if the impetus to adopt TQM comes from pressure from a customer or desire to win an award.

No Upfront Assessment: Companies often fail to measure current performance and compare it to goals.

Training as a Miracle Cure: Training, on its own, will not produce results. There must be infrastructure, a plan, followup, and management support.

Lack of Role Definition: Every person in the organization must be able to define what quality means for him or her.

Failure to Address Individual Management Style: Dictatorial management styles will prevent teams from working effectively.

Bumping Heads with the Company's Infrastructure: Unless the quality initiative is linked to performance appraisal and career development, quality will not be a part of the operational areas of the company.

Disconnect between Strategic Objectives and Quality Improvement: If quality improvement efforts are not tied directly to business objectives, employees will see them as ill-conceived.

Mismanaging the Transition: Companies often underestimate the amount of inertia keeping old systems in place, and preventing new ones from taking over.

Giving It Up Too Soon: Initiatives often slow after initial dramatic improvements. Efforts may appear stalled, and become a self-fulfilling prophecy.

Source   T. E. Benson, "Quality: If at First You Don't Succeed. . . ," *Industry Week*, July 5, 1993, 48–59.

SMITH-TAYLOR MEMORIAL REVISITED

After deciding to write off the 20 percent charges to patients, the Smith-Taylor Board of Trustees demanded that Allen identify why concentrating on the quality of patient care resulted in inaccurate record keeping. Do you think there was a conflict between patient care and accuracy of records? Why do you think chart accuracy declined?

How might Allen design an accuracy improvement system? Should he first determine which types of records are being charted wrong or omitted? Could a training program help, or is it possible that further training would not work because record keeping is merely a low priority for staff? How might the accuracy of charts be monitored to prevent inaccuracies, rather than detect after-the-fact inaccurate charts?

QUESTIONS FOR REVIEW

1. Describe the contributions of each of the quality gurus.
2. Describe the TQM framework. Discuss how its components are related.
3. Describe the eight dimensions of product quality.
4. How does Shewhart's P-D-C-A cycle contribute to continuous improvement?
5. What are the four phases of QFD? How does QFD take into account the customers' needs?
6. How is the house of quality used in the QFD process?
7. Describe the seven traditional and seven new quality tools.
8. What is the importance of benchmarking?
9. Describe how process improvement occurs using the QI story format.
10. Why is quality more difficult to measure in the service sector than in manufacturing?
11. Describe the four classes of quality costs.
12. How does the impact of a local perspective on decision making differ from that of a global perspective?

QUESTIONS FOR THOUGHT AND DISCUSSION

1. What are the negative aspects of an award program like the Malcolm Baldrige Award?
2. Why do you think the QI story concept was developed?
3. Can the P-D-C-A cycle be applied to personal productivity improvement? How?

INTEGRATIVE QUESTIONS

1. How does QFD contribute to value?
2. Why, from a strategic perspective, must TQM be a cross-functional commitment?
3. How can TQM be included in the strategic decision-making process?

SUGGESTED READINGS

Berry, L. L., Parasuraman, A., and Zeithaml, V. A. "The Service-Quality Puzzle." *Business Horizons* 31 (September-October 1988): 35–43.

Burt, D. N. "Managing Product Quality through Strategic Purchasing." *Sloan Management Review* 30 (Spring 1989): 39–47.

Clausing, D. "The House of Quality." *Harvard Business Review* 66 (May-June 1988): 63–73.

Crosby, P. B. *Quality Is Free.* New York: McGraw Hill, 1979.

Duncan, W. J., and Van Matre, J. G. "The Gospel According to Deming: Is It Really New?" *Business Horizons* 33 (July-August 1990): 3–9.

Finkelman, D., and Goland, T. "The Case of the Complaining Customer." *Harvard Business Review* 68 (May-June 1990): 9–24.

Forker, L. B. "Quality: American, Japanese, and Soviet Perspectives." *Academy of Management Executive* 5 (November 1991): 63–74.

Garvin, D. A. "How the Baldrige Award Really Works." *Harvard Business Review* 69 (November-December 1991): 80–93.

Juran, J. M. *Juran on Planning for Quality.* New York: Free Press, 1988.

Leonard, F. S. "The Case of the Quality Crusader." *Harvard Business Review* 66 (May-June 1988): 12–20.

Reichheld, F. F., and Sasser, W. E., Jr. "Zero Defections: Quality Comes to Services." *Harvard Business Review* 68 (September-October 1990): 105–111.

Smith, M. R. "Improving Product Quality in American Industry." *Academy of Management Executive* 1 (August 1987): 243–245.

Taguchi, G., and Clausing, D. "Robust Quality." *Harvard Business Review* 68 (January-February 1990): 65–75.

Walton, M. *Deming Management at Work.* New York: Putnam, 1990.

QUALITY MANAGEMENT TOOLS

  **Eric's Diner**

Eric's Diner is a low- to medium-priced restaurant that caters to business commuters on their way in and out of a large eastern city. Its breakfast buffet is one of its most popular features. The restaurant is owned and managed by Eric Davis. ■ For the third time in as many days, Eric overheard a customer complaining as she paid her bill. This complaint was no different from the other two. She was a longtime customer who stopped here two or three days a week for breakfast on the way to work. She told the cashier that she was not planning to return because it was just taking too long to get breakfast. ■ Eric grimaced as he watched her walk out but attempted to greet the next group with a smile. "Four of you for the buffet? We'll have you seated in just a few minutes," Eric said in as cheerful a tone as he could. He knew that they should not have to wait for a seat at all. ■ That evening at home, as he pondered the problem, he recalled a group of customers discussing an improvement process they were using at work. One of the group members was a local woman, Val Ballard. Eric decided to ask her for advice the next time that he saw her. As luck would have it, Val showed up for breakfast the next morning. Eric offered her free breakfast if she would respond to his problem. She agreed. ■ "We know our customers are getting less and less satisfaction," Eric said. "They're waiting longer, but we're not sure what to do about it. We've examined the kitchen activities and are certain the buffet is well stocked. Every morning things go great for a while, and then, all of a sudden, things get backed up. How would you suggest we go about finding the root of this problem?" ■ "Before you can take any action, you must carefully define the problem," Val said. "We use a well-known process for solving problems at work, and it starts with developing a clear definition of what we're trying to accomplish." Val looked around for something to write on and after pulling a pen from her purse, turned over a paper placemat. "Here's the process we follow," she said, as she began to write the following list on the placemat:

1. Define the problem.
2. Study the situation.
3. Identify potential causes.
4. Implement a solution.
5. Check the results.
6. If the results are good, standardize the change throughout the organization.
7. Establish plans for future improvements.

■ "Thanks for the help!" Eric called as she left. ■ "I know what the problem is," thought Eric, "but I'm not sure I really understand the situation well enough to be certain of the cause. I don't want to 'fix' something that isn't broken." ■ In order to gain a better understanding of the situation, Eric decided to get information from his customers. For the next week, he collected information through a survey. He was correct in his early prediction that customers were unhappy with the time they spent waiting, but that was not the only thing they were unhappy about. The results of his survey showed that there were the following problems:

Complaint	Frequency
Had to wait for seats	70
Buffet table disorganized	60
Table not clean	41
Had to wait too long for coffee	12
Missing utensil at place setting	5
No sweetener provided	4

■   Eric decided to focus on the waiting problem and to try to identify potential causes. This proved to be more difficult than he imagined. As a last resort, he assigned his assistant manager to greet customers while he took a seat at the table in the far corner. After an hour spent studying the activity, he began to understand what was going on.   ■

Source   Adapted from M. Gaudard, R. Coates, and L. Freeman, "Accelerating Improvement," *Quality Progress* (October 1991): 81–88.

Quality tools perform a variety of functions that have been designed to ensure that customers are satisfied. Some of these tools are quality or performance indicators that compare actual performance with expected performance in order to identify areas for improvement. One procedure, known as statistical process control (SPC), is used to determine if the process or system is in control. Routine adjustments to the system are made if corrective action is required. If the system is in need of further improvement, another tool, the quality improvement (QI) story, may be used to improve the system. The concept of acceptance sampling is also presented.

Quality tools are designed to enhance the product or service provided and directly improve the competitiveness of the organization. Quality methods also improve other aspects of an organization's activities or functions because quality improvement applies to all aspects of an organization. Thus, quality can enhance a firm's ability to design, produce, and deliver a product or service.

STATISTICAL PROCESS CONTROL

STATISTICAL PROCESS CONTROL (SPC)

A procedure used to distinguish between random variability and variability that has an assignable cause.

Statistical process control (SPC) typically monitors the output of a system by sampling the output and comparing actual output with expected output through control charts. From a statistical perspective, the concept of *control* suggests that the way in which a measure might be predicted to vary in the future can be used to prevent defects. That is, when probabilistic measures are used to describe behavior, variation is predictable. Variations that can occur may be due to chance, or they may be due to some assignable cause.

Variations due to chance, also referred to as random or common variations, are built into the system as designed by management. New designs or improvements in the system can change the amount of chance variation possible in the system.

Variations due to some assignable cause, sometimes called special variations, can be identified and removed. These variations are capable of being controlled and require action. They must first be detected, then the cause must be identified, and finally the cause must be eliminated. Some examples of assignable causes include machines that are out of order, poor product design, improper training or instruction of a worker, inadequate lighting, a change in raw materials, and inappropriate work environments.

CONTROL CHARTS

Charts that monitor production operations by plotting data.

The process of detecting variation due to assignable causes is accomplished through the use of statistically developed **control charts.** Control charts cannot be developed until the process to be monitored produces consistent output. If a process is initially not stable, materials, machines, raw material, or worker skill may need to be adjusted with the goal of developing consistent output. Once consistent output is obtained, a control chart may be used to monitor and improve the process.

All control charts are similar in design. The process of developing a control chart starts by identifying and measuring an important characteristic of a product or service. For ex-

Production operations at Betz Laboratories use Betz Action Alert—a statistical process control package that monitors the quality of water, wastewater, and process systems. Samples from production runs undergo more testing in Betz's quality assurance lab, shown here. The results of constant monitoring and lab testing, which are subjected to computer-generated statistical analysis, guarantee consistent product quality.

Source   Courtesy of Betz Laboratories, Inc.

ample, pizza deliveries may be timed or the number of students who get first choice on class schedules may be counted. These measures are then plotted and compared with the mean or center line for the data under consideration (see Figure 6.1). The amount of variation is measured using statistical tools to establish an upper and lower control limit for the data.

The two basic types of control charts are variables charts and attribute charts. A **variables chart** measures values along a continuum, such as the width of a shaft, the height of a cylinder, or the time it takes to deliver a pizza. When data are discrete, or countable,

VARIABLES CHART
A control chart based on data that are measured along a continuum.

FIGURE 6.1   **Control Chart Format**

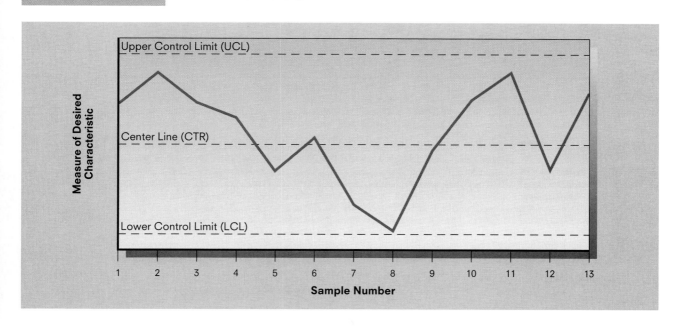

ATTRIBUTE CHART
A control chart based on data that are counted.

attribute charts are used. Such charts may measure the fraction that are defective, the number defective, or the number of defects per unit. Attribute data may take on only two values—that an order is on time or late or that a batter did or didn't receive a hit. Often the choice for these two values is to accept an item as good or reject it as bad.

VARIABLES CHARTS

X-BAR CHART
A type of variables chart used in monitoring the means of a sample group of items.

R CHART
A type of variables chart used to monitor process variability within a sample group.

There are two commonly used variables charts: *X*-bar charts and *R* charts. The **X-bar chart** measures the mean or average values of a subgroup of items. The **R chart** measures the range of values from high to low in a subgroup. Both charts are necessary because it is possible that the mean of a process may not change while the variability does. This variability would be indicated by the *R* chart. It is also possible that the mean of a process may change while the variability remains constant. The *X*-bar chart would detect this change.

The *X*-bar chart is formed by first computing the mean of each subgroup. A subgroup size is small, typically from 2 through 5 items. When the subgroup size exceeds 10, the *X*-bar and *S* (sample standard deviation) charts are used. If a subgroup consists of 4 items, the mean of these 4 items is determined. A total of 25 or more samples, each containing 4 items, may be selected and plotted. The mean, $\bar{X}_1$, is

$$\bar{X}_1 = \frac{x_1 + x_2 + \cdots + x_n}{n} \tag{6.1}$$

where *n* is the subgroup size. The grand mean $\bar{\bar{X}}$, or center line, in the control chart is found by averaging the means for each subgroup. Thus $\bar{\bar{X}}$ is

$$\bar{\bar{X}} = \frac{\bar{X}_1 + \bar{X}_2 + \cdots + \bar{X}_k}{k} \tag{6.2}$$

where *k* is the number of samples of size *n*.

The range, R_1, for subgroup 1 is determined by subtracting the smallest value in a subgroup from the largest value. The mean of the ranges, $\bar{R}$, is

$$\bar{R} = \frac{R_1 + R_2 + \cdots + R_k}{k} \tag{6.3}$$

The upper control limits (UCL) and lower control limits (LCL) for the *X*-bar chart are

$$\text{UCL} = \bar{\bar{X}} + A_2\bar{R} \tag{6.4}$$

$$\text{LCL} = \bar{\bar{X}} + A_2\bar{R} \tag{6.5}$$

3-SIGMA
Denotes three standard deviations (the square root of the variance) on each side of the mean.

where A_2 is a constant that is based upon the subgroup size, and provides a **3-sigma** (3 standard deviations on each side of the mean) control limit for *X*-bar when multiplied by *R*-bar. (See Box 6.1.)

For the *R* chart, the center line is $\bar{R}$, and the upper and lower control limits are

$$\text{UCL} = D_4\bar{R} \tag{6.6}$$

$$\text{LCL} = D_3\bar{R} \tag{6.7}$$

Table 6.1 presents values for A_2, D_3, and D_4. Note that these values depend upon the subgroup size and are based upon the assumption that the sample means are normally distributed. These factors provide 3-sigma control for *X*-bar and *R*.

OPERATIONS OUTLOOK

BOX 6.1

Is 3-Sigma Enough?

With normal random fluctuation, any process will produce approximately 2,700 parts per million outside (99.7 percent inside, 0.3 percent outside) of the 3-sigma limits. Three-tenths of 1 percent seems insignificant, but it can result in serious problems. For example, a product with 1,200 parts would be ex-pected to have, on average, 3.24 defects per unit. Some units would have more, some would have less. Out of every 1,000 units produced, only 40 would be expected to have no defects. This translates into only 4 percent defect free.

Source "Motorola Inc.," *Profiles of Malcolm Baldrige Award Winners* (Boston: Allyn and Bacon, 1992).

USES OF CONTROL CHARTS

Control charts provide a look at the past performance of a process and can provide insight into potential problem areas. Whenever the results appear to be nonrandom, there is the potential that an assignable cause may be found for the nonrandomness. The nonrandom nature of the data may present itself in several different formats. Some of the patterns suggesting nonrandom activity include the following:

- 1 point is either above the upper or below the lower control limit
- 2 of 3 successive points are between 2 and 3 standard deviations from the center line
- 4 of 5 successive points are between 1 and 3 standard deviations from the center line
- 8 successive points are all above or all below the center line

TABLE 6.1   **Factors for Computing 3-Sigma Control Limits for *X*-Bar and *R* Charts**

Number of Observations in Subgroup (n)	Factor for *X*-Bar Chart (A_2)	Lower Control Limit (D_3)	Upper Control Limit (D_4)
2	1.880	0	3.268
3	1.023	0	2.574
4	0.729	0	2.282
5	0.577	0	2.114
6	0.483	0	2.004
7	0.419	0.076	1.924
8	0.373	0.136	1.864
9	0.337	0.184	1.816
10	0.308	0.223	1.777
15	0.223	0.348	1.652

Source   Adapted from "1950 ASTM Manual on Quality Control of Materials," American Society for Testing and Materials, in J. M. Juran, ed., *Quality Control Handbook* (New York: McGraw-Hill 1974), Appendix II, 39; and D. Delmar and G. Sheldon, *Introduction to Quality Control* (New York: West 1988), 498.

FIGURE 6.2	**Nonrandom Patterns**

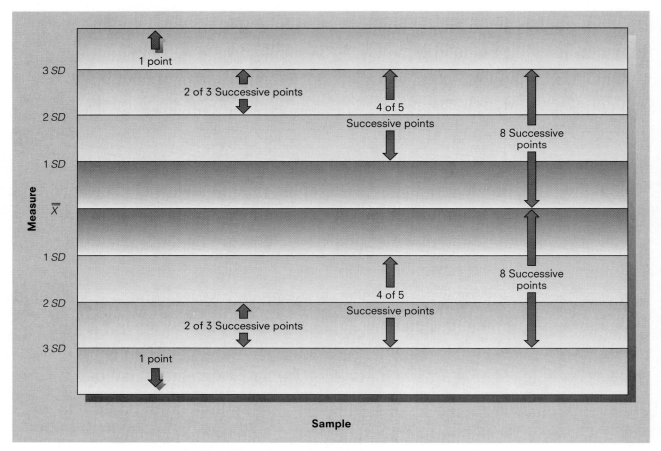

Source   B. Brocka and M. S. Brocka, *Quality Management: Implementing the Best Ideas of the Masters* (Homewood, Ill.: Business One Irwin, 1992), 281.

■   6 or more successive points are continually increasing or decreasing

Most of these patterns are shown in Figure 6.2 and are valid for any type of control chart having 3-sigma control limits.

EXAMPLE 6.1	

Constructing and Interpreting *X*-Bar and *R* Charts

The diameter of a shaft that is used to connect two sections of the shell of a microcomputer is designed to be 50 millimeters. Twenty-five samples, each of which has 4 separate measures, were taken directly from the process producing the shafts (see Table 6.2). Develop *X*-bar and *R* charts for this process.

SOLUTION

Table 6.2 shows the measures and values for *X*-bar and *R* for each sample. The value of *X*-double bar is determined to be 50.00 millimeters, and the value of *R*-bar is 6.88 mil-

TABLE 6.2

Sample Number	1	2	3	4	X-Bar	R
1	49	47	52	48	49.00	5
2	48	48	54	49	49.75	6
3	49	49	51	47	49.00	4
4	47	47	50	51	48.75	4
5	51	51	57	52	52.75	6
6	52	54	54	54	53.50	2
7	54	57	45	57	53.25	12
8	51	52	49	53	51.25	4
9	52	51	42	54	49.75	12
10	54	52	41	51	49.50	13
11	49	45	48	52	48.50	7
12	48	47	45	50	47.50	5
13	47	49	51	54	50.25	7
14	52	51	54	49	51.50	5
15	54	50	43	48	48.75	11
16	55	47	42	49	48.25	13
17	54	46	48	46	48.50	8
18	51	44	46	47	47.00	7
19	52	41	51	51	48.75	11
20	49	49	50	52	50.00	3
21	48	48	54	46	49.00	8
22	47	52	55	52	51.50	8
23	51	57	52	50	52.50	7
24	50	52	52	51	51.25	2
25	51	50	49	51	50.25	2

$$\overline{\overline{X}} = 50.00$$
$$\overline{R} = 6.88$$

limeters. The upper and lower control limits for *X*-bar are found by using equations 6.4 and 6.5:

$$\mathrm{UCL} = \overline{\overline{X}} + A_2\overline{R}$$

$$= 50.00 + (0.729)(6.88)$$

$$= 55.02$$

$$\mathrm{LCL} = \overline{\overline{X}} - A_2\overline{R}$$

$$= 50.00 - (0.729)(6.88)$$

$$= 44.98$$

The control chart for *X*-bar is shown in Figure 6.3. In order to construct the lines at 1 and 2 standard deviations above or below the mean, the width of the interval from the center line is divided by 3. Because this width is $(0.729)(6.88) = 5.02$, those values above the

| FIGURE 6.3 | *X*-Bar Control Chart |

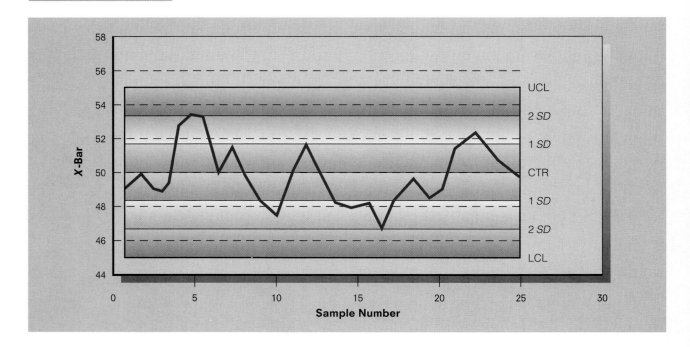

center line would be drawn at $50 + 1.67 = 51.67$, and $50 + (2)(1.67) = 53.34$. Those below the center line would be done using the same procedure. Note that all of the points fall within the control limits.

The *R*-chart is shown in Figure 6.4. The center line is *R*-bar. The upper and lower control limits are computed using equations 6.6 and 6.7:

$$UCL = D_4\bar{R}$$

$$= (2.282)(6.88)$$

$$= 15.70$$

$$LCL = D_3\bar{R}$$

$$= (0)(6.88)$$

$$= 0$$

where D_3 and D_4 are found in Table 6.1 and where the subgroup size is 4.

A question may arise as to why both *X*-bar and *R* charts are necessary. The *R* chart describes the variation in measures within the subset. Thus from Table 6.2, for sample number 1, a range value of 5 states that the difference between the high and low value within the set of 4 measures is 5. Thus the sample mean may be acceptable, but variation between each reading may be unacceptable. By measuring and graphing the range, an acceptable level of variation can be measured and monitored.

FIGURE 6.4   **Range Control Chart**

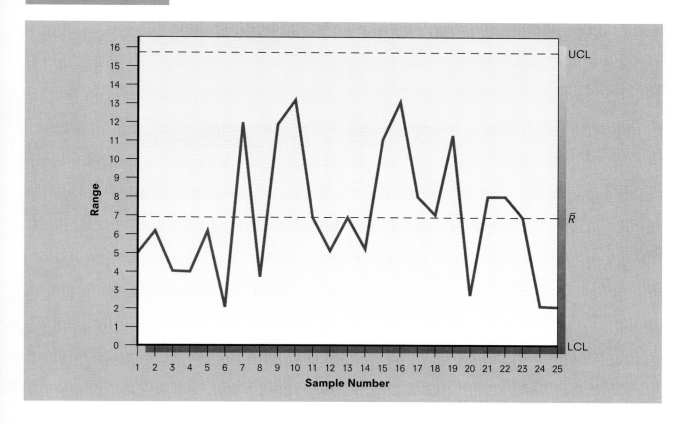

ATTRIBUTE CHARTS

The **p chart** is the most commonly used attribute chart. The chart is used to evaluate whether the proportion unacceptable, or nonconforming, produced by the system is in control from a statistical perspective. Because attribute charts involve yes-no type of decisions, the statistical distribution involved is the binomial distribution, and the standard deviation for the binomial distribution is used to determine the control limits for the p chart. A variety of business activities fit the yes/no format, including, for example, whether materials were filed incorrectly, catalogs were mailed late, products were improperly labeled, bills gave the wrong account number, and percent of customers was seated on time.

P CHART
A control chart for attributes used to monitor the proportion of defectives in a process.

The center line, p-bar (or $\bar{p}$), is the proportion defective, where

$$p\text{-bar} = \frac{\text{total number defective}}{\text{total number inspected}} \qquad \textbf{(6.8)}$$

The 3-sigma upper and lower control limits are computed using the following format:

$$\text{UCL} = \bar{p} + 3S_p \qquad \textbf{(6.9)}$$

$$\text{LCL} = \bar{p} - 3S_p \qquad \textbf{(6.10)}$$

and

$$S_p = \sqrt{\frac{\bar{p}(1 - \bar{p})}{n}} \tag{6.11}$$

represents the standard deviation of the sample. Example 6.2 demonstrates the use of a *p* chart.

EXAMPLE 6.2

Constructing and Interpreting *p* Charts   A medical insurance company is analyzing the promptness of its claims department in responding to customer claims. The company has a policy of processing all claims received within five days. In order to determine how well the organization is doing, data were gathered to determine the proportion of time the claims were mailed late. A total of 25 sets of 100 samples each was made from which the proportion of claims that were mailed within the five-day limit was determined. These data are presented in Table 6.3. Determine 3-sigma control limits and construct a *p* chart.

TABLE 6.3

Sample number	1	2	3	4	5	6	7	8	9	10	11	12	13	14	15	16	17	18	19	20	21	22	23	24	25
Number late	12	14	18	10	8	12	13	17	13	12	15	21	22	19	17	23	24	21	9	20	16	11	8	20	7

SOLUTION

From equation 6.8:

$$p\text{-bar} = \frac{\text{total number defective}}{\text{total number inspected}}$$

$$= \frac{382}{25(100)}$$

$$= 0.1528$$

Using equation 6.11, the standard deviation is

$$S_p = \sqrt{\frac{\bar{p}(1 - \bar{p})}{n}}$$

$$= \sqrt{\frac{(0.1528)(1 - 0.1528)}{100}}$$

$$= 0.035979$$

Using equations 6.9 and 6.10, the control limits are

FIGURE 6.5   *p* **Control Chart**

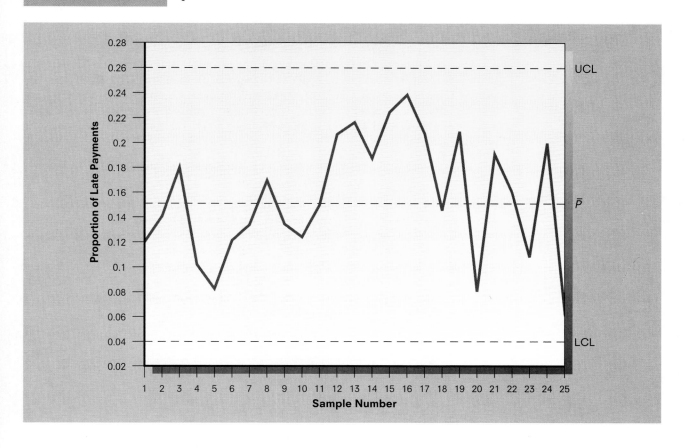

$$\text{UCL} = \bar{p} + 3S_p$$

$$= 0.1528 + (3)(0.035979)$$

$$= 0.2607$$

$$\text{LCL} = \bar{p} - 3S_p$$

$$= 0.1528 - (3)(0.035979)$$

$$= 0.0449$$

These control limits and the control chart are presented in Figure 6.5.

PROCESS CAPABILITY

The capabilities of a process cannot be determined until the process is in control. If a process is stable and it is approximately normally distributed, the process capability can be easily analyzed. **Process capability** describes whether a process can meet a customer's specifications. A process may be in statistical control and still not be able to consistently meet the specifications required. This inability may be due to excessive variability and requires a reexamination of the items that may cause variability such as raw material, workers, machines, environment, and setup.

Many businesses have improved their processes to the extent that they can claim 6-sigma accuracy as opposed to the more common 3-sigma control. (See Box 6.2.)

One straightforward way to determine if the process is able to meet the specification limits is to compare a customer's upper and lower specification limits with the standard deviation. If the control limits are $\pm 3\sigma$, then the difference between the upper and lower tolerance limits divided by 6σ should be greater than 1 to satisfy the specification limit. Often a value of 1.33 is used as a minimum acceptance level. The formula for computing the process capability index is

$$C_p = \frac{\text{Upper specification limit} - \text{lower specification limit}}{6\sigma} \qquad \textbf{(6.12)}$$

where σ is the standard deviation. Values for $C_p \leq 1$ are not acceptable because only part of the process output meets the specification. The rest would be unacceptable. It is also important to note that the process must be properly centered in order to use the capability index. Results obtained when the process is not centered are unacceptable.

Suppose the specifications of one dimension of a part require that the length be within 4 millimeters of 100 millimeters. The standard deviation for the process is 1.67 millimeters. The upper specification limit would be 104 millimeters, and the lower specification would be 96. The value for C_p using formula 6.12 is

$$C_p = \frac{\text{Upper specification limit} - \text{lower specification limit}}{6\sigma}$$

$$= \frac{104 - 96}{(6)(1.67)}$$

$$= 0.80$$

OPERATIONS OUTLOOK

BOX 6.2

Is 6-Sigma Really Necessary?

Motorola was one of the first U.S. companies to embrace a goal of 6-sigma quality. Six-sigma quality means 99.9999998 percent accuracy. That's two defects out of one billion! One might ask, Why is 6-sigma accuracy needed? It seems that 99.7 percent accuracy (3-sigma) would be sufficient. In some situations, just because of sheer numbers, 3-sigma accuracy would be totally unacceptable. For example, with only 99 percent quality there would be

- 20,000 wrong drug prescriptions each year
- More than 15,000 newborn babies accidentally dropped by doctors and nurses each year

- Unsafe drinking water for almost an hour each month (but you wouldn't know which hour)
- At major U.S. airports, two short or long landings each day
- Nearly 500 incidents per week of the wrong surgical procedure performed on patients in the United States
- 2,000 lost articles of mail each hour in the United States

Source "Six Sigma: Motorola's Quest for Zero Defects," *APICS— The Performance Advantage* (July 1991): 36–40.

This solution suggests that the process must be changed because it has too much variability, and consequently a significant number of shafts manufactured will not meet the specifications.

PROCESS IMPROVEMENT AND ANALYSIS TOOLS

FLOWCHARTS

The first step toward improving a process is gaining a clear understanding of what is to be accomplished. In many cases, it is useful to construct a flowchart of the process under consideration. A **flowchart** provides a pictorial representation of the various operations of the process and essentially documents the procedure used. Figure 6.6 is an example of a flowchart for a university's telephone registration process. The process starts when a student has determined the appropriate schedule for the next semester. The next step occurs when the student phones in the schedule. A student can only call in the schedule during

FLOWCHART
A pictorial representation of the various operations of a process that documents all procedures used.

FIGURE 6.6	**Flowchart for Registration Process**

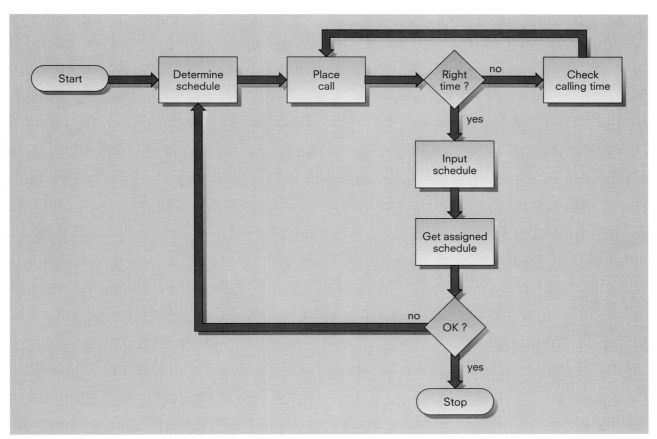

designated hours that are based on the number of credit hours the student has completed. If the call is not at the right time, it will not be accepted and the student must call at a later time. If the time of the call is correct, the student's schedule may be accepted. After several days, the student receives a hard copy of the schedule of courses that the computerized system assigned. If this schedule is acceptable, the scheduling process is complete. If the schedule is not acceptable, the student must determine a new schedule and proceed through the process until an acceptable schedule is generated.

CHECK SHEETS

In many environments, the search for potential causes of quality problems begins by examining subjective data. Statistical tools provide an objective method of determining which of the potential causes for a problem can be validated. They provide a method of validating a hypothesized cause.

CHECK SHEETS
A statistical tool (often a predesigned form) that facilitates the collection of data that will be used in detecting possible causes of quality problems.

Check sheets are a statistical tool that facilitates the accurate collection of data. Check sheets are usually predesigned forms on which data are recorded by using a checkmark or symbol.

Data are normally collected about a clearly defined objective or problem. In manufacturing processes, the data are often linked to the production of a part or product. Whenever data are collected, the question of their reliability must be dealt with because a wrong conclusion can result if data are not reliable. In collecting data about services performed, for example, the quality indicator is determined through verbal methods such as an interview. If two people were collecting data, the results would need to be independent of who collected the data.

Check sheets can be used in conjunction with data that have been designed to measure variables or attributes. For example, a check sheet might record the diameter of a shaft and

---

FIGURE 6.7   **Process Capability Check Sheet**

						Count										
						5				10				Frequency
Upper specification	9.0													
	8.9	X												1
	8.8	X	X											2
	8.7	X	X	X										3
	8.6	X	X	X	X	X								5
	8.5	X	X	X	X	X	X	X	X	X				9
	8.4	X	X	X	X	X	X	X	X					8
	8.3	X	X	X	X	X								5
	8.2	X	X	X										3
	8.1	X												1
Lower specification	8.0													
Total														37

TABLE 6.4							Defect Check Sheet

Type of Defect							Total
Burned	|||||	|||||	|||||	|||||	|||||	||		27
Broken	|||||	|||						8
Dark	|||||								6
Hard	|||||							5
Light	||							2
Soft	||							2
Total								50

determine whether the measures fall within the upper and lower specification limits for this process. In Figure 6.7, individual measures are recorded to determine whether the process capability of a machine is within the specifications. In this case, the upper specification is 9.0 units and the lower specification is 8.0 units. The data collected indicate the process variation is acceptable.

Check sheets may also be used to classify defects according to type. For example, in the manufacture of cookies, defects may be tallied according to the number that are burned, the number that are too dark, the number that break, and the number that are too soft. This type of classification provides another way to stratify the data. Table 6.4 provides an example of this type of application of a check sheet.

HISTOGRAMS

We can also use histograms to describe both variable and attribute data. The data provided in Table 6.4 are attribute data and are converted to a histogram by using a bar chart. The corresponding histogram is presented in Figure 6.8. The process of constructing a histogram from variable data is normally a part of descriptive statistics and is not presented here.

PARETO ANALYSIS

Data that have been tabulated in a check sheet format according to the type of defect can be analyzed using Pareto analysis. Table 6.5 lists the data required to construct a Pareto diagram. **Pareto analysis** provides a way to focus on the vital few rather than the trivial many. Analysis of quality problems often requires the data to be viewed or stratified from many perspectives. In Table 6.5, data are sorted by type of defect. The data could also be

PARETO ANALYSIS
A technique that classifies problem areas according to the degree of importance of the detected defect.

| **TABLE 6.5** | | Data Sheet for a Pareto Chart | | |

Type	Number of Defects	Cumulative Total	Percent of Total	Cumulative Percent
Burned	27	27	54	54
Broken	8	35	16	70
Dark	6	41	12	82
Hard	5	46	10	92
Light	2	48	4	96
Soft	2	50	4	100
Total	50			

sorted by the oven used, the cook involved, or the day of the week. In each case, a different view of the problem would be created and a better understanding of the problem would be obtained.

The Pareto chart in Figure 6.9 provides a graphic display of the type of cookie defects and indicates that burned cookies are a significant part of the problem. Pareto charts are often used to show a before and after view of an attempt at quality improvement. Usually the

| **FIGURE 6.8** | Histogram of Cookie Defects (June 1 to June 6) |

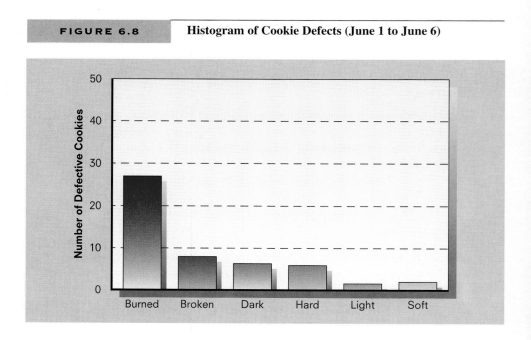

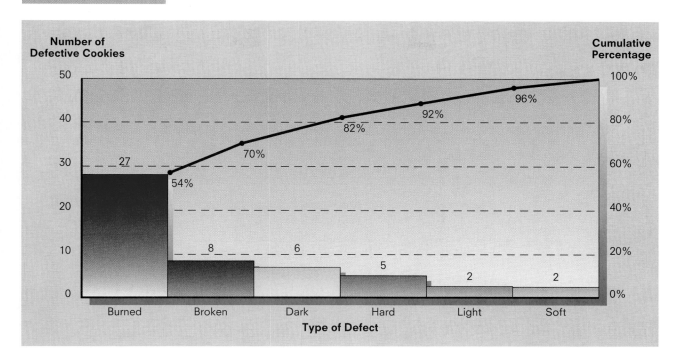

FIGURE 6.9　　**Pareto Chart of Cookie Defects (June 1 to June 6)**

before and after charts are drawn using the same axis and the same scale. If the problem with burned cookies were resolved, for example, the after picture would show the improvement that had occurred.

CAUSE-AND-EFFECT DIAGRAMS

Cause-and-effect, or fishbone, diagrams organize all of the known causes of a problem into a direct cause-and-effect relationship. The process of constructing a fishbone diagram begins by writing the problem statement in the head of the fish. For example, in the cookie making process presented earlier, the problem would appear to be the number of burned cookies. The process of identifying all levels of causes is accomplished by brainstorming or directed group discussion.

CAUSE-AND-EFFECT DIAGRAMS
A tool for analyzing data by organizing all the known causes of a problem into a direct cause-and-effect relationship.

　　Causes are typically identified in a group using a round-robin approach in which discussion is kept to a minimum and criticism of ideas is not acceptable. The causes are written on removable, adhesive-backed notes, with one cause per note. The notes are displayed on the wall. The next stage is the development of an affinity diagram. This is done by silently moving the notes into logical groups that have a common theme. If one cause appears to belong to two groups, a second note is written and the cause can be in both groups.

　　A key word is used to define each of the groups. The key words are used to form the major bones in the fishbone diagram. Recalling the cookie problem, some of the key words might be the oven, ingredients, cook, and procedures used throughout the process. Table 6.6 shows these key words and the causes that were grouped under each heading.

TABLE 6.6	Results after Brainstorming and Establishing Affinity Relationships
Oven	Uneven heating in different parts of the oven Temperature is not constant Airflow in oven not uniform Thermostat not working
Cook	Cookies baked at the wrong height in the oven Cook set temperature incorrectly Cook removed cookies from oven too late Ingredients mixed in different order Materials not mixed thoroughly Wrong type of pan is used Size of cookies is not uniform
Ingredients	Different sources of raw materials are used Ingredients not fresh
Procedures	Temperature setting is too high Cooking time is too long No policy about the correct pan to use Materials not mixed properly Different proportion of ingredients are used Ingredients mixed in different order

These data are shown in the fishbone diagram in Figure 6.10. Note that the head of the fish describes the problem. Each of the major bones of the fish is made up of the major headings in Figure 6.10.

BRAINSTORMING

BRAINSTORMING
A technique for generating a large number of ideas from a group of people in a relatively short period of time.

Brainstorming is an effective procedure used to generate a large number of ideas in a relatively short amount of time. The process usually begins by providing each person in the group with a chance to suggest an idea about the problem. Individuals may elect to give up

At MagneTek facilities, brainstorming sessions aimed at identifying, analyzing, and eliminating work process problems take place regularly. Problem prevention is an important part of T.E.A.M.—Total Excellence at MagneTek.

Source Courtesy of MagneTek, Inc.

| FIGURE 6.10 | Fishbone Diagram: Why Cookies Are Burned |

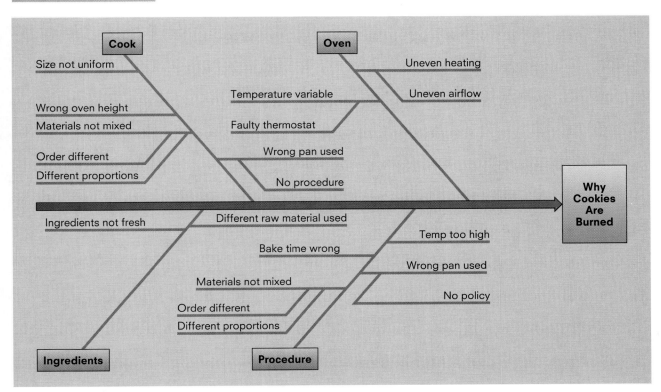

their turn in one round and contribute in the following round. It is important not to criticize but to allow individuals to express their points of view. Discussion other than clarification should be avoided. Clarification should be done by the owner of the idea. Ideas are recorded for everyone to see. Usually new ideas are extensions of, or related to, old ideas.

Multivoting   Multivoting is a procedure used to reduce the number of items under consideration in a discussion to a reasonable number, usually three to five, with good support from the group. Multivoting often follows a brainstorming session in which many ideas have been generated. The process is begun by providing everyone with a chance to vote for the items under consideration. Group members may vote for as many items as they wish, but they cannot vote for an item more than once.

After the votes have been counted, a smaller list is formed from those items receiving the most votes. The choice of how many items are on the list is made by looking for where a natural break occurs or by selecting only those items that have received at least half the votes. The process continues until the number of items have been reduced to an acceptable number. At each stage, when a new list is formed, it is important to make sure that everyone in the group can identify with at least one item on the list. If someone cannot identify strongly with one of the items on the list, that person can add one item to the list before the next stage begins.

THE QI STORY

Although the analysis tools are used separately, several different procedures have been developed to use these tools in a systematic process. The quality improvement (QI) story, which was described briefly in the previous chapter, is one such method. A more complete description follows. Companies usually utilize QI stories after a system they use has been documented, and some type of monitoring has indicated a problem. Monitoring may take the form of a control chart, or it may be customer feedback through some other means. The QI story is a systematic approach to problem solving that also serves as a well-defined communication vehicle within and outside of the quality improvement team.

QI story teams consist of small groups of people, usually from as few as four or five to as many as a dozen. The makeup of the team depends on whether the problem to be solved is departmental or broader. It should include representatives from the areas involved.

At the heart of the QI story is the scientific method. The decisions made are based on a blend of subjective and objective data. The approach identifies a problem that needs to be solved, validates that the problem really exists, explores alternative solutions, selects a solution, validates that the solution provides the desired results, and then standardizes the solution throughout the organization. The process is then repeated with another problem. The types of problems that are solved may be related to a manufacturing process, a service provided, or another system that is a part of the organization. Table 6.7 provides a summary of the seven steps in the QI story.

In step 1, a significant problem is identified and objective data are used to validate selection of that problem.[1] A quality indicator is also identified, which provides an objective measure of the significance of the problem and a sense of how much improvement is needed. Problem areas may be identified by surveying internal or external customers, recognizing special causes identified through SPC processes, or by reviewing departmental or organizational indicators of quality.

Step 2 is understanding the problem. Brainstorming is sometimes used by a group of people to generate, clarify, and evaluate a number of different issues or problems. When several potential problem areas arise, a single problem needs to be identified. Multivoting may be used to reduce the number of problems to just a few. A selection matrix is often used to make a final decision about the problem to pursue. The selection matrix focuses on the impact the problem has on customers and the need to improve the process or system. For each problem area, each team member rates the customer impact on a scale of 1 through 5 (1 = none, and 5 = extreme) and the need to improve on a scale of 1 through 5. These results are multiplied, and the overall winner is the highest product. This step is important because if others in the organization do not perceive the problem to be important, implementation of a solution to the problem may not happen. The other tools are used to help present data in an objective way so as to define the problem more clearly.

The purpose of step 2 is to fully understand the problem so that factors that cause the problem can be discovered. Skilled criminal investigators often return to the scene of the crime to understand who committed the crime. The same is true in problem solving. The problem should be viewed from as many points of view as possible. For example, are there more defects in the morning or afternoon? Are there more defects on Monday or Tuesday or some other day of the week? Are all defects in a specific section or subassembly of a product? Are there more defects for one type of product? Are there more defects for one type of customer? Are the defects all of the same type?

---

[1]These sections are based in part on H. Kume, *Statistical Methods for Quality Improvement* (Tokyo: 3A Corporation, 1985), 191–207.

TABLE 6.7   The Seven Steps in the QI Story

Step 1: Problem Identification

Activities	*Tools Commonly Used*
Identify a significant problem	Selection matrix
Identify an indicator of performance	Graph
Express concretely the undesirable results of the performance	Histogram
	Control chart
	Flowchart
	Check sheet
	Brainstorming
	Multivoting

Step 2: Understanding the Current State

Activities	*Tools Commonly Used*
Investigate by stratifying the problem from many points of view	Pareto chart
Select a subset of the problem for more focus	Histogram
Write a problem statement	Control Chart
Select a target level	

Step 3: Analysis of Causes

Activities	*Tools Commonly Used*
Identify and select root causes	Fishbone diagram
Validate root causes with objective data	Pareto chart
	Check sheets
	Scatter plots

Step 4: Corrective Actions

Activities	*Tools Commonly Used*
Evaluate proposed solutions that attack verified root causes	Brainstorming
Select a course of action and obtain support from those involved	Multivoting
	Selection matrix

Step 5: Check Results

Activities	*Tools Commonly Used*
Confirm the effects of the countermeasures (solutions)	Pareto charts
Use before and after comparisons of data in the same format	Graphs
	Scatter plots
	Control charts
	Histograms

Step 6: Standardization

Activities	*Tools Commonly Used*
Specify who, what, where, why, when, and how the procedure has changed	Control charts
Make changes a part of the standard operating procedure	Histograms

Step 7: Conclusion/Next Steps

Activities	*Tools Commonly Used*
Explore remaining problem	Brainstorming
Identify future topics for investigation	Seven traditional tools

After the problem has been fully explored and understood, a clear statement of the problem is made. This statement is derived from the objective data generated in viewing the problem from many perspectives. After the problem has been identified, a target should be set to indicate the improvement expected. Sometimes targets are linked to what the customers want. In other cases, benchmarking may be used to establish targets.

In step 3 the main causes of the problem are identified and validated. The process may be viewed as building a hypothesis about the cause and testing the hypothesis to validate the cause. Generally speaking, the problem must be consistently present when the cause is present, and the problem must be consistently absent when the cause is absent. However, it must be ascertained that the cause is the root cause. If your car does not start, for example, you may hypothesize that the cause is a dead battery. Replacing the battery may start the car, but the root cause may have been a faulty alternator. Until the alternator is repaired, the problem will exist because the root cause was not identified and eliminated. Normally, new data need to be generated to verify root causes.

Verification of root causes can be done in several ways. For example, the strength of a relationship can be expressed through a correlation coefficient, analysis of variance, or the use of a Pareto chart. Relationships may also be identified via a cause and effect diagram. A useful tool in finding the root cause is to ask the question "Why?" For example, why does the car not start? A possible cause is the battery. Why doesn't the battery work? One of several possible causes is the alternator. Why does the alternator not work? The process of asking why continues until the reasons are out of the immediate control of the investigator. For example, if the alternator does not work because the manufacturer used faulty material, the root cause is out of your control.

In step 4 solutions that will attack the root cause are developed and compared. The advantages and disadvantages of the proposed solutions may be compared with respect to costs and benefits and impact on the customer. The solution selected must be the one agreed to by the people involved.

Step 5 is to determine if the solutions really worked. Before and after comparisons must be made using data presented in the same format. If a Pareto chart had been used in the earlier steps, then a Pareto chart should be used again. If the results do not indicate progress toward the target and undesirable results continue at an unacceptable level even after all the corrective actions have been taken, then the problem-solving efforts have failed and it is necessary to return to step 2 and start again.

In step 6, action ensures that the root cause and the problem will not recur. The specific changes are incorporated into the standard operating procedure of the system. Making sure that those involved in the process understand why the changes are necessary is an essential part of the standardization process. Proper preparation, training, and communication are essential when new standards or procedures are introduced. Procedures must also be put in place to gather data, such as the use of control charts, to ensure the changes are actually adopted by those involved.

Step 7 analyzes and evaluates any problems that were not solved and establishes plans for how to deal with them. The work of the committee is reviewed and any lessons learned or ways to improve the process are noted.

EXAMPLE 6.3

A QI Story Application   An employee put a note in a company suggestion box requesting that the organization take advantage of invoice discounts. A committee consisting of people directly involved was formed to study this suggestion and act on it.

Step 1: *Problem Identification*

About 50 percent of the invoices paid each week were eligible to receive discounts of between 1 and 4 percent. The problem was that more than 90 percent of the invoices that were eligible for a discount were not paid on time, and so no discount was received. To be eligible for a discount, the invoice had to be paid within five days of receipt.

Step 2: *Understanding the Current State*

In attempting to understand the problem, it was discovered that there were three basic reasons why the invoices were not paid on time: the in-plant administrative processes, incorrect invoices, and shipping or materials problems. A Pareto chart of a random sample of orders exceeding the time limit indicated that 70 out of 90, or 77.8 percent, of the problems were due to in-plant administration problems (see Figure 6.11).

The in-plant administrative processes were broken down into the six separate steps, shown in Figure 6.12. A sample of invoices with vendor discounts was analyzed using a Pareto chart to determine the amount of time spent on each step. The first task, which takes up 75 percent of the time, is the primary source of the problem. After careful analysis it was felt that a target of two days for step 1 would be a reasonable place to start. Two days was the fastest time for this process of any of the samples checked.

Step 3: *Analysis of Causes*

Figure 6.13 on page 151 shows a fishbone diagram with a list of possible root causes. After considerable discussion, the group decided to

---

FIGURE 6.11   **Pareto Analysis of Possible Causes**

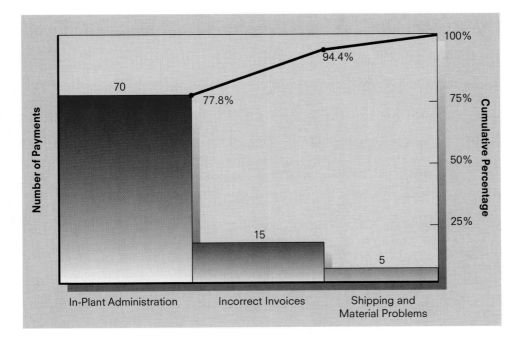

| FIGURE 6.12 | Pareto Analysis of Possible In-Plant Causes |

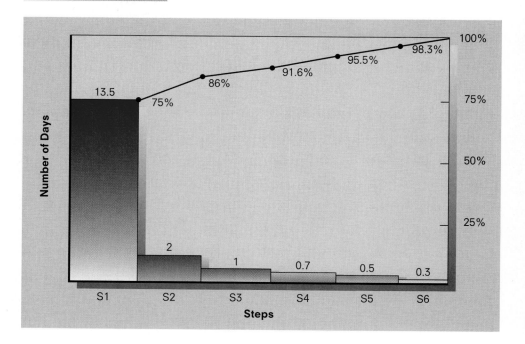

concentrate on several root causes. The members decided to determine first if there was an in-plant procedure for vendors' payments that were eligible for a discount, and second to determine the extent of training of the people involved.

Members of the team discovered that the time required to process an invoice depended on the individual doing the work. The organization used a job rotation system, and the output per week varied by more than 40 percent. Figure 6.14 (page 152) shows that samples 4, 5, and 6 were not processed by the same person who processed samples 7, 8, and 9. Samples 11, 12, 13, 14, and 15 were processed by yet another person. The team discovered that invoices were paid at different times, and the person performing this task was occasionally on loan to help with other pressing matters and not processing invoices. There was also evidence that different workers performed the tasks differently. The group did not find evidence of an in-plant procedure for identifying invoices eligible for a discount.

Step 4: *Corrective Action*

Two solutions were proposed: a procedure to process eligible invoices that would be in agreement with corporate guidelines, and uniform training for all workers. A backup system was proposed in the event the employee who processed invoices was asked to perform other functions temporarily. If all invoices were processed on time, the annual dollar savings possible was estimated to be about $40,000 per year. The QI story team

| FIGURE 6.13 | **Fishbone Diagram of Possible Causes** |

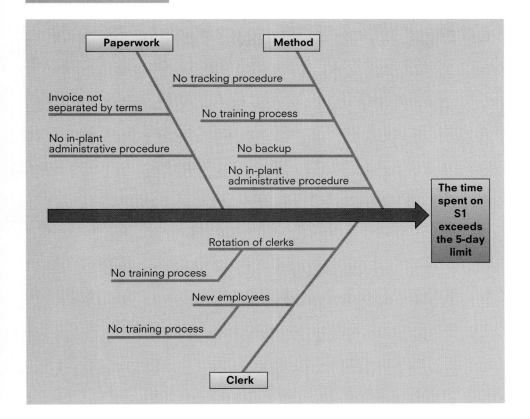

included representatives from the areas involved, and there was unanimous agreement on the proposed course of action.

Step 5: *Check Results*

The effects of the countermeasures, or solutions, were measured using the Pareto charts that were used in the earlier stages. The before and after comparisons showed that although about 10 percent of the orders did not get processed in time, the average time to process the invoices at S1 dropped from 13.5 days to 2.5 days, an 11-day improvement. Compare Figure 6.12 with Figure 6.15 to note these differences. Figure 6.16 provides a before-and-after view of the run time to process each invoice.

Step 6: *Standardization*

The solutions proposed in step 4, and validated in step 5, were submitted for acceptance as standard operating procedure to the administrative council. The procedures were accepted and are currently standard operating procedures.

Step 7: *Conclusion/Next Steps*

The proposed solution to the problem made a significant contribution to resolving the problem. Although the problem had not been completely

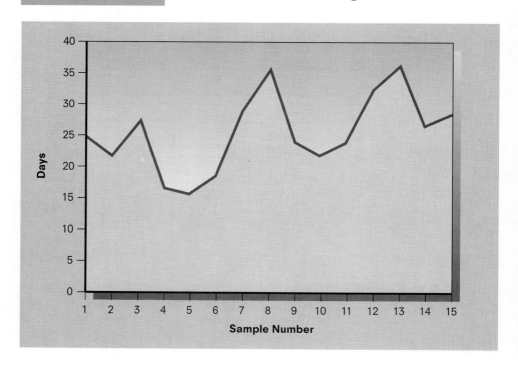

FIGURE 6.14   **Run Chart of Invoice-Processing Time**

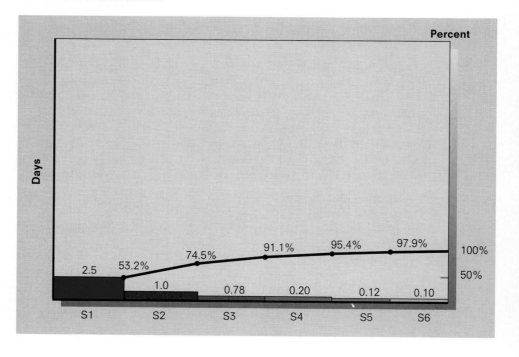

FIGURE 6.15   **Pareto Chart of Results after Changes**

| FIGURE 6.16 | **Before-and-After Run Chart of Processing Time** |

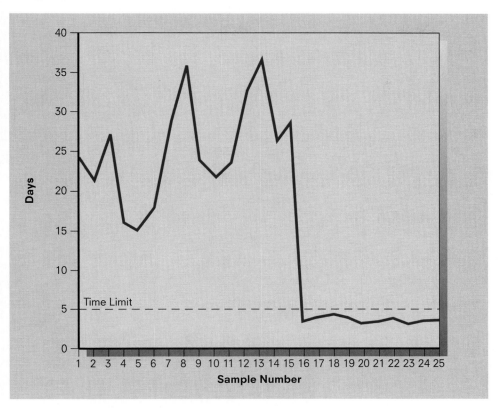

Before 1–15; after 16–25

---

resolved, it was felt that operating and training procedures in other departments should be evaluated next.*

BUYER/SUPPLIER RELATIONSHIPS

A critical link in the production of quality products exists between the suppliers who sell raw materials and component parts to manufacturers who produce an end product. In many organizations manufacturers have strengthened this link by working with a small number of regular suppliers. These manufacturers promote quality by developing long-term buyer/supplier relationships that are based on statistical evidence of quality and strive for continuous improvement.

One such approach, outlined in Figure 6.17, describes the relationship between Florida Power and Light and its suppliers. At the heart of this improvement effort are vendor quality improvement teams that use the QI story and the P-D-C-A cycle as tools for improvement. The vendor in Figure 6.17 eventually becomes a quality vendor. This is the first of a

---

*This example is based in part upon work completed by Florida Power and Light.

FIGURE 6.17   **The Quality Vendor Process**

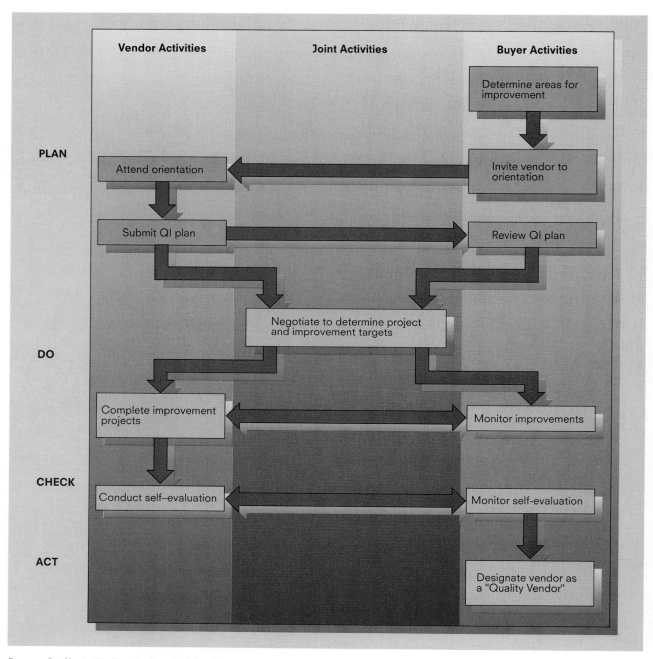

Source   Profiles in Quality (Needham Heights, Mass.: Allyn and Bacon, 1991), 124.

Allied Signal, which buys from preferred dealers who support its productivity goals, trains suppliers in techniques that improve quality and reduce costs. Here, an Allied Signal Automotive team conducts a Total Quality Speed workshop for Ashtabula Rubber Company, a supplier of components for Allied Signal truck brakes. This training helped Ashtabula implement a one-step spray-coating process that reduced its order-to-delivery time by one-third.

three-step process. The remaining two levels are certified vendor and excellent vendor. As vendors proceed through these steps, they provide manufacturers—their customers—with process capability data and statistical process control data, and they concentrate their efforts on controlling variation.

Many manufacturers are directly involved in supplier development activities. The success of these programs depends on both the manufacturers' and suppliers' commitment to become involved in joint problem-solving activities. Lascelles and Dale provide clear guidelines for supplier development activities. They describe the following steps for a supplier development program:

1. Establish and articulate program objectives
2. Set priorities for action
3. Identify key suppliers as long-term partners and make plans to reduce the supplier base
4. Communicate the program objectives and methodology to key suppliers
5. Assess the capability of suppliers to meet purchase requirements
6. Engage in quality planning with suppliers
7. Formally recognize suppliers that achieve preferred status
8. Develop an ongoing quality improvement relationship with suppliers, based on a free exchange of information[2]

Some suppliers provide manufacturers with process control charts or other statistical evidence about the quality of incoming materials. Whenever manufacturers do not know

---

[2]D. M. Lascelles and B. G. Dale, "The Buyer-Supplier Relationship in Total Quality Management," *Journal of Purchasing and Materials Management* 25 (Summer 1989): 10–19.

the quality of incoming materials, they have to determine it themselves. One technique they use is acceptance sampling, which requires that a sampling plan be developed to determine an acceptable quality level.

ACCEPTANCE SAMPLING

ACCEPTANCE SAMPLING
A type of inspection that manufacturers use to infer a level of quality for a population based on the level of quality of a sample.

ACCEPTABLE QUALITY LEVEL (AQL)
The percentage level of defects specified by the producer but acceptable to the consumer.

LOT TOLERANCE PERCENT DEFECTIVE (LTPD)
The threshold (or upper limit) of percentage defects that the consumer is willing to accept.

PRODUCER'S RISK
The probability of rejecting a "good" lot, that is, a lot that meets or exceeds the acceptable quality level.

CONSUMER'S RISK
The probability of accepting a "bad" lot, that is, a lot that is at the LTPD or worse.

Manufacturers use **acceptance sampling** to evaluate items that they have received from a supplier or from another part of the organization. It is based upon a sampling plan that specifies that one or more samples be taken and that from that sample, the manufacturer assesses the quality of the order. In this section a sampling plan based upon the evaluation of one sample is developed.[3]

A single sampling plan is determined by two key values, n and c. The sample size is referred to as n. The largest number of defects allowed in a sample considered to be acceptable is represented by c. Because every random sample is not an exact replica of the population that is being sampled, there are risks involved for both the producer of the item and the consumer of the item. In order to discuss these risks, the concept of acceptable and unacceptable quality levels needs to be defined.

The **acceptable quality level (AQL)** is specified by the producer and agreed to by the consumer. Lots are viewed as good if they are of AQL quality level or better. The unacceptable quality level is called the **lot tolerance percent defective (LTPD)**. The LTPD is specified by the consumer and agreed to by the producer, and it represents a threshold quality level that the consumer cannot accept. Both the AQL and LTPD are positive decimals, but some consumers may demand that the quality level be as good as fewer than 10 defects per million, creating very small values for AQL and LTPD. In terms of risk, the producer is concerned about a sampling plan that would reject a lot that contains an AQL level of quality or better. This risk is known as the **producer's risk** and has a probability of α of occurring. That is, the probability that a good lot is rejected is equal to α. The consumer is concerned with accepting a lot containing a LTPD or higher of defective goods. This risk is known as the **consumer's risk** and has a probability of β of occurring. Thus the probability of having a bad lot accepted is equal to β.

THE SAMPLING PLAN

The values for α, β, AQL, and LTPD are mutually agreed upon and provide the input for determining the values for n and c. These values can be used to derive the values of n and c through a trial and error process, using either the binomial distribution, or if $n > 20$ and $p < 0.05$, the Poisson distribution. Typically, organizations use standard references such as MIL STD 105D (one of many government publications related to quality) or the civilian version ANSI/ASQC Z1.4 to develop sampling plans.[4]

An operating characteristic (OC) curve is a graph of how well a sampling plan performs. The Poisson distribution can be useful in constructing OC curves because the values are easy to compute. In Figure 6.18 the operating characteristic curve for AQL = 0.02,

---

[3]For information on other sampling plans, see A. Duncan, *Quality Control and Industrial Statistics,* 5th ed. (Homewood, Ill.: Irwin, 1986).
[4]Duncan, 217–248.

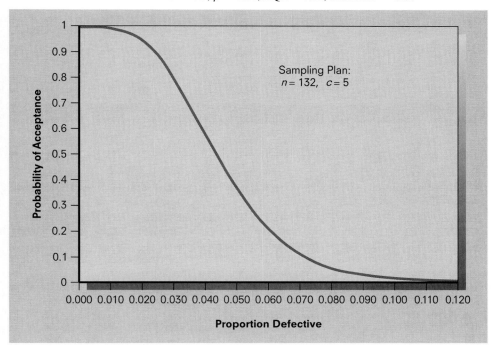

FIGURE 6.18

OC Curves
$\alpha = 0.5$, $\beta = 0.10$, AQL $= 0.02$, and LTPD $= 0.07$

LTPD $= 0.07$, $\alpha = 0.05$, and $\beta = 0.1$ is provided. The sharpness of the curve between the AQL value and the LTPD value indicates how well the sampling plan discriminates. The OC curve passes through the points (AQL, $1 - \alpha$) and (LTPD, β).

The sampling plan specified for the values given in Figure 6.18 results in values of n and c, which are $n = 132$ and $c = 5$. After 132 units have been inspected, a decision to accept or reject the entire lot is made based upon the number of nonconforming items found in the lot. If the number of nonconforming items is less than or equal to 5, the lot is accepted. If the number is greater than 5, the lot is rejected.

SUMMARY

The quality movement has taken root in many U.S. companies. Although many companies have successful quality programs, the popular press reports many companies whose results have been less than satisfactory. Most of the quality tools used for improvement in the United States have been a part of the success of the Japanese since the 1980s. When these tools are understood and used properly, U.S. firms will also find them successful in satisfying customers.

The tools for continuous improvement apply equally well to services and manufacturing organizations, as the QI story case presented in this chapter shows. Improvement projects have become much broader than they were only a decade ago. Not only can processes be improved, but systems and subsystems that plan, organize, and control processes can also be improved. The goal of all improvement efforts is customer satisfaction, which leads to competitive advantage.

ERIC'S DINER REVISITED

CROSS-LINKS The cause-and-effect analysis of Eric's Diner showed that during busy times, the table staff were unable to clean and set tables fast enough to keep up with arriving customers. The kitchen help and hosts had no trouble keeping the buffet stocked and customers' drinks filled. Further analysis showed that the tables farthest away from the kitchen were the ones that seemed to take the longest to bus. A discussion with the table staff convinced Eric that the time it took to bus the tables wasn't the problem. Carrying the dirty dishes back to the kitchen, however, *was* a problem—this chore took more time than clearing the table. So Eric ordered four new bussing carts. Two weeks later, the four carts arrived and one cart was placed in each of the far two corners of the restaurant during busy periods. As each cart was filled by the table staff, it was brought into the kitchen and replaced by an empty cart. Carts were to be emptied by kitchen help as time allowed.

With this problem solved, Eric decided to look at the next most frequent complaint: the disorganized buffet. How would you utilize the QI story to better organize the buffet? What type of information would you need? How could this information be collected?

QUESTIONS FOR REVIEW

1. What is SPC?
2. What is the difference between variation due to chance and variation due to an assignable cause?
3. What is the purpose of a control chart?
4. What is the likelihood that a point will fall outside the control limits if 3-sigma control limits are used?
5. Explain the difference between attributes and variables and give an example of each.
6. What does the process capability index measure? How is this information used?

7. Which step(s) in the QI story deal with problem identification?
8. Which steps in the QI story deal with identifying and evaluating solution alternatives?
9. In the QI story, how is it determined that the problem has been solved?
10. When is SPC useful?
11. Describe how an acceptance sampling plan is developed.

QUESTIONS FOR THOUGHT AND DISCUSSION

1. Where does the customer fit in the QI story?
2. Suppose you deliver pizza and you would like to make more money from tips. By using a fishbone diagram and/or a cause and effect analysis, identify the major causes that might keep you from making more money.

3. One problem is more important than another problem facing an organization. How should the next problem to attack be selected when using the QI story?

INTEGRATIVE QUESTIONS

1. Identify the capabilities an organization gains by developing a TQM philosophy. How might these capabilities be useful in other ways in the future?

2. If an organization develops and implements a TQM philosophy, what else must it do in order to be successful?

PROBLEMS

1. Consider the *X*-bar chart shown in the figure below. Identify as many ways as you can to show that the data are nonrandom.

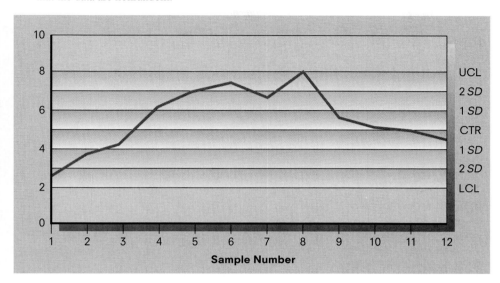

2. Consider the *X*-bar chart shown in the figure below. Identify as many ways as you can to show that the data are nonrandom.

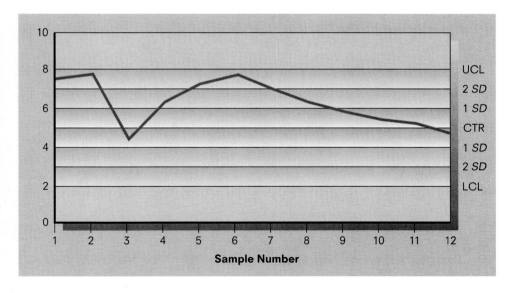

3. Consider the following 12 sets of data with each subgroup consisting of 5 individual measures.

1	2	3	4	5	6	7	8	9	10	11	12
20	17	21	16	21	26	24	21	23	21	25	26
21	15	16	22	14	19	27	23	25	28	24	19
21	17	18	12	24	28	28	25	27	22	25	19
22	15	12	22	18	24	21	27	14	26	18	25
18	19	17	18	19	20	19	16	17	22	19	21

   a. Determine X-bar for each subgroup.
   b. Determine X-double bar.
   c. Determine the range for each subgroup.
   d. Determine R-bar.
   e. Determine the control limits for an X-bar chart and the R chart.
   f. Graph each data set.

4. A registration-by-phone system has drawn significant criticism from students. Initial studies indicated that only one in four was able to get through without a busy signal on the first call. Consequently, the administration has made several attempts to improve the system. In order to assess the situation, researchers took 25 samples, each containing 25 interviews with students who had used the system. These students were asked whether they were able to get through without a busy signal on their first call. The number of students saying yes out of the 25 interviewed in each sample is shown below.
   a. Construct 3-sigma confidence intervals for this process using a p chart, with $\bar{p} = \frac{1}{4}$.
   b. Construct control charts and plot the data.
   c. Based upon these data, has there been any improvement?

Sample Number	Response	Sample Number	Response
1	9	14	5
2	4	15	3
3	5	16	4
4	6	17	7
5	7	18	5
6	6	19	8
7	13	20	6
8	4	21	9
9	5	22	10
10	3	23	9
11	8	24	5
12	4	25	6
13	6		

5. The specifications for a part are 30.0 ± 1.5 millimeters. The process used to make this part has a standard deviation of 0.298 millimeters. Assuming the process is centered, calculate the process capability index and make a recommendation regarding the variation in this process.

6. The specification for the height of a part is 20 ± 0.05 millimeters. The process used to make this dimension has a standard deviation of 0.018 millimeters.
   a. What is the process capability index?
   b. What fraction of the items produced will not meet the specifications?

7. A major league manager of a baseball team is planning to use SPC to monitor the performance of his star baseball player. The player has had an average of about .300 over the past four years. The manager has decided to count the number of hits the batter makes in 50 at-bats. He has taken a total of 25 samples, each of 50 at-bats, over the past four years. His data are shown below. Based upon this information, what is the fewest number of hits the batter may receive before there would appear to be an assignable cause for his poor performance? Use a 3-sigma control limit.

Sample No.	Number of Hits	Sample No.	Number of Hits
1	22	14	17
2	20	15	13
3	22	16	10
4	9	17	7
5	12	18	17
6	21	19	16
7	14	20	10
8	15	21	17
9	10	22	24
10	18	23	20
11	21	24	10
12	9	25	11
13	10		

8. A pizza company is having difficulty with late deliveries. So management has kept track of when a late delivery was made as well as who the driver was in the chart below.

Time	Monday	Tuesday	Wednesday	Thursday	Friday
4–6	AC	AAB	AABCCC	A	ABC
6–8	BCC	ABCC	ABCCC	BBCC	ABBBCCC
8–10	AC	BB	BBCCC	BCC	AABBCCC
10–12	BC	BBCC	ABBCCC	BC	BBC

For example, an AC in the 4–6 slot on Monday means driver A and driver C each had one late delivery during that period. In order to further analyze this problem, construct bar charts for the following:

a. The number of late deliveries by each driver
b. The number of late deliveries by day of the week
c. The number of late deliveries by time of day

What do these charts suggest about the possible problem for this pizza company?

SUGGESTED READINGS

Gaudard, M., R. Coates, and L. Freeman. "Accelerating Improvement." *Quality Progress* (October 1991): 81–88.

Harrington, H. J. *The Improvement Process.* New York: McGraw-Hill, 1987.

Kume, H. *Statistical Methods For Quality Improvement.* Tokyo: 3A Corporation, 1985.

Mizuno, S. *Management for Quality Improvement: The 7 New Tools.* Cambridge, Mass.: Productivity Press, 1988.

Pyzdek, T. *What Every Manager Should Know About Quality.* Milwaukee: ASQC Quality Press, 1991.

Shores, A. Richard. *A TQM Approach to Achieving Manufacturing Excellence.* Milwaukee: Quality Press, 1990.

Tomasek, H. "Improve Process with the Quality Journal." *Quality Progress* (July 1992): 49–54.

THE JUST-IN-TIME PHILOSOPHY

Mama's Finest

Mama's Finest is a producer of fruit spreads, jams, and jellies. It has a small share of the market with its own label, but most of its sales come from private label products that the company produces for several large grocery store chains. Recently, it began to sell a 64-ounce jar of grape jelly to a large warehouse club chain. Management sees the warehouse club market as having the greatest potential for growth in the near future. Mama's Finest's processes are quite simple. Several raw materials, the most significant being fruit, pectin, and corn syrup, are blended, cooked, and then jarred. Filled jars are then labeled, boxed, and shipped. Raw materials delivered daily include jars, lids, and labels. Fresh and frozen fruit is contracted annually. Corn syrup or other sugar substitutes are purchased through the commodity markets. ■ Allison Foster, production manager for Mama's Finest, was pleased to see the increase in orders for the 64-ounce grape jelly and believed the relationship with the warehouse club was going to payoff handsomely. Not only was she happy because of the increase in orders, but she was also pleased because it was for the 64-ounce size. Despite the fact that the markup was small, the volume was going to make up for it. ■ Everything seemed to run smoothly when Mama's Finest was filling 64-ounce jars. It was the best of both worlds for equipment efficiency. The filler (the machine that transferred the jelly into the jars) went through product more quickly than it did for smaller sizes, but the jars moved more slowly. The high volume of product resulted in fewer setups per ton of product. The slower speed resulted in less breakage of jars and less maintenance expense. Allison's cost per case equivalent was its lowest when the company ran 64-ounce jars. ■ Purchasing had come through for

her on this one, too. She had convinced Tom Crawford, purchasing manager, that the demand for the 64-ounce jar was increasing and that he should try to negotiate a high volume discount. He had been pleased to announce to her the day before that a four-months' supply of 64-ounce jars was on its way. ■ Two weeks later, she started using the new 64-ounce jars. The last thing Allison wanted to do was to have to turn down a quick turnaround order from one of the warehouse chains. With a four-month shelf life of the product, she knew she could afford to build up a substantial finished-product inventory that would allow her to respond quickly and build up confidence in Mama's Finest's performance. She instructed the number four filler line that until further notice it would be dedicated to 64-ounce grape. After two weeks of uneventful production on the number four line, the supply of 64-ounce grape was sufficient to meet four weeks of demand at its current level. Allison felt relieved that she was now buffered from any disasters. Production could now just back off to the rate of demand and maintain the four-week level of finished product. Any call from a warehouse club could be satisfied out of the large buffer of finished product. Her confidence was not to last long, however. ■ On Monday, just two days after she had filled her finished product buffer, she strolled by the number four filler. She saw the line foreman and Tom Crawford engaged in what seemed to be a heated discussion. As she approached them, she saw Ellis, the foreman, holding a 64-ounce jar and heard him say, "This is the third bead we've found this week, Tom. I think we need to check this out further." ■ Tom replied, "All of the beads were small, I don't think there is any reason to be concerned." ■ Allison immediately asked, "What's going on?" ■ Ellis responded, "You're aware of the problems we sometimes have with breakaway beads. Small pieces of glass are sometimes attached to the inside bottom of the jar. Sometimes they are solidly attached and just form a bump in the jar. Other times they break loose, resulting in a piece of glass in the product. They are very difficult to spot. Sometimes they don't break loose during the jar wash but do break loose during the filling process itself. We've been finding a lot of beads in this batch of jars. Most have been breaking off during the jar wash. I am concerned that some may be making it through the jar wash and break off at the filler, or they may break off when a customer bumps them with a knife. In either case, there will be a loose piece of glass mixed in with the jelly." ■ Allison faced a difficult decision. There was a two-and-a-half months' supply of 64-ounce jars remaining from the initial large order. It was from this order that the quality problem was originating. A call to the supplier was of little use. Because it was a certified supplier, its lot had not been inspected. It had produced the entire quantity in one run, so any of the jars could be a problem. The supplier would be unable to replace the entire lot for several weeks. ■ Mama's Finest had two alternatives. It could return all of the unused jars to the supplier and halt production of the 64-ounce jelly until the supply of jars was replenished. This solution could mean missing orders from warehouse clubs. The second alternative was to gear up for a full inspection of the unused 64-ounce jars. This step would require shutting down one of the other filler lines and moving personnel to a temporary inspection station. Allison knew that both measures were really only stopgap. Because of the size of the lot and the amount of time that had passed before Mama's Finest had found the defect, it was unlikely that the supplier could find the cause of the defect and prevent it from happening again. Because of the number of jars they had already filled and the fact that with either alternative they would all have to be destroyed, Allison knew that any near-term profit from warehouse clubs would be offset by increased costs related to the defective jars. ■

JUST-IN-TIME (JIT)
A management philosophy, which originated in Japan, that focuses on the elimination of waste.

Most U.S. consumers are aware of the competitive forces of Japan. When shopping for a camera, stereo, TV, VCR, computer, microwave oven, camcorder, or automobile, an American sees evidence of Japanese manufacturers' success everywhere. Many differences exist among Japanese manufacturers, but they have some common approaches that have had significant influence on U.S. manufacturing and that are beginning to influence services as well. A group of beliefs and management techniques, known as **just-in-time (JIT),** is associated with Japanese manufacturing management, although not all aspects of it originated in Japan. The dominant goal of JIT can be summed up quite simply: eliminate waste.

Waste can be considered any effort or expenditure that doesn't add value to a service or product. Fujio Cho of Toyota describes waste as "anything other than the minimum amount of equipment, materials, parts, space, and workers' time, which are absolutely essential to add value to the product."[1] Toyota has identified the following seven types of waste:

Waste from overproduction: Overproduction is caused by producing more than is needed, or producing items early. Both practices result in excess inventory.

---

[1]Kiyoshi Suzaki, *The New Manufacturing Challenge* (New York: Free Press, 1987), 8.

Waste of waiting time: Waiting time results from orders for products and partially completed products that are in the system but spending a great deal of time waiting to be processed. In this situation the amount of time spent in the physical production system may be much greater than the time required for the actual processing.

Transportation waste: Transportation waste within the system is caused by excessive handling and movement of material from one place to another, usually resulting from an ineffective layout and/or process design.

Processing waste: Unnecessary steps in the production process are the most common form of processing waste.

Inventory waste: Inventory results from producing at a rate faster than the rate of consumption. Excess inventory is money invested in something that yields no return. It may exist for a number of reasons and may cause many other problems as well.

Waste of motion: Waste of motion results from poorly designed jobs that do not effectively utilize workers' energies and skills.

Waste from product defects: Product defects not only waste materials, but they also waste time. Defects must be identified and corrected. For many firms, fixing what was not done correctly the first time consumes a significant portion of the operating budget.[2]

There are other types of waste as well. Unnecessary paperwork and the time and effort spent in associated tasks are significant for many companies. JIT seeks to eliminate waste at both the macro and micro levels of a business. One of the most common types of waste, from which JIT gets its name, is excess inventory caused by making things before they are needed.

In JIT, waste is eliminated in many ways. One common approach to identifying waste is to expose problems so that they can be solved by eliminating things that conceal them. Managers often work on short-term solutions that really aren't solutions at all. They're merely coping mechanisms that make it easier to tolerate a problem by reducing its effects. Treating symptoms rather than the real causes of problems is common in business because it often costs less in the short term. JIT eliminates the so-called noise that often prevents managers from seeing the real problems. Although this approach may increase the short-term impact of the problem, it also creates an opportunity for long-term improvement by exposing the problem. Through this approach, JIT accomplishes a number of specific objectives. Figure 7.1 demonstrates how JIT strives to reduce inventory, improve productivity, improve quality, and increase the level of worker involvement in decision making, all within an environment of continuous improvement. The result is a never-ending cycle of exposing and conquering problems.

Although JIT has four seemingly autonomous objectives, its function as a system can best be understood from the standpoint of what contributions JIT makes to the management of resources within the operations function. Recall that processes, inventory, work force, and facilities and equipment are the four resource categories within the operations function. The elimination of waste has direct implications for these resources. From the perspective of these four resource categories, the waste elimination objectives of JIT are

To simplify and increase the productivity of processes

To reduce inventory

---

[2]Suzaki, *The New Manufacturing Challenge,* 12.

FIGURE 7.1   **Objectives of JIT**

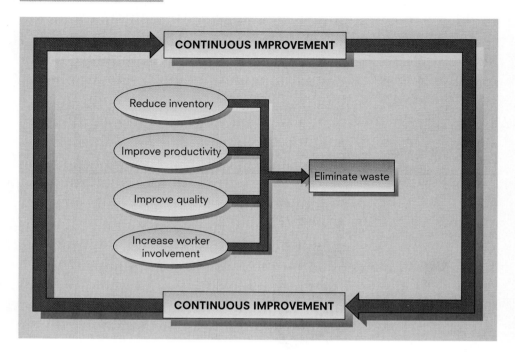

To involve the work force in decision making

To increase flexibility of facilities and equipment

These objectives are achieved through the application and interaction of a variety of techniques, which provide benefits on their own or work in conjunction with each other. All the techniques have a primary benefit that contributes to one objective and tangential benefits that contribute to the accomplishment of others.

The remainder of this chapter is devoted to an overview of the approaches JIT uses to accomplish its eliminate-waste mission in each resource category and the linkages between these approaches and the competitive priorities of price, quality, dependability, flexibility, and time. The chapter concludes with an overview of the impact JIT has on other business functions.

SIMPLIFYING AND INCREASING PROCESS PRODUCTIVITY

WHAT IS PRODUCTIVITY?

PRODUCTIVITY
The ratio of outputs per unit of input.

Productivity is generally viewed as a ratio of output per unit of input, as shown in equation 7.1:

$$\text{Productivity} = \frac{\text{outputs}}{\text{inputs}} \qquad (7.1)$$

It might be a measure as specific as units per hour or as global as return on investment. Processes, as described in chapter 1, refer to the actions that are taken to convert inputs to

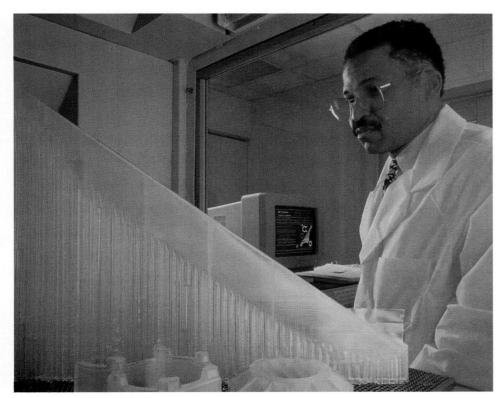

Ford Motor Company is sharpening its global competitive edge by using new technology to improve the efficiency of its processes. It usually takes about six weeks to handcraft a prototype part of wood, metal, or plastic. Ford, however, makes prototypes in a matter of hours by using a new process called stereolithography. The stereolithography system's computer reads data from a design engineer's computer model of a new part, then builds the part by firing a laser beam that hardens a liquid resin into a solid object. Here a Ford engineer looks at parts made by its rapid-prototype system.

Source Courtesy of Ford Motor Company.

outputs and are generally composed of specific procedures. An increase in process productivity is a natural outcome of the elimination of waste. Elimination of waste means eliminating efforts or expenditures that do not add value. Stalk and Hout report that in traditional manufacturing systems, products receive value for only 0.05 percent to 5 percent of the time that they are in the system.[3] Elimination of efforts or expenditures that do not add value to processes results in a reduction of the amount of resources (money, labor, materials, and the like) required to get the same outputs.

As the denominator of the productivity equation is reduced, productivity is increased. Outputs are primarily the products or services the company sells. Inputs vary from company to company, but they are generally categorized by the four resource categories from chapter 1—process, inventory, work force, and facilities and equipment. For many firms, facilities, equipment, and inventory make up most of the product costs. Inventory, for example, can account for as much as 60 percent of a product's cost.

PROCESS PRODUCTIVITY IMPROVEMENT APPROACHES

Several JIT techniques combine to increase overall process productivity, as shown in Figure 7.2. One approach to eliminating waste is to eliminate unnecessary steps in the production of a service or product. Unnecessary steps include such things as unnecessary mo-

---

[3]G. Stalk, Jr., and T. M. Hout, *Competing Against Time* (New York: Free Press, 1990), 49.

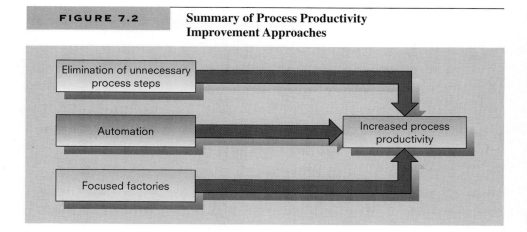

| FIGURE 7.2 | **Summary of Process Productivity Improvement Approaches** |

tion, unnecessary transportation, or unnecessary waiting time. More attention to the physical layout of work centers to reduce unnecessary production or service steps is also a major contributor to eliminating waste.

GROUP TECHNOLOGY
The process of grouping products with similar processing requirements into manufacturing cells.

Group technology, the process of grouping products with similar processing requirements into manufacturing cells, is often used to reduce unnecessary movement of materials. JIT encourages the development of a flow of products through processes by using product-oriented layouts and cells instead of the more traditional functional layouts found in many U.S. factories. Better layouts result in a one-way flow of materials with material deliveries made directly to the shop floor, reducing transportation and material movement costs. This is often accomplished by starting and ending all lines near exterior walls and having numerous delivery accesses so delivery trucks can feed material directly to production lines. Many of the planning and control tasks are simplified because of the elimination of wasted steps and the development of a flow.

JIT also strives to increase productivity by increasing the outputs. As the numerator of the productivity equation (7.1) increases, productivity increases. JIT makes use of automation and robotics. It supports the belief that using machines rather than people to do tedious, unpleasant, or dangerous tasks not only increases outputs but also demonstrates respect for workers by freeing them to make more valuable contributions.

At more of a macro level, JIT also encourages process focus—"Do what you do well." It advocates concentrating on a narrow spectrum of products or services rather than on a broad spectrum or concentrating on a narrow spectrum of processes by producing products that may differ but have similar processes. With this approach, expertise is increased and attention can be given to perfecting a narrow span of processes rather than attaining mediocrity across a large variety of processes. In order to attain this focus, JIT companies tend to have networks of small focused factories or several focused factories in one facility rather than a few huge factories, as has often been the case in the United States. Many U.S. firms have adopted this approach with existing facilities by reorganizing large manufacturing plants into several smaller units under one roof.

Unlike U.S. manufacturers, Japanese manufacturers have traditionally offered fewer options on products. They have also maintained a pattern of shorter model cycles (a cycle is the lifespan of a specific product model) than U.S. competitors. The trend in Japan now is to further restrict product variety and in an attempt to reduce costs, to lengthen model cycles.

To eliminate waste and to provide better quality than competitors, JIT espouses a **quality at the source,** or total quality management (TQM), mentality. Every employee is responsible for quality, and quality is a part of every step in the production of a good or service. To make all workers responsible for their own quality means that they must also be given the authority to stop the production line if there is a problem. This quality mentality and the worker empowerment that must accompany it are known as **jidoka** and are a part of the TQM philosophy, described in chapter 5. TQM and JIT support each other, and TQM is generally considered a prerequisite to JIT. Quality is important in a JIT system because with it comes a reduction of inventories, as will be discussed later in this chapter. Work centers can very quickly be shut down for lack of materials if the small quantity of inventory is found to be defective.

In TQM, the quality focus is on acting to ensure quality production. Defects should not be produced. This is accomplished through an attitude of "do it right the first time" and techniques that make it happen. A number of techniques, including statistical process control and poka yoke, an emphasis on making processes foolproof, contribute to accomplishing this objective. In the United States, the quality focus has historically been one of detection rather than prevention: find the defects before they get to the market. This has changed drastically in recent years as U.S. manufacturers have increased their commitment to TQM.

QUALITY AT THE SOURCE
A concept of JIT making each employee responsible for the quality of his or her work.

JIDOKA
A form of worker empowerment that gives workers the power to stop production processing if they believe something is not as it should be.

PROCESS PRODUCTIVITY IMPROVEMENT AND COMPETITIVE PRIORITIES

Improving the ratio of outputs to inputs has the potential to reduce the cost associated with producing a given quantity of outputs. Cost savings are obtained by eliminating unnecessary steps; from group technology, automation and robotics, process focus, and TQM; and through reductions in material costs made possible by changing relationships with suppliers. This cost savings can be passed on to customers to provide a company with a competitive price advantage, or the savings can be added to profit. The effort to improve quality not only increases productivity, thereby contributing to cost reduction, but it also improves a company's ability to compete on the basis of quality. Process focus, as well as the use of automation and robotics, may also enhance quality. Increases in process productivity and improvements in quality contribute to increased dependability, by eliminating last-minute problems, such as the discovery of defects, that can result in late orders. Dependability is also improved by eliminating unnecessary steps in the process and by the predictable flows that result from group technology. The use of automation and robotics can also enhance dependability. Reducing the throughput time, the total amount of time a product is in the system, by eliminating unnecessary steps in the process, increases a company's flexibility to respond to last-minute customer demands and market changes. Increasing productivity is often achieved by reducing the time it takes to produce a product by eliminating unnecessary steps as well as improving the remaining steps. Although other aspects of JIT also contribute to the reduction of throughput time, productivity improvements play a major part. They often result in a much shorter response time, which translates into quicker turnaround for the customer and the associated competitive advantage. Reduced throughput time is also enhanced by better communication between product design and manufacturing so that new products are more manufacturable.

INVENTORY REDUCTION

THE PROBLEMS WITH HIGH LEVELS OF INVENTORY

Inventory is probably the most common coping mechanism in business. It is used to hide the symptoms of many problems rather than eliminate the cause of the problem. JIT advocates a reduction of inventory for the purpose of exposing a company's problems. An analogy to a boat helps to describe how this reduction works. Figure 7.3 shows the boat (the company) protected, at least for now, from the damaging rocks (unreliability) by a high water (inventory) level. The JIT philosophy says the water should be lowered to expose the rocks. This change in water level may result in short-term problems but would enable the rocks to be located and eliminated, making the harbor safer in the long run even at lower water levels. Reduction of inventory has the same effect. It may cause problems to manifest themselves but facilitates their elimination, resulting in a long-term improvement.

THE COSTS OF CARRYING INVENTORY

Although excess inventory is listed as an asset on U.S. balance sheets, U.S. companies are beginning to recognize the negative impact it can have. The financial carrying cost of inventory, for example, can be significant. Some estimates are as high as 35 percent of the average dollar value of the inventory. If a company maintains an average level of inventory worth $3 million, for example, it may incur an associated annual cost of more than $1 million dollars. Inventory carrying costs consist of such things as insurance, obsolescence, damage, warehousing costs, and lost opportunity on the dollars invested in inventory. Other negative effects of carrying excessive inventory will be described below.

TURNOVER ADVANTAGE
The financial advantage gained from rapid turnover of inventory.

Inventory should be treated like an investment, and like any investment, the return should be maximized. One way to do that is through **turnover advantage,** which Stalk and

---

FIGURE 7.3   **"Boat and Rocks" Analogy for Inventory and Problems**

Hout describe.[4] Suppose a retailer pays $75 for an item and resells it for $150. A gross margin of $75, 50 percent of the sales price, results. This margin pays the retailer's expenses, including the inventory carrying costs. Suppose this retailer's inventory turns over three times per year. In other words, on the average, an item remains in inventory for four months before it is sold. The gross margin on the inventory investment is 300 percent per year. If the retailer could receive orders from suppliers the day after ordering, the level of inventory could be reduced. Suppose through quick response from suppliers, the average amount of time an item is in inventory is reduced to one month. Turns are now increased to 12. Gross margin on the inventory investment increases to 1,200 percent.

INVENTORY REDUCTION TECHNIQUES

Raw materials (RM) inventory, which consists of the material inputs to the transformation process, must not enter the physical system at a rate faster than outputs are exiting the system, or inventory will accumulate. Traditionally in the United States, raw materials have been purchased periodically in large quantities, rather than more frequently in smaller quantities. Purchasing managers have adapted this process for three basic reasons. First, many suppliers offer discounts for larger quantities. Second, if purchasing managers locate a raw material for an attractive price, it may seem economically logical to buy a large quantity to take advantage of the opportunity. Third, and the most important reason for maintaining large quantities of raw materials, purchasing managers buy them to protect against an unreliable supply. If only a small RM inventory is held, a disruption in supply could be devastating. Retailers with low RM inventories, for example, often find themselves stocking out within a few days during a Teamsters strike when independent truckers refuse to haul goods as well. Large raw material inventories buffer a company against the immediate impact of undependable suppliers. Companies have held large raw material inventories to enhance the competitive capabilities of dependability without increasing the dependability of suppliers. Firms that use natural resources as raw materials are particularly vulnerable to disruptions in supply. During the summer of 1994, for instance, L. L. Bean found itself with just one month's supply of cotton—instead of its usual six months' supply—when boll worms threatened the cotton crops of China and Pakistan.[5] The large raw material inventory does not eliminate the basic problem of unreliable suppliers, however; it simply hides it.

The raw material reduction objectives of JIT cannot be adequately addressed without discussing the buyer/supplier relationships in JIT. Typically, one approach to developing a more reliable supplier base is to reduce the number of suppliers. Stronger relationships are built with suppliers through a system called partnering. These linkages support the objectives of more frequent deliveries, shorter lead times, and lower inventory levels. They are enhanced by electronic data interchange (EDI) and paperless transactions designed to reduce the administrative costs associated with frequent deliveries, as well as supplier quality certification which eliminates incoming quality inspections.

A prerequisite to eliminating inventory is to ensure that all phases of the transformation process are accomplished at the rate the product is consumed by the market. JIT applies this strategy to the reduction of raw material inventories by requiring very frequent deliveries of small quantities of raw materials. Rather than a delivery of one month's supply once a month, receive a delivery of a half day's supply at 8 AM and at noon. This type

RAW MATERIALS (RM) INVENTORY
Material inputs to the transformation process, prior to any processing.

---

[4]Stalk and Hout, 96.
[5]"Insect Swarms Threaten Asian Cotton Crop," *The Wall Street Journal,* July 18, 1994, C, 1.

of schedule has numerous logistical implications. It may mean that the supplier has to be located close to the customer, that small trucks have to be used rather than rail transportation, and that the paperwork processing must be changed to reduce the amount of paperwork per delivery. It will certainly mean that unreliable suppliers or suppliers of less than top quality goods can no longer be tolerated.

Reducing RM inventory will expose the unreliable suppliers and may result in downtime for the service or manufacturer until the problems can be eliminated or new, reliable suppliers can be found. Because of the adjustments that must be made by suppliers, relationships between customers and suppliers must change. The new relationships are typically of longer duration and companies reduce the number of suppliers for items. (See Boxes 7.1 and 7.2.)

OPERATIONS OUTLOOK

BOX 7.1

The Decline of Coalitions in Japan

Large Japanese manufacturers have traditionally formed *keiretsu*, a Japanese term for "groups of subcontractors," to supply them with needed components. The resulting network of producers has helped them compete globally. In the traditional keiretsu system, a manufacturer takes care of only a small portion of the production processes, and a chain of subcontractors takes care of the rest. In fact, more than 50 percent of the small- and medium-sized Japanese companies supply parts to manufacturers. The large manufacturers guarantee the subcontractors long-term relationships. In return, the subcontractors assist with quality assurance issues and provide dependable and appropriate deliveries. This approach has worked well in the past and has provided manufacturers with responsive suppliers committed to quality and dependability.

As international demands for automobiles, electronics, and electric machinery have dropped, these coalitions have been changing. Large manufacturers have pressured subcontractors to reduce production costs or be excluded from the keiretsu. In response, many subcontractors are pursuing business outside of their keiretsu or are changing their status as subcontractors and becoming independent. The keiretsu system is changing from its current pyramid-type coalition to one that may be more of a horizontal network of parts suppliers and manufacturers. As many subcontractors are seeking to become independent from keiretsu, they are also improving their use of technology and production capabilities. Some are seeking new business partners outside their groups, and others are becoming independent specialists in specific types of processing.

This trend has increased since 1985 when the yen strengthened against the dollar, causing an economic boom in Japan that initiated a labor shortage and a surge in land prices. Many subcontractors capable of technological development relocated to rural areas. At the same time, large Japanese manufacturers shifted production overseas and began to advance into overseas markets, supplying parts to overseas manufacturers and training local employees as well. The result is an expected internationalization of the JIT approach.

As many large Japanese manufacturers are seeing demand and profits drop, they are initiating various cost-cutting programs, including a reduction in work hours, a simplification of model lines, and lengthened model change cycles. These cutbacks are expected to continue, particularly as the Japanese automakers' foreign market share continues to decline. These changes are hurting subcontractors, which are laying off workers, streamlining production systems, and supplying parts to manufacturers outside their industry, such as those in the electric machinery industry. As another cost-cutting measure, many Japanese firms are purchasing parts from American suppliers. In the computer industry, Japanese firms use U.S. chips to a great extent, and in the automotive industry, General Motor's automotive components group is selling approximately $75 million worth of antilock breaking systems to Toyota, Isuzu, and Suzuki. Japanese manufacturers are even going outside their keiretsu when purchasing from other Japanese firms. Nissan, for example, recently chose Tokai Rika, a Toyota affiliate, to supply automatic transmissions.

The result is expected to be a horizontal network of suppliers who deal across industries, rather than the current pyramid shape of keiretsu within specific industries.

Sources "New Trends in the Keiretsu System," *The Wall Street Journal*, November 16, 1992, sec. A, 12. "Doing the Unthinkable," *Business Week*, January 10, 1994, 52–53.

OPERATIONS OUTLOOK

BOX 7.2

The Rise of Coalitions at Home

Many U.S. companies in the digital information industry are forming the American equivalent of the Japanese *keiretsu.* Firms are seeking alliances primarily to reduce risk in uncertain markets, to spread costs, and to help establish technical standards. Alliances are taking place among leaders in five industries: computing, communications, consumer electronics, entertainment, and publishing. Companies have one overriding issue in mind: to convey video, sound, graphics, and text in digital form inexpensively. They expect that the industry will evolve into three distinct segments: content of data transmissions; delivery of information over telephone lines, cable, or satellite; and manipulation of information with PCs, TV controllers, and special software. Companies are betting that the right combination of these segments will result in products that will dominate a market that Apple Chairman John Sculley estimates could be worth $3 trillion by the year 2000.

Numerous alliances are forming around the two largest cable operators: Time-Warner and Tele-Communications Inc. (TCI). These rival companies have entered into an agreement to develop hardware and software standards for interactive TV.

In other alliances, Microsoft is working with Intel and Compaq. Apple, AT&T, Motorola, Sony, Matsushita Electric Industrial Co., and Philips Electronics NV own equal shares of General Magic Inc. Motorola and AT&T are archrivals in wireless networks and devices. Sony, Matsushita, and Philips are competitors in consumer electronics. Kaleida Labs, which is an Apple and IBM alliance, has alliances with Motorola and Scientific Atlanta to develop converters and networks needed to manipulate information over interactive TV. Time-Warner's alliance with US West includes interests in cable TV, movie and music production, magazine publishing, and regional telephone service. US West has an alliance with TCI in England.

The cooperation fostered by keiretsu is expected to enhance the U.S. position in global advance-technology markets. Concerns exist, however, over the potential the keiretsu have for eliminating competition and closing markets to new entrants.

Sources "Digital Media Business Takes Form as a Battle of Complex Alliances," *The Wall Street Journal,* July 14, 1993, sec. A, 1, 6. "Media Mania" *Business Week,* July 12, 1993, 110–119.

RM inventory can also be reduced through redesign or an improved design of products to reduce the number of components and standardize parts across product lines. By standardizing parts across products as much as possible, component variety is reduced, fewer items must be inventoried, and fewer suppliers are needed. Although manufacturers are under increasing pressure to offer more variety, many of them have eliminated variety that does not seem to add value from customers' perspectives. (See Box 7.3.)

Work-in-process inventory (WIP) is the goods within the production system. The inventory is no longer raw materials because it has undergone some of the processing, but it isn't finished goods yet because it hasn't completed the processing. A technique known as batching has significant impact on the amount of WIP in the system. To gain economies of scale, manufacturers and services often prefer to process a large number of items before changing equipment to process something else or before passing the items on to the next processing step. Insurance claims, for example, are sometimes processed in batches, and catalog orders from mail-order retailers are frequently batched. When an order is called in, the order is placed with a group of orders until the number of orders is sufficient to warrant sending them all to the warehouse to be pulled and shipped. The accumulation of orders increases the time that customers wait for a product because it increases the amount of time the order is in the system.

When one machine performs several manufacturing functions, large batches of one type of an item are processed before the machine is changed to perform another process.

WORK-IN-PROCESS INVENTORY (WIP)
Inventory within the production system, no longer raw material, but not yet a finished product.

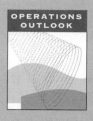

OPERATIONS OUTLOOK

BOX 7.3

The Manufacturers' Choice

Throughout the 1980s and early 1990s we saw product variety used as a competitive weapon. Even Japanese manufacturers, who in the early 1980s marketed very few options in their products, had succumbed to consumers' desires for choice. This trend is reversing, however, as Japanese auto manufacturers have faced many of the problems encountered by U.S. automakers. Mazda, for example, has significantly reduced product variety to concentrate on variety that adds significant value. The table below compares the options available on a 1992 Mazda RX-7, with those of the RX-7 from 1991 and before.

Option	1992	1991 and Earlier
Engine	Turbocharged only	Turbocharged or standard
Hood	Aluminum with air scoop only	4 options
Steering wheel	With or without airbag; both are 3-spoke leather	9 options
Wheels	16-inch aluminum only	6 options
Body color	5 options	7 options
Seats (including shapes, fabrics, colors)	15 options	79 options
Body type	Coupe only	Coupe or convertible
Total	19 variations	67 variations

For its 929 luxury car, Mazda has reduced its variations from 96 to 23. Other manufacturers are following suit.

Efforts to increase the number of common parts, in order to reduce tool changes and inventory, are also being introduced. Nissan's entire product line utilizes 500 different sizes, shapes, colors, and textures of steering wheels, 110 types of radiators, 1,200 types of floor carpets, 437 types of dashboard meters, and more than 300 varieties of ashtrays. Nissan has ordered designers to slash the number of unique parts by 40 percent. Model variations will be rolled back by 35 percent. An example of the waste caused by the excess component variety is seen at the Murayama plant north of Tokyo, where the Laurel is made. Eighty-seven different types of steering wheels were offered for the Laurel in 1993, but 70 of them accounted for a total of only 5 percent of the total installed. Steering wheel types have been slashed to 10. Model types have been cut from 23 to 10, and floor carpets have been reduced from seven to two. Yukio Miyamori, the president of Calsonic Corp., one of Nissan's suppliers, is cheering the action. According to Miyamori, mindless variation forces Calsonic to manufacture more than 2,000 kinds of mufflers, most of which are used at the rate of only a few units per year. The presses, dies, and inventory on all the muffler types must be maintained for the lifetime of the cars.

This trend is not confined to the auto industry. Matsushita, well-known in the United States for its Panasonic brand, is reducing the number of models of television sets by 30 to 40 percent. Sony, which produces 12 different sizes of television sets, has dropped its 27- and 31-inch models and may drop several smaller sizes as well. Model cycles are lengthening also. Japanese auto manufacturers have traditionally introduced new models after four years, compared to five to ten years in Europe and the United States. Japanese manufacturers are starting to lengthen the model cycle to five years or longer. The model cycle for Japanese-made televisions has increased from an average of 12 to 13 months to 14 months. The number of models offered has been reduced by approximately 9 percent. The model cycle for VCRs has increased from 9 or 10 months to an average of 12. The number of models has been reduced from 97 to 72, a 25 percent decrease.

It is likely that this trend is resulting from two strong influences. First, it is an effective means of reducing costs. Economic sluggishness has reduced sales, and cost reductions are one means of dealing with profitability problems. It also appears that consumers' desires are becoming more focused on the genuine quality of the product instead of product options.

Sources A. Pollack, "Japan Eases 57 Varieties Marketing," *The New York Times,* October 15, 1992, sec. C1, 7; C. Chandler and M. Williams, "A Slump in Car Sales Forces Nissan to Start Cutting Swollen Costs," *The Wall Street Journal,* March 3, 1993, sec. A1, 4.

The time required to make the necessary changes is known as setup, or changeover, time. Larger batches, and their longer production runs, are attractive in manufacturing because they result in fewer changeovers, thus making more time available for processing. With a larger batch size, however, the greater is the WIP inventory, and the longer it takes for a

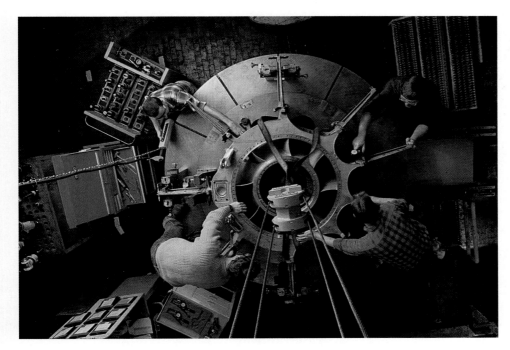

This complex seven-axis machining center, which is used to manufacture fan case assemblies at United Technologies' Pratt & Whitney plant in Middleton, Connecticut, once required three hours of setup time. But a team of shop floor workers and their supervisors reduced that time to just ten minutes. Productivity initiatives like this one are helping United Technologies gain a cost advantage in the marketplace.

Source ©John Madere 1992 for United Technologies Corporation. Used with permission.

unit of product to go through the system. A large batch size appears to be at odds with JIT's requirements that batches be made as small as possible. Large batches are sometimes justified, however, when long or expensive setups are required.

For small batches to be economically feasible, changeover time must be reduced. Companies have instituted a variety of changes to reduce changeover time. Better design of processes and components has resulted in greater standardization of components, fewer components, and fewer changeovers. Better organization and training of workers have made changeovers easier and faster. Improved designs of equipment and fixtures also have improved the changeover process, reducing the time required. The use of interchangeable dies and better organized lines has greatly contributed to the reduced changeover time necessary for small-batch production. This area has traditionally received so little attention in the United States that substantial improvements have come through minimal effort and have often resulted in improvements by as much as a factor of 100. Many firms, for instance, have adopted a technique known as *single-minute exchange of dies,* or SMED, a process developed at Toyota to reduce die-changeover times to less than 10 minutes. The increased use of automation in machines and material handling systems has also contributed to reduced WIP inventory levels.

A smaller batch size decreases the time each item spends moving through the system because each item spends less time waiting until the entire batch is completed before proceeding to the next step in the process. This faster pace improves a company's response time and flexibility. Reduced levels of WIP reduce inventory carrying costs, resulting in savings that can be passed on to customers or to increased profits. Smaller batches also improve quality feedback time. Quality problems are often detected by the user of a component, who is often the employee responsible for the next step in the production process. If a large batch of components is manufactured and then transferred to the next step in the production process, the potential exists for a large number of defects to be produced before they are discovered. The smaller the batch size, the fewer the defects produced before discovery.

| | TABLE 7.1 | | Large-Batch Production and Inventory Levels | | | |

Day	Demand A	Demand B	Production A	Production B	Inventory A	Inventory B
1	100	100	200	0	100	900
2	100	100	200	0	200	800
3	100	100	200	0	300	700
4	100	100	200	0	400	600
5	100	100	200	0	500	500
6	100	100	200	0	600	400
7	100	100	200	0	700	300
8	100	100	200	0	800	200
9	100	100	200	0	900	100
10	100	100	200	0	1000	0
11	100	100	0	200	900	100
12	100	100	0	200	800	200
13	100	100	0	200	700	300
14	100	100	0	200	600	400
15	100	100	0	200	500	500
16	100	100	0	200	400	600
17	100	100	0	200	300	700
18	100	100	0	200	200	800
19	100	100	0	200	100	900
20	100	100	0	200	0	1000
21	100	100	200	0	100	900
22	100	100	200	0	200	800
23	100	100	200	0	300	700
24	100	100	200	0	400	600
25	100	100	200	0	500	500

Not only must batch sizes be reduced, but each step in the process must also be linked to the demand for the final product to prevent inventory from accumulating. Companies use a so-called pull system to authorize the movement of inventory from one work center to the next. This system, known as a **kanban system,** will be discussed in detail in chapter 15, "Scheduling Operations." Kanban, a Japanese term that translates into "visible record" or "signal," operates under a simple rule: Do not produce an item unless it is needed by the succeeding step in the production process. This system prevents inventory from being pushed into the system to keep workers busy. The JIT philosophy maintains that it is better for an employee to be paid for doing nothing than to be paid for producing excess inventory. Because no business wants to pay employees to sit idle, however, JIT promotes cross-training, or teaching workers many different skills. At Caterpillar, for example, a cross-trained worker who is not needed in one work center for a certain amount of time can be moved to another where there is a need for production. Cross-trained workers could also perform preventive maintenance tasks, practice changeovers, or work on housekeeping chores. The service sector has adapted cross-training to its needs, teaching workers to do many tasks as a means of providing more flexibility with fewer workers. Salary levels are frequently tied to the number of jobs a worker can perform.

Reducing the WIP inventory that exists between work centers exposes those work centers that are prone to breakdowns. If a work center does not have a large buffer of WIP

KANBAN SYSTEM
In just-in-time, a system used to link production of each item to the market demand.

Day	Demand A	Demand B	Production A	Production B	Inventory A	Inventory B
26	100	100	200	0	600	400
27	100	100	200	0	700	300
28	100	100	200	0	800	200
29	100	100	200	0	900	100
30	100	100	200	0	1000	0
31	100	100	0	200	900	100
32	100	100	0	200	800	200
33	100	100	0	200	700	300
34	100	100	0	200	600	400
35	100	100	0	200	500	500
36	100	100	0	200	400	600
37	100	100	0	200	300	700
38	100	100	0	200	200	800
39	100	100	0	200	100	900
40	100	100	0	200	0	1000
41	100	100	200	0	100	900
42	100	100	200	0	200	800
43	100	100	200	0	300	700
44	100	100	200	0	400	600
45	100	100	200	0	500	500
46	100	100	200	0	600	400
47	100	100	200	0	700	300
48	100	100	200	0	800	200
49	100	100	200	0	900	100
50	100	100	200	0	1000	0
			Daily Average Inventory Levels		500	500

inventory, it may not be able to continue its work if there is a breakdown at a preceding work center, and an entire production line may stop soon thereafter. JIT responds to this problem by greatly increasing the amount of preventive maintenance. As the reliability of work centers improves, large amounts of inventory do not have to move from one work center to another, and inventory levels can be further reduced. With the elimination of this inventory, defects are also quickly exposed, and their causes can then be eliminated.

Finished goods (FG) inventories can be reduced by tying the production rate directly to the rate of consumption. If the production rate is greater than the consumption rate, even for a short period of time, inventory will result. For example, suppose a manufacturer produces two models of cars, model A and model B. Each has a customer demand of 100 units per day. All of the equipment is used on both models, so the managers find it useful to produce model A for two weeks, then produce model B for two weeks, thereby reducing the amount of time and effort required to perform changeovers. Each month, they produce one month's supply of each model, but they're producing them at a rate twice that of consumption. They produce a month's supply of model A in two weeks, and for the next two weeks, while they're producing model B, demand for model A is supplied from inventory. The average daily level of inventory is 500 units. (See Table 7.1.)

FINISHED GOODS (FG) INVENTORIES
Finished products that have not yet been sold.

| | **TABLE 7.2** | | **Small-Batch Production and Inventory Levels** | | | |

Day	Demand A	Demand B	Production A	Production B	Inventory A	Inventory B
1	100	100	200	0	100	100
2	100	100	200	0	200	0
3	100	100	0	200	100	100
4	100	100	0	200	0	200
5	100	100	200	0	100	100
6	100	100	200	0	200	0
7	100	100	0	200	100	100
8	100	100	0	200	0	200
9	100	100	200	0	100	100
10	100	100	200	0	200	0
11	100	100	0	200	100	100
12	100	100	0	200	0	200
13	100	100	200	0	100	100
14	100	100	200	0	200	0
15	100	100	0	200	100	100
16	100	100	0	200	0	200
17	100	100	200	0	100	100
18	100	100	200	0	200	0
19	100	100	0	200	100	100
20	100	100	0	200	0	200
21	100	100	200	0	100	100
22	100	100	200	0	200	0
23	100	100	0	200	100	100
24	100	100	0	200	0	200
25	100	100	200	0	100	100

If, rather than produce a month's supply at a time (batches of 2,000), management decided to produce batches of 400, they would produce model A for two days and then switch to model B for two days, as shown in Table 7.2. This change would have a substantial impact on the average level of inventory. The daily average level of inventory would drop to 100 units.

To produce at the consumption rate, however, would require that the correct proportion of the two models be produced every day. In fact, the production schedule would need to produce one A, then one B, then one A, then one B, repeating this cycle for as long as the demand for A and B remained in a one to one proportion. This approach is known as **mixed model production.** If mixed model production were implemented, production would be very close to the rate of consumption. This would mean that finished goods would be consumed almost immediately after they were produced, resulting in no finished goods inventory. Processing WIP in very small batches and taking frequent delivery of small batches of raw materials allows this "production to the rate of consumption" to govern all aspects of the conversion process, clear back to the input of raw materials.

One main reason for holding large quantities of finished goods inventories, however, is that it allows companies to better cope with seasonal demands. It is difficult for manu-

MIXED MODEL PRODUCTION

In JIT, the practice of alternating models in production to match the rate of consumption as closely as possible.

Day	Demand A	Demand B	Production A	Production B	Inventory A	Inventory B
26	100	100	200	0	200	0
27	100	100	0	200	100	100
28	100	100	0	200	0	200
29	100	100	200	0	100	100
30	100	100	200	0	200	0
31	100	100	0	200	100	100
32	100	100	0	200	0	200
33	100	100	200	0	100	100
34	100	100	200	0	200	0
35	100	100	0	200	100	100
36	100	100	0	200	0	200
37	100	100	200	0	100	100
38	100	100	200	0	200	0
39	100	100	0	200	100	100
40	100	100	0	200	0	200
41	100	100	200	0	100	100
42	100	100	200	0	200	0
43	100	100	0	200	100	100
44	100	100	0	200	0	200
45	100	100	200	0	100	100
46	100	100	200	0	200	0
47	100	100	0	200	100	100
48	100	100	0	200	0	200
49	100	100	200	0	100	100
50	100	100	200	0	200	0
			Daily Average Inventory Levels		100	100

facturers to chase demand by increasing and decreasing output rates to coincide with seasonal demand fluctuations. It would require a great deal of hiring and firing and would also result in much of the firm's equipment being idle during low demand periods. In reaction to this fluctuation, manufacturers typically have built up inventories during low demand times and have met high demand by supplying out of inventory and off the production line. Because high levels of finished goods inventories are taboo under JIT, this practice is limited. JIT companies strive to lock into a **level load** on the plant for as long as possible. This stable load on the plant does not necessarily come from a steady demand for one product. Several products with offsetting seasonal demand cycles may be produced. Figure 7.4 shows the approaches used to reduce inventories and which inventories are targeted by each approach.

LEVEL LOADING
In JIT, the practice of stabilizing the load on the production processes for long periods of time.

INVENTORY REDUCTION AND COMPETITIVE PRIORITIES

The reduction of inventory levels can contribute significantly to the development of differentiating capabilities through the direct linkages to price, quality, dependability, flexibility, and time. Because of the carrying costs, excessive inventory can result in costs being

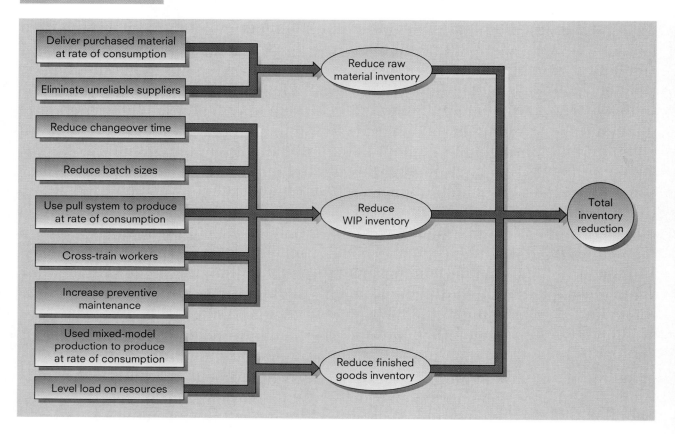

FIGURE 7.4   **Combined Effect of JIT Inventory Reduction Approaches**

passed on to the customer in the form of price increases or cutting into profit margins. Reduction of inventory levels reduces carrying costs, and consequently, cost savings can be passed on to the customer or used to enhance profits. Despite the substantial cost savings that result from inventory reduction, many JIT experts contend that the effect inventory reduction has on quality, dependability, flexibility, and time is even more important.

Inventory can be subject to increasing levels of damage the longer it is stored. Quality levels improve with reduced inventory levels. The biggest effect on quality, however, manifests itself in what is known as quality feedback time. Quality feedback time is the amount of time it takes to determine that a defect has been produced and change the process to eliminate the problem. Quality problems sometimes go undetected until the inventory is actually used. When raw materials are purchased in large quantities relatively infrequently, there are potentially more defective raw materials than there would be if the order quantity were low. Also, because the purchases are made infrequently, the supplier may have produced the raw material a long time ago. If there is a defect, the supplier may have produced many more defects since then, and even if that is not the case, the lack of immediate feedback makes it much more difficult for the supplier to identify the cause of the quality problem and prevent it from recurring. Quality feedback is also enhanced as WIP and finished goods are reduced through batch-size reduction.

Inventory is often kept to eliminate threats to dependability. In fact, until the causes of the lack of dependability are eliminated, inventory does help. However, the more inventory in the system, the greater and the more variable the throughput time. Longer throughput times compounded by variable throughput times make it very difficult to develop accurate estimates of completion dates for orders and result in missed due dates, negatively affecting dependability. Long delivery lead times from the supplier, on the other hand, result in a need for higher levels of raw materials inventory for the buyer.

Inventory has a profound effect on flexibility. Consider the predicament of an Italian restaurant that negotiated an extremely low price on canned tomato paste used in its spaghetti sauce. The price was so good that the business manager decided to buy a three-month supply. Shortly after the purchase, however, the chef discovered that the sauce could be improved if the recipe were changed to use whole cooked tomatoes instead of tomato paste. The flexibility of the restaurant has been diminished by the large purchase quantity. Should the restaurant change the sauce recipe to increase customer satisfaction and market share? If it does, what will it do with the tomato paste? Should the restaurant use up the paste and then change the recipe? If it does that, it would delay the introduction of the improvement by three months and lose three months of improved customer satisfaction. The impact of high inventory levels on the flexibility of manufacturers is similar. In industries where technical or marketing changes are frequent, flexibility and ability to be the first in the market with an improvement are very important.

Inventory level affects time because of its role in determining throughput time. WIP inventory, in particular, often exists in the form of queues of work in front of work centers. The longer the queues, the longer each order spends waiting in each queue. This increases the throughput time and can prevent a company from providing quick customer turnaround.

THE WORK FORCE AND DECISION MAKING

WHY INCREASE WORKER INVOLVEMENT?

The JIT philosophy recognizes the abilities and value of workers and, consistent with its ideology to eliminate waste, seeks to make the best use of their talents and knowledge. To have access to the valuable resources of worker knowledge and talent and not to use them would be wasteful. The JIT perspective also embraces the benefits of labor/management cooperation. With this increased involvement comes a more committed and loyal work force.

TECHNIQUES TO INCREASE WORKER INVOLVEMENT

Managers employ several techniques, as presented in Figure 7.5, to increase worker involvement and make the best use of worker talent. Managers acknowledge that the workers who spend hours every day running a particular machine probably know more about how to improve it than anyone else. One of the ways JIT takes advantage of the knowledge and abilities of the workers is to involve them in making productivity and quality improvements. This is typically accomplished through organized groups of employees who are brought together for the specific purpose of making improvements. These groups are often known as quality circles. Through the use of analysis and problem-solving techniques, they develop improvements or solutions to problems and make formal presentations to management. Because of the sophisticated nature of many of the analysis techniques, many employees undergo intensive training to develop these skills. Quality circles result in productivity and quality improvements, and the increased involvement in decision

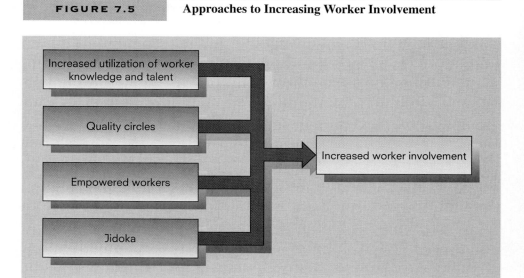

FIGURE 7.5   **Approaches to Increasing Worker Involvement**

making enhances the sense of ownership workers feel for their company and its products and increases the level of labor-management cooperation.

If management increases workers' responsibilities, it must also increase their authority and empower them to use their abilities and knowledge. Jidoka, discussed earlier, is one form of worker empowerment. Jidoka gives all workers the power to stop the production process if they believe something is not as it should be.

WORKER INVOLVEMENT AND COMPETITIVE PRIORITIES

Improvements in productivity and quality brought about through quality circles have a positive impact on production costs and price. Employee suggestions for improvements can also affect quality, dependability, flexibility, and time, depending on the nature of the improvement. The ability and responsibility for employees to identify defects at the source is one of the underpinnings of TQM. In addition to this direct impact, the pride and feeling of ownership brought about by involving and empowering the work force enhance productivity and quality, reduce absenteeism, and increase the likelihood that the goals of management and labor will be similar.

INCREASING FLEXIBILITY OF FACILITIES AND EQUIPMENT

Successful companies must have the ability to adapt quickly to changes. Traditionally, U.S. manufacturers relied on inventory to help them react to unanticipated demand, and stocks of raw materials and work-in-process buffered them from unanticipated disruptions. To allow for the elimination of inventory under JIT, these problems must be addressed and minimized. Some unexpected demand is still likely to occur, and it may be welcome. Despite efforts to eliminate their causes, some internal and external disruptions will occur as well. Capacity flexibility provides a means by which a business can cope with these unexpected

Quality teams at Public Service Enterprise Group, a gas and electric utility, work to improve procedures designed to increase efficiency and enhance customer satisfaction. This Customer Expectation Team is analyzing ways to reduce the number of steps required to complete new-customer gas-supply connections. During 1993, shortened cycle times initiated by quality teams resulted in cost savings of $15 million and improved customer relations.

Source   Courtesy of PSE&G.

occurrences. The JIT approach requires a level of protective capacity to provide flexibility. Protective capacity is not committed in planning stages and exists to enable the firm to absorb unexpected disruptions and demand changes without damaging customer service. Because U.S. manufacturers often use capacity utilization as a performance measure, they often strive to eliminate capacity that is not used at a high enough level. They often do so by laying off employees. Firms frequently find that as they reduce their capacity to the point at which it is close to that required by demand, they begin to have problems meeting due dates and with customer service. As these problems become severe, workers that have been laid off are brought back. Many companies repeat this cycle over and over. JIT companies have recognized the trade-off of excess inventory for a level of protective capacity and do not use utilization as the sole measure of equipment and labor performance.

Companies committed to the JIT philosophy have also found that it is often beneficial to purchase several small-scale pieces of equipment instead of one large one. Smaller scale equipment makes it easier to produce at the consumption rate, increases the flexibility by enabling the processing of more than one type of product at a time, and contributes to a more efficient layout of lines and group technology cells.

CAPACITY FLEXIBILITY AND COMPETITIVE PRIORITIES

An increase in capacity flexibility profoundly increases a firm's flexibility and enhances its dependability by increasing its ability to respond to unexpected events. Capacity flexibility may also help firms to compete on the basis of response time. A company with protective capacity has the flexibility to successfully complete an order in an unusually short time frame if absolutely necessary. This can solidify the relationship with a longtime customer or open doors to new ones.

JIT AS A SYSTEM

Many of the components of JIT support more than one of the JIT objectives. The matrix in Table 7.3 lists the individual components of the JIT system, their resource category target, and the relationships among the competitive capabilities. Many of the techniques have a primary impact on one competitive capability and a secondary impact on several others. The JIT philosophy provides a system of organizing management activities.

The specific techniques of JIT provide patterns of actions that not only support the JIT objectives, shown in Figure 7.1, but also provide capabilities for reaching a business's more general goals. The objectives of JIT are consistent with business goals, but because they are more specific, they provide a guide for reaching those goals. (See Box 7.4.)

Figure 7.6 illustrates how the JIT philosophy provides direction across all management tasks and resource groups and provides intermediate objectives that, if met, are consistent with global goals.

CONTINUOUS IMPROVEMENT

All of JIT's objectives and approaches described up to this point exist in an environment of continuous improvement where perfection, although unachievable, is the ultimate goal. JIT champions a constant effort to improve on all objectives and problems are viewed as op-

---

TABLE 7.3   **Links between JIT Techniques and Competitive Priorities**

Technique	Primary target	Relationship to Competitive Priorities*				
		Price	Quality	Dependability	Flexibility	Time
Eliminate unnecessary steps	Process productivity	P	S	S	S	S
Group technology	Process productivity	P	S	S	S	S
Automation and robotics	Process productivity	P	S	S	S	S
Process focus	Process productivity	P	S			
Total quality management	Process productivity	S	P	S		S
Frequent deliveries	RM inventory reduction	P	S		S	
Supplier relationships	RM inventory reduction	P	S		S	
Reduction in supplier numbers	RM inventory reduction	P	S	S	S	
EDI, Paperless transactions	RM inventory reduction	P		S		
Design and part standardization	RM inventory reduction	P	S	S	S	S
Small batch production	WIP, FG inventory reduction	P	S		S	
Reduced changeover times	WIP, FG inventory reduction	P	S		S	
Kanban	WIP, FG inventory reduction	P	S	S	S	S
Cross-training workers	WIP, FG inventory reduction	P	S	S	S	
Increased preventive maintenance	WIP, FG inventory reduction	P	S	S		
Mixed model production	FG inventory reduction	P	S	S	S	S
Level loading	FG inventory reduction	P		S		
Quality circles	Work force involvement	S	P	S	S	S
Protective capacity	Equipment flexibility			S	P	S
Small-scale equipment	Equipment flexibility			S	P	S

*P = Primary link; S = secondary link.

BOX 7.4

A JIT Success Story

John Crane Belfab produces edge-welded bellows and bellows seals and generates $20 million in revenues from four business units. All four businesses are housed in one facility, using a cellular structure to provide quick response to changes in customer needs.

In what started as merely an inventory reduction effort, Belfab found itself adding numerous progressive practices to improve all aspects of the business. The practices include quick-change dies, statistical process control, point-of-use inventory storage, a kanban-based supply system, and a cross-trained work force.

Improvements are numerous. Domestic market share has increased from 12 percent in 1985 to 22 percent in 1992. Inventory turns have increased from 1.7 to 30 on some product lines. First-pass yields are 99.95 percent, a threefold reduction in scrap as a percentage of sales (0.5 percent). Belfab's on-time delivery rate is 99.67 percent. Inventory levels are down 51 percent since 1987.

Five levels of management staff were reduced to two. All of the work force, including the unionized laborers, is now salaried. Almost two-thirds of the work force participate in small group improvement activities in which cross-functional groups address specific problems. Each of these employees receives 38 hours of training per year through a curriculum developed with Daytona Beach Community College. Training is free for Belfab employees, and they receive half pay for time spent in class.

Customer response to these improvements has been significant. Since 1990, two of Belfab's largest customers have increased sales volumes 188 percent and 1,280 percent respectively. In 1991 Belfab was named supplier of the year by Applied Material Inc. In 1992 it earned elite-supplier certifications from Pratt & Whitney, Rockwell International, and Allied-Signal's Engine Division.

Source   "John Crane Belfab," *Industry Week,* October 18, 1993, 37–38.

portunities. For example, if no production line stoppage were to occur, there would be no opportunity to improve. Managers committed to the JIT philosophy might reduce WIP levels in that situation. By reducing WIP levels further and further, eventually a problem will surface. When it does, numerous engineers and specialists will descend upon it because it offers an opportunity to improve.

JIT IN THE UNITED STATES

There has been much debate about the viability of JIT in the United States. Many critics contend that significant improvements cannot be obtained in this country because its culture is so different from that of Japan. Some people maintain that cultural differences make some aspects of JIT impossible to implement here. Still other people contend that JIT is universally adaptable and not culturally based. Although there have been some failures, the implementation of JIT in the United States has had a tremendous impact on manufacturing. The objectives of reducing inventory, increasing productivity, and improving quality have resulted in significant improvements to the extent that thousands of firms have enjoyed its benefits. (See Boxes 7.5 and 7.6.)

JIT did not develop in Japan as a conscious decision, as it did in this country. Rather, many of the aspects of JIT evolved from circumstances. Small frequent deliveries, for example, were necessary because only narrow roads and small vehicles were available after World War II. Inventory had to be minimized because the premium on space was so high. Business space could not be wasted on something as unproductive as a warehouse. Keep in mind that Japan, a country roughly the size of California, has more than 110 million inhabitants. Because much of the land is mountainous, most of the population lives around

FIGURE 7.6	**JIT's Influence on the Task/Resource Model of Operations Management**

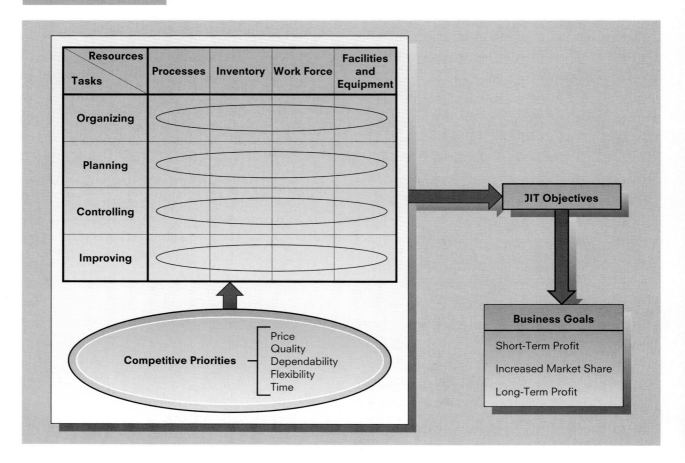

the perimeter. The group and team emphasis on problem solving and reward systems may be culturally based. Highly populated, more crowded conditions require a more cooperative, group orientation than often prevails in the United States.

Despite the attractiveness and overall success of JIT in the United States, some components of the JIT system have not been implemented with the same success as others. For example, U.S. workers tend to be less team-oriented and more concerned with individual reward than their Japanese counterparts. This orientation has affected the way quality circles function. For some manufacturers, job shops in particular, kanban just isn't appropriate because of the jumbled routings.

U.S. manufacturers have found many of the JIT techniques function quite well on their own and have often used a pick and choose approach to implementing aspects that are most compatible with their particular situation. For example, some companies benefit from reducing changeover times and the resulting batch-size reduction.

Some aspects of the JIT approach are beginning to affect the service sector because many service businesses interact with manufacturers. While the overall eliminate-waste mentality espoused by JIT is attractive to services, many are choosing particular components for implementation. Services are seeing particular benefit from the inventory reduction strategies used in JIT and the cost reduction and flexibility enhancement that follow. The employee involvement techniques, including quality circles, have also proved to be at-

BOX 7.5

JIT Pros . . .

A Carrier Corporation plant in Arkadelphia, Arkansas, presents a look at what may be the future for U.S. manufacturing. It looks very much like JIT. The plant is a small one-story structure that employs only 150 workers. The factory is quiet and spotless. Although it may look like an insurance office, it produces the most important component of Carrier's air conditioners—the compressor. It intends to produce each compressor for $35 less than it currently pays to buy them. At full production of 750,000 per year, this will result in a savings of $26.3 million. The plant is highly automated and makes no finished goods inventory. Compressors are made only to fill orders.

Although the physical system is compatible with JIT, the approach to workers is even more so. The hiring process is extremely selective. Applicants who advance past the interviews take a six-week course that meets five nights per week for three hours each night and on a couple of Saturdays. The attendees are not paid and are not guaranteed a job. Most are working elsewhere during the training process. Those that successfully finish the training process are hired.

Once hired, they have an unusual amount of authority. They have the authority to shut down production lines if they suspect problems, to communicate directly with suppliers, to order some of their own supplies, and even to interview prospective supervisors. When the plant opened, the first employees suggested that they install their own machines. Management agreed. Their work not only saved the company $1 million in installation costs, but it also instilled in the employees a sense of ownership that has lasted. When workers realized that they could work more productively if the layout of machines was changed, they were allowed to rearrange the equipment. Carrier management believes that the quality levels of compressors will result in selling compressors from Arkansas to Japan.

The example set by Carrier Corporation isn't unique. Many firms are opening small plants that require highly educated work forces. Intel, for example, is constructing a computer-chip plant in Santa Clara, California, which will eventually employ 25 workers. Many of the small plants are being built near major customers to facilitate frequent deliveries and long-term relationships. M. A. Hanna Co., for example, is building near a customer in Phoenix a 60-employee plant to make color concentrates for plastics. The small plants are flexible, responsive, able to change production schedules quickly, and are easier to manage.

Source "Small, Flexible Plants May Play Crucial Role in U.S. Manufacturing," *The Wall Street Journal,* January 13, 1993, sec. A 1, 2.

tractive to the service sector. As TQM makes more of an impact on services and manufacturing, the JIT philosophy will follow.

For many services, the implementation of a so-called lean and mean mentality, similar to that of JIT, has taken the form of **reengineering,** a radical improvement process in which all aspects of a business are redesigned to gain a more productive organization.

Many companies that have successfully implemented JIT approaches have found it necessary to change performance measures so they do not conflict with JIT objectives. Performance measures based on traditional cost accounting techniques frequently create barriers that prevent managers from implementing JIT. Some common approaches that must be changed to approaches compatible with JIT objectives include the following:

1. Heavy reliance on standards
2. Emphasis on variance from standards and efficiencies
3. Heavy reliance on direct labor as a basis for overhead cost allocation
4. Extensive tracking of inventory
5. Inappropriate measures for performance[6]

REENGINEERING
A radical improvement process in which all aspects of a business are redesigned to gain a more productive organization.

[6]F. B. Green, F. Amenkhienan, and G. Johnson, "Performance Measures and JIT," *Management Accounting* (February 1991): 50–53.

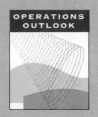

OPERATIONS OUTLOOK

BOX 7.6

. . . and JIT Cons

Allen-Edmonds Shoe Corporation, a manufacturer of expensive shoes, tried JIT, but failed miserably. It attempted to reduce product lead time from eight weeks to five days, increase production, cut costs, and increase customer satisfaction. After losing a reported $1 million on the project, the company has resumed its traditional approaches. Allen-Edmonds makes 41,000 variations of men's and women's shoes in small quantities, resulting in many equipment changeovers and not enough volume for long production runs. A 1988 JIT implementation at the company's main plant, where soles and uppers are sewed together, was successful. It freed up over $400,000 in capital by reducing inventory, and production lead time dropped from three and one-half days to eight hours.

One difficulty it had in implementing JIT was to get suppliers to cooperate. Suppliers of soles agreed to change from monthly to weekly deliveries, but tanneries supplying leather for uppers refused to provide weekly batches for a customer as small as Allen-Edmonds. The company still carries $1 million in inventories of hides, which could be cut to $250,000 if weekly shipments could be made.

The biggest blow to JIT came at the Lake Church Plant, six miles from the main plant in Port Washington, Wisconsin. Piecework pay systems were changed to hourly pay. Worker productivity dropped and employee discipline dropped as well. Piecework was reinstated in 1991, and productivity shot back up. The company was profitable again in 1991.

Allen-Edmonds is not the only firm to resume its old ways after trying JIT. Federal-Mogul Corporation has re-duced automation at an auto-parts plant, as has General Motors. Whirlpool Corporation has become dissatisfied with quality circles, as has General Electric and Corning. Some companies have also rethought the concept of having suppliers deliver in small batches only as needed.

The problems encountered by some U.S. firms can be tied to several factors. Many misapplied the Japanese techniques. Others went too far in automating processes, increasing speed of production but losing valuable flexibility. In 1992, Federal-Mogul removed robots, production-line computers, and automated conveyor systems. The plant has tripled its variety and reduced batch sizes as a result of the increased flexibility.

General Electric's Appliance Division found that kanban resulted in inventories that were too low, preventing it from responding quickly to customers. It increased its inventory of parts with long delivery lead times by 24 percent. This change made possible a response time reduction from 18 weeks to 3.6 weeks.

Skill-based pay has also encountered problems in the United States. Firms can end up paying employees for skills that aren't needed or for skills that quickly become obsolete. Employees also become frustrated, and productivity declines if promotions don't quickly follow the learning of new skills.

Sources "Allen-Edmonds Shoe Tries 'Just-in-Time' Production," *The Wall Street Journal,* March 4, 1993, sec. B, 2. "Some Manufacturers Drop Efforts to Adopt Japanese Techniques," *The Wall Street Journal,* May 7, 1993, sec. A 1, 12. "Many Companies Try Management Fads, Only to See Them Flop," *The Wall Street Journal,* July 6, 1993, sec. A 1, 8.

One of the most significant changes in performance measurement brought about by JIT has been the shift from hourly pay to salaried employees. The fact that direct labor is such a small portion of total product cost and not directly proportional to the number of units produced has resulted in some firms, such as Hewlett-Packard, regarding labor as another component of factory overhead.[7]

JIT AND OTHER BUSINESS FUNCTIONS

The adoption of the JIT philosophy has had far-reaching effects on all business functions. The purchasing function of any business adopting JIT principles and practices takes on an entirely new role. Rather than annual contracts going up for bid, the purchasing department

---

[7]Green, Amenkhienan, and Johnson, 52.

establishes long-term, mutually beneficial relationships with suppliers. The numbers of suppliers are usually reduced, but the risks associated with using one source, that is, *sole-sourcing,* place added responsibilities on the purchasing function. In many cases, companies must assist suppliers in meeting quality standards. Often, incoming quality inspections are eliminated in favor of a vendor certification program. The process of certifying vendors adds to the enhanced role of purchasing.

Marketing must recognize the improvements in competitive capabilities and market them rather than just a product. Marketing must also acknowledge the need to stabilize the plant load and assist with this by appropriately planning promotions.

The role of logistics changes in a JIT environment particularly if customers also require JIT delivery. If raw materials inventories are at low levels, missed shipments can be disastrous. Reliability of transportation and delivery takes on a new level of importance for the firm producing and supplying others JIT.

Cross-training employees, quality circles, and increased levels of employee involvement place added training responsibilities on the human resource management function. Many companies have a professional staff completely devoted to the facilitation of quality circle groups. All of these techniques require the significant involvement of labor unions in unionized firms. Expanding the role of individual workers to include many tasks goes against traditional work rules associated with labor unions. Recognizing the need for increased productivity, many unions have begun to relax demands for strict work rules as contracts are renegotiated. The human resources implications for JIT also change the role of the supervisor, who must encourage worker involvement and responsibility and take on more of a coaching role to support the team atmosphere. Cross-training has also increased the necessity of ongoing training of workers.

Because of significant changes made in buyer/supplier relationships, purchasing must adapt to fewer suppliers, different types of transactions, more frequent deliveries, and different contractual structures. Because of the increased expectations put on suppliers, JIT buyer/supplier relationships must become more long-term and cooperative. It is common for buyers to tell suppliers their production schedules to aid them in their scheduling process. Quality management personnel frequently interact and often assist suppliers in solving quality problems.

Accounting must adapt to JIT in its cost accounting and performance measurement responsibilities. Traditional cost accounting allocates overhead to products based on the amount of direct labor used. This has not proved to be an accurate way of allocating overhead. Some JIT companies allocate overhead based on the amount of time the product is in the system. Labor, in a JIT system, is essentially treated as a fixed cost rather than a variable cost, as has been commonly done in the United States. Because it is better for a worker and equipment to be idle than to produce excess inventory, the use of equipment utilization as a performance measure is eliminated under JIT. Utilization, as a performance measure, encourages the running of equipment and production of unneeded inventory.

Finance must consider many previously unrecognized, nonfinancial benefits of capital investments. Of the five competitive priorities, only factors associated with price can easily be quantified. Equipment purchases might appear to be bad investments when judged solely on cost savings. But when examined from the standpoint of improved flexibility, increased dependability, and reduced response time, the investment may well be justified. This is particularly true when the flexibility advantages of buying several identical smaller scale pieces of equipment are compared with those of one large one.

Engineering must also adapt to JIT. Process engineers must become more attuned to simplifying and making processes foolproof. Product engineers must become attuned to the process in a JIT environment and consider manufacturing capabilities when they design new products. Process and product engineers often work together on product development

CONCURRENT ENGINEERING
The linking of product and process engineering to create products that better match manufacturing capabilities.

in JIT companies using a process known as **concurrent engineering,** which matches product design to manufacturing capabilities.

SUMMARY

Once thought to be merely a fad, JIT has had tremendous impact on U.S. manufacturing and is beginning to infiltrate the service sector. Combined with TQM, it is responsible for much of the improvement in U.S. manufacturing and its improving position in the world's marketplace. Although it appears to be a complex system when fully implemented, its components are logical, simple, and often inexpensive to adopt. It has become clear that its philosophy and impact are here to stay.

MAMA'S FINEST REVISITED

CROSS-LINKS

Mama's Finest must deal with two separate issues. First, the firm must resolve the immediate problem of what to do with the 4-week inventory of potentially defective and dangerous product. Second, it must develop a way to prevent the problem from happening again.

Regarding the immediate problem, should Mama's Finest destroy the 4-week inventory of 64-ounce grape jelly? What are the alternatives, and what are their advantages and disadvantages?

Allison downgraded the glass supplier's certification so that the supplier would have to inspect final product before delivery and provide Mama's Finest with the records of the results of these inspections. Given the alternative (losing Mama's Finest's business), the supplier did not object. How can Mama's Finest help the supplier resolve the problem?

What should Mama's Finest do with the remaining 2½ months' worth of unfilled 64-ounce jars?

QUESTIONS FOR REVIEW

1. What is the overriding goal of JIT?
2. What are the objectives of JIT from the perspective of the operations resource categories?
3. What techniques does JIT employ to improve process productivity?
4. Why is inventory reduction important to JIT?
5. What techniques are used to reduce RM, WIP, and FG inventories?

6. Describe the meaning of the phrase *produce at the consumption rate* and its effect on inventory.
7. How do batch-size reduction and mixed model production relate to producing at the consumption rate?
8. Why does JIT strive to involve the work force in decision making? How is this related to eliminating waste?
9. Why is training so important to empowerment efforts?
10. What are the benefits of increasing capacity flexibility?

QUESTIONS FOR THOUGHT AND DISCUSSION

1. Identify JIT applications that would improve familiar areas within your university.
2. Identify a service with which you are familiar. What JIT techniques would be appropriate to it?
3. What effects does JIT have on concepts and techniques used in your major?
4. How can governmental agencies gain from the use of JIT?

5. What cultural resistance would you expect when implementing JIT?
6. What is the effect on product costs if a supplier accomplishes JIT deliveries but still produces in large batches, that is, merely stores the products in finished goods and delivers in small frequent deliveries? Is there any real savings?

INTEGRATIVE QUESTIONS

1. Compare and contrast JIT with TQM.
2. Why is TQM often thought to be a prerequisite to JIT?
3. How does inventory reduction improve quality?

4. What problems would you expect to result from a JIT implementation without the presence of a commitment to quality?
5. Can a pull system be appropriate for a make-to-stock environment?

6. What are the potential areas for implementing JIT in make-to-stock versus make-to-order environments?

7. What are the effects of JIT on each of the five competitive priorities?

8. Which JIT components would be most applicable in the service sector?

SUGGESTED READINGS

Alonso, R. L., and C. W. Frasier. "JIT Hits Home: A Case Study in Reducing Management Delays." *Sloan Management Review* 32 (Summer 1991): 59–67.

Billesbach, T. J., and M. J. Schneiderjans. "Applicability of Just-in-time in Administrations." *Production and Inventory Management Journal* 30 (3rd Quarter 1989): 40–45.

Burt, D. N. "Managing Suppliers Up to Speed." *Harvard Business Review* 67 (July-August 1989): 127–135.

Coates, N. "Determinants of Japan's Business Success: Some Japanese Executives' Views." *Academy of Management Executive* 2 (February 1988): 69–72.

Helper, S. "How Much Has Really Changed between U.S. Automakers and Their Suppliers?" *Sloan Management Review* 32 (Summer 1991): 15–28.

Karmarkar, U. "Getting Control of Just-in-Time." *Harvard Business Review* 67 (September-October 1989): 122–131.

Krafcik, J. F. "Triumph of the Lean Production System." *Sloan Management Review* 30 (Fall 1988): 41–52.

Lyons, T. F., A. R. Krachenberg, and J. W. Henke, Jr. "Mixed Motive Marriages: What's Next for Buyer-Supplier Relations?" *Sloan Management Review* 31 (Spring 1990): 29–36.

Mansfield, E. "Technological Creativity: Japan and the United States." *Business Horizons* 32 (March-April 1989): 48–53.

McMillan, J. "Managing Suppliers: Incentive Systems in Japanese and U.S. Industry." *California Management Review* 32 (Summer 1990): 38–55.

Sakai, K. "The Feudal World of Japanese Manufacturing." *Harvard Business Review* 68 (November-December 1990): 38–45, 48.

Schmenner, R. W. "The Merit of Making Things Fast." *Sloan Management Review* 30 (Fall 1988): 11–17.

Schonberger, R. J. *Japanese Manufacturing Techniques: Nine Hidden Lessons in Simplicity.* New York: Free Press, 1982.

Skinner, W. "The Focused Factory." *Harvard Business Review* 52 (May-June 1974): 113–121.

White, M. I. "Learning and Working in Japan." *Business Horizons* (March-April 1989): 41–47.

CONSTRAINT MANAGEMENT

Numbers Tell the Real Story at SportSeat

SportSeat is an original equipment manufacturer (OEM) of seats for ski boats, bass fishing boats, and top-end cigarette boats. The family-owned business was purchased in 1983. Since that time, it has become the sole supplier of seats to two major manufacturers and the backup supplier for SlimCraft, a third boat manufacturer. Permanent business from SlimCraft, would be a major coup for SportSeat. SlimCraft is located only 350 miles away, and SportSeat is certain it could prove itself if only given a chance. ■ Recent investments in technology have greatly increased SportSeat's capacity. The seat manufacturing process is relatively simple, but a large amount of product variety cuts into equipment and labor efficiency. The boat manufacturers' requirements for option packages to meet customer demand result in short runs and significant amounts of downtime for changeovers. ■ The manufacturing of boat seats consists of three parallel production processes—one for the seat frame, one for the foam back and seat, and one for the fitted upholstery cover. The frame is cut from plywood. There are just a few different frames for the entire range of seats. Seat and back pads are cut from foam to meet the specifications of different seats. Most of the variety comes from the contour or thickness of the pads and the type and color of upholstery. Upholstery is cut to shape and sewn together. In the assembly process, upholstery is stretched over the foam pads and frame and stapled into place. ■ The large amount of variety in the upholstery cutting process, combined with a chronic capacity shortage in this area, prompted the owners to invest in two programmable numerically controlled (NC) cutting machines. The NC cutters, as they are known, cut upholstery at a constant rate to match the seat patterns. The preceding work center, known as the feeder, cuts the upholstery in 48-by-48-inch squares from its 52-inch bolt. In order to keep the NC cutters working, the operator of the feeding work center begins work at 7:00 AM. The NC cutters are turned on at 8:00 AM. Even with the NC cutters, no excess capacity exists for cutting. If fed consistently, each NC cutter can automatically cut upholstery at a rate of 40 seats per hour, giving the plant a maximum capacity of 640 seats per day, unless short runs require excessive changeovers. One week's supply of frames and foam pads is typically stocked in inventory. Early on a recent Monday morning, SportSeat got the opportunity it had been waiting for: a call from SlimCraft for a rush order. ■ Sandra McKenna, director of sales, was beaming as she rushed into the office of Production Manager Jim Washington. "This is it!" she exclaimed. "SlimCraft is finally in a bind, and they need us. This is our chance to cut into Sunval's market share!" ■ Jim was just as excited. "What happened? Why do they need our seats all of a sudden?" ■ "According to their purchasing manager," replied Sandra, "Sunval subcontracts its deliveries to a small local trucking firm. There have evidently been intermittent labor problems. Last night everything came to a head, and the drivers walked out. Sunval's seats are sitting on the loading dock. The company's dockworkers are refusing to load them on any truck out of sympathy for the striking drivers." ■ "What's the order?" Jim asked. ■ "We need 320 seats there by tomorrow morning," Sandra said. "I know it will cost a lot to get overnight delivery, but this order's worth it. The truck must be loaded by 6:00 PM. The question is, can we finish 320 seats by then? The changeover for the NC cutter will be completed by 1:30. That gives us four and a half hours to complete the order. Pads and frames are available in inventory. The real problem is the NC cutter. It'll be close, but with luck we should be able to do it. All cutting must be done by 5:30." ■   At 4:30, Sandra walked through the plant to see how the order was progressing. As she passed the NC cutter, she asked the operator how it was going. "No problems. The cutters are working great!" the operator said. Congratulating herself, she went back to her office. ■   Still a little nervous at 5:00, Sandra went to the end of the assembly line to check the progress. With one hour remaining, they were short 120 seats! Sandra was in shock. The assembly foreman said they had been keeping up all afternoon. Before going any further, Sandra called the trucking firm and convinced them (with a hefty bonus) to pick up the order after 6:00 PM. At 5:30 she returned to the NC cutters. A stockpile of forty 48-inch squares lay in front of them. An examination of the log told an interesting story. From 1:30 to 2:30 and from 2:30 to 3:30, the NC cutters had completed only 60 units per hour. Thereafter they had produced at the maximum 80 units. The NC-cutter operator explained that although he had had no problems, he couldn't run the cutters at full speed early on because there weren't enough squares from the feeder. ■   The feeder operator didn't know why Sandra was so upset. He showed her his log:

Hour	Quantity
1:30–2:30	60
2:30–3:30	60
3:30–4:30	100
4:30–5:30	100

He had clearly met his quota of 320 for the afternoon—an average of 80 seats an hour. ■

In this chapter, the third of three trends in operations management is examined—constraint management. Although constraint management is not as well-known or as widely used as TQM or JIT, its use has grown since the mid-1980s and it has provided direction for many firms interested in improvement. Depending on the company implementing the techniques, constraint management is sometimes referred to as synchronous manufacturing, synchronous management, or theory of constraints.

Constraint management has a colorful and unusual history. Unlike JIT and TQM, constraint management has been developed primarily through the efforts of one individual. In the early 1980s Eli Goldratt, a Ph.D. physicist from Israel, developed a computer software package called Optimized Production Technology (OPT) to be used for scheduling complex manufacturing systems. Goldratt's company at that time, Creative Output, sold, maintained, and provided technical support for companies that purchased OPT. Those companies were never told precisely how the software worked. This so-called black-box approach to selling the software was controversial, and because many managers will not use a tool they do not understand, it probably reduced the use of the software.

In 1984 Goldratt wrote *The Goal,* a book that translated the general logic embedded in OPT software into the fictional account of a plant manager who solves production quality and delivery problems.[1] To further develop the concepts introduced in *The Goal* and to help

---

[1]E. M. Goldratt and J. Cox, *The Goal* (Croton-on-Hudson, N.Y.: North River Press, 1992).

U.S. businesses compete worldwide, Goldratt founded the Avraham Y. Goldratt Institute, which is devoted to educating managers. The institute labeled his philosophies and approaches the Theory of Constraints (TOC). Many managers and consultants have adopted these principles, modified them, and applied them to a variety of settings.

In the early 1990s the Goldratt Institute began moving away from operations-related applications of its theories and started focusing instead on the development of better thinking and problem-solving processes. The transition was controversial and in 1993, some staff members who were more interested in the business applications of constraint management left the institute. The institute's current understanding of TOC is that it is a thought process that can be applied to many aspects of everyday life and is not just an approach for running a business. Because of the changes at the Goldratt Institute and the confusion about the definition of terms, the applications and techniques associated with the Theory of Constraints, *The Goal,* and other related concepts will be referred to as constraint management techniques. The techniques that have the most specific application to operations will receive the most attention.

Constraint management, as it applies to business systems, is based on two premises: *(a)* The goal of a business is to make more money now and in the future; and *(b)* a system's constraints determine its output. A **constraint** is defined as anything that inhibits a system's performance toward its goals. Thus any problem that affects output is a constraint. For example, managers at Howmet Turbine's components manufacturing plant in La Porte, Indiana, noticed that production was backing up at six injection molding machines. After determining that the constraint was the result of an insufficient number of workers operating the machines, management took steps to eliminate the problem. An extra worker was assigned to each of the six machines, increasing output by 40 percent. As business systems have become increasingly complex, their resources have become more difficult to plan, schedule, and utilize effectively. Constraint management helps decision makers separate the important few from the trivial many in these complex environments. (See Box 8.1.) Constraint management techniques also include a structured process for solving problems and a scheduling system that links schedules directly to the capabilities of the constraint.

CONSTRAINT MANAGEMENT
A management philosophy based on two premises: that the goal of a business is to make more money now and in the future and that a system's constraints determine its outputs.

CONSTRAINT
Anything that inhibits a system's performance toward its goals.

CUTTING-EDGE COMPANIES

BOX 8.1

A Monster Improvement

Noel Lee—the Head Monster—is the inventor of and creative genius behind Monster Cable Products Inc. In ten short years, Monster Cable evolved from a two-person, spare-room operation to a business with annual sales of more than $20 million. Although his company was already a success, when Lee read *The Goal* in 1990 he began making changes to implement what he had learned. *Throughput,* rather than output, became the new goal. Monster Cable had been manufacturing products faster than it could get them out the door. Under the new regimen, batch sizes were reduced to one, thereby lowering inventory levels and decreasing response time. Irene Baran, Monster's operations manager, claims that in two years the company reduced the time it took to produce and ship an order from ten days to less than one. The company now receives an order in the morning and ships it that night. Service aspects of the company have improved as well. In the past, a customer with a problem would deal with different people in sales, customer service, and credit departments. Now each customer deals with just two people at Monster, and either person can take care of any problems the customer might have. Lee has also focused on the constraints in his sales forces, by concentrating on, what he calls, the "weakest links."

Source Michael Maren, "The Monster Method," *Success,* June 1992, 43–49.

Having examined the worldwide deployment of its chemical and pharmaceutical operations, the Global Facilities Optimization Task Force of Merck's Manufacturing Division has rearranged production and packaging to create centers where technology and teamwork combine to make optimum use of each Merck facility. Each center is now an integral part of a global manufacturing network designed to achieve an optimal balance of technology resources, inventory levels, capital utilization, and manufacturing costs. The Ballydine, Ireland, plant shown here is the worldwide manufacturing center for Merck's new drug for treating osteoporosis.

Source Michael Sheil, Photographer for *Black Star.* Courtesy of Merck & Co., Inc.

In order to effectively examine the implications of constraint management, the coverage of this topic will be divided into two sections. The first section will examine constraint management implications specifically related to manufacturing and service operations management. The second will provide an overview of the thinking processes involved in the development of these techniques.

MANUFACTURING AND SERVICE OPERATIONS MANAGEMENT

Constraint management techniques emphasize the differences between global and local performance improvement. Global improvement means that performance toward overall organizational goals has improved. Local improvement acknowledges better performance in certain parts of an organization such as a department or work center. It may or may not result in global improvement. **Global optimization** means that the entire system is functioning at the best level that it can.

Local optimization, or the perfecting of local performance, does not necessarily result in global improvement. There are many examples of local optimization that does not have a global impact. Most sales commission systems, for example, are designed to give a salesperson a percentage of the sales price, thus encouraging the sale of more expensive items. This incentive may result in a large increase in total sales dollars, but it may not cause profit to grow. The most expensive items are not necessarily the most profitable because the profit margin is not the same from item to item. Even if the difference between cost and selling

GLOBAL OPTIMIZATION
Maximizing the performance of the system toward its goals.

LOCAL OPTIMIZATION
Maximizing part of the system in terms of a local measure of performance.

price was greatest for the most expensive item it might not be desirable to increase production of that item because another product mix might be more profitable.

Another example of local optimization is the creation of production schedules that make the best use of individual work centers. This approach typically results in high levels of inventory because the production rates of individual work centers are treated independently. For example, office-furniture maker JOFCO Inc. at one time had built up a six-year supply of pencil trays—simply because one operator wanted to keep his machine busy. (After implementing constraint management techniques the company reduced work-in-process inventory by 23 percent while increasing overall revenues by nearly one-third.) The number of units shipped over a given period is an often-used local measure of output that, when optimized, can directly oppose the maximization of profit. When outcome is measured in units shipped, sales are often pulled forward from future periods to increase the current period's output. Management bonuses are often calculated on a units-shipped basis, or simply a dollars-shipped basis. This practice also results in pulling orders from the next period. (See Box 8.2.)

PERFORMANCE MEASURES

Constraint management takes a global perspective of decision making and emphasizes that decisions should be made for the good of the entire system. Its view is that managers should focus on a system's constraints as a basis for making the right decisions because they cannot have a precise view of an entire complex system. Consider as an analogy how to strengthen a chain. You would look for the weakest link in the chain, and by strengthening it, you would strengthen the entire chain. This is precisely what constraint management advocates. By focusing on the weakest link, the greatest improvement can be realized. As the weakest link becomes strengthened, another link becomes the new weakest link.

Strengthening a link that isn't the weakest, however, is common in business decision making. Many companies have invested in technology that has not resulted in improved performance toward their goals. For example, investments in automation that are intended to increase the output of particular departments may improve the performance of those departments but not the system. The investment may increase the quantity of inventory in the

CUTTING-EDGE COMPANIES

BOX 8.2

New Measurements at Follet Corporation

Follet Corporation produces beverage dispensers, ice bins, and other related products. Follet's inventory levels were high, but the company also had frequent shortages of specific materials. The company was concerned about the use of departmental efficiencies as performance measures: It recognized the need to view the business from a system perspective because the traditional measures were distorting decisions. By creating more of a so-called pull system, Follet managed to reduce inventory and lead times 70 percent. Keeping inventory levels down enabled the company to implement product changes and upgrades quickly with no need to work off old inventory. Increases in throughput resulted not only in faster flow through the production processes but also in more timely delivery to meet commitments.

Source V. Lippa, "Measuring Performance with Synchronous Management," *Management Accounting* (February 1990): 54–59.

system, but that doesn't mean sales will also increase. To help managers understand the impact that local decisions have on global performance, constraint management proposes three new measures of global performance.[2] These mearsures are

THROUGHPUT
The rate at which the system generates money through sales.

INVENTORY
The money invested in purchasing things the system intends to sell.

OPERATING EXPENSE
The cost of turning inventory into throughput.

Throughput (*T*): The rate at which the system generates money through sales

Inventory (*I*): All the money invested in purchasing things the system intends to sell

Operating Expense (*OE*): All the money the system spends in turning *inventory* into *throughput*

Goldratt's definitions differ significantly from the conventional definitions of these terms. The constraint management definition for throughput is a prime example. In conventional usage, *throughput* means the rate at which the system is making products. Constraint management considers a business analogous to a money-making machine; until an item is sold, it is not throughput, it is merely inventory. The formula for determining throughput, based on the constraint management definition, is "sales minus the purchased materials used in the specific items sold."[3]

The constraint management definition of inventory includes money invested in equipment because ultimately equipment is saleable. So is the facility. Advocates of constraint management do not recognize the value-added component of inventory accounting. Rather, finished goods are valued according to the price paid for the raw materials, and value added by the system—even the direct labor consumed to make the goods—is not taken into account. Using this approach eliminates the practice of moving of expenses from one period to another by attaching them to inventory as investments, thereby enhancing net profit figures. According to constraint management, it is not acceptable to consider inventory values in a way that not only increases WIP and finished goods but also may result in contrived improvements in net profit.

Constraint management defines *operating expense* simply as the cost of turning inventory into throughput.[4] The use of the word *cost,* however, is not advocated because *cost* has too many different meanings. The definition of operating expense, then, is simple and makes arbitrary distinctions difficult. For example, it does not distinguish between the salaries of a production line worker or salesperson and that of the CEO's chauffeur. Constraint management avoids these distinctions because allocating these costs would require that a cost be converted into an investment and that profit figures be distorted.

Although constraint management's global measures are significantly different from traditional measures, they can be equated with the more traditional performance measures in the following ways:

$$\text{Net profit} \; = \; \text{throughput} \; - \; \text{operating expense} \qquad \textbf{(8.1)}$$
$$= T - OE$$

$$\text{Return on Investment} = \frac{\text{throughput} - \text{operating expense}}{\text{inventory}} \qquad \textbf{(8.2)}$$

$$= \frac{T - OE}{I}$$

---

[2]E. M. Goldratt and R. E. Fox, "The Fundamental Measurements," *The Theory of Constraints Journal* 1 (August-September 1988): 4.

[3]Goldratt and Fox, 5.

[4]Goldratt and Fox, 4.

$$\text{Inventory turns} = \frac{\text{throughput}}{\text{inventory}} \qquad \textbf{(8.3)}$$

$$= \frac{T}{I}$$

$$\text{Productivity} = \frac{\text{throughout}}{\text{operating expense}} \qquad \textbf{(8.4)}$$

$$= \frac{T}{OE}$$

Constraint management presumes that a company will be profitable if it can increase throughput and at the same time reduce inventory and operating expenses. In fact, some firms like Monster Cable (see Box 8.1) have found that this shift in measurement has resulted in significant improvement. Although the use of T, I, and OE makes global performance measurement more concrete and provides managers with some guidance for making local decisions, it does not provide them with enough direction to be confident in all their local decision-making activities. Constraint management advocates the use of the following three measures for local control of throughput, inventory, and operating expense.

Throughput dollar-days: A measure of due-date performance equal to the summation, for each late order, of the dollar value (sales price) of the order times the number of days it is late

Inventory dollar-days: A measure of inventory equal to the value of the inventory (raw material cost) times the number of days until it will be sold

Local operating expense: The operating expense over which the department or managerial unit has full control

Throughput dollar-days can be used internally among departments as well as among functions within the same department, such as engineering and manufacturing or MIS and accounting. This measure acknowledges that a late order's importance is influenced by two factors, the dollar value of the order and how late it is.

Inventory dollar-days gives appropriate focus to inventory reduction efforts. Inventory carrying costs are a function of the amount of money invested in inventory and the amount of time it is held. In a sense, constraint management looks at inventory as a loan made to a plant.[5] The plant borrows money to make or buy inventory, but it must pay the money back when the inventory is sold.

The unit of measure for the cost of a loan (interest) is not just dependent on the sum borrowed, it also includes the amount of time until it is repaid. It is common for managers involved in inventory reduction efforts to cut the inventories that have high dollar values. If these items move fast, however, they may be contributing less to inventory costs than the low-dollar items that move very slowly. An analysis of the interest payments on a car loan will lead to similar conclusions. Consider how the term and the principal act together to determine the total cost of borrowing. The raw material value of the inventory is multiplied by the number of days until it will be sold to derive the dollar-day measure. The number of days until the inventory is sold may be determined precisely if the inventory was built to satisfy a specific order, or it can be calculated from demand forecasts.

THROUGHPUT DOLLAR-DAYS
A measure of due date performance that is the dollar value of an order (sales price) multiplied by the number of days the order is late.

INVENTORY DOLLAR-DAYS
The dollar value of the inventory (raw materials costs) multiplied by the number of days until it will be sold.

LOCAL OPERATING EXPENSE
The operating expense over which a department or managerial unit has full control.

---

[5]Goldratt and Fox, 19.

Local operating expense consists of costs incurred that are within the control of the local unit being measured. The costs are examined in total and are not allocated to particular products or activities. Traditional local performance measures, like efficiency, equipment utilization, and cost per unit, are not directly related to the traditional global measures of net profit or return on investment or to the constraint management global performance measures.

Critical conflicts between traditional local and global measures of performance are evident in business. Most businesses show a typical pattern, known as the **end-of-the-month syndrome.**[6] During the early stages of their reporting periods (monthly, quarterly, and the like), most companies evaluate performance using traditional local performance measures, such as efficiency and utilization of individual workers, work centers, or departments. The commitment to local measures early in the period results in excess inventory of some items and shortages of others depending on whether work centers are used at high efficiencies. During this part of the reporting period, output is relatively stable and managers stress "keeping efficiency and utilization numbers up." As the end of the period looms near, management begins to take notice of another important measurement of performance—orders (or dollars) shipped. Suddenly this becomes the new most important measure. In some businesses managers scramble to identify customers that will take early delivery on the items that have been overproduced just to increase that period's shipments, knowing full well that they are simply borrowing sales from the next period.

This desperate and inane behavior is also an example of succumbing to a local measure of maximizing sales for a period rather than maximizing long-term profits. By essentially throwing out local performance measurement approaches during the last few days of the period, output goes up drastically in order to meet shipping goals, resulting in a pattern similar to that shown in Figure 8.1.

When local and global measures conflict, management cannot perform well. Most managers know intuitively that if they really want output, they must occasionally ignore traditional measures. Unfortunately, consistent reinforcement to do otherwise can, over time, eliminate intuition.

END-OF-THE-MONTH SYNDROME
The tendency for businesses to increase output near the end of an accounting period in order to maximize sales for that period, rather than concentrating on long-term profits.

UTILIZATION OR ACTIVATION

Traditionally, utilization has been defined as the time a particular work center is producing divided by the total amount of time available. Constraint management recognizes that it is possible to produce without contributing to throughput. Constraint management defines production that contributes to throughput as **utilization.** Production that does not contribute to throughput is known as **activation.** Activation is not desired because it not only fails to increase throughput, but it also increases inventory and operating expense. Recall that this is consistent with the JIT philosophy.

Both philosophies stress that it is better to be idle than to produce excess inventory. Workers at the auto parts manufacturer HS Automotive, for example, were making large quantities of parts even when the company had no new orders. Using constraint management techniques, the company shut down some machines and idled workers in order to focus on throughput. The result was a $300,000 reduction in the cost of inventory and a healthy increase in profits.

UTILIZATION
The use of resources for production that contributes to throughput.

ACTIVATION
Production that does not contribute to throughput.

---

[6]M. L. Srikanth and M. U. Umble, *Synchronous Manufacturing* (Cincinnati: South-Western Publishing, 1990), 12–13.

FIGURE 8.1	End-of-the-Month Syndrome

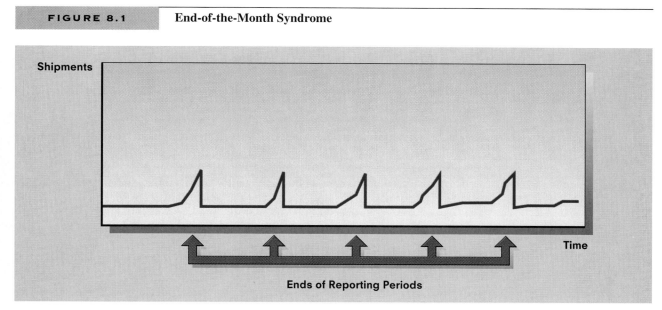

Source   Adapted from M. L. Srikanth and M. U. Umble, *Synchronous Manufacturing* (Cincinnati: South-Western, 1990), 12.

Figure 8.2 presents an example of how excess inventory could be produced if the production rate of the constraint is not used as a guide for all work centers. It shows a simple production system with six steps, one at each work center (WC1, WC2, . . . , WC6) and the time to complete each one. In this example, all products are sold as soon as they complete WC6. Demand is greater than can be supplied by the system, so all finished units are sold immediately. Products must be processed by all six work centers in the correct sequence.

The slowest step in the process, the constraint, is WC4. Because WC4 processes products in 2.1 minutes, products will leave WC6 every 2.1 minutes. Although WC5 and WC6 process more quickly, they can only receive a unit every 2.1 minutes. WC4 is the only work center that can be *utilized* 100 percent. If material is provided to WC1, WC2, or WC3 at a rate faster than one unit every 2.1 minutes, material will enter the system at a rate that is faster than the rate at which it can leave the system. Any work center producing at a rate faster than one unit every 2.1 minutes will not be contributing to throughput; it will merely be contributing to increasing inventory in the system.

WC1, for example, can only be utilized 71.4 percent of the time (1.5 minutes out of every 2.1 minutes). It will work 1.5 minutes and then will be idle for 0.6 minutes before

FIGURE 8.2	Constraint in a Production System

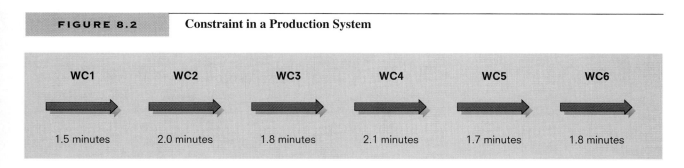

again being utilized. Running WC1 greater than 71.4 percent of the time is not utilization. It is merely activation and will increase operating expense and inventory while not increasing throughput. WC2 can be utilized 95.2 percent of the time because it will work 2 minutes and be idle 0.1 minutes. The utilization of WC3 can be no greater than 85.7 percent. Because WC5 receives products every 2.1 minutes, it will work for 1.7 minutes and then will be idle for 0.4 minutes, giving it a utilization of 80.9 percent. The utilization of WC6 will be 85.7 percent.

Recognizing the difference between utilization and activation is important. Because a salary is being paid to its operator, an idle work center contributes to operating expense without adding value to the product. However, a work center being activated results in the same operating expense (salary) plus increased levels of inventory.

This phenomenon has serious implications for the use of equipment utilization as a measure of performance. Because of constant pressure to lower cost per unit, U.S. manufacturing and service businesses typically define equipment utilization as a performance measure. Cost per unit is a local measure. Efforts to minimize it assume that if cost per unit is reduced, total costs are being reduced, and profits are increased. This logic presumes that as equipment costs are spread out among more products, the cost for each is reduced. Thus, this reasoning goes, maximizing utilization maximizes the number of units produced and minimizes the cost for each. This is not the case, however. Reducing cost per unit when additional units merely add to inventory will not result in a reduction of total costs and thus will not increase profit. This practice is futile because the level of utilization (contribution to throughput) of a work center is determined by the capacity of the system constraint and not by each work center. The irrationality of using utilization as a performance measure is not only recognized by constraint management but is also fundamental to JIT's success.

The system constraint, however, should be fully utilized. Because the constraint determines system throughput, the cost of a constraint that is idle is equivalent to shutting down the entire system. An idle constraint has numerous implications for costs. Whether the constraint breaks down, is shut down for an operator's lunch break or because of a changeover, or is used to work on an item that is already defective, the costs are all far greater than might have been thought. It also has some implications for costs associated with nonconstraints. The downtime costs of a breakdown on a nonconstraint, for example, are nonexistent as long as the breakdown doesn't cut into that work center's utilization. Investment to increase the output of a nonconstraint will not increase the output of the system.

Recognizing the difference and the interaction between constraints and nonconstraints, constraint management also acknowledges two different types of batch sizes. **Process batch** is defined as the quantity produced before the work center changes over to produce something else. **Transfer batch** is defined as the quantity of items produced before the items are moved to the next step in the process.

Traditional U.S. manufacturing has assumed that process batch and transfer batch are the same. In other words, it has been common to transfer parts to the next processing step only after the entire process batch has been completed. If an order was late, requiring special treatment or expediting, this tradition was typically broken and a practice known as lot splitting was invoked. Lot splitting simply means that partial batches were transferred even if the entire batch wasn't completed. This is an example of intuition taking over in a crisis, doing the right thing even if it means violating standard operating procedures.

Constraint management advocates using excess time available on nonconstraints to do additional setups, thereby reducing the process batch size to its minimum and reducing overall levels of inventory without reducing throughput. The process batch size on the constraint must be large or the setup time very small in order to reduce constraint downtime brought on by changeovers. Transfer batches should be as small as possible in all situations

PROCESS BATCH
The quantity of items produced before equipment is set up to produce something else.

TRANSFER BATCH
The quantity of items produced before the items are moved to the next processing stage.

to bring about a more even flow and reduce the probability that a nonconstraint has to wait so long for material that it consumes all available idle time and becomes a temporary constraint.

THE FOCUSING PROCESS

According to constraint management, system improvement means improvement in the performance toward a system's goals and not just toward local goals. When the refrigerator division of Premarks Food Equipment Group adopted this principle at its Kansas City facility, the plant manager helped employees understand the concept by telling them to think like baseball players. "You never saw George Brett walk off the field a winner while the rest of the Royals lost," she said.

Constraint management utilizes a five-step focusing process to obtain ongoing improvement in a system's performance toward its goals.[7]

Step 1: Identify the System's Constraint(s)   A constraint may be a physical resource, such as time on a particular work center or raw materials. It might be money. It might also be a policy or regulation or the market. Most constraints in system performance turn out to be policies. For example, a company could create a constraint by issuing an edict that limited production to one 8-hour shift per day.

Step 2: Decide How to Exploit the System's Constraint(s)   Exploitation of a constraint requires that its output, relative to a system's goals, must be maximized. If the constraint is physical, it must be used to produce the greatest contribution to the system's goals. If the system's goal is to make money and the constraint is a work center, exploitation would mean that the most money possible should be obtained from each minute of the constraint's time. If the constraint is the availability of a particular raw material, the most money per unit of raw material would be desired. The general approach is to maximize the return per constraint unit.

If the constraint is a policy, exploitation means that the policy must be changed or eliminated so that better performance toward the system's goals can be achieved.

Step 3: Subordinate Everything Else to That Decision   Subordination often deals with the process of scheduling. Typically this means that the work must be started and sequenced in such a way that the constraint can always work.

One subordination technique companies use is known as **drum-buffer-rope** (DBR). DBR establishes buffers of inventory just before the constraint and at several other key points in a process to ensure that the constraint is never idle because of a shortage of material. The buffers also provide a link between the material input rate and the pace of the constraint. The system is similar to the kanban system of JIT except that the input rate in DBR is linked to the rate of production of the constraint rather than directly to market demand. Both systems are discussed in detail in chapter 16.

DRUM-BUFFER-ROPE
A subordination technique that establishes buffers of inventories just before the constraint and at other key points in the process to ensure the constraint is never idle because of a shortage of material.

Step 4: Elevate the System's Constraint(s)   Elevating the constraint means identifying ways that will improve the performance of the system relative to its goals. If the constraint is a work center, elevation might include additional preventive maintenance, or it might involve purchasing additional machines to increase capacity.

[7]E. M. Goldratt, *Theory of Constraints* (Croton-on-Hudson, N.Y.: North River Press, 1990), 7.

GPM Gas Corporation, the gas and gas liquids business of Phillips Petroleum, plans to achieve its growth goals in part by applying technology to reduce costs. Facing capacity constraints in New Mexico, where its natural gas processing plants were operating at full capacity, GPM's ability to compete for new gas supplies was limited. To ease these constraints, an employee team built a new, fully automated, remote-controlled plant, which not only reduced operating costs but also will serve as a prototype for GPM's future plants.

Source   Courtesy of Phillips Petroleum Company.

Step 5: If a Constraint Has Been Broken in the Previous Steps, Go Back to Step 1   For many companies, the elimination of a constraint starts a chain of improvements as a new constraint surfaces. (See Box 8.3.) There is always something limiting an organization's performance toward its goals. If the current constraint is broken or eliminated, there must be another constraint.

If all internal constraints are broken, then the constraint may be in the marketplace. A constraint is said to be in the market if sales are limiting the organization's performance toward its goals. There are few market constraints, but there are many marketing policy constraints. A true market constraint would exist only if a company controlled 100 percent of the worldwide market for a product. (See Box 8.4.)

Step 5 prevents inertia from stopping improvements and turns a simple improvement process into a continuous improvement process. The five-step focusing process can be used to improve large systems as well as small subsystems and is just as applicable in the service sector as it is in manufacturing. Consider the following example of one way to apply the five-step focusing process in a small production system.[8]

---

[8]This system as well as similar problems at the end of the chapter are adapted from E. M. Goldratt, *The Haystack Syndrome* (Croton-on-Hudson, N.Y.: North River Press, 1990), 66–78.

BOX 8.3

Eliminating Constraints at Pratt & Whitney

At the Middletown, Connecticut, Pratt & Whitney engine housing plant, a grinding machine that took 32 hours to set up was identified as a constraint. After the set-up time was reduced to 2 hours, other constraints were identified and successively eliminated. In the yearlong process, the production lead time was reduced from 20 weeks to less than 10. Work-in-process inventory has dropped by 77 percent as a result.

Pratt & Whitney Canada has also begun to implement constraint management techniques. The company set a goal of reducing lead time and inventory by 50 percent while improving on-time deliveries to 100 percent. Between September 1990 and June 1991, it increased on-time deliveries from 40 percent to 60 percent, cut inventory by 25 percent, and reduced lead time by 38 percent. Part of the culture change was the replacement of the traditional measures of efficiency and hours produced with throughput, inventory, and operating expenses.

Dover Casting, a Pratt & Whitney supplier, is applying the same approach. It has cut the lead time on Pratt & Whitney castings from 16 to 4 weeks and has reduced inventories by 40 percent.

Northwest Airlines, a customer of Pratt & Whitney, has adopted similar techniques in its repair shop. Northwest's Atlanta repair shop has reduced the time it takes to refurbish an engine by 28 percent. This reduction has created sufficient capacity to enable the repair shop to repair engines for other carriers and is expected to make a profit next year.

Sources "The Responsive Factory," *Business Week Enterprises Issue,* 1993, 48–53. "Synchronous Manufacturing: New Methods, New Mind-Set," *The Journal of Business Strategy* (January/February 1992): 53–56.

BOX 8.4

Crayolas and Constraints

Binney & Smith, the manufacturer of Crayola brand crayons, was forced by a major retailer to take a serious look at its ability to respond quickly to customer orders. In a discussion of a potential partnership, the retailer stated that at first Binney & Smith would be expected to respond to orders in three days, but that would be reduced to two and then to one.

Binney & Smith management had been implementing incremental improvements, incorporating employee involvement techniques, JIT, and TQM. After this meeting, it recognized a need for a revolution rather than an evolution. Its solution was to achieve high velocity manufacturing by combining various aspects of JIT, TQM, constraint management, and employee involvement. More than 300 employees were trained in various components of the different philosophies they were drawing on. Binney & Smith adopted the measures of throughput, inventory, and operating expense as well as the five-step process to focus on constraints and maximize impact. The company identified the customer and the market as its constraints. All decisions were subordinated to focusing on the customer.

The result has been significant success. During 1991 and 1992, an extremely slow economic time, Binney & Smith has maintained double-digit growth.

Source J. M. Roberts and D. W. Tretter, "Competing with Crayolas: Manufacturing as a Competitive Weapon at Binney & Smith," *National Productivity Review* (Spring 1993): 183–191.

EXAMPLE 8.1

An Application of the Five-Step Focusing Process

Consider a small production system for manufacturing two products, P and Q, as shown in Figure 8.3. The goal of this system is to maximize profit. Each week there are demands for 110 units of product P and 60 units of product Q. The production of 1 unit of product P requires 1 unit of raw material 1 (RM1) at a cost of $20, 1 unit of raw material 2 (RM2) at a cost of $20, and 1 unit of a purchased component at a cost of $5. The production of product Q requires 1 unit of RM2 at a cost of $20 and 1 unit of RM3 at a cost of $25. Each work center—A, B, C, and D—must accomplish two tasks. Work center A, for example, processes both the RM1 needed for P (15 minutes per unit) and the RM3 needed for Q (10 minutes per unit). In addition to the cost of raw materials and purchased parts, it takes $6,000 to operate the system, including all labor costs, utility costs, and the like. Product mix does not affect operating expense.

	P	Q
Demand per week	110	60
Selling price	$90	$100
Raw material costs		
RM1	$20	
RM2	$20	$ 20
RM3		$ 25
Purchased part	$ 5	

Time available on each work center: 2,400 minutes
Operating expense per week: $6,000

FIGURE 8.3   **Production System for Producing P and Q**

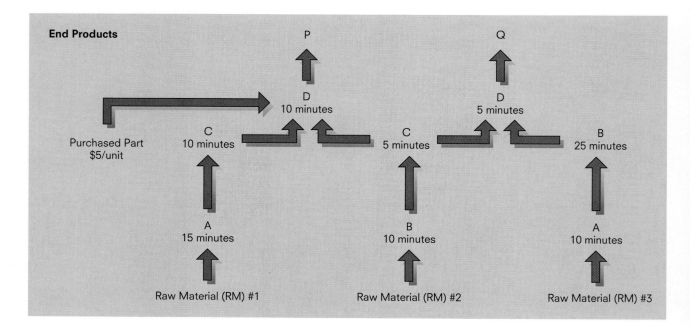

TABLE 8.1   Potential Profit of Production System

	P	Q	Totals
Market demand	110 units	60 units	4
Selling price	$90	$100	
Raw material cost	$45	$45	
Contribution (selling price minus raw material cost)	$45	$55	
Total (market demand times contribution)	$4,950	$3,300	$8,250
Operating expense			$6,000
Net profit per week			$2,250

As detailed in Table 8.1, the system has the potential of making a net profit of $2,250 per week. Maximizing profit takes on a new level of difficulty when it is recognized that the system cannot meet demand, as is demonstrated by the calculations in Table 8.2.

Step 1: Identify the system's constraint(s). In Table 8.2 the capacity required at each work center to produce the number of products necessary to meet demand is determined and compared to the capacity available at each work center. Notice that the required capacity of work center B is 133 percent of that available. This means that in order to produce all of P and Q the capacity on work center B would need to be increased by 33 percent. The current level of capacity on B is insufficient to produce all units of P and Q that would be required to meet demand. Work centers A, C, and D have sufficient capacity to produce all of the demand for both products. Step 1, Identify the constraint, has been accomplished by this analysis. Time available on work center B is the constraint.

TABLE 8.2   Capacity Analysis of Production System

Work Center	Load for P	Load for Q	Total Time Required	Time Available	Percent Required
A	1,650*	600	2,250	2,400	94%
B	1,100	2,100	3,200	2,400	133%
C	1,650	300	1,950	2,400	81%
D	1,100	300	1,400	2,400	58%

*Each P requires 15 minutes on work center A, and market demand is 110. Therefore, the load is
15 × 110 = 1,650 minutes on A.

Step 2: Decide how to exploit the system's constraint(s).   We know that exploitation of the constraint means maximizing the system's output relative to the system's goals. Because the goal of the system is expressed in terms of profit (dollars) and the constraint is measured in time (minutes) on work center B, exploitation means determining how to get the greatest amount of dollars per minute of use of this work center. Both P and Q utilize work center B. No matter what combination of P and Q is produced, all of the time available (2,400 minutes) on work center B will be utilized. In order to maximize profit, work center B must be used in the most profitable way possible. Table 8.3 shows the calculations required to determine the return per constraint minute for products P and Q. As is shown in this table, product P has a greater return, $4.50 per minute on B, than does product Q at $1.57 per minute on B. Thus, work center B should be used to make as many units of product P as possible, and the remaining time available will be used to make product Q.

Consider some of the more traditional measures of a product's profitability. The contribution margin of product Q is greater than that of product P ($55 versus $45). This frequently used measure of a product's profitability would suggest that the demand for Q should be met first, and then any remaining capacity should be used for production of P. The more global measure of return per constraint minute, however, identifies what products P and Q do for the system. Contribution and sales price are merely local measures.

Because product P contributes the most to the system's goals, all of the demand for P (110 units) should be met. Any remaining capacity on B will be used to produce as many Qs as possible. Table 8.4 presents the calculations necessary to determine the actual product mix and, from that, the expected weekly profit.

Exploitation of the constraint provides a product mix of 110 Ps and 37.1 Qs that will maximize net profit. (*Note: The situation becomes more complex when two or more resources require greater than 100 percent of capacity. But these conditions are beyond the scope of this text.*)

Step 3: Subordinate everything else to the above decision.   As in most companies, the employees in this example are always striving to improve performance. Any attempt to improve performance—or, for that matter, to change anything—must be considered from the perspective of its potential impact on the constraint. Any impact on the constraint is, by definition, an impact on the system. Thus, unlike steps 1 and 2, step 3 can never be completed. It is ongoing, even as step 4 is undertaken.

Step 4: Elevate the system's constraint(s).   Suppose an engineer who recognized the importance of elevating the constraint presented management with the following puzzling proposal to modify the system:

- Decrease work center B's operation time on RM2 from 10 to 5 minutes. This modification will require equipment changes costing $1,000.

TABLE 8.3	Calculating Return per Constraint Minute

Product	Contribution Margin	Time on B	Return per Minute on B
P	$45	10 minutes	$4.50
Q	$55	35 minutes	$1.57

TABLE 8.4	**Product Mix and Expected Net Profit**

Time required on B for P

Time on B for each P	Market demand for P	P's load on B
10 minutes	× 110 units	= 1,100 minutes

Remaining time on B to make Q

Total time available	Time required for P	Time available for Q
2,400 minutes	− 1,100 minutes	= 1,300 minutes

Quantity of Qs that can be produced

Time available	Time required per Q	Quantity of Qs possible
1,300 minutes	÷ 35 minutes	= 37.1 Qs

Expected weekly net profit

	P	Q	Total
Production units	110	37.1	
Contribution margin	$45	$55	
Total	$4,950	$2,040.50	$6,990.50
(market demand × contribution)			
Operating expense			$6,000.00
Net profit per week			$ 990.50

- Increase work center C's operation time on RM2 from 5 to 10 minutes to take on part of work center B's current load. This modification will require equipment changes costing $500.
- Change work center D's operations to accommodate the differences in processing RM2. These changes can be done at no cost but will result in a 2-minute increase in the time it takes D to perform its work on both P and Q.

That is, the engineer is suggesting that the company spend $1,500 to decrease time on work center B from 10 to 5 minutes, increase time on work center C from 5 to 10 minutes, and increase both operation times on work center D by 2 minutes, with a net increase of 2 minutes in direct labor for both P and Q. These proposed changes are shown in Figure 8.4.

Because the time required by work center B has been reduced, the throughput should increase and more time should be available to produce product Q. It is also possible that the constraint has been broken and a new constraint will exist, which would require a return to step 1. Thus, the capacity analysis must be performed for the new system. If the constraint has changed, we must recalculate the return per constraint minute, refigure our product mix, and determine if the profit potential has increased before a decision can be made on this proposal.

Step 5: If in the previous steps a constraint has been broken, go back to step 1.   Table 8.5 presents the new capacity analysis. It shows that elevating work center B has broken that constraint, so we return to step 1.

FIGURE 8.4 **Proposed Production System for Producing P and Q**

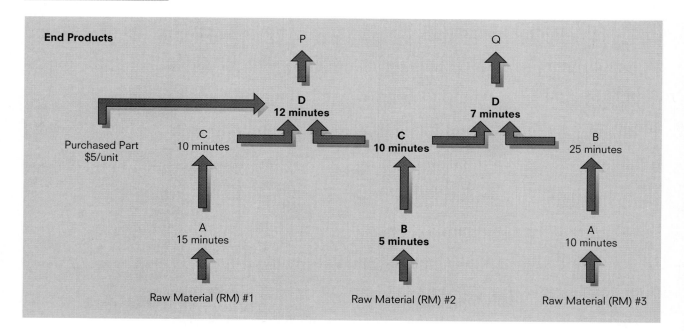

Step 1: Identify the new constraint. Table 8.5 shows that work center C is the new constraint, and Table 8.6 shows the new analysis of the return per constraint minute. The change in the constraint has had a dramatic effect on this analysis. Product Q now utilizes the constraint to the greatest benefit, returning $5.50 per constraint minute compared to $2.25 for P.

With the new scenario, all of the demand for Q is met first, and any remaining capacity on work center C is used to produce P. The analysis in Table 8.7 shows that to produce 60 units of Q, work center C uses 600 minutes, leaving 1,800 minutes available for the production of P. Ninety units of P can be produced in 1,800 minutes. Thus the new product mix

TABLE 8.5 **Capacity Analysis for Proposed Changes**

Work Center	Load for P*	Load for Q	Total Time Required	Time Available	Percent Required
A	1,650	600	2,250	2,400	94%
B	550	1,800	2,350	2,400	98%
C	2,200	600	2,800	2,400	117%
D	1,320	420	1,740	2,400	73%

*Each P requires 15 minutes on the A work center, and market demand is 110. Therefore, the load is
  15 × 110 = 1,650 minutes on A.

TABLE 8.6	**Calculating Return per Constraint Minute for Proposed Changes**

Product	Contribution Margin	Time on C	Return per minute on C
P	$45	20 minutes	$2.25
Q	$55	10 minutes	$5.50

TABLE 8.7	**Product Mix and Expected Net Profit of Engineer's Proposal**

Time required on C for Q

Time on C for each Q	Market demand for Q	Q's load on C
10 minutes ×	60 units =	600 minutes

Remaining time on C to make P

Total time available	Time required for Q	Time available for P
2,400 minutes −	600 minutes =	1,800 minutes

Quantity of Ps that can be produced

Time available	Time required per Q	Quantity of Qs possible
1,800 minutes ÷	20 minutes =	90 Ps

Expected weekly net profit

	P	Q	Total
Market demand (units)	90	60	
Contribution Margin	$45	$55	
Total (market demand × contribution)	$4,050	$3,300	$7,350
Operating expense			$6,000
Net profit per week			$1,350

is 60 units of Q and 90 units of P, which yields a weekly net profit of $1,350—an increase of $359.50 over that of the original system. This means that the $1,500 investment would be repaid in slightly over 4 weeks.

Despite the fact that the engineer recommended increasing overall labor content, which would increase cost per unit if direct labor were included in the cost calculation, an increase in net profit is generated. The five-step focusing process helped identify work center C as the constraint for the system, thereby allowing management to make the appropriate decision.

All departments within the organization must make decisions based upon what the constraint is and which product contributes the most per constraint unit. If the pay structure for the sales force ignores this information and the sales force develops its own policies, performance will be less than ideal and a policy constraint will have been created.

THE TOC THOUGHT PROCESS

Constraint management, like JIT and TQM, espouses a philosophy of continuous improvement through the continual application of the five-step focusing process. Although physical systems constrained by work center capacity can frequently be improved using the five-step focusing process, constraint management recognizes that improvement does not always come that easily. Goldratt contends that any improvement requires change.[9] He provides three questions that must continually be answered in order to achieve continuous improvement:

1. What should be changed?
2. What should it be changed to?
3. How can I cause this change to happen?

The five-step focusing process often provides direction in answering the first question, "What should be changed." Because the constraint determines system performance, identifying what should be changed to provide system improvement will likely be directly related to the constraint. The answer to the second question, "What should it be changed to," is not always easy. For example, suppose customer lines at a branch bank got so long on Friday afternoons that people were beginning to take their business to another bank. If available capacity at the teller windows was identified as what to change, identifying what to change to may be as straightforward as changing to a higher level of capacity. Suppose, however, that all employees are already working and all teller windows are in use. It is no longer easy to determine what to change to. United Electric Controls Co. faced even more complex challenges after it began implementing the constraint management theories outlined in Goldratt's *The Goal.* But since each of the company's 45 employees had been given a copy of the book, management was able to draw on the expertise of the entire workforce in determining what to change. The improvements were so impressive that in 1990 United Electric was awarded the coveted Shingo prize for its gains in manufacturing productivity.

To help companies address complex improvement problems, a problem-solving process, known as the theory of constraints (TOC) thought process, has been developed. It utilizes several other techniques and tools to provide answers to the three questions posed above.[10] The techniques include current reality trees, effect-cause-effect, evaporating clouds, future reality trees, prerequisite trees, transition trees, and a so-called buy-in procedure.

---

[9]Goldratt, *Theory of Constraints,* 7–9.

[10]The descriptions of these techniques are based on notes taken during the 1990 JONAH conferences held in Grand Rapids, Michigan, and Orlando, Florida, and the 1991 JONAH conference held in Dayton, Ohio. All were sponsored by the Avraham Y. Goldratt Institute.

TOC TECHNIQUES

Effect-Cause-Effect　Determining what should be changed requires the identification of core problems. Core problems are identified using *current reality trees* to describe cause-and-effect relationships in the present environment and a process known as *effect-cause-effect* (ECE) to aid in developing these trees. The ECE process begins by identifying several undesirable effects or conditions. For example, a company might have a problem with missed customer due dates, excess work-in-process inventory, and defective end products. Improvement would be obtained if these undesirable effects could be eliminated.

The next step in the ECE process is to hypothesize a cause for each of the undesirable effects that have been identified. Missed customer due dates, for instance, might be caused by chronic shortages of raw materials or by lack of staff in the shipping department. In order to verify a cause, ECE tests hypotheses by identifying additional effects that would be present if the hypothesized cause were valid. Once validated, a cause, such as a shortage in raw materials, is treated as an undesirable effect and *its* causes are further hypothesized. It might be, for example, that raw-material shortages arise from unreliable deliveries. This effect-cause-effect process of hypothesis and validation continues until the various causes, or branches, begin to converge into one or two root causes.

Typically, it is easy to identify six or eight undesirable effects; and when their causes are hypothesized, it becomes obvious that some undesirable effects share causes. When these causes are themselves treated as undesirable effects and their causes identified, it is seen that even more causes are shared. Thus the tree, as it is constructed from top to bottom, shows the convergence of a few true causes for a set of undesirable effects. Managers, however, may not be able to resolve a true root cause because their authority is limited. Rather, managers may address core problems—the lowest level causes within their authority to tackle.

Current reality trees often reveal a core problem that identifies *what* to change and what to change *to* at the same time. Suppose, for example, that missed customer due dates were all linked to a core problem of one unreliable supplier of raw materials. Clearly, the solution to "what to change" is the supplier, and the solution to "what to change to" is a reliable supplier. But sometimes identifying what to change to is not so easy. In fact, even if the answer is readily apparent, implementing the appropriate change may seem impossible because resources are scarce or conflicts are involved. It is not uncommon, however, that seemingly impossible problems can be solved if the underlying assumptions are exposed and evaluated.

Evaporating Clouds　Evaporating clouds can be used to expose faulty assumptions and resolve conflicts. The process consists of several steps. First, identify the objective, which should be the opposite of the core problem identified in the current reality tree. For example, suppose the core problem is identified as an unreliable supplier. The opposite is the objective: get a reliable supplier. Next, define the requirements of this objective, the prerequisites, and the relationships between them as well as the conflicts that prevent action. One requirement for a reliable supplier, for example, might be that it must be someone new, not the current unreliable one. The second requirement could be that the new supplier must be able to make daily deliveries. We now have an objective and two requirements. Suppose, however, that the current supplier is the only one within one day's travel time. The problem appears to be unsolvable. But the relationships between the prerequisites, requirements, and objective are all based on assumptions. The third step is to articulate and challenge all assumptions necessary for the existence of these relationships. An assumption found to be invalid will cause the conflict to evaporate. For example, one assumption might be that a supplier must be located less than one travel day in order to provide daily deliveries. That is not true as long as the company can provide the supplier with necessary requirements more than one day ahead of time. As soon as the assumption is invalidated, the conflict between needing a new supplier and having only the old one to choose from evaporates. In order to invalidate an assumption, it is typically necessary to change the environment in such a way as to make the assumption invalid. This change is called an *injection,* and its role is to eliminate, or *cure,* the conflict.

Future Reality Trees   The future reality tree is used to develop the linkages between the injection identified in the evaporating cloud and undesirable effects. The injection is placed at the base of the tree, and opposites of the original undesirable effects are placed at the top of the tree. Using the causal relationships of the current reality tree as a guideline, the tree is rebuilt from bottom to top. This process helps to identify other actions or other injections that may be necessary. It is an important part of this process to take a devil's advocate role in challenging all relationships to bring out any weaknesses. As an example, consider the unreliable supplier problem. To construct the future reality tree, the opposites of all original undesirable effects are placed at the top of the branches. The bottom of the tree is the new, but longer distance, supplier. Using the cause and effect relationships identified in the current reality tree, we reconstruct the tree from bottom to top, identifying any additional undesirable effects that may be related to the longer distance supplier and including the injections needed to eliminate them.

Most managers agree that identifying what to change and what to change to is not nearly as difficult as effecting the change. Effecting change involves people, and people tend to resist change. Recall the example of United Electric, which implemented many of the concepts explained in *The Goal.* Since the company was already doing well financially, managers encountered resistance among workers who wondered why change was necessary. Constraint management advocates the use of prerequisite trees, transition trees, and a buy-in procedure to accomplish this task. We will limit our discussion to prerequisite trees, because the other two concepts are complex and beyond the scope of this text.

Prerequisite Trees   Prerequisite trees are built from the bottom to the top. Starting at the base of the prerequisite tree, with the original injection from the evaporating cloud and additional injections from the future reality tree, we proceed upward toward the objective of the evaporating cloud (the opposite of the undesirable effects) at the top of the prerequisite tree, identifying obstacles that stand in the way of achieving the objective. Then we identify additional objectives that will eliminate each of these obstacles. This process is stopped when an objective that can be attained immediately is identified. Continuing the example of the unreliable supplier, the base of the tree is the acceptance of a supplier farther away than one day's travel plus any new injections identified in the future reality tree. Proceeding upward to the top of the tree, which lists all of the opposites of the original undesirable effects, we identify those conditions that might inhibit accomplishments. For example, with increased distance to a supplier, and consequently more inventory "in the pipeline," weather conditions may now create delays that didn't exist with a nearby supplier. Additional injections may be needed to eliminate this obstacle.

After identifying the objective that can be achieved immediately at the top of the prerequisite tree, we work back down the tree, identifying other actions that will begin to move us toward the next objective and eliminate the next obstacle. This process is repeated until each obstacle is overcome and the injection at the bottom of the prerequisite tree is reached.

Constraint management recognizes that resistance to change is prevalent in most organizations and advocates, as much as possible, a Socratic (dialog) approach to develop a sense of ownership in others and reduce that resistance. A sense of ownership may be accomplished through several methods, including explaining the current reality tree and allowing others to improve upon the future reality trees.

CONSTRAINT MANAGEMENT CROSS-LINKS

Constraint management and TOC thought processes affect a variety of business functions. Constraint management has implications for managerial accounting practices, particularly with such local measures as cost per unit and utilization and the conflicts that exist between them and global measures.

Constraint management also has implications for financial decisions, particularly those involving investments in capital equipment. Basing decisions on cost per unit reductions (often through direct labor savings) can mislead managers, particularly if the investment increases capacity of a work center that is not the constraint. Increasing the capacity of a nonconstraint has the effect of increasing the amount of idle time of the work center.

By focusing on the entire system rather than on local optimization, constraint management has implications for marketing as well. Its approach to determining the contribution a product makes to the system rather than local measures, such as a product's contribution margin or sales price, leads to sale commission systems that are more consistent with system goals and sales efforts that support the desired product mix. Constraint management also has implications for product pricing, particularly for items that do not use the constraint. For products that do not utilize the constraint, variable costs associated with production are, for the most part, limited to materials costs because the work centers have idle time anyway. Prices can reflect these costs and present opportunities for breaking into markets with prices significantly lower than those of competitors.

CONSTRAINT MANAGEMENT AND COMPETITIVE PRIORITIES

The constraint management objective of increasing throughput while reducing inventory and operating expense has a direct impact on costs and, therefore, price. Focusing on the constraint, through the five-step focusing process, often results in lowering costs of system improvement because money spent has a more immediate result than if it were spent on nonconstraining resources.

Inventory reduction, through transfer and process batch reduction, results in shorter response time and smoother flows, enhancing the competitive capabilities of flexibility and time, just as in a JIT system. Although product quality is not specifically addressed by constraint management, dependability and service quality are frequent benefits of the improvement process because of the inventory reduction and better flow of material. The use of drum-buffer-rope provides a means of ensuring more predictable lead times and more reliable promise dates, and it enhances the dependability of delivery. Like TQM and JIT, constraint management's influence can span all resource categories and enhance performance of all competitive priorities, as shown in Figure 8.5. Through its five-step focusing process and performance measures, constraint management provides local direction for management decisions to increase the likelihood that they will be consistent with business goals.

FIGURE 8.5   **Constraint Management's Influence on the Task/Resource Model of Operations Management**

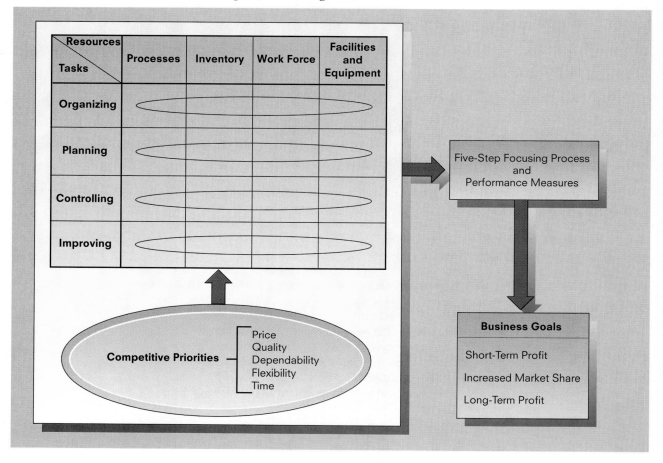

TQM, JIT, AND CONSTRAINT MANAGEMENT APPROACHES: A COMPARISON

The increased interest in and implementation of new management philosophies have had dramatic effects on U.S. services and manufacturers. Most of these effects have come from TQM and JIT, but an increasing number of businesses are implementing constraint management approaches. Like new and controversial approaches in any other field, these philosophies have engendered disagreements about which is best. Some people have become so committed to one approach over the others that their support has almost taken on religious overtones. There are, in effect, TQM, JIT, and constraint management disciples.

The overall objectives of JIT, TQM, and constraint management are similar, but their focuses differ. While JIT emphasizes "leanness," the elimination of waste, TQM stresses "doing it right the first time" to keep customers from ever being dissatisfied. Constraint management, on the other hand, concentrates on the "constraint"—anything that limits the achievement of major goals. All three broadly advocate continuous improvement, but each accomplishes continuous change differently. TQM uses the quality improvement (QI) story, JIT uses inventory reduction, and constraint management uses the five-step focusing process. These different focuses and techniques, however, often overlap. In fact, TQM is considered necessary for the successful implementation of JIT, and much of the constraint management philosophy is consistent with TQM and JIT. Moreover, all three philosophies espouse increased worker involvement as well as process improvement and simplicity.

It is not the purpose of this text to try to determine if one approach is better than another. In fact, trying to make such a determination is absurd. An analogous task would be to try to determine which is better, a hammer or a screwdriver. Would you rather hire a mechanic who was a hammer expert or a screwdriver expert, or one who had a large tool box full of tools and knew how to use all of them appropriately? The answer is obvious. TQM, JIT, and constraint management provide managers with the equivalent of tool boxes. Each contains a number of useful tools. In some cases, a tool in one box may be similar to a tool in another; in other cases one box may offer a tool to accomplish a task that cannot be substituted with a tool from another box.

Making a commitment to TQM or JIT or constraint management techniques to the exclusion of all others places unnecessary limits on what managers can accomplish. The most effective companies and managers have a thorough understanding of all approaches and use the most appropriate technique or the one that works best for them. Many companies find that they can incorporate TQM, JIT, and constraint management into their improvement processes and utilize a full range of tools.

SUMMARY

The five steps of the focusing process of constraint management form a basis for making improvements that will result in the greatest system benefit. The application of this approach is intuitively attractive for many managers. It remains to be seen, however, if the TOC thought processes actually result in better decisions and faster rates of improvement. Comparative studies have not been done. The complete process, including all its steps, appears to violate a traditional rule for useful managerial models: "K.I.S.," or *keep it simple.* Managers tend to use techniques that are straightforward and easy to understand, primarily because the results of such techniques are easier to explain to others. If the thought processes are shown to result in better decisions and faster rates of improvement, however, they may become more widely accepted and more commonly used.

Examination of the TQM, JIT, and constraint management approaches reveals some differences as well as some common ground. Most important, they all point to the need for continuous improvement—and therefore continuous change—as a norm, rather than an exception.

SPORTSEAT REVISITED

CROSS-LINKS

Even though the order was shipped later than planned, it was delivered on time. Sandra received a valuable lesson in scheduling, however, and realized that some important changes needed to be made.

How should Sandra determine shipping times for orders in the future? What role does the constraining operation play?

The results of this experience convinced Sandra that the performance measurements used for nonconstraining work centers, like the feeder, were not appropriate. What type of performance should be encouraged at the feeder? How could a performance measurement system encourage this behavior?

Sandra also realized that she needed to reduce the direct dependency the NC Cutter had on the feeder. How might this be accomplished?

QUESTIONS FOR REVIEW

1. What are the performance measures espoused by constraint management? How do they differ from traditional performance measures?
2. Describe the end-of-the-month syndrome.
3. Compare utilization and activation from a constraint management perspective.
4. What is the significance of transfer batch and process batch?
5. What are the five steps of the constraint management focusing process?
6. How does the five-step focusing process work if the constraint is a policy?
7. What three questions must be answered in order to maintain continuous improvement?
8. What implications does constraint management have for managerial accounting? For marketing?
9. How does constraint management affect the competitive capabilities of a firm?

QUESTIONS FOR THOUGHT AND DISCUSSION

1. In the application of the constraint management focusing process, to what level could the price of Q be lowered in an effort to stimulate demand for Q and have Q still remain the most profitable product?
2. How do you define *throughput* as it relates to your personal productivity?
3. What are your constraints?
4. How can your personal constraint(s) be exploited?
5. How is *throughput* defined for a university?
6. How would you define *inventory* in a university setting?
7. How would you define *throughput* and *inventory* for a bank? For an insurance company? For the criminal justice system?
8. What are the constraints that must be eliminated in order to attain continuous improvement of a system you are familiar with?

INTEGRATIVE QUESTIONS

1. Compare the five-step focusing process to the QI story. How is it similar? How is it different? What are the advantages and disadvantages of each?
2. Are the three global measures of throughput, inventory, and operating expense in conflict with JIT? Explain.
3. JIT reduces set-up times throughout the system to allow for batch size reduction. What would be the constraint management approach to reducing set-up times?
4. How can buffers be used to protect service sector constraints from being idle? Provide examples.

PROBLEMS

1. Using the five-step focusing process, maximize profit for the following production system:

	P	**Q**
Demand per week	110	60
Selling price	$ 90	$100
Raw material costs		
RM1	$ 20	
RM2	$ 20	$ 20
RM3		$ 25
Purchased part	$ 5	

Time available on work centers
A, B, C, and D: 2,400 minutes each

Supply of raw materials: Unlimited, except for RM2, which is limited to 155 units per week

Operating expense per week: $6,000

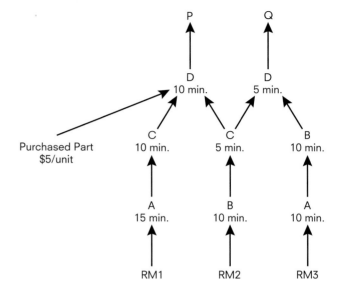

2. Using the five-step focusing process, maximize profit for the following production system:

	P	**Q**
Demand per week	110	70
Selling price	$110	$ 75
Raw material costs		
RM1	$ 20	
RM2	$ 24	$ 24
RM3		$ 20
Purchased part	$ 5	

Time available on work centers
A, B, C, and D: 2,400 minutes each

Supply of raw materials: Unlimited

Operating expense per week: $6,000

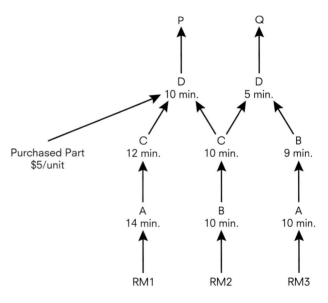

3. Using the five-step focusing process, maximize profit for
the following production system:

	P	Q
Demand per week	240	160
Selling price	$ 65	$ 55
Raw material costs		
RM1	$ 10	
RM2	$ 10	$ 10
RM3		$ 12
Purchased part	$ 5	

Time available on work centers
A, B, C, and D: 2,400 minutes each

Supply of raw materials: Unlimited

Operating expense per week: $6,000

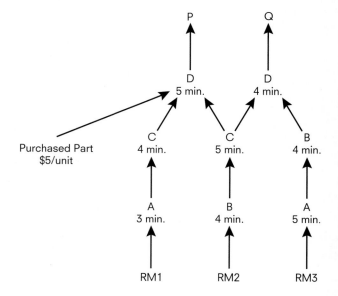

4. Using the five-step focusing process, maximize profit for
the following production system:

	P	Q
Demand per week	130	180
Selling price	$110	$ 75
Raw material costs		
RM1	$ 20	
RM2	$ 24	$ 24
RM3		$ 20
Purchased part	$ 12	

Time available on work centers
A, B, C, and D: 2,400 minutes each

Supply of raw materials: Unlimited, except for
RM2, which is
limited to 200 units
per week

Operating expense per week: $6,000

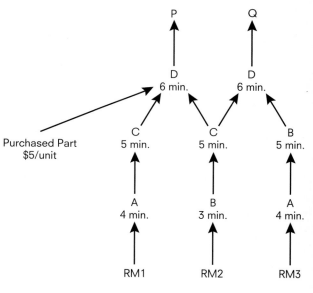

SUGGESTED READINGS

Fry, T. D., and J. F. Cox. "Manufacturing Performance: Local versus Global Measures." *Production and Inventory Management Journal* 30 (2nd Quarter 1989): 52–57.

Goldratt, E. M., and R. E. Fox. *The Race.* Croton-on-Hudson, N.Y.: North River Press, 1986.

Goldratt, E. M., and J. Cox. *The Goal.* 2nd ed. Croton-on-Hudson, N.Y.: North River Press, 1992.

Goldratt, E. M. *Theory of Constraints.* Croton-on-Hudson, N.Y.: North River Press, 1990.

———. *The Haystack Syndrome.* Croton-on-Hudson, N.Y.: North River Press, 1990.

Lambrecht, M. R., and L. Decaluwe. "JIT and Constraint Theory: The Issue of Bottleneck Management." *Production and Inventory Management Journal* 29 (3rd Quarter 1988): 61–65.

Lundrigan, R. F., and J. R. Borchert. *The Challenge.* Croton-on-Hudson, N.Y.: North River Press, 1988.

Spencer, M. S. "Using 'The Goal' in an MRP System." *Production and Inventory Management Journal* 32 (4th Quarter 1991): 22–28.

PART III

PLANNING FOR OPERATIONS

"**W**hat do ya suppose management is using for brains? You'd think *some-body'd* figure out that the packing and shipping department needs to be near the door. It's a real hassle hauling everything to one central location, only to haul it right back out again!" ■ "We can't keep working 10-hour days 7 days a week! Wouldn't it be cheaper to hire more short-order cooks, just to get us through the summer season?" ■ "I know the price of crude keeps fluctuating. But how much oil do we have to pump just to keep our refineries operating at an effective level?" ■ "Did you order enough paper so we can print all the spring catalogs? Can we do them in one print run, or do we need to run several smaller lines?" ■ Every minute of every day, managers throughout the United States and the world are facing these and other, even more difficult questions. The common factor among all such questions is planning. ■ Plans are like maps. Without them, we might know where we want to go, but we wouldn't know how to get there. Plans, then, are maps or guides to competitive success. Contrary to popular belief, the ownership of resources doesn't guarantee that a firm will achieve a competitive edge: It's the way resources are used that separates winners from losers. ■ In many businesses, the operations function controls 70 percent of the firm's resources, including inventory, facilities, plant and equipment, and much of the labor force. In Part III we examine the role operations plays in developing and implementing plans that allow management to anticipate business conditions and arrive at contingencies to cover them. Well developed plans for the use of resources offer alternatives that can reduce costs and increase short-term profit. They can also enhance quality and service in ways that will increase market share and create a loyal customer base. ■

FORECASTING DEMAND

A Sales Manager Eats Crow

CompuSmart is a small but growing manufacturer of personal computers. Sales have doubled each year since the company was founded in 1990. Much of the success has been credited to Simon Baxter, sales manager and close friend of the company founder. ■ The latest monthly figures for CompuSmart were on sales manager Simon Baxter's desk when he arrived at 7:00 Monday morning. He looked at the last page summary before examining any of the detailed product breakdowns. A comparison of the past month's customer service to that of the previous two months caught his eye. It showed more missed deliveries. Something was wrong. Before he could e-mail the other managers that he wanted to meet with them about this matter, his phone started ringing. ■ The first call was from an independent computer retailer in the southern part of the state. Last Thursday she had ordered 64 standard 486 computer systems. The shipment had arrived too late Friday night for proper checking, and when she counted the packages this morning, she found that she had been shipped only 30 systems. Because each of the shipments was to fill a customer order, she knew she was going to have to do some fast talking to prevent this from costing her sales. No sooner had Simon promised her delivery by morning and hung up than the phone rang again. By 8:00 he had talked to seven angry customers. He immediately e-mailed Celeste Richardson, the production manager, with instructions to call him as soon as she got in. ■ Simon then made a telephone call to the shipping department. The only information he could get was that they had shipped everything that was on the dock when the truck had to leave. Simon's second call was to the finished goods warehouse. MaryAnn Krogh, the warehouse manager, assured him

that on Friday the warehouse had pulled every system available, but it did not have the stock to fulfill all orders. ■ "This is beginning to be a Monday morning ritual," thought Simon. "No one is willing to take responsibility for this screwup." Before he could call anyone else, Celeste called. He immediately began blasting her with questions. "Why were the systems not at the shipping dock on time? Why weren't they in the warehouse? Where are they now? Why didn't you. . . ." Celeste interrupted with some questions of her own. ■ "Why are you mad at me? Have you compared the customer order total to the projection you gave me last Monday? You know our production lead time is 5 days, yet you continue to promise customers that they can order on Friday morning and receive shipment by Monday morning. What do you expect?" Fortunately for Simon, Celeste's secretary interrupted, and she had to hang up. ■ Simon pulled last week's file and looked at the projection for standard 486 systems. The total was 531, the same demand as the week before, but customer orders totaled 578. He looked at last month's report and saw a pattern. Projections were below actual orders for each week of the month except the last. It was worse the first week of the month. Orders were usually high the first week of each month and low the last because customers tried to deplete inventory at the end of a month. Orders were being missed, resulting in declining on-time deliveries. ■ There was another problem too. Systems were costing more to produce because, in response to Simon's Monday morning tirades, Celeste was using overtime to get the computers out as soon as possible, usually by Tuesday morning. Overtime, at time and a half the normal labor rate, was increasing the total production costs of the 486 by 7 percent. If costs continued to rise at this rate, Simon knew that prices would have to be increased. The use of overtime seemed ridiculous because he knew there was excess capacity in the production department late in the week. He also knew, however, that if Celeste had not used overtime to fill the orders as quickly as she could, the customers would have canceled the orders. ▪ Examination of the monthly reports for the previous 3 months showed a similar pattern, which had been getting worse. Simon groaned in frustration. Sales were increasing at a wonderful rate, but customer service was declining at an equal rate. He knew it was just a matter of time before customers looked for more reliable suppliers. That would be the end of CompuSmart's growth. ▪

WHY FORECAST?

The resources managed by the operations function consist of processes, capacity, inventory, and work force. The need for changes in any of these resources is often driven by changes in product or service demand. Planning for these resources, therefore, is often contingent on forecasts of product demand. To understand the role of forecasts, it is helpful to understand how the relationships between plans, forecasts, and the **planning horizon,** which is how far in the future one must plan, relate to one another.

The minimum planning horizon is determined by the lead times of any actions that may need to be taken in order to meet plans. Consider, for example, a restaurant that determines it must increase its capacity to meet demand. To increase capacity the restaurant would have to undergo construction that would take 6 months. That restaurant's minimum horizon for capacity planning would be 6 months. If the restaurant only plans capacity 3 months into the future and identifies a shortage, the 6-month lead time on completing construction would mean that the capacity increase would be completed too late and would result in the restaurant's not meeting demand during a 3-month period.

Managers cannot depend on actual orders from customers to provide a basis for plans because the lead times required to carry out those plans are frequently much longer than the delivery times promised to customers. For example, when demand for pickups, minivans, and sport-utility vehicles unexpectedly shot up in early 1994, the Big Three automakers quickly made plans to boost production. General Motors and Chrysler began running factories around the clock, while Ford started switching some car plants to truck production. The plans were not implemented fast enough to satisfy dealers, however, who complained that their supply was not keeping up with demand.[1] To avoid this kind of problem, firms must accurately predict what their orders will be in the future. This process is known as **demand forecasting.**

Forecasts provide a basis for planning. Once a firm estimates the demand for a product or service, it can determine other planning functions, such as raw material requirements, work force size, capacity and equipment needs, and cash flow requirements. (See Box 9.1.) Figure 9.1 shows how forecasting affects planning across all resource categories of the task/resource model of operations management.

Forecasting provides a basis for short-, medium-, and long-term planning. Without an estimate of what the demand will be for a product or service, many aspects of planning cannot occur. The accuracy of forecasts are, to a great extent, influenced by two factors. First, the farther into the future the forecast, the less accurate it will be. Thus, forecasting can be

PLANNING HORIZON
The number of periods of time for which an organization will schedule its production.

DEMAND FORECASTING
The process of predicting future demand for products or services as a means to schedule production.

---

[1] James Treece and Kathleen Kerwin, "Detroit Highballing It into Trucks," *Business Week,* March 7, 1994, 46.

| FIGURE 9.1 | **Relationship between Forecasting and the Task/Resource Model** |

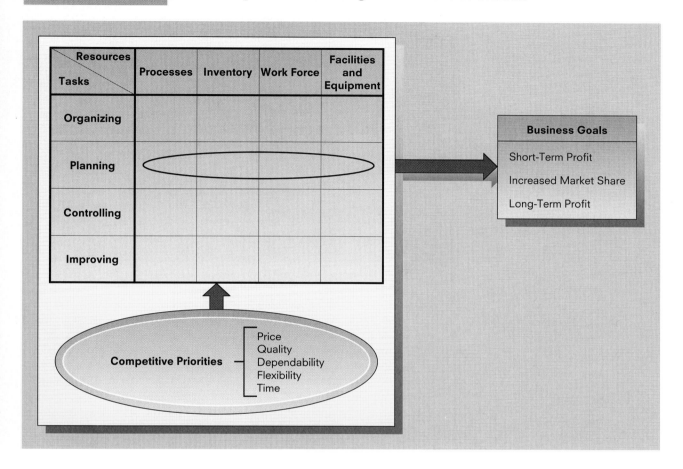

improved by shortening the lead times needed to accomplish tasks. Second, the more aggregate the demand being forecasted, the more accurate the forecast will be. However, with aggregation the values for individual products are not available.

Specific planning activities are often linked to a certain time frame. Long-range, or long-term, planning activities focus on strategic issues such as capacity requirements, the number and location of facilities, new product lines or services, and financial resources required for capital expenditures. Long-term forecasting, upon which many long-term plans are based, typically extends 4 years or more into the future. Years ago television makers like Zenith Electronics Corp. had to rely on long-term forecasting to determine whether to invest the time and money required to develop high-definition televisions, which are not expected to be available in stores until 1996.[2] Because long-term forecasting of this type is likely to be inaccurate, aggregate forecasts are used to increase accuracy. Rather than forecasting the demand for each product, managers typically forecast the total demand for all products, using an aggregate term such as *units, tons,* or *dollars of sales* as the all-encompassing unit.

---

[2] "1–2 million HDTVs in 1996—Pearlman," *Television Digest,* November 15, 1993, 15.

Long-term plans focus on strategic issues. Reynolds Metals' long-term transportation strategy includes increasing plant capacity to strengthen its position as an automotive supplier. Aluminum usage in cars grew from an average of 130 pounds in 1981 to 191 pounds in 1991 and is expected to increase to 350 pounds by the year 2000. To meet this demand, Reynolds built a $26 million plant for producing such automotive components as bumper systems, and it has increased production capacity by 50 percent at its aluminum wheel plant. In this photo, Reynolds' marketing managers explain aluminum applications in Chrysler, Ford, and General Motors cars to Reynolds' employees.

Source Courtesy of Reynolds Metals Company.

Medium-term planning involves planning for 1 to 3 years and is often based on forecasts of a similar time frame. More specific requirements for production, such as work force, cash, inventory and specific work center requirements, are aggregated to a lesser degree at this level. Managers will often forecast the demand for a particular product family rather than for a specific model. This type of forecast increases the accuracy and still provides sufficient specificity to make necessary decisions. Managers at Zenith, for example, forecast in 1992 that demand for various models of the company's color television sets would increase by 7 percent the following year, reaching 24 million units. The production department then used that projection to ensure the company had an accurate supply of products.[3]

Forecasting in the short term is more finely tuned to the specific needs of individual products or services and is typically for periods shorter than 1 year. For example, rather than plan for general work force needs, a company like Zenith would determine the specific skill levels or skill types required to produce a particular television model. In the short term, the needed level of forecast accuracy can be achieved without aggregation. Short-term forecasting is the primary focus of this chapter.

DEMAND MANAGEMENT AND FORECASTING

DEMAND MANAGEMENT
The function of recognizing and managing all of the demands for products to ensure the master scheduler is aware of them.

Demand management is defined by the *APICS Dictionary* in the following way:

The function of recognizing and managing all of the demands for products to ensure the master scheduler is aware of them. It encompasses the activities of forecasting, order entry, order promising, branch warehouse requirements, interplant orders, service parts requirements.[4]

---

[3]Nancy Brumback, "Zenith Sees Big Color-TV Year," *HFD—The Weekly Home Furnishings Newspaper,* May 17, 1993, 70.

[4]J. F. Cox, J. H. Blackstone, and M. S. Spencer, eds., *APICS Dictionary,* 7th ed. (Falls Church, Va.: American Production and Inventory Control Society, 1991), 13.

OPERATIONS OUTLOOK

BOX 9.1

Forecasting Demand for Magnetic Resonance Imaging

In the early days of Magnetic Resonance Imaging (MRI) technology, little was known about its potential applications to specific diagnoses and it was difficult to forecast demand for it. Its application was primarily focused on neurologic diseases, but it was also effective in imaging all types of soft tissue, particularly in areas invisible to more conventional X-ray technology, such as those in which tissue was obscured by bone. MRI was also superior in imaging in high-risk patients who could not be exposed to radiation from traditional imaging technologies.

Because of the high cost of MRI technology, hospitals had to be confident that they would use the equipment to near capacity before they invested in it. Three community hospitals in Omaha, Nebraska, developed a detailed method of forecasting MRI demand in order to receive the State Certificate of Need approval required for purchasing the technology.

Medical staffs from the three hospitals defined the types of disease that would benefit from MRI imaging. This list was then reviewed and refined by physicians and medical records professionals. A weight, representing the applicability of MRI to patients, was given to each possible diagnosis within a diagnostic category. For example, it was estimated that 90 percent of all multiple sclerosis patients would have MRI scans. It was estimated that only 25 percent of patients with migraine would need MRI scans. Migraine and multiple sclerosis are both neurologic diseases, but they were given different weights based on their characteristics. Four weights were used: 25 percent, 50 percent, 75 percent, and 90 percent.

After the weight of the MRI applicability was determined, an estimate was made of when MRI imaging would be used in each diagnosis. MRI applicability research was at various stages in different diagnostic categories. For exam-ple, based on research results, MRI was expected to be used immediately for diagnosis of prostate cancer, but it was estimated that MRI would not be routinely used for the diagnosis of Hodgkin's disease because of the lack of research available. Three levels of applicability were used: Level I indicated that MRI would be used immediately; Level II meant that it would be used within 2 to 3 years; and Level III indicated that although MRI would eventually be applied, no time frame was projected.

The forecast of the number of patients requiring MRI scans was calculated by identifying the number of patients discharged from the three hospitals during the previous year who fell into each diagnostic category. The number of patients in each category was multiplied by the appropriate weight (25 percent, 50 percent, 75 percent, or 90 percent). These estimates were then distributed among the appropriate time periods (Levels I, II, and III) and added.

This forecast was for 2,381 Level I scans, compared to the expected annual capacity of an MRI unit, which was 2,740 based on an estimated one patient per hour and 2,740 hours available per year. This finding resulted in an expected 87 percent utilization for the first year.

Learning curve effects were expected to increase the capacity to 1.5 patients per hour by the second year, where it would level off, reducing the expected utilization to only 58 percent. However, because most of the Level II diagnoses could be added during the second year, expected demand was an additional 1,099 scans for a total projection of 3,480 scans (85 percent utilization). In year three, the remaining Level II diagnoses and some Level III diagnoses would require MRI and further increase the utilization.

Source J. S. Carnazzo, "Demand Forecasting for Magnetic Resonance Imaging Services," *Hospital and Health Services Administration* (March-April 1985): 84–94.

Even before a company receives an order for a product or service, the linkage between operations and the customer is established through demand management via forecasting. Demand management activities vary depending on the nature of the company. The role and linkage of forecasts to operations depends on whether the organization is make-to-stock (MTS); make-to-stock/assemble-to-order (MTS/ATO); or make-to-order (MTO). Because of competitive pressures, MTS firms, such as manufacturers of everything from computers to packaged foods, often hold finished goods in stock for immediate delivery. Forecasting activities would be required to determine everything needed for the production of items or services before the receipt of any order. If the forecasts are inaccurate, it can lead to lost sales as when Apple Computer Inc. could not keep up with demand for its Powerbook 180 and 145 portables. The company's distributors worried that the product shortages would turn customers away from the Macintosh and toward systems offered by rivals.[5]

On the other end of the spectrum, pure MTO firms such as makers of custom goods complete production of the product or service only after receiving an order. For example, the auto parts produced by Edgewood Tool and Manufacturing Co., headquartered outside Detroit, are based on custom orders from car makers. Since requests involve such specialty items as hinges for a particular car model, the company cannot begin production until after it receives an order.[6] These firms must perform long-range planning to have the facilities and capacity available to meet customer demand. They must forecast specific product demand only if the promised customer delivery time is shorter than the production lead time. In that case some of the production process must be completed before the order is received. This must be based on a demand forecast. In most cases, products are customized and although there may be a few common raw materials whose need must be established through forecasting, the rest of the needs are not forecasted. (See Figure 9.1.)

If an MTO firm stocks many of the components and assemblies that go into the final product, an MTS/ATO environment is created. For example, furniture makers often assemble frames, then attach upholstery fabric once a customer order is received. Forecasting demand in this environment provides the basis for capacity and facility planning and for raw materials and subassembly planning but not for finished goods planning because they are assembled to order. Table 9.1 provides an overview of the basis for forecasting customer demand in the three manufacturing environments.

The key point in this discussion about MTO, MTS, and MTS/ATO firms is that each type of firm has different forecasting needs and different time frames in order to develop the required linkage between operations and the customer. In some cases, the forecast is for an end item with virtually no customer lead time, as is true for an MTS firm. In others, as is true with pure MTO firms, the customer may have to wait a long time for delivery after ordering a customized product. MTS firms are the most dependent on forecasts, and MTO are the least dependent.

FORECAST ACCURACY

Forecast accuracy is defined as how close the forecast of demand matches actual demand. Forecast accuracy is usually quantified using measures of forecast error. The forecast error of different forecasting techniques can be measured and compared, making it possible to identify the best techniques for the specific situation. **Forecast error** is determined by calculating the difference between the actual demand and the forecast demand for a given period using the following formula:

FORECAST ERROR
Actual demand minus
forecast demand.

$$E_t = A_t - F_t \qquad (9.1)$$

where E_t is the error for time period t, A_t is the actual demand for period t, and F_t is the forecast of the demand for period t. Forecast error will be positive when the forecast is too small, and negative when the forecast is too large. By using the forecast error, several procedures for measuring forecast accuracy can be defined.

A measure of forecast accuracy is obtained by analyzing how well a forecasting technique matches the forecast to the demand over a period of time. This is accomplished by

---

[5]James Daly, "Apple Latest Victim of PC Shortage," *Computerworld,* December 7, 1992, 4.
[6]John S. DeMott, "Strength in Numbers," *Nation's Business,* August 1993, 53–55.

TABLE 9.1	Overview of Forecasting in Three Manufacturing Environments		

| | Environment | | |
Use in Planning	MTO	MTS/ATO	MTS
Capacity	Yes	Yes	Yes
Raw Materials	Sometimes	Yes	Yes
Subassemblies	No	Usually	Yes
Finished Goods	No	No	Yes

measuring two components of forecast error. The first component of forecast error is the inclination or bias of the error. Forecast bias is the tendency for the forecast to be, on the average, high or low. An unbiased forecast will be high as often as it will be low, and the sum of the errors will equal zero. Forecasts can be biased for a number of reasons. Errors in developing an accurate model can result in unintentional bias. Biases can also be intentional and related to the source of the forecast and the agendas of the forecaster. For example, sales managers generally prefer underestimated numbers because bonuses are often based on the performance toward a quota and quotas are derived from forecasts. Production managers typically favor overestimated numbers because they prefer being overstocked rather than understocked. Marketing managers also favor overestimated numbers because advertising budgets usually depend on forecasts. New product managers expect each product to take the market by storm and often create high forecasts.[7]

The **mean forecast error (MFE)** is a common approach to measuring forecast bias. The MFE is the average error over time. The formula for the MFE is

$$\text{MFE} = \sum_{t=1}^{n} \frac{(A_t - F_t)}{n} \tag{9.2}$$

where n is the number of periods under consideration.

The **running sum of forecast error (RSFE)** is also sometimes used as a measure of forecast bias. It is obtained by summing the errors for all the periods in which forecasts were determined. Obviously, the closer the RSFE is to zero, the better.

The bias that exists in the forecasting approach is represented by a positive or a negative MFE, so the MFE is sometimes called the "bias." Thus, if the MFE is negative, forecasts are, on average, too large; if the MFE is positive, forecasts are, on average, too small. Because the errors in an unbiased forecast sum to zero, the closer the MFE is to zero, the better the forecast.

The second component of forecast error is the magnitude of the error. The magnitude is simply the size of the difference between the forecast and the demand, $A_t - F_t$. A common measure of the magnitude of the forecast error is called the **mean absolute deviation (MAD).** The MAD provides a measure of the size or magnitude of the error, without considering whether the error is positive or negative. To compute the MAD, we determine the

MEAN FORECAST ERROR (MFE)
The mean of the difference between actual demand and forecast demand.

RUNNING SUM OF FORECAST ERROR (RSFE)
The sum of the differences between actual demand and forecast demand.

MEAN ABSOLUTE DEVIATION (MAD)
The average of the absolute values of the differences between actual demand and forecast demand.

[7]L. J. Chaman, and T. P. Chen, "The Role of Judgment in Business Forecasting," *Industrial Management* 34 (November/December 1992): 1–3.

absolute value of each error, $|A_t - F_t|$, and then we calculate the average of the absolute errors. The smaller the average magnitude of the error, the smaller the MAD. The formula for the MAD is

$$\text{MAD} = \sum_{t=1}^{n} \frac{|A_t - F_t|}{n} \tag{9.3}$$

An alternative measure of the magnitude of the forecast error is the mean squared error (MSE). To calculate the MSE, we first determine the error for each period, square those values, and sum them. Then we divide by the number of values (n) minus 1. The formula for the MSE is

$$\text{MSE} = \sum_{t=1}^{n} \frac{(A_t - F_t)^2}{n - 1} \tag{9.4}$$

PERCENT ERROR
For each time period, the absolute error divided by the actual demand.

MEAN ABSOLUTE PERCENT ERROR (MAPE)
The mean, over time, of the percent errors.

A fourth measure of forecast accuracy uses calculations of the **percent error,** the absolute error divided by the actual demand for each time period. This measure, the **mean absolute percent error (MAPE),** does not measure the bias or the average magnitude of the error, but instead, computes an average of the absolute values of the errors as a percent of the demand. This is quite useful because often the size of the error relative to the size of the demand is more important than the size of the error alone. The MAPE is calculated by dividing the absolute error for each period by the demand for each period. Next, compute their average. The formula for computing the MAPE is

$$\text{MAPE} = \frac{100}{n} \sum_{t=1}^{n} \frac{|A_t - F_t|}{A_t} \tag{9.5}$$

The following example demonstrates how the MFE, MAD, MSE, and MAPE measures of forecast error are computed.

EXAMPLE 9.1

Measuring Forecast Accuracy

Green Acres Inc. is a small firm that produces lawn mowers. The actual demand and forecast for Green Acres lawn mowers over a 10-week period are listed below:

Period	1	2	3	4	5	6	7	8	9	10
Demand	146	150	144	147	152	153	142	139	147	152
Forecast	142	148	149	148	149	153	150	146	141	144

Determine the RFSE, MFE, MAD, MSE, and MAPE for these weeks.

SOLUTION

The given demand and forecast data are shown in columns 1, 2, and 3 in Table 9.2. The data in columns 2 and 3 are used to determine the values for the remaining columns. The actual error (column 4) is determined by using the formula $E_t = A_t - F_t$ (eq. 9.1) for each period, the absolute error (column 5) is simply the absolute value of each entry in column 4, and the squared error (column 6) is the square of each entry in column 4. The absolute percent error (column 7) is the absolute error (column 5) divided by the actual demand (column 2).

| TABLE 9.2 | | | **Lawn Mower Demand and Forecast** | | | |

Period (1)	Actual Demand A_t (2)	Forecast F_t (3)	Actual Error $A_t - F_t$ (4)	Absolute Error $\|A_t - F_t\|$ (5)	Squared Error $(A_t - F_t)^2$ (6)	Absolute Percent Error $\dfrac{\|A_t - F_t\|}{A_t}$ (7)
1	146	142	4	4	16	2.7%
2	150	148	2	2	4	1.3%
3	144	149	−5	5	25	3.5%
4	147	148	−1	1	1	0.7%
5	152	149	3	3	9	2.0%
6	153	153	0	0	0	0.0%
7	142	150	−8	8	64	5.6%
8	139	146	−7	7	49	5.0%
9	147	141	6	6	36	4.1%
10	152	144	8	8	64	5.3%
		Totals	2	44	268	30.2%

The RFSE is easily obtained—it is the sum of all the forecast errors in column 4, which is shown in the Totals row; that is,

$$RFSE = \sum_{t=1}^{n}(A_t - F_t)$$

$$= 2$$

And when we add the entries in each column, we get the sums (shown in the Totals row) necessary for calculating the MFE, MAD, MSE, and MAPE. Then we use formulas 9.2, 9.3, 9.4, and 9.5, as follows:

$$MFE = \sum_{t=1}^{n}\frac{(A_t - F_t)}{n}$$

$$= \frac{2}{10}$$

$$= 0.2$$

$$MAD = \sum_{t=1}^{n}\frac{|A_t - F_t|}{n}$$

$$= \frac{44}{10}$$

$$= 4.4$$

$$\text{MSE} = \sum_{t=1}^{n} \frac{(A_t - F_t)^2}{n - 1}$$

$$= \frac{268}{9}$$

$$= 29.8$$

$$\text{MAPE} = \left(\frac{100}{n}\right) \sum_{t=1}^{n} \frac{|A_t - F_t|}{A_t}$$

$$= \left(\frac{100}{10}\right) 30.2$$

$$= 3.02\%$$

The results suggest that this forecasting approach shows very little bias. The magnitude of the forecast error as measured by the MAD is relatively small at 4.4, and the MAPE is low at 3.02%. Also MFE = 0.2 and RFSE = 2. Recall that since the errors in an unbiased forecast sum to zero, the closer to zero the MFE and RSFE are, the less biased the forecast.

If the forecast errors are normally distributed with a mean of zero, which implies that the MFE is zero, the standard deviation of the errors and the MAD are closely related. The MAD is approximately equal to 0.8 standard deviations. If the data are biased, the MSE is not a good estimate of the forecast error variability. For example, a forecast that is constantly 5 units smaller than demand should have zero variability, but it doesn't—it has an MFE of 5.

FORECASTING APPROACHES

There are two basic approaches used to forecast customer demand: qualitative techniques and quantitative techniques. Long-term forecasting typically involves the use of qualitative or judgment techniques. Qualitative techniques, which allow for the use of opinion or information that is often difficult to quantify, include the Delphi method, market research, executive opinion, and sales force estimates.

A group of quantitative techniques known as time series analysis is useful in short-term and medium-term forecasting and forms the basis for short- and medium-term plans. Time series models are based upon the belief that it is useful to know historical demand for predicting future demand. Another group of quantitative techniques known as causal models are used more often for medium-term planning activities and identify underlying relationships or causes that affect demand.

Both causal and time series methods require a significant amount of data that is not always available, particularly with new products or those that involve rapidly changing technologies or pricing strategies that will affect demand significantly. In addition, quantitative methods do not effectively incorporate judgment or executive opinion in the models. In some circumstances, the amount of time available limits the type of forecast to be used, and qualitative techniques may be the only available choice.

QUALITATIVE FORECASTING APPROACHES

In general, qualitative forecasts are beneficial tools for strategic or long-term decisions. This is true for each of the qualitative approaches that follow.

Delphi Method   The **Delphi method** uses expert opinion to reach consensus about a decision regarding a future event. A panel of experts, often from different parts of the country, respond individually to the issue in question. A questionnaire format is often used. The results of the questionnaire are tabulated and summarized statistically by a coordinator, who sends the summations back to the participants to give them an opportunity to modify their responses. Responses that differ significantly from the norm are often asked to be justified. The data collection process is then repeated. Usually a consensus can be reached in two to four rounds. Participants usually do not meet and may not know one another.

DELPHI METHOD
A qualitative forecasting method which uses a panel of experts.

Market Research   Market research is important for such activities as the development or adaptation of products and the establishment of a business that will perform a new service. Market research is conducted through surveys to test hypotheses about the market for a product or service. These surveys are administered by telephone, through mailings, or in personal interviews to a representative sample of the market of interest.

Market research tests demand for goods and services. To learn about what customers want in merchandise and services, Amoco built an experimental "Customer-Driven Facility" service station in Indianapolis. This station—which includes the McDonald's restaurant shown here—allows Amoco to test various merchandise and service options while gauging customer satisfaction.

Source   Courtesy of Amoco Corporation.

OPERATIONS OUTLOOK

BOX 9.2

Value Pricing through Market Research

Many manufacturers have adopted the concept of value pricing for use with products that traditionally offered many options. IBM, for example, has successfully used this approach in packaging memory size, hard drive size, and internal clock speed on personal computers with its Value Point line of 486SX PCs. General Motors (GM) has also begun a significant move in this direction.

GM's value pricing program, which began in early 1993, seeks to sell a series of so-called special-edition cars and trucks that are fitted with popular options. The prices are set far below what these cars would cost if the options were purchased individually. GM will offer 46 value-priced models in California, and if the experiment is successful, it will expand the value-priced line to the rest of the country.

Value pricing at GM is based on its experience with Saturn and the close attention paid to customer service and customer feedback. Using information obtained through market research, GM manufacturing experts package the kinds of options that most likely interest customers and set the prices they are willing to pay.

Source "Barabba Helps GM Tune in," *USA Today*, August 25, 1993, sec. B, 5.

The formulation and administration of the survey and the interpretation of the results require a high level of skill. For example, market researchers must know how to interpret results depending on the survey return rate. Surveys take time to conduct, but those done correctly can produce excellent forecasting results. Market research has become increasingly important as manufacturers and service firms try to create packages of goods and services most appealing to customers. (See Box 9.2.) The results tend to be less valuable over time as the situation that affected the market changes, or modifications occur in a company's competitive position or products.

Executive Opinion   When a new product or service is being considered, upper management may have to forecast the demand for the product or service because there is no historical data or because political and economic times have changed since a similar study was conducted. Upper management typically reviews and modifies other forecasts that have been derived through such methods as market surveys. Judgment is crucial for successful forecasting. Although it would be nice to be able to completely mechanize the forecasting process, most successful businesses recognize this will never happen. Even when initial forecasts are developed through quantitative techniques, judgment is often used to adjust and improve these forecasts. (See Box 9.3.) The knowledge and experience of top people in areas such as marketing, manufacturing, engineering, and finance bring their considerable expertise to establish or verify a forecast for a product or service. Long-range forecasting is also commonly done at this level in the organization. A potential for bias exists, however, in that the opinion of one individual may dominate the decisions reached or a group may make decisions based on intuition rather than facts.

Sales Force Estimates   The sales force is sometimes used to forecast demand for a product based on its experience and contacts with customers. In many ways, the sales force may know more about what customers will do than anyone else in the organization.

Reliance on the sales force has several potential limitations. Salespeople may incorporate their own biases into the forecast, and they may only know what the customer would like to buy and not what the customer will buy.

OPERATIONS OUTLOOK

BOX 9.3

Judgment Can Improve Forecasts

In a survey of a number of large businesses, including Coca-Cola, E.I. Dupont de Nemours, AT&T, McCormick & Company, Howmedica, Lever Bros., and S.C. Johnson Wax, none of those surveyed thought that a completely mechanized forecasting system would ever be used. The amount of judgment used varied substantially, however. Judgment accounts for 50 percent of the aggregate level forecasts and 75 percent of the product level forecasts for Lever Bros., for example.

Different companies have different reasons for using judgment to adjust quantitative forecasts. AT&T uses judg-

ment when a dramatic shift in the market is expected, when the consequences of wrong forecasts are severe, when the company's forecasts are out of line with those of competitors, and when forecasts just don't make sense.

McCormick & Company adjusts final forecasts when it expects changes in pricing strategies or trends in fad items. Coca-Cola and Howmedica use judgment if they expect that there will be cannibalization of products (that is, some products will take demand from others).

Source L. J. Chaman and T. P. Chen, "The Role of Judgment in Business Forecasting," *Industrial Management* 34 (November/December 1992): 1–3.

Because it draws from a wide variety of expert sources, the Delphi method stimulates creative thinking and results in a large array of alternatives. It is especially useful in forecasting long-range technological breakthroughs. For example, a company might ask a panel of experts to predict major technological innovations likely to occur over the next 10 years. The information could then be used to develop a five-year strategic plan. The Delphi method can be time-consuming, however, and result in less-than-optimal compromises.

Market research, conducted and interpreted correctly, can reveal changes in patterns of consumer preference, as well as identify demand for new products. The main drawback to this method of forecasting is that costs increase with the level and sophistication of the methods employed. There is also no guarantee that the results will support the company's desired outcome.

When cost is a major consideration, a company may choose to use executive opinion and sales force estimates as forecasting tools. Both approaches are relatively inexpensive because they rely on in-house resources. But managers must guard against using forecasts that reflect individual biases.

QUANTITATIVE FORECASTING APPROACHES

Time Series Analysis   Time series analysis is based on the concept that the past demand for a product provides an indication of what the future demand will be. A **time series** is simply a historical record of demand at fixed time intervals. The time intervals can be of any length, from hours to years. For example, an organization's monthly sales for the past 12 months would form a time series, as would a 24-hour listing of the hourly demand on an automatic teller machine.

The time series provides the basis for the analysis that is performed. Typically, a manager would perform an analysis by plotting the points that make up the time series and examining it visually, looking for patterns. The major components in a time series are trend, seasonality, cycles, and random variations. These components are shown in Figure 9.2.

If the data being analyzed consist of sales figures, the **trend** component describes whether sales over time are generally increasing, decreasing, or flat. If sales were flat, there

TIME SERIES
A historical record of demand at fixed time intervals.

TREND
A gradual, long-term movement in data that indicates an increasing, decreasing, or flat pattern of demand.

| FIGURE 9.2 | **Components of a Time Series** |

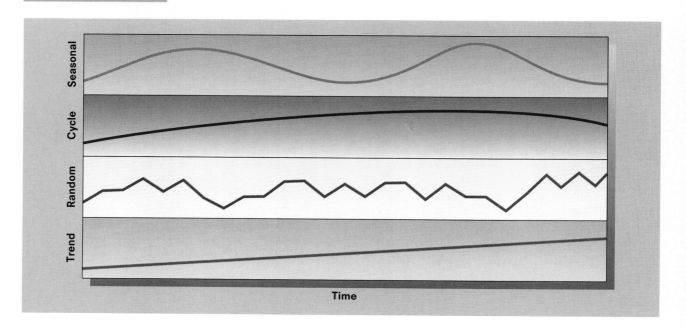

would be no trend component, and the slope of the trend line would be zero. If sales were increasing, the slope of the trend line would be positive; if sales were decreasing, the slope would be negative.

SEASONALITY
Repetitive short-term variations in demand.

Seasonality refers to short-term variations in demand that are repetitive. Sales for snowmobiles, for example, are greater in winter than in summer, and that pattern could be expected to continue into the future. Sales of pizzas on Friday evenings are and will continue to be greater than sales on Tuesdays. Factors such as the weather and holidays all tend to create similar repeating patterns.

CYCLICAL PATTERNS
Repetitive variations that occur less frequently than once every year.

Cyclical patterns in demand are those that recur after more than a year. Cyclical patterns are difficult to detect, in part because they extend over a long time frame. Cycles are often related to other business patterns or economic conditions. For example, the sales of houses are usually linked to long-term interest rates, which follow a cyclical pattern. Product demand forecasts do not typically utilize time series that are long enough to include cycles. For this reason, forecasting techniques that incorporate the use of cycles are outside of the scope of this text.

RANDOM PATTERNS
Variations that do not follow an identifiable pattern.

Random patterns in demand are fluctuations that do not follow an identifiable pattern. Demand for canned items like peaches and beans, for example, fluctuates for no predictable reason, as does that for bread and toilet tissue. One approach to forecasting in an environment involving only random variation is the simple moving average.

SIMPLE MOVING AVERAGE
Average of data with equal weight.

Simple Moving Average Forecasts   The **simple moving average** uses data from previous periods to provide a forecast for the next period. For example, a forecast for October may be based on demand data for July, August, and September. Three time periods are used to create a 3-period moving average. The forecast for November would be based on the demand data for August, September, and October. In this way, the averaged data move to include the most recent known demand data to forecast the next month's demand. The number of periods in a simple moving average varies from 2 to 10 or more. As more periods are included, the forecast becomes more stable and less responsive to a change in demand. Example 9.2 illustrates how simple moving averages are developed.

Weighted Moving Average Forecasts   The simple moving average approach gives equal weight to each data point, but a **weighted moving average** assigns different weights to different data points. For example, in some environments more recent data may be a better predictor of demand than older data. It would provide better accuracy to weight the immediate past period's demand more heavily than data from two periods back. A weighted moving average assigns weights as desired, provided the sum of the weights is equal to 1. Example 9.3 demonstrates how weighted moving averages are developed.

WEIGHTED MOVING AVERAGE
Average of data with unequal weight.

EXAMPLE 9.2

Procom Communications, which manufactures cellular telephones, has seen the following pattern of demand for the last 18 months:

Simple Moving Average Forecasts

Period (month)	1	2	3	4	5	6	7	8	9	10	11	12	13	14	15	16	17	18
Demand	185	178	169	176	190	174	184	188	180	184	174	190	189	182	195	189	192	187

Provide 3-period and 6-period simple moving average forecasts for cellular telephones and graph the results.

SOLUTION

The forecast for period 4, using a 3-period moving average, is determined by averaging the demand from periods 1, 2, and 3. Thus, we have $(185 + 178 + 169) \div 3 = 177.33$, as a forecast for period 4. The 3-period moving average forecast for period 5 is found by averaging the demand data from periods 2, 3, and 4. The forecast for periods 6 through 18 are computed in the same manner.

The forecast for period 7, using the 6-period moving average, is found by computing the average of the first 6 periods. For each of the remaining periods, the pattern is repeated. The oldest data point is dropped and the newest data point is added to the computation as values are averaged for each period. The results of the computations are shown in Table 9.3 on page 240.

Figure 9.3 (page 240) is a graph of the demand and forecasts. The magnitude of the change in the forecast depends on the size of the shift in demand and on the number of periods in the average. The 6-period moving average is somewhat smoother and less responsive than that of the 3-period moving average because each data point carries less weight. The 3-period moving average appears more responsive because each data point contributes one-third of the average. The moving average always lags behind the actual demand and any changes in demand, so it is not an appropriate forecasting technique if the data have a significant trend or seasonal component. If demand for a product is fairly stable, however, a long time span can be used for calculating the moving average.

TABLE 9.3   3-Period and 6-Period Moving Average Forecasts

Period (Month)	Cellular Telephone Demand	3-Period Moving Average	6-Period Moving Average
1	185		
2	178		
3	169		
4	176	177.33	
5	190	174.33	
6	174	178.33	
7	184	180.00	178.67
8	188	182.67	178.50
9	180	182.00	180.17
10	184	184.00	182.00
11	174	184.00	183.33
12	190	179.33	180.67
13	189	182.67	183.33
14	182	184.33	184.17
15	195	187.00	183.17
16	189	188.67	185.67
17	192	188.67	186.50
18	187	192.00	189.50

FIGURE 9.3   Graph of 3-Period and 6-Period Moving Average Forecasts

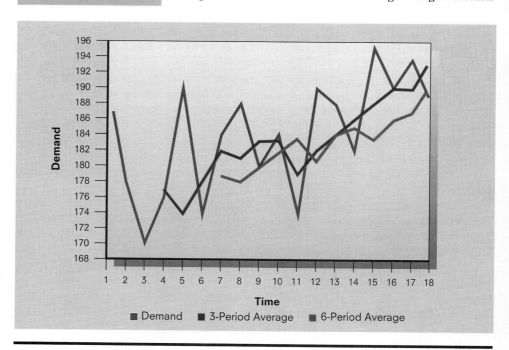

EXAMPLE 9.3

Weighted Moving Average Forecasts

In addition to selling cellular telephones, Procom Communications also carries a line of pagers. Using the four weekly demands for the pagers and the weights provided below, compute a weighted moving average forecast for period 5.

Week	1	2	3	4
Pager Demand (A_t)	100	120	105	125
Weight (W_t)	0.10	0.20	0.30	0.40

SOLUTION

The forecast for period 5, F_5, is computed by multiplying the demand by the weight in each period, then summing; that is,

$$F_5 = 0.10(100) + 0.20(120) + 0.30(105) + 0.40(125) = 115.5$$

The weighted moving average is an improvement over the simple moving average because of the flexibility available in varying the influence of past data. It provides the capability to increase or decrease the responsiveness of the forecast. The 3-period moving average forecast is more responsive than the 6-period moving average forecast because the most recent demand carried more weight. The weighted moving average can be more responsive because it allows the user to base the calculations on as many periods as is desirable and give the most recent periods whatever weight provides the desired level of responsiveness. The weighted moving average is most appropriate as a forecasting tool in an environment where only random variations (no trend or seasonal component) exist.

Simple Exponential Smoothing   **Simple exponential smoothing** (SES), like the moving average, provides a forecast for the next period but does not require historical data to make the forecast. It uses only the current forecast and current demand for the item. The exponential smoothing approach bases the next period's forecast on this period's forecast plus some fraction of the forecast error in the current period. The forecast is calculated by adding this period's forecast to the product of this period's forecast error and a smoothing constant. The formula is

$$F_{t+1} = F_t + \alpha(A_t - F_t) \tag{9.6}$$

where α is a constant that may take on any value between 0 and 1. Some people find the following alternative, equivalent formula helpful in understanding exponential smoothing:

$$F_{t+1} = \alpha(A_t) + (1 - \alpha)F_t \tag{9.7}$$

If $\alpha = 0$, the next period's forecast is equal to the current forecast. If $\alpha = 1$, the next period's forecast equals the current period's demand. When the next period's forecast is the same as the current period's demand, it is called the *naive forecast*. The exponential smoothing forecast is a sophisticated weighted moving average, as a close examination of equation 9.7 shows. The larger the value of α, the greater is the weight placed on the most immediate demand and the less is the weight placed on the forecast. Because that forecast was calculated in the same manner, it was based on the immediate past demand and the immediate past forecast, both weighted by the effect of the α. Thus, the exponential

SIMPLE EXPONENTIAL SMOOTHING
A forecasting method based on the previous forecast plus some fraction of forecast error.

smoothing technique creates a weighted moving average whose responsiveness can be easily adjusted by changing the value of α. The technique has the added benefit of not requiring the accumulation of historical data. Consider the following example.

EXAMPLE 9.4

Exponential Smoothing Forecast

Suppose this period's demand for Procom pagers is 100, and the forecast for this period was 90. Compute the next period's forecast using $\alpha = 0.2$.

SOLUTION

Using formula 9.6:

$$
\begin{aligned}
F_{t+1} &= F_t + \alpha(A_t - F_t) \\
&= 90 + 0.2(100 - 90) \\
&= 92
\end{aligned}
$$

Or, using formula 9.7:

$$
\begin{aligned}
F_{t+1} &= \alpha(A_t) + (1 - \alpha)(F_t) \\
&= .2(100) + .8(90) \\
&= 92
\end{aligned}
$$

Note that the new forecast is 2 units higher than the previous forecast of 90. This makes sense because the previous forecast had underestimated demand, but the weight given to the most recent demand was only 0.20.

Figure 9.4 shows two different forecasts for the same set of demand data given in Example 9.3. Both of these forecasts are calculated using exponential smoothing, one with $\alpha = 0.3$ and the other with $\alpha = 0.8$. Note that the forecast with $\alpha = 0.8$ tends to follow the demand pattern more closely than the forecast that uses $\alpha = 0.3$. The forecast that uses $\alpha = 0.3$ tends to be smoother or less jagged than the $\alpha = 0.8$ forecast. These variations are a result of the different weights given the most recent demand and most recent forecast. Determining which value for α produces the optimum forecast depends upon the demand data. A value for α that works in one environment may not be successful in another. In general, the choice of the value of α is related to the stability of the demand. If demand is stable and a change in demand usually represents a true change in demand rather than just a random spike, a higher value of α is used. If the demand is unstable with a great deal of fluctuation and a sudden increase may not mean demand is really changing, a smaller value of α is probably more appropriate. Comparing forecasts to determine the best α is done using the accuracy measurement approaches—the mean forecast error, mean absolute deviation, mean squared error, running sum of forecast error, or mean absolute percent error.

Like all moving averages, exponential smoothing forecasts lag behind the demand and changes in demand, so these techniques may not be as useful if demand has a significant trend or is seasonal. Methods to deal with these demand components are discussed next.

Using Least Squares Regression to Incorporate Trends into Forecasts   Trend represents the general direction that time series data are moving over time. Recall, for example, that if the data being analyzed are sales, the trend component would describe whether sales over time

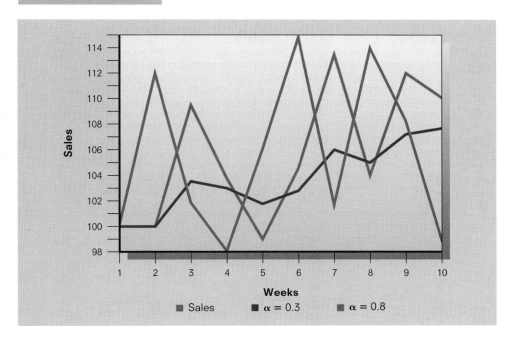

| FIGURE 9.4 | **Exponential Smoothing Using Different Values of α** |

are generally increasing, decreasing, or flat. In order to estimate the trend value, a method that identifies the linear relationship between the data and time is needed. This relationship is established by determining the slope of the line and its *Y* intercept. We know that in an *X,Y* coordinate system, the slope is the change in the *Y* value for each unit change in the *X* value. If the *X* axis represents months and the *Y* axis represents sales, the slope would represent the change in sales per month. The *Y* intercept is the point where the line intercepts the *Y* axis.

The method most commonly used to estimate the slope and *Y* intercept of a line is known as **least squares regression** (LSR). The general linear equation is

$$Y_x = a + bx \tag{9.8}$$

where *a* is the *Y* intercept of the line and *b* is the slope of the line.

When the least squares regression equation is used to identify a trend equation, it is often written as $Y_t = a + bt$, where *t* is the unit of time defined by the data. The values for *a* and *b* are given by the following equations:

$$a = \frac{\Sigma y - b\Sigma t}{n} \tag{9.9}$$

and

$$b = \frac{n\Sigma ty - \Sigma t \Sigma y}{n\Sigma t^2 - (\Sigma t)^2} \tag{9.10}$$

The following example demonstrates how the values of *a* and *b* are computed and how the equation is used to forecast demand.

LEAST SQUARES REGRESSION
A forecasting method that incorporates trend by identifying a linear relationship between data and time.

EXAMPLE 9.5

Using Least Squares Regression

A Cincinnati-based microcomputer company is attempting to forecast sales for a line of computers. This is the second year this product has been on the market. Sales for the past 12 months are given in Table 9.4. The data suggest that sales have increased and a least squares regression approach may be an appropriate tool to predict sales. Graphically verify the existence of what appears to be a linear trend. Then develop a trend equation based on the least squares regression model that can be used to predict sales for the coming year.

SOLUTION

The graph of actual demand presented in Figure 9.5 provides support for the idea that a trend equation is an appropriate tool to use because it shows demand is generally increasing over time.

The least squares regression equation is of the form $Y_t = a + bt$, where a and b must be determined using equations 9.9 and 9.10, as follows:

$$b = \frac{n\Sigma ty - \Sigma t \Sigma y}{n\Sigma t^2 - (\Sigma t)^2}$$

$$= \frac{12(264,700) - (78)(39,880)}{12(650) - (78)^2} = \frac{3,176,400 - 3,110,640}{7,800 - 6,084}$$

$$= 38.32$$

and

$$a = \frac{\Sigma y - b\Sigma t}{n}$$

$$= \frac{39,880 - 38.32(78)}{12}$$

$$= 3,074.25$$

The trend equation is therefore $Y_t = a + bt = 3,074.25 + 38.32t$.

The forecast for the first month of next year—the thirteenth month—is determined by substituting 13 for t in the trend equation to obtain

$$Y_{13} = a + bt$$
$$= 3,074.25 + 38.32(13)$$
$$= 3,572.4$$

DOUBLE EXPONENTIAL SMOOTHING
Exponential smoothing method that includes a trend component.

Using Double Exponential Smoothing to Incorporate Trend into Forecasts **Double exponential smoothing** (DES) provides another approach to forecasting demand that has a trend component. Double exponential smoothing is sometimes referred to as trend adjusted exponential smoothing or forecast including trend (FIT). This model is based on the simple exponential smoothing model examined earlier in this chapter, but it adds a trend component. Double exponential smoothing utilizes two smoothing constants. In addition to α, a second constant, β, is used to smooth the trend component. The double exponential

TABLE 9.4	**Computer Sales for 12 Months**

Month t	Sales y	t^2	ty
1	3,000	1	3,000
2	3,200	4	6,400
3	3,140	9	9,420
4	3,300	16	13,200
5	3,340	25	16,700
6	3,390	36	20,340
7	3,260	49	22,820
8	3,400	64	27,200
9	3,450	81	31,050
10	3,380	100	33,800
11	3,470	121	38,170
12	3,550	144	42,600
$\Sigma t = 78$	$\Sigma y = 39,880$	$\Sigma t^2 = 650$	$\Sigma ty = 264,700$

FIGURE 9.5	**Actual Demand for Computers**

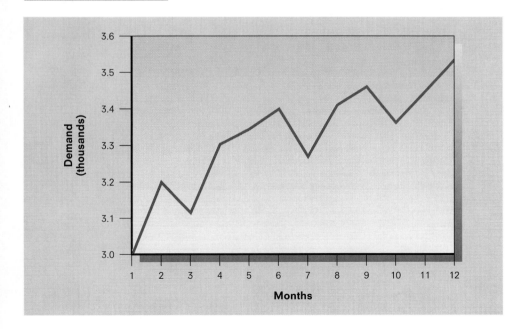

smoothing model consists of two distinct parts which are represented in the following equations:

$$FIT_{t+1} = F_t + T_t \tag{9.11}$$

where F_t is the smoothed forecast and T_t is the current trend estimate and

$$F_t = FIT_t + \alpha(A_t - FIT_t) \tag{9.12}$$

$$T_t = T_{t-1} + \beta(FIT_t - FIT_{t-1} - T_{t-1}) \tag{9.13}$$

where α and β are smoothing constants. Example 9.6 demonstrates how these formulas are used.

EXAMPLE 9.6

Using Double Expontential Smoothing

The past 12 weeks' demand for cars at a rental car company are shown below:

Week (t)	1	2	3	4	5	6	7	8	9	10	11	12
Demand (A)	144	154	146	158	150	158	156	164	167	162	169	172

James Freedmen, the company manager, believes this pattern will continue and would like to develop a forecast using the exponential smoothing model with a trend adjustment (FIT). Develop such a model using $\alpha = 0.1$ and $\beta = 0.9$. Use an initial trend value of 2 and an initial forecast of 144.

SOLUTION

The initial values, where $t = 1$, are $F_1 = 144$ and $T_1 = 2$. Based on these values, we can compute $FIT_{t+1} = FIT_2$ using equation 9.11:

$$FIT_2 = F_1 + T_1$$
$$= 144 + 2$$
$$= 146$$

To determine FIT_3, the values for F_2 and T_2 must be determined using the equations 9.12 and 9.13, as shown below:

$$F_2 = FIT_2 + \alpha(A_2 - FIT_2)$$
$$= 146 + 0.1(154 - 146)$$
$$= 146.8$$

$$T_2 = T_1 + \alpha(FIT_2 - FIT_1 - T_1)$$
$$= 2 + 0.9(146 - 144 - 2)$$
$$= 2$$

Therefore:

$$FIT_3 = F_2 + T_2$$
$$= 146.8 + 2$$
$$= 148.8$$

Continue this process by finding F_3 and T_3 and then computing FIT_4. These values along with the results of the remaining computations are shown in Table 9.5.

TABLE 9.5		Computation Results for FIT		

Week (t)	Demand (A)	F	T	FIT$_t$
1	144	144.00	2.00	144.00
2	154	146.80	2.00	146.00
3	146	148.52	2.72	148.80
4	158	151.92	2.47	151.24
5	150	153.95	3.08	154.39
6	158	157.13	2.68	157.03
7	156	159.43	2.77	159.81
8	164	162.38	2.43	162.20
9	167	165.03	2.59	164.81
10	162	167.06	2.79	167.62
11	169	169.77	2.29	169.85
12	172	172.05	2.22	172.06

FIGURE 9.6		Car Rental Demand and Forecasts

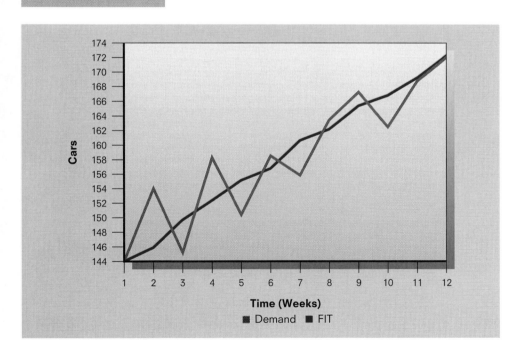

The graph in Figure 9.6 compares the forecasts with the actual demand, and demonstrates how appropriate this technique is for forecasting demand when the time series has a trend component.

As Examples 9.5 and 9.6 show, both the FIT model and the least squares linear regression model are useful as forecasting tools when a time series exhibits a trend.

Incorporating Seasonality into a Forecast   Seasonal patterns are typically related to the time of the year, time of the month, time of the week, or even time of day for products or services that are influenced by repeating factors. The seasonal factor, or **seasonal index,** corresponding to each time period is found by computing the average demand over a given time horizon and then dividing the actual demand for each period by that average demand. The seasonal index calculated in this way shows the relationship between the demand for that specific period and the average demand. A seasonal index of 1.2 means that the demand during that period is 1.2 times the average demand. A seasonal index of 0.7 means that the demand during that specific period is 0.7 times the average demand. The use of seasonal indices is demonstrated in the following example.

SEASONAL INDEX
A seasonal factor found by computing the average demand over a given time horizon and then dividing the actual demand for each period by that average demand.

EXAMPLE 9.7

Incorporating Seasonality into the Demand Forecast

Suppose this week's pizza sales were 700 units and the daily sales are as shown in Table 9.6. As is evident, pizza sales are highly seasonal, and the seasonal pattern is related to the day of the week. Use the data provided in the table to compute the seasonal index for each day of next week. The total expected demand for next week is 910.

SOLUTION

If the total sales for next week are expected to be 910, the expected average daily demand is $910/7 = 130$. To forecast the demand for each day, multiply the expected average demand by the seasonal index, as Table 9.7 shows.

TABLE 9.6   **Calculation of Seasonal Indices**

Day	Demand	Average Demand	Seasonal Index*
Sunday	120	100	1.2
Monday	70	100	0.7
Tuesday	60	100	0.6
Wednesday	80	100	0.8
Thursday	80	100	0.8
Friday	150	100	1.5
Saturday	140	100	1.4
Total	700	700	7

*Notice that the seasonal indices sum to 7 here. If calculated correctly, the sum of the seasonal indices will equal the number of "seasons." (If seasonal indices were calculated for each of the 12 months in a year, they would sum to 12.)

TABLE 9.7		Calculation of Forecasts Using Seasonal Indices		

Average Daily Demand	Seasonal Index	Calculation		Forecast
130	1.2	130 × 1.20	=	156
130	0.7	130 × 0.70	=	91
130	0.6	130 × 0.60	=	78
130	0.8	130 × 0.80	=	104
130	0.8	130 × 0.80	=	104
130	1.5	130 × 1.50	=	195
130	1.4	130 × 1.40	=	182
Total 910	7			910

Notice that the daily forecasts sum to the expected weekly demand, 910. Checking to make sure that the daily forecasts sum to the season forecast is a good way to verify your calculations.

Incorporating Trend and Seasonality into a Demand Forecast   Although there are many different approaches to forecasting when a time series has both a trend and seasonal component, the two basic models are the *additive* and *multiplicative* approaches. The additive model assumes that if the time series includes both a trend and seasonal component, the forecast can be found by adding these pieces together. The multiplicative model assumes that the relationship between the seasonality and the trend is multiplicative—an approach similar to the one used in Example 9.7, where forecasts are made by multiplying the seasonal index by the average daily demand; that is, the relationship between the average demand and the seasonal influence is assumed to be multiplicative. An additive approach would have been to develop seasonal indices by subtracting the average demand from the actual demand rather than dividing. These seasonal indices would then be added to the average demand. With a multiplicative model, the seasonal effect increases as the average demand increases; but with the additive model, the seasonal effect does not change with an increase in demand.

Because the approach we used to generate seasonal indices in Example 9.7 was multiplicative, the model we present here focuses on a multiplicative relationship between the trend component and seasonal component; thus the forecast takes the form

$$F = T \times S \tag{9.14}$$

where T is the trend component for the period and S is the seasonal index for the same period. The steps required to use this approach are illustrated in Example 9.8. First, an average seasonal index is computed for each period. The average seasonal index is the average of seasonal indices for corresponding seasons. The seasonal indices are used to remove the seasonal patterns from the data—that is, to deseasonalize the data. The deseasonalized data are analyzed using least squares regression to determine a trend equation. The forecast is then determined by multiplying the value from the trend equation for the period in question by the corresponding average seasonal index for that period.

EXAMPLE 9.8

Incorporating Seasonality and Trend into the Demand Forecast

Consider the time series provided in Table 9.8, where quarterly demand (Q1–Q4) for the past 3 years is shown. The average quarterly demand is given as 600 units. The seasonal indices, calculated by dividing the actual demand for each period by 600, are shown in the Seasonal Index column. The seasonal indices for corresponding seasons are averaged to create one average seasonal index for each quarter. The deseasonalized demand is computed by dividing each period's demand by the corresponding average seasonal index for the quarter.

Use these data to determine the trend component and make demand forecasts.

TABLE 9.8   **Deseasonalized Data**

Season		Period (t)	Demand (A_t)	Seasonal Index (S)	Average Seasonal Index $(\bar{A}_i)$	(y) Deseasonalized Data $(A_t/\bar{A}_i)$
YR1	Q1	1	420	0.700	0.739	568.34
	Q2	2	650	1.083	1.161	559.86
	Q3	3	695	1.158	1.216	571.55
	Q4	4	495	0.825	0.883	560.59
YR2	Q1	5	450	0.750	0.739	608.93
	Q2	6	710	1.183	1.161	611.54
	Q3	7	740	1.233	1.216	608.55
	Q4	8	525	0.875	0.883	594.56
YR3	Q1	9	460	0.767	0.739	622.46
	Q2	10	730	1.217	1.161	628.77
	Q3	11	755	1.258	1.216	620.89
	Q4	12	570	0.950	0.883	645.53

Average Demand $\bar{A} = 600$

*The average seasonal index, $\bar{A}_i$, is the average, by quarter, of the seasonal indices for the 3 years, calculated as follows:

$$\bar{A}_i = \frac{(Q1 \text{ for YR1}) + (Q1 \text{ for YR2}) + (Q1 \text{ for YR3})}{3}$$

Thus

	YR1	YR2	YR3	$\bar{A}_i$
Q1	0.700	0.750	0.767	0.739
Q2	1.083	1.183	1.217	1.161
Q3	1.158	1.233	1.258	1.216
Q4	0.825	0.875	0.950	0.883

SOLUTION

The deseasonalized data from Table 9.8 are used as the dependent variable y and the time periods as the independent variable t to determine the trend component. By using the calculations in Table 9.9 and the regression equations 9.9 and 9.10, the values for a and b are determined to be

$$b = \frac{n\Sigma ty - \Sigma t\Sigma y}{n\Sigma t^2 - (\Sigma t)^2}$$

$$= \frac{12(47,841.28) - 78(7,201.57)}{12(650) - (78)^2} = 7.21$$

$$a = \frac{\Sigma y - b\Sigma t}{n}$$

$$= \frac{7,201.57 - 7.21(78)}{12} = 553.27$$

The trend equation thus becomes $Y = a + bt = 553.27 + 7.21t$. The result of this equation is multiplied by the appropriate average seasonal index to generate the forecasts for periods 13 through 16. Using the multiplicative model, $F_t = T_t \times S_t$, we get

$$F_{13} = T_{13} \times S_{13} = Y_{13} S_{13} = (a + bt)_{13} S_{13}$$
$$= [553.27 + 7.21(13)]0.739$$
$$= 478$$

The forecasts as shown in Tables 9.9 and 9.10 are computed in the same manner.

TABLE 9.9   **Trend Equation Calculations**

Season		Period (t)	(t^2)	Deseasonalized Demand (y)	ty
YR1	Q1	1	1	568.34	568.34
	Q2	2	4	559.86	1,119.72
	Q3	3	9	571.55	1,714.65
	Q4	4	16	560.59	2,242.36
YR2	Q1	5	25	608.93	3,044.65
	Q2	6	36	611.54	3,669.24
	Q3	7	49	608.55	4,259.85
	Q4	8	64	594.56	4,756.48
YR3	Q1	9	81	622.46	5,602.14
	Q2	10	100	628.77	6,287.70
	Q3	11	121	620.89	6,829.79
	Q4	12	144	645.53	7,746.36
Totals		$\Sigma t = 78$	$\Sigma t^2 = 650$	$\Sigma y = 7,201.57$	$\Sigma ty = 47,841.28$

TABLE 9.10		Forecasts Using Regression and Multiplicative Seasonal Indices				
Season	Period (*t*)	Trend Line Values (*T*)	×	Average Index (*S*)	=	Demand Forecast (*F*)
YR4 Q1	13	646.780		0.739		477.97
Q2	14	653.980		1.161		759.27
Q3	15	661.180		1.217		804.66
Q4	16	668.380		0.883		590.18

CAUSAL FORECASTING APPROACHES

CAUSAL FORECASTING
Using the relationship to an external variable to predict demand.

LEADING INDICATOR
An external variable that is a good predictor of demand.

From a forecasting perspective, it is useful to establish a relationship between two variables so that the independent variable can be used in predicting a dependent variable. The use of an external variable to predict demand is called **causal forecasting.** Changes in demand for a product can be the result of a number of factors, many of which are measurable. (See Box 9.4.) One factor may be, for example, the prediction of significant snowfall for the winter months, which would increase the sale of snowmobiles and snowblowers. In this case, the heavy snowfall prediction is called a **leading indicator.** The key in the process is to identify the real causes of changes in demand.

In many cases, there are several independent or predictor variables for a dependent variable or result. For example, the amount of liquid refreshment consumed at a professional baseball game is probably related to attendance and the temperature at game time, so attendance and temperature would both be needed to predict consumption. Problems with two or more variables related to a third variable require the use of multiple regression techniques, which exceeds the scope of this book. The focus here is on causal relationships between one independent variable or leading indicator and a dependent variable in which the

CUTTING-EDGE COMPANIES

BOX 9.4

Pizza Sociology

Domino's Pizza has frequently surveyed its drivers to correlate their observations with sales data for particular periods of time. They have found relationships between pizza consumption and various demographics as well as news and economic events. For example, the survey showed that although Los Angeles residents typically preferred vegetarian toppings, following disasters, such as earthquakes and riots, 64 percent of the sales were for meat toppings. Domino's also found that when a report on the fat content of Chinese food was made public dur-

ing the fall of 1993, Sunday evening pizza sales in New York increased 34 percent.

Domino's initially became interested in what it calls pizza sociology during the Reagan administration, when a Washington, D.C., franchise owner began to predict when a crisis was brewing by the amount of nighttime pizza orders placed by White House and CIA staff. Pizza orders at the CIA dried up after that correlation was made public.

Source   W. M. Bulkeley, "If Clinton Orders Double Cheese and All the Toppings, It's a Crisis," *Wall Street Journal,* December 7, 1993, sec. B, 2.

relationship between the variables is approximately linear and thus the least squares regression model can be used.

The general linear equation for least squares regression was given in equation 9.8 as $Y_x = a + bx$, where a is the Y intercept of the line, b represents the slope of the line, and x is the independent variable.

The values for a and b in terms of x and y are

$$a = \frac{\Sigma y - b\Sigma x}{n} \tag{9.15}$$

$$b = \frac{n\Sigma xy - \Sigma x\Sigma y}{n\Sigma x^2 - (\Sigma x)^2} \tag{9.16}$$

EXAMPLE 9.9

Using Least Squares Regression for Causal Relationships

The Atlanta Braves and the San Francisco Giants are about to have a 3-game series in Atlanta, and the games have been sold out for weeks. Because the Braves have been successful in recent years, attendance has been very good. In fact, most of the games this year have been sellouts. A significant amount of data exists on sellout games. The data for 15 sellout games are presented in Table 9.11, which shows the sales, in thousands of dollars, of liquid refreshments compared to the temperature that day. The temperature for the game this Saturday is expected to be 95°F. Forecast the sales of liquid refreshments for Saturday's game.

TABLE 9.11 **Causal Forecast Calculations**

Temperature x	Refreshment Sales (in thousands) y	x^2	xy
81	135	6,561	10,935
75	130	5,625	9,750
59	100	3,481	5,900
80	138	6,400	11,040
79	125	6,241	9,875
58	95	3,364	5,510
69	118	4,761	8,142
89	150	7,921	13,350
82	140	6,724	11,480
66	110	4,356	7,260
91	155	8,281	14,105
93	158	8,649	14,694
65	115	4,225	7,475
78	125	6,084	9,750
73	120	5,329	8,760
$\Sigma x = 1,138$	$\Sigma y = 1,914$	$\Sigma x^2 = 88,002$	$\Sigma xy = 148,026$

SOLUTION

Because the attendance is not a variable but constant (all were sellouts), it is possible to use a least squares linear regression model to predict sales of liquid refreshments. Consider the data in Table 9.11.

Using equations 9.16 and 9.15 the values of b and a are

$$b = \frac{n\Sigma xy - \Sigma x \Sigma y}{n\Sigma x^2 - (\Sigma x)^2}$$

$$= \frac{15(148{,}026) - (1{,}138)(1{,}914)}{15(88{,}002) - (1{,}138)^2} = 1.69$$

$$a = \frac{\Sigma y - b\Sigma x}{n}$$

$$= \frac{1{,}914 - 1.69(1{,}138)}{15} = -0.61$$

Thus the least squares regression equation is

$$y = -0.61 + 1.69x$$

If the temperature is 95° at game time, the sales forecast is

$$y = -0.61 + 1.69(95) = 159.94$$

The sales for liquid refreshments should be about $159,940.

WHICH FORECAST METHOD IS BEST?

There may not always be one forecast that best predicts the demand for a particular product. In practice, organizations may use a number of different forecasting techniques to forecast demand for the next period. An employee of American Hardware Supply, Bernard Smith, developed the concept of **focus forecasting,** which selects the best forecast from a group of forecasts generated by simple techniques, including some of the approaches discussed in this chapter.

FOCUS FORECASTING
Employing several forecasting techniques simultaneously and selecting the one that performs best.

The types of techniques used include methods such as: next month's forecast will be the same as last month's demand, next month's forecast will be the same as demand last year at that time, or next month's forecast will be 10 percent more than the demand was last year for the same month. Six or more forecasting techniques may be used.

By using historical data, the technique that performed the best on recent data can be identified, and that technique would be chosen to be used to forecast demand for the next period. All of the techniques would be evaluated each month, and based on this evaluation, a different technique might be selected for the following month. Some general relationships as well as possible appropriate forecasting techniques for different situations are shown in Table 9.12.

MONITORING FORECASTS

TRACKING SIGNAL
A statistical calculation used to monitor the accuracy of a forecast.

In many organizations, the demand forecasting process has become automated, requiring sophisticated procedures to monitor its accuracy. One such approach for monitoring accuracy is through a **tracking signal.** A tracking signal (TS) allows forecast accuracy to be tracked using statistical process control charts. There are several approaches to calculating a tracking signal. One common method is to divide the running sum of forecast errors

TABLE 9.12	Choosing the Appropriate Technique

Forecast Horizon	Forecast Period	Nature of the Data	Possible Forecasting Technique
Long range	Year	Aggregated	Qualitative methods
Medium range	Year	Aggregated	Regression, qualitative methods
Short term	Day, week, month, quarter	Trend and seasonal component	Multiplicative model
Short term	Day, week, month, quarter	Trend component	Double exponential smoothing, simple linear regression
Short term	Day, week, month, quarter	Random (no discernible pattern)	Moving average, weighted moving average, simple exponential smoothing

(RSFE) by the mean absolute deviation (MAD). The RSFE, as described earlier in this chapter, is a cumulative total of the forecast errors. A tracking signal of 2, for example, means that the running sum of forecast errors totals 2 MADs. If the tracking signal continues to move, in the same direction over time, becoming more positive or more negative, the forecasting approach is becoming more biased, suggesting that a change in forecasting procedure is required. The tracking signal is computed using the following formula:

$$TS = \frac{RSFE}{MAD} \qquad (9.17)$$

If the forecast errors are normally distributed and unbiased, control limits can be established based on the relationship that 1 MAD = 0.8 standard deviations. Using the data from a normal curve found in the Z table in Appendix A, the likelihood of obtaining a value greater than 1, 2, or 3 standards deviations from the mean can be determined. Because the MAD is equal to 0.8 standard deviations, the same Z table can be used to determine the probability of obtaining a tracking signal value greater than 1, 2, 3, or 4 MADs. Process control charts establish control limits to allow the user to distinguish between random fluctuations of forecast error and fluctuations that have an assignable cause. They can be applied to this setting with substantial benefits. Table 9.13 shows that the probability of the tracking signal's being ± 4 MADs is 99.86% if the forecast is unbiased and errors are

TABLE 9.13	Probabilities of Tracking Signals at Specified MADs

MAD	Standard Deviations	Proportion of Area within Control Limits (%)
±1	±0.8	57.62
±2	±1.6	89.04
±3	±2.4	98.36
±4	±3.2	99.86

normally distributed. If a tracking signal was observed to be greater than 4, one could conclude with high confidence that the errors were no longer normally distributed and/or the forecast was no longer unbiased, or both. If the tracking signal were greater than 4, it would be said that the forecast was no longer in control. As Table 9.13 shows, it is highly unlikely that the tracking signal will be larger than 3 if the data are unbiased.

EXAMPLE 9.10

Computation of Tracking Signal

Table 9.14 provides the actual demand and forecasts for 5 periods. The forecast error is computed using equation 9.1, $E_t = A_t - F_t$. The RSFE is computed by adding the error from period 1 to that of period 2, and so on. The absolute error column is the absolute value

TABLE 9.14   **Tracking Signal Calculations**

Period t	Actual Demand (A_t)	Forecast (F_t)	Error $(A_t - F_t)$	Absolute Error $(|A_t - F_t|)$	RSFE	MAD	Tracking Signal
1	520	500	20	20	20	20.00	1.00
2	460	510	−50	50	−30	35.00	−.86
3	430	440	−10	10	−40	26.67	−1.50
4	450	430	20	20	−20	25.00	−0.80
5	500	460	40	40	20	28.00	0.71

FIGURE 9.7   **Control Chart for Tracking Signals**

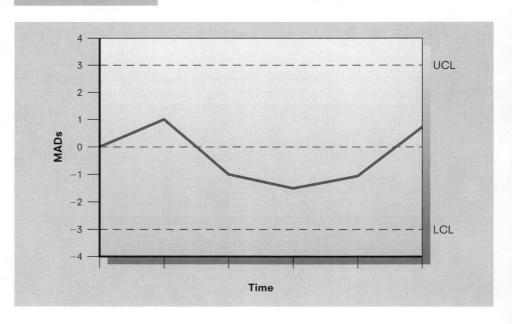

Capacity planning is directly dependent on demand forecasts. The demand for prescription drugs is expected to grow substantially, largely owing to an aging population and to the extended prescription coverage included in national health-care legislation. Walgreens is expanding its pharmacy service to new markets by opening pharmacy-only RxPress stores in areas that cannot support full-size stores. RxPress stores extend Walgreens' geographic coverage, which is especially important to third-party prescription plan customers with members across the country. The drive-through windows at RxPress stores provide the ultimate in customer convenience.

Source   Courtesy of Walgreen Co.

of the error column. The MAD and tracking signal are computed in period 2, based on the data from periods 1 and 2. In period 3, the MAD and tracking signal are computed based upon the first three periods, and so on.

Because the tracking signal ranges from a high of 0.71 to a low of −1.50, the forecasting process appears to be in control and no changes would be recommended. A control chart is provided in Figure 9.7. The values are clearly within the control limits of ±3 MADs. If a value for the tracking signal falls outside the control limits, corrective action would be required.

FORECASTING CROSS-LINKS

FORECASTING AND OTHER BUSINESS FUNCTIONS

Forecast accuracy and other business functions have a critical link. Until actual demand is known, either after the fact or from customer orders, the forecast provides the only projection of the product demand. The long lead times associated with many activities that are prerequisites to the production of goods and services make forecast accuracy crucial. Not only are there strong dependencies between successful materials and inventory planning and the demand forecast, but there are also critical links to the planning of other resources. Capacity planning, in all time frames, is directly dependent on the demand forecast, and the success of capacity planning decisions is frequently a result of forecast accuracy. Long-term forecasts of demand, although usually aggregate forecasts, are nevertheless important for identifying potential capacity problems far enough in the future to allow for them to be addressed. Addressing these problems also often involves hiring and training or laying off employees, which directly involves the personnel or human resources function. Bringing on additional employees to satisfy labor requirements places a demand on the human resources function. If forecasts are low and the human resources function is forced to respond quickly, the quality of the work force and amount of training possible may suffer.

Marketing is so dependent on a demand forecast that, in many companies, it is responsible for creating the forecast. Approximately 50 percent of firms conduct demand forecasting in the marketing department and then plan accordingly. For example, Weight Watchers Food Company's marketing department forecast in 1993 that the natural-foods segment of the frozen-foods market would grow at an annual rate of 5 to 6 percent. The forecast enabled the company to begin making plans to meet this expected increased demand from health-conscious consumers.[8] Other organizations forecast in operations, finance, or accounting.[9]

Manufacturers and services must be able to forecast demand accurately to maintain acceptable levels of customer service. This task can be particularly difficult when forecasting the demand for products that incorporate promotions as a marketing tool, as many food industries do. Promotions not only increase demand by amounts that are difficult to foresee but also cause a postpromotion lag that is difficult to predict.

The purchasing and logistics functions of manufacturing and service firms are heavily dependent on forecasts. Orders for raw materials and outsourced parts are usually based on short- and medium-term forecasts for demand; long-term forecasts are sometimes necessary to assist the purchasing department in establishing long-term supplier relationships, which increase the likelihood of obtaining price advantages. For some businesses, raw materials are purchased on the global commodity markets and can only be purchased at certain times of the year. For these industries, an accurate medium- or long-term forecast is crucial. For logistics, the outflow of products must be predictable in order to allow for planning of transportation. Last-minute changes to transportation requirements can easily result in higher transportation costs that eat into profit margins.

The financial aspects of a firm also depend heavily on accurate forecasts. Demand forecasts provide an important input for sales forecasts, which form the basis for cash-flow forecasts at many firms. Financial planning, such as payroll, equipment expense, and maintenance projects, are often scheduled to coincide with cash-flow forecasts. Sequoia Systems Inc. is one company that learned the importance of sales forecasts the hard way. In May 1992, the company forecast sales of $85 million for fiscal year 1992. Three months later it reported a sales forecast of $71 million and then restated it at $65.7 million. By October 1992, Sequoia stock had plummeted to $2.75, down from $18.37 a year earlier. Shareholders filed suit and the Securities and Exchange Commission (SEC) launched an investigation.[10]

---

[8]Stephen Dowdell, "A Natural Entree, Weight Watchers Expects Increasing Demand for Nutrition to Be Healthy Source of Growth," *Supermarket News,* September 13, 1993, 10A.

[9]T. A. Davidson, "Forecaster: Who Are They? Survey Finding," in *A Managerial Guide to Judgmental Forecasting,* ed. C. L. Jain (New York: Greaceway Publishing, 1987), 51–53.

[10]John R. Wilke, "Sequoia Systems Remains Haunted by Phantom Sales," *Wall Street Journal,* October 30, 1992, sec B, 8.

FORECASTING AND COMPETITIVE CAPABILITIES

The links between demand forecasts and competitive capabilities are numerous. Prices are affected by demand forecast accuracy through the purchasing function and as a result of investments in capital equipment, which are necessary to meet forecasted changes in demand. The overriding issue is that forecasts form the basis for most business plans. Plans provide managers with an increased number of alternatives. Poor forecasts mean poor plans, and poor plans mean that managers may have to make last-minute decisions with few alternatives, which do not permit them to take advantage of cost savings. The ability to anticipate change far in advance allows management to consider more options in adapting to the change. (See Box 9.5.) The more options that are available, the more choices there are. The fewer the options, the more likely it is that options will be expensive.

Quality is influenced by forecasts through the impact forecast accuracy has on inventory levels. Demand forecasts that are too high often result in the production of excess inventory. Excess inventory gets damaged as it is moved around, and ultimately it becomes obsolete. Demand forecasts that are too low result in expediting, or speeding up production of an order, which often results in less than adequate attention being paid to quality. Low forecasts may also result in material shortages that force purchasing to request that

---

OPERATIONS OUTLOOK

BOX 9.5

Forecasting in the Environmental-Services Industry

After used syringes and other hospital waste appeared on the New Jersey shore in 1988 and numerous reports were broadcast about hospital waste at landfills, it was reasonable to anticipate that the public reaction would result in stringent new regulations of medical waste disposal. Two companies, Waste Management Inc. and Browning-Ferris Industries Inc., invested heavily in the business, betting, in effect, that their speculation would be correct.

Anticipating regulations is not uncommon in the environmental-services industry. In fact, almost all successful plant investments in the industry result from regulations that have specified certain ways in which wastes must be handled. For example, hazardous waster incinerators have increased in value because of increased regulation of landfills. Modern garbage dumps, with plastic liners and sophisticated treatment of contaminated water, are more valuable because old-fashioned dumps are being phased out.

In anticipation of the medical waste regulations, the two companies adopted different strategies. Waste Management invested almost entirely in medical-waste incinerators that turn needles into an unrecognizable ash, which then goes to a landfill. Browning-Ferris invested in steam-cleaning autoclaves, which use steam and pressure to sterilize waste products. Autoclaved needles, unless shredded, can still prick someone. Waste Management also anticipated that

incineration would be seen as more environmentally responsible. It turned out, however, that some environmental groups support autoclaving over incineration because of the toxic materials emitted during incineration. The toxins that are released into the air include dioxin and heavy metals.

The demand for off-site medical waste disposal is increasing for several reasons. The plastic that is increasingly being used in disposable medical products burns too hot for many older in-site incinerators. Many medical procedures are now done in doctors' offices rather than at a hospital. Most doctors' offices do not have on-site waste disposal facilities. Despite past growth and projected growth at a rate of greater than 6 percent per year, increasing numbers of competitors are even making it difficult for Browning-Ferris, despite its correct technology choice. Competitors have aggressively cut prices to the point that hospitals pay as much as 50 percent less per pound of waste than they paid in the late 1980s.

The regulations anticipated by Waste Management didn't materialize. Many new regulations were passed, but incineration is required for only a small portion of medical waste. This, combined with the greater expense for incineration than autoclaving, has put Waste Management at a serious competitive disadvantage.

Source "How Two Garbage Giants Fought over Medical Waste," *The Wall Street Journal,* November 17, 1992. sec. B, 6.

suppliers expedite, which sometimes results in lower quality, or switch to a second choice supplier if first choice suppliers can't meet the demand.

Forecast accuracy also affects the dependability of delivery. Forecasting too low in the short term results in stocks that are not sufficient to meet demand, causing back orders and dissatisfied customers. Capacity shortages brought about by medium- and long-term forecasts that are too low result in orders that are missed because of capacity shortages or force sales reps to decline orders that they know cannot be satisfied from existing low levels of capacity. This loss encourages customers to go elsewhere and directly hurts market share. For example, Nabisco underestimated demand for its new line of fat-free chocolate and marshmallow cookies. Even though Nabisco had three production lines running overtime and planned to add another, it still could not keep up with demand for its Snackwell's Devil's Food Cookie Cakes. The result was angry customers and lost sales.[11]

The flexibility that is so important to being able to adapt quickly to changes is made possible by the ability to anticipate changes in the marketplace. The ability to anticipate is enhanced by accurate forecasts not only of demand but also of economic trends and changes in customer preference. These changes and trends lend themselves to qualitative and/or quantitative forecasting techniques.

Like flexibility, response time is also enhanced by the ability to accurately forecast demand. A classic example is that of the make-to-order manufacturer. The MTO manufacturer can reduce the amount of time a customer must wait by performing preliminary operations prior to receiving the order. The ability to accurately forecast demand and start early processing steps allows the manufacturer to promise a delivery time to the customer that is less than the total time it takes to manufacture the item. This has the potential to win orders from companies that must be flexible and that need suppliers who can contribute to this flexibility.

SUMMARY

In many environments, the demand forecast is one of the most important pieces of information available to management. Many of the important decisions in operations and in other business functions depend on its accuracy. Long-term forecasting provides information necessary for making strategic decisions, and medium- and short-term forecasts guide decisions relative to work force needs, raw material needs, assembly needs, cash flow needs, and so on. Forecast accuracy is a critical requirement, but predicting the future will always result in some degree of error. For this reason, it is important to realize that lead time reduction will often contribute more to forecast accuracy than will efforts to improve quantitative techniques. Lead times establish the minimum planning horizon, and the planning horizon determines how far into the future we must forecast. If we reduce lead times, we can reduce the planning horizon, improving the accuracy of our forecasts and plans.

Quantitative forecasting techniques, particularly time series techniques, have received the greatest attention in this chapter. Specific components of a time series have been identified, and the presence of each has been linked to one or more forecasting techniques. Several methods of measuring and monitoring forecast accuracy have also been presented. The quantitative techniques presented in this chapter are effective when used appropriately. Quantitative techniques will never replace good judgment, however, which plays an important role in forecasting. When good judgment is combined with specific tools, an excellent basis for planning results.

---

[11]Kathleen Deveny, "Man Walked on the Moon but Man Can't Make Enough Devil's Food Cookie Cakes," *Wall Street Journal,* September 28, 1993, sec. I, 1–2.

COMPUSMART REVISITED

CROSS-LINKS At the beginning of this chapter, we met Simon Baxter, the sales manager for CompuSmart, which manufactures personal computers, including a popular 486 system. Simon had a problem with forecasting. The company seemed to be increasingly unable to fulfill orders on time and/or on budget. Close examination of Simon's files for the previous three months revealed a pattern: His projections of orders for the

486 computer system were consistently below actual orders for the first three weeks of every month. These projections are shown below, along with the number of actual orders and the quantities of on-time and late deliveries.

What forecasting method has Simon been using and why is it not very effective? What other forecasting methods should he consider? Which method would you recommend?

Week	Orders	Forecast	On Time	Late
1	463	400	424	39
2	410	463	410	0
3	432	410	416	16
4	440	432	436	4
5	480	440	459	21
6	464	480	464	0
7	491	464	491	0
8	513	491	499	14
9	525	513	520	5
10	481	525	481	0
11	520	481	490	30
12	531	520	524	7
13	578	531	508	70

QUESTIONS FOR REVIEW

1. What are the four components of a time series?
2. Identify at least three ways forecasts are used.
3. What are the advantages of the use of qualitative forecasts?
4. What is the difference between forecast error and forecast accuracy?
5. How is forecast accuracy measured?
6. Compare the responsiveness of a simple 3-week moving average forecast to a simple 5-week moving average forecast.
7. What is the advantage of using a weighted moving average forecast instead of a simple moving average forecast?
8. What effect does the value of α have on the responsiveness of a simple exponential smoothing forecast?
9. Explain what is meant by a seasonal index.
10. Identify two useful forecasting methods for an environment in which a trend component is present.
11. If data have no trend, seasonal, or cyclical components, which forecasting techniques would be appropriate?
12. What types of forecasts are most appropriate for long-range decisions?
13. What is a tracking signal? How is it used?
14. How can control charts be used to monitor tracking signals?

QUESTIONS FOR THOUGHT AND DISCUSSION

1. The meteorologists on channel 6 and on channel 12 both claim to be able to provide the most accurate forecast for tomorrow. Describe how you would go about determining who is the most accurate.
2. What assumptions about the data must be met for 1 MAD = 0.8 standard deviations?
3. How can demand be influenced? What type of organizations with which you are familiar have the capability of influencing demand?
4. What are the implications of a negative tracking signal?
5. Can least squares regression be appropriately used on a time series? Explain.
6. Describe the contribution that the MFE, RSFE, MAD, MSE, and MAPE make to measuring forecast accuracy.
7. Suppose you are forecasting in an environment in which a trend exists and you are using a simple moving average. What results would you expect?
8. For what types of businesses would you expect simple exponential smoothing to be appropriate?

INTEGRATIVE QUESTIONS

1. What could be the quality implications of a low forecast of product demand?
2. When would forecasting product demand be important in a make-to-order environment?
3. At what points in the strategy formulation process is forecasting important? What would need to be forecast at these points?
4. Is forecasting necessary in a JIT system? Why or why not?

PROBLEMS

1. Two different forecasting techniques have been used by an organization to forecast demand for the past 8 weeks. By using the MAD and MFE approaches, determine which of the two techniques appears to be performing better.

Week	Demand	First Forecast	Second Forecast
1	312	290	300
2	324	300	310
3	320	320	313
4	331	330	320
5	304	335	330
6	312	320	320
7	330	318	325
8	319	325	340

2. Given the following time series and two separate forecasts, determine the MFE, MAD, and MSE for each forecast. Which of these forecasts appears to be better? Why?

Week	Demand	First Forecast	Second Forecast
1	156	170	165
2	171	165	160
3	167	170	180
4	190	165	175
5	169	180	182
6	177	170	172
7	185	175	178
8	180	177	182

3. The past 6 months' demand for a new ice cream dessert is given below. Construct a forecast for August using each of the following techniques.
   a. A 3-period moving average
   b. A 4-period moving average with weights of 0.4 for July, 0.3 for June, 0.2 for May, and 0.1 for April
   c. A simple exponential smoothing model with $\alpha = 0.2$, and 2,100 as the forecast for April
   d. The naive forecast

Month	Demand
January	2,250
February	2,150
March	2,125
April	2,220
May	2,160
June	2,230
July	2,280

4. The quarterly demand for a dishwasher detergent is shown below:

Quarter	Spring	Summer	Fall	Winter
Demand	8,320	8,260	8,340	8,230

Construct a forecast for spring using the following techniques.
   a. A 3-period moving average
   b. A 4-period weighted moving average with weights of 0.4 for winter, 0.3 for fall, 0.2 for summer, and 0.1 for spring
   c. A simple exponential smoothing model with $\alpha = 0.4$, assuming that the forecast for winter was 8,250
   d. The naive forecast

5. The following is the actual demand for the previous 4 quarters of microwave oven sales at an electronics store. There is no evidence to suggest the demand has been seasonal, and there does not appear to be an increase in sales over the previous year.
   a. Develop two forecasts for this spring using simple exponential smoothing model with $\alpha = 0.4$ and $\alpha = 0.2$. The forecast for spring of last year was 3,850.
   b. Determine the MAD for both forecasting techniques. Which forecast seems to be better?
   c. Discuss the size of the MAD. Does exponential smoothing seem to be an acceptable technique to be used in this environment?

Quarter	Spring (last year)	Summer	Fall	Winter
Demand	3,890	4,100	4,060	4,200

6. Bicycles Incorporated is in the process of estimating the sales of bicycles for the next year. Quarterly sales records have been kept for the past 3 years. Sales have increased each year. A trend equation has been developed to aid in the effort. The equation is $Y = 1.7t + 89$, where $t = 1$ corresponds to quarter 1 of year 1. The demand for the bicycles is also seasonal.
   a. Determine the quarterly seasonal average for each quarter.
   b. Using the multiplicative model forecast the demand by quarter for the next year.

YR1	Demand	YR2	Demand	YR3	Demand
Q 1	120	Q 1	130	Q 1	136
Q 2	100	Q 2	105	Q 2	110
Q 3	70	Q 3	77	Q 3	82
Q 4	80	Q 4	90	Q 4	100

7. The owner of a small motel has been keeping occupancy records for the past 6 years and would like to know what the room occupancy is likely to be next year. Use least squares regression to provide an estimate.

Year	Occupancy
1988	7,100
1989	7,300
1990	7,200
1991	7,700
1992	7,900
1993	7,800

8. Use least squares regression to develop a trend equation for the following data. What is the forecast for period 13?

Month	Demand
1	186
2	209
3	197
4	210
5	214
6	204
7	225
8	231
9	221
10	223
11	241
12	245

9. Using the double exponential smoothing model (FIT) with $\alpha = 0.7$, determine the best value of β based on the MAD and MFE. Narrow your search of the best β to 0.26, 0.41, 0.78, and 0.89 ($F_1 = 413$ and $T_1 = 2$). Which value results in the best forecast?

Month	Sales
1	413
2	421
3	434
4	422
5	437
6	445
7	430
8	455
9	462
10	470
11	451
12	475

10. The demand for a product during the past 12 months suggests that a trend approach may be appropriate, as shown below. Develop a forecast for each month using the FIT model with $\alpha = 0.5$, $\beta = 0.3$, $T_1 = 3$, and $F_1 = 245$. Also develop a forecast for each month using simple exponential smoothing with $\alpha = 0.6$. Compare your results using the MAD.

Month	Demand
1	246
2	254
3	265
4	260
5	255
6	265
7	261
8	271
9	274
10	268
11	277
12	275

11. The past year's demand for garden tractor sales in a midwestern state is given below.
   a. Determine the seasonal index for each quarter.
   b. If sales are expected to average 800 units per quarter next year, what is your forecast for each of the next 4 quarters?

Quarters	Spring	Summer	Fall	Winter
Demand	1,250	1,000	300	550

12. The data shown below are believed to contain both trend and seasonal components. Graph the data to verify this. Using a multiplicative model, develop the 4 forecasts for 1995.

1993	Spring	145
	Summer	135
	Fall	150
	Winter	121
1994	Spring	160
	Summer	140
	Fall	170
	Winter	140

13. The sales for the past 10 weeks of a product are given below:

   a. Using a simple exponential smoothing model with $\alpha = 0.5$, develop a forecast for each of these periods. Assume the forecast for period 1 was 313.
   b. Compute the tracking signal for periods 2 through 10. Comment on whether this forecasting approach works.

Period	Sales
1	315
2	325
3	299
4	314
5	320
6	327
7	312
8	321
9	295
10	333

14. The sales for the past 12 months for a product are given below.
   a. Using a simple exponential smoothing model with $\alpha = 0.9$, develop a forecast for each of these periods. Assume the forecast for period 1 was 4,150.

   b. Compute the tracking signal for periods 2 through 12. Comment on whether this forecasting approach is working.

Month	Sales
1	4,100
2	4,150
3	4,075
4	4,130
5	4,200
6	4,160
7	4,180
8	4,080
9	4,140
10	4,200
11	4,090
12	4,120

15. The data provided below identifies the gas mileage obtained by a specific vehicle traveling at the specified miles per hour (mph). Use these data to develop a relationship between the speed that this vehicle travels and the gas mileage obtained. What would the gas mileage be if the vehicle traveled 70 miles per hour?

Speed	Mileage
56	35
61	33
60	34
45	41
51	37
35	45
53	37
40	40
47	38
64	31

SUGGESTED READINGS

Bowerman, B. L., and R. T. O'Connell. *Time Series Forecasting.* Boston: Duxbury Press, 1986.

Box, G. E. P., and G. Jenkins. *Time Series Analysis: Forecasting and Control.* San Francisco: Holden Day, 1970.

Chambers, J. C., S. K. Mullick, and D. D. Smith. "How to Choose the Right Forecasting Technique." *Harvard Business Review* 49 (July-August 1971): 45–74.

Gardner, E. S. "Exponential Smoothing: The State of the Art." *Journal of Forecasting* 4 (March 1985): 1–38.

Makridakis, S., S. C. Wheelwright, and V. E. McGee. *Forecasting: Methods and Applications.* 2d ed. New York: John Wiley, 1983.

SPREADSHEET APPLICATIONS
FOR DEMAND FORECASTING

Many of the forecasting techniques presented in this chapter are easily done using a spreadsheet, such as Lotus 1-2-3. Several examples are provided in this section to demonstrate how a spreadsheet can simplify the process of forecasting.

FORECAST ACCURACY

The first spreadsheet, Exhibit 9S.1, demonstrates how forecast error is computed. This exhibit provides product demand and forecasts for a 5-weeek period. The data in cells A2 to A7, B2 to B7, and C2 to C7 have all been entered manually. The error, absolute error, and squared error can then be computed for each period by using the cell formulas shown in line 8. Once a cell formula has been entered, the remaining relevant entries for the column are copied. For example, the forecast error ($A_t - F_t$; see equation 9.1) in cell D7 is computed using the formula +B7−C7 shown in cell D8. The absolute error ($| A_t - F_t |$) is computed using the formula @ABS function shown in cell E8. And the squared error [$(A_t - F_t)^2$] is computed using the formula +D7^2, where ^2 squares the entry in D7.

The formulas for computing the MAD, MFE, and MSE (see equations 9.2, 9.3, and 9.4) are shown in the lower left-hand corner of Exhibit 9S.1. Note that in Lotus, the notation D3 . . D7 indicates the inclusive range D3, D4, D5, D6, and D7. Thus the formulas for finding the MAD, MFE, and MSE are, respectively, @AVG(D3 . . D7), @AVG(E3 . . E7), and @SUM(F3 . . F7)/4, where @AVG is the average function and @SUM is the summation function.

EXPONENTIAL SMOOTHING

In a spreadsheet there is really only one formula required to perform simple exponential smoothing. The simple exponential smoothing formula +C7+$E$1*(B7−C7) is presented in row 9 of Exhibit 9S.2. The cell location E1 has the $ symbol linked to both the E and the 1. The $ symbol is used so that a formula may be copied, but the values associated with the $ will remain unchanged. In this formula cell location E1 is where the value for α is given, and this placement should not change when this formula is copied in column C. Because the value for α is in a separate cell, its value can be changed and a new forecast for each week will automatically be computed. This feature provides the capability to easily examine other values of α, and perform what-if analysis.

EXHIBIT 9S.1   **Spreadsheet View of Forecast Accuracy Measurement***

	A	B	C	D	E	F
1						
2	Period	Demand	Forecast	Error	Abs Error	Sqr Error
3	1	95	85	10	10	100
4	2	85	90	−5	5	25
5	3	89	85	4	4	16
6	4	69	88	−19	19	361
7	5	94	82	12	12	144
8		FORMULAS FOR LINE 7 →		+B7−C7	@ABS(D7)	+D7^2
	MFE: @AVG(D3..D7) =			0.4		
	MAD: @AVG(E3..E7) =			10		
	MSE: @SUM(F3..F7)/4 =			161.5		

*Data entered manually are shaded in gray. Values that have been computed are shaded in yellow. Comments that provide directions, formulas, and the like are shaded in brown.

EXHIBIT 9S.2   **Spreadsheet View of Simple Exponential Smoothing**

	A	B	C	D	E
1	Weeks	Demand	Forecast	Alpha =	0.4
2	1	125	120.00		
3	2	129	122.00		
4	3	115	124.80		
5	4	132	120.88		
6	5	119	125.33		
7	6	130	122.80		
8	7	124	125.68		
9	FORMULA FOR LINE 8 →		+C7+$E$1*(B7−C7)		
10					

LEAST SQUARES REGRESSION

The least squares regression line calculation in Lotus 1-2-3 is aided by a built-in function that does most of the work. In Exhibit 9S.3, sales for the previous 12 months have been provided. A forecast is required for month 13 based on a least squares model. The specific key strokes required to generate the regression output are shown below.

Lotus Prompt	Keystrokes Required
Call Regression	/DR
X Range	A3 . . A14 <Enter>
Y Range	B3 . . B14 <Enter>
Output Range	A18 <Enter>
Intercept Compute	<Enter>
Go	<Enter>

The output shown on line 18 and below will result from these commands. The regression equation is of the form $Y = a + bX$, where a is the value of the constant (line 19) and b is represented by the X coefficient (line 25). The equation becomes $Y = 657.06 + 8.35X$. The formula used to determine the forecast for the 13th month is shown in cell C17. This formula is copied from cells C3 through C14 to determine the points that would form the regression line.

TREND AND MULTIPLICATIVE SEASONAL MODEL

Exhibit 9S.4 demonstrates how to use the multiplicative seasonal model in order to forecast for data that have both a trend and seasonal component. The first step is to determine the average demand. The average given in cell B1 is the result of using the @AVG function. This result is necessary to determine the quarterly index. The specific tasks in sequence as well as the formulas and data ranges are provided in Exhibit 9S.5. Examples of most formulas appear on lines 11 and 20 of the spreadsheet.

| EXHIBIT 9S.3 | | **Spreadsheet View of Least Squares Regression** | |

	A	B	C	D
1				
2	Months	Sales	Trend Line	
3	1	670	665.41	
4	2	690	673.76	
5	3	656	682.11	
6	4	705	690.46	
7	5	710	698.81	
8	6	690	707.16	
9	7	700	715.51	
10	8	730	723.86	
11	9	740	732.21	
12	10	715	740.56	
13	11	760	748.91	
14	12	770	757.26	
15			Forecast	
16	13		765.61	
17		Formula for cell C16 →	657.06+A16*8.35	
18		*Regression Output*		
19	*Constant*			*657.06*
20	*Std Err of Y Est*			*16.96*
21	*R Squared*			*0.78*
22	*No. of Observations*			*12.00*
23	*Degrees of Freedom*			*10.00*
24				
25	*X Coefficient(s)*		*8.35*	
26	*Std Err of Coef*		*1.42*	

EXHIBIT 9S.4 — Spreadsheet View of Trend and Multiplicative Seasonal Model

	A	B	C	D	E	F	G	H
1	AVG =	93.5						
2	Period	Demand	Demand/ 93.5	Deseason- alized Data	Regression Output			
3	1	95	1.016	84.595	Constant			78.04
4	2	85	0.909	85.919	Std Err of Y Est			5.187
5	3	89	0.952	83.633	R Squared			0.754
6	4	69	0.738	83.786	No. of Observations			8
7	5	115	1.230	102.400	Degrees of Freedom			6
8	6	100	1.070	101.080				
9	7	110	1.176	103.370	X Coefficient(s)		3.435	
10	8	85	0.909	103.210	Std Err of Coef		0.800	
11	Formulas for line 10 →	+B10/93.5	+B10/C19					
12								
13								
14								
15	Period	Trend	Average Index	Forecast				
16	9	108.936	1.123	122				
17	10	112.371	0.989	111				
18	11	115.806	1.064	123				
19	12	119.241	0.824	98				
20	Formula for line 19 →	78.04+3.435 *A19	(C6+C10)/2	+B19*C19				
21								

EXHIBIT 9S.5 — Multiplicative Seasonal Model Building Tasks

Tasks	Formulas or Functions	Data Range
Determine average demand	@AVG	B3..B10
Compute quarterly index	+B10/93.5	C3..C10
Deseasonalize data	+B3/C16	D3..D10
Perform Regression Analysis—See previous section		X Range A3..A10
		Y Range D3..D10
Determine trend values	78.04+(3.435*A19)	B16..B19
Determine average index	(C6+C10)/2	C16..C19
Compute forecast	+B19*C19	D16..D19

LEARNING OBJECTIVES

Upon completing this chapter, you should be able to explain

- what the purpose of aggregate planning is and how it fits with the strategic plan of the organization
- what the relevant costs associated with aggregate planning decisions are
- how a chase and a level strategy differ
- what the implications of the learning curve in aggregate planning decisions are
- how aggregate planning in services differs from aggregate planning in manufacturing organizations
- how to construct an aggregate plan using a chase strategy, a level strategy, and a mixed approach
- what role other functional areas have in the aggregate planning process

CHAPTER 10

AGGREGATE PLANNING

CROSS-LINKS **It's a Wrap**

Southern Atlantic produces a large variety of paper products. The Madison Mill, one of the smallest plants in the company, produces three product lines of tissue paper. The industrial line produces tissue for manufacturers, many of which are in the steel industry and insert tissue paper between sheets of stainless steel to prevent scratching. The retail line provides tissue paper for use in the packaging of clothing. Most of it is custom printed with the retailer's logo. The consumer line consists primarily of gift wrap for birthdays and holidays. Demand in the industrial line is stable, but the retail and consumer lines are seasonal. ■ As Jill Montgomery entered the conference room for the Madison Mill's annual review meeting, she was surprised at how upbeat everyone was. Every year the managers met on the morning of the first day of the new year to review the past year's successes and failures. She knew the company had had a good year, but she was also aware of several problems that were sure to get worse if they were not solved. Jill's colleagues did not always believe she understood the paper business because of her position as director of personnel recruitment and training. However, her 6 years' experience as a technical sales representative gave her a knowledge of the product line and customer base that was greater than anyone else's in management. ■ Jill's presentation was the third on the agenda. She listened to the first presentation with keen interest as the leader of the plant's three artists described how each new gift wrap print had done and outlined upcoming design changes. Sales manager Steve Thomas made the second presentation. He provided a concise overview of sales for the three

product lines. Jill, who had worked for Steve when she started with Southern Atlantic, was not surprised when his graphs showed a leveling off and slight decline of demand in the retail and consumer lines. Although Steve tried to attribute it to the slow economy, he was stopped short by Ed Bowden. Ed was vice president for finance. He was one of the surliest people Jill had ever met and one of the sharpest. Ed always ran this meeting, and no one could ever get anything past him. His comments to managers were always direct, accurate, and usually quite humbling. ■ "Isn't it true," asked Ed, "that one of the reasons behind the softening of demand is a series of quality problems in our seasonal product lines?" ■ "We did have some minor difficulties on the second and third shifts," replied Steve. "But with the new shift supervisors, I'm confident that that problem's been eliminated. Isn't that right, Tom?" Steve looked to production manager Tom Arlington for support. ■ "Yes, that's correct, Steve," Tom said. "We moved two stars from first shift at the end of November. They had second and third shifts running smoothly in no time." ■ "Right!" thought Jill, sarcastically. "Everything will run smoothly for a while. We'll cut back to two shifts again in February, so the third shift will cause no problems. In March we'll drop the second shift and we'll run one shift until August. Everyone here knows that the problems will start again when we begin to add shifts." Before she could finish her thought, Ed Bowden asked her to present her annual summary. ■ Jill began, somewhat nervously, by summarizing the bad news. "This was the most difficult time we've had trying to recruit and train laborers for the second and third shifts. In June we began interviewing for positions that would open when we started second shift operations in August. As you know, our first step is to contact everyone who worked for us last year. We got very few hits from this pool this year. It seems that most of our former employees had gone to work for one of our competitors. As you know, training people to use this equipment is difficult. It really helps to get experienced workers, but they're getting harder and harder to find. We finally filled our second shift, but the quality and commitment of the work force was lower last year than I've ever seen it. The July and August push for the third shift operation beginning in September was even worse. Besides, more than half of the third shift laborers live over 40 miles away. Absenteeism has been high, so we've had to move people around to cover jobs. Turnover has also been higher than ever before. In short, our hiring and training costs were up 60 percent for last year, and even with that we had a less skilled group of workers. I'm convinced that our inability to attract a skilled work force for the second and third shift operations will make the quality problems Ed mentioned even worse next year. Contacts from my days as a tech-rep tell me that several of our retail and consumer line customers are nosing around for backup suppliers. If I'm right, we may lose some customers. I am open to any suggestions that will improve this situation." ■ Jill looked to Ed, expecting an immediate reaction. For the first time since she'd known him, he had nothing to say. ■

Organizations need to look ahead periodically and plan how they are going to meet the future demand for their products or services. Because changes in demand often require changes in capacity, equipment, or the size of the work force, planning must be done far enough in advance to allow appropriate changes to be made. Marketing and forecasting identify what should be produced. How the goods and services are efficiently produced, in line with the organization's goals, is the objective of **aggregate planning**.

AGGREGATE PLANNING
A plan devised to determine how resources will be used to satisfy the demand for goods and services.

OBJECTIVES OF AGGREGATE PLANNING

The process of aggregate planning incorporates the goals of the organization and the projected demand from marketing and forecasting in developing a game plan, or strategy, for the future. This game plan is designed both to make efficient use of resources and to satisfy anticipated demand. Time horizons for aggregate planning vary from as short as 6 months to 18 months and longer. This game plan specifies what to produce as well as the work force and capacity requirements necessary to make it happen. It must also satisfy specific goals relating to cost, quality, dependability, flexibility, and time. In order to provide the most accurate projection of the needs for resources, the demand data are normally combined, or aggregated, by product group. For example, if an organization manufactures two different sizes of tricycles and three different designs for each size, the aggregate planning process would combine the manufacturers' total needs, such as those for the work force and raw materials, for all tricycles rather than specific requirements for each of the six different alternatives. In Table 10.1 the two types of tricycles are S and L and the designs are 1, 2, and 3. The aggregation of hours required is presented for the month of January. This process would be done for all months in the planning period. Four hours are required per tricycle. For planning purposes, the six tricycle types would be viewed as one product requiring 2,280 hours in January.

TABLE 10.1	The Aggregation Process for January		
Type	**Design**	**Demand**	**Hours Required**
S	1	200	800
S	2	100	400
S	3	50	200
L	1	80	320
L	2	40	160
L	3	100	400
Total			2,280

Requirements projected in this manner are more accurate than if they were developed individually. You may recall that an aggregate forecast is more accurate than forecasts for individual items, particularly when forecasts are made far into the future, as is the case when developing demand projections for an aggregate plan. Aggregate planning also requires less time and effort for many organizations than the planning that would be required for each item.

LINK TO THE STRATEGIC PLAN

An aggregate plan must support and be consistent with the strategic plan, which identifies how an organization plans to compete. The structural strategic decision categories, such as capacity, facilities, and process technology, define the framework in which the aggregate plan must function. Infrastructural decision categories, such as quality, organizational structure, and human resources, further define the nature of the decisions that must be made at this level of planning.

Structural restrictions, such as specific facilities, capacity, and technology choices, are generally fixed during an aggregate planning period. The aggregate plan must fit into the existing framework defined by the structural component of the strategic plan, but it may signal a need for more facilities or capacity sometime in the future. The aggregate plan provides a way of identifying discrepancies between existing resources and the resources required to meet strategic objectives. In that way, it affects the strategic plan. Cooper Tire and Rubber Co., for example, identifies growth prospects as part of its planning process. It then refits existing plants to meet the new capacity requirements. A new plant is built only when a major study indicates it is necessary to meet long-term demand.[1]

The aggregate plan also must adhere to infrastructural restrictions. For example, there are many approaches to effectively integrating work force policies into an aggregate plan. Human resources issues specify how the organization will identify, hire, and train the work force as well as what the organization's policy is with regard to laying people off, firing members of the work force, or using overtime. Some organizations have a permanent work force that satisfies 80 percent to 90 percent of the work force needs. A temporary work force can be hired to deal with variations in demand and allow for increases and decreases in the number of employees. Some organizations may choose to give workers overtime, but others may hire and lay off staff as needed to cope with the variability in demand. Rhino

---

[1]Jennifer Reese, "America's Most Admired Corporations," *Fortune*, February 8, 1993, 44–72.

At Coca-Cola Enterprises, the world's largest bottler of Coca-Cola Company products, ongoing development of information systems supports the company's growth strategy, which includes package innovations, such as the 20-ounce bottle in the contour shape shown here. By providing managers with real-time information on sales and gross profits sorted by customer, channel, product, and package, information systems allow managers to analyze promotional and pricing strategies immediately. The sales information is integrated with production scheduling and raw material needs to manage just-in-time inventory and ensure manufacturing efficiency.

Source   ©Flip Chalfant. Will Sumpter & Associates.

Foods, a specialty-dessert maker in Burlington, Vermont came up with an innovative solution when it experienced a decline in demand. Rather than temporarily laying off workers, the company arranged to contract out idle employees to other local businesses. The employees were pleased they were still earning money. And once demand picked up again, Rhino asked them to come back to work and even hired its own contract workers to handle a year-end rush.[2]

The focus provided by the competitive priorities of price, quality, dependability, flexibility, and time must also be included in the aggregate plan. Price generally receives a lot of attention in most aggregate plans. Depending on other goals, cost reduction activities involve examining the tradeoffs between finished goods inventory holding costs, hiring and firing costs, and overtime costs. The cost emphasis often conflicts with other issues. For example, minimizing finished goods inventory reduces costs but may result in poorer customer service. Sometimes it is less costly to hire and fire workers than to accumulate finished goods inventory. But the hiring/firing policies may hurt morale and lead to less worker commitment and a lower quality product. Cost advantages of specific plans translate into competitive price advantage.

Organizations trying to compete on the basis of quality will emphasize work force stability and inventory-related alternatives. A stable work force is usually better trained and more committed to the organization than a labor pool with frequent fluctuations. This sta-

---

[2]"Employee Swapping," *Inc,* December 1993, 65.

bility helps ensure that customers receive on-time delivery of items that meet or exceed their expectations.

An organization competing on the basis of dependability must ensure its products consistently meet high standards. It also must deal with a concept referred to as backordering. A backorder is an order that cannot be filled on time. A dependable company keeps its promises to its customers and thus must focus on eliminating backorders. With a good aggregate plan, backorders can be prevented.

Flexibility is often measured by the ability of the aggregate plan to adjust to changing markets or demand patterns. For example, a firm is at a competitive advantage if it can easily customize products to meet consumer demand. An organization competing on flexibility also needs to have quick access to additional capacity or the ability to change the amount of capacity quickly. Some of the ways to change capacity in the short term include overtime, adding additional shifts, changing the work force size, or subcontracting. Organizations that are currently fully staffed and running two or more shifts have a limited amount of flexibility.

Organizations competing on the basis of time must develop an aggregate plan that not only allows for reliable deliveries but also provides extremely quick deliveries. These goals typically require more on-hand finished goods inventory and quick access to additional capacity which would enable a firm to meet unexpected demand.

INFORMATIONAL SOURCES FOR AGGREGATE PLANNING

Aggregate planning depends on information from most of the functional areas within an organization. Marketing provides valuable information about the demand for current products and future products. It also provides information about the behavior of competitors, consumer preferences, and the general economic conditions in the markets served. Finance presents required cost and cash flow data. Engineering presents projected changes in product design, requirements for new products, and changes in equipment and process design. Purchasing or materials management provides data about raw material costs, availability, suppliers, subcontracting alternatives, and existing inventory levels. Human resources provides information about the availability of key labor skills in the area as well as worker training needs and costs and the ability of the organization to meet these needs. Operations must provide information on the capacity of the equipment, the staffing requirements, the productivity level of the current work force, and the capacities of the machines to be used during the planning period. All these factors serve as crucial information for the aggregate planning process.

MODIFICATIONS OF DEMAND

The forecasted demand pattern may have such significant peaks and valleys that the likelihood of developing a feasible plan is low. Firms whose demand patterns exhibit large swings normally need significant overtime, frequent hiring and firing, or substantial finished goods inventory, all of which are costly.

One approach to this problem is to smooth demand by using a **pricing strategy** that levels demand for goods and services. This approach provides an opportunity for operations and marketing to work together. For example, long-distance telephone companies employ a marketing strategy that offers lower rates after 5 P.M. and on weekends to increase usage during what are ordinarily off-peak times. Other alternatives include offering rebates or using more advertising at key points within the planning period. Some promotional efforts include financial incentives to make the process of buying an item easier. Such ef-

PRICING STRATEGY
An approach to demand smoothing that uses increases or reductions in prices to level the demand for goods or services.

forts are often identified with such advertising slogans as "no money down" and "no interest for the first year." Other incentives include low interest rates. Companies sometimes use a combination of promotions to boost demand. Consumer electronics retailer Best Buy Co., for instance, tries to attract customers by offering to sell products with no money down, no payments for six months, and no interest. On selected items it also offers rebates of up to $150, which it pays in "Best Buy Bucks." Customers can use the rebates to purchase additional products in the store.[3] Thus, advertising efforts can shift demand from a high demand period to a lower demand period.

Another approach to smoothing demand is to produce a secondary line of products whose demand peaks and valleys complement those of existing products. For example, Honda Power Equipment makes lawn mowers for the international markets at its plant in Swepsonville, North Carolina. But during the summer months—the traditional trough in the lawn mower production cycle—the plant produces automotive transmission housings.[4]

A third approach would be not to meet all the demand. It may be possible, for instance, to subcontract during peak demand periods. Or, owing to cost or quality issues, a firm may set an upper limit on the number of units that can be produced. Such adjustments lower the peaks and fill the valleys in the demand pattern and make it more feasible.

LINK TO HUMAN RESOURCES

From most perspectives, it is advisable to maintain a constant work force with few fluctuations. With a stable work force size, companies keep a constant flow of raw materials, work-in-process, and finished goods. This approach allows for more consistent management of batch sizes, machines and the work force in general. Organizations can focus on improving delivery time or being more flexible in an environment where there is no change in production levels. Employees maintain a stronger commitment to the organization, and quality issues can be dealt with much more effectively if the work force is not continually changing. Spartan Motors of Charlotte, Michigan, illustrates the potential benefits of a stable work force. The company, which makes custom chassis for fire trucks, motor homes and other heavy-duty vehicles, has a no-layoff policy even though it competes in an industry fraught with plant closings. But while its competitors have been struggling financially, Spartan has earned a reputation for high-quality products. As a result revenues and earnings have increased more than sixfold in a five-year period.[5]

Whatever type of aggregate plan is adopted, several steps can be taken to ensure the best use of human resources. If the plan contains significant demand variability, adjustments should be made early in the planning period to match vacation times with low demand periods. In some environments it is possible for the work force to vary the weekly work hours so that during low demand periods they work perhaps as few as 35 hours and get paid for 40 hours, with the understanding that they will work additional hours during peak periods to compensate for the hours that had previously not been worked.

Although layoffs appear to be a fact of life, organizations that develop systems that protect a large percentage of their work force from future layoffs have the potential to create a work environment that will foster and support improvement methods such as total quality management or just-in-time. Efforts to improve quality or productivity will not be as likely to occur in environments where the work force does not feel secure.

---

[3]Best Buy Co., 1994.
[4]Gary S. Vasilash, "People Who Like Lawn Mowing," *Production* (July 1991): 38.
[5]Edward O. Welles, "The Shape of Things to Come," *Inc,* February 1992, 66–74.

Ted Castle (center), president of Rhino Foods, celebrates with employees who suggested lending workers to neighboring businesses that needed help on a short-term basis.

Source ©Alan Jakubek.

RELEVANT COSTS

Aggregate planning activities include an analysis of several different types of labor costs. The first of these is the **regular-time cost,** which includes the wages and benefits workers receive for working normal hours. Health-care costs are a significant component of employee benefits. Although there are exceptions, **overtime costs** are normally 150 percent of regular time wages except for Sundays and holidays, when they are 200 percent of regular time. **Hiring costs** focus on the costs required to identify, select, and train the work force, and **layoff costs** are those associated with exit interviews and severance pay. **Inventory costs,** which refer to the cost of holding an item in inventory, also must be considered. These costs are influenced by the dollar value of the inventory and the storage and warehouse costs associated with the items, which include insurance, taxes, obsolescence, and theft. **Backorder costs,** or stockout costs, are associated with not satisfying a customer's order. These costs vary with the product but often lead to lost sales and may result in a loss of goodwill between the customer and the organization. The cost of loss of goodwill is almost impossible to assess accurately. In some environments, a backorder can merely result in the costs required to expedite the order. These costs are also difficult to measure.

In cases where the productivity of the work force does not depend on the aggregate plan, the regular-time salary paid is often not computed because this cost will not change.

REGULAR-TIME COSTS
Costs of wages and benefits that workers receive for working normal hours.

OVERTIME COSTS
Additional costs associated with working longer hours than normal.

HIRING COSTS
Costs associated with identifying, selecting, and training the work force.

LAYOFF COSTS
Costs associated with exit interviews and severance pay.

INVENTORY COSTS
All costs of holding items in inventory.

BACKORDER COSTS
Costs associated with not satisfying a customer order.

The relevant costs to consider are only those that change from one version of an aggregate plan to another alternative plan. Frequently, the only relevant costs are for hiring and firing, overtime, and inventory.

TYPES OF AGGREGATE PLANS

There are essentially three types of aggregate plans: plans that use a chase strategy, plans that use a level strategy, and plans that use a mixed strategy. The chase and level strategies are sometimes called pure strategies.

CHASE STRATEGY
Aggregate planning strategy that strives to produce exactly what is needed each period to meet the demand of that period.

A **chase strategy** means that production will "chase," or follow, demand and involves producing exactly what is needed each month. The chase strategy involves adjusting an organization's ability to produce, normally by changing the size of the work force or by using overtime to meet the monthly demand requirements. Inventory level is usually fixed at a specified level, and inventory costs are minimized within the constraints established by the organization. Hiring and firing costs or overtime costs tend to be high with a chase strategy. Because the work force is often changing on a monthly basis, concerns about commitment of the work force and quality may surface. The chase strategy is attractive, however, in low-paying, low-skill level jobs that require little training and where there is an abundant supply of labor. This approach is also useful for the production of items with a short shelf life, such as dairy products, or those that are likely to quickly become obsolete, such as sophisticated computer components.

LEVEL STRATEGY
Aggregate planning strategy that strives to produce the same quantity each period.

A **level strategy** means that production will be constant. The firm produces the same amount each day over the planning period and deals with variations in demand through the use of inventory or overtime. During part of the planning period, the amount produced will exceed demand, and inventory will accumulate. When the demand exceeds the rate of production, the accumulated inventory will be used to satisfy demand. A level strategy fixes the number of workers and other resources needed to produce at the same level throughout the period. Although hiring and firing costs are reduced, the financial and nonfinancial costs of carrying high levels of finished goods inventory generally increase with this strategy. The level strategy has much to offer in highly labor intensive environments in which workers are highly skilled and hard to replace and quality is extremely important. Companies like Motorola or Texas Instruments, which invest heavily in worker training and development, often are reluctant to see employees leave their jobs.

MIXED STRATEGY
In aggregate planning, a combination of chase and level strategies.

A **mixed strategy** uses a combination of level and chase strategies. A mixed strategy may be used to produce at the same level for several months and then to adjust production to another level and produce at that level for several more months. For example, Harbor Sweets candy company lays off many of its employees in spring and summer since a sweet tooth tends to be a seasonal urge centered around holidays. When production shifts back into high gear in the fall and winter, the company puts workers back on the payroll.[6] By not changing levels each month, the hiring and firing costs are reduced, and by changing production levels more often than in the level strategy, the amount of finished goods inventory can also be reduced. This strategy is typically better than the chase strategy from a cost and flexibility perspective, but it may not be as appropriate as the level strategy from a quality perspective.

---

[6]Martha Mangelsdorf, "Managing the New Work Force," *Inc,* January 1990, 78–83.

SOLVING AGGREGATE PLANNING PROBLEMS

The approaches used to solve aggregate planning problems vary significantly. Many organizations use nonquantitative approaches. These usually involve using rules of thumb or trial-and-error approaches that are linked to the previous aggregate plan.[7] The **cut-and-try method** is essentially a trial-and-error approach that can be significantly enhanced in a spreadsheet environment.

Whether an organization is using a chase, level, or mixed strategy, there are several relationships that need to be identified. In all plans it is necessary to determine the size of the work force, the average inventory level per period, and any changes in work force size. Other information, such as the daily production rate, is necessary for the level production strategy.

All plans presented begin with the number of labor hours needed per planning period. Most will require the calculation of a number of values and are aided by the following formulas.

$$\text{Labor hours per period} = (\text{demand for period})(\text{hours per unit}) \tag{10.1}$$

$$\text{Work force size} = \frac{\text{total hours required per planning period}}{\text{hours worked per worker during planning period}} \tag{10.2}$$

$$\text{Daily production rate} = \frac{\text{total hours worked per day}}{\text{hours required per unit}} \tag{10.3}$$

$$\text{Ending inventory} = \left(\begin{array}{c}\text{beginning}\\\text{inventory}\end{array}\right) + \left(\begin{array}{c}\text{monthly}\\\text{production}\end{array}\right) - \left(\begin{array}{c}\text{monthly}\\\text{demand}\end{array}\right) \tag{10.4}$$

$$\text{Inventory cost} = (\text{average inventory level})(\text{monthly cost per unit}) \tag{10.5}$$

where the beginning inventory for one month is the ending inventory for the previous month, and the average inventory level is the average of the beginning and ending inventory for the month.

CUT-AND-TRY METHOD

In Example 10.1 a problem is proposed and solved using the cut-and try approach in combination with a chase strategy, a level strategy, and a mixed strategy.

EXAMPLE 10.1

Cut-and-Try Aggregate Planning

Genesis Music Co., which has a work force size of 100, has a planning horizon of the next 12 months. The demand for its top-of-the-line stereo system is shown in Table 10.2, as well as the number of workdays available each month. Each stereo takes 12 hours of direct labor to manufacture, and the organization requires at least 750 stereos in finished goods inventory, which is normally equivalent to about 2 weeks' demand. A total of 19,800 stereos must be manufactured in 260 workdays. Hiring costs are $400 per person, and firing costs

---

[7]F. L. Dubois and M. D. Oliff, "Aggregate Production Planning in Practice," *Production and Inventory Management Journal* 32 (1991): 26–30.

TABLE 10.2	Workdays per Month and Demand Projection

Months	Days	Demand
January	21	1,400
February	20	1,500
March	23	1,600
April	22	1,700
May	21	1,800
June	23	1,900
July	22	2,000
August	21	1,800
September	22	1,600
October	22	1,700
November	21	1,400
December	22	1,400
Total	260	19,800

are $500 per person. The cost of holding an item in inventory is $10 per unit per month. Wages average $16 per hour plus benefits. Additional costs associated with overtime production (over 40 hours per week) are based on 1.5 times the regular wage, or $8 per hour. During overtime, production averages 13 hours per unit rather than the normal 12 hours per unit. Additional costs associated with overtime production are $8 × 13 = $104 per unit. Subcontracting is not possible for this product.

SOLUTION 1: CHASE STRATEGY

The chase strategy matches product demand with the work force required each month and adjusts the work force accordingly. Using the specific data shown in Table 10.2 and equations 10.1 and 10.2, we get the hours worked per month and the size of work force required:

$$\text{Labor hours for January} = (\text{monthly demand})(\text{hours per unit})$$
$$= (1,400 \text{ units/month})(12 \text{ hours/unit})$$
$$= 16,800 \text{ hours/month}$$

$$\text{Work force size for January} = \frac{\text{total hours required for January}}{\text{hours worked per worker in January}}$$

$$= \frac{16,800 \text{ hours}}{(8 \text{ hours/day})(21 \text{ days/worker})}$$

$$= 100 \text{ workers}$$

Using these formulas for each month, along with the fact that the starting work force size for the previous month was 100, we can calculate all of the columns in Table 10.3. Adjustments to the work force are noted in the columns headed Hires or Fires. The costs associated with hiring and firing are summarized at the bottom of Table 10.3. Since the work force is changed to match the demand, it is assumed that there is no change in inventory level. The cost for this plan is $142,400.

TABLE 10.3	Costs for Chase Strategy

Original Work Force = 100   **Starting Finished Goods Inventory = 750**

Months	Days	Demand	Hours/Month	Work Force	Hires ($400)	Fires ($500)
January	21	1,400	16,800	100	0	0
February	20	1,500	18,000	113	13	0
March	23	1,600	19,200	105	0	8
April	22	1,700	20,400	116	11	0
May	21	1,800	21,600	129	13	0
June	23	1,900	22,800	124	0	5
July	22	2,000	24,000	137	13	0
August	21	1,800	21,600	129	0	8
September	22	1,600	19,200	110	0	19
October	22	1,700	20,400	116	6	0
November	21	1,400	16,800	100	0	16
December	22	1,400	16,800	96	0	4
Total	260	19,800	237,600		56	60

Inventory	Hires	Fires
Costs: 750 × 12 × $10 = $90,000	56 × $400 = $22,400	60 × $500 = $30,000

Total Costs of Plan: $142,400

SOLUTION 2: LEVEL STRATEGY

The level strategy maintains a stable work force and uses finished goods inventory to deal with variability in demand. The key to this approach is to determine the daily production rate required to manufacture 19,800 units in the 260 days available. So we use equations 10.1 through 10.5 to calculate the figures shown in Table 10.4, as follows:

$$\text{Labor hours for the year} = (19,800)(12 \text{ hours})$$
$$= 237,600 \text{ hours}$$

$$\text{Work force size} = \frac{237,600 \text{ hours}}{(8 \text{ hours/day})(260 \text{ days/year})}$$
$$= 115 \text{ workers}$$

$$\text{Daily production rate} = \frac{(115 \text{ workers})(8 \text{ hours/day})}{12 \text{ hours/unit}}$$
$$= 76.67 \text{ units/day}$$

The monthly output is determined by multiplying the daily output by the number of days in each month. Thus, for January, which has 21 days, the monthly output is

$$(76.67 \text{ units/day})(21 \text{ days}) = 1,610 \text{ units}$$

Then, since the beginning inventory is 750 and the demand is 1,400 for January,

$$\text{Ending inventory} = 750 \text{ units} + 1,610 \text{ units} - 1,400 \text{ units}$$
$$= 960 \text{ units}$$

				Beginning	Ending	Average	Inventory
Month	**Days**	**Demand**	**Output**	**Inventory**	**Inventory**	**Inventory**	**Costs ($)**
January	21	1,400	1,610	750	960	855	8,550
February	20	1,500	1,533	960	993	977	9,770
March	23	1,600	1,763	993	1,156	1,075	10,750
April	22	1,700	1,687	1,156	1,143	1,150	11,500
May	21	1,800	1,610	1,143	953	1,048	10,480
June	23	1,900	1,763	953	816	885	8,850
July	22	2,000	1,687	816	503	660	6,600
August	21	1,800	1,610	503	313	408	4,080
September	22	1,600	1,687	313	400	357	3,570
October	22	1,700	1,687	400	387	394	3,940
November	21	1,400	1,610	387	597	492	4,920
December	22	1,400	1,687	597	884	741	7,410
Total	260	19,800	19,934				90,420

TABLE 10.4   **Level Production Strategy with 115 Workers**

Finally, the monthly inventory costs are

$$\text{Inventory cost per month} = \left(\frac{750 + 960}{2}\right)(\$10)$$

$$= \$8550$$

In Figure 10.1 we see how the chase and level strategies compare in terms of work force requirements. The level strategy requires a constant 115 workers whereas the chase strategy requires a variable number, from a high of 137 workers to a low of 96.

The level production strategy shown in Table 10.4 is unacceptable, however, because the amount of inventory drops below the 750 level to 503 at the end of July and to a low point of 313 at the end of August. The identification of such violations of policy is an integral part of the cut-and-try process.

In order to solve this inventory problem, Genesis is willing to explore two of three possible alternatives: using overtime, providing additional inventory before the start of the planning period, or hiring more workers. In this situation, management is unwilling to hire additional workers unless a clear change in demand occurs.

Overtime   The cost of the overtime alternative includes (1) the additional manufacturing cost and (2) any additional inventory carrying costs.

1. Since the lowest inventory level is 313, the total amount of additional inventory needed is found by subtracting 313 from 750, so 437 units would have to be produced. The additional cost to manufacture these items is (437)($104) = $45,448.

2. To find the additional inventory costs, we start with the first shortfall, which occurs at the end of July. To resolve that shortfall, only 750 − 503 = 247 additional units would need to be available by the end of July. The remaining 190 units would have to be available by the end of August, when the low point of 313 occurs. These items will be in inventory for the remaining

FIGURE 10.1   **Comparison of Work Force Requirements for Chase and Level Strategies**

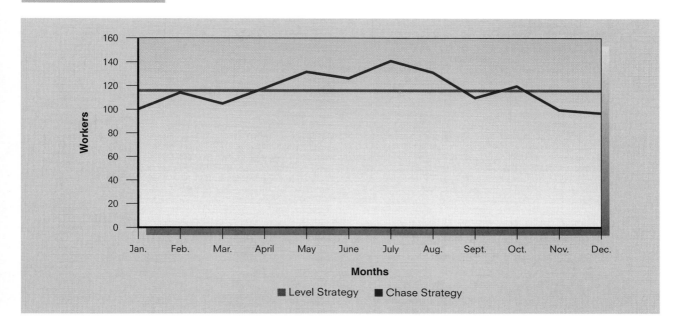

months. Using this method, the inventory costs will be (247 units) ($10) (5 months) = $12,350 plus (190 units)($10)(4 months) = $7,600, for a total additional inventory cost of $19,950.

When these cost changes are added to the original production costs shown in Table 10.4, the result is $90,420 + $45,448 + $19,950 = $155,818.

Providing Additional Inventory at the Start of the Period   To anticipate the low point of 313 at the end of August, the beginning inventory for January would have to be 750 + 437 units = 1,187. These additional units would be available every month, adding an additional (437)($10 per month)(12 months) = $52,440 in inventory carrying costs. The cost of this plan is $52,440 + $90,420 = $142,860, assuming production costs had been assigned to the previous planning period.

In Figure 10.2 a graph of the monthly finished goods inventory under the second alternative of the chase strategy is compared to the monthly finished goods inventory of the level strategy. Figures 10.1 and 10.2 graphically show the major differences between the two strategies. In Figure 10.1, the chase strategy provides for tremendous variation in work force size, while the level strategy holds the work force size at 115. In Figure 10.2, the level strategy has a significantly greater amount of finished goods inventory than the 750 units that the chase strategy provides.

SOLUTION 3: MIXED STRATEGY

Table 10.5 illustrates how the mixed strategy is a combination of the other two. The data it presents are aggregated by quarters to simplify the mixing of the level and chase approaches. For the mixed strategy, decisions are made on the basis of both the work force

| FIGURE 10.2 | **Finished Goods Inventory: Chase versus Level Strategy** |

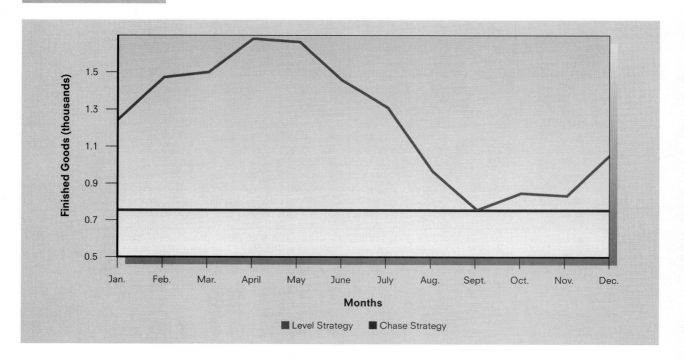

requirements and inventory levels for each quarter. The result is much like four separate level strategies, one for each quarter. At the beginning of each quarter, a change in work force requirements is possible, as it is each month when using the chase strategy.

The values in Table 10.5 are computed using equations 10.1, and 10.2:

$$\text{Labor hours for quarter 1} = \text{(quarterly demand)(hours per item)}$$
$$= \text{(4,500 items)(12 hours per item)}$$
$$= 54,000 \text{ hours}$$

$$\text{Work force size for quarter 1} = \frac{\text{total hours required for quarter 1}}{\text{hours worked per worker in quarter 1}}$$

$$= \frac{54,000 \text{ hours}}{\text{(8 hours)(64 days)}} = 105.46$$

or

$$= 106 \text{ workers}   \text{(rounded up)}$$

Thus, six people must be hired to change the number of workers from 100 to 106 in quarter 1.

The inventory levels associated with this decision are provided in Table 10.6. Although the inventory at the end of each of the four quarters is at or above the required 750 unit level, the inventory levels at the ends of the months within the quarters are unacceptable. For example, the inventory level drops to a low of 567 units at the end of August. This occurs because the average demand for the quarter is exceeded during the first 2 months of the quarter.

TABLE 10.5		Mixed Strategy: Hire and Fire Costs				

Quarter	Work Days	Demand per Quarter	Hours per Quarter	Workers Needed	Hires	Fires
1	64	4,500	54,000	106	6	0
2	66	5,400	64,800	123	17	0
3	65	5,400	64,800	125	2	0
4	65	4,500	54,000	104	0	21
Total	260	19,800			25	21

Costs: Hires: $10,000   Fires: $10,500
Total Costs: $20,500

The unacceptable inventory levels can be resolved by increasing the work force size during the first three quarters of the planning period and decreasing it during the fourth quarter. This allows additional inventory to accumulate early in the year, preventing the inventory from falling below 750. An additional worker provides an average of 65 days × 8 hours per day = 520 hours per quarter. Because each item requires 12 hours to produce, a total of 520 ÷ 12 = 43.3 products would be generated per worker each quarter. Thus, five additional workers, working one quarter each, are needed to produce the 183 units required to satisfy the inventory policy. Although there are several ways of assigning these workers, the option chosen here is to hire one additional worker during the first quarter, three additional workers in the second quarter, and one additional worker in the third quarter. (See Table 10.7.)

TABLE 10.6		Mixed Strategy: Inventory Costs					

Month	Work Days	Monthly Demand	Output	Beginning Inventory	Ending Inventory	Average Inventory	Inventory Cost ($)
January	21	1,400	1,484	750	834	792	7,920
February	20	1,500	1,413	834	747	791	7,910
March	23	1,600	1,625	747	772	760	7,600
April	22	1,700	1,804	772	876	824	8,240
May	21	1,800	1,722	876	798	837	8,370
June	23	1,900	1,886	798	784	791	7,910
July	22	2,000	1,833	784	617	701	7,010
August	21	1,800	1,750	617	567	592	5,920
September	22	1,600	1,833	567	800	684	6,840
October	22	1,700	1,525	800	625	713	7,130
November	21	1,400	1,456	625	681	653	6,530
December	22	1,400	1,525	681	806	744	7,440
Total	260	19,800	19,856				$88,820

| TABLE 10.7 | | Revised Mixed Strategy: Hire/Fire Costs | | | | | |

Quarter	Work Days	Demand per Quarter	Hours per Quarter	Workers	Hires	Fires
1	64	4,500	54,000	107	7	0
2	66	5,400	64,800	126	19	0
3	65	5,400	64,800	126	0	0
4	65	4,500	54,000	100	0	26
Total	260	19,800			26	26

Costs: Hires: $10,400   Fires: $13,000
Total Costs: $23,400

The addition of these workers increases by 1 the total number of hires for the year. Because these workers are hired to generate additional inventory and not because demand has increased, the number of workers used during the fourth quarter will be reduced so the overall production for the year will match the demand. Thus a total of 100 workers is required for the fourth quarter.

Table 10.8 summarizes the inventory costs by month. The cost associated with this plan includes $102,690 inventory cost and $23,400 for hiring and firing, for a total of $126,090.

The cut-and-try approach provides a feasible solution to the aggregate planning problem, but is not an optimizing approach. The results of the alternative plans evaluated are presented in Table 10.9. Genesis may choose the low-cost plan, which would be to use a

| TABLE 10.8 | | Revised Mixed Strategy: Inventory Costs | | | | | |

Month	Work Days	Monthly Demand	Output	Beginning Inventory	Ending Inventory	Average Inventory	Inventory Cost ($)
January	21	1,400	1,498	750	848	799	7,990
February	20	1,500	1,427	848	775	812	8,120
March	23	1,600	1,641	775	816	796	7,960
April	22	1,700	1,848	816	964	890	8,900
May	21	1,800	1,764	964	928	946	9,460
June	23	1,900	1,932	928	960	944	9,440
July	22	2,000	1,848	960	808	884	8,840
August	21	1,800	1,764	808	772	790	7,900
September	22	1,600	1,848	772	1,020	896	8,960
October	22	1,700	1,467	1,020	787	904	9,040
November	21	1,400	1,400	787	787	787	7,870
December	22	1,400	1,467	787	854	821	8,210
Total	260	19,800	19,904				$102,690

TABLE 10.9	**Cost Summary of the Three Plans**			

Strategy	Inventory Costs	Overtime Costs	Hire/Fire Costs	Total Cost
Chase	$ 90,000		$52,400	$142,400
Level				
Using overtime	$110,370	$45,448		$155,818
Additional finished goods inventory	$142,860			$142,860
Mixed	$102,690		$23,400	$126,090

mixed strategy to meet the inventory policy. Or management might identify other alternatives that may perform better. Keep in mind that the total costs compared do not represent the total cost of the entire 12-month plan. Only those costs that change from one plan to the next are considered when comparing alternatives. Cut-and-try is appropriate for any of the three strategies and can be further adjusted to reduce costs and more nearly attain the organization's goals.

In practice, whether the organization uses a chase, level, or mixed strategy depends upon a number of variables, the most important of which is often the variability of demand. Products that have no distinct seasonal pattern and little demand variability provide the best opportunity for a level strategy. When product demands are highly seasonal, attempts are often made to configure loads on resources, such as equipment and staff, in such a way as to reduce the seasonal effect.

OTHER APPROACHES TO SOLVING AGGREGATE PLANNING PROBLEMS

Although they are not used extensively in aggregate planning, several quantitative modeling techniques are available. Linear programming is perhaps the most commonly used of such techniques. Linear programming models seek to optimize a single objective, such as minimizing costs or maximizing profits, within constraints of the system. The constraints of the system are usually capacity limitations, staffing limitations for both regular time and overtime, and inventory restrictions. These constraints as well as the objective function must be expressed in a linear relationship for linear programming to be appropriate. A special linear programming model, the transportation method, is useful when hiring or firing costs are not a factor. It is particularly useful in evaluating overtime, subcontracting, inventory, and backordering decisions.[8]

Another aggregate planning approach, the linear decision rule,[9] is based on a quadratic cost function and the identification of linear equations that represent the work force size

[8]E. H. Bowman, "Production Planning by the Transportation Method of Linear Programming," *Journal of the Operational Research Society* 4 (February 1956): 100–103.
[9]C. C. Holt, F. Modigliani, J. F. Muth, and H. A. Simon, "A Linear Decision Rule for Production and Employment Scheduling," *Management Science* (October 1955): 1–10.

and production rate that would minimize that cost function. A third approach, the search decision rule,[10] does not limit the form or type of functions that describe the cost relationships. The search decision rule searches for the minimum points on total cost curves. A final aggregate planning method is called the management coefficients model.[11] This model analyzes historical data, typically using regression techniques. The regression equations are then used to make decisions for the future. Neither the search decision rule nor the management coefficients model guarantee that the best solution will be found. Linear programming and the linear decision rule are optimizing models.

LEARNING CURVE THEORY

Aggregate planning for new products and government contracts as well as for products involving significant organizational or technological improvements is often difficult because of the uncertainty in predicting how much time will be required to complete the necessary tasks and in predicting demand. There is a significant need to incorporate the concept of learning in the planning process for new products.

LEARNING CURVE THEORY
Theory based on the idea that the time required to produce an item decreases successively.

The consideration of learning in aggregate planning models is fairly common.[12] The general idea of the **learning curve theory** is that the time required to produce a second item is less than that required to produce the first, and the time required to do the third is less than the second, and so on. This time per unit may be reduced because of the learning curve of the individual performing the processes or movements required to do the job. It may also be due to process or technology improvement, better product designs, or the result of continuous improvement activities at the organizational level. As products move through the product life cycle and the focus is more on standardization, the learning curve concepts may not be as applicable because learning levels off and output is more constant.

LEARNING RATE
The rate of improvement from producing the first item, to the second, to the third, and so on.

Learning curve theory can be traced from the 1930s and the manufacture of airplanes. It was found that the time required to produce successive planes decreased proportionally. The proportion was related to the **learning rate.** If the learning rate was 0.80, and the 1st unit took 100 hours, then the 2nd unit required 80 hours. The 4th unit would take 64 hours, the 8th unit would take 51.2 hours, and so on. This pattern is shown in the table below:

Unit Number	Time (hours)
1	100
2	80
4	64
8	51.20
16	40.96
32	32.77
64	26.21
128	20.97
256	16.77

[10]W. H. Taubert, "A Search Decision Rule for the Aggregate Scheduling Problem," *Management Science* (February 1978): 343–359.

[11]E. H. Bowman, "Consistency and Optimality in Managerial Decision Making," *Management Science* 9 (January 1963): 310–321.

[12]P. Dileepan and L. P. Ettkin, "Learning: The Missing Ingredient in Production Planning Spreadsheets," *Production and Inventory Management Journal* 29 (1988): 32–35. R. Ebert, "Aggregate Planning with Learning Curve Productivity," *Management Science* 23 (October 1976): 171–182.

Tandy Corporation spent two years planning its new product—Incredible Universe—the world's first consumer electronics "gigastore." The concept has progressed quickly since the first store opened in 1992. Growth plans call for six new stores in 1994, eight in 1995, and a total of 50 by the year 2000. The experience of opening the first two stores has helped Tandy reduce the construction costs of the new buildings by as much as 15 percent.

Source   ©The Tandy Corporation.

Because the number of repetitions must be doubled to gain the reduction in time, the rate of improvement flattens out after a large number of repetitions.

A learning curve is a graph or equation that identifies the time required to produce the nth unit, given that the time to produce the 1st unit, and the learning rate, are known. The general equation for the learning curve is

$$T_n = T_1 n^r \tag{10.6}$$

where T_n = the time in hours to produce the nth unit, T_1 = the time in hours to produce the 1st unit, n = the number of the unit being computed, and $r = \log l / \log 2$ where l is the learning rate.

The values shown in the preceding table and graphed in Figure 10.3 were determined using equation 10.6. For example, to find T_4 with $l = 0.8$, $n = 4$, and $T_1 = 100$, we have

$$T_n = T_1 n^r$$
$$T_4 = 100(4)^{\log 0.8/\log 2}$$
$$= 100(4)^{-0.322}$$
$$= \frac{100}{4^{0.322}}$$
$$= 64$$

Figure 10.3 compares the graphs for 70 percent and 80 percent learning curves. Although the amount of change that occurs after the first 25 units is not dramatic, change is still observable after 64 units have been produced.

The use of the learning curve as an aid in aggregate planning is appropriate when significant learning is expected to occur and the learning will influence time or resources required to complete the plan. Example 10.2 shows how learning affects the aggregate plan.

FIGURE 10.3	**Comparison of 0.70 and 0.80 Learning Curves**

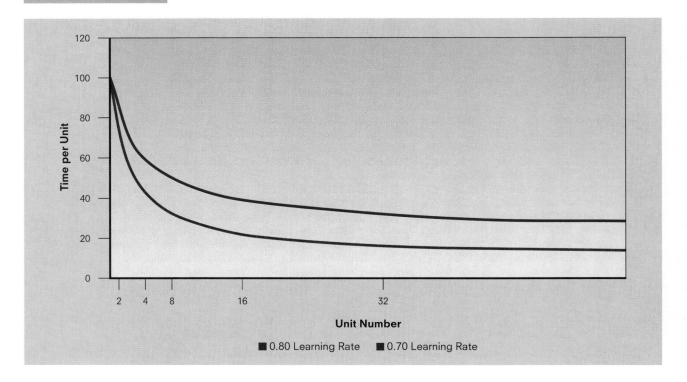

EXAMPLE 10.2

Aggregate Planning Application of Learning Curve Theory

DNB Enterprises is in the process of planning for the production of 50 special terrain vehicles that must satisfy government specifications. The total time required to produce the first special vehicle was 1,500 hours, and previous work in this area suggests that the learning rate for this project will be about 85 percent.

Management has posed several questions:

1. How many hours per month must be committed to this project in order to complete it in 12 months?
2. In which month will each of the units be ready for delivery?
3. If the learning rate is slower than expected, say 90 percent, how late will the project be, and how many additional direct labor hours will be required?

SOLUTION

1. The total hours required to complete the project can be computed using the table found in Appendix B, the 85 percent learning rate, and the completion time for the first unit. For 50 units at a learning rate of 85 percent, a value of 25.51 is obtained from Appendix B. The 25.5131 represents the time to do the 50 units if the 1st unit takes 1 hour. Because the 1st unit took 1,500 hours, the total time is estimated to be (25.5131)(1,500) = 38,269.65 hours. A monthly

commitment of 38,269.65/12 = 3,189 hours is required to complete the 50 units in 12 months.

2. In Table 10.10 (pages 292–293), which is based on a learning rate of 0.85 and 3,200 hours per month, equation 10.6 is used to compute the time required for each unit. These times are listed in the first column, and a cumulative total is provided in the second column. When the cumulative time for the units produced during that month exceeds 3,200 hours, the next month begins, then the next, and so on. The month in which each unit can be completed is given in the third column.

3. With a learning rate of 0.90 and 50 units, the table value from Appendix B is 32.1420. The total hours required would be (32.1420)(1,500) = 48,213 hours, which is 9,943 hours more than expected with a learning rate of 0.85. With 3,200 hours committed to this project per month, the additional hours would require that the project run into the 16th month. Note that the completion time is 25.99 percent above the original estimate.

The fact that a small change in learning can produce a significant change in completion time is significant. In fact, completion time is tied not only to direct labor hours but also to overhead costs and hence total project costs. It has been suggested that an interval— or range—rather than a point estimate be used to predict the learning curve effect and avoid errors of the magnitude seen in Example 10.2.[13] This method is particularly effective when preparing bids that must take learning into account. An error in projecting the completion time (and thus direct labor costs) can easily mean the difference between a profit and a loss on a particular bid.

AGGREGATE PLANNING FOR SERVICES

Aggregate planning in services differs from that in the manufacturing environment in that inventory usually cannot be used to cope with variability in demand. In some environments, however, changes in demand can be predicted and adjustments to the size of the work force can be made. In retail stores, for example, personnel is often added during the Christmas holidays. Most organizations, however, must find means to better utilize the existing work force during peak periods. One common approach is to develop a multifunctional work force that is capable of performing tasks not directly related to the customer during slack times. A bank or retail store, for example, can more easily match demand if the tellers or clerks can perform tasks other than helping customers.

The skill level required of the work force creates another problem in some service organizations. If a high degree of skill or training is required to provide the service, staff cannot easily be replaced. Because of these additional personnel-related costs, a chase strategy may not be appropriate for many service organizations. If the skills of the work force are important and not readily available, a form of level strategy is often used in which slack times in the demand pattern are absorbed by management rather than by hiring and firing

---

[13]B. J. Finch and R. L. Luebbe, "Risk Associated with Learning Curve Estimates," *Production and Inventory Management Journal* 32 (1991): 73–76.

TABLE 10.10	Learning Curve Data

Hours to produce first unit = 1,500
Learning rate = 0.85

Unit Number	Time per Unit	Cumulative Time	Month of Completion
1	1,500.00	1,500.0	1
2	1,275.00	2.775.0	1
3	1,159.37	3,934.4	2
4	1,083.75	5,018.1	2
5	1,028.51	6,046.6	2
6	985.47	7,032.1	3
7	950.48	7,982.6	3
8	921.19	8,903.8	3
9	896.10	9,799.9	4
10	874.23	10,674.1	4
11	854.91	11,529.0	4
12	837.65	12,366.7	4
13	822.07	13,188.7	5
14	807.91	13,996.6	5
15	794.95	14,791.6	5
16	783.01	15,574.6	5
17	771.96	16,346.6	6
18	761.68	17,108.2	6
19	752.09	17,860.3	6
20	743.10	18,603.4	6
21	734.64	19,338.1	7
22	726.67	20,064.7	7
23	719.14	20,783.9	7
24	712.00	21,495.9	7
25	705.22	22,201.1	7

staff. Peaks in demand are handled by using overtime wherever possible. The following example demonstrates the role that overtime might play in a service environment using a level strategy.

EXAMPLE 10.3

Application of a Level Strategy for a Service

A-1 Repair, a company that services cash registers for retail stores, has found that each service call averages 9 hours. The quarterly demand is as follows:

Quarter	1	2	3	4
Demand	700	630	670	770

Each employee is paid at the rate of $10 per hour for a total of 520 hours per quarter. Determine the number of workers required and the payroll costs if no overtime is used. How will these costs compare if 15 percent overtime is used (at time-and-a-half) each quarter?

	Hours to produce first unit = 1,500 Learning rate = 0.85		
Unit Number	Time per Unit	Cumulative Time	Month of Completion
26	698.76	22,899.9	8
27	692.61	23,592.5	8
28	686.73	24,279.2	8
29	681.10	24,960.3	8
30	675.71	25,636.0	9
31	670.53	26,306.5	9
32	665.56	26,972.1	9
33	660.77	27,632.8	9
34	656.16	28,289.0	9
35	651.72	28,940.7	10
36	647.43	29,588.2	10
37	643.28	30,231.4	10
38	639.27	30,870.7	10
39	635.39	31,506.1	10
40	631.63	32,137.7	11
41	627.99	32,765.7	11
42	624.45	33,390.2	11
43	621.01	34,011.2	11
44	617.67	34,628.9	11
45	614.43	35,243.3	12
46	611.27	35,854.6	12
47	608.19	36,462.8	12
48	605.20	37,068.0	12
49	602.28	37,670.2	12
50	599.43	38,269.7	12

SOLUTION

Consider Table 10.11. The Total Hours column shown in Table 10.11 is found by multiplying the number of calls by 9, the average number of hours per call. The Workers Required column is determined by dividing the data in the Total Hours column by 520 hours, the hours per quarter available for each worker. (*Note:* These values are typically rounded up.)

TABLE 10.11	Quarterly Demand

Quarter	Service Calls	Total Hours	Workers Required
1	700	6,300	13
2	630	5,670	11
3	670	6,030	12
4	770	6,930	14

TABLE 10.12		Plan If Overtime Is Allowed			
Quarter	Service Calls	Total Hours	Workers Required	Available Regular Hours	Overtime Hours
1	700	6,300	11	6,240	60
2	630	5,670	10	6,240	
3	670	6,030	11	6,240	
4	770	6,930	12	6,240	690
Total					750

TABLE 10.13	Comparison of the Costs of the Two Plans	
	No Overtime	15% Overtime
Regular work force	$291,200 (14 workers)	$249,600 (12 workers)
Overtime		$ 11,250
Total	$291,200	$260,850

Because the workers are valuable and cannot easily be replaced, the number of workers required for the entire year is 14, the number required during the peak period.

The wages for this plan are

(14 workers)($10/hour)(520 hours/quarter)(4 quarters/year) = $291,200

Table 10.12 presents the plan if overtime is used. The Total Hours column is again computed by multiplying the number of calls by 9. The Workers Required column takes into account that up to 15 percent overtime is possible per quarter. Therefore the available hours per worker total (1.15)(520 hours), or 598 hours per quarter. Thus, the values in the Total Hours column are divided by 598 to obtain the number of workers. The Available Regular Hours are (520 hours)(12 workers) = 6,240 hours. A comparison can now be made between the total hours and the available hours. When the total hours exceed the available hours, overtime is required.

The costs for both alternatives are compared and summarized in Table 10.13. Note that the overtime plan saves more than $30,000 a year.

SUMMARY

Aggregate planning provides a broad view of what an organization's game plan will be for the planning horizon. It links the strategic initiatives of the organization to the medium range plans of the organization. Two pure strategies are commonly used in aggregate planning. The chase strategy tends to minimize finished goods inventory by using overtime or hiring and firing to produce what is needed. The level strategy maintains a constant work force and uses finished goods inventory and overtime to deal with variations in demand.

Most organizations use a combination of both the chase and the level strategies, called a mixed strategy.

Although there are quantitative modeling approaches in use, the cut-and-try approach presented in this chapter is one of the most commonly used approaches. Learning curve theory must often be integrated with aggregate planning because of the effect learning has on plans.

THE MADISON MILL REVISITED

CROSS-LINKS After Jill's presentation, the other managers began to open up about quality problems they anticipated. For what may have been the first time in his career, Ed Bowden just sat back and listened. He could read the handwriting on the wall. The company was in trouble. Finally, he suggested that the managers examine the possibility of a new plan for meeting the seasonal demands of their products. The current approach is presented below:

	Jan.	Feb.	March	April	May	June
Shifts	2	2	1	1	1	1

	July	Aug.	Sept.	Oct.	Nov.	Dec.
Shifts	1	2	3	3	3	3

Demand projections in tons of paper for the upcoming year are presented below:

	Jan.	Feb.	March	April	May	June
Industrial	425	410	428	430	430	422
Retail	321	360	130	110	100	110
Consumer	347	345	120	180	130	118
Total tons	1,093	1,115	678	720	660	650

	July	Aug.	Sept.	Oct.	Nov.	Dec.
Industrial	422	435	430	425	429	414
Retail	114	256	560	530	520	510
Consumer	105	415	510	565	634	580
Total tons	641	1,106	1,500	1,520	1,583	1,504

What would you suggest as an alternative for the Madison Mill to examine?

QUESTIONS FOR REVIEW

1. What is the purpose of aggregate planning?
2. What is a chase strategy?
3. What is a level strategy?
4. Identify four ways that an organization can change its capacity in the short run.
5. How is aggregate planning for services different from aggregate planning for manufacturing?
6. Under what conditions is a level strategy a good choice?
7. What are the relevant costs associated with the aggregate planning process?
8. How is the ending inventory for a time period calculated?
9. How is the number of workers needed for a chase strategy determined?
10. What is a learning curve?
11. How does the learning curve help the aggregate planning process?

QUESTIONS FOR THOUGHT AND DISCUSSION

1. Discuss the strengths and weaknesses of the chase strategy.
2. Discuss the strengths and weaknesses of the level strategy.
3. Your organization is competing by emphasizing quality. How would this emphasis affect your aggregate plan?
4. Discuss the link between the strategic plan and the aggregate plan.
5. Discuss the impact forecasting might have on the aggregate plan. What steps might be taken to compensate for a poor forecast?
6. What are the key variables in the aggregate planning process?
7. Why does a mixed strategy often result in lower overall costs?
8. How is the aggregate plan related to marketing? Finance?
9. What human resource issues surface in the aggregate planning process?
10. How does the aggregate plan benefit the organization?
11. Hiring and firing practices often destroy worker morale. Discuss ways this problem might be solved.
12. How might you use the MAD and the tracking signal for the past planning period to improve the aggregate plan for the next planning period?

INTEGRATIVE QUESTIONS

1. When constructing an aggregate plan, how might the impact of expected forecast error be considered and included in the plan?
2. What is the relationship between the level loading done in a JIT environment and the level strategy of aggregate planning? Do JIT environments accomplish the level production in the same manner that is typically used in the aggregate planning level strategy? How is level production accomplished in JIT?
3. Can learning rate change the location of a system constraint? Considering learning curve theory and constraint management principles, where should training dollars be spent?
4. What impact could a chase strategy have on quality?

PROBLEMS

1. An organization is in the process of developing an aggregate plan for the next four quarters. The demand for its product, by quarter, is given below. Each product requires 6 hours of direct labor.
    a. What size work force is required if a level strategy is used?
    b. What will the daily production rate be?
    c. How much inventory is needed at the start of the quarter to avoid a stockout during the second quarter?

Quarter	Demand	Days/Quarter
1	5,500	65
2	6,800	65
3	6,000	65
4	4,600	65

2. A small manufacturer has recently received information from marketing about the projected sales for next year. The demand, by quarter, is provided below. Each product requires 5 hours of direct labor. There are 65 days in each quarter.
    a. What size work force is required if a level strategy is used?
    b. If a chase strategy is used, how many employees are needed each quarter?
    c. If a level strategy is used, how much inventory is needed at the start of the first quarter to avoid a stockout during the second quarter?

Quarter	1	2	3	4
Demand	7,800	9,000	8,800	7,400

3. A product's demand for the next 4 quarters is shown below. Each quarter has 65 workdays. It takes 20 hours of direct labor to produce a product. The additional cost for the use of overtime is $7 per hour, or $140 per product. Beginning inventory is 150 units. There is no minimum level of inventory required, but backorders are not acceptable. It costs $20 per quarter to hold an item in inventory. A level strategy is being planned with overtime being used only as needed to protect from backorders. Determine the work force size, the costs for overtime, and the finished goods inventory carrying costs for this plan.

Quarter	1	2	3	4
Demand	1,200	1,400	1,600	1,000

4. A manufacturer of concrete products uses a chase strategy to meet demand. Sixteen hours of direct labor are required per product. There are currently 70 employees. Each quarter has 65 working days. Use the demand data provided below to determine the number of hires and fires for each of the next 4 quarters. Determine the hiring and firing costs if it costs $300 for each hire and $400 for each fire.

Quarter	1	2	3	4
Demand	2,200	2,000	2,800	2,400

5. The concrete manufacturer in problem 4 is also considering a level strategy. The current inventory level is 100 units. It costs $10 to hold a unit in inventory for a quarter. Hiring costs are $300 and firing costs are $400.
    a. Develop a level strategy without overtime and determine the inventory of this plan.
    b. Compare the inventory costs of this plan with the hiring and firing costs of problem 4. Which plan is cheaper?

Quarter	1	2	3	4
Demand	2,200	2,000	2,800	2,400

6. A service organization that repairs copying equipment is planning its work force needs for the next 6 months. The expected number of service calls is provided below. Each service call averages a total of 15 hours, including travel time. The skills of the work force are important and difficult to replace. Each worker is paid for 520 hours per quarter at a rate of $10 per hour. Each worker works 160 hours per month, or 480 hours per quarter, with the remaining hours being used for vacations and holidays.
    a. Determine the work force requirements for each month.
    b. If the work force size is determined by the number of workers required during the peak period, what will the annual payroll be?

c. If the same conditions in part b hold and overtime of up to 20 percent during the peak period is allowed, what will be the annual payroll costs if the overtime rate is $15 an hour?

Months	1	2	3	4	5	6
Calls	400	430	480	440	400	390

7. A large office repair service is developing an aggregate plan for the next 6 months. The organization does not fire workers during slack periods. A plan is to be devised that will provide the lowest direct labor cost per service call. Each call averages 12 hours, including travel time. Two plans are being considered. The first uses the number of workers required during the peak month as the work force size. The other alternative is to allow up to 20 percent overtime during the peak period. The projected number of calls for the next 6 months is provided below. Workers have an average hourly wage of $9. Each worker works 160 hours per month, and the overtime rate is $13.50 an hour.
   a. What plan would you recommend?
   b. What is the average cost per service call for that plan?

Months	1	2	3	4	5	6
Calls	560	450	480	600	640	580

8. Develop a level production strategy for the following demand. Specify the work force size and the inventory and overtime costs associated with your decision. Use overtime only if the inventory level will fall below 50 units. Finished goods inventory is currently at 50 units. It takes 40 hours to produce each item. The cost to carry an item in inventory is $10 per month, and overtime costs are $300 per unit.

Months	Jan.	Feb.	March	April	May	June
Days	21	20	23	22	21	23
Demand	75	70	70	65	60	55

Months	July	Aug.	Sept.	Oct.	Nov.	Dec.
Days	22	21	22	22	21	22
Demand	60	70	85	120	110	95

9. Develop a level strategy and a chase strategy for the following demand data. Overtime is allowed only with the level strategy and can be used only to deal with shortages in finished goods inventory below 200 units. Each item takes 10 hours of direct labor. The current inventory level is 200 units. Inventory costs are $25 per unit per month. Overtime production costs an additional $70 per unit. Hiring and firing costs are $500 and $600 per person, respectively, and 40 people are employed at the start of the period. Which plan is cheaper?

Months	Jan.	Feb.	March	April	May	June
Days	21	20	23	22	21	23
Demand	700	800	650	700	750	800

Months	July	Aug.	Sept.	Oct.	Nov.	Dec.
Days	22	21	22	22	21	22
Demand	600	900	700	750	659	700

10. For the given demand data, use a mixed strategy in which the data are aggregated into quarterly periods and the work force size is determined for each quarter. Compute the inventory cost per month (see Table 10.6). It takes 18 hours to produce each item. Hiring and firing costs are both $500 per person, and 30 people are employed at the start of the period. The cost to carry an item in inventory is $20 per month, current inventory stands at 100 units, and inventory cannot fall below 75 units.

Months	Jan.	Feb.	March	April	May	June
Days	21	20	23	22	21	23
Demand	330	340	350	360	390	400

Months	July	Aug.	Sept.	Oct.	Nov.	Dec.
Days	22	21	22	22	21	22
Demand	320	310	300	300	290	280

11. A bid is being prepared to manufacture 40 units of a particular item. It required 400 hours to make the 1st unit. A learning rate of 85 percent exists. A work force equipped to work 800 total hours per week will be assigned to this project. The direct labor costs will be $15 per hour per employee. Overhead costs for this project will average $4,000 per week.
   a. What are the total costs for this project?
   b. What week can delivery for each of the 40 items be promised?

SUGGESTED READINGS

Abernathy, W. J., and K. Wayne. "Limits of the Learning Curve." *Harvard Business Review* 52 (September-October 1974): 109–119.

Bowers, M. R., and J. P. Jarvis. "A Hierarchical Production Planning and Scheduling Model." *Decision Sciences* 23 (January/February 1992): 144–159.

Bowman, E. H., and R. B. Fetter. *Analysis for Production and Operations.* 3rd ed. Homewood, Ill.: Richard D. Irwin, 1957.

Dileepan, P., and L. P. Ettkin. "Learning: The Missing Ingredient in Production Planning Spreadsheet Models." *Production and Inventory Management Journal* 29 (3rd Quarter 1988): 32–35.

Leong, G. K., M. D. Oliff, and R. Markland. "Improved Hierarchical Production Planning." *Journal of Operations Management* 8 (1989): 90–114.

Mcleavy, D. W., and S. L. Narasimhan. *Production Planning and Inventory Control.* Boston: Allyn and Bacon, 1985.

Miller, T. C. "Integrating Current End-Item Inventory Conditions into Optimization-based Long-Run Aggregate Production and Distribution Planning." *Production and Inventory Management Journal* 32 (1991): 74–80.

Oliff, M. D., and E. E. Burch. "Multi-Product Production Scheduling at Owens-Corning Fiberglass." *Interfaces* 15 (1985): 24–34.

Schroeder, R. G., and P. Larson. "A Reformulation of the Aggregate Planning Problem." *Journal of Operations Management* 6 (1986): 245–256.

Taubert, W. H. "A Search Decision Rule for the Aggregate Scheduling Problem." *Management Science* (February 1978): 343–359.

Yelle, L. E. "The Learning Curve: Historical Review and Comprehensive Survey." *Decision Sciences* 10 (April 1979): 302–328.

PERFORMING AGGREGATE PLANNING IN A SPREADSHEET ENVIRONMENT

Spreadsheets are applicable to the aggregate planning problem, particularly because of their "what if" capabilities. Because spreadsheets allow us to compute values automatically, we can easily change the value of any variable to meet any contingency—without having to go through several sets of onerous calculations. In this section, we'll look at a spreadsheet approach to implementing a chase strategy and a level strategy. We'll also use a spreadsheet approach to solving learning curve problems.

A SPREADSHEET APPROACH TO IMPLEMENTING A CHASE STRATEGY

Company A manufactures widgets; it takes 10 hours to make each widget, and the initial work force consists of 120 workers. The monthly demand for widgets is shown in cells C4 to C15 in Exhibit 10S.1, and the months and days are shown in cells A4 to A15 and B4 to B15, respectively. These given data have all been entered manually into the spreadsheet; the values in the remaining columns have been calculated using spreadsheet functions. Comments have been added to give direction; these comments do not usually appear in a spreadsheet document.

SPREADSHEET CALCULATIONS

Hours/Month (D)   The values in the Hours/Month column are computed by multiplying the demand values in column C by 10, the number of hours required to make each widget. Thus the formula for cell D4 is 10*C4, where the asterisk indicates multiplication. These values would be copied through D15. (The formula for the final cell in this column is shown in line 16.)

Workers (E)   The method for finding the number of workers is to divide the total number of hours by the hours per worker during the period. For cell E15, then, the formula for this calculation is +D15/(8*B15), where D15 is the work that must be completed in the month, B15 is the number of days in the period, and 8 is the number of hours in each day. Then, in order to guarantee that the number of workers will always be a whole number, we use the rounding function, @ROUND(X,N). In general, @ROUND(X,N) rounds any number X to N places. In this case, $N = 0$ because a whole number is required, and the X value 0.499 is added so that the number will always be rounded up. This rule of rounding ensures

EXHIBIT 10S.1	Layout for a Chase Strategy*

	A	B	C	D	E	F	G
1			Minimize Inventory—Produce to Meet Demand				
2							
3	Months	Days	Demand	Hours/Month	Workers	Hires	Fires
4	Jan	21	2100	21000	125	5	0
5	Feb	20	2400	24000	150	25	0
6	Mar	23	2700	27000	147	0	3
7	Apr	22	2800	28000	160	13	0
8	May	21	2900	29000	173	13	0
9	Jun	23	3000	30000	164	0	9
10	Jul	22	2800	28000	160	0	4
11	Aug	21	2700	27000	161	1	0
12	Sep	22	2600	26000	148	0	13
13	Oct	22	2400	24000	137	0	11
14	Nov	21	2000	20000	120	0	17
15	Dec	22	2100	21000	120	0	0
16	Formula, cell D15: 10*C15					57	57
17	Formula, cell E15: @ROUND(D15/(8*B15)+.499,0)					@SUM(F4..F15)	@SUM(G4..G15)
18	Formula, cell F15: @IF(E15>E14,E15−E14,0)						
19	Formula, cell G15: @IF(E15>E14,0,E14−E15)						

*The data in columns shaded in yellow are calculated using spreadsheet formulas. Comments are shaded in brown, and data entered manually are shaded in gray.

that we'll always have enough workers for the period. The cell formula for E15, shown in line 17, is therefore @ROUND(D15/(8*B15)+.499,0).

Hires (F)   If the work force requirements in one month are greater than the work force requirements in the previous month, the number of hires is the difference between the work force requirements in the two months. Thus, for example, the work force requirement in February, E5, is greater than E4 in January, so the formula for the number of hires is E5−E4 or 150 − 125 = 25. This seems simple enough, but there's a catch. What happens in March, when the work force requirement E6 is less than E5 in February? The spreadsheet formula must take this possibility into account. Using cell values, it must first be determined if E6 is greater than E5. If it is, the number of hires is E6−E5; otherwise, the value must be 0. To make this decision, we use the function @IF(CONDITION,X,Y). This function gives a value X if the condition is true, and a value Y if the condition is false. Thus, the formula for F15, shown in line 18, is @IF(E15>E14,E15−E14,0). For March, then, we see that because E6 = 147 and E5 = 150, E6 < E5, so there will be no new hires in this month.

Fires (G)   The values in column G, Fires, are similar to those of Hires in column F. Thus, for March, where E6 is less than E5, there would be no hires, but E5−E6 fires. In this case, however, the condition for hires is reversed, and the entry in cell G6 would be computed using the formula @IF(E6>E5,0,E5−E6). Because the condition E6>E5 is not true, the value for this cell is E5−E6 = 3.

The remaining values, the sums in cells F16 and G16, are determined using the @SUM function, shown in line 17.

SPREADSHEET APPROACH TO IMPLEMENTING A LEVEL STRATEGY WITH OVERTIME

Company B manufactures gizmos. The time required to manufacture each gizmo is 10 hours, and it costs an additional $150 to produce each gizmo using overtime. Finished goods inventory is initially 750 and cannot drop below that number. The demand and production days are entered in cells B4 to B15 and C4 to C15 in Exhibit 10S.2.

SPREADSHEET CALCULATIONS

Size (C19)   The first step in a level production plan is to determine the size of the work force needed, a number that can be found by using the same principle employed in the chase spreadsheet to find the work force requirement for each period. In this case we need the total demand and total workdays for the planning period, which are calculated using the @SUM function. These totals are shown on line 16 in columns B and C. The formula for the work force size, @ROUND(C16*10/B16*8)+.499,0), is shown in cell D19. As in the chase spreadsheet, the @ROUND function is used, and the number of workers is equal to the total work required for the planning period divided by the quantity of work a single worker can perform during the whole period.

Output (D)   The output per month also uses the @ROUND function, without rounding up. For instance, the formula for cell D5, @ROUND(119*8*B5/10,0), computes the available hours and divides those by 10, the hours per gizmo, as follows: (119 workers × 8 hours/day × 20 days/month)/10 hours = 1,904.

Beginning Inventory (F)   The beginning inventory (F) is 750 units, and the beginning inventory for the other periods is the ending inventory for the previous period. Thus the entry for cell F5 is the value +G4.

Ending Inventory (G)   The ending inventory (G) is the beginning inventory (F) plus output and overtime for the month (D and E) minus the monthly demand (C). Thus for G5 the cell formula is +F5+D5−C5+E5.

EXHIBIT 10S.2 **Level Production with Overtime**

	A	B	C	D	E	F	G	H	I
1			Level production strategy with overtime						
2						Inventory	Inventory	Inventory	Inventory
3	Months	Days	Demand	Output	Overtime	Beginning	Ending	Average	Cost
4	Jan	21	1500	2000	0	750	1250	1000	10000
5	Feb	20	1600	1904	0	1250	1554	1402	14020
6	Mar	23	1700	2190	0	1554	2044	1799	17990
7	Apr	22	2400	2095	0	2044	1739	1892	18920
8	May	21	2300	2000	0	1739	1439	1589	15890
9	Jun	23	2500	2190	0	1439	1129	1284	12840
10	Jul	22	2700	2095	226	1129	750	940	9400
11	Aug	21	2300	2000	300	750	750	750	7500
12	Sep	22	2150	2095	55	750	750	750	7500
13	Oct	22	1900	2095	0	750	945	848	8480
14	Nov	21	1900	2000	0	945	1045	995	9950
15	Dec	22	1800	2095	0	1045	1340	1193	11930
16	Total	260	24750	24759	581				144420
17		@SUM(B4..B15)	@SUM(C4..C15)	@SUM(D4..D15)	@SUM(E4..E15)				@SUM(I4..I15)
18	WORKFORCE								
19	Size		119	←@ROUND(C16*10/(B16*8)+.499,0)					
20									
21	OT Costs		87150	←$150*E16					
22	Inventory Costs		144420	←+ I16					
23	Total Costs		231570	←@SUM(C21..C22)					
24	Formula for Cell I5: $10*H5								
	Formula for Cell D5: @ROUND(119*8*B5/10,0)								
	Formula for Cell E5: @IF(D5+G4−C5<750,@MIN(380,750−D5−G4+C5),0)								
	Formula for Cell F5: +G4								
	Formula for Cell G5: +F5+D5−C5+E5								
	Formula for Cell H5: @AVG(F5..G5)								

Average Inventory (H)   The average inventory (H) is the average of the beginning and ending inventory and is computed using the @AVG function.

Overtime (E)   Overtime is used only when the ending inventory does not meet the 750 minimum. The amount of work that can be done is limited. In this example, the number of units is 380 units a month, which is 20 percent of regular production during the shortest month in the planning period. If the ending inventory is projected to be less than 750, over-time will be used, up to a maximum of 380 units for the month, to maintain a proper inventory level. To determine whether overtime is necessary, we use the following reasoning process: If production for the current month (D) plus ending inventory for the previous month (G) minus demand for the current month (C) is less than 750, then overtime is required. For cell E5, then, the formula for this process is D5+G4−C5<750.

To calculate the amount of overtime needed, we subtract from 750 the production from the current month and the inventory from the previous month. Thus the formula for cell E5 is 750−D5−G4+C5. But since this amount cannot exceed 380, we need to use the @MIN(X,Y) function. This function selects the minimum values of *X* or *Y*.

Finally, to combine all of these formulas and decisions, we need to use an @IF statement. For cell E5, the formula thus becomes @IF(D5+G4−C5<750,@MIN (380,750−D5−G4+C5),0). This formula simply says that if fewer than 750 units are in inventory at the end of the 5th period, then as many extra units, up to a total of 380, should be produced as are needed to bring the inventory to 750.

Inventory Costs (I)   Inventory costs are calculated simply by multiplying the average inventory (H) by $10, the cost per unit. Thus the formula for cell I5 is 10*H5.

Overtime, Inventory, and Total Costs   Overtime costs are computed by multiplying the cost per unit $150 by the sum of the units produced by overtime. This sum is shown in cell E16, so the formula is 150*E16 = $87,150. The total cost, $231,570, is the sum of the overtime costs and inventory costs, @SUM(C21..C22).

LEARNING CURVE

The learning curve is a complex mathematical equation that is not always fully understood. By using a spreadsheet to solve learning curve problems, the application is simplified, creating an opportunity for greater understanding. Sensitivity analysis is also easy to perform, which is particularly important when working with learning curves because significant changes can result from a small error in estimating the learning rate.

In Exhibit 10.S3 the time required to make the first unit is given as 100 hours and the learning rate is given as 0.80. The formula to compute the time to copy the second unit is shown in line 8. This is the LOTUS version of equation 10.6. In LOTUS, dollar signs, $, are used to fix values so that when these values are copied they will not change. The carat, ^, is used to raise a quantity to any power, and @LN(X) represents the natural log (ln) of *X*. Thus the first unit is $E$3, and the learning rate is $E$4. This formula shown in line 8 can be copied from E8 through E38.

The Cumulative Hours column begins with 100 hours, the time to produce the first unit, and then adds the hours required for the next item. Thus for cell C9, the value is +C8+B9. This should also be copied through C38.

Because both the time for the first unit and the learning curve rate are easily changed, the impact of small errors in these values can be easily determined. For example, if the

EXHIBIT 10S.3 **Learning Curve Analysis**

	A	B	C	D	E	F
1			LEARNING CURVE ANALYSIS			
2						
3		Hours for first unit			100	
4		Learning curve rate			0.80	
5	Unit	Unit	Cumulative			
6	Number	Time (hours)	Hours			
7						
8	1	100.00	100.00	Cell B9: $E$3*A9^(@LN($E$4)/@LN(2))		
9	2	80.00	180.00	Cell C9: +C8+B9		
10	3	70.21	250.21			
11	4	64.00	314.21			
12	5	59.56	373.77			
13	6	56.17	429.94			
14	7	53.45	483.39			
15	8	51.20	534.59			
16	9	49.29	583.89			
17	10	47.65	631.54			
18	11	46.21	677.75			
19	12	44.93	722.68			
20	13	43.79	766.47			
21	14	42.76	809.23			
22	15	41.82	851.05			
23	16	40.96	892.01			
24	17	40.17	932.18			
25	18	39.44	971.62			
26	19	38.76	1010.37			
27	20	38.12	1048.49			
28	21	37.53	1086.02			
29	22	36.97	1122.99			

| EXHIBIT 10S.3 | Continued |

	A	B	C	D	E	F
30	23	36.44	1159.43			
31	24	35.95	1195.38			
32	25	35.48	1230.86			
33	26	35.03	1265.89			
34	27	34.61	1300.50			
35	28	34.21	1334.71			
36	29	33.82	1368.53			
37	30	33.46	1401.99			
38	31	33.10	1435.09			

learning rate were 0.82, changing the value in E4 to 0.82, the subsequent values would automatically be computed. Also, because total hours are available, the number of weeks could be obtained, given the direct hours available for the project, and the changes in weeks or months and any associated overhead costs per week can be determined.

CHAPTER 11

PLANNING FACILITY LOCATIONS

CROSS-LINKS **Ranch House Steaks: When It's Time for a Move**

Ranch House Steaks is a fast-growing restaurant franchise, specializing in steaks that are extremely lean and well trimmed. The franchise headquarters is in Los Angeles, where the first restaurant was located. ■ Steve Lawson, owner and developer of the Ranch House concept, has been under increasing pressure to move the headquarters out of the Los Angeles area. The company is growing at a rate of 24 new restaurants per year, and this rate is expected to increase. The headquarters is used for 2-week training courses as well as quarterly training updates for all franchise owners. It also is used for storage and distribution of supplies and food for all the restaurants. It has become obvious that the current facility is not large enough to accommodate the increasing numbers. As the business expands out of California to neighboring states, the high costs associated with a Los Angeles location are also becoming more difficult to justify. With a new location, Steve hopes to maintain a model restaurant next door where he can test new dishes and practices. The restaurant would also serve as a training ground for new franchisees. ■ Steve scheduled a preliminary meeting with his immediate staff. Rosita Arroya, an equipment specialist, was opposed to the move because she preferred living in a metropolitan area and was afraid the company would move to a small town. Mike Anderson, a marketing manager, favored the move because he was tired of the congestion and traffic of Los Angeles. Tony Luchessi, a legal expert, was in favor of the move because he thought it would be to the company's advantage legally to locate outside of California. Head chef Pat Williams was concerned about the availability of good produce and meat outside of Los Angeles. Currently, all supplies were centrally purchased, and franchisees were required to buy them from the parent company. ■ In a long and stressful meeting, the group identified the most important criteria for selecting a new location. The new site should be

1. central to the expected market area as projected for 1998
2. near (within 30 miles) a major airport and interstate highways
3. within a block of a large hotel
4. large enough to accommodate a restaurant on the same property
5. in an area with sufficient traffic to support a restaurant

Steve requested that each group member come to the next meeting with nominations for two communities that met criteria 1 and 2 and had the potential to satisfy criteria 3, 4, and 5. ■ "We'll start with that list, plus two cities I nominate, and work down to a short list of four cities," he announced to the group. All staff members were pleased with the amount of input they would have. ■ "This won't be as bad as I expected," thought Rosita, as she assembled her notes and prepared to leave. ■ "Hold on a second," Steve said, trying to regain control of the group. "We've got an even bigger issue to deal with." The group suddenly got quiet, expecting bad news. ■ "It's not bad news!" Steve said. "But it will require serious consideration. We've been approached by a very wealthy investor who would like to take the franchise to Europe. He wants to start by opening three restaurants in the United Kingdom. I want to maintain control of the Ranch House concept wherever it goes so I will not relinquish control. I would sell him a number of franchises. But I need to decide if this concept can work in Europe. There are dozens of issues to consider. The Ranch House concept is tied to the U.S. western culture. The ingredients in our dishes are linked to what's available here. I would like each of you, based on your own areas of expertise, to brainstorm and identify as many issues as you can that must be considered in this decision." ■ Steve continued, "This investor's interest has convinced me that it's time to plan our growth beyond the West Coast region. I'd like to begin examining a new region for expansion. Let's evaluate the southeastern United States first. I'd like to initiate plans for restaurants in Atlanta, Orlando, and Nashville. We'd probably use Atlanta as the regional headquarters, on a trial basis, to handle training and supplies. If we were to expand in that region, we would need to identify the top 20 markets and decide where to locate the headquarters permanently. Next week, after we discuss the European expansion, let's talk about potential markets in the Southeast." ■

FACILITY LOCATION DECISIONS

Location decisions are long-term commitments: They cannot be changed easily or cheaply. Moreover, location can be a determining factor in a firm's ultimate success because it has a direct impact upon its competitive capabilities. Businesses in both the manufacturing and service sectors typically make location decisions under the following circumstances.

- ■ *Planning New Enterprises* Choosing the appropriate site for a new business can be crucial to its success. For example, when Outback Steakhouse, an Australia-themed restaurant chain, was established in 1987, the restaurants were all located close to residential neighborhoods rather than in business districts. Outback is now one of the fastest growing U.S. businesses, and its founder, Chris Sullivan, attributes much of the chain's success to this location decision. He says that it's cheaper to buy real estate where people live than where they work and that a dinner business is more lucrative than a lunch crowd.[1]

- ■ *Relocating an Existing Business* Relocation can be an opportunity for a business to improve operations, or it may be a necessity to maintain current operation levels. Cost cutting is a common factor in relocation decisions. Manufacturers may decide to relocate because of changes in system inputs, such as the availability of raw materials and/or the cost of energy. Or the decision may be driven by changes in operating costs, such as lease agreements, or by changes in economic conditions, such as taxes and government regulation. By choosing a new site that allows them to take advantage of differences in shipping and transportation costs, as well as lower utility or labor costs, firms can try to position themselves as low-cost producers. This is particularly im-

---

[1]Andrew E. Serwer, "America's 100 Fastest Growers," *Fortune,* August 9, 1993, 40–56.

At this plant in Zambia, Colgate-Palmolive manufactures toothpaste tubes and toothbrushes. The Colgate-Palmolive Company is expanding its production capacity by building new plants in Latin America, Asia, Africa, and Central Europe to meet increased consumer demand for its products in these emerging markets.

Source Courtesy of Colgate-Palmolive; Richard Alcorn, photographer.

portant as markets become globalized. For example, Cypress Semiconductor of San Jose, California, decided to relocate offshore in 1992. By opening a plant in Thailand, this firm was able to save $17 million in costs and free itself of time-consuming government regulation. According to Chief Executive Officer T. J. Rodgers, it took less time to get the Bangkok plant operating than it would have taken to get approval to install an awning in California.[2]

For businesses in the service sector, relocation may be desirable or necessary because of a shift in the market or because of changes in the location of competitors, economic conditions, or operating costs. Service firms may also relocate because they wish to take advantage of some new development or because new, more desirable sites become available. Businesses may also be compelled to relocate because of a merger or acquisition. The accounting firm, Coopers & Lybrand, for instance, moved 5,500 staff members from 13 different sites to one central office in London after its merger with Deloitte, Haskins, and Sells.[3]

■ *Expanding Capacity* When businesses need to add to their capacity, they may decide to relocate if the costs and benefits of moving to a new site compare favorably to the costs and benefits of adding to an existing facility. If the

---

[2]John DeMott, "California's Economic Crisis," *Nation's Business* (July 1993): 16–22.
[3]Sarah Grey, *Journal of Accountancy* (May 1993): 65.

existing site cannot be expanded economically, a firm often has no choice except to purchase or build a new facility. Or, under certain conditions, a firm may do both. For instance, Intel Corporation—the largest manufacturer of semiconductors in the United States—has made plans to build huge microchip factories in Arizona and New Mexico in addition to spending $400 million to expand its chip-making plant near its Santa Clara, California, headquarters.[4]

The expansion decision is a complex one, including many factors that are difficult to quantify. Building new facilities can be costly, both in time and money. But if a business decides to expand a current facility, it may not be able to take advantage of the newest and most efficient technology available because any new equipment they install would have to be compatible with current equipment. Thus, the firm may be yielding an advantage to competitors. Moreover, adding new facilities is often seen as advantageous, even when there is no need for added capacity. Particularly in the service sector, new facilities often act as barriers to entry, making it more difficult for competing firms to enter or dominate a market.

LOCATION DECISIONS AND COMPETITIVE PRIORITIES

Location is one of the most important decisions a firm has to make: It has a direct effect on all five competitive priorities.

Price   Because location affects the cost of producing goods or services, it has a significant influence on the price that is passed on to a customer. Location affects both fixed costs—taxes, utilities, and the purchase price of land or facilities—and variable costs—materials, labor, and transportation, as we see in Box 11.1. Moreover, firms that wish to respond quickly to customers often find proximity to suppliers helpful because it allows them to keep inventory levels low and costs down.

 Quality   Location affects the quality of a product or service in several ways. First, it often determines the availability of skills in the work force. Worker skills are translated into quality during the design, development, and production of the product or service. For some firms, particularly those that utilize high levels of technology, the educational and cultural characteristics of a community become important location criteria. For example, Alfa-Laval Thermal Company, a Swedish manufacturer of heat-transfer equipment, had originally located its production plant in Poughkeepsie, New York. Recently, that site was sold and the facility relocated in Richmond, Virginia, where the company was assured of access to a high-quality, manufacturing-oriented work force.[5]

The availability and cost of raw materials can also be quality factors dictated by location. Manufacturers whose products have short shelf lives, for instance, find it advantageous to be near customers. And for businesses in the service sector, where time is often an integral part of the "good" being sold, long distances translate into inferior products.

---

[4]DeMott, "California's Economic Crisis"; Larry Hall, "Intel Spends Billions on Plant," *Journal of Commerce* (March 1994), sec. A, 6.
[5]Joyce Santora, "How Alfa-Laval Got Its Employees Moving," *Personnel Journal* (January 1991): 38–42.

Dependability   Locations distant from customers and suppliers pose the risk of inter-ruptions in delivery systems. Inclement weather, for instance, is more likely to disrupt the flow of raw materials into or finished goods out of a manufacturing concern when long dis-tances must be traversed. Distance can also pose logistical problems. Alfa-Laval, for in-stance, solved a real long-distance problem when it selected Richmond, Virginia, as the site for its U.S. plant. In order to bring products in from Sweden, it chose a city within a day's travel of a major seaport. Service-sector firms also find that proximity to customers in-creases reliability and convenience. All other things being equal, customers usually prefer convenient suppliers they can count on to be available.

Flexibility   Quick access to raw materials and other inputs to the production system, like skilled employees and adequate transportation, can enhance a firm's ability to respond rapidly to customers. This fact has implications for decentralization. Although a central lo-cation may offer economies of scale, multiple decentralized sites may be more profitable because the increased flexibility improves customer service enough to offer a competitive advantage. In the plastics industry, for example, many firms are seeking increased flexibil-ity through geographic diversification. Manufacturers in this industry are finding that, in-stead of maintaining one large plant, building several smaller plants in different areas around the country can shield the whole firm from the economic downturns that may strike in a particular region. Moreover, such geographic diversity encourages the introduction of variations in management approaches and changes in technology, which may ultimately enhance the company's competitive position.[6]

Time   Quick response times, often necessary in JIT environments, are all but impossi-ble to attain if products and services are not located near customers. The time it takes to transport inputs and products is included in lead times, so shorter travel distances result in shorter total lead times. Customers benefit not only because they receive orders more quickly but also because they do not have to order so far in advance. Thus they gain the ad-vantage of using short-term forecasts, which tend to be more accurate and more sensitive to current conditions than long-term forecasts. Customers are often willing to pay premium prices to the supplier who, because of speedy response times, offers them protection from unexpected demands and stockouts.

Figure 11.1 shows how location decisions fit into our task/resource model. As we can see, location decisions affect the tasks of planning and organizing primarily in the areas of work force and facilities and equipment.

LOCATION DECISIONS IN MANUFACTURING

Manufacturers must evaluate so many alternatives and criteria before they choose a loca-tion that they need to minimize the number of options before making a decision. One im-portant initial approach is classify the location decision either as *input driven* or *customer driven*. A location decision is driven by inputs when it depends heavily on inputs, such as the cost and availability of labor, transportation, raw materials, and energy. Location decisions are customer driven when proximity to customers is of more importance than

---

[6]P. A. Toensmeier, "Site Selection Options and Benefits Multiply as Locales Seek Jobs Growth," *Modern Plastics* (September 1993): 98–110.

OPERATIONS OUTLOOK

BOX 11.1

Location and the Bottom Line

The location of a manufacturing facility can have a big effect on operating costs. The accompanying table, prepared by Boyd Co. Inc., location consultants from Princeton, New Jersey, compares costs of operating a hypothetical 100,000 square feet injection molding plant in 16 cities. The plant employs 250 hourly workers, and the labor costs include base pay and fringe benefits for nonexempt labor. The locations compared include major California cities and others that could ship to a western market in the United States. All costs are expressed in $1,000s. The difference between the high and low cost location is $4.2 million annually, which could mean the difference between profit and loss.

Source P. A. Toensmeier, "Site-Selection Options and Benefits Multiply as Locales Seek Jobs Growth," *Modern Plastics* (September 1993): 100–101.

Location	Annual Labor Cost (Avg. $/hr.)	Electric Power Cost	Natural Gas Cost	Occupancy Costs (amortization, property tax, air conditioning)	Shipping Costs	Total Annual Operating Costs
Los Angeles/ Long Beach	8,191 (12.56)	222	570	1,035 199 79	333	10,599
Anaheim/ Santa Ana	8,758 (13.43)	222	570	1,035 111 67	272	11,035
San Diego	8,837 (13.55)	138	493	798 113 43	335	10,758
Bakersfield	8,966 (13.78)	180	570	862 95 106	320	11,119
San Francisco	9,456 (14.50)	180	531	1,201 148 86	328	11,910
San Jose	10,564 (16.20)	180	531	1,074 117 63	327	**12,856**

nearness to inputs. The decision to locate near customers may result from service aspects closely linked to the product; for example, such proximity is desirable when it is not economical to transport finished products over long distances because of their weight or bulk or because they are perishable.

We can clarify the relative importance of specific issues in relocation decisions by examining them from the perspectiove of the production cycle. Recall that there are four stages in the production cycle: the basic producer, the converter, the fabricator, and the assembler. In each of these stages different criteria are possible.

■   Basic producers are likely to be located near raw materials. Because of the great bulk and/or weight of their outputs, they need to be near sources of in-

Location	Annual Labor Cost (Avg. $/hr.)	Electric Power Cost	Natural Gas Cost	Occupancy Costs (amortization, property tax, air conditioning)	Shipping Costs	Total Annual Operating Costs
Sacramento	9,163 (14.05)	164	531	876 90 86	311	11,221
Oakland	10,193 (15.63)	180	531	957 130 63	324	12,378
Phoenix	8,152 (12.50)	175	547	757 229 123	358	10,341
Denver	9,000 (13.80)	138	499	738 209 128	456	11,168
Salt Lake City	8,086 (12.40)	123	410	716 126 111	296	9,858
Seattle	9,716 (14.90)	106	552	1,042 142 113	448	12,119
Reno/ Sparks	8,915 (13.67)	150	436	789 87 108	294	10,779
Albuquerque	7,213 (11.06)	189	344	733 99 93	439	9,110
Dallas	7,610 (11.67)	124	602	752 180 103	744	10,115
Sioux Falls	6,535 (10.02)	111	385	649 171 128	707	**8,686**

expensive transportation, such as waterways or railroads. And because their operations require high energy use, they need to locate in areas where utility costs are low or cheap power sources are available. The nature of the labor force and the level of automation is such that specific skills are generally not critical in these industries, so location decisions would not likely be made on the basis of the availability of a skilled labor force.

■ Converters, which generally take in inputs of high bulk and volume, tend to use the same criteria that basic producers do, frequently locating near their basic "feeding" producer.

■ Fabricators, which are less generic than converters and produce more specialized end products, may also choose locations on the basis of proximity to

FIGURE 11.1 **Location Decisions and the Task/Resource Model of Operations Management**

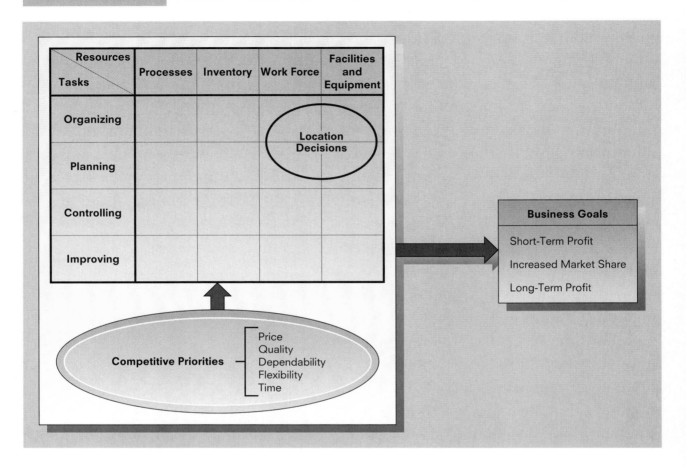

their suppliers. Because fabricators' inputs are the end products of converters—and because their inputs are few compared to the variety of their ouputs—fabricators often find sites near their converters most cost-effective.

- Assemblers, which use multiple inputs, cannot be located near all their suppliers—not unless they are powerful enough to compel suppliers to locate near them, as has been the case in the U.S. auto industry. On the whole, however, assemblers frequently choose to locate near their customers.

It should be clear that transportation costs are often the determining factors in location decisions, and that the relative importance of proximity to raw materials or to customers depends largely on the type of manufacturing concerned. Some manufacturers locate near raw material sources because they use inputs that are heavy or bulky and therefore costly to transport. Others can easily transport raw materials, but produce products that can't be transported long distances, so they locate near customers. (See Box 11.2.) Still other manufacturers, such as those that make bricks or precast concrete products, cannot economically transport either raw materials or finished products. These manufacturers tend to serve relatively small regional markets located near their raw material sources.

BOX 11.2

Location Strategies for Breweries and Soft Drink Bottlers

Although the finished product and much of the production process may seem similar, differences between the production of carbonated soft drinks and beer have led to significant differences in facility location strategies. The megabreweries of major beer brands tend to have regional locations. Despite the weight, they transport finished products up to several hundred miles. Soft drink bottlers, on the other hand, have facilities that serve much smaller areas, greatly reducing transportation costs for getting their finished products to customers. This difference has evolved because soft drink manufacturers can ship an important raw material, in the form of concentrated syrup, to local bottlers much more cheaply than they can ship the heavy, bulky, finished product. Shipping syrup over long distances and finished product over short distances results in lower total transportation costs.

Beer manufacturers, because of the processes involved, must complete the product on site. They cannot ship a concentrated form of beer to a more widely distributed network of bottlers in order to reduce transportation costs. Thus, beer distributors minimize total transportation costs by transporting inputs by rail and outputs by truck to large geographic regions.

Historically, the location of several kinds of manufacturing concerns can be traced to the transportation problem. Consider, for example, the furniture industry that developed in Hickory and Lenoir, North Carolina, near an abundance of hardwood forest. This location was an obvious choice because timber is harder to ship than tables and chairs. Similarly, the automobile industry originally developed in the Great Lakes region because cities in this area had ready access both to inexpensive water transport and to major steel factories.

Manufacturers may also locate in a particular area because of the availability of potential employees with certain skills. The computer industry in California's Silicon Valley and the Research Triangle in North Carolina, for example, evolved because of an abundant supply of workers with expertise in computer hardware and software. In addition to availability of labor, the labor climate may also be critical to a location decision. Depending on the type of industry, different regions, and even different communities within regions, offer varying degrees of labor/management harmony. Labor climate can also be a determining factor in the choice between adding to an existing facility and building a new one. If the labor climate in the current location is poor, companies are likely to build elsewhere.

Several other factors may also influence location decisions. Many firms move to specific locations to gain market access. They must often follow the industries they supply. As JIT has become more widely used, many manufacturers have found that they must be near both suppliers and customers in order to receive frequent deliveries (to minimize raw material inventories) and deliver frequently to customers (to minimize both finished goods inventories and customers' raw materials). Some major corporations actually restrict their suppliers' locations to within specific geographic distances. This trend has already had a significant impact on the hundreds of suppliers in the U.S. auto industry. Many suppliers have had to relocate to sites closer to assembly plants in order to deliver as required without incurring unacceptable cost increases.

Avoiding regulation has become an increasingly important factor in the relocation decision-making process. For example, many companies have been moving out of California and setting up new sites in states that have access to the large California market. Custom Stamping, Inc., is a case in point. This manufacturer of metal parts for the computer and telecommunication industries decided to leave California in 1993 and build a new $12 million factory near Carson City, Nevada. Among the reasons cited for the move were excessive regulation and an expensive workers' compensation system.[7] Increasing costs and time delays resulting from government regulations have prompted many companies to adjust their approach to choosing sites.[8] The following are five typical adjustments:

1. Increasing use of on-site expansion rather than new-site building
2. Placing more than one division on a single site
3. Procuring sites in advance of any need and holding them in a "land bank," which can be accessed any time a new site is needed
4. Maintaining an up-to-date library of preliminary studies on numerous potential sites across a wide geographic range, thereby reducing the time required to identify the most desirable new sites
5. Performing detailed engineering for a new plant while the site selection process is going on

Historically, quality of life has been considered a secondary factor in location decisions. But as crime rates are seen to rise and as pollution and traffic continue to increase, quality-of-life issues have become linked to actual costs.

During periods of slow economic growth, community and state governments are often willing to offer incentives to attract manufacturing concerns seeking new locations in order to increase the job base of the area. These incentives frequently include tax breaks, but may include other, less tangible incentives as well. Such incentives can play a major role in the location decision if all other important criteria are satisfied. For example, Stride Rite Corporation decided to consolidate its distribution facilities in Louisville, Kentucky, after government officials offered the company a $23 million tax break.[9] On their own, however, incentives rarely convince a company to relocate in a particular community.

Two regions that have been particularly successful at attracting new business are the upper Midwest and the South, as Table 11.1 shows. Between 1986 and 1990, capital spending per worker was 9 percent higher in the Midwest that anywhere else in the United States. Ohio and Wisconsin, as well as Minnesota and Iowa, known traditionally as farm states, have promoted their low labor cost, good work ethic, low taxes and utility rates, and general quality of life. Many companies look favorably on their characteristics.[10] Like the Midwest, the South has also been attracting new manufacturing businesses because of its low labor costs and good labor/management relations. With the added advantage of a favorable climate, states like Arkansas, the Carolinas, and Texas have brought in many new facilities. (See Box 11.3.)

LOCATION DECISIONS IN SERVICES

Location decisions can be more critical for firms in the service sector than for manufacturers because completed services cannot be stored and transported. For services, location decisions tend to be customer, rather than input, driven. Services such as food and beverage

---

[7]DeMott, "California's Economic Crisis."

[8]R. W. Schmenner, *Making Business Location Decisions* (Englewood Cliffs, NJ: Prentice-Hall, 1982), 40–41.

[9]Tom McNiff, Jr., "Haulers Weigh Effect of Shift in Stride Rite Distribution," *Journal of Commerce and Commercial,* January 15, 1993, sec. A, 1.

[10]"Once the Rust Belt, Midwest Now Boasts Revitalized Factories," *The Wall Street Journal,* January 3, 1993, sec. A, 1, 4.

TABLE 11.1	Locations of Expansions and New Facilities for 1992

State	Number of New Sites or Expansions
Texas	405
North Carolina	405
Ohio	319
Florida*	252
California	221
Louisiana	168
Wisconsin	161
Indiana	159
Georgia	148
Virginia	131

*Florida led the United States from 1988 to 1991.

Source   Industrial Development Research Council and Conway Data, as reported in "North Carolina, Texas Gain the Most Corporate Sites," *Nation's Business,* November 1993, 54.

sales, retail sales, and automobile services are highly dependent on convenience factors related to location and traffic patterns, as we see in Box 11.4.

The relative importance of various location criteria can be examined from the perspective of the degree of customer interaction or customization and the degree of labor intensity of the serivces. Recall that

Service factories have low levels of labor intensity and low levels of customer interaction and customization

Service shops have low levels of labor intensity and high levels of customer interaction and customization

Mass services have high levels of labor intensity and low levels of customer interaction and customization

Professional services have high levels of labor intensity and high levels of customer interaction and customization

Service factories include such businesses as airlines, trucking firms, hotels, resorts, and recreation centers. Location decisions for these businesses are driven by the location of the demand. They must offer the service in popular destinations where it is needed, such as large cities, centers of commerce, and tourist attractions. Service shops are somewhat more specialized in their services and will locate for convenience. They also recognize, however, that an area of specialty will bring in customers from some distance away. Mass services, such as retailing, offer little in the way of customization, so they cannot easily differentiate themselves from their competition. For this reason, convenience and traffic flow are critical in their location decision. Professional services, such as doctors and lawyers, must select a location that is convenient and also in an area where there is not already an oversup-

CUTTING-EDGE COMPANIES

BOX 11.3

Buying BMW

In early 1992, the luxury German automaker BMW was considering building a new $1 billion factory 15 miles south of Spartanburg, South Carolina. The United States was a likely sight for expansion for several reasons. Labor costs were low and BMW believed it could attain its quality requirements. In 1991 the average German manufacturing worker received $24.36 per hour compared to $15.39 paid to American workers. Also the United States has the largest consumer market in the world, and BMW believed it could increase sales.

Spartanburg really wanted this plant. The factory was expected to bring an additional 1,800 jobs to a state that already led the nation in per capita foreign investment. During the previous 25 years, low labor costs, right-to-work laws, good transportation, and generous tax incentives had led foreign companies like Michelin, Hoechst Celanese, and Adidas USA to invest more than $1.5 billion in a county with a population of just over 225,000. But the BMW plant would be larger than anything Spartanburg County had ever seen.

In April 1992, South Carolina Gov. Carroll A. Campbell, Jr., signed a bill to provide $35 million worth of incentives aimed at luring BMW to Spartanburg. This package was in addition to $5 million in state income tax credits. South Carolina businesses added another $3 million to help train future BMW employees. The incentive package also included $25 million in bonds to buy and improve the 500-acre site that the state would lease to BMW for a nominal fee. An airport extension was also included. An additional $10 million was earmarked for improving roads near the site. Area real estate developers contributed five rent-free floors of a downtown office building. The value of all the incentives totaled over $150 million. The location of the proposed site was also attractive. It was along the I-85 corridor and within a 1.7-million-person TV market. In addition, there were 3,000 local workers trained in Deming's quality improvement techniques.

South Carolina had committed to doing whatever it took to attract industry, despite the fact that it had some of the lowest high school graduation rates in the United States. The state's Special Schools Program was started in 1961, to provide training courses at South Carolina's 16 technical colleges or at plant sites. In fiscal year 1992, 6,500 workers, at more than 120 plants participated in the training programs. As a result the state could guarantee BMW five qualified candidates for each job opening.

BMW decided to choose Spartanburg for the new plant. The South Carolina State Development Board predicted that suppliers would follow, generating over $1 billion in investments and creating 10,000 jobs in the next 20 years.

Sources "Could Anything Be Finah Than to Be in Carolina?" *Business Week,* June 1, 1992. "German Manufacturers Try 'Made in the USA' " and "Giddy about Plant," *USA Today,* June 24, 1992, sec. B, 1. "Why Foreigners Flock to South Carolina," *Fortune,* November 2, 1992, 48. "Workers Trained to Order—At State Expense," *Business Week,* September 27, 1993, 102.

ply. They can safely expect customers to travel some distance, however, if they provide a specialty service that is in short supply.

Customer contact proves to be another interesting perspective from which to examine location decisions. Different services have varying degrees of customer contact. The location of back-office activities, those that do not require customer involvement, can be separated from high customer contact activities and can be located elsewhere. For example, a software developer can operate from a back-office site, while sending field representatives to the customer site. Pulling back-office activities away from the customers to a less expensive site often provides an opportunity to reduce fixed and variable costs.

LEVELS OF LOCATION DECISIONS

Both manufacturers and services typically progress through several decision levels before they choose where to locate. It is common for this progression of decisions to start with the selection of the region of the country or even a specific country, if international locations

OPERATIONS OUTLOOK

BOX 11.4

Location May Indeed Be Everything

The parent companies of the businesses listed below have described the characteristics of their biggest or highest volume outlets. In many cases the outlet's location is a major reason behind its success. Notice the variety of factors that contribute to successful locations.

Source "Location, Luck, Service Can Make a Store Top Star," *Wall Street Journal*, February 1, 1993, sec. B, 1.

Store	Biggest Location	Characteristics
Amoco Gasoline	Whiting, Indiana	Located on Illinois/Indiana border, taking advantage of a \$.13 per gallon tax difference Sometimes needs three tanker deliveries per day
Florsheim Shoes	New York City	Herald Square, across from Macy's Serves 28,000–30,000 patrons per year
Wal-Mart	Laredo, Texas	U.S./Mexico border Over 151,000 square feet (three football fields) 350 associates
Chevrolet Automobiles	Ed Morse Chevrolet Lauderhill, Florida	Fleet sales to Alamo and Avis Over 100,000 cars sold in 1992 50 sales people Averages 600 Chevrolets on the lot
Hertz Rent-A-Car	Los Angeles International Airport	West Coast's busiest airport Averages 2,000 rentals per day 36 acres of parking lots and maintenance facilities
Domino's Pizza	U.S. Marine Corps base near Twenty-Nine Palms, California	Only on-base pizza parlor for 11,000 marines and their families Often sells 4,000 pizzas per week 1991 post–Desert Storm sales of over \$1 million
Baskin-Robbins	Royal Hawaiian Shopping Center Honolulu, Hawaii	Year-round warm weather Only food outlet in the Honolulu mall 1992 annual gross of \$925,000
Radio Shack	Dadeland Mall Miami, Floria	Many sales to Puerto Rico and other offshore destinations High volumes and generous commissions, which attract good employees
Lexus Automobiles	Margate, Florida	Palm Beach high-income area 1992 sales of nearly 2,200 Often runs out of cars each month 22-Bay service center open until midnight
McDonald's	Darien, Connecticut	On I-95 near New York/Connecticut border Serves nearly 3 million customers per year Averages 8,000 meals per day 19 cash registers, 12-foot fry grill, 32 phones

Valley Bancorporation brings the convenience of full-service banking to consumers when and where they shop, 7 days a week. Its supermarket banking branches are open 60 hours a week, rather than the standard 45 hours for a bank.

Source Courtesy of Valley Bancorporation, headquartered in Appleton, Wisconsin.

are considered. Once the region is decided, a more local decision on the community must be reached, and this is typically followed by a decision on the actual site. But this progression is not universal: There are often exceptions. For example, suppose a company wishes to purchase a warehouse. If the company is simply looking for a 3-acre site on which to build a new warehouse, the decision-making process would probably proceed through the typical series of levels. But if it wishes to purchase an existing warehouse of approximately 100,000 square feet, with rail access, this site issue would probably be considered simultaneously with the community decision because of the limited number of options.

CRITERIA FOR LOCATION DECISIONS

Regional criteria include such issues as proximity to markets, nearness to raw materials or other inputs, climate, tax issues and incentives, transportation costs for inputs and for outputs, labor climate, and availability of work force skills. Regional decisions are often dominated by economic concerns. Community criteria include such cost issues as local taxes, local business climate, and by-product waste disposal. In addition, community choices may include such subjective criteria as quality-of-life issues and community support.

Site criteria include such specific issues as utility costs, zoning requirements, traffic patterns, availability of transportation (expressways, railroads, airports), fire protection,

TABLE 11.2	**Important Relocation Criteria**

Factors	Level
Regulatory environment	Regional, community
Cost of labor	Regional, community
Community image	Community
Tax climate	Regional, community
Utility availability	Community, site
Cost of real estate	Regional, community, site
Access to markets	Regional, community
Utility costs	Regional, community
Quality-of-life issues	Regional, community
Business services/technical support	Regional, community
Incentives	Regional, community
Education system/training infrastructure	Community
Labor force issues	Regional, community
Transportation issues	Community, site
Availability of real estate	Community
Proximity to suppliers of raw materials	Regional, community
University resources	Community

and potential for future expansion. These issues are related to costs as well as to such other criteria as safety and government regulations.

Although the relative significance of individual criteria depends on the situation, it is common to find a number of factors that are consistently considered to be important decision-making criteria. Table 11.2 presents a summary of factors, at both the regional and community level, that are important in relocation decisions.

INTERNATIONAL LOCATION DECISIONS

For many U.S. citizens, the swell of nationalism of the early 1990s, immediately following the U.S. military involvement in the Persian Gulf, engendered a strong desire to "buy American." However, many individuals came to realize that it was not easy to identify what was actually manufactured in the United States and what wasn't. Some automobiles purchased from U.S. manufacturers were built in another country. Some automobiles purchased from Japanese manufacturers were made completely in this country. That means a Mercury Tracer may have been built in Mexico, while a Nissan may have been manufactured in Smyrna, Tennessee.

As U.S. businesses have been forced to recognize that their competition and their markets extend beyond U.S. borders, they have realized that resources are also available outside their own country.

The role U.S. businesses play in the global market has shifted dramatically since the mid-1970s. This change can be attributed to the increasing number of imports into U.S. markets, the increase in foreign-owned capacity in the United States, and the increase in foreign competition in almost every industry. Outside of the borders of the United States the shift in the role of U.S. business can be attributed to a reduction in the U.S. share of the

Baxter International Inc. is expanding rapidly in international markets with high market-growth potential. In 1993, Baxter opened this surgical-instruments manufacturing plant in Russia, where only one-third of the demand for these products is being met currently. Baxter believes that markets outside the United States will account for more than a third of its revenue by the year 2000.

Source Courtesy of Baxter International Inc. © Robert Wallis/SABA.

global gross domestic product (from 40 percent in 1965 to 30 percent in 1987.)[11] During the same two-decade period, the growth rate of private consumption outside the United States exceeded that within this country. In many developing markets, projected rates of market growth far exceed those of the United States.

Many manufacturers have found that as product life cycles have become shorter, the need to speed products to market has become more critical. The need to simultaneously introduce new products globally has resulted in a requirement to locate facilities throughout the world.

Many U.S. manufacturers have discovered that for some operations, particularly those that are labor intensive and not requiring high skill levels, work can be done more economically in other countries. Unfortunately, many manufacturers have also realized that cheaper labor does not necessarily result in lower total costs, particularly when high levels of turnover or low product quality reduce productivity levels. (See Box 11.5.) Strategies based on low labor costs are not likely to be successful, primarily because labor costs make up such a small portion of total costs. In most industries it accounts for less than 15 percent, and in high-tech industries it rarely exceeds 10 percent and is often under 5 percent.[12]

For manufacturers and some services, locations for new facilities or relocation of current operations will likely include international alternatives. While advantages of locating in another country may be obvious, disadvantages may be more difficult to foresee. Because of the higher initial costs associated with a location outside of the United States, the decision is even more critical and mistakes are potentially more costly. Many issues related

---

[11]National Research Council, *The Internationalization of U.S. Manufacturing: Causes and Consequences* (Washington, D.C.: National Academy Press, 1990).

[12]National Research Council.

OPERATIONS OUTLOOK

BOX 11.5

Moving South and Moving North

With the passage of the North American Free Trade Agreement (NAFTA), there has been great speculation about the mass movement of U.S. manufacturers to Mexico. The full impact of NAFTA will not be known for quite some time, but some things that have already occurred may be surprising.

Quality Coils is a manufacturer of electromagnetic coils. In 1989 CEO Keith Gibson shut down a Quality Coils factory in Connecticut and opened one in Ciudad Juarez, on the Mexican side of the U.S.–Mexican border. He knew he would have to pay Mexican workers only one-third as much as their U.S. counterparts. Quality Coils contracted with a company that supplied laborers at a rate of $3.35 per hour, as well as providing factory space and utilities. All signs pointed to an extremely profitable operation.

Despite the expectations, Quality Coils consistently lost money in Mexico because of high absenteeism, low productivity, and problems with long-distance management. Further investigation of the Mexican plant showed that employees increased production rates when they were being observed, but their production fell as soon as close monitoring stopped. Turnover was high because many Mexican workers traveled long distances to work in the plant and became homesick.

Quality Coils also started having trouble meeting customers' expectations. To keep inventories low, customers expected quick response in filling small orders on a wide variety of products. Unfortunately, the Mexican operation never developed the flexibility required to produce in short production runs (small batches). Shipments of components bound for the Mexican plant would often be delayed at the border for weeks. According to Ned Dougherty, president of Pentex Enterprises (the company that set up Quality Coil's Juarez facility), materials supply problems made short-run production practices, an important component of just-in-time manufacturing, unmanageable in Mexico.

In April 1993 the Juarez operation was moved back to Stonington, Connecticut. Gibson learned that it took three workers in Mexico to accomplish what one worker could do in Connecticut. With salaries at the Juarez operation due to go up to $5.38 Gibson decided that it would be advantageous to move the plant back because Connecticut workers made less than three times the $5.38 wage of Mexican workers.

Many manufacturers have discoverd that wage levels are only one of many issues to consider when making an international relocation decision. The level of worker skills, the availability and quality of transportation, and the access to necessary technology also must be considered.

Some companies have closed down Mexican plants for other reasons. McIlhenny Co. located a Tabasco sauce factory in Mexico City in the 1950s to avoid the tariffs and regulations that blocked imports into Mexico from the United States. As those tariffs and regulations were lifted in the 1980s, the need for the Mexican location disappeared. McIlhenny closed its Mexico City plant in 1989 and expanded its Louisiana operation. Tabasco sauce could be bottled four times faster in the Louisiana plant than the Mexico City plant, and the company could maintain better quality control in Louisiana.

Haworth Inc., a Holland, Michigan, office-furniture manufacturer has evaluated the costs of producing in Mexico twice and has concluded both times that it can produce at lower costs in Michigan for the Mexican market. The company calculated that even if Mexican labor only cost $1 per hour, total costs would still be 25 percent less in Michigan. Haworth also examined the possibility of purchasing electronic components from a supplier that manufactured them in Mexico. The manufacturer opted to produce the components in-house in Michigan because it could save 20 percent and have a 3-day lead time rather than a lead time of two weeks. The reduced lead time contributed to lower inventory levels.

NAFTA has had an impact on companies south of the border as well. A significant number of Mexican businesses have started expanding into the United States. For example, a new Elasticos Selectos plant is expected to create 400 jobs in McAllen and Garland, Texas, will get an additional 400 jobs from a tile plant. Other transplants include candy, tortilla, apparel, steel, tire, cement, and auto manufacturers, as well as banks, broadcasters, and resorts.

Sources "Some U.S. Firms Find Mexico No Bargain," *The Wall Street Journal,* September 15, 1993, sec. A, 1, 16. "Some Mexicans Charge North in Nafta's Wake," *The Wall Street Journal,* February 22, 1994, sec. B, 1, 14.

to operations management are affected by globalization. Because these issues affect all aspects of operations management, their implications must be considered part of the location decision.

Political factors have also resulted in pressures for U.S. businesses to globalize and for foreign firms to increase their presence in the United States. The impact of the North American Free Trade Agreement will certainly increase these trends, but to what extent is still unclear. Eastern Europe and the former Soviet Union present examples of markets that are now open and have potential for rapid growth.

Changes in economic conditions, political relationships, and technological capabilities have resulted in a business climate that forces all companies to consider other countries as a marketplace, as possible location sites, and as the home of some of their competitors.

MAKING THE BEST LOCATION DECISION

Recall that because of the huge number of options available to a company in the midst of a location decision, the field of alternatives is typically narrowed to a reasonable number. A more detailed analysis is then performed on this short list. The actual location decision is often the result of qualitative analysis and judgment as well as quantitative analysis. The importance that firms place on qualitative analysis versus such easily quantified factors as transportation costs or taxes varies because the priority of these issues differs from company to company and manager to manager. It can be safely said, however, that the result of the decision-making process is usually at least as much dependent on qualitative reasoning and judgment as it is on the use of quantitative analysis.

Most firms recognize that there is no optimal solution to most location problems. There are certainly some locations that will be better than others, however, and these should be identified. Several tools can be used to aid in the decision-making process. The linear programming (LP) method is an optimization approach. A quantitative technique, LP is used to minimize or maximize an objective within specifically stated constraints. Linear programming will not be covered in this text, but is typically included in introductory management science courses. Three other approaches—the factor rating approach, decision trees, and break-even analysis—are often helpful in narrowing the field down to a manageable short list and selecting one best location from that list.

It is important to recognize that competitive priorities must be closely linked to the decisions that result in a short list as well as in the final location decision.

THE FACTOR RATING APPROACH

FACTOR RATING
An approach to evaluating location decisions that includes both qualitative and quantitative inputs.

The **factor rating** approach provides a means of converting qualitative information to quantitative information to help the decision maker reach a conclusion more objectively. The factor rating approach involves a four-step process. First, all relevant factors must be identified and given a rating of importance. This importance rating, or weight, should reflect the relative importance of that factor compared to all of the other factors. The sum of all of the importance ratings must equal 1.00. Second, for each alternative location, each factor must be scored, typically on a scale of 1 to 100, with 100 going to the best site and appropriate lower scores going to the others. For each location alternative, each factor's score is then multiplied by the factor's weight. These products are then summed to yield a total score for each location. The highest scoring location is the one that best satisfies the criteria.

This process is essentially a weighted average of the scores. It must be stressed that just because it is a quantitative approach to decision making, it is not necessarily objective.

The weights given to the factors play a key role in determining the outcome of this process, and biases may affect what weights are given. If the decision is going to be made by a group or project team, the weights can be created as an average to reduce individual bias. The weights must be consistent with the goals of the organization.

To create weights, simply collect, from each team member, weights that they feel accurately reflect the level of importance of each factor, based on the firm's goals. The average of these weights, for each factor, can then be used as the factor weight. If the decision is not being made by a group, an individual simply assigns appropriate weights to each factor. Example 11.1 demonstrates the use of the factor rating process in identifying a solution to a location problem.

EXAMPLE 11.1

Using the Factor Rating Method in Location Decision

Brumlee's Waste Disposal is in the process of designing a new recycling center. The site location team is made up of four managers who have reduced the number of alternative sites to a short list of four 2-acre sites that do not conflict with zoning regulations. The team identified the following factors as important considerations in deciding on the site of the new recycling center:

1. Lack of traffic congestion problems and ease of truck entry and exit
2. Nearness to the center of the company's pickup area
3. Nearness to the truck maintenance center
4. Cost of the land plus utility hook-up costs

In a secret ballot procedure each manager proposed the weights for each factor, and these weights were then averaged. The factors and average weights are presented in Table 11.3.

SOLUTION

Using a 1- to 100-point scoring system, the team reached consensus on a score on each factor for each site. The weighted factor scores for each site were then obtained by multiplying the factor weight averages by the appropriate factor scores. The four weighted factor scores for each site were summed to obtain the composite score. The composite scores

TABLE 11.3	Factor Weight Results

	Factor Weights			
	Traffic	**Centrality**	**Maintenance**	**Site Costs**
Manager A	0.4	0.2	0.2	0.2
Manager B	0.3	0.1	0.3	0.3
Manager C	0.5	0.2	0.2	0.1
Manager D	0.4	0.1	0.3	0.2
Factor Weight Averages	0.4	0.15	0.25	0.2

TABLE 11.4	Factor Scores			

	Consensus Factor Scores			
	Traffic	**Centrality**	**Maintenance**	**Site Costs**
Site #1	100	80	40	60
Site #2	90	100	60	40
Site #3	50	30	30	100
Site #4	70	60	100	80

TABLE 11.5	Weighted Factor Scores and Composite Scores				

	Weighted Factor Scores				
	Traffic	**Centrality**	**Maintenance**	**Site Cost**	**Composite**
Site #1	40.0	12.0	10.0	12.0	74.0
Site #2	36.0	15.0	15.0	8.0	74.0
Site #3	20.0	4.5	7.5	20.0	52.0
Site #4	28.0	9.0	25.0	16.0	78.0

were then compared to each other to determine the most desirable site. Tables 11.4 and 11.5 show the results of this process.

Again, caution should be used. Even though factor rating is a quantitative technique, it is not necessarily objective. Objectivity in establishing weights cannot be assumed. Great care must be taken to ensure the weights accurately reflect the firm's strategic objectives.

THE DECISION TREE APPROACH

DECISION TREE
Diagram that provides a structured approach to decision making that incorporates uncertainty of outcome and expected revenues.

A **decision tree** is a diagram that provides an effective way to organize and analyze a problem that involves a sequence of decisions with uncertain outcomes and expected revenues. This type of approach to a location problem is useful because a significant degree of uncertainty affects the measure of success of the decision in the final analysis. Uncertainty typically exists in the expected sales at a new location or the expected increase in sales at a current location. In addition, expansion alternatives, which are usually linked to location decisions, are often examined in phases. These sequential events fit nicely with decision tree logic. The decision tree allows for the development of an expected value for revenues, based on estimates of the probability that certain events will occur. Example 11.2 illustrates the use of a decision tree in a location problem.

EXAMPLE 11.2

Dennise Schlegel, the owner of Schlegel's Bagels, has a dilemma. Dennise opened her shop 7 years ago, and business has been good except for a rough first year of operation. Her shop is on the fringe of an area that is growing rapidly and is expecting another major development within the next year. Unfortunately, she has lost her lease on this site. She has identified two possible sites for locating within new development areas. Site A will entail an initial cost of $80,000. It is not big enough to handle demand that may exist in the future, but it could be expanded at a cost of $75,000 if the demand materializes. Site B is large enough to handle any future demand. It will cost $130,000 up front, but will never need an expansion. Dennise wishes to use a decision tree to help in making her decision and is assuming the following.

An Application of Decision Trees in a Location Decision

1. The initial cost of Site A is $80,000. If demand is high, which she estimates to have a probability of 0.6, and Site A is not expanded, she estimates her yearly revenue to be $80,000. If demand is high and Site A is expanded, an additional $90,000 per year could be generated. If demand is low, which she thinks has a likelihood of 0.4, her expected revenue would be $80,000.
2. Site B will cost $130,000 initially. With a high demand (likelihood of 0.6), she expects revenues of $180,000 per year. With a low demand (probability of 0.4), she expects revenues of only $70,000 per year.

FIGURE 11.2   **Decision Tree for Schlegel's Bagels**

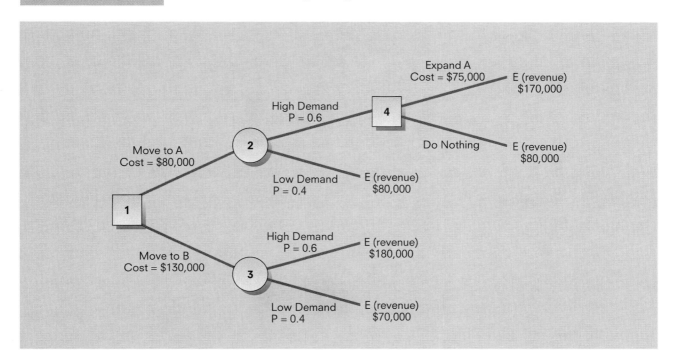

SOLUTION

Figure 11.2 presents the decision tree for this problem. Each intersection of branches represents a decision point (a box node) or a chance occurrence (a circle node). Notice that there are two decision points (nodes 1 and 4) and two chance events (nodes 2 and 3).

To solve the decision tree, start at the final outcome, or the "leaves," and work from right to left back to the first node or "trunk" of the tree. First determine the best decision to make in the second decision (node 4) by calculating the return for each possible alternative. The revenue generated by expanding Site A is

$$\$170,000 - \$75,000 = \$95,000$$

and the revenue generated by doing nothing is $80,000. Because expansion has a higher expected value, it would be chosen. The Do Nothing alternative would be pruned from the decision tree.

The next step is to determine the expected values for moving to Site A or Site B. The expected values of chance occurrences are calculated by summing the products of the probabilities and the expected values branching from each circle node. That means the expected value of moving to Site A is calculated by summing the products of the demand probabilities and the expected revenues for each demand, as shown below:

$$(0.6 \times \$95,000) + (0.4 \times \$80,000) = \$57,000 + \$32,000 = \$89,000$$

To determine the expected value of moving to Site A, subtract the $80,000 initial cost:

$$\$89,000 - \$80,000 = \$9,000$$

To calculate the expected value of moving to Site B, sum the products of the probabilities of the demands multiplied by the expected revenues.

$$(0.6 \times \$180,000) + (0.4 \times \$70,000) = \$108,000 + \$28,000 = \$136,000$$

The expected value would be

$$\$136,000 - \$130,000 = \$6,000$$

Moving to Site A has a higher expected value.

Caution should be used when relying on the outcomes of decision trees. Heavy reliance on the computed value for expected revenue is somewhat risky and should serve as only one of several criteria in the decision-making process. Demand projections are, after all, forecasts: The fact that the probabilities yield an expected revenue of a certain amount does not mean that the expectations will be borne out. If it were possible for the same scenario to repeat itself 100 times, very likely the average amount of revenue would be quite close to the expected revenue.

BREAKEVEN ANALYSIS
Technique for evaluating several alternatives by determining the total cost of each and deciding on the basis of cost.

THE BREAKEVEN ANALYSIS APPROACH

Breakeven analysis is a frequently used technique for evaluating and deciding among several alternatives. Alternatives to a particular decision may result in different costs. For each alternative there will be both fixed and variable costs and, possibly, differences in revenues.

Because of the different costs of the various alternatives, one alternative may result in lower total costs at one production or service volume, but another alternative may result in lower costs at another volume. By plotting the total cost curve for each alternative, and comparing the total costs of each alternative at the forecasted number of units or volume of service at the new facility, a comparison can be made that aids in the location selection. Example 11.3 demonstrates this technique.

EXAMPLE 11.3

An Application of Locational Breakeven Analysis

Suppose there are four possible alternatives for expanding a business in order to increase capacity. Three call for relocating the business at different sites, and one calls for expanding the current site. The four options have construction costs. These costs are fixed and unrelated to the volume of output. Because of the different locations and resultant differences in labor costs and costs to transport raw materials, variable costs also differ among the alternatives. The fixed and variable costs are presented in Table 11.6.

The total cost curves for each of the alternatives are assumed to be linear and can be created by using the basic formula for a line:

$$y = a + bn$$

where a is the Y intercept (total fixed costs), b is the slope (total variable cost per unit), n is the number of units produced, and y is the total cost for producing n units.

TABLE 11.6   **Fixed and Variable Costs**

Site	Fixed Costs	Labor/ Unit	Materials/ Unit	Total Variable Cost per Unit
A	$435,000	$ 6.50	$6.30	$12.80
B	$396,000	$ 9.00	$8.00	$17.00
C	$420,000	$10.20	$7.50	$17.70
Expand	$388,000	$14.00	$6.60	$20.60

TABLE 11.7   **Total Cost Curve Formulas**

Site	Total Cost Curve Equation
A	$y = 435{,}000 + 12.8n$
B	$y = 396{,}000 + 17n$
C	$y = 420{,}000 + 17.7n$
Expand	$y = 388{,}000 + 20.6n$

| FIGURE 11.3 | **Graph of Total Cost Curves** |

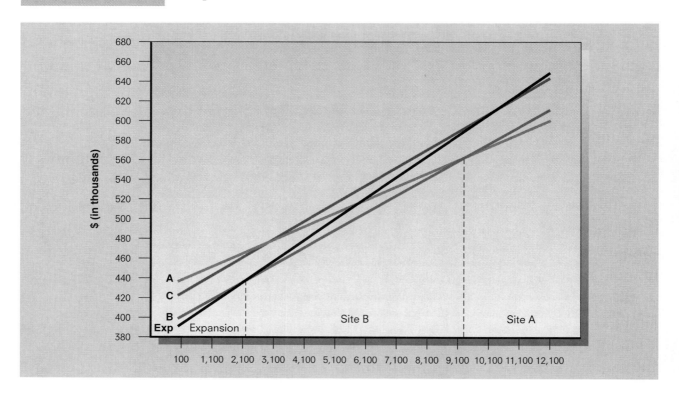

| TABLE 11.8 | **Calculations of Intersection of Total Cost Curves** |

Intersection for Site B and the expansion alternative:

$$396,000 + 17n = 388,000 + 20.6n$$
$$8,000 + 17n = 20.6n$$
$$8,000 = 3.6n$$
$$2,222.22 = n$$

Intersection for Site A and Site B:

$$435,000 + 12.8n = 396,000 + 17n$$
$$39,000 + 12.8n = 17n$$
$$39,000 = 4.2n$$
$$9,285.71 = n$$

The formulas for the total cost curves of each alternative are presented in Table 11.7. The breakeven analysis can be done in two steps. First, the intersections of the total cost curves can be identified graphically by identifying two points to determine the line described by each equation. The lines can then be drawn, as in Figure 11.3. The figure shows that expansion offers the lowest total costs for volumes under approximately 2,200. For volumes of approximately 2,200 to 9,300, site B offers the lowest total costs. For volumes greater than 9,300, site A offers the lowest total costs.

The identification of the exact points of intersection of the total cost curves can be determined by setting the appropriate pairs of cost curves equal to each other, and solving for n, as is done in Table 11.8.

Based on these results, if volumes are projected to be less than 2,222, expansion of the current site would be the best alternative. For volumes between 2,222 and 9,285, site B would present the best alternative. For volumes greater than 9,286, the best choice would be Site A. Site C is not a low-cost alternative at any volume.

In some applications, the expected revenues would differ from one site to another, so rather than graphing just cost curves, costs would be subtracted from revenues.

It is appropriate to identify three cautions for this technique. First, the projected volume is a forecast. As has been stated previously, forecasts are frequently wrong. There would always be a chance that the decision was based on a projected volume that was too high or too low. For this reason, it is beneficial to identify a likely range of volume for comparison. Second, this technique does not allow for the introduction of uncertainty into the problem. There is often uncertainty in fixed and variable cost estimates, as well as forecasts of volumes of products or services. Third, this approach assumes that the relationships between costs and volumes are linear. In fact, the cost per unit often changes as the volumes increase. This can be the result of changes in labor content of each unit, resulting from learning curve effects, or changes in the cost of materials for each unit because of quantity discounts offered by suppliers. Nevertheless, break-even analysis often provides another piece of useful information for solving the complex location problem.

TECHNOLOGICAL INFLUENCES

Many manufacturers and services realize that the location of a facility does not necessarily place limits on the location of its employees. In almost every industry and for many positions, workers are able to fulfill responsibilities at home, by using information technologies such as a personal computer and a modem. As a result, workers are not bound to live near their place of employment. It has also improved the ability of managers in isolated locations to communicate more directly with peers and supervisors. The improved level and accuracy of communication technologies have had a dramatic impact on many fields. (See Box 11.6.)

LOCATION DECISION CROSS-LINKS

For manufacturers and services, location decisions have significant financial implications particularly during the decision-making process. The investment in an expanded or new facility is probably one of the biggest investments a firm will make. This decision must be

OPERATIONS OUTLOOK

BOX 11.6

Musicians Don't Need to Be Present for Concerts

Many industries are increasingly relying on technology to eliminate the barriers created by distance. The music industry is a prime example.

In May 1993, Graham Nash, formerly of Crosby, Stills, and Nash, played the piano at his home in Hawaii for a concert in a San Francisco auditorium, while his duet partner appeared on stage. The two were linked by new telephone technology that can transmit sound with the quality of a CD. The same technology is now used in the recording industry. Musicians no longer have to travel to studios and can more easily collaborate with other musicians.

Source S. Shellenbarger, "Some Thrive, but Many Wilt Working at Home," *The Wall Street Journal,* December 14, 1993, sec. B, 1, 16.

closely linked to financial considerations such as tax implications and facility and capital equipment purchases.

Whenever a firm plans a new facility it has an opportunity to improve technologies. Decisions related to technology changes should be made in close consultation with engineering as well as with market research staff who have a good idea of future product innovation requirements.

In manufacturing and to an even greater degree in services, the location decision has significant impact on the marketing function. Because services cannot be stored and transported, location is probably the most important marketing decision. It is important to involve marketing in this decision so that issues such as population demographics can be included in the selection of a location.

Since location affects the cost of system inputs, particularly purchased raw materials, it will greatly influence the bargaining power of the purchasing function. It also will establish the extent to which purchasing and traffic control staff will be able to negotiate and control transportation costs for raw materials and finished products.

Another key system input affected by location is the availability of specifically trained workers. This factor, along with the labor climate, will affect the human resources function significantly, including hiring, training, and labor/management relations efforts.

SUMMARY

For manufacturers and services, the location of facilities controls such important competitive aspects as price, dependability of delivery, flexibility, and time, all crucial capabilities in today's business environment. Because of the expense required to relocate, the location decision is one of the most crucial and, to a great extent, irreversible decisions top management can make. As time-based competition and customer service become more important, the location decision can be expected to become even more critical.

RANCH HOUSE STEAKS REVISITED

CROSS-LINKS At the next week's meeting, the Ranch House Steaks staff examined the list of ten suggested cities. How would you recommend that the group move from the ten nominated cities to a short list of four? What criteria should they use to eliminate or select from the list? In your opinion, what criteria have been left out?

The expansion into the United Kingdom has many potential problems. Identify the issues that must be considered in the expansion. Some initial questions might include the following: Will the concept work abroad? Will the menu transfer successfully? How can these and other questions be addressed?

Suppose Ranch House decides to open three restaurants—one each in Atlanta, Orlando, and Nashville—and possibly expand into the Southeast in the future. Where should they locate the headquarters? How might this decision be made?

QUESTIONS FOR REVIEW

1. What competitive capabilities are influenced by a facility location decision? How are these capabilities affected?
2. What are the differences between input driven and customer-driven location decisions?
3. What are some examples of inputs that must be considered in location decisions?
4. Describe location criteria related to region, community, and site.

5. What issues must be considered when examining a relocation to another country?
6. What are the potential biases of using factor rating to aid in location decisions?
7. What are the weaknesses of relying too heavily on the results of decision trees?
8. Describe the three weaknesses of break-even analysis.

QUESTIONS FOR THOUGHT AND DISCUSSION

1. Identify a successful service business in your community. What role does location play in the business's success?
2. Identify a business that has, in your opinion, failed because of a poor location decision. Evaluate the location chosen.
3. Identify, for your community, excellent locations for the following businesses: a cookie shop; a 20-minute oil change shop; an automatic teller machine (ATM); and a remote sack lunch pickup window for university food service meal ticket holders. Explain why your chosen location is preferable to others.

INTEGRATIVE QUESTIONS

1. What effect has JIT had on location decisions?
2. Describe the effect location decisions have on competitive priorities.
3. Compare how location affects value for manufacturers and services.

4. How can location be used as a resource to combine with others and form competitive capabilities?
5. How can location be used to enhance quality for services and manufacturing?
6. Can location of a facility be a constraint? If so, how?

PROBLEMS

1. The post office of a small town in Iowa currently consists of approximately 25 mail boxes grouped together under a little awning. The town council has decided to relocate the post office based on the results of a factor rating process. Four sites have been evaluated on the basis of three criteria. Which site should be chosen?

Criteria	Weight
1. Nearness to the center of town	0.4
2. Nearness to the rural mail carriers current delivery route	0.1
3. Absence of traffic that would make it difficult to pick up mail	0.5

Scores for each site, as assigned by town council

	Site			
Criteria	A	B	C	D
1	70	50	90	40
2	55	70	100	90
3	40	80	65	40

2. Brittany Westmore, owner of Pets Unlimited, has lost her lease and is evaluating four potential locations. All are suitable in terms of size, parking availability, and layout. She wishes to use a factor rating approach to aid in the decision-making process. She has identified the following factors on which the sites differ and has assigned a rating to each.

Criteria	Weight
1. Passing traffic	0.3
2. Aesthetics of the building	0.1
3. Rent	0.2
4. Nearness of competition	0.4

Brittany has scored each of the four sites on each factor:

	Site			
Criteria	A	B	C	D
Passing traffic	80	65	90	75
Aesthetics of the building	90	80	50	65
Rent	80	80	70	100
Nearness of competition	30	80	90	85

Which site should be selected?

3. Philip Engough, owner of Sudsy's Gas and Car Wash, has decided to expand his business by adding a new location. Three sites are currently available. He has described the potential of each site as follows:

Site A

Cost: $320,000

High revenue potential: $160,000 per year for 4 years, probability 0.7

Low revenue potential: $84,000 per year for 4 years, probability 0.3

Site B

Cost: $320,000

High revenue potential: $210,000 per year for 4 years, probability 0.4

Low revenue potential: $95,000 per year for 4 years, probability 0.6

Site C

Cost: $75,000

High revenue potential: $100,000 per year for 4 years, probability 0.3

Low revenue potential: $50,000 per year for 4 years, probability 0.7

Using a decision tree, evaluate the expected return over the 4-year period. Ignore the time value of money. Which site should be chosen?

4. Using a decision tree, evaluate three alternative locations that are described as follows:

Site A

Cost: $320,000

High revenue potential: $120,000 per year for 4 years, probability 0.65

Low revenue potential: $96,000 per year for 4 years, probability 0.35

Site B

Cost: $320,000

High revenue potential: $150,000 per year for 4 years, probability 0.55

Low revenue potential: $125,000 per year for 4 years, probability 0.45

Site C

Cost: $290,000

High revenue potential: $145,000 per year for 4 years, probability 0.3

Low revenue potential: $110,000 per year for 4 years, probability 0.7

5. Pierre, owner of Pierre's Hockey Supply, is being evicted because he refused to pay his rent when he was informed of a rent increase. Pierre has two options. Site A is a small shop near the ice arena that can be bought cheaply but will need to be expanded if demand reaches Pierre's expectations. Site B is more expensive but is large enough to accommodate future demand. Pierre plans to go back to the Yukon in 4 years, so he is interested in choosing the site with the best 4-year return. Ignore the time value of money.

Site A
Initial cost: $60,000

Expansion cost: $110,000

High demand (probability = 0.7): $120,000 per year expanded; $80,000 not expanded

Low demand (probability = 0.3): $70,000 per year

Site B
Initial cost: $135,000

High demand (probability = 0.7): $155,000

Low demand (probability = 0.3): $110,000

6. Using locational breakeven analysis, evaluate the following four alternatives for a small factory location. Graph the total cost curves. Then, identify the precise ranges of volumes for the sites with the lowest total costs.

Site	Fixed Costs	Variable Costs per Unit
A	$345,000	$10.15
B	$323,000	$12.50
C	$310,000	$17.70
D	$395,000	$15.40

7. Stanley McConnell's precast concrete company manufactures various concrete products including end stops for parking spaces, feed bunkers for cattle, and slatted floor units for swine confinement buildings. He has identified four possible sites for an additional plant in a new geographic region. Given the projected costs shown here for each site, graph the total cost curves and identify the ranges of volumes for the sites with the lowest total costs.

Site	Fixed Costs	Labor/Unit	Materials per Unit
A	$222,000	$3.20	$5.40
B	$246,000	$4.50	$5.50
C	$230,000	$3.10	$4.16
D	$255,000	$1.80	$3.22

SUGGESTED READINGS

Schmenner, R. W. *Making Business Location Decisions.* Englewood Cliffs, N.J.: Prentice-Hall, 1982.

Upon completing this chapter, you should be able to explain

- what the general strategic alternatives for facility layout are and how their competitive strengths and weaknesses compare
- which competitive criteria are important in facility layout decisions
- how to use line balancing to maximize efficiency in product-oriented layouts
- how to incorporate the cut-and-try approach to minimizing material-handling costs and the simplified systematic layout planning (SSLP) approach to solving process-oriented layout problems
- what the linkages between layout decisions and other business functions are

CHAPTER 12

PLANNING FACILITY LAYOUTS

CROSS-LINKS

Tensile Products: Excess Capacity, but Poor Performance

Tensile Products manufactures two product lines that use similar processes but are for distinctly different markets. A number of problems, which seem to have their roots in the facility layout, have caused Drew Durham, manager of manufacturing engineering, and Brian Wilcox, operations manager, to consider major layout changes. ■ One product line is a variety of point-of-sale (POS) racks used by retailers to display snack items, magazines, and other impulse items sold near their cash registers. Most racks are manufactured to the specifications of the retail chain ordering them. Business in this market is booming as a result of the major refurbishing of a number of large department and discount store chains. The racks are made of heavy-gauge steel wire that is formed, welded, and coated with plastic. ■ The second product line consists of six models of crates that are made to stock and sold to several pet store chains. Like the POS racks, the pet crates are also manufactured from heavy-gauge steel wire that is formed and welded. Although the crates are not coated in plastic, they do require a metal-formed tray that is fitted into the bottom and some hardware for the door. These components are purchased from an outside vendor and assembled with the formed and welded crate. ■ Drew and Brian met early one morning to try to summarize the current problems. ■ "As I see it," began Drew, "one of our biggest problems is increasing production lead times. Lead times for POS racks have been getting longer and longer as queues in the form-

ing and welding departments lengthen. Lead times for pet crates are getting longer, too. The increased batch size means it takes longer for a line to cycle through the six crate models. When we get an order, it can sometimes be several weeks before we manufacture the model again. If stocks are low, we can't provide good delivery promises." ■ "I agree," responded Brian. "But what makes it look even worse is that our equipment utilizations are not very high. We've got redundant capacity in a lot of places, but we can't produce as much or as quickly as we need to. It seems that when we're short on welding capacity for POS displays, it is available over on crate lines. Unfortunately, the permanent fixtures prevent us from setting it up for use. The same thing happens in forming." ■ After a short pause, Drew summarized, "As things stand right now, we have enough capacity, but it's not flexible enough to allow us to use it where we need it. We're also having problems with queue lengths and long production runs resulting from long changeovers. It seems to me that one way to improve this situation is to take a completely different look at the way the equipment is organized. We've currently separated the plant into two distinct parts, one for POS displays and one for crates. Many of the processes are the same and, in fact, can be done on the same equipment. With the exception of the plastic coating department, the two separate parts of the plant are essentially the same." ■ "Drew, I agree completely, but I really don't know where to start," replied Brian. ■

FACILITY LAYOUT DECISIONS

Facility layout decisions, like location decisions, involve both long- and medium-term commitments, but they are seldom as difficult or expensive to change as locations. Several types of layouts (first described in Chapters 2 and 3) are reviewed here.

MANUFACTURING

PRODUCT-ORIENTED LAYOUT
A flow shop in which equipment is arranged in the sequence it is used to produce a specific product.

A **product-oriented layout** is a flow shop in which dedicated equipment is arranged in the same sequence as the routing, or product flow. Typically, the machinery used in this layout is quite specialized and the workers perform the same tasks repetitively. This layout is predominantly used for manufacturing high volumes of products in environments where routings are fixed and customization is not desirable. Automobile assembly lines, for example, are frequently product-oriented layouts. Characterized by relatively low costs per unit, the product-oriented layout is designed to permit a firm to compete on the basis of price.

In Figure 12.1, we see an example of a product-oriented layout for EZSeat Manufacturing, Inc., which produces three models of upholstered chairs. Notice that each of the three flow lines is self-contained: Each line assembles just one model and all the resources to make that model are present on a single line.

FIGURE 12.1   **Product-Oriented Layout for Chair Manufacturing**

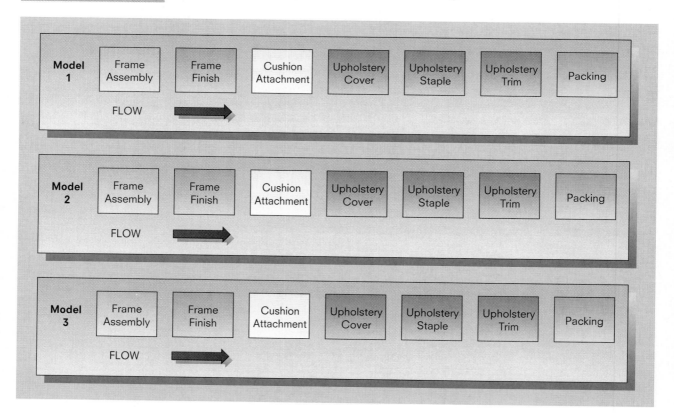

A **process-oriented layout** is a functional layout that can accommodate variable routings. In this type of layout, departments are created with dedicated functions, requiring that a product move from one to another to complete the routing steps. Compared to the product-oriented layout, the equipment used in this layout is typically more generalized, capable of the modifications required for customization, and the work force tends to be more highly skilled. Although manufacturers employing the process-oriented layout are not as efficient in producing high volumes of products, they are more capable of competing on the basis of flexibility.

Figure 12.2 shows a process-oriented layout for our chair manufacturer, EZSeat. Notice that all three chair models must go through a single functional department. Thus each department must have equipment that can be changed enough to accommodate the differences between the models, as well as workers trained to adapt their tasks to those differences.

Cellular manufacturing, which combines the advantages of product- and process-oriented layouts, has become increasingly popular in recent years. This type of layout requires the use of numerous small cells that contain all the machinery necessary to produce a family of products. The equipment used in this layout permits more customization than is possible in product-oriented layout because it is generally less narrow in function. It is also

PROCESS-ORIENTED LAYOUT
A layout in which equipment that performs similar functions is grouped together to facilitate varied processing requirements.

CELLULAR MANUFACTURING
A layout in which machinery is grouped into numerous small cells that can process a family of products.

FIGURE 12.2   **Process-Oriented Layout for Chair Manufacturing**

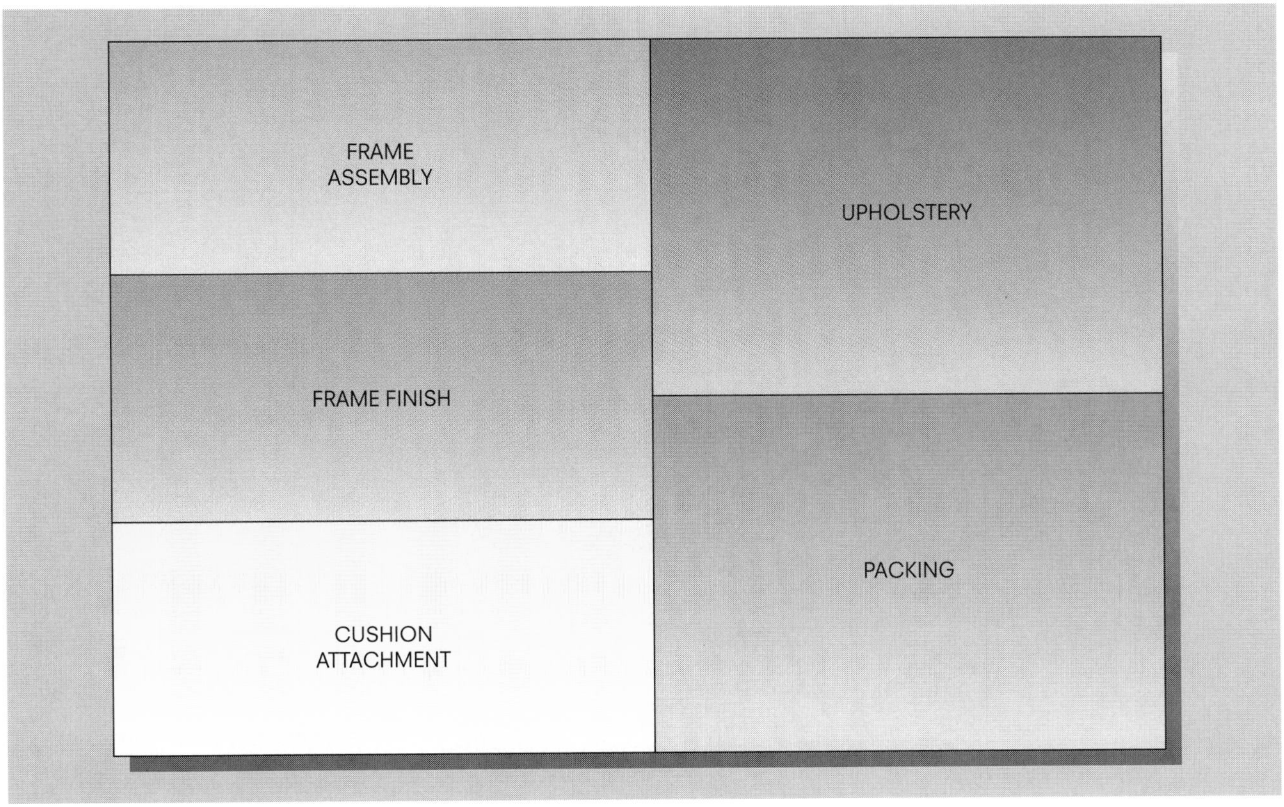

smaller in scale than that used in the process-oriented model, and the cellular arrangement eliminates the need to move material from one department to another.

Figure 12.3 shows a cellular layout for EZSeat. Notice the similarities between this layout and the product- and process-oriented layouts—each model is produced by one cell, which is functionally organized. The difference, however, is that the cells can produce products with variable routings, an advantage over product-oriented layouts. This can be accomplished without the material handling costs and long queues of the process-oriented layout.

One manufacturer that uses the cellular layout is the Fisher-Rosemont plant in Chanhassen, Minnesota. In this plant, teams of up to eight employees are positioned at work stations with all the parts necessary for assembly of modular transmitters. They work in a U-shaped cell that enables them to communicate with each other and respond quickly to production and material changes.[1] Many other manufacturers have been able to incorporate the use of cells for both high- and low-volume production when some flexibility is needed. Not surprisingly, however, changeover time becomes a factor when high variety and low volumes are involved. (See Box 12.1.)

FIXED-POSITION LAYOUT
An arrangement of equipment in which resources are brought to the product.

A fourth layout type, the **fixed-position layout,** is used in large-scale manufacturing when the product cannot be moved. In this type of layout, resources are brought to the

---

[1]Michael A. Verespej, "America's Best Plants: Fisher-Rosemont," *Industry Week,* October 18, 1993, 52–55.

| FIGURE 12.3 | **Cellular Layout for Chair Manufacturing** |

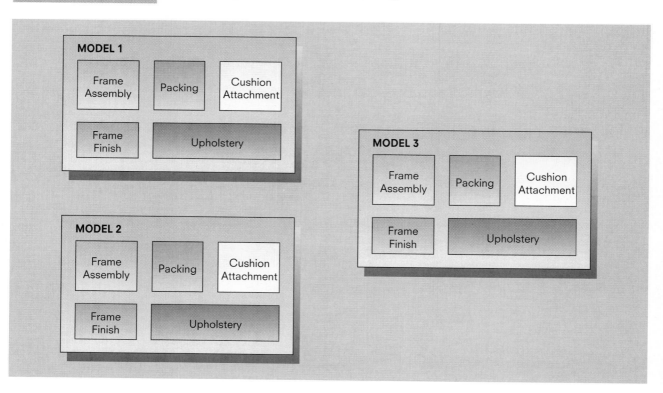

The Ingalls division of Litton Industries uses a fixed-position layout in the production of ships for the U.S. Navy and allied nations. Ingalls' advanced computer-aided engineering systems are used to design and plan construction for ships in various stages of production to provide on-schedule, on-budget deliveries. Shown here is a guided missile destroyer under construction at the shipyard.

product, often arranged in concentric rings to ensure their timely availability. Although obviously inappropriate for manufacturing chairs, this layout is suitable for producing large items like jet aircraft or ships. For example, Aerospatiale uses a fixed-position layout at its final assembly plant for Airbus Industrie A320s. Teams of workers move to the aircraft, rather than waiting for A320s to move to them on a linear production line.[2]

For most manufacturers, the choice between process-oriented, product-oriented, cellular, or fixed-position layout has implications far beyond just the arrangement of work centers. The general layout requirement is established by the type of equipment needed to fulfill strategic objectives and, to a great extent, by the basic nature of the business. Once a firm chooses a general layout type, it can decide on specific alternatives within the framework of that particular layout type.

SERVICES

Services can also utilize product-oriented, process-oriented, cellular, or fixed-position layouts. The healthcare industry, for example, makes good use of a variety of layout types. Clinics specializing in child and infant immunization use product-oriented layouts. These

---

[2]"Modular Final Assembly Facility Boosts Flow of A320 Transports," *Aviation Week & Space Technology,* April 1, 1991, 23.

CUTTING-EDGE COMPANIES

BOX 12.1

Cellular Manufacturing at Cummins Engine

Cummins Engine, a manufacturer of diesel engines, had held onto a 50 percent market share until it faced increased competition from Komatsu and Caterpillar in the late 1970s and early 1980s. With increasing competition, customers began to demand greater variety, and with that came a need for greater production flexibility. Cummins was forced to cut new product prices up to 40 percent to maintain market share. It was also necessary to reduce lead times to remain competitive.

Like many manufacturers of a great variety of machined products, Cummins was using a process-oriented layout. Lathes were situated together, grinders were together, and so on. The process-oriented layout brought with it, however, complex flows of material, high levels of WIP inventory (in queues waiting for processing), and long lead times.

Cummins reorganized its factories into cells—small, product-oriented lines that can produce a family of parts. In the Columbus, Indiana, plant, for example, there are 15 cells. One cell produces a variety of flywheels, another makes water pumps, and another is responsible for manifolds, and so on. Unlike many companies that have adopted cellular manufacturing to produce low volumes, Cummins also produces some parts in high volumes. Some lines tend to be disrupted by the extremely low volume parts. Even an aggressive changeover reduction effort has not eliminated all problems. Designation of different cells to deal with issues of high versus low volume, high versus low design stability, and high versus low predictability of demand have increased flexibility substantially.

Results of these efforts in a flywheel housing cell included a labor efficiency increase from 42 percent to 96 percent, a reduction in the number of employees from 49 to 20, a throughput time reduction of 1.83 days to 40 minutes, a 43 percent reduction in product cost, a 99 percent reduction in manufacturing scrap, an increase in on-time delivery from 30 percent to 100 percent, raw material reduction from 6 days to 1 day, WIP inventory reduction from 1.4 days to 1 hour, and finished goods inventory reduction from 4 days to 1 day.

Cellular layouts, combined with a team approach, extensive employee training (math, statistical process control, and engine study), cross-training of workers, and union cooperation, have created a flexible and productive plant.

Source Ravi Vankatesan, "Cummins Engine Flexes Its Factory," *Harvard Business Review* (March-April 1990): 120–127. "Once the Rust Belt, Midwest Now Boasts Revitalized Factories," *The Wall Street Journal,* January 3, 1994, sec. 1, 4.

types of clinics are often set up on a temporary basis in schools or churches for a few days each month. Parents bring their children, who enter a flow, which takes them through a series of workstations, where needs are recorded, shots and vaccines are administered, and records updated.

Process-oriented layouts are also very common in health care. Many hospitals are organized around functional areas: admission, emergency, X-ray, orthopedics, coronary care, intensive care, and the like.

Close approximations to cellular layouts are found in many dentists' or doctors' offices. The patient is moved from the waiting area to a treatment room, which is equipped with the necessary resources. Many dentists who have three or four treatment rooms equip each one with X-ray capabilities, anesthetic-delivery systems, and all other equipment necessary for their procedures. The alternatives would be a product-oriented layout or a process-oriented layout. The product-oriented layout would move the patient through a series of work centers, requiring each patient to go through the same steps, and limiting the dentist to a few common types of treatment; the process-oriented layout would provide an X-ray department, a cleaning department, a drilling department, and so on, which would be very inconvenient for patients.

It is even possible to identify a fixed-position layout in the health-care industry. Individual patients in most intensive care units (ICUs) are treated using this type of approach.

Instead of moving patients, which could be dangerous, resources specific to individual conditions are brought to patients in the ICU.

Just as material movement is a major contributor to costs in a manufacturing layout, customer movement can be problematic in a service layout. Although material or customer movement is reduced in a product-oriented layout, these layouts lack the flexibility required to customize according to customer expectations. The ability to produce or serve large volumes cheaply under this type of layout, however, is an advantage when customization is not necessary. Flexibility is enhanced in a process-oriented layout, but it is not as efficient for producing or serving high volumes. The cellular layout can represent a compromise for services and manufacturers. It decreases the amount of material handling or customer movement and offers increased opportunities for customization. For most services and manufacturers, the fixed-position layout is inappropriate, but it may be the only feasible alternative when the product or customer cannot be moved. Because of the relatively infrequent use of the fixed-position layout, it will not be discussed in detail here.

COMPETITIVE IMPORTANCE OF LAYOUT DECISIONS

Facility layout decisions, at the general level of process-oriented, product-oriented, cellular, or fixed-position, must be consistent with the competitive thrust of the business. The strategic decision of general layout type is often a tradeoff between *flexibility* and *cost,* but it has implications for all competitive priorities as Figure 12.4 illustrates. The process-oriented layout offers opportunities to compete on the basis of flexibility. The product-oriented layout lacks flexibility, but competes well on the basis of price. The decision between these layout types often depends on four factors: (1) the current stage in the product's life cycle, (2) how rapidly products will move through that life cycle, (3) which competitive capability—flexibility or price—will best differentiate the firm in the marketplace, and (4) the number or type of products produced. It is important to recognize that none of these factors is known for certain, but must be predicted using the best data and judgment available.

In addition to price and flexibility, quality is another key criterion in the general layout decision. Quality problems can manifest themselves in consistency problems, low worker motivation, and generally poor performance. Product-oriented layouts, because of their fixed routings, provide high levels of consistency from one product to the next. On the other hand, the process-oriented and cellular layouts are often better able to satisfy customization requirements.

Dependability can also be an important consideration in examining layout alternatives. Although well-managed layouts of any type can deliver in a dependable fashion, some layouts are easier to manage than others. The nature of product-oriented layouts, with their fixed routings, dedicated work centers, and repetitive tasks, makes them more predictable and easier to manage in service and manufacturing environments than process-oriented layouts. As soon as customization and variable routings are needed, however, the ability to predict how long a product or customer will be in the system becomes questionable.

Time can also be an important factor to consider when choosing a general layout type. For example, extremely quick response to customers who want standard products may best be achieved through a product-oriented layout and a make-to-stock approach. In fact, even if volumes are small, the quickest response to orders can probably be achieved by satisfying customers from an inventory of finished products. Similarly, in the service sector, the quickest service can probably be provided by offering a specialized service that is organized for high volume and low levels of customization. You can get an oil change from an auto dealer service center, for example, but a "quick-lube" facility would probably do it faster because it does not offer the variety of service work done at the dealer.

FIGURE 12.4 Layout Decisions in the Task/Resource Model of Operations Management

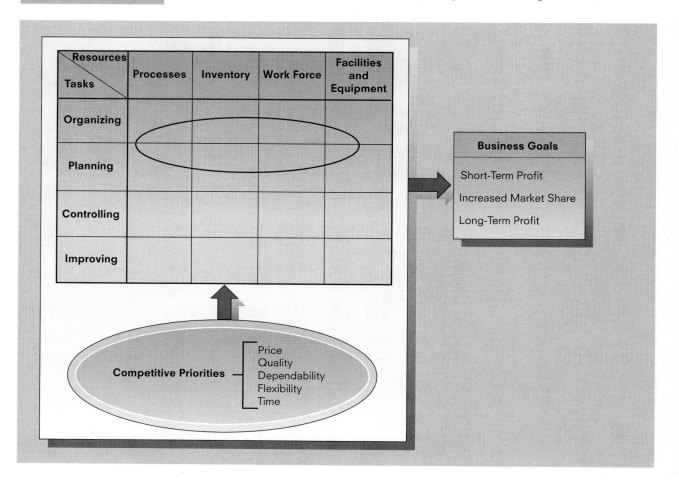

Throughout the service sector, random arrivals of customers often result in lines or queues, particularly in process-oriented layouts. Because specialized services organized in a product-oriented layout usually offer more consistent servicing times, long queues are less of a problem. In a process-oriented service, however, where customization is a competitive advantage, customers can spend more time waiting in queues than they spend being processed. Longer queue times make it much more difficult to predict how long it will take to move through the system and complete an order.

After the strategic decision of general layout type is made, services and manufacturers must still make many specific layout decisions. Much of this fine-tuning must be adapted to market needs and variations in processes. For the product-oriented layout, many of the more specific decisions affect costs. The decisions to be made center on assigning specific tasks to specific work centers in ways that can accomplish the necessary tasks and make the best use of equipment.

For the process-oriented layout, specific decisions also affect cost. Because of the flow of materials and/or customers from one functional department to the next, financial and nonfinancial costs of product or customer movement are of concern.

For the cellular layout, decisions related to the composition of each cell must be made to maximize flexibility and make the best use of capital investments in equipment. This is done through the appropriate grouping of products into cells to bring products with similar processing steps and routings together. At most firms, cellular layouts account for just 10 percent of total production.[3] Some processes do not have the volumes necessary to justify their dedication to an individual cell. Moreover, cellular arrangements are often inappropriate for highly automated processes, which do not benefit as much from teamwork or added flexibility.

The types of specific layout decisions made for each general layout type, and some examples of techniques for making these decisions, are discussed in the following sections.

PRODUCT-ORIENTED LAYOUTS

LINE BALANCING

Product-oriented layouts are common in high-volume manufacturing as well as in service factories because the linear flow of materials or customers presents an opportunity for maximizing efficiencies. This potential, however, can be maximized only through a process known as **line balancing.** Consider the simple production line presented in Table 12.1. This line could represent the manufacturing steps in six work centers (WC) required for producing a product, or it could represent the steps involved in processing forms in a service operation. In either case, it is a series of sequential steps, each with specified tasks or elements to complete and processing times that average to the amounts shown.

The constraint, or bottleneck, of this line is WC4, which takes the longest amount of time per unit: Because WC4 processes units at an average time of 2.1 minutes, products can leave the line every 2.1 minutes. The frequency of completion of each unit by the entire

LINE BALANCING
The process of assigning tasks to work centers in such a way as to balance the processing times and minimize delay.

---

[3]N. Gaither, G. V. Frazier, and J. C. Wei, "From Job Shops to Manufacturing Cells," *Production and Inventory Management Journal* 31, no. 4 (Fourth Quarter 1990): 33–36.

TABLE 12.1	**Simple Production Line**

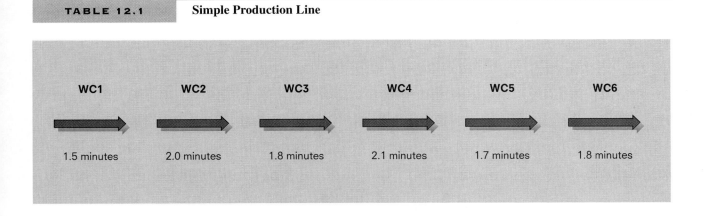

CYCLE TIME
The time (usually maximum time) allowed at each work center to complete its set of tasks on a unit.

PRODUCTION LEAD TIME
The total amount of time a unit spends in a production system.

system is known as the **cycle time** (C); for this line C is 2.1 minutes. Unless it is allowed to build up large supplies of inventory, WC1 can be operated only 1.5 minutes out of every 2.1 minutes. It will work 1.5 minutes, then be idle for 0.6 minutes before it can be utilized again. Similarly, WC2 can run 2.0 minutes out of every 2.1 minutes, WC3 can run 1.8 minutes out of 2.1, WC5 can run 1.7 minutes out of 2.1, and WC6 can run 1.8 minutes out of 2.1. The total amount of time each unit spends in the system is its **production lead time** and is determined by multiplying the cycle time (C) by the number of work centers (N). For the example in Table 12.1, production lead time is computed as follows:

$$\text{Production lead time} = C \times N = (2.1 \text{ minutes}) \times 6 = 12.6 \text{ minutes}$$

Some of the time each unit spends in the system is used unproductively because of the amount of time the unit may spend waiting for the next work center to become available. For example, after a unit completes WC1, it will wait 0.5 minutes before WC2 is available. The total time (T) actually spent performing the tasks needed to produce the product or service is determined by summing the times (t) for each task:

$$T = \Sigma t = 1.5 + 2.0 + 1.8 + 2.1 + 1.7 + 1.8 = 10.9 \text{ minutes}$$

This lack of balance not only results in the product's spending time waiting in the system, but also results in some work centers' being idle part of the time. The time a work center is used for actual production divided by the total time available is known as **theoretical utilization.** The utilization (U) of the line is calculated by the following equation:

THEORETICAL UTILIZATION
Traditionally, in line balancing, the sum of the task times divided by the production lead time.

$$\text{Utilization} = \frac{\text{Sum of the task times}}{(\text{number of work centers}) (\text{cycle time})}$$

or

$$U = \frac{T}{N \times C} \tag{12.1}$$

For this production line, the utilization is 10.9/12.6 = 86.5 percent. To improve the utilization of this line, it is necessary to reduce the amount of idle time. This can be done through line balancing, that is, designing the line and the jobs so that the times required at the work centers are as closely balanced as possible. If each work center takes exactly the same amount of time, the idle time is eliminated and the utilization approaches 100%. To rebalance a line that already exists or to construct a new balanced line requires the following steps:

1. Determine the precedence relationships between the tasks that need to be completed. This requires a detailed analysis of the tasks and their prerequisites, usually in the form of a precedence chart and diagram.
2. Determine the cycle time (C) needed to satisfy capacity requirements by using the following formula:

$$C = \frac{\text{Production hours available per day}}{\text{Units of output required per day}} \tag{12.2}$$

3. Determine the theoretical minimum number of work centers (N_{min}) by using the following formula:

$$N_{min} = \frac{T}{C} \tag{12.3}$$

4. Assign the tasks to work centers. (This can be done using any of a variety of approaches.)
5. Evaluate the utilization of the line using equation 12.1.
6. Rebalance if necessary.

Example 12.1 demonstrates the line-balancing process.

EXAMPLE 12.1

A Line-Balancing Application

Natural Beauty, a small woodworking, furniture repair, and refinishing shop, has established a line of attractive cutting boards made of native and exotic hardwoods with patterns of contrasting colors. Initially the idea was to make cutting boards only during periods when the demand for the workers' refinishing expertise was low. The cutting boards also offered an opportunity to use small pieces of scrap wood, particularly hard maple and black cherry, left over from other projects. Since introducing the cutting boards at several art shows, Ron Stevens, the shop owner, received a large number of requests from gift shops and a chain of upscale kitchen shops. Currently, he has orders totaling 3,500 standard cutting boards, all due on November 1, which gives him 70 workdays to get them done. If sales are good, he expects additional monthly orders for approximately 800 standard boards a month.

To meet his commitments, Ron must now purchase wood specifically for making cutting boards. To maximize the use of wood that may have knots or imperfections, Ron has also chosen to make small cutting boards that match the designs on the standard boards, so they can be sold as a matched set.

The standard cutting board is 10 inches wide, 17 inches long, and $\frac{7}{8}$ of an inch thick. After much experimentation, Ron has developed fairly precise methods for accomplishing each of the tasks required to make the standard board. These tasks are presented in Table 12.2.

The fabrication steps will not be done as a part of the production line responsibilities. Ron has purchased two gravity-feed roller conveyors that will move the fixtures from one worker to the next. A slow-turning horizontal carousel will be used to store the fixtures and boards during the glue curing time.

SOLUTION

Step 1 The first step in the line-balancing process is to establish the precedence relationships among the tasks. To do this, we use a *precedence table* and then a **precedence diagram.** After the prerequisites for each task are specified in the precedence chart, the precedence diagram can be constructed. The precedence table for this example is shown in Table 12.3. The precedence diagram in Table 12.4 identifies which tasks must come before others, which tasks can be done simultaneously, and which are indifferent to sequence.

PRECEDENCE DIAGRAM
A diagram showing a sequence of tasks.

Step 2 The cycle time (*C*) needed to satisfy capacity requirements must be determined. Ron has 70 workdays remaining until the November 1 due date. In order to keep up with his refinishing and restoration commitments, he prefers to have his 60 workers devote 4 hours per day to cutting board production and the remainder of their time to normal

TABLE 12.2	**Tasks Required for Cutting Board Production**

Fabrication Tasks

1. Plane both sides of 8′ × 1⅛″ × 12″ boards down to a thickness of exactly ⅞″.
2. Rip each planed 8′ board into 1″ strips.
3. Cut strips into standard 18″ lengths.

Assembly and Finishing

Task	Time t (minutes)
1. Line glueing fixture with waxed paper.	0.20
2. Select eleven 18″ strips based on desired color pattern.	0.50
3. Position strips in fixture according to desired color pattern.	0.60
4. Rearrange so that like woods are similar in grain and appearance. Replace any strips that do not match.	0.50
5. Turn each strip, except for the bottom one in the fixture, a quarter turn away from the worker.	0.20
6. Apply a bead of glue to the top surface of each strip.	0.40
7. Spread each glue bead with a small brush.	0.80
8. Turn all but the bottom strip a quarter turn toward the worker, firmly pressing strips together.	0.40
9. Apply the center clamp. Tighten it until glue begins to squeeze out.	0.50
10. Apply the right end clamp to moderate tightness.	0.50
11. Apply the left end clamp to moderate tightness.	0.50
12. Tighten each clamp one quarter turn.	0.40
13. Tighten each clamp another one quarter turn.	0.40
14. Repeat cycle of tightening each clamp until all are tight.	1.20
15. After 30 minutes' curing time, remove clamps.	0.20
16. Plane both sides, until thickness is ⅞″.	1.20
17. Cut 1″ off each end, so the board is 17″ long.	0.60
18. Disk-sand ends smooth.	1.30
19. Hand-sand lightly to knock off sharp corners.	0.80
20. Brand bottom with logo	0.40
21. Wipe with oil.	0.40
22. Install 4 rubber feet.	1.40
Total assembly and finishing time	$T = 13.40$

refinishing and restoration work. The required cycle time (C) is determined by using equation 12.2:

$$C = \frac{\text{Production hours available per day}}{\text{Units of output required per day}}$$

$$= \frac{4 \times 60}{50 \text{ units}}$$

$$= 4.8 \text{ minutes}$$

TABLE 12.3	**Precedence Table**

Task	Required Predecessors*
1	0
2	0
3	1 **2**
4	1 2 **3**
5	1 2 3 **4**
6	1 2 3 4 **5**
7	1 2 3 4 5 **6**
8	1 2 3 4 5 6 **7**
9	1 2 3 4 5 6 7 **8**
10	1 2 3 4 5 6 7 8 **9**
11	1 2 3 4 5 6 7 8 **9**
12	1 2 3 4 5 6 7 8 9 **10 11**
13	1 2 3 4 5 6 7 8 9 10 11 **12**
14	1 2 3 4 5 6 7 8 9 10 11 12 **13**
15	1 2 3 4 5 6 7 8 9 10 11 12 13 **14**
16	1 2 3 4 5 6 7 8 9 10 11 12 13 14 **15**
17	1 2 3 4 5 6 7 8 9 10 11 12 13 14 15 **16**
18	1 2 3 4 5 6 7 8 9 10 11 12 13 14 15 16 **17**
19	1 2 3 4 5 6 7 8 9 10 11 12 13 14 15 16 17 **18**
20	1 2 3 4 5 6 7 8 9 10 11 12 13 14 15 16 17 18 **19**
21	1 2 3 4 5 6 7 8 9 10 11 12 13 14 15 16 17 18 19 **20**
22	1 2 3 4 5 6 7 8 9 10 11 12 13 14 15 16 17 18 19 20 **21**

*Immediate predecessors are boldfaced.

Step 3   The theoretical minimum number of work centers is determined by using equation 12.3:

$$N_{min} = \frac{\Sigma t}{C}$$

$$= \frac{13.4}{4.8}$$

$$= 2.79 \text{ work centers}$$

Because there cannot be 2.79 work centers (a fractional work center), the theoretical minimum number of work centers is 3. The theoretical utilization of this line can be calculated by dividing the theoretical minimum number of work centers (2.79) by the actual number of work centers (3). Thus the theoretical utilization of the line is 2.79/3 = 93%.

Step 4   Tasks must be assigned to each work center. Although there are numerous sophisticated approaches to accomplishing this, we'll use an uncomplicated approach known as the *longest task time heuristic*. (A heuristic

TABLE 12.4	Precedence Diagram

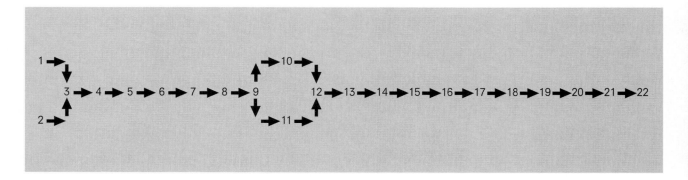

is a rule of thumb, or a simple, procedure. Heuristics do not generally guarantee the best possible solution, but they provide a pattern of outcomes that is predictable and satisfactory.) In this approach, tasks are assigned to work centers starting with the first task and proceeding to the next until the sum of the task times assigned is equal to the cycle time. If the last task assigned to a work center results in a sum of task times greater than the cycle time, then that last task cannot be assigned to that work center. If, according to the precedence diagram, there is a choice about which task to assign to a work center next, the task with the longest time is assigned unless it results in the sum of the task times greater than the cycle time.

Beginning with task 2—because it takes longer than task 1—tasks can be added to work center 1 until the cycle time, 4.8 minutes, is reached. This time is reached when either of tasks 10 or 11 is added to the list. Because the times for tasks 10 and 11 are the same (0.50 minutes), it does not matter which is added. Task 10 will be included, arbitrarily, for WC1. (Task 11 will then be assigned to WC2.) The total of the task times for WC1 is 4.6 minutes. Beginning with task 11, tasks are assigned to WC2. Using the same approach, WC2 will be responsible for tasks 11 through 17, giving it a total of 4.5 minutes. The remaining tasks, 18 through 22, will be assigned to WC3, giving it a total of 4.3 minutes. The final assignment of tasks to work centers is illustrated in Figure 12.5.

Step 5   The cycle time for the balanced line, based on the desired output of 3,500 units, is 4.8 minutes. The line is capable of a 4.6-minute cycle time, however, based on the pace of the slowest work center. Work center 1, which takes 4.6 minutes, is the constraint, or bottleneck, work center and has established 4.6 minutes as the shortest possible cycle time. This time, however, would result in an output greater than that desired. Based on the 3,500 unit output, work center 1 will be idle 0.2 minutes out of every 4.8, for a utilization of 4.6/4.8 = 95.83%. Work center 2, taking 4.5 minutes, will be idle 0.3 minutes out of every 4.8 minutes, for a utilization of 4.5/4.8 = 93.75%. Work center 3 will be idle 0.5 minutes out of every

FIGURE 12.5   **Final Assignment of Tasks to Work Centers**

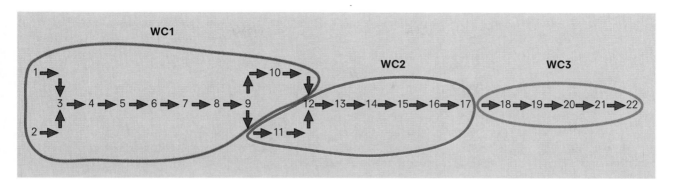

4.8, yielding a utilization of 4.3/4.8 = 89.58%. The utilization of the entire line is calculated by using equation 12.1:

$$\text{Utilization} = \frac{T}{N \times C}$$

$$= \frac{13.4}{3(4.8)}$$

$$= 93.05\%$$

Step 6   Although this line is satisfactorily balanced, other considerations may require rebalancing. For example, lines occasionally need to be balanced with maximizing output as a goal. In this case, the number of work centers is not a concern, but minimizing cycle time is. The minimum cycle time is determined by the longest task time. In this case, the shortest possible cycle time would be 1.4 minutes because the time associated with task 22 is the longest. It sets the lower limit for cycle time. The line would be balanced by grouping tasks together and trying to balance each work center at 1.4 minutes.

Caution   Line-balancing calculations cannot be completely accurate, and they are subject to change. Actual utilization rates do not always equal those computed during the line-balancing process for a number of reasons. The task times used are averages, so the actual times can be higher or lower than those calculated. In addition, variation can occur that affects the amount of time work centers spend waiting for their predecessors to supply them with work, as well as the amount of inventory that accumulates between work centers. Workers may accomplish tasks at an average rate equal to the times used in the analysis, but they are not robots—their times vary, causing the balance to fluctuate.

Worker absenteeism also affects the balance of the line. The line can be fine-tuned by moving workers from one work center to another and even by reassigning tasks. Suppose, for example, that the workers on WC2 averaged 4.7 minutes per board for the first hour of work, 4.5 minutes per board for the second and third hours of work, and 4.3 minutes per board for the fourth hour. Then WC3 could not process boards faster than one every 4.7 minutes during the first hour; the rate at which boards arrive thus limits WC3's output, despite the fact that the total task time for WC3 is only 4.3 minutes.

Continuous improvement efforts intended to enhance processes may reduce the balance in the line, making it necessary to rebalance it. Engineering changes can also result in a need for rebalancing.

Although utilization can be an important measure of the productivity of a capital investment, it is not an exact measure of the performance of an individual work center. Utilization rates are not completely within the control of a single work center. They are the result of that work center's relationships to other work centers within the system.

Line balancing is frequently an ongoing process. The variability between work centers and continuous improvements often unbalance the line and require that it be adjusted frequently in order to maintain the balance.

JIT IMPLICATIONS

The influence of the JIT philosophy has probably been greatest in operations that utilize a product-oriented layout. Companies ascribing to the JIT philosophy must strive to minimize inventory and produce at a rate close to market demand. This results in the minimization of raw materials, work-in-process, and finished goods inventories. The ability to produce at the market rate is greatly enhanced by mixed model production. Mixed model production requires that, for each day, production volumes match those of demand. To accomplish mixed model production, many firms adapt their lines so that one product can be produced for a short period of time, and then another product can be produced. This system adds a level of complexity to the line-balancing problem. Line balancing for a mixed model

Ametek's Lamb Electric Division, which produces vacuum cleaner motors, installed a fully automated U-shaped production line for armatures and fields. This layout reduces cycle time, allowing the division to offer customers shorter lead times on large and small orders. Shown here is a segment of the robotic line where metal shafts, laminations, and windings are fed at one end, and finished armatures are produced at the other end.

Source Courtesy of Ametek, Inc.

production line requires that the proportions and sequence of products must first be established. After this has been done, the line can be balanced for each product.

JIT environments also frequently arrange lines in a U shape to improve communication between workers and reduce the distance for material handlers. This configuration also enables firms to locate the beginning and end of a line adjacent to a building exit, making frequent deliveries of raw materials and pickup of completed products much easier and less costly. In Figure 12.6, for example, we see a U-shaped line that EZSeat, the chair manufacturer, might set up to facilitate its operations. Schonberger and Knod[4] describe five advantages of U-shaped lines:

Staff flexibility: A single cross-trained worker can more easily operate more than one work center when a co-worker is absent or if demand is low.

Teamwork: Communication and joint problem solving are enhanced when workers are closer together.

Rework: Rework can more easily go directly back to the work center that created the problem.

Passage: Long lines make passage of people and equipment more difficult.

---

[4]R. J. Schonberger and E. M. Knod, *Operations Management* (Plano, Texas: Business Publications, 1988), 721.

| **FIGURE 12.6** | **U-Shaped Line for Chair Manufacturing** |

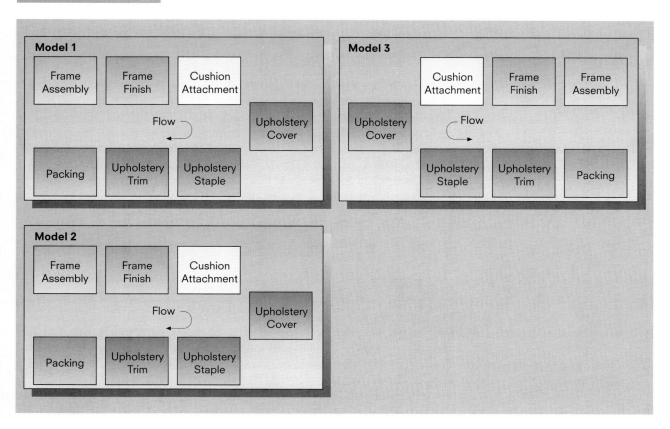

Material and tool handling: Delivery and pickup paths for raw materials and finished products are shorter and can be accomplished with one stop, rather than two stops a great distance apart.

PROCESS-ORIENTED LAYOUTS

The primary advantage of the process-oriented, or functional, layout is its flexibility. For many manufacturers and services, the negative aspect of the functional layout—inefficiency at producing high volumes—is offset by its capacity to accommodate customization. Because the work centers are arranged by function rather than by a product's routing or inflexible steps in a service, each product or customer may take a different route through the functional departments.

The functional layout requires that products or customers move from one department to another. A good layout is important in this environment in order to minimize material handling costs or, in the case of many services, customers' frustration over what they may perceive as getting the runaround.

There are two general approaches to designing the process-oriented layout, but neither is guaranteed to provide an optimal solution. The first approach is to try to minimize movement of material or people. Numerous techniques and algorithms have been designed to create a layout that achieves this objective. The second general approach to the layout problem is to use a system that rates the desired closeness of each pair of work centers. The objective of this approach is to develop a layout that satisfies a firm's requirement that departments be near each other.

MINIMIZING MATERIAL HANDLING OR CUSTOMER MOVEMENT

It may appear simple to lay out a process-oriented facility, but evaluating the various possibilities requires a comparison of the total material handling costs of each alternative. The number of alternative layouts for even a small facility can be quite large. For example, assigning six departments to six locations involves 6!, or 720, possible layouts. It is not practical to evaluate every alternative, so the objective is to determine a good layout, not necessarily the best layout. The cut-and-try approach to minimizing material handling requires the initial construction of two matrices, one showing the frequency of interactions between each pair of departments and the other showing the distances between all departments. These matrices are used to compute a total daily distance value for each alternative layout. Typically, this approach starts out with a first try at a layout, which is followed by modifications that attempt to improve upon it. Each adjusted layout can be compared to the original by comparing the total daily distance required. Example 12.2 presents this approach to minimizing materials handling costs or customer movement.

EXAMPLE 12.2

Minimizing Materials Handling Costs in a Process-Oriented Layout: A Cut-and-Try Approach

Patricia Vanderhoff, owner of a small plastic molding company, plans to move her business to a building she recently purchased. She was attracted to the facility for many reasons, but the deciding factor was that it was already configured for six separate departments—exactly the number needed for her operation. The rough floor plan of the building is shown in Figure 12.7.

The six departments in Patricia's small factory are briefly described in Table 12.5. Patricia must assign each of these departments a location on the rough floor plan. To facilitate this, she has developed two matrices. The first matrix, shown in Table 12.6, shows the dis-

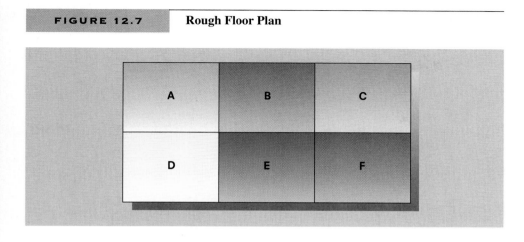

FIGURE 12.7   **Rough Floor Plan**

TABLE 12.5

Department	Description
Receiving (Rec.)	Incoming raw materials and packaging materials are received.
Molding (Mld.)	Actual production takes place on molding presses.
Regrinding (Reg.)	Waste plastic and defective items are ground into pellets so that they can be reused.
Packing (Pck.)	End products are sorted and packaged to meet customer requirements.
Shipping (Shp.)	Boxes of products are palletized and loaded on trucks.
Management (Mgt.)	All management personnel work in an open-office configuration.

tances, from center to center, between each pair of locations. The second matrix, shown in Table 12.7, presents the average number of fork-truck trips per day between each pair of departments at the current location. This pattern is expected to continue at the new location. Patricia must determine which layout minimizes material handling costs. Total daily distance traveled will be considered the best measure of material handling costs in this example because all material movement is done using a fork truck and the cost is the same no matter what material is being moved.

Table 12.8 summarizes the number of interactions between departments. Shipping and Packing have the most. Thus, to minimize the distance traveled, Shipping and Packing should be close to each other.

SOLUTION

As a first try at this layout, Shipping will be assigned to location A, and Packing will be assigned to location D. Packing and Molding also interact frequently, so it would be appropriate to locate Molding close to Packing, in location E. There also is frequent interaction

TABLE 12.6			Distance Matrix (in feet)			

To:		A	B	C	D	E	F
From:	A	0					
	B	40	0				
	C	80	40	0			
	D	35	75	115	0		
	E	75	35	75	40	0	
	F	115	75	35	80	40	0

TABLE 12.7		Trips Matrix					

To:		Rec.	Mld.	Reg.	Pck.	Shp.	Mgt.
From:	Rec.	0	30	0	14	0	0
	Mld.	0	0	8	45	0	0
	Reg.	0	5	0	0	1	0
	Pck.	0	0	0	0	65	0
	Shp.	0	0	0	0	0	0
	Mgt.	0	0	0	0	0	0

TABLE 12.8	Department Pairs with Most Interaction

Department Pairs	Number of Interactions
Shipping and Packing	65 interactions per day
Packing and Molding	45 interactions per day
Receiving and Molding	30 interactions per day
Packing and Receiving	14 interactions per day
Molding and Regrind	13 interactions per day
Regrind and Shipping	1 interaction per day

between Receiving and Molding. If Receiving is situated in location B, the distance between it and Molding is minimized. Regrind also interacts with Molding, but not to the same degree as Receiving and Packing. Regrind can be positioned at location F. (This position doesn't minimize Regrind's distance from Molding, but the two are still reasonably close.) Location C will be given to Management. The result of the first try at this layout is presented in Table 12.9.

To compare this layout with other attempts, the total daily travel distance must be computed. This computation is done by multiplying the number of trips per day for each pair of interacting departments by the distance between them and summing the results. The results for this layout are presented in Table 12.10.

TABLE 12.9	**Result of the First Try**

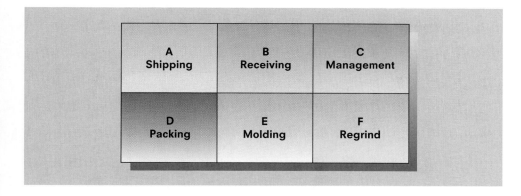

TABLE 12.10	**Total Daily Distance Traveled**

Interacting Departments	Number of Interactions	Distance	Total
Shipping and Packing	65	35	2,275
Packing and Molding	45	40	1,800
Receiving and Molding	30	35	1,050
Packing and Receiving	14	75	1,050
Molding and Regrind	13	40	520
Regrind and Shipping	1	115	115
Total distance traveled per day for this layout:			6,810 feet

Particularly with more complex layouts, the first try often yields a less than satisfactory result. Further inspection often identifies modifications that can be made to improve the layout. After adjustments are made, comparisons between alternative layouts can be made by comparing the total daily distance traveled. The layout with the lowest total distance would be the best layout.

CLOSENESS RATINGS

Closeness ratings, a relative measure of how desirable it is for departments to be close together, may be used in various ways to help develop process-oriented layouts. One of the most commonly used approaches is the **simplified systematic layout planning (SSLP)** procedure, developed by Muther and Wheeler.[5] Although the SSLP process is not new, it provides an excellent example of how a system based on closeness ratings can be designed. SSLP is a structured six-step process for developing process-oriented layouts:

Step 1.   Chart the relationships between every pair of departments

Step 2.   Establish space requirements for each

SIMPLIFIED SYSTEMATIC LAYOUT PLANNING (SSLP)
A structured approach to identifying satisfactory facility layouts by using ratings of desired closeness.

---

[5]R. Muther and J. D. Wheeler, *Simplified Systematic Layout Planning* (Kansas City, Mo.: Management and Industrial Research Publications, 1961).

Step 3.   Diagram activity relationships

Step 4.   Draw space relationship layouts

Step 5.   Evaluate alternative arrangements

Step 6.   Detail the selected layout plan

Step 1 of SSLP requires that the desired closeness of each pair of departments be given a rating. Rating alternatives in SSLP are AEIOUX: A (absolutely necessary), E (especially important), I (important), O (ordinary closeness OK), U (unimportant), and X (undesirable). An undesirable closeness rating may result because of safety concerns, such as fire hazards (welding next to painting) or contamination (dusty processes next to processes that must be clean). Step 2 requires that the space requirements be established, usually in terms of square feet, as well as any other specific physical features such as floor support or ceiling height. Step 3 uses a diagram of activity relationships to begin the process of developing the actual layout. First, select pairs of departments from the relationship chart that have A-rated closeness requirements. Each pair should be labeled on the drawing and connected to each other by four parallel lines. E-rated pairs are then added, connected by three parallel lines. I-rated pairs are added next, connected by two parallel lines. O-rated pairs are added, connected by one line. X-rated relationships are added last and connected by wavy lines. At each addition of a pair, the diagram can be rearranged as needed. The result of step 3 is a diagram that shows positional relationships, but space criteria have not been included. Step 4 involves geographically arranging the space available for all activities within the locational guidelines established in the previous step. Steps 1 through 4 are often repeated to create several alternatives. Step 5 involves the use of a factor rating process, like the one used in evaluating alternative locations, to determine a score for each alternative. The selected layout is then drawn in detail in step 6.

Example 12.3 provides a demonstration of steps 1 through 4 of the SSLP approach to layout planning.

EXAMPLE 12.3

Using SSLP for Process-Oriented Layout Planning

Assume that the building to which Patricia Vanderhoff was going to move her plastic molding factory does not have any interior walls. Patricia would need to determine where and how large each department would be within the confines of the exterior walls.

Note: In this example, there are no instances in which it would be undesirable to have departments in close proximity to each other.

SOLUTION

Patricia has developed the table of closeness ratings, presented in Table 12.11, based on the SSLP guidelines.

The next step is to diagram the A-rated relationships. This is done, according to the SSLP guidelines, in Figure 12.8.

The next step is to include the E-rated relationships in the diagram. There is only one in this example—Receiving and Packing. This is done by connecting 1 and 4 in the diagram, as shown in Figure 12.9.

Any necessary adjustments should be completed at this time. The next step is to add any I-rated departments to the diagram, as shown in Figure 12.10.

The next step is to add any O-rated departments. Shipping and Regrinding have an O-rated relationship, as does Management with each other department. Figure 12.11 shows the diagram with all relationships included. Notice that an adjustment was made to the

TABLE 12.11   **Closeness Ratings**

	1	2	3	4	5	6
	Rec.	Mld.	Reg.	Pck.	Shp.	Mgt.
1 Receiving	—	—	—	—	—	—
2 Molding	A	—	—	—	—	—
3 Regrinding	U	I	—	—	—	—
4 Packing	E	A	U	—	—	—
5 Shipping	U	U	O	A	—	—
6 Management	O	O	O	O	O	—

FIGURE 12.8   **Diagram of A-Rated Departments**

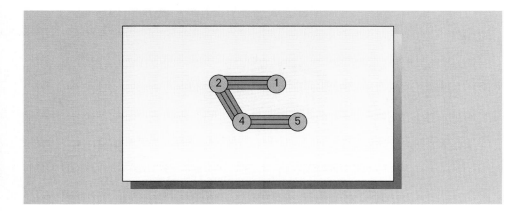

FIGURE 12.9   **Diagram Including E-Rated Departments**

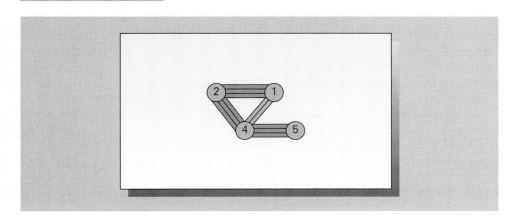

FIGURE 12.10	Diagram Including I-Rated Departments

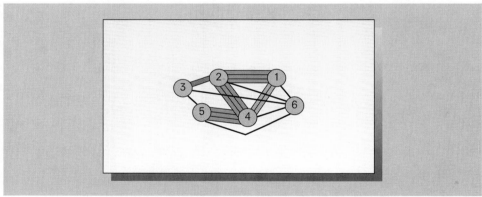

FIGURE 12.11	Diagram Including O-Rated Departments

positioning of Regrinding and Shipping. Figure 12.11 shows O-rated relationships in addition to those that are I-, E-, and A-rated. Like the cut-and-try approach demonstrated in the previous example, SSLP is *not* an optimization procedure. It is an iterative process involving the decision-maker's best judgment.

After any U-rated or X-rated relationships have been added to the diagram, it is converted into an actual floor plan. The size requirements must be taken into consideration at this time also. Figure 12.12, based on the outcome of the SSLP process in this example, shows the final floor plan in which each department is the same physical size. Several alternatives could be generated by repeating the process. After the development of several alternatives, step 5 would evaluate them using the factor rating approach. The best layout could then be selected.

Notice that the result of this example, which incorporates closeness ratings to aid in the layout process, is different from the result of Example 12.2, which used a cut-and-try approach to minimizing material handling costs. Both layouts are acceptable and accomplish the objective of developing a good layout that takes into consideration the relationships among the various departments.

FIGURE 12.12   **Final Layout Using SSLP**

A Regrind (3)	B Molding (2)	C Receiving (1)
D Shipping (5)	E Packing (4)	F Management (6)

Either layout approach could be applied to a service that was departmentalized, such as the main floor of a hospital or the main administration building of a university.

CELLULAR LAYOUTS

Cellular layouts, combined with group technology, allow many firms to maintain high efficiencies, reduced levels of WIP inventory, shorter lead times, and improved quality while reducing the materials handling costs typically associated with process-oriented layouts. Rather than route different products through functional departments, cellular layouts incorporate smaller scale equipment in cells. The facility layout consists of a number of cells, each designed to be sufficient for a product family. The advantages of cellular layouts are numerous.

When compared to product-oriented systems, cellular layouts have greater flexibility and can accommodate variable routings. Cells may also provide workers with more responsibility and a greater role in decision-making if designed with this objective. This empowerment can translate into improved employee commitment and product quality.

When compared with process-oriented layouts, cellular layouts reduce materials handling and production lead times because they cut the time needed to transport material from one department to another. Work-in-process inventory levels are reduced, decreasing the lengths of queues and the corresponding waiting time, further reducing lead times. Reduced movement of materials results in less damage and improved quality. Reduction in queue times results in more predictable lead times and more reliable delivery performance. In some cases, cellular approaches to manufacturing represent a compromise that captures the best aspects of process- and product-oriented manufacturing.

Layout solutions for product-oriented layouts, process-oriented layouts, and cellular layouts have been made more accessible with the development of computer software packages that can more easily analyze large, complex environments. Although the methods presented in this text offer good techniques to analyze layout alternatives, they could become too complex to deal with if the facility had a large number of work centers or departments. The computer applications remove some of the tedium associated with a large-scale layout analysis, but the logic is similar to that used in this chapter's analyses.

Danaher Corporation uses a cellular layout with machine process control to produce chucks for portable consumer drills. The cell produces the chuck in one-tenth the space required for conventional equipment. As shown here, this layout requires only one cell operator, whose principal responsibility is to ensure the quality of the process. The computer measures concentricity and results are verified automatically by the computer-controlled recorder that collects data directly for customer analysis and certification.

Source   Courtesy of Danaher Corporation.

SERVICE AND MANUFACTURING LAYOUTS

The layout approaches described in this chapter have been addressed from both general service and manufacturing perspectives. However, it is useful to identify the different types of layouts that best fit the strategic objectives for any firm, manufacturer or service. Table 12.12 summarizes the type of layout (product-oriented, process-oriented, or cellular) that is most common and best supports the strategic objectives of several different types of manufacturers. Notice that for some manufacturers, more than one layout type works.

Services have also been classified on the basis of differentiating characteristics. Table 12.13 summarizes the four general types of services and identifies the most commonly used layout choice to accomplish strategic objectives. In services, it is sometimes necessary to consider the issue of customer movement rather than material movement. In general, the greater the level of customization, the more likely a process-oriented layout will be needed.

In recent years, some firms have become quite sophisticated in the way they collect data for use in layout decisions. For example, retailers base their layout decisions on the link between the location of items within a store and customer traffic patterns. (See Box 12.2.)

FACILITY LAYOUT CROSS-LINKS

The strategic decision of the general layout type has tremendous implications for marketing because it dictates, to a large extent, whether the company will compete on the basis of flexibility or price. If the manufacturer or service selects a strategy in which the most important competitive priority will be price, the product-oriented layout will most likely be selected. The decisions made within that framework, regarding, for example, U-shaped

TABLE 12.12	Manufacturing Classification and Layout

Manufacturing Type	Most Commonly Used Layout
Production Cycle	
Basic Producer	Product-oriented
Converter	Product-oriented
Fabricator	Process-oriented
Assembler	Product-oriented, cellular
Processing Method	
Discrete Manufacturing	Product-oriented, process-oriented, cellular
Nondiscrete Manufacturing	Product-oriented
Volume	
High	Product-oriented
Low	Process-oriented
Demand Information Source	
Make-to-stock	Product-oriented
Make-to-order	Process-oriented, cellular
Make-to-stock/assemble-to-order	Product-oriented, cellular

lines, line balancing, and mixed model production, will further affect costs and price through the determination of such concerns as efficiencies, utilization, materials handling, and quick response to problems.

The tendencies for the system to build up work-in-process inventories will also be influenced by specific decisions made when setting up the product-oriented layout. If a firm selects a process-oriented layout because of the need for flexibility and the capability to customize products or services, marketing will be affected because of the nature of the equipment chosen and its capabilities relative to customization. Companies often differentiate themselves from the competition based on how they provide a product or service to their customers. For example, the speed of product delivery or the atmosphere and convenience of a service may be just as important as what they provide and how much they charge for it. The general layout type, as well as the way it is implemented, helps to determine how the product or service is produced and delivered.

Facility layout decisions are also closely linked to the engineering function. Production and service processes must be developed in a manner that is closely coordinated with the layout decision. Product engineering and new product development must also be coupled with the layout decision when the initial layout is determined as well as any time changes being considered.

TABLE 12.13	Service Type and Layout Choice

Service Type	Most Commonly Used Layout
Service factory	Product-oriented
Mass service	Product-oriented
Service shop	Process-oriented
Professional service	Process-oriented

OPERATIONS
OUTLOOK

BOX 12.2

Prying Eyes in the Supermarket

Close tracking of customers has given several retailers new insights into how traffic patterns can be used to change store layouts. By observing customers from catwalks, Marsh Supermarkets has determined that many shoppers stay in the periphery of the store, concentrating on the produce, dairy, and meat sections and rarely venture into the interior dry-goods portion of the store. The chain's inner aisles accounted for only 13 percent to 30 percent of the traffic, while the periphery received as much as 80 percent of the traffic. Other studies have shown that when shoppers do go into a store's interior, they leave their carts on the periphery. This practice, known as dipping, concerns retailers because without their carts, shoppers' purchases are limited by what they can carry.

A Procter & Gamble study showed that sales could be increased significantly if items like coffee and toothpaste were placed outside their normal display aisles. And Pepsi-Co concluded that only 35 percent of shoppers traveled through the soft-drink aisle. To reach out to the other 65 percent, the company began branching into the better-traveled bakery department by placing Pepsi displays beside picnic-oriented items in the unused space under bakery tables.

Retailers have also identified so-called dead spots in stores. These are areas that for one reason or another don't get traffic. Some retailers have found that certain features of stores unintentionally divert traffic from other areas.

Source "James Bond Hits the Supermarket: Stores Snoop on Shoppers Habits to Boost Sales," *The Wall Street Journal,* August 25, 1993, sec. B, 1, 8.

Performance measures, primarily those related to equipment utilization, such as cost per unit, must take the type of layout into account. Layout selection will influence the number of changeovers and, thus, affect utilization rates. The effectiveness of the line-balancing efforts dictates how work centers are utilized, often in ways that are out of the control of each work center. In many businesses, a line supervisor's performance evaluation would be negatively affected by poor utilization rates, even if these rates were caused by processing time variation outside of his or her influence. These issues have implications for performance appraisal, incentive systems, and to some extent, managerial accounting procedures.

Although the general layout decision tends to be long term and strategic in nature, the decisions that are made within each general layout must be evaluated on an ongoing basis. Continuous improvement efforts and a changing competitive environment require that management be aware of possible improvements to processes. For example, as product mix changes, patterns of material movement among various departments of a functional layout also are likely to change, requiring a new analysis of the layout. As engineering improvements are made, the processing times in a product-oriented layout change, requiring a re-balancing of lines. As new products are brought on board, the grouping of products in a cellular layout may need to be reexamined. Like all aspects of a business, layout is subject to continuous evaluation and improvement.

SUMMARY

The selection of a general layout type is a long-term decision which helps a firm establish the foundations of what it can and cannot offer its customers. Specific layout decisions, within each general layout type, establish how effectively the firm will utilize the layout and greatly influence competitive priorities. As new approaches and new philosophies gain popularity, their effect on layout decisions will become more pronounced, increasing the need for firms to compete on the bases of cost and flexibility rather than on one or the other.

TENSILE PRODUCTS REVISITED

 CROSS-LINKS Do you agree with Drew's assessment of the problem? How would you recommend that Brian and Drew analyze the situation in order to better understand possible changes? Does a functional layout appear to be better for both product lines? Do you think a product-oriented approach is likely to provide enough flexibility to customize point-of-sale displays?

The large production batches are contributing to Tensile's problems. How might Tensile Products eliminate some of the large batch problem and make better use of equipment capacity that, because of current fixtures, isn't flexible enough to be used in more general ways?

What type of layout do you think offers the greatest potential for Tensile Products to improve?

QUESTIONS FOR REVIEW

1. Compare process-oriented and product-oriented layout types. What are the competitive strengths and weaknesses of each?
2. Why is the cellular approach to layout becoming more popular?
3. Why does the presence of variable processing times reduce the effectiveness of line balancing?

4. Describe how mixed model production aids in reducing inventory levels.
5. What are the benefits of U-shaped lines?
6. Describe the cut-and-try approach to minimizing materials handling in a process-oriented layout.
7. Compare the cut-and-try approach with the use of closeness ratings.

QUESTIONS FOR THOUGHT AND DISCUSSION

1. Compare the layouts of Wendy's, McDonald's, and Subway restaurants. Why are they so different?

2. How have services begun to adopt cellular approaches?

INTEGRATIVE QUESTIONS

1. What value can be added through the effective layout of a service?
2. Which tools associated with TQM can be used to improve a layout?

3. Compare the implications for competitive priorities that layout has for manufacturing and services.

PROBLEMS

1. In an effort to increase the output of insurance claims processed per day, a large insurance company has decided to establish a line approach to the preliminary steps in claim processing instead of the current functional layout. The 14 steps in the process take the following amounts of time:

Step	1	2	3	4	5	6	7	8	9	10	11	12	13	14
Time (in minutes)	0.5	0.8	0.3	0.6	0.2	0.5	1.2	0.9	0.2	0.4	0.6	0.3	0.9	0.7

All steps must be done in the sequence shown. The line must have the capacity to process 350 claims in an 8-hour day.
a. What is the required cycle time to meet the capacity requirements?
b. What is the theoretical minimum number of work centers?
c. What is the theoretical utilization of the line?

d. Assign the tasks to work centers using the longest task time heuristic.
e. What is the utilization of the balanced line?
2. A manufacturer of electronic games must develop an assembly line for its latest development. A table of tasks, task times, and precedence relationships is shown on the following page:

Task	Task Time (in minutes)	Immediate Predecessors
A	3	—
B	2	A
C	2	B
D	4	C
E	4	A B
F	4	E
G	5	A B
H	3	G
I	4	H
J	4	D F H
K	3	J
L	5	J
M	4	K L
N	4	M

Current projections of demand show that the line must be able to produce 50 units per day (480 minutes per day).

a. Construct a diagram showing the tasks, including precedence relationships and task times.

b. Determine the cycle time necessary to meet the capacity requirements.

c. Determine the theoretical minimum number of work centers.

d. Determine the theoretical utilization of the line.

e. Assign the tasks to work centers using the longest task time heuristic.

f. Determine the actual utilization of each work center and of the balanced line.

g. What is the line's daily capacity (480 minutes in a day)?

h. What would be the line's daily capacity if the shortest possible cycle time were used?

3. Carson's Machine Shop is converting from a functional layout to a cellular layout. One cell will be used to clean and refurbish molds used by other companies that manufacture injection molded plastic items. The cell will house the following five work centers:

1. Incoming rack   4. Hone
2. Milling machine   5. Outgoing rack
3. Surface grinder

The daily interactions among each of the five work centers are shown below:

To: From:	Incoming	Milling	Grinder	Hone	Outgoing
Incoming	—	18	13	10	0
Milling	0	—	7	9	11
Grinder	0	11	—	24	14
Hone	0	13	4	—	24
Outgoing	0	0	0	0	—

a. Which work center should be closest to the outgoing rack?

b. Which work center should be closest to the incoming rack?

c. Of the milling machine, surface grinder, and hone, which two should be close to each other?

d. For ease of fork truck access, incoming and outgoing must be in locations 1 and 2, respectively. Using the cut-and-try approach, assign the remaining three work centers to the rough layout shown below:

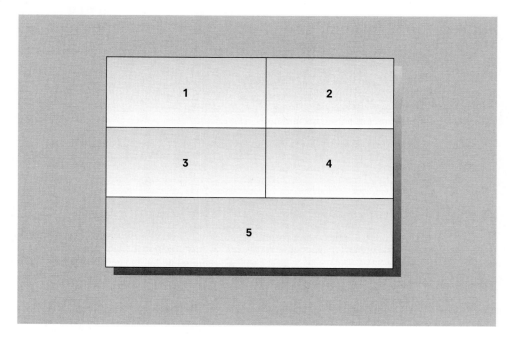

4. Seven architectural departments must be arranged in the C-shaped office building diagrammed below. Most of the interaction between departments can be accommodated by e-mail, but, because of the complexity of some of the design projects, a significant amount of face-to-face interaction must occur. Architects have complained lately because of the amount of walking they must do in order to meet with others. A recent decision has been made to reassign offices in a manner that reduces the amount of walking architects must do if they meet with others frequently. Meetings that have been necessary over the past 2 months have been recorded and are shown in the diagram.

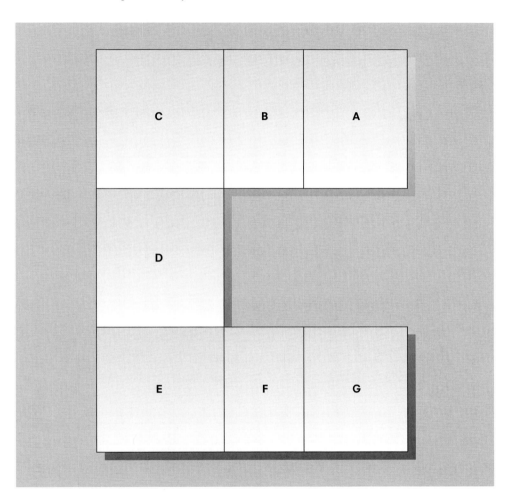

a. Define four pairs of architects that appear to have very close working relationships.
b. Using the cut-and-try approach, assign architects to the offices.

Architect	1	2	3	4	5	6	7
1	—	—	—	—	—	—	—
2	15	—	—	—	—	—	—
3	0	8	—	—	—	—	—
4	5	5	16	—	—	—	—
5	3	9	14	2	—	—	—
6	4	2	5	18	6	—	—
7	7	6	4	3	5	15	—

5. Taking the interactions established in problem 4 into consideration, use the SSLP approach to assign architects to the locations in the office building shown in the diagram below. The relationships from Problem 4 have been transformed into ratings as shown in the accompanying table.

Architect	1	2	3	4	5	6	7
1	—	—	—	—	—	—	—
2	A	—	—	—	—	—	—
3	U	E	—	—	—	—	—
4	I	I	A	—	—	—	—
5	O	E	A	O	—	—	—
6	O	O	I	A	I	—	—
7	E	I	O	O	I	A	—

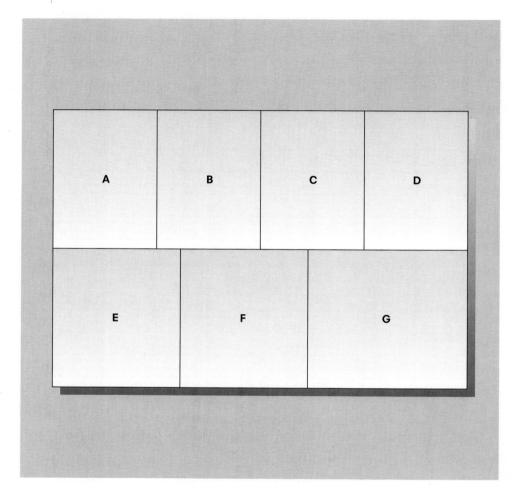

6. Arrange in the following layout the six departments whose interactions are presented in the accompanying table:

Department	1	2	3	4	5	6
1	—	—	—	—	—	—
2	A	—	—	—	—	—
3	U	A	—	—	—	—
4	O	U	O	—	—	—
5	O	U	U	O	—	—
6	E	I	E	U	A	—

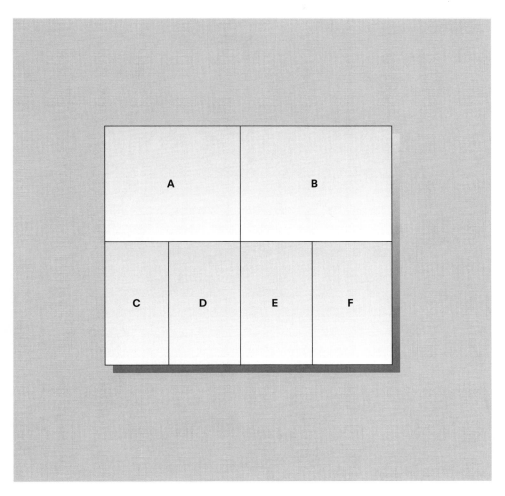

SUGGESTED READINGS

Choi, M. "Manufacturing Cell Design." *Production and Inventory Management Journal* 33 (Second Quarter 1992): 66–69.

Fry, T. D., M. B. Wilxon, and M. Breen. "A Successful Implementation of Group Technology and Cell Manufacturing." *Production and Inventory Management* 28 (Third Quarter 1987): 30–35.

Green, T. J., and R. P. Sadowski. "A Review of Cellular Manufacturing Assumptions, Advantages, and Design Techniques." *Journal of Operations Management* 4 (February 1984): 85–97.

Hyer, Nancy L., and U. Wemmerlov. "Group Technology and Productivity." *Harvard Business Review* 62 (July-August 1984): 140–149.

Shin, D., and H. Min. "Flexible Line Balancing Practices in a Just-in-time Environment." *Production and Inventory Management Journal* 32 (Fourth Quarter 1991): 38–41.

Urban, T. L. "Combining Qualitative and Quantitative Analysis in Facility Layout." *Production and Inventory Management Journal* 30 (Third Quarter 1989): 73–77.

CHAPTER **13**

PLANNING FOR PROJECTS

 CROSS-LINKS

**Beating the Competition
to the Market**

*Totco manufactures electronic video
game hardware and software, primarily for children. In this industry,
the time it takes to get a product to the marketplace
can mean the difference between a major success and
a major failure. Typically, software concepts are developed for use with the most advanced hardware format available. New hardware products are always in
developmental stages with accompanying software
following closely behind. Unlike software, new hardware must be developed by both product and process
engineers so that the completed design can be manufactured economically. Totco has decided it must reduce its time to market by incorporating more parallel
tasks during development. Product and process engineering, the two product development tasks that take
the longest, are going to be done simultaneously for
the latest hardware product.* ■ Marci Schmidt,
vice president for product development, has developed the following time estimates for the development
of the next generation of game controller. The figures
are based on average times for product developments
over the past 5 years.

Steps	Time
1. Data collection market survey and focus groups	2 months
2. Technology survey	1 month
3. Product design	3 months
4. Process design	3 months
5. Equipment appropriation and modification	2 months
6. Supplier negotiation	2 months
7. First production run	1 month

Steps 1 and 2 can be done in parallel, as can steps 3
and 4. Steps 5 and 6 can also be done at the same time.
What used to take 14 months should be accomplished
in 9 months with parallel tasking. ■ Eager to get
the process under way, Marci launched the project by
announcing its scheduled completion date. Marketing
immediately began gathering the latest information on
customer desires and current technology levels. Both
surveys were finished on time. ■ Marci expected
product and process design tasks to be much easier
than some parallel tasks because both were housed in
the engineering department. Communication between
the two groups would be much easier. Engineering had
submitted time estimates for the product and process
design phases based on information from the marketing and technology surveys. It expected product design to take 2,400 hours and process design to take
2,880 hours. ■ After product and process design
had been in full swing for 6 weeks, Marci checked on
the progress. When she examined the flow chart used
to monitor the project, she immediately noticed that
the work was behind schedule. As Ron Foster, chief
engineer, came into the design suite she said, "I don't
understand this, Ron. You assured me that the hourly
projections were accurate. You guaranteed me 2,400
hours for product design and 2,880 hours for process
design. But when I look at your progress, it is obvious
that you're at least a week behind!" ■ "I'll stand
by those numbers, Marci, but because I'm not allowed
to use overtime, my engineers can only work 40-hour
weeks. I have only 8 engineers!" ■

Some businesses produce products and services that are so customized that each one is unique. Others launch efforts aimed at changing or improving the way they do business. For example, a company might decide to implement a new computer system or adopt JIT or TQM techniques. Civic, corporate, government, and not-for-profit organizations all periodically become involved in these types of large-scale enterprises or sets of activities. Activities that are directed toward a specific purpose and take several months or more to complete are frequently known as **projects.** The activities within projects are often interrelated, with some activities having to precede others.

Almost every type of business or organization and all business functions have projects. An accounting department may implement a new cost accounting system. Financial managers may develop a new financial strategy. Operations may design a new layout consistent with JIT. Human resources may hire and train workers for a new shift. All of these tasks could be considered projects. Other examples of projects include such large-scale efforts as making a site location decision, hiring key figures in an organization, purchasing and installing new equipment, conducting a marketing study to determine customers' needs, opening a new store, or constructing a bridge or building.

In some cases projects are performed entirely within one functional department. In many cases, though, projects span several functional areas within one business and require the efforts of people from marketing, operations, engineering, finance, and management information systems as well as outside vendors, suppliers, or service personnel. For example, when Ford Motor Company decided to redesign its classic Mustang, it assembled a team made up of 450 workers from various departments. The Mustang team took 36 months to develop the fourth-generation 1994 model. This type of project is known as a cross-functional project, and it requires a managerial perspective that is project-oriented and global, rather than narrow and functionally oriented. Companies often use a matrix-type of orga-

PROJECT

A set of activities, directed toward a specific purpose, whose completion time extends over several months or more.

Some projects span several functional areas. The Dial Corp's Household & Laundry division uses specialized training, cross-functional teams, and accelerated project management to bring new products to market. This project-oriented approach has helped the division reduce by half the time required to develop and introduce new products.

Source The Dial Corp.

nization in which team members are on loan to the project leader and are responsible to both the project leader and the head of their own functional department.

As businesses become more dependent on continuous improvement approaches that require constant appraisal and change, like JIT, TQM, and constraint management, the use of cross-functional project teams is likely to increase. Projects undertaken for the sake of improvement also may include anything from a strategic decision to relocate to the development of a new product. These projects frequently are aimed at helping an organization achieve its mission. The increasing use of cross-functional project teams and the rapid rate of change in organizations make it more important than ever to manage people effectively.

Many Japanese and U.S. corporations describe respect for people as one of their organization's goals. According to Katzenbach and Smith the way a team is organized, makes decisions, shares responsibility and authority, and measures performance affects its ultimate success.[1] Teams that work together to make joint decisions, are individually and collectively accountable, and share authority and responsibility perform better than those teams that use more traditional lines of authority and responsibility. Johnsonville Foods' chief executive officer Ralph Stayer learned this first-hand when he was asked by a large food company to manufacture sausage under a private label. Since the added production would push plant capacity to the limit, he gave worker teams the authority to decide whether the contract should be accepted. They not only agreed to the extra work, they also took on the responsibility for the plant expansion project.[2]

Managing a project is different from many manufacturing or service activities for several reasons. Each project is unique. Unlike most product- and service-oriented activities, which are repetitive, a project, once it has been completed, will probably never be repeated. This means that a project has greater potential for surprises and unexpected problems. The uniqueness of the project requires working with new and different suppliers and with a special work force that quite likely has never worked together before. Members are likely performing tasks for which there are few established guidelines or procedures and no benchmarks for comparison.

The success or failure of many projects depends on the selection of the project team and project manager. The manager's skills must include the ability to communicate and motivate team members. The manager must be flexible, a good listener, assertive, and a problem solver who can both convey the project goals and manage the process of accomplishing them.

Team members must have a clear understanding and be supportive of and committed to the project's goals. They must be willing to work with others in a team environment, sharing responsibility and authority, and be able to complete tasks on time. Team members must be valued and respected and have the technical competence to get the job done. A project team at NCR Corp. that successfully developed the system 3000 Model 3445 floorstand computer exhibited all of these characteristics. As a result, it was able to come up with a system that required fewer assembly operations, contained fewer parts, and cost less to produce than a previous model.[3] In some environments, team members may be on loan or shared with a department. This requires that those team members be able to work under two bosses.

---

[1] Jon R. Katzenbach and Douglas K. Smith, "The Discipline of Teams," *Harvard Business Review* 71 (March-April 1993): 111–120.

[2] Ralph Stayer, "How I Learned to Let My Workers Lead," *Harvard Business Review* 69 (November-December 1990), 66–83.

[3] "An NCR Team That Could," *Industry Week*, June 17, 1991, 52–53.

Some projects have an impact on cost. To achieve synergistic savings, NBD Bancorp consolidated and converted its 12 Indiana banks with about 200 offices and $9.5 billion in assets into a single entity—NBD Bank, N.A. The cross-functional team shown here helped plan and schedule the project, which involved 1,935,000 deposit and loan accounts and 210 major software applications.

Source Courtesy of NBD Bancorp, Detroit, MI.

PROJECT MANAGEMENT AND COMPETITIVENESS

The process of *planning, scheduling,* and *controlling* projects is called project management. The types of projects managed by businesses can be divided into two groups—those that undertake projects for their own firms, and those that perform projects for others. Many projects are intended to change things within the firm. For example, IBM announced in 1994 that it was reorganizing its sales and marketing staff into 14 industry types as part of its efforts to boost profitability. The work force was previously organized by geographic location. Successfully managing these types of projects is important because the changes are typically intended to improve the firm's performance. The competitive priority specifically affected would depend on the type of project. Some projects have an impact on cost and price, and others affect quality. Still others could result in the improvement of dependability, flexibility, or response time.

Some manufacturers and services contract to perform projects for other businesses. For example, financially ailing Euro Disney hired advertising giant Ogilvy & Mather to develop a new ad campaign for the theme park. The development of the campaign is a project. The firms' timely completion of these projects affects their competitiveness because a customer would view a business's inability to complete a project on time as a lack of dependability.

Organizations that are able to shorten the lead time required for product development can gain a significant competitive advantage. According to McKinsey & Co., a consulting firm, the cost of arriving late to market with a product can be great and may reduce gross profit by as much as 10 percent. Profits and market share are both linked to timely delivery of a product. For example, Procter & Gamble lost a significant share of the disposable diaper market to rival Kimberly-Clark because it was late in introducing a thin diaper to compete with the successful Huggies UltraTrim. Project management can make a difference in managing the time-to-market process. (See Box 13.1.)

PROJECT MANAGEMENT APPROACHES

Two similar approaches used to help manage projects are the **critical path method (CPM)** and **program evaluation and review technique (PERT).** Both approaches were developed in the 1950s. CPM was developed by J. E. Kelly, who worked for Remington-Rand, and M. R. Walker, who worked for DuPont, to schedule maintenance shutdowns in chemical processing plants. PERT was developed by the U.S. Navy and other organizations as part of the Polaris missile project. Both approaches can be viewed as networks that visually represent the tasks to be completed in graphic format, sequenced from left to right across the page. Over the years, PERT and CPM have grown so similar that they are often used interchangeably or as a more generic technique called PERT/CPM. The original differences between the two approaches, however, were that CPM could not accommodate variations in activity times, but PERT could. For the purposes of this text, this distinction will be continued.

THE NETWORK REPRESENTATION

In order to use a network representation as a project model, several assumptions must be satisfied. First, the project must be broken up into small well-defined tasks, or activities. Second, the specific activities must have a definite beginning and end, independent of other activities, and a reliable estimate of the time required to complete each activity. Third, the activities must follow a specific order or sequence. When all activities have been completed, the project must be completed.

CRITICAL PATH METHOD (CPM)
An approach to planning and coordinating large projects by directing managerial focus to the project's most critical aspects and providing an estimate of its duration.

PROGRAM EVALUATION AND REVIEW TECHNIQUE (PERT)
An approach to planning and coordinating large projects in which time estimates for activities are uncertain. Three time estimates are required: optimistic, pessimistic, and most likely.

OPERATIONS OUTLOOK

BOX 13.1

The Role of Project Management in Product Development

New products can get to market more quickly when managed properly. Project management can help in several ways. First, the methods and principles of project management can help managers identify projects or parts of projects that are poorly defined or lack direction. They also can help everyone involved in the project create a common vision and establish a clear direction. The breakdown of the work provides a picture of exactly what is required to get the product to market. Because the vision, direction, and steps required are all evident, the project can be viewed as a whole. This encourages teamwork and good communication across departments and also shows the interdependence and importance of individual tasks in completing the project on time.

As the project unfolds, project management methods require managers to be proactive and make adjustments based on actual outcomes of the project to date. Managers can determine the impact of actual adjustments in terms of time and resources and can consider other alternative plans. This capability provides the opportunity to ask "what-if" types of questions related to both time and money.

Source Adapted from R. Wallace and W. Halverson, "Project Management: A Critical Success Factor or a Management Fad," *Industrial Engineering* (April 1992): 48–50.

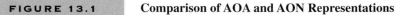

FIGURE 13.1 Comparison of AOA and AON Representations

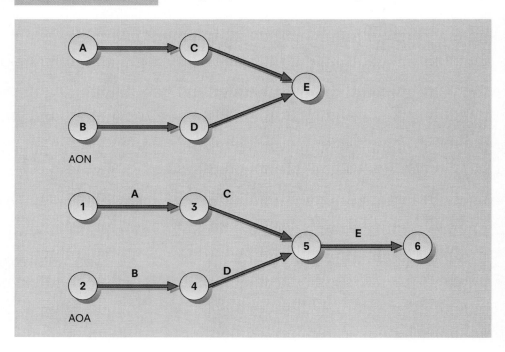

There are two approaches to representing a project using a network. The network representation consists of combinations of arrows and nodes for both approaches. One approach, called the **activity-on-node** (AON) representation, shows each specific task with a node or circle. Arrows represent the sequencing of the activities. The second approach is called the **activity-on-arrow** (AOA) network. In this approach, the arrows or arcs represent the activity, and the nodes represent events. Figure 13.1 compares these two network representations. Both illustrate the same sequence of activities. Although both types of networks are used in practice, the activity-on-node representation will be used exclusively in this text.

ACTIVITY-ON-NODE
A project network convention that identifies project activities with a node or circle. Sequencing is represented with arrows.

ACTIVITY-ON-ARROW
A project network convention that identifies project activities with arrows. Events are represented with nodes or circles.

THE CRITICAL PATH METHOD

Critical path method (CPM) provides a useful approach for determining overall project relationships by directing managerial focus to the project's most critical aspects and providing an estimate of its duration. Example 13.1 demonstrates how a project can be modeled in an AON network format. By incorporating CPM, the expected duration of the project can then be determined.

EXAMPLE 13.1

A CPM Application Sean Jones is starting an electronics company and has selected a site for it. Sean has identified the activities he feels must be completed before opening the business. These activities are listed in Table 13.1, as is the immediate predecessor of each activity. Using this information, construct an activity-on-node network that correctly sequences the activities to be completed prior to the grand opening. When can the grand opening be scheduled?

TABLE 13.1	Activities and Precedence Relationships		
Activity	**Description**	**Immediate Predecessor(s)**	**Time (days)**
A	Purchase facility	—	60
B	Prepare facility	A	25
C	Hire manager	A	10
D	Select merchandise to be sold	C	8
E	Purchase and receive merchandise	D	10
F	Display merchandise	E, H, B	14
G	Hire work force	C	10
H	Train work force	G, J	4
I	Select equipment	C	5
J	Purchase and receive equipment	I	10
K	Prepare for opening day	F	2

SOLUTION

Note that activity C is the immediate predecessor for activities D, G, and I. None of these activities can begin until activity C has been completed. Activities F and H have more than one predecessor. When an activity has two or more predecessors, each predecessor must be completed before the activity begins. Figure 13.2 (page 378) shows how the activities are represented in the AON format.

Figure 13.2 also shows many of the situations that are typically encountered when constructing networks. For example, there are situations in which an activity must be completed before another activity can begin. This is demonstrated by the relationship between A and B. In fact, A must precede both B and C. Another common relationship is demonstrated by the relationships of H to G and J. Both J and G are listed as immediate predecessors of H. Thus H cannot begin until both J and G are completed. The relationships among E, H, B, and F are similar except that the three activities must precede F.

Finding the Critical Path   A network representation of a project shows the work flow from left to right, but it does not provide specific information about the project's duration or which activities are most important to its successful completion. To answer these questions, the concept of a path must be developed. A path is a sequence of activities that originates at the start of the project and stops at the end of it. The number of paths depends on the project's complexity. In Figure 13.2, ACIJHFK is an example of a path. Other paths are ACDEFK, ACGHFK, and ABFK, for a total of four different paths in this network. The **critical path** determines the duration of the project because it is the path in the network that takes the longest amount of time. There may be more than one critical path. Activities on the critical path must be completed on time, or the project will be delayed. A day lost by any activity on the critical path is a day lost for the project.

An important part of successfully managing a project is the management of the critical path. The focus provided by this path gives management an opportunity to concentrate on the aspects of the project that are most critical to its successful and timely completion.

CRITICAL PATH
The path through a project network that takes the longest amount of time.

FIGURE 13.2 **CPM Network Representation (Example 13.1)**

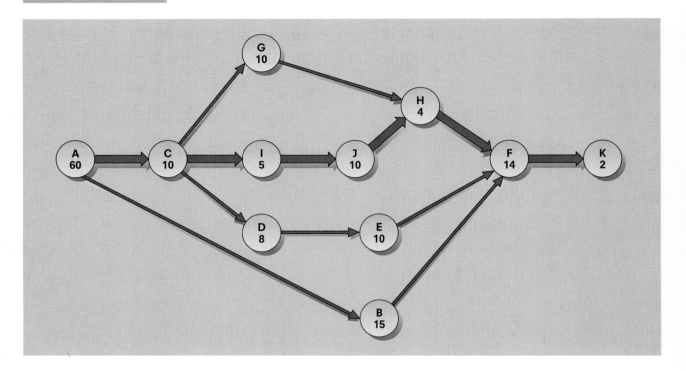

Activities not on the critical path can often be delayed without negatively affecting the project's completion time. An activity's **slack** is the amount of time that an activity may be delayed without affecting the project's completion time. For activities on the critical path, the slack is always zero. One approach to identifying the critical path is to identify activities that have no slack. If an activity not on the critical path is delayed for more than its available slack, a new critical path is created, extending the duration of the project.

An activity's slack is determined by computing four different values for each activity. These values are the early start (ES), early finish (EF), late start (LS), and late finish (LF). The early start is the earliest an activity can begin. For the first activity in the network, the ES is usually 0. The early finish time is the early start time plus the time required to complete the activity. If the time required to complete the activity is t, then

$$EF = ES + t \tag{13.1}$$

The ES time for any activity other than the first is computed by moving from left to right through the network. The ES time is equal to the EF time of the immediate predecessor. If there is more than one predecessor, the ES time is the largest, or maximum, of the EF times of the immediate predecessors because the activity cannot begin until all predecessors have been completed. The computation of the ES and EF values is known as the *first pass,* the *forward pass,* or the *early start schedule.* After the ES and EF times have been computed, the LS and LF values can be determined.

The notation used to designate $ES, EF, LS,$ and LF is displayed in Figure 13.3. The ES and EF times have been computed for the previous example and are shown in Figure 13.4. Note that activity H cannot start until both activity G and activity J are completed.

FIGURE 13.3   **Network Notation Format**

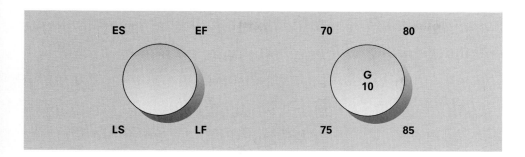

Computing the *LS* and *LF* values begins with the last activity and moves from right to left across the network. It is frequently known as the *backward pass*. It is also referred to as the *late start schedule* or *backward scheduling*. The *LF* for the last activity is set equal to the *EF* of the last activity. The *LS* for the last activity is found by using the following equation:

$$LS = LF - t \tag{13.2}$$

where *t* is the time required to complete the last activity.

Following through the example, the *LF* for activity F is the *LS* from activity *K,* or 103, because *F* is the predecessor of just one activity. If *F* had been the predecessor of more than

FIGURE 13.4   **Results of CPM First Pass**

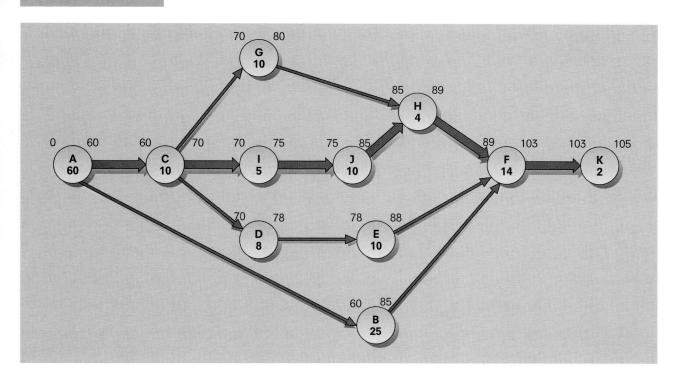

one activity, the *LF* would be equal to the smallest *LS* time of all activities that immediately follow that activity (or alternatively the smallest *LS* of all arrows that exit the specific activity). For example, activity C is the predecessor of more than one activity. The *LF* for activity C is the smallest of the *LS* for activities I, G, or D. That is, the smallest of 70, 75, and 71. The *LS* and *LF* times have been computed for each activity in the example network and are shown in Figure 13.5.

The project duration is 105 days. The values for *ES, EF, LS,* and *LF* are shown in Table 13.2. Slack is computed for each activity by either *LS* − *ES* or *LF* − *EF,* as shown in the table. Those activities with zero slack are A, C, I, J, H, F, and K, which make up the critical path. If each of the activities on the critical path is completed on time, and the remaining activities are done within the available slack time, the project will be completed in 105 days. The critical path is identified as ACIJHFK, as shown in Figure 13.5.

Identifying, sequencing, and scheduling the activities that make up a project are clearly important management tasks. However, the ability to monitor the activities and compare actual performance to planned performance is probably the biggest advantage in using a network approach. The activities on the critical path must be monitored carefully because any activity not completed on time will extend the duration time for the project. Other activities must be monitored closely as well because the failure of an activity to be completed within its slack time may create a situation in which two or more paths become critical. For example, if activity D takes 9 days instead of 8 days, an additional critical path would be formed (ACDEFK). If two critical paths exist, any activity on either path that is not completed on time will delay the completion of the project. The existence of two critical paths would make the project more difficult to manage.

| FIGURE 13.5 | **Results of Backward Pass** |

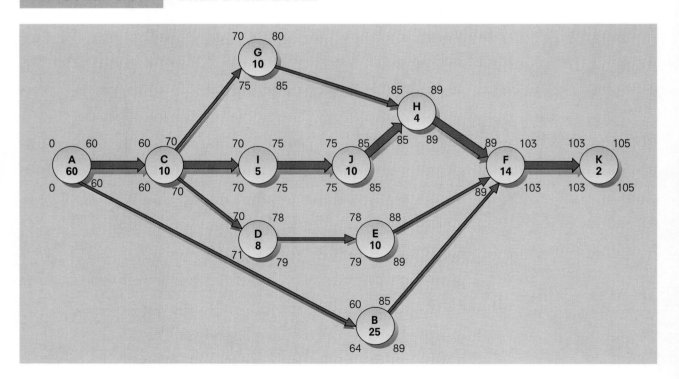

TABLE 13.2	Slack Computations				
Activity	*ES*	*EF*	*LS*	*LF*	**Slack**
A	0	60	0	60	0
B	60	85	64	89	4
C	60	70	60	70	0
D	70	78	71	79	1
E	78	88	79	89	1
F	89	103	89	103	0
G	70	80	75	85	5
H	85	89	85	89	0
I	70	75	70	75	0
J	75	85	75	85	0
K	103	105	103	105	0

In addition to the critical path information, slack computations are also useful in monitoring and controlling projects. The start time of activities with slack can often be modified slightly, allowing resources to be reallocated to complete a critical path activity. The slack available in activities B, D, E, and G, for example, provides management with flexibility to make adjustments to resources.

PROGRAM EVALUATION AND REVIEW TECHNIQUE

In many projects the duration of each activity is not known with a high degree of certainty, and that uncertainty can present significant problems. The program evaluation and review technique (PERT) can deal with projects in which time estimates for activities are uncertain. For example, if there is significant variability in the duration of several activities, the critical path may change. The PERT approach requires three different time estimates. These estimates are denoted *o, m,* and *p,* where

> *o* is an optimistic estimate that reflects the time required under optimum conditions
> *p* is a pessimistic estimate that reflects the time required under the worst case scenario
> *m* is the most likely time estimate

Using these three estimates, the mean and variance of the time estimates can be computed. The beta distribution is often used to compute the mean and variance of the time estimates. The expected time T_e is computed using the following equation:

$$T_e = \frac{o + 4m + p}{6} \tag{13.3}$$

Note that T_e is essentially a weighted average of *o, p,* and *m* (the most likely time estimate), with *m* receiving four times as much weight as *o* or *p.*

The variance for single activity, σ^2, is

$$\sigma^2 = \left(\frac{p - o}{6}\right)^2 \tag{13.4}$$

The standard deviation for the critical path is given by

$$\sigma_p = \sqrt{\Sigma(\text{variances on the critical path})} \qquad \textbf{(13.5)}$$

The variance and standard deviation provide a means to measure the uncertainty related to the time estimates. If it is assumed that the completion times of the critical path are normally distributed, the probability of completing the path by a certain time, T, can be computed. Then $T - T_e$ yields the difference between the expected completion time and the time in question. This difference, divided by the standard deviation, σ_p, yields the number of standard deviations T is from T_e. This value is commonly referred to as Z, as shown in the following equation:

$$Z = \frac{T - T_e}{\sigma_p} \qquad \textbf{(13.6)}$$

By using a standard normal probability table like the one in Appendix A, the value of Z can be used to determine the probability that the project date T can be met. The following example demonstrates how this is done.

EXAMPLE 13.2

A PERT Application   In the solution to Sean's opening day problem, the time values used were actually estimates of the time required to complete each activity. Sean has determined an optimistic (o), pessimistic (p), and most likely time (m) for each of these activities. These values are shown in Table 13.3. The values for T_e are computed using equation 13.3. Although the values for T_e vary slightly from those provided in the original example, the critical path for these activities is the same. The project completion time, 105 days, is the same as well. The variances for all activities, computed using equation 13.4, are also provided in Table 13.3.

The variance for the critical path consists of the sum of the variances of the activities ($\Sigma\sigma_p^2$) along the critical path ACIJHFK. Thus,

$$\begin{array}{ccccccc} \text{(A)} & \text{(C)} & \text{(I)} & \text{(J)} & \text{(H)} & \text{(F)} & \text{(K)} \end{array}$$
$$\Sigma \sigma_p^2 = 25.00 + 0.69 + 0.44 + 1.78 + 0.11 + 0.44 + 0.03$$

$$= 28.49$$

TABLE 13.3		Expected Values and Variances			

Activity	o	m	p	T_e	$\sigma_p^2 = [(p - o)/6]^2$
A	45	60	75	60.00	**25.00**
B	21	25	32	25.50	3.36
C	8	10	13	10.17	**0.69**
D	4	8	10	7.67	1.00
E	6	10	16	10.33	2.78
F	12	14	16	14.00	**0.44**
G	9	10	14	10.50	0.69
H	3	4	5	4.00	**0.11**
I	3	5	7	5.00	**0.44**
J	6	10	14	10.00	**1.78**
K	1	2	2	1.83	**0.03**

and from equation 13.5

$$\sigma_p = \sqrt{\Sigma \, \sigma_p^2}$$
$$= \sqrt{28.49}$$
$$= 5.34$$

With this information, it is possible to answer questions about the likely completion time of the project. For example, to determine the likelihood that the critical path will be at least 5 days late (completed on or after day 110), equation 13.6 would be used.

$$Z = \frac{T - T_e}{\sigma_p}$$
$$= \frac{110 - 105}{5.34}$$
$$= 0.94$$

So, the probability that T is greater than or equal to 110 is equal to the probability that Z is equal to or greater than 0.94; that is, $P(T \geq 110) = P(Z \geq 0.94)$. By using the standard normal probability table found in Appendix A, the value for Z is found to be 0.3264. In Figure 13.6, the area of interest lies to the right of $Z = 0.94$, and because the area under one-half the normal curve (or from 0 to the right) is 0.5, the probability that the project will take at least 110 days is $0.5 - 0.3264 = 0.1736$. Thus, there is a 17.4% probability that the project would be at least 5 days late.

FIGURE 13.6   **Area under the Normal Curve to the Right of $Z = 0.94$**

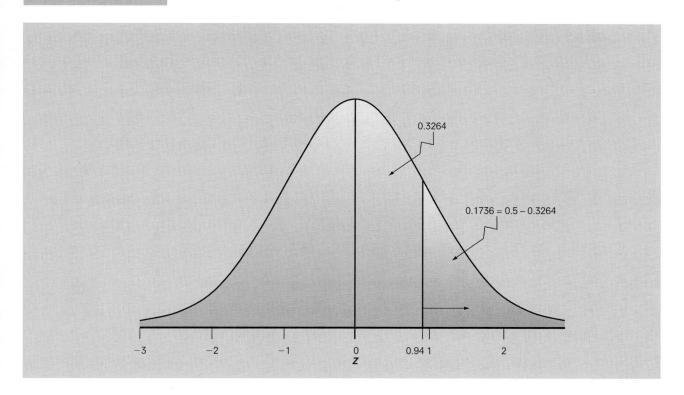

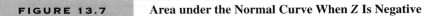

FIGURE 13.7   **Area under the Normal Curve When Z Is Negative**

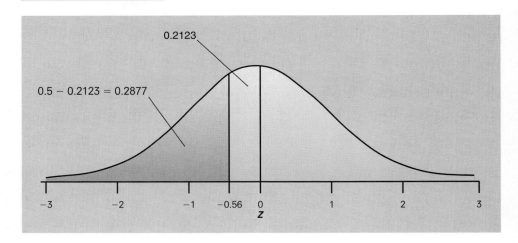

If the goal is to finish early, that is, before day 105, the value for Z would be negative. For example, to determine the probability of finishing at least 3 days ahead of time, equation 13.6 would be used. The value for Z is

$$Z = \frac{T - T_e}{\sigma_p}$$

$$= \frac{102 - 105}{5.34}$$

$$= -0.5618$$

In Figure 13.7, the area to the left of -0.5618 represents the probability that the job will be finished at least 3 days early. This area is $0.5 - 0.2123 = 0.2877$. Thus, the probability the job will be done at least 3 days early is 0.2877.

Notice in Table 13.3 that the variation in the example project is almost completely a result of the variability of activity A. If the time for activity A were known with more certainty, the variability associated with the completion time could be largely eliminated. If no variability existed in activity A, the variance for the project would be reduced from 28.49 to 3.49, and σ_p would be $\sqrt{3.49} = 1.87$. Using this value for σ_p would significantly change the probability that the project would be 5 days late. If the variability of activity A could be eliminated, the new value of Z would be

$$Z = \frac{T - T_e}{\sigma_p}$$

$$Z = \frac{110 - 105}{1.87}$$

$$= 2.67$$

If $Z = 2.67$, then $P(T \geq 110) = P(Z \geq 2.67)$. From the table in Appendix A, a value of $Z = 2.67$ yields a value of 0.4962. Thus, $P(T \geq 110) = 0.5000 - 0.4962 = 0.0038$. The probability of being at least 5 days late is approximately 0.38%. In other words, this project would be 5 days or more late in about 4 cases out of 1,000.

The management focus on the PERT network should not only be on the critical path activities but also on the critical path activities having the most variability. These activities will provide the greatest potential savings in terms of project duration. TQM's quest for the elimination of variability is a valuable approach when applied to project activities on the critical path. Eliminating variability within activities eliminates uncertainty from the overall project and provides more confidence in the project's duration time.

In Example 13.2 the first activity is the one with the most variability. Probabilities could be recomputed after the first activity has been completed by using the variances of the remaining activities on the critical path. This later computation would provide a much more accurate projection of the likelihood of completion by a certain date because most of the variability would be gone. After activity A is completed, the variability in the network would almost be eliminated and the project completion time would become much more predictable.

It is important to point out that not all efforts to reduce variability in activities are equal. Elimination of variability should be focused toward those activities with the greatest amount of variability and on eliminating variability of activities on the critical path. Investments in technology or special help designed to eliminate variability on activities off the critical path will not reduce the variability of the project duration, unless the critical path changes.

CRASHING PROJECTS

In many situations, failure to complete a project on time results in a penalty, like a monetary fine for each day a construction project is late. In other cases, the penalty takes the form of weakened competitive position, as a result of poor customer service, lost sales, or a general reputation for being unreliable. The relative importance of completing a project on time may vary, but because projects are usually one of the ways organizations accomplish their goals, on-time completion is important for achieving those goals. The process of **crashing** is designed to identify the best ways to reduce project duration.

CRASHING
A process used to identify the best ways to reduce project duration.

Crashing is accomplished by reducing the time required to complete at least some of the activities on the critical path. It is an approach designed to help management decide which activities to reduce and how best to invest money in these activity time reductions.

Consider the network presented in Figure 13.8. The project duration is 35 days, and the critical path is ABEG. Suppose it is important that the project be completed in as close to 30 days as possible.

Crashing a network is complicated by the fact that, as activity times on the critical path are reduced, the critical path may change or more than one may be formed. If more than one critical path is formed, all the critical paths must be reduced in order to reduce the project duration, making it more difficult for management to focus on the appropriate activities and more likely that competition for resources will affect activities on the critical path. Selecting which activities to reduce in the crashing process is critical to allow management to get the most project improvement for its investment.

Some aspects of the crashing process may seem familiar because of their similarity to the line-balancing process described earlier in this text. Recall that in order to eliminate idle time in the line, an attempt was made to balance the total time for each work center. This was done by grouping tasks in such a way as to not have some work centers with total times that were significantly different from others. Constraint management correctly

FIGURE 13.8	**Example Network for Crashing**

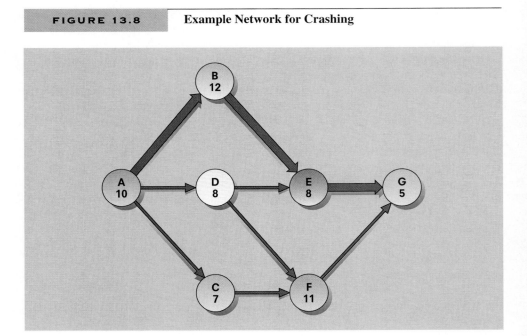

points out that reducing the time required on any of the work centers with idle time will not improve the cycle time. However, if the time on the constraint work center, the one that has no idle time and sets the cycle time, were reduced, the cycle time would be reduced. The role of the critical path is similar to the role of the constraint work center. The critical path sets the time of the project and, in a sense, is the constraint for the network.

Table 13.4 provides data related to the activities from Figure 13.8. The normal time required to complete the activity is presented, along with a crash time, which is an absolute minimum time required to complete the activity and can only be obtained through increased costs. The daily crash cost for each activity, which is in addition to normal costs, is also provided. Crash costs consist of any additional costs that would be incurred in order to reduce the activity time. They might include such costs as additional labor or special or additional equipment.

TABLE 13.4	**Crash Data**

Activity Name	Normal Time (days)	Crash Time	Cost (cost/day)
A	10	9	400
B	12	11	300
C	7	4	300
D	8	5	350
E	8	7	500
F	11	9	400
G	5	4	500

Crashing a network begins with an examination of all the activities on the critical path. The project is reduced 1 day at a time by reducing the times of those activities that will require the least additional cost and still reduce the overall length of the project by 1 day. Because the critical path consists of activities A, B, E, and G, the additional costs associated with reducing each of those activity times are compared. To do this computation, refer to Table 13.4. Because activity B requires the least cost to obtain the 1 day reduction, it will be reduced from 12 days to 11 days, at a cost of $300, reducing the critical path to 34 days.

Initially, only one critical path existed, thus the only activities of concern were on that path. As the project is shortened, however, other paths may also become critical. Table 13.5 identifies the four possible paths in the network and the length of each after the reduction of activity B by 1 day. Paths ABEG and ADFG are now critical paths. Therefore, both paths must be shortened simultaneously in order for the project duration to be reduced. To get the most reduction for the least cost, it is logical to seek out activities that are on both critical paths so that reducing one activity time would result in a reduction in both critical paths.

The choices available are to consider the additional costs of activities common to both paths, such as A or G, or to reduce E from path ABEG and also reduce D or F from path ADFG. (Note that B cannot be reduced further because it is already at the absolute minimum time required to complete the activity.) From Table 13.4 it can be seen that reducing a single activity, such as A or G, is the least costly alternative and that A, at $400, is preferable to G, at $500. Because activity A is reduced to 9 days, and A is also a part of all four paths, the time required for each path has also been reduced by 1 day. No additional critical paths are created. The project length is now 33 days. Again, for the next reduction, reducing a single activity that is common to both critical paths is cheaper than reducing two different activities. G, at a cost of $500, is the only remaining choice. When G is reduced, the critical path becomes 32 days.

Further reduction is more difficult because the common activities, A and G, cannot be reduced further. For critical path ABEG, E is reduced at a cost of $500. For critical path ADFG, D is reduced at a cost of $350. Both D and E have been reduced to 7 days. Because none of the activities on ACFG has been reduced, there are now three critical paths: ABEG, ADFG, and ACFG. Figure 13.9 shows the current network. The project duration is now 31 days.

The project cannot be reduced to fewer than 31 days because all of the activities on path ABEG have been reduced as far as possible. Table 13.6 summarizes the decisions that were made and the relative costs involved.

TABLE 13.5	**New Network Paths**				

Path		Duration in Days			
A B E G	35	34	33	32	31
A D E G	31	31	30	29	27
A D F G	34	34	33	32	31
A C F G	33	33	32	31	31
Activity crashed		B	A	G	D and E
Crash cost		$300	400	500	850
Cumulative cost		$300	700	1,200	2,050

FIGURE 13.9   **Network Times after Crashing**

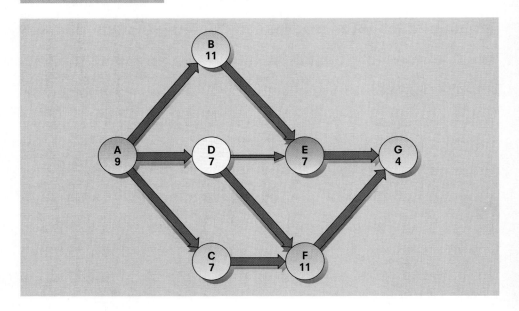

LIMITED RESOURCES

For the networks presented to this point, a major assumption has been that the resources required to complete the network activities were not a factor in deciding the order and timing of the activities, and resource shortages did not extend the project duration. But these assumptions are not always true. Limited resources affect the completion time of a project whenever different activities within the project need the same resource at the same time. Limited resources may be almost anything: the size of the work force, the number of trucks available, the number of units of a specific type of equipment, the number of electricians, the number of computers, or the number of trained interviewers. For smaller projects, identifying limited resources is not difficult. In large projects with many activities occurring at the same time, however, identifying limited resources becomes much more difficult. Ignoring the effects of limited resources can result in a project not being completed on time.

TABLE 13.6   **Results of the Crashing Process**

Feasible Activities	Lowest Cost	Project Duration (days)	Critical Path(s)			Total Crash Cost ($)
A ,B, E, G	B	34	A B E G	A D F G		300
A, G, E and (D or F)	A	33	A B E G	A D F G		700
G, E and (D or F)	G	32	A B E G	A D F G		1,200
E and (D or F)	E, D	31	A B E G	A D F G	A C F G	2,050
			Total Cost			4,250

| FIGURE 13.10 | **Example Network with Limited Resources** |

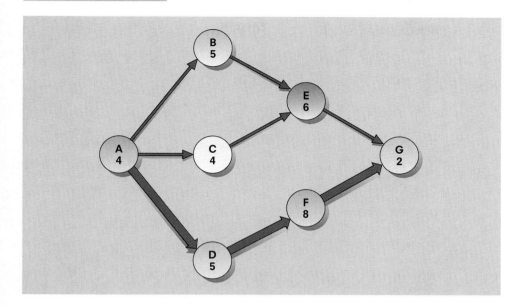

Consider the network provided in Figure 13.10. There are three paths in this network. The critical path is ADFG. The project duration is 19 days.

Management must consider the time required for each activity in this network, as well as worker limitations. Table 13.7 displays the worker requirements per activity. The total number of workers available for this project is 12. As activity A is completed, activities B, C, and D are all eligible to start. If these three activities were begun simultaneously, they would require a total of 14 workers. Only 12 workers are available. Because activity C will have to be postponed until B or D is completed, the project duration is extended an additional 5 days, and the new critical path will pass through C, E, and G. Without special attention paid to the requirements and availability of the resources, PERT/CPM would not identify this problem and the new critical path would not be identified.

When resource unavailability prevents activities and the project from being completed on time, an entirely new set of problems arises. To minimize the project duration, the key issue for management is determining which activities should be scheduled first, second, and so on. This new problem is essentially a scheduling problem. Unfortunately, just as there was no guaranteed method for assigning job tasks to work centers in the line-balancing problem, there is no general way of assigning activities to guarantee a schedule that will minimize project duration.

The fundamental decision to be made whenever an activity has been completed is which eligible activity should be next?

| TABLE 13.7 | **Worker Requirement per Activity** |

Activity	A	B	C	D	E	F	G
Worker Requirement	10	4	2	8	6	9	5

TABLE 13.8		Scheduling Activities
Feasible Activities	**Selected Activities**	**Reason for Selection**
A	A	Precedence
B, C, D	D	Zero slack (on the critical path)
B, C	B	Least amount of slack
C, F	C	C is now on the critical path
F	F	C and F can be done simultaneously before E
E	E	
G	G	

An intuitive method is presented that provides a satisfactory, but not necessarily optimal, solution. Under this method, the activity with the least amount of slack follows the activity that has been completed. Recall that slack is the amount of time an activity can be delayed without affecting the project's completion time. If ties exist, the tie breaker would be to choose the activity with the longest completion time. This method supplements the precedence relationships required by the project.

There are other alternatives as well. For example, one alternative would be to schedule the activity with the least variance first or to schedule the activity requiring the shortest amount of time first. Many methods used to cope with these situations are similar to priority or dispatching rules used in traditional job shop sequencing.

Table 13.8 shows how the activities are scheduled by choosing the activities with less slack first. Recall that the critical path is ADFG. Activity A must be completed first, followed by D, which is on the critical path and thus has no slack. B is chosen over C because it has less slack. After activities A, D, and B are completed, C is chosen because it is on the new critical path of ACEG and has no slack. F is the next choice because it is the only feasible alternative. For the remaining activities, E must precede G.

The load profile is a useful tool for services and manufacturers to use when planning projects with resource availability problems. It shows how much of a given resource is needed and when it is required. A load profile for workers in this project is shown in Figure 13.11. The profile is constructed from the data provided in Figure 13.10 and Tables 13.7 and 13.8. Activities are entered in Figure 13.11 based on the scheduling sequence shown in Table 13.8. Activities are started in sequence as long as the total work force required at one time does not exceed 12. Table 13.7 shows the number of workers required for each activity. Note that the project duration is 25 days instead of the initially expected 19 days. Clearly, limited resources affect project duration.

If planning allowed the project to begin early enough to take into account the effects of limited resources, competition between activities for the same resource could be avoided and the project could be completed by the appropriate time.

STRENGTHS AND WEAKNESSES OF PERT/CPM

PERT and CPM networks offer managers an opportunity to better understand and manage projects. They give managers the ability to identify the specific activities and relationships within a project and estimate the time required to complete each activity. This helps them

FIGURE 13.11   **Load Profile of Workers**

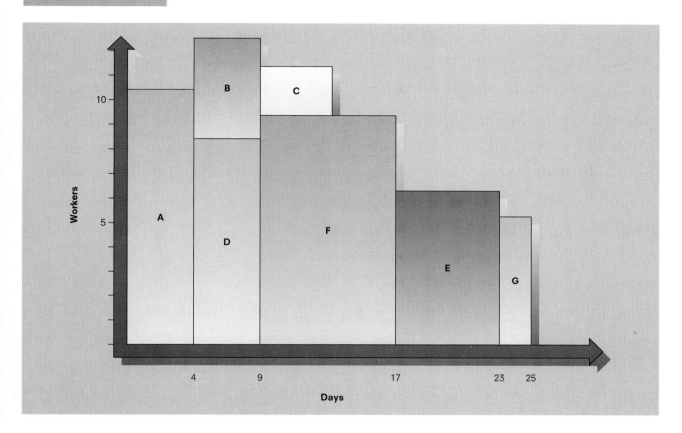

view the whole project rather than just small pieces. By identifying the critical path, PERT/CPM provides management a focus as the project is being monitored. Additionally, the networks provide a graphic model of the project and its key activities. One weakness with networks is that they do not allow for the possibility that some activities may not be completed at all, throwing the time projection for the project into disarray. Some structured processes for developing contingency plans can minimize the impact of such occurrences.

PERT/CPM can consider uncertainty in activity completion time but not uncertainty about whether actual completion will occur. Risk of completion exists in such activities as research and development and in the reengineering of processes, where some attempts will not be successful. Risk of completion time means the duration may be longer or shorter than expected, but it will be completed.

In addition to the PERT/CPM network, the process decision program chart (PDPC process) can be incorporated into the project planning process.[4] This starts as a macro-level flow chart of the project's activities. For each activity there may be more than one approach leading to completion. Each of these approaches may have more than one possible outcome, depending on problems encountered, environmental issues, or other difficult-to-

---

[4]D. L. Kimbler, "Operational Planning: Going Beyond PERT with TQM Tools," *Industrial Management* (September/October 1993): 26–29.

OPERATIONS OUTLOOK

BOX 13.2

TQM Tools in Project Management

The current emphasis on quality highlights several factors directly related to project management. First, the increased emphasis on building quality through effective design increases the emphasis placed on how research and development projects are conducted. Second, the increased use of reengineering as one approach to process improvement creates projects related to the redesign of processes. Third, many of the tools associated with TQM have been found useful in project planning. The first two factors demonstrate the increased need for effective project management because there are more projects to manage. The third provides a useful addition to the standard tool kit for project managers. The application of several TQM tools to project management is summarized below:

Source   Adapted from D. L. Kimbler, "Operational Planning: Going Beyond PERT with TQM Tools," *Industrial Management* (September/October 1993): 26–29.

Project Planning Task	TQM Tools to Apply	Project Planning Task	TQM Tools to Apply
Define objectives	Use affinity diagrams to synthesize results of discussions and brainstorming, within the guidance of an overall theme.	Specify deployment of key tasks	Use flow charts with an added dimension of responsibility.
Define organization	Use a tree diagram to illustrate the structure of the problem being addressed.	Define project structure	Use the Process Decision Program Chart (PDPC process) or PERT/CPM.
Define key relationships	Use the interrelationship diagram to show the causal relationships between pairs of objectives and to depict bottlenecks.	Model implementation	Use a matrix of targets and means to align tasks structure with goals.
		Model task alignment	Use a run chart to track progress and align lower-level tasks with goals.
Model macro structure	Use a flow diagram to model the solution structure.	Feasibility review	Use matrices and checklists to look at tradeoffs between resources.
Establish and organize current knowledge	Use cause-and-effect, Pareto, and matrix diagrams to increase detail in the model of the macro structure.	Periodic review	Extract key documents to guide reviews and help establish a review schedule.
Establish operational requirements	Use Pareto and matrix diagrams to organize information requirements and definitions.		

predict influences. Some of the possible outcomes may be undesirable and lead to a failure of completion.

For each possible outcome, a contingency plan is defined for one of two possible states. First, we might choose to allow the outcome to occur and define ways to recover or react to it, so that the activity and project can continue to completion. Alternatively, we might choose to prevent the outcome because its impact would be so severe.

Options, possible outcomes, and potential contingency plans are studied thoroughly before each activity is undertaken. Once the activities and relationships have been defined using PERT/CPM and the range of possible outcomes and contingency plans have been developed through PDPC, the potential for unexpected outcomes leading to risk of completion is reduced.

A model, however, is only as good as the data that have served as input. Activities are sometimes sequenced improperly, time estimates may be inaccurate, and activities may be omitted entirely. Managers must recognize that time estimates are forecasts, and forecasts are frequently wrong. The most costly errors are typically not clerical errors but those that occur because the project wasn't understood completely. Computer software designed for project management is often necessary for complex projects. Even software cannot help management identify, before the fact, all activities that must be completed on a project that has never before been attempted. This can only come from managerial expertise and foresight. The success of the project planning effort can be increased by integrating the PERT/CPM techniques discussed here with other known successful approaches to managing tasks, such as the TQM tools. (See Box 13.2.)

SUMMARY

PERT and CPM are two commonly used approaches for managing projects. The network approaches provided by these techniques enhance management's ability to plan, schedule, and monitor complex projects. By identifying the project duration through the critical path, managers separate the important few from the trivial many and focus their attention on the most important activities. A process known as crashing can often be used to shorten the length of projects. Crashing is accomplished by shortening the critical path activities as well as other activities that may become critical as the project length is cut.

The use of PERT/CPM has been the target of criticism in recent years. Part of the problem is related to management's failure to acknowledge the effects that limited resources have on project duration. Some experts suggest that focusing on the critical path activities is less important than focusing on activities that have the greatest variability. Using forecasts of activity times as the basis for a firm commitment for project duration is also viewed by some as suspect. Because of the uncertainty typically associated with such forecasts, frequent updating is essential for successfully monitoring and predicting completion dates.

TOTCO REVISITED

CROSS-LINKS Marci has clearly made some false assumptions when developing the schedule for this project. What aspects of project management did Marci neglect? How could this be avoided in planning for future projects?

Given current staffing levels and a 20 working-day month, how long will it take to finish product and process design?

Could this time be shortened? How? What would be the disadvantages of using outside help to restore the resource conflict and shorten the lead time? Devise a process to identify, in advance, the problem that has resulted in this project's taking longer than expected.

QUESTIONS FOR REVIEW

1. Compare PERT and CPM.
2. What is slack? How is it used?
3. What requirements must be satisfied before CPM or PERT could be used?
4. What are the major advantages of the network (PERT/CPM) approach?
5. What are the three major activities that make up project management?
6. What are the disadvantages of the network (PERT/CPM) approach?
7. Why is the critical path important in project management?
8. How is the critical path determined?
9. Define crashing.
10. What is the effect of creating more than one critical path in the crashing process?
11. How do limited resources affect project management?

QUESTIONS FOR THOUGHT AND DISCUSSION

1. How can PERT/CPM be improved?
2. Discuss the crashing process. What weaknesses are present in this process?

3. How would you manage a project in which the completion times of the activities were just estimates?

INTEGRATIVE QUESTIONS

1. How can constraint management principles be applied to project management?
2. How does the concept of the critical path relate to the concept of a constraint?
3. How can project management be used to help implement

TQM or JIT? What resources might be involved? Would any of them be limited?

4. How might project management be used in identifying a new business location?

PROBLEMS

1. Given the following set of activities and precedence relationships, construct an AON network.

Activity	Predecessors	
A	—	
B	A	
C	—	
D	B	
E	C	
F	B	
G	C	
H	E	G
I	D	F
J	H	I

2. Construct an AON network based upon the following information.

Activity	Predecessors		
A	—		
B	A		
C	A		
D	A		
E	B		
F	B		
G	C		
H	E	F	
I	D	G	F
J	H	I	

3. Determine the critical path and the amount of slack for each activity in the network shown below.

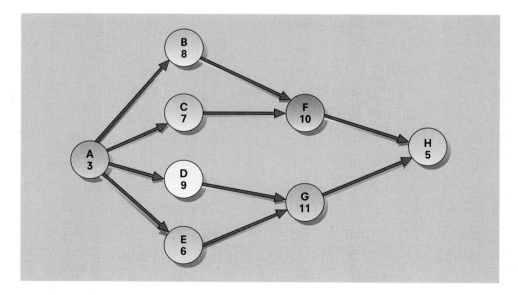

4. Determine the critical path and slack for each activity in the network provided.

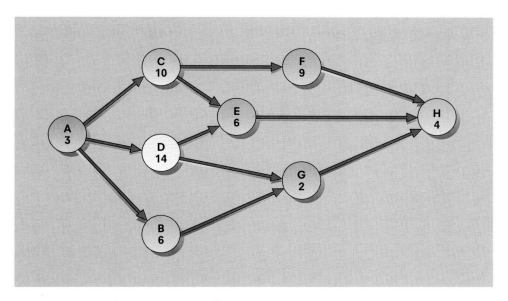

5. The accompanying table gives the pessimistic, most likely, and optimistic times as well as the precedence relationships for all activities in a project. Determine the critical path and construct the network. What is the likelihood the project will be completed in 60 days?

Activity	Predecessors	Optimistic (*o*)	Most Likely (*m*)	Pessimistic (*p*)
A	—	12	15	18
B	—	14	16	20
C	A	9	12	16
D	B	6	10	16
E	C	9	12	15
F	C D	4	5	6
G	D F	7	11	14
H	E G	10	15	19

6. The time estimates for a PERT network as well as precedence relationships are given in the accompanying table. Determine the critical path and construct the network. What is the probability the project will be completed by day 67?

Activity	Optimistic (*o*)	Most Likely (*m*)	Pessimistic (*p*)	Predecessor
A	4	4	4	—
B	9	10	12	—
C	12	16	18	A
D	12	17	20	B
E	14	17	21	B
F	8	11	15	C
G	7	10	12	C D
H	16	18	21	D E
I	21	24	26	F G H

7. A project is defined below by the activities and the completion times provided in the table. Crash times and the daily cost to crash each activity are also provided.

    a. Determine the project duration and the critical path.
    b. If the project needed to be reduced by 5 days, what would you do?

Activity	Predecessors	Normal Time	Crash Time	Crash Cost/Day ($)
A	—	10	8	500
B	A	12	9	600
C	A	8	7	400
D	A	14	11	350
E	C D	18	15	550
F	B E	7	5	450
G	D	9	7	275
H	G E	8	7	475
I	F E H	10	9	700

8. The accompanying network has been solved, and the critical path is ACDF with a project duration of 33 days. Using the crash data provided, reduce the project duration as much as possible.

Activity	Normal Time	Crash Time	Crash Cost ($)
A	10	8	250
B	12	10	300
C	6	5	200
D	8	7	400
E	5	5	
F	9	8	350

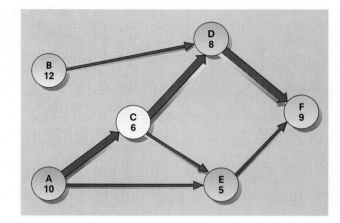

9. The project has a critical path of 33 weeks. The critical path is ABFG. This construction project requires the use of cranes. The minimum number of cranes needed at any given time is shown in the table. A total of 5 cranes is available. How will the crane requirement affect the length of the project?

Activity	A	B	C	D	E	F	G
Cranes	0	3	2	4	3	2	0

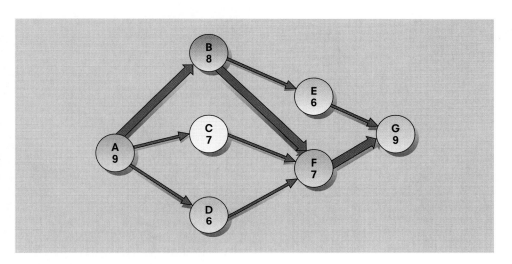

SUGGESTED READINGS

Aquilano, N. J., and D. E. Smith. "A Formal Set of Algorithms for Project Scheduling-Material Requirements Planning." *Journal of Operations Management* 1 (1980): 57–67.

Weiss, J. W., and R. K. Wysocki. *5-Phase Project Management.* Reading, Mass.: Addison-Wesley, 1992.

Weist, J. D., and F. K. Levy. *A Management Guide to PERT/CPM.* 2nd ed. Englewood Cliffs, N.J.: Prentice-Hall, 1977.

PART IV

MANAGING THE
PHYSICAL SYSTEM

We can imagine that about five thousand years ago, when some Grand Manager of Construction in ancient Egypt finally figured out a way to set one row of 30-ton limestone blocks on top of another, he must have insisted that all the workers use the same technique. This may have been the beginning of standard operating procedures. As workers learned that some ways of doing things were better than others, policies and procedures were born. And, as organizations became more complex, day-to-day and minute-by-minute decisions became more important and more difficult. ■ In Part IV we examine the techniques and designs for systems that managers may use in making thousands of resource decisions every day. And we see that merely making these resource decisions is not enough. Decisions reached must be consistent with a firm's business objectives, and they must be supported by all the firm's business functions. ■

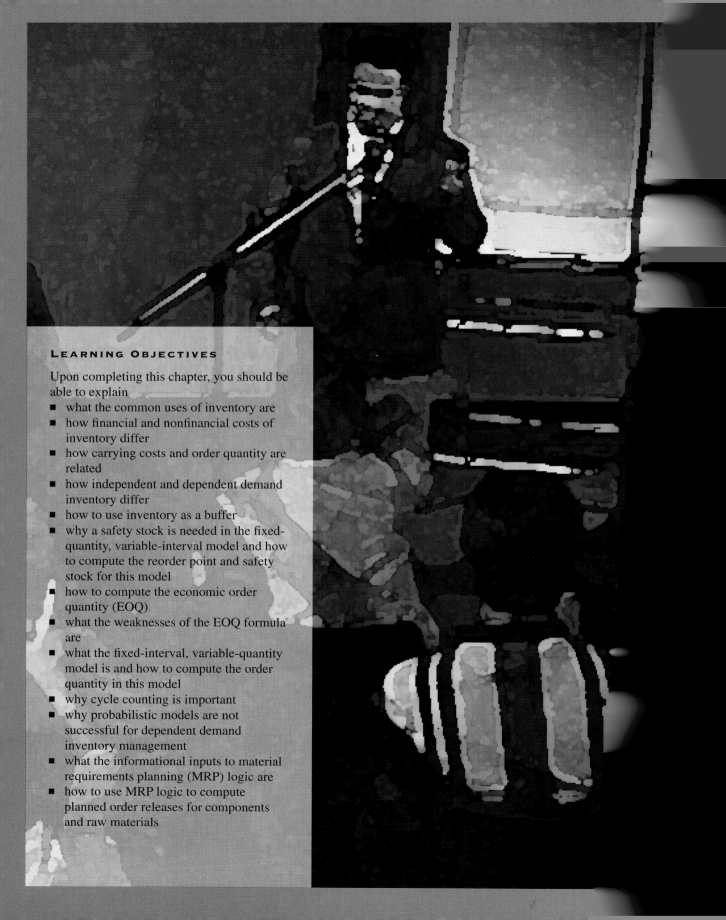

MANAGING INVENTORY

Proof Positive

Waterproof Outdoors is a manufacturer of a number of outdoor sports-related accessories, many of which were designed for use around and in water. The products include neoprene eyeglass straps, so-called dry bags for storage of items while canoeing or boating, neoprene wading shoes, wrap-around nylon and Velcro watch bands, and waterproof wallets. Waterproof Outdoors products are sold through outfitters, sporting goods stores, and marinas. ■ Kyle Packard, V.P. for sales, scheduled his monthly meeting of sales reps for Monday morning. As usual, everyone was there early. Kyle could tell from the informal chatter that all was not well with the group. Kyle heard people say "backorders," "late deliveries," and "get their act together" a number of times. ■ At 9:05, Kyle called the meeting to order and opened the same way he always did, with a question to the group, "How's it going?" ■ The response was somewhat overwhelming. Of the 12 reps, at least 8 were talking at the same time. Kyle held up his hands and shouted "One at a time, please!" ■ Elana Brant was the first to speak. "Out of 70 customers, 22 have had backorders this past week! Last week it was 16. The week before it was 12. If this trend continues, they'll have no product to sell. We're already turning over 20 percent of our customers to our competitors each year. Time we spend recruiting new customers cuts into the time we spend with those we already have. It's a vicious cycle that is being made much worse with these poor delivery practices." ■ Other reps jumped in with comments of their own, but none were substantively different from Elana's. It was clearly a serious problem and one that was likely to cost the company in the short and long term. Kyle decided he should cancel the planned agenda and concentrate on this problem. He told the group to take a 20-minute break while he tried to arrange to bring in Stanley Pierce, the inventory manager. ■ Stan was not that surprised when Kyle described the situation. In fact, he was well aware of the problem and was willing to explain to the reps what was being done to correct it. ■ Kyle called the meeting back to order and introduced Stan to the group, even though everyone knew him. Stan began his informal presentation. "I know all of you are upset with the poor delivery practices we've been encountering lately. I want you to know that we're aware of it, and we think we have gotten a temporary handle on the problem. As a stopgap measure, we're doubling our production of the fastest moving items. That should eliminate 90 percent of the backorders you've been experiencing. The long-term solution is much more difficult, however. The roots of the problem are in the way we determine what to produce. We're certain that that's the problem, but we're not sure of a solution. We're hiring a consulting firm to help us identify the best course of action. Let me explain what we think the problem is." ■ Stan began by sketching a simple diagram on the easel. "We produce to fill two separate inventories, represented by these two circles. The first is the finished goods inventory, which you all know about. The second is our component inventory, which contains all of the partially completed items, components, and raw materials. We forecast the demand for each inventory type based on demand from 2 weeks before. For example, this week's demand for every item in each inventory was forecast a week ago last Friday based on that week's demand. These numbers provided the basis for last week's production. Last Friday all of the completed stock was transferred to finished goods inventory. All components were put into the component inventory. It's really that simple." ■ Stan went on with the description. "We are finding that as we have increased the product variety, our demand forecasts have been less accurate. Sometimes we're high, sometimes we're low. Demand for components is becoming especially difficult to predict. The variability of component demand has become enormous. Some weeks the demand is zero; the next week it's in the hundreds. We think we may have to manage these two different inventories with completely different approaches, but we're really not sure. That's what we're hoping to get from the consultants. As I mentioned, the increased production will eliminate many of the backorders, but it will also inflate our inventories far beyond what we can endure for the long term. It cannot be a long-term solution." ■ Kyle stopped Stan at that point and thanked him for coming in. ■

The JIT philosophy describes excess inventory as one of the key wastes to eliminate. Excess inventory diminishes a firm's ability to compete and particularly affects the competitive priorities of price, quality, flexibility, and time. Appropriately placed inventory, in appropriate quantities, is important, however, and ensures that the customer can be served reliably and promptly. Appropriate levels of inventory enhance all the competitive priorities because they protect a business from disruptions that could hinder its operation. If all suppliers were perfectly dependable, if machines never broke down, and if demand could be forecast with perfect accuracy, inventory needs would diminish. Excess inventory frequently exists, however, not only to prevent disruptions from hindering operations, but also as a result of poor decision making.

Inventory is always the result of a decision—it doesn't just "happen." It may be the result of a purchasing decision or a production schedule. If unwanted inventory exists, it must be the result of a poor decision or of unanticipated changes in demand. But effective inventory management requires a difficult balancing act because firms are trying to achieve two conflicting objectives. They want to have enough inventory on hand to provide an acceptable level of customer service, while also maintaining inventory levels low enough to keep costs down.

It is useful to think of inventory as stored capacity. Excess inventory protects firms from many of the same disruptions that would otherwise be absorbed with excess capacity. A large finished goods inventory or excess capacity can enhance a firm's ability to respond quickly to a customer order, for example. A manufacturing firm with excess inventory must either have excess capacity or it must produce some items in excess while creating shortages in others.

Inventory is often measured as if it were capacity. For example, many companies describe their quantity of finished goods inventory in *days of production* or *days of demand.* "Twelve days of finished goods" simply means that the amount is equivalent to 12 days of demand. "Twelve days' supply of raw materials inventory" means that the raw materials are sufficient to last for 12 days of production.

WHY CARRY INVENTORY?

Firms carry inventory for a number of reasons, most commonly to meet customer demand, eliminate direct dependencies (decoupling) to minimize the effect of disruptions, absorb demand fluctuations, or take advantage of volume economies. These reasons are discussed in more detail below.

The Grainger Division of W. W. Grainger, Inc., is a distributor of maintenance, repair, and operations products. Contractors are typical of Grainger customers, who must often make urgent, unplanned purchases. They rely on Grainger to have what they need, when they need it. To meet customer needs nationwide, the division has more than 330 branch locations and inventories thousands of MRO items.

Source Courtesy of W. W. Grainger, Inc.

Meeting customer demand is an important use of inventory. The success of major retailers like Toys 'Я' Us, Home Depot, and Computer City depends on their ability to satisfy the customer immediately. Make-to-stock (MTS) firms also compete on the basis of quick response to a customer order. For an MTS firm, a stockout often translates directly into a lost sale, so it must achieve a balance between maximizing customer service and minimizing costs associated with finished goods inventory.

Make-to-order and make-to-stock/assemble-to-order firms also carry inventory, but it is more likely to be work-in-process (WIP) than finished goods. Nevertheless, response time is important to the customer. Often partially completed products will be kept in stock to reduce the time between a customer's order and delivery. Maintaining finished goods and WIP inventory to reduce a customer's lead time can be very important to the firm's competitive position by improving response time and dependability of delivery.

Eliminating direct dependencies between processing steps, or **decoupling,** as it is often known, helps protect against idle capacity. Consider, for example, the sequence of events when 2,300 workers walked off the job at a Lordstown, Ohio, tool-and-die plant operated by General Motors Corp. Lordstown supplied key components to twelve other assembly plants. Within a week, seven of those plants closed their doors as well, not because their workers were on strike but because of a lack of components. In all, nearly 35,000 workers were idled.[1] Raw materials inventory acts to decouple a manufacturer or service firm from direct dependence on its suppliers.

DECOUPLING
Reducing the direct dependency a process has on those that supply it with material.

---

[1]Kathleen Kerwin, "The UAW Fires a Shot across GM's Bow," *Business Week,* September 14, 1992, 28.

One of the most common uses of decoupling inventory is to *buffer against disruptions.* Raw materials, WIP, and finished goods are often used as buffers. Raw materials might be added to buffer against an unreliable trucking firm. Additional quantities of work-in-process might protect downstream work centers from the effects of a work center that frequently breaks down. Firms might order extra finished goods inventory because they don't think inventory counts are accurate enough to depend on. All are common uses of inventory to buffer against problems. A buffer of inventory that has completed one process but not another decouples the second process from the first. If the first process breaks down, the second process can continue to produce until the inventory is exhausted. Without the inventory, the second process would stop as well as the first.

In most cases, the solution is to correct the problem creating the disruption rather than covering it up with inventory. Buffers allow managers to cope with disruptions but do not force management to eliminate them. Murphy's Law is alive and well in business: Disruptions inevitably occur. But they should be minimized to reduce the need for this type of inventory.

Maintaining inventory, particularly finished goods, to *absorb demand fluctuations* is important for many manufacturers, especially those whose demand is seasonal. For example, since more soup is consumed in January than in July, Campbell Soup Company keeps enough inventory on hand to ensure it can meet the seasonal spikes in demand.[2] The use of inventory to absorb fluctuations in demand is a tradeoff between building up and selling down inventory on the one hand, and changing capacity by hiring and firing on the other. Although this use of inventory is universal, and for many businesses, absolutely necessary, it is not merely the result of uneven demand for products. It is also brought about by the uneven demand on capacity and the unwillingness of management to have excess capacity during periods of low demand. If the load on the capacity were smoothed by manufacturing products with complementary demand cycles, the inventory and work force level could be stabilized.

QUANTITY DISCOUNTS
Price reductions for buying large volumes.

Inventory levels, particularly raw material inventories, have often been inflated because of **quantity discounts** offered by suppliers. Purchasing agents frequently buy in larger quantities to get a price reduction. These agents must balance the money saved through the quantity discount with the additional carrying costs associated with a large order. As we'll see in the following section, however, financial carrying costs are not the only costs resulting from large order quantities.

As JIT has become more popular, quantity discounts have been more closely scrutinized. Even though the cost per unit may be lower, purchasers are less inclined to buy the larger quantity, because they have recognized the danger of excess inventory. Suppliers may be less likely to offer quantity discounts because the changes they have made to produce JIT have eliminated many of the costs associated with producing in small quantities.

COSTS OF INVENTORY

FINANCIAL COSTS

Traditionally, the costs associated with inventory have been identified as the following:

- carrying costs
- order costs and setup/changeover costs
- stockout costs

---

[2]Nanette Byrnes, "Inventory Management, Campbell Soup," *Financial World,* September 28, 1993, 52.

Carrying costs, also known as *holding costs,* are those expenses associated with stocking goods in inventory. They include insurance costs; storage facility costs, such as rent, building maintenance, and security; pilferage; obsolescence; material handling; and the opportunity cost of the dollars that could be invested in something other than inventory.

Carrying costs are often related directly to the dollar value of the inventory. Annual carrying costs typically amount to 25–35 percent of the average value of the inventory. In other words, the cost of carrying inventory that has an average value of $1 million ranges from $250,000 to $350,000 per year. The average value of the inventory, or average inventory level, is significantly influenced by the size of the order quantity. An important lesson from JIT is that the most effective way to reduce inventory is to produce at the rate of consumption. For example, the specialty steel manufacturer Quanex keeps almost no inventory at its Fort Smith, Arkansas, plant since every batch is sold before it is produced.[3] When ordering raw materials or purchased components from a supplier or ordering manufactured components from a production department, the smaller the order quantity is, the more closely the input rate of the inventory can match its output rate.

Figure 14.1 compares two retailers that both get annual demands of 6,000 units of a product. In Case A, the retailer has chosen to replenish the stock monthly, placing 12 orders per year of 500 units each. The retailer in Case B orders weekly, placing 52 orders of 115 units each.[4] Assuming that each retailer can receive each order the day it is placed and that the demands are smooth and at a constant rate, the average level of inventory in each case is the order quantity divided by 2. That is,

$$\text{Average inventory level} = \frac{Q}{2} \qquad\qquad \textbf{(14.1)}$$

where Q is the order quantity.

For Case A, the average inventory level would be 250 units, and for Case B it would by 57.5 units. Carrying costs for Case B would be less than one-fourth of the carrying costs for Case A. This straightforward example shows why reducing the order quantity while increasing the frequency of ordering is a popular approach to lowering carrying costs. Carrying costs increase a firm's operating expenses. These increased expenses must be passed on to the customer in the form of a price increase, thereby adversely affecting a firm's competitive position, or they must be absorbed, adversely affecting profit.

Order costs are principally the administrative overhead associated with placement of an order. Order costs include the cost of forms, multiple copies, telephone calls, and the time required by staff to place orders. Costs associated with a particular order are typically fixed, regardless of the size of the order. The total order costs for a year are calculated by multiplying the cost per order by the number of orders placed per year:

$$\text{Annual order costs} = (\text{cost/order}) \times (\text{number of orders/year}) \qquad\qquad \textbf{(14.2)}$$

The number of orders expected per year can be computed by dividing the annual demand by the order quantity. A reduction in annual order costs can be accomplished by reducing the administrative effort required to create an order or by reducing the total number of orders. Firms like Sears have reduced administrative paper-handling costs by using electronic data interchange (EDI), a standardized system for sending information from one component to another. The system, which Sears implemented in 1989, links buyers and

CARRYING COSTS
Costs associated with holding inventory, including such costs as insurance, storage, damage, and opportunity cost of the dollars invested.

ORDER COSTS
Cost, usually administrative, associated with placing an order for more inventory.

---

[3]Peter Nulty, "The Less-Is-More Strategy," *Fortune,* December 2, 1991, 102–6.
[4]In order to match the 6,000 units ordered per year in Case B, 115.3 units would be required per week. Because a fractional unit can't be ordered, this value was rounded to 115 units per week.

Relationship between Order Quantity and Average Inventory Level

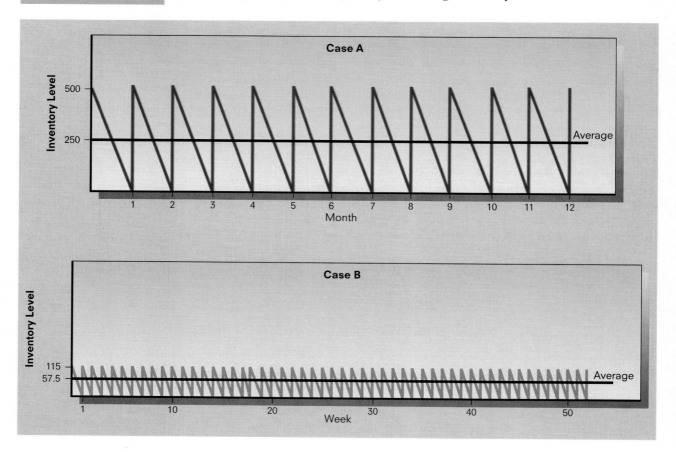

suppliers in a way that reduces the expense of placing an order.[5] If demand remains the same, reducing the number of orders would require that the number of items requested in any one order be increased. This would decrease the costs associated with ordering but also increase inventory carrying costs. As Figure 14.1 shows, the number of orders placed is four times greater in Case B than in Case A. Smaller, more frequent orders result in less inventory but greater ordering costs. This relationship creates the classic tradeoff between inventory carrying costs and order costs.

Setup, or changeover, costs are analogous to order costs but exist when the item ordered is manufactured in-house. Whenever an item is manufactured (except for those instances when dedicated equipment is used), machinery must be adjusted and prepared to produce that specific item. The cost to perform the changeover is known as the **setup cost.** The tasks to be accomplished in a changeover may include changing tools on a machine, adjusting a machine, or cleaning lines and tanks to avoid batch contamination in liquid- or powder-oriented manufacturing. The greater the variety of items produced on a machine, the more time is spent on setups or changeovers and the less time in actual production.

SETUP COSTS
The costs associated with changing equipment from producing one product to producing another.

---

[5]"Sears Takes Direct Approach," *Chain Store Age* (March 1994), 168–9.

Setup cost is usually determined by calculating the value of the production lost while the setup is being accomplished. It is debatable, however, that this is an actual cost for most setups. Constraint management has brought a significant amount of attention to this issue. If a machine is not a constraint, it will by definition be idle part of the time to avoid building up excess inventory. If the machine is going to be idle anyway, setup time may not contribute to a loss of productive capability. Cutting setup costs requires lowering the cost of an individual setup or reducing the number of setups. Current theory, consistent with JIT, is that great potential lies with reducing setup time. In fact, the smaller batch sizes made possible by the decrease in setup times have probably contributed as much to inventory reduction in JIT systems as any other factor.

Carrying costs, order costs, and setup costs are financial costs associated with ordering inventory or having inventory on hand. Stockout costs are financial costs associated with not having inventory. The stockout cost is the expense incurred when inventory is not available to meet demand. For lack of a particular finished product, the customer may go elsewhere, resulting in a lost sale. Or if the customer is forced to wait for the product, goodwill may be lost because of the inconvenience and perceived poor service. A stockout that results because a component is not available may mean that production of the end product is likely to be delayed. This will likely result in a stockout of the end product. As a result, customer service and competitive advantage suffer.

NONFINANCIAL COSTS

Another factor that has contributed to the universal trend toward inventory reduction in recent years is the identification of nonfinancial costs of inventory. These costs can best be examined through their effects on competitive priorities that cannot easily be measured in financial terms—quality, dependability, flexibility, and time.

High levels of inventory have a negative effect on quality. Inventory affects quality through its impact on **quality feedback time,** which is the period between when a defect is produced and when it is identified. Frequently, a defective component is not identified until it is used in subsequent stages of manufacture. If, for example, the average inventory level of a specific component is 3 weeks, there will be 3 weeks between the production of the component and its use. That means a 3 week supply of defective components might be produced before the problem is identified. This flawed production will increase the level of scrap, thereby wasting labor, capacity, and material. If the defects are reparable, the level of rework will increase, causing production costs to rise, potentially to a point that they absorb any profit margin. In some cases, the problem is not identified until after the finished product is sold, making it even more expensive to correct. Reducing the batch size, and the resulting reduction in inventory levels, shorten the quality feedback process and help prevent the production of defective products.

QUALITY FEEDBACK TIME
The time between producing a defect and finding out that a defect has been produced.

Excessive amounts of inventory also reduce a firm's flexibility. The greater the amount of inventory, the longer it takes to introduce an improvement to the market because the inventory on hand must be consumed first. Engineering changes that can increase market share if they get to the market quickly are stifled by raw materials, work-in-process, or finished goods that must be consumed before introducing the change. The electronic components manufactured by Marshall Industries, for example, have a new-product life cycle of only 12 to 18 months. Keeping excess stock on hand is costly for Marshall because prices can plummet so fast that inventory values sometimes drop as much as 50 percent in 6 months.[6]

[6]Leland Montgomery, "Inventory Management, Marshall Industries," *Financial World,* September 29, 1992.

Dependability of delivery and response time to customer orders are enhanced by appropriate levels of raw materials, work-in-process, and finished goods inventory. However, excess work-in-process inventory does not contribute in a positive manner. In fact, it may have an adverse impact on both competitive priorities. Work-in-process inventory frequently exists in the form of queues in front of work centers, particularly in job shops or process layouts. The time each order spends in queue, known as **queue time,** may make the lead time longer and difficult to predict. If lead times become difficult to predict, order promise dates become inaccurate and delivery becomes unreliable.

QUEUE TIME
Time that an order spends waiting between processing steps.

STRATEGIC USES OF INVENTORY

INVENTORY AS BUFFER

Using inventory as a buffer against disruptions—one of the most important ways inventory can be used strategically—is common practice. Appropriate use of buffers can reduce overall inventory levels. Establishing a **maximum buffer size,** the maximum quantity allowed in an inventory buffer, provides an effective way to keep inventory levels low while protecting against upstream disruptions. This approach can be applied to raw materials, work-in-process, and finished goods. Just-in-time and constraint management approaches utilize buffers extensively.

MAXIMUM BUFFER SIZE
In a just-in-time kanban system, the maximum quantity allowed in an inventory buffer.

The JIT kanban system makes use of small buffers between processes and departments and even between suppliers and customers. Although there are many variations of the kanban approach, each essentially consists of buffers prior to every step in the process. A work center, department, or feeding plant is authorized to produce only if the buffer prior to the next step in the process is below its maximum quantity.

Constraint management takes a different approach to the use of buffers in its drum-buffer-rope (DBR) system. Because the approach focuses on the utilization of the constraint, it places a constraint buffer prior to the constraint, a shipping buffer prior to the market, and an assembly buffer at any work center combining a part that has gone through the constraint with a part or parts that haven't. The **constraint buffer** is placed immediately before the constraint, and it serves to protect the constraint from being idle as a result of an upstream disruption. A **shipping buffer** protects the market from disruptions that could take place between the constraint buffer and the last step in the process. An **assembly buffer** is used to ensure that once a part has been processed by the constraint, it will not have to wait prior to an assembly because other parts are missing. The assembly buffer consists of nonconstraint parts and helps maintain a smooth flow of product.

CONSTRAINT BUFFER
A buffer placed immediately prior to the constraint to ensure that it will be supplied with material.

SHIPPING BUFFER
A buffer placed immediately prior to shipping to absorb disruptions that could delay shipment.

ASSEMBLY BUFFER
A buffer of nonconstraint parts placed prior to an assembly with constraint parts.

All constraint management buffers are known as **time buffers.** A time buffer consists of orders or material equivalent to a specific amount of time. These buffers protect against disruptions because the size of a disruption is typically measured in units of time. If the worst-case disruption could restrict material from reaching the constraint for 12 hours, a 12-hour time buffer would protect the constraint. Orders would be released into the system to maintain a 12-hour buffer prior to the constraint and at the rate the orders in the constraint buffer are processed.

TIME BUFFERS
Orders or materials measured in terms of a specific amount of time to protect against disruptions prior to processing at the constraint, at assembly, or at shipping.

In JIT and constraint management, material flows into the system at the rate it flows out of buffers. Because of the use of buffers throughout production in the kanban system, it is described as a "pull system." Inventory ordered from the last buffer in the system authorizes production by the preceding processing step, which must withdraw material from its buffer, and so on. In other words, material is produced only if it is ordered. In drum-buffer-rope, a pull system exists between the first step in the process and the constraint buffer. A separate pull system exists between the constraint work center and the shipping buffer. (JIT kanban systems and the drum-buff-rope system used in constraint management are discussed in detail in Chapter 16.)

Buffers can also be used strategically at other points in manufacturing or service systems. To reduce customer lead time and maintain low levels of finished goods, buffers are often placed just prior to diverging points in the production process.[7] Figure 14.2 shows that material placed just prior to points of divergence is not committed to a specific finished good and reduces customer lead time by the time of processing up to the buffer.

INDEPENDENT VERSUS DEPENDENT DEMAND INVENTORY

There are two types of inventory—independent demand and dependent demand inventory. **Independent demand inventory** consists of inventory that is consumed by the market, and is independent of the demand for other inventoried items. Independent demand inventory consists of finished goods and any raw materials or work-in-process that is sold directly to the market as replacement or repair parts for equipment. Independent demand must be forecast if production or ordering must begin before the demand occurs. **Dependent demand inventory** is consumed by the manufacture of independent demand

INDEPENDENT DEMAND INVENTORY
Inventory whose demand is determined by the market.

DEPENDENT DEMAND INVENTORY
Inventory whose demand is determined by the demand for other items.

[7]Byron J. Finch and James F. Cox, "Strategic Use of WIP Inventory: The Impact of Bill of Material Shape and Plant Type," *Production and Inventory Management Journal* 30 (1989).

| **FIGURE 14.2** | **Use of Buffers at Divergent Points in Material Flow** |

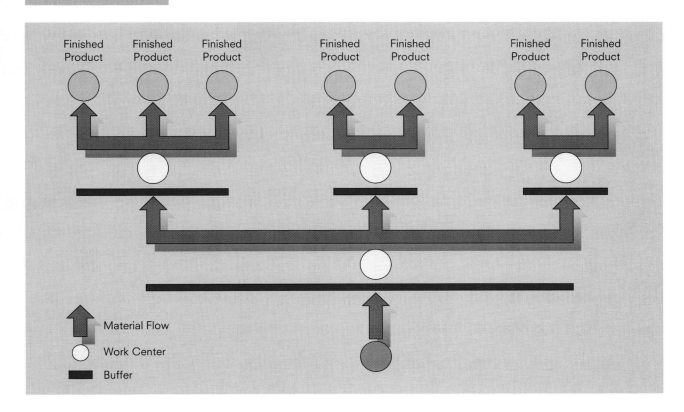

inventory. For example, Gateway 2000 of North Sioux City, South Dakota, assembles computers using components purchased from other companies. Its demand for hard drives and keyboards is dependent on the demand for computers.[8] Dependent demand inventory usually consists of raw materials, components, and work-in-process inventory. If the independent demand has been forecast, the dependent demand can be calculated.

It is possible for a component—the rim for a bicycle wheel, for example—to have both independent and dependent demand. Repair shops and bicycle owners purchase the rims directly to replace damaged rims (independent demand), and rims are used to manufacture new bicycles (dependent demand).

Maintenance, repair, and operating (MRO) inventories are consumed in the production of most services and manufacturing processes. In manufacturing, they consist of such items as cleaning supplies, machine repair parts, and lubricants. In a service such as banking, MRO inventory could consist of forms, paper, cleaning supplies, pencils and pens, and copy machine toner. MRO inventories are considered independent demand inventories because their demand is determined by a market (the workers) and is not directly proportionate to the demand for any other item. Their future demand must also be forecast.

Because independent demand is forecast with some degree of error but dependent demand can be calculated exactly, the techniques used to manage the two types of inventory differ significantly.

INDEPENDENT DEMAND INVENTORY MANAGEMENT TECHNIQUES

Independent demand inventory exists in the finished goods warehouse of a manufacturer and includes the inventory of distribution firms, wholesalers, and retailers. From a management perspective, the most important characteristic of independent demand inventory is that its demand is probabilistic. Demand can never be certainly predicted and must, therefore, be forecast.

Two questions must be answered in managing independent demand inventory: *when* to order and *how many* to order. These issues are not independent of each other. Recall the relationship between carrying costs and order costs: Frequent ordering reduces carrying costs but raises order costs. Similarly, large order quantities reduce order costs but increase carrying costs.

SERVICE LEVEL
The percentage of orders satisfied from stock.

INVENTORY TURNOVER
The number of times a firm's inventory cycles (or moves through the system), computed by dividing annual cost of sales by the average inventory level (dollars).

The decisions on order quantity and order timing are made with two objectives. First, the firm must maintain an acceptable ability to satisfy demand. The ability to satisfy demand is typically measured using the **service level,** which is defined as the percentage of orders that can be satisfied from stock.[9] Second, inventory levels must be as low as possible to reduce the financial and nonfinancial carrying costs.

Inventory level may be measured as a dollar value or by using a relative measure known as inventory turns or inventory turnover. **Inventory turnover** is defined as the annual cost of sales divided by the average inventory level (in dollars).[10] Inventory turnover measures the number of times a firm's inventory "cycles," that is, the relative speed at which material moves through the system. It is directly related to lead time. For example, if a manufacturing firm claims that it is able to achieve 12 inventory turns, its average lead

---

[8]Joshua Hyatt, "Betting the Farm," *Inc.* (December 1991), 36–45.

[9]J. F. Cox, J. H. Blackstone, and M. S. Spencer, eds., *APICS Dictionary* 7th ed. (Falls Church, Va.: American Production and Inventory Control Society, 1992), 45.

[10]Cox, Blackstone, and Spencer, 23.

Thomas & Betts, a manufacturer of electrical products, uses a computerized inventory management approach that analyzes daily sales updates and historical trend data to forecast its distributors' inventory needs. Called Distributor/ Manufacturer Integration, the service reduces distributors' inventories and handling and order-processing costs. The business research team shown here developed the DMI approach.

Source Used with permission of Thomas & Betts Corporation/Gloria Baker Photography, Inc., 1994.

time must be 1 month. If a supermarket is able to achieve 52 turns, its inventory averages only 1 week on the shelf. Firms often have even higher inventory turnover. Edy's Grand Ice Cream of Fort Wayne, Indiana, for instance, has 65.5 annual inventory turns.[11]

There are numerous approaches to determining the timing and order quantity for independent demand inventory. Two approaches are commonly used to determine when to reorder: (a) ordering when inventory drops to a specific level or (b) ordering at fixed time intervals.

If additional inventory is ordered when the inventory drops to a specified level, known as the **reorder point** (ROP), the time between orders will fluctuate if the demand varies. Thus, using a reorder point model implies that the time interval between orders is variable. Because the inventory level is the same each time the order is placed, the order quantity remains the same also.

REORDER POINT
A predetermined level to which inventory drops and a replenishment order is placed.

If an order is placed at fixed time intervals, demand between orders would probably fluctuate, and thus the inventory level at the time the order was placed would vary. As a result, the order quantity would vary also. Thus, there are two general approaches that must be examined:

1. Fixed-quantity, variable-interval systems
2. Fixed-interval, variable-quantity systems

---

[11]Tracy Benson Kirker, "Edy's Grand Ice Cream," *Industry Week,* October 18, 1993, 29–32.

A FIXED-QUANTITY, VARIABLE-INTERVAL SYSTEM

A common implementation of the fixed-quantity, variable-interval system is the *reorder point (ROP) model.* In the ROP model, inventory is monitored every time inventory is removed; thus it is often referred to as a continuous-review or perpetual-review model. The reorder point is the level to which inventory is allowed to drop before a replenishment order is placed, that is, the "trigger" that activates the ordering process. Management must determine two parameters to establish the ROP model: the reorder point and the order quantity.

Determining the Reorder Point   Figure 14.3 provides a general view of the ROP model. It shows that demand consumes inventory and that eventually the reorder point is reached, triggering the placement of a replenishment order. The order does not arrive immediately, however, and demand continues to consume inventory during the replenishment lead time. The order quantity is the same for each order. But because the demand during the lead time varies, inventory levels at the time the orders are received vary and the peak levels of inventory during each order cycle differ.

The reorder point is used to provide inventory that will satisfy demand during lead time. If an order is not placed until the inventory level reached zero, demand during lead time cannot be satisfied. Because inventory is monitored continuously in the ROP model, the only chance for a stockout is while waiting for the replenishment order to arrive. This fact provides direction for establishing the reorder point value.

Keeping in mind that the reorder point must be set high enough to satisfy the demand during lead time, consider how large the reorder point must be. Several factors will affect its size, including the level and variability of demand during lead time and the length of the lead time. To determine the reorder point the expected demand during lead time must be forecast.

The simplest approach to forecasting demand during lead time would be to use the average demand. If the demand during lead time is normally distributed, then actual demand

---

FIGURE 14.3   **The Reorder Point Model**

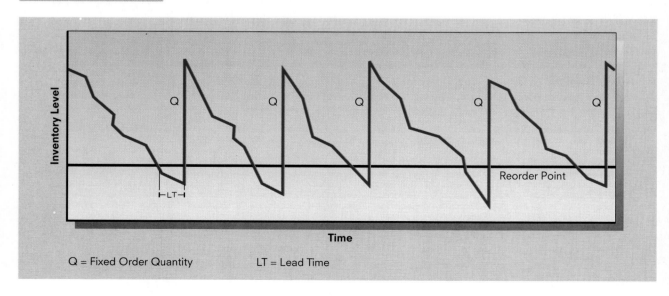

Q = Fixed Order Quantity   LT = Lead Time

will be greater than average 50 percent of the time and less than average 50 percent of the time. When actual demand is less than average, all demand can be satisfied. When actual demand turns out to be greater than average, a stockout occurs.

As Figure 14.4 illustrates, using the average demand during lead time as the reorder point results in stocking out during 50 percent of the lead times. This may not be an acceptable level of customer service. One way of improving the service level under the ROP model is through the use of **safety stock**—inventory aimed at protecting against unexpectedly high demand.

The relationship between the standard deviation, a measure of demand variability, and the probability of a specific demand level makes it possible to develop a reorder point that will provide a desired service level. To achieve that service level, the reorder point must consist of two parts: the average demand during lead time ($\bar{d}_{LT}$) and a safety stock. The safety stock is computed by first determining the desired service level, and multiplying the standard deviation of demand during lead time (σ_{LT}) by the appropriate Z value from a standard Z table, as provided in Appendix A. The general formula for the reorder point is:

SAFETY STOCK
Stock that is held in excess of expected demand to protect against unexpectedly high demand.

$$\text{Reorder point} = \text{Average demand during lead time} + \text{safety stock} \qquad \textbf{(14.3)}$$

or

$$\text{ROP} = \bar{d}_{LT} + \sigma_{LT} Z \qquad \textbf{(14.4)}$$

where $\bar{d}_{LT}$ is the average demand during lead time, σ_{LT} is standard deviation of demand during lead time, and Z is the number of standard deviations above the mean required to achieve the desired service level.

If the variability of daily demand is known but the lead time is longer than 1 day, adjustments must be made in computing σ_{LT}. For example, if the demand rate is given per day and the lead time is 4 days (assuming the variance for each day, σ_{day}^2, is independent and equal), then σ_{LT} is calculated as follows:

$$\sigma_{LT}^2 = \sigma_{\text{day}}^2 + \sigma_{\text{day}}^2 + \sigma_{\text{day}}^2 + \sigma_{\text{day}}^2 \qquad \textbf{(14.5)}$$

FIGURE 14.4   **Service Level Using Average Demand during Lead Time as the Reorder Point**

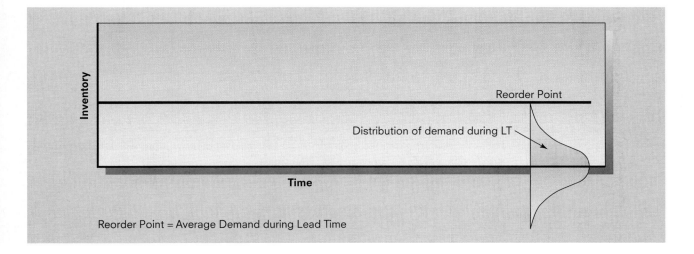

FIGURE 14.5   **Reorder Point with Safety Stock**

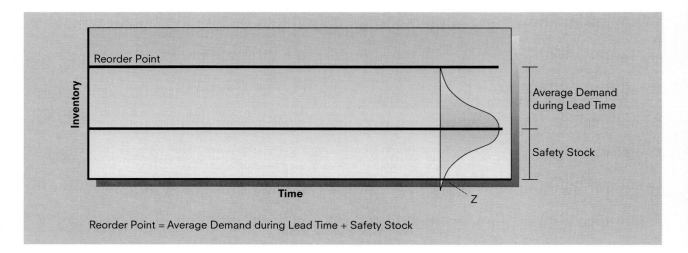

Reorder Point = Average Demand during Lead Time + Safety Stock

and

$$\sigma_{LT} = \sqrt{\sigma^2_{day} + \sigma^2_{day} + \sigma^2_{day} + \sigma^2_{day}} \tag{14.6}$$

The effect this approach has on the level of service provided by a reorder point is shown in Figure 14.5. Notice that inventory is added in the amount needed to shift the reorder point so that it satisfies demand to a greater level of probability.

EXAMPLE 14.1

Computing the Reorder Point

Smith's Outfitters tries to maintain an inventory of book bags to supply the student demand. The supplier is reliable and provides 1 week delivery. Average weekly demand $\bar{d}$ is 22 bags, with a standard deviation σ of 2.2. Compute the appropriate reorder point to ensure that Smith can satisfy all orders for 97 percent of the lead time periods.

SOLUTION

Appendix A shows that 0.9699 (that is, 97%) of the area under the normal curve is contained to the left of 1.88 standard deviations above the mean. Thus $Z = 1.88$. Using equation 14.4, the reorder point is

$$\begin{aligned} \text{ROP} &= \bar{d}_{LT} + \sigma_{LT}\,Z \\ &= 22 + (2.2 \times 1.88) \\ &= 26.1 \end{aligned}$$

If Smith reorders when the inventory drops to 26 bags, there will be sufficient inventory to satisfy demand 97 out of every 100 lead times.

A simple average is not the most accurate means of forecasting, especially if trend or seasonality is present in the data. Consider the example above. If book bag demand is highly seasonal (and it most likely would be) the "average weekly demand" would not be representative of the demand for the first week of school. Actual demand could be many times the average, and if the reorder point calculation did not reflect the seasonality, many sales could be lost because of a stockout. Because a simple average is not representative, companies often use their best forecast for demand as a basis for the reorder point. When they do, the safety stock ($\sigma_{LT} Z$) must be calculated in a different manner.

If average demand during lead time ($\bar{d}_{LT}$) is used as the forecast, a stockout could result from demand fluctuation around the mean, which is measured by the standard deviation (σ_{LT}). The greater the demand fluctuation, the greater the necessary size of the safety stock. If the firm's best forecast for the demand during lead time is used as a basis for the reorder point, a stockout would be the result of forecast error. The greater the forecast error, the larger the required level of safety stock.

The measure of forecast error that is used to develop an appropriate safety stock is the mean absolute deviation (MAD). The MAD is the mean of the absolute values of the forecast errors. Fortunately, there is a constant relationship that approximately equates the MAD with the standard deviation (σ_{LT}), allowing us to use the Z table to calculate safety stocks when the MAD is used. This relationship is

$$\sigma_{LT} = 1.25 \times \text{MAD}$$

Thus, to calculate the safety stock, $\sigma_{LT}Z$, we multiply the MAD from the forecast by 1.25, then multiply the product by the appropriate Z value for the desired level of service. That is

$$\text{ROP} = \bar{d}_{LT} + Z(1.25\text{MAD}) \qquad \textbf{(14.7)}$$

EXAMPLE 14.2

Calculating Reorder Point When MAD Is Used in the Safety Stock

Suppose that Smith's Outfitters identified a seasonal pattern in its book bag demand and was forecasting the demand using multiplicative seasonal indices. The forecast for the first week in September was for 125 bags. Smith monitored the forecast accuracy and maintained a steady MAD of 4.0. Compute the reorder point to be used to achieve a lead time service level of 97 percent.

SOLUTION

As in Example 14.1, $Z = 1.88$ (from Appendix A). Thus, using formula 14.7,

$$
\begin{aligned}
\text{ROP} &= \bar{d}_{LT} + Z(1.25\text{MAD}) \\
&= 125 + 1.88 \, (1.25 \times 4) \\
&= 125 + 9.4 \\
&= 134.4
\end{aligned}
$$

If Smith reorders when the inventory drops to 134 units, the demand during the first week in September would be covered with 97 percent confidence.

There are two important points to recognize about this particular approach. First, the reorder point is dynamic. In other words, it changes in response to changes in the demand forecast. This requires additional effort and cost. Second, it assumes that the forecast is not biased. This may need further clarification.

A large MAD could exist in several situations. The MAD could be high, but bias could be zero. In this situation, using a reorder point of just the forecast, with no safety stock, would satisfy demand during 50 percent of the lead times. Demand would be greater than the forecast half the time, and less than the forecast half the time if the forecast were unbiased. A large MAD could also be the result of a biased forecast. Because the MAD is calculated using absolute values, the direction of the bias would not be evident from the MAD. If, for example, the forecast were biased negatively, it would be consistently greater than actual demand.

Consider what would happen if the forecast were so biased that it was always greater than the actual demand. Would the actual demand be greater than the forecast 50 percent of the time? Of course not. If the forecast were always greater than the demand, the demand could never be greater than the forecast. In that situation, adding a safety stock based on a calculation of the MAD would be unnecessary. By the same token, if the bias were such that the forecast tended to be low, a safety stock calculated by this method would not provide the desired level of service.

Determining the Order Quantity   In many inventory management systems, including the ROP model, a fixed order quantity is used. The determination of this order quantity is important because of the effect it has on order costs, carrying costs, and nonfinancial costs of carrying inventory.

ECONOMIC ORDER QUANTITY (EOQ)
The point at which holding costs and order costs are equal and total inventory costs are minimized.

A common approach to determining the order quantity has been to use the **economic order quantity (EOQ)** model. The EOQ is the point at which holding costs and order costs are equal and the point at which total inventory costs are minimized. Recall that the annual inventory carrying costs are equal to the average inventory level ($Q/2$) multiplied by a rate, often a percentage of the value of the inventory, or by a cost per unit per time period. The annual order costs are equal to the cost per order times the number of orders per year. The number of orders per year can be computed by dividing the annual demand by the order quantity. These combined costs for carrying and ordering inventory can be expressed by the following formula:

$$\text{Total costs} = \text{carrying costs} + \text{order costs}$$

or

$$TC = H\frac{Q}{2} + S\frac{D}{Q} \tag{14.8}$$

where TC is the total cost, H is the holding cost, Q is the order quantity, S is the order cost, and D is the annual demand.

Sometimes companies determine H (holding cost) as a function of the purchase price (P) and a percentage of that price (i). In this situation, the holding cost is defined by

$$H = iP \tag{14.9}$$

The total cost curve, which represents total cost as a function of the order quantity, has the general shape shown in Figure 14.6. Notice that the bottom of the total cost curve is relatively flat. Small changes in order quantity do not result in large changes in cost, so many firms round off to order quantities that are more easily used. The minimum point on the total cost curve can be found by using calculus to take the first derivative of equation 14.8 with respect to Q. The resulting formula is

$$\text{EOQ} = \sqrt{\frac{2DS}{H}} \tag{14.10}$$

where D is the annual demand, S is the order cost per order, and H is the annual holding cost per unit.

The EOQ formula is based on the following assumptions:

1. Only one product is being considered.
2. Lead time is constant and known.

FIGURE 14.6   **Total Cost Curve**

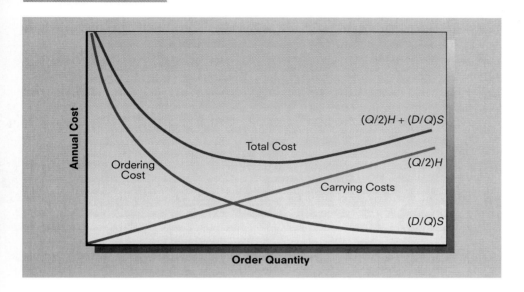

3. There are no quantity discounts.
4. Demand is even and constant.
5. Annual demand is known.
6. Orders are delivered in single deliveries.

EXAMPLE 14.3

Steven's College Center sells supplies for students, including the ever-popular reading pillow. The demand for reading pillows is 1,200 per year. Pillows are purchased from a supplier for $9 each. Order costs are $10 per order. Annual carrying costs are $2.50 per unit. Thus

$$D = 1,200$$
$$S = \$10$$
$$H = \$2.5$$

Compute the economic order quantity.

Computing the Basic Economic Order Quantity

SOLUTION

Using equation 14.10

$$EOQ = \sqrt{\frac{2DS}{H}}$$

$$= \sqrt{\frac{2(1,200)(10)}{2.5}} = \sqrt{\frac{24,000}{2.5}}$$

$$= 97.98$$

Steven's College Center should therefore order in quantities of 98 units.

Violation of any of the assumptions will result in order quantities that are suboptimal, but because the bottom of the total cost curve is flat, minor violations of the assumptions do not have serious impact.

The basic EOQ model can be modified when specific assumptions do not apply. One commonly used alteration is made to cope with quantity discounts. Suppliers usually offer discounts by providing different prices for various order sizes. For example, one price per unit may be given for orders of 0 to 500 units, another price per unit for orders of 501 to 2,000 units, and a third price per unit for orders greater than 2,000 units. If quantity discounts exist, finding the least cost order quantity becomes an iterative process. Because the purchase cost varies with different order quantities, purchase cost must be included in the total cost formula, as shown in equation 14.11:

$$TC = H\frac{Q}{2} + S\frac{D}{Q} + PD \qquad (14.11)$$

where TC is the total cost, Q is the order quantity, D is the annual demand, H is the holding or carrying cost, P is the purchase cost per unit, and S is the order cost.

Because the total cost curve varies from one discount range to another, a different total cost curve exists for each discount range. To identify the low-cost order quantity, use the following steps:

1.   Compute the basic EOQ using equation 14.10. The EOQ will fall within one of the discount ranges offered by the supplier.
2.   If the EOQ falls within the discount range having the lowest per-unit price, it is the optimal order quantity. Compute the total cost of ordering at that quantity using equation 14.11.
3.   If the basic EOQ does not fall within the range of the lowest unit price, all ranges having lower per unit prices must be evaluated. Compute the total cost using equation 14.11 for the lowest possible order quantity in each range.
4.   Compare the total cost of ordering the EOQ with the total cost of ordering at the other price breaks and select the quantity providing the lowest total cost. If the holding costs are a function of the item costs as represented in equation 14.9, where $H = iP$, then the EOQ is computed beginning with the lowest per-unit price until a feasible solution is found. A feasible solution occurs when the EOQ for a given price falls within the discount range in which the price is valid. Once a feasible solution is found, proceed to step 2 above.

EXAMPLE 14.4

Identifying the Low-Cost Order Quantity When Quantity Discounts Exist

Steven's College Center has identified a new supplier of reading pillows—one that offers quantity discounts. The demand for reading pillows is 1,200 per year. Order costs are $10 per order, annual carrying costs are $2.50 per unit, and the prices are

Orders	Price per unit
1 to 30	$9
31 to 100	$8.80
101 or more	$8.50

Compute the economic order quantity.

SOLUTION

Since the new supplier offers quantity discounts, the applicable formula for calculating total cost is 14.11, which includes the purchase cost as a factor. To use this formula, we follow the prescribed steps:

Step 1: Calculate the basic EOQ: Using equation 14.10, the basic EOQ = $\sqrt{2DS/H} = \sqrt{[2(1,200(10)]/2.5}$, which is unchanged from the previous example; thus, EOQ is 98 units.

Step 2: Compute the total cost of ordering at the EOQ:

$$TC = H\frac{Q}{2} + S\frac{D}{Q} + PD$$

$$= 2.5\left(\frac{98}{2}\right) + 10\left(\frac{1,200}{98}\right) + 8.80(1,200)$$

$$= 122.5 + 122.4 + 10,560$$

$$= \$10,804.90$$

Step 3: The EOQ of 98 units does not fall within the discount range having the lowest price per unit, so we have to evaluate the discount range of 101 or more. The total cost for ordering 101 units, using equation 14.11 is

$$TC = H\frac{Q}{2} + S\frac{D}{Q} + PD$$

$$= 2.5\left(\frac{101}{2}\right) + 10\left(\frac{1,200}{101}\right) + 8.50(1,200)$$

$$= 126.25 + 118.8 + 10,200$$

$$= \$10,445.05$$

Step 4: The total cost of ordering in quantities of 101 is less than the cost of ordering in quantities of 98, so 101 is the optimal order quantity.

Note: If carrying costs had been expressed as a function of the purchase price (P), carrying costs would vary from one discount range to another, as purchase price changed.

Quantity discounts are not as popular as they once were, however, not only because purchases of large quantities result in higher inventory levels and associated costs, but also because most manufacturers are now producing in smaller batches. Meeting an order for a large quantity does not necessarily result in a savings for producers. In fact, for small-batch producers, delivering infrequently in large batches may require them to maintain higher levels of finished goods inventory to meet large orders. Once a firm has made the changes necessary for small-batch production, it may not be economically attractive to produce in large batches, and the firm may have no reason to encourage customers to purchase in large quantities. Small retailers, however, often consider quantity discounts a way to reduce costs.

Another modification of the basic EOQ model relaxes the assumption that orders are delivered in single deliveries. In many manufacturing settings, inventory is delivered gradually, as it is produced. This model, known as the production lot size, has become less popular as manufacturers have recognized the nonfinancial costs of large batch sizes.

Limitations of the EOQ formula   The benefits of using the EOQ formula must be weighed against the nonfinancial costs of ordering large quantities. Since the inventory reduction strategies accompanying JIT began to take form in the early 1980s, the EOQ formula has come under close scrutiny and, in many cases, has been abandoned.

Although the numbers generated by the EOQ formula are correct, the validity of the assumptions upon which it rests is debatable. Several assumptions, such as that of a smooth demand, are essential for the formula to provide the true low-cost solution: but other, more basic assumptions, such as the accuracy of the total cost formula from which the EOQ formula is derived, are questionable. Many firms consider the nonfinancial costs of inventory, including reduced flexibility, increased quality feedback time, and increased lead time, as more critical than the savings of carrying and order costs. Despite the high costs of carrying inventory, many managers claim that the least significant benefit of inventory reduction has been the reduction in carrying costs. They say the other nonfinancial benefits are more important because of their broad strategic implications. Retailers, distributors, and manufacturers benefit from the flexibility gained from inventory reduction. For example, even though Archway Cookies sells 64 varieties of cookies with a short shelf life, good inventory management helps ensure high product quality. Thanks to low inventory levels, product rotation time in the finished goods warehouse is 48 hours.[12] Because all the nonfinancial costs of carrying inventory increase as order quantity increases, the resulting order quantity would be smaller if such costs could be included in the total cost equation. Many theorists assert that the heavy reliance on the EOQ formula has resulted in the so-called large batch mentality that exists in the United States—a mentality that has contributed significantly to problems related to quality and flexibility.

A FIXED-INTERVAL, VARIABLE-QUANTITY SYSTEM

An alternative to the fixed-quantity approach is to order at fixed time intervals. The fixed-interval model is not a continuous-review approach. The inventory level is checked periodically, and a quantity is ordered to bring it back up to a target level. For example, a vendor might visit a retailer on a weekly basis to check stock levels and place the appropriate orders. Unlike the ROP model, in which increasing demand results in more frequent orders, increasing demand in the fixed-period model results in larger order quantities. From a cost-monitoring standpoint, the periodic review is less expensive because inventory isn't monitored continuously. Although the periodic model often provides less control than the ROP model, it can provide a high level of reliability if the review is frequent enough. (See Box 14.1.)

Because inventory levels are constantly monitored under the ROP approach, items are exposed to the risk of stockout only during the replenishment lead time. Under the fixed period model, however, a stockout may occur during the lead time and during the period between inventory checks; thus there is a greater need for safety stock in this model. Management must make two decisions in order to implement the fixed-interval approach. First, management must determine the frequency of orders, which is known as the *order interval.* Managers may make this determination on the basis of convenience, or as a way to group orders together that go to the same supplier. Second, management must determine the or-

---

[12]"Archway Cookies Meets Increased Product Demand," *Industrial Engineering* (September 1992), 18.

CUTTING-EDGE COMPANIES

BOX 14.1

Electronic Inventory Management at Wal-Mart

Founded in 1962 by Sam Walton, Wal-Mart has become the most sophisticated, state-of-the-art network of stores in the world. In the early days Walton had trouble persuading suppliers to deliver to the small, out-of-the-way towns where his stores were located. Now, however, Wal-Mart has the clout to persuade its suppliers to assist in inventory management, including buying, ordering, and inventory control.

Owing to its $500 million information system, Wal-Mart has given increasing responsibility for its operations to suppliers, which now stock Wal-Mart's shelves on the basis of purchase orders and sales reports received electronically. Suppliers also have a greater say in what Wal-Mart sells, often eliminating the middleman function of buyers and sales representatives.

Wal-Mart's objective is to minimize expenses while keeping shelves stocked. Wal-Mart's expenses as a percentage of sales are currently 16 percent, compared to K mart's 18.5 percent and Sears, Roebuck and Co.'s 29 percent.

VF Corporation, which makes Lee and Wrangler jeans and Vassarette lingerie, is a major Wal-Mart supplier. An ex-amination of VF's linkage to Wal-Mart reveals a relationship typical of the Arkansas retailer's suppliers. VF receives daily sales figures through its computer linkages from each of Wal-Mart's stores—more than 2,000 of them. Using bar code scanners at check-out counters and hand-held wireless computers, Wal-Mart compiles the data automatically, and VF replenishes Wal-Mart's shelves based on those data. Most products are shipped within 24 hours. The result is a daily periodic review system with more than 2,000 separate inventories for each item in each store. For VF, the system has meant a 33 percent increase in sales for the first 9 months of 1992. For Wal-Mart, it has reduced expenses and kept empty shelves to a minimum.

In addition to the information provided to suppliers by the new system, part of the electronic data interchange (EDI) system lets Wal-Mart send purchase orders and invoices through the computer. It also allows the retailer to communicate plans for promotions and needs for specially priced products through an e-mail system.

Source "Wal-Mart Goes Electronic," *The Cincinnati Enquirer,* January 17, 1993, sec. d, 2.

---

der quantity, which depends on the demand during the order interval plus the amount of safety stock needed to maintain the desired service level. As each order interval passes, the amount to order is calculated using the following formula:

$$\text{Quantity} = \begin{pmatrix} \text{Forecast demand} \\ \text{during the interval} \\ \text{and lead time} \end{pmatrix} + (\text{Safety stock}) - \begin{pmatrix} \text{Amount of} \\ \text{inventory available} \end{pmatrix}$$

or

$$Q = \bar{d}_{OI+LT} + \sigma_d \, Z \sqrt{(OI + LT)} - A \qquad \textbf{(14.12)}$$

where $\bar{d}_{OI+LT}$ is the average demand during the order interval and lead time, σ_d is the standard deviation of daily demand, Z is the number of standard deviations required for the desired level of service, OI is the order interval in days, LT is the lead time in days, and A is the current inventory level.

As in the ROP model, normally distributed demand is assumed. Figure 14.7 presents a diagram of the fixed-interval, variable-quantity model.

FIGURE 14.7	**Fixed-Interval, Variable-Quantity Model**

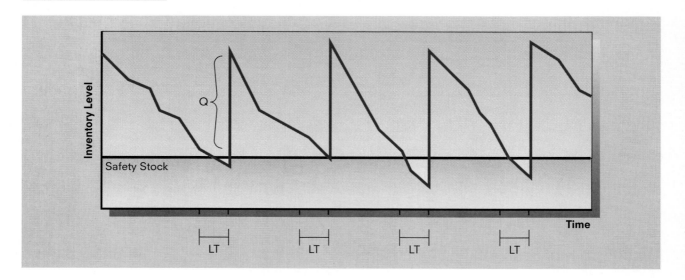

EXAMPLE 14.5	

Computing Q in the Fixed-Interval, Variable-Quantity Model   Les's Hardware orders a number of its products from the same distributor and prefers to group these orders together by using a fixed-interval approach to replenishing inventory. Given the following data, calculate the reorder quantity for the current order interval:

$$\begin{aligned} \text{Average demand } \bar{d} &= 12 \text{ units/day} \\ \text{Lead time } LT &= 4 \text{ days} \\ \text{Standard deviation } \sigma_d &= 2 \text{ units/day} \\ \text{Current inventory level } A &= 51 \text{ units} \\ \text{Service level required } Z &= 95\% \\ \text{Order interval } OI &= 10 \text{ days} \end{aligned}$$

SOLUTION

Since the average demand ($\bar{d}$) is 12 units per day and the lead time (LT) plus the order interval (OI) is 4 + 10 days, the demand during the interval and lead time, $\bar{d}_{OI+LT}$, is 12(10+4) = 168 units. And for a 95 percent service level the number of standard deviations is 1.645 (from Appendix A). Using formula 14.12

$$\begin{aligned} Q &= d_{OI+LT} + \sigma_d Z \sqrt{OI + LT} - A \\ &= 168 + (2 \times 1.645)\sqrt{14} - 51 \\ &= 168 + 3.29(3.74) - 51 \\ &= 129.3 \end{aligned}$$

Having calculated the order quantity as 129.3, Les should reorder at 130 units.

THE COSTS OF SAFETY STOCK

It is important to recognize the effect that safety stocks have on inventory levels because most independent demand inventory management models use them. To better understand the impact of safety stocks, consider the ROP system as it was described earlier. Recall that using the average demand during lead time as the reorder point resulted in stocking out during 50 percent of the lead times. Suppose the reorder point is calculated by adding a safety stock to the average demand during lead time. Fifty percent of the lead times would have a demand sufficient to dip into the safety stock (see Figure 14.5). The other 50 percent would not require safety stock to meet demand. On the average, the safety stock is not used because the average demand is satisfied without its use. Thus, the inventory level at the end of the "average" lead time would be equivalent to the safety stock. Over time, the average inventory level is approximately equal to $Q/2$ plus the safety stock. It is necessary, therefore, to focus on minimizing disruptions and sources of variability because maintaining additional safety stock directly affects inventory levels, resulting in competitive disadvantages.

Choosing the Appropriate Inventory Management Tool   A firm's inventory usually consists of materials or products that span several price ranges. Radio Shack stores, for example, stock everything from batteries that cost under $1 to computers priced at several thousand dollars. It makes sense to manage low-priced inventory differently from big-ticket items.

ABC analysis is often used to aid in identifying appropriate inventory management approaches. It is based on the "80-20 rule," which says that approximately 80 percent of the dollar usage is linked to 20 percent of the items. ABC analysis requires that the inventory be classified in order of importance. "Importance" is usually measured as dollar usage, but other measures of importance, such as the replenishment lead time, may be appropriate in some circumstances. Three classifications are typically used: A (very important), B (medium level of importance), and C (least important).

The A category typically consists of only 5 percent to 10 percent of the inventory items, but it may account for more than 60 percent of the dollar usage. These items are the most important, and as a result, would justify the most sophisticated and costly inventory management approaches. The B items may account for up to 30 percent of the items, but only 10 percent to 20 percent of the dollar usage. C items often consist of a large percentage of the items (50 percent to 60 percent) but only 10 percent to 20 percent of the dollar usage. ABC analysis provides focus for managers and aids them in choosing appropriate inventory management systems.

ABC ANALYSIS
An approach to classifying inventory based on three classes of importance.

DEPENDENT DEMAND INVENTORY MANAGEMENT TECHNIQUES

Dependent demand inventory must be managed differently from independent demand inventory for several reasons. Paramount among those is the fact that the pattern of dependent demand differs markedly from that of independent demand. Independent demand inventory, unlike dependent demand inventory, is typically removed from stock in a relatively smooth manner. Consider, for example, the situation that results when a manufacturer stores end product A in a finished goods warehouse and manages the inventory

FIGURE 14.8 **Inventory Profile of End Product A**

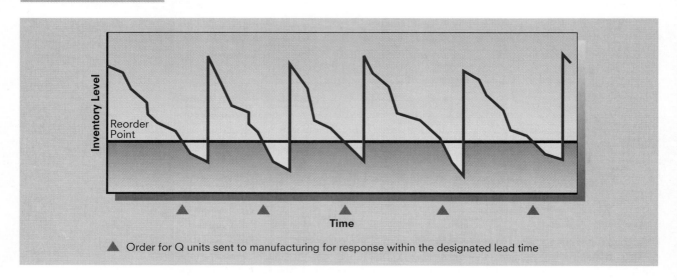

▲ Order for Q units sent to manufacturing for response within the designated lead time

with a reorder point system. The inventory profile of A, which is a typical independent demand inventory pattern, is shown in Figure 14.8 while Figure 14.9 shows the product structure of end product A.

When the reorder point for A is reached, an order is immediately sent to manufacturing so that the supply of product A will be replenished. Upon receipt of the order to make a batch of A, the supervisor authorizes the removal of the necessary quantity of required components from their respective inventories so that the process of assembling A can begin. The pattern of inventory of component B, which depends upon the demand for end product A, is shown in Figure 14.10.

The pattern in Figure 14.10 is based on the assumption that when the inventory of B runs out or reaches a predesignated reorder point, more units will be ordered. This order would again go to manufacturing, requesting that a batch of product B be produced. For manufacturing to fulfill this order, the right number of components D and E would be

FIGURE 14.9   **Product Structure of A**

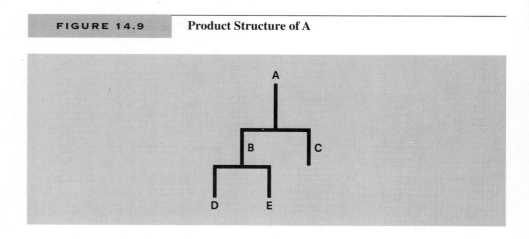

| **FIGURE 14.10** | **Inventory Profile of Component B** |

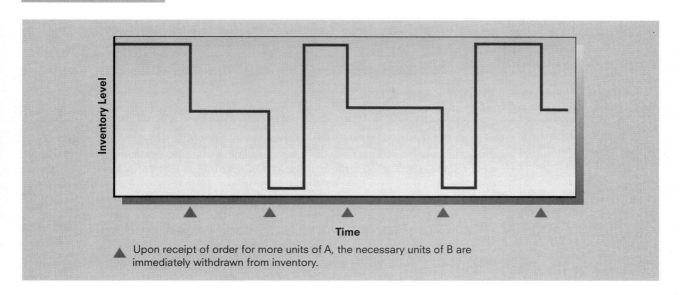

▲ Upon receipt of order for more units of A, the necessary units of B are immediately withdrawn from inventory.

pulled from inventory to produce the required quantity of B. The inventory pattern for D and E would be similar to that of B because the inventory would also be withdrawn in batches. This pattern is typical of dependent demand inventory and is known as **lumpy demand.** If component B were also used in the manufacture of other end products, the demand for D and E would be even lumpier.

If the daily demand for component B is examined, the difference between it and the independent demand for A is apparent. During most days, the demand for B is zero. Occasionally, however, the demand is very large. In this case, if no other end product used component B, the average daily or weekly demand for B would be the same as that of A, but it would clearly have a different distribution.

The distribution of the demand is much more important than just the average over a time period because of the way the appropriate level of safety stock is determined. Keep in mind that the Z values are based on the area under a *normal* curve. Because the lumpy demand pattern is extremely variable, but not normal, safety stocks of the parent item would need to be extremely large to provide a reasonable service level.

The lumpy pattern of dependent demand inventory sets it apart from independent demand inventory, but further analysis reveals an even more important reason why the two types of inventory are managed differently. Independent demand inventories are managed using probabilistic approaches because their demand is uncertain. The decisions about when to order and how much or how many to order are made based on a forecast of demand, or what management thinks will happen. Because accuracy is always in question, the independent demand management system must use safety stock to protect against potential forecast errors.

There is no uncertainty about dependent demand. Once the schedule for production of the end products is known (either from orders generated by customers or independent demand inventory management systems), the necessary level of dependent demand inventory items can be calculated precisely, eliminating the need for forecasts and safety stock. For dependent demand inventory, the approach used to calculate when to order and how much

LUMPY DEMAND
A demand pattern characterized by time periods of little or no demand followed by time periods of very high demand.

MATERIAL REQUIREMENTS PLANNING (MRP)
An approach used to determine the timing and size of orders for dependent demand inventory.

BACKWARD SCHEDULING
A technique for determining when to order dependent demand inventory that starts at the due date and schedules back to determine the start date.

FORWARD SCHEDULING
A technique for determining when to order dependent demand inventory that begins with the start date and schedules forward to the due date using expected lead times.

or how many to order is known as **material requirements planning (MRP).** This approach to inventory management can result in tremendous benefits. When Philadelphia Mixers Corp. adopted MRP techniques, it boosted on-time deliveries to 95 percent, eliminated a 10-week backlog, and improved inventory accuracy to 98 percent.[13]

MATERIAL REQUIREMENTS PLANNING LOGIC

To determine when to order dependent demand inventory, managers use **backward scheduling,** or, as it is sometimes called, time-phasing. Backward scheduling is a straightforward approach used to determine when a task should be started. The first step in backward scheduling is to identify when the task must be completed. Next, based on the expected lead time, schedule backwards from the future due date, toward the present, to identify the necessary start date. The opposite of backward scheduling is forward scheduling. **Forward scheduling** is used to determine the completion date when the start date is known. To forward schedule, identify the start date, and, based on the expected lead time, schedule in a forward direction (toward the future) to determine the expected completion date.

Backward scheduling is used in MRP at each level in the structure of the end product. If an end product must be completed on day 20, for example, and it has an assembly lead time of 10 days, backward scheduling indicates that assembly must be started on day 10. In order to start the assembly of the end product on day 10, all components must be available by then. This dependent relationship between end product and components establishes the due dates for components. Once the due dates for components are known, backward scheduling is used to establish their start dates. The start dates for these components provide the due dates for components on the next lower level.

Figure 14.11 provides a product structure diagram for a simple end product, product P. The following lead times for end product P and each component can be considered with the product structure illustrated in Figure 14.11 to aid in understanding the relationship between parent start dates and component due dates:

$$P = 1 \text{ week}$$
$$Q = 2 \text{ weeks}$$
$$R = 1 \text{ week}$$
$$S = 2 \text{ weeks}$$
$$T = 1 \text{ week}$$
$$U = 2 \text{ weeks}$$
$$V = 2 \text{ weeks}$$
$$W = 3 \text{ weeks}$$

The lead times have been incorporated into a horizontal view of the product structure of end product P in Figure 14.12.

After incorporating the lead times into the product structure diagram, the relationship between the start date for parents at one level of the product structure and the due dates for components at the next lower level becomes apparent. The question of when to order can be answered by backward scheduling from the due date. For the end product (independent demand item), the due date is established when the order is received. The start date is determined by backward scheduling. For all components, the due date is established by the start date for the parent. Backward scheduling is then used to determine when assembly of components must begin.

---

[13]Walter E. Goddard, "Focus on the Fundamentals of MRP II," *Modern Materials Handling* (December 1993), 35.

| FIGURE 14.11 | Sample Product Structure |

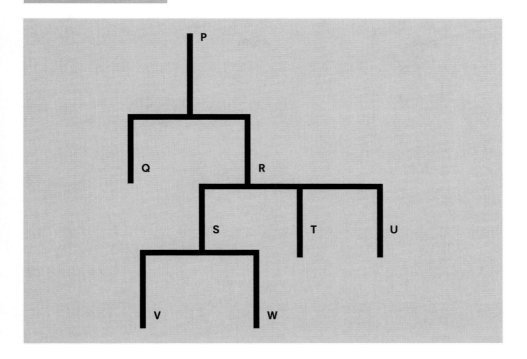

While backward scheduling is used to determine when to order dependent demand inventory, a process known as netting is used to determine how much to order. **Netting** is the process of determining net requirements by subtracting projected beginning on-hand inventory quantities from gross requirements. The netting process is most easily described by starting with the requirements for the end product. Suppose 300 units of end product P were required by Friday of week 8 (*T*). From Figure 14.12 it is clear that 300 Qs and 300 Rs will be required by the Friday of week 7 (*T* − 1). The requirements for Q and R are gross requirements. They describe how many units are needed. This may not be the quantity that must be manufactured, however, because there may be some in inventory already.

Suppose there were already 100 of Q and 100 of R in inventory. The net requirements for Q and R would be 200 units each. By Friday of week 7, the net requirements (200 units each) of Q and R will need to have completed the manufacturing process. When combined with the 100 units of Q and R that are already in inventory and any scheduled receipts, the newly manufactured products will satisfy the gross requirements for Q and R. The general formula for computing net requirements, assuming no safety stock, is

$$\text{Net requirements} = \left(\begin{array}{c}\text{Gross}\\\text{requirements}\end{array}\right) - \left(\begin{array}{c}\text{Beginning}\\\text{on-hand}\\\text{inventory}\end{array}\right) - \left(\begin{array}{c}\text{Scheduled}\\\text{receipts}\end{array}\right) \quad \textbf{(14.13)}$$

MRP combines the logic of time-phasing and netting into a structured approach that enables management to determine when to place orders. But several pieces of information are needed to successfully use this approach. The time-phasing process requires product structure and lead time information. The netting process requires accurate inventory counts for all end products, components, and raw materials. MRP also requires product structure

NETTING
The process of determining net requirements (actual amount needed in each time period) of materials by subtracting beginning on-hand inventory from gross requirements (the total expected demand during a time period).

FIGURE 14.12   **Product Structure with Lead Times**

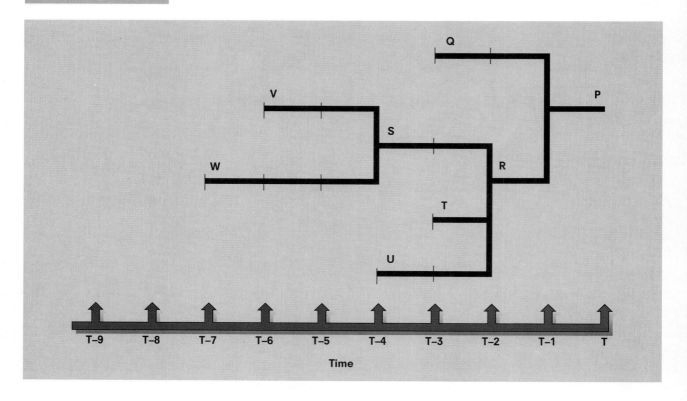

information for the quantity of components required per end product. The gross requirements for the end products are also required to complete the gross-to-net calculations.

BILL OF MATERIAL (BOM)
A listing of quantities of all raw materials, parts, and assemblies that go into an end item.

Product structure information is provided by the **bill of material (BOM).** It is analogous to a recipe for a meal if the meal is considered to be an end product and each ingredient is a component. The BOM not only describes the components required to produce the end product, but it also details how many of each are required and their respective levels in the product structure. It is a structure similar to the diagram and parts list that accompanies a bicycle, gas grill, or other product that must be assembled.

MASTER PRODUCTION SCHEDULE (MPS)
A statement of the quantity and timing of requirements for finished products.

The **master production schedule (MPS)** is a statement of quantity and timing of the production of end products. Using the meal analogy, the MPS would be similar to the week-by-week menu used by many college food-service operations. The role of the MPS is to provide gross requirements of the end products (independent demand inventory items) to MRP logic. Once the quantity of end products needed is known, the calculations for component order releases can be done.

The exact process used to develop the master production schedule varies from company to company, but it is typically developed from both forecast and order information. Forecasts provide information for time periods that are too far into the future to show actual orders. Near-term periods are based more heavily on actual orders. Once the requirements from the forecasts and orders are generated, these quantities are compared to quantities on hand. The MPS quantity is the difference between these quantities.

For make-to-stock firms, the orders that provide input to the MPS would be the orders released from the finished goods warehouse, such as those created by a reorder point system like the one discussed earlier in this chapter. For make-to-order firms, orders would come directly from customers. For make-to-stock assemble-to-order firms, the MPS would state the requirements and due dates for the stocked assemblies, those major assemblies that are made in advance and stored, rather than the actual end item. The orders for these assemblies would be generated by an inventory system similar to one used by a make-to-stock firm. The schedule for the actual assembly of the end items is called a final assembly schedule, and it is driven directly by customer orders.

The **inventory record** is a computer record that provides current information on the quantities of all items inventoried as well as information on lead time, suppliers, and the like. Figure 14.13 shows the relationship between MRP logic and its informational inputs.

The primary outputs of the MRP logic process are **planned order releases**—quantities that must be ordered to satisfy net requirements—for components and raw materials. MRP is typically done by computer, but the logic can be accurately duplicated through the use of a time-phased record and elementary arithmetic. Figure 14.14 shows a typical time-phased record.

A time-phased record is used with each end product and each component or raw material. Understanding the systematic logic utilized in MRP requires an understanding of two sets of relationships. First, relationships among cells within a time-phased record must be established. Second, relationships among the various time-phased records associated with each component must be established.

Figure 14.14 shows seven rows in the time-phased record. Gross requirements for the end product consists of the quantities and timing taken directly from the master production schedule. For components and raw materials of the same end product, gross requirements are derived from the planned order releases of each component's parent. This will be described in more detail as the relationships among different time-phased records are addressed. Inventory levels are projections. Beginning on-hand inventory is the projected inventory level at the beginning of the period and is equal to the projected inventory level at the end of the previous period. Projected ending on-hand inventory must be calculated. Only two types of changes can affect projected beginning inventory levels to result in a different projected level at the end of the period. The projected inventory level can be

INVENTORY RECORD
A computer file containing information on each item inventoried, including lead time, quantity on hand, supplier, and the like.

PLANNED ORDER RELEASE
The quantity to order in each period to satisfy net requirements.

FIGURE 14.13	**MRP and Informational Inputs**

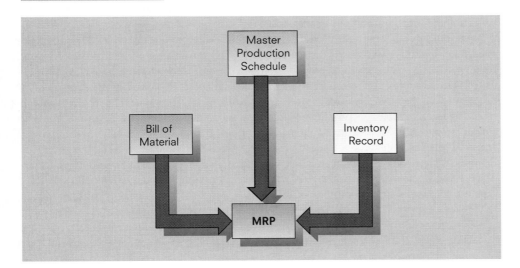

| FIGURE 14.14 | Sample Time-Phased Record |

Week:	1	2	3	4	5	6	7	8
Gross requirements								
Beginning on-hand								
Ending on-hand								
Scheduled receipts								
Net requirements								
Planned order receipts								
Planned order releases								

PLANNED ORDER RECEIPT
The quantity of each material that is to be received in each time period.

increased as a result of a **planned order receipt** or a scheduled receipt, or it can be decreased, as a result of a gross requirement. Thus, the formula for calculating the ending on-hand inventory is

$$\begin{matrix} \text{Ending} \\ \text{on-hand} \\ \text{inventory} \end{matrix} = \begin{pmatrix} \text{Beginning} \\ \text{on-hand} \\ \text{inventory} \end{pmatrix} + \begin{pmatrix} \text{Scheduled} \\ \text{receipts} \end{pmatrix} + \begin{pmatrix} \text{Planned} \\ \text{receipts} \end{pmatrix} - \begin{pmatrix} \text{Gross} \\ \text{requirements} \end{pmatrix}$$

NET REQUIREMENT
The amount of material and the timing of the needed materials that must be provided by either production or purchasing, calculated by subtracting on-hand inventory from gross requirements.

The **net requirement** is the quantity that must be produced and that will satisfy gross requirements when combined with on-hand inventory. It is equal to the gross requirements minus beginning on-hand inventory. Planned order releases are equal to the net requirement that appears one lead time into the future if planned order release quantities are to be for the exact amount of the net requirement. If planned order releases are equal to net requirements, the procedure is known as **lot-for-lot ordering.** If planned order release quantities are to be for amounts greater than the net requirement, other order policies must be used.

LOT-FOR-LOT ORDERING
In material requirements planning, ordering in quantities equal to the net requirements.

The use of order policies other than lot-for-lot is frequently the result of quantity discounts, high changeover costs, inflexible container sizes, or an attempt to balance inventory carrying costs with order or setup costs.

Various approaches to developing "lowest cost" order policies have been tried. The issues are essentially the same as discussed in the EOQ formula—minimizing the order and holding costs. Various attempts have been made at using derivations of the EOQ formula as well as other more sophisticated algorithms. Most experts agree that as small batch manufacturing has become widely accepted as a means of improving competitive advantage, many of the incentives to producing large batches as a way to drive down costs are no longer appropriate. Most progressive manufacturers attempt to produce as small a quantity as possible. In fact, the production batch size may even be smaller than the net requirement. Several smaller batches may be used to fulfill a planned order release for 100 units, for example. Although small batches have become more common, for many manufacturers fixed quantity lot sizes will be common because of the need to fill containers or trucks.

Lot sizing decisions may also be influenced by changeover practices. For example, some manufacturers perform changeovers "off shift," after production employees have gone home. Production lot sizes are frequently dictated by the quantity that can be produced in an 8-hour shift.

The planned order receipt is simply the acknowledgment of the receipt of the planned order release and is shown to occur one lead time after the planned order release.

The time-phased records are schedules that "scroll" as time passes. As each week passes, week 2 becomes week 1, week 8 becomes week 7, and a new week 8 appears. As week 2 becomes week 1, it is said to mature. Week 1 is the "current" week. All of the planned order releases in week 1 must be reviewed and decisions must be made to actually release the orders to production or in the event of a purchased item, to the supplier. When an order is actually released, it is not considered a planned order release any more. It is called an **open order.** Rather than having a corresponding planned order receipt, open orders have a corresponding **scheduled receipt.** So, when a planned order is actually released, the planned order receipt becomes a scheduled receipt.

The relationships among the various time-phased records are defined by the parent-component relationships that exist in the product structure. With the exception of the end product, gross requirements for all time-phased records are derived from the planned order releases of the parent and the number of components required for each parent, taken from the bill of material. For example, if in Figure 14.12 three Rs were required to produce one P, a planned order release for 100 Ps in week 6 would create a gross requirement for 300 Rs in week 6. If R were used as a component for several other end products, it would receive gross requirements from their planned order releases as well.

In most MRP systems the master production schedule is netted against finished goods inventory prior to providing the gross requirements of the end product to MRP. To simplify the discussion of MRP logic, and because the complexities of master production scheduling techniques are beyond the scope of this text, we have chosen to compute net requirements for the end product exactly as is done for all components and raw materials, that is, as part of MRP.

Example 14.6 provides a demonstration of MRP logic.

OPEN ORDER
In material requirements planning, an order that has been placed, but not yet filled.

SCHEDULED RECEIPT
In material requirements planning, the receipt that corresponds to an open order.

EXAMPLE 14.6

Consider two end products, X and Y, which are manufactured and have the master production schedule shown below. Product structures are presented in Figure 14.15.

Material Requirements Planning Logic

Week	1	2	3	4	5	6	7	8
X	100	130	50	80	40	60	110	90
Y	210	80	79	90	60	85	90	130

FIGURE 14.15   **Product Structures of X and Y**

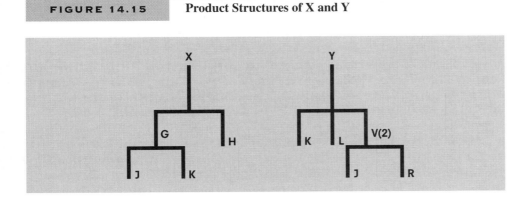

TABLE 14.1	Lead Times and Beginning Inventory Levels	

Item	Lead Times	Inventory Level
X	1 week	200 units
Y	1 week	200 units
G	1 week	50 units
H	2 weeks	80 units
L	2 weeks	170 units
V	2 weeks	410 units
J	2 weeks	400 units
K	1 week	200 units
R	1 week	355 units

Lead times and current inventory levels for the end products and components are provided in Table 14.1. Table 14.2 (pages 434–35) provides the nine time-phased records for this example.

LOW LEVEL CODE
Restructuring the bill of materials so that all occurrences of an item are made to coincide with the lowest level of the structure in which the item appears.

Several points must be made to enhance the understanding of the MRP logic. First, notice the sequence of the time-phased records in Example 14.6. X and Y are first, followed by G, H, and L, while V, J, K, and R are last. This sequence is in order of the **low level codes** of the items. The low level code is the lowest level that an item will appear in any product structure (see Figure 14.15). The low level code of X and Y is 0. The low level code of G, H, L, and V is 1. The low level code of J, K, and R is 2.

Notice that K appears at both levels 1 and 2. Because its lowest level is 2, its low level code is 2. The calculations are done in order of low level code to accommodate situations like that of K, which appears in more than one level. K gets its gross requirements from two places because it has two parents, G and Y. By computing the gross requirements of K after the computation of the planned order releases of G, the gross requirements of K can include planned order releases of G and Y. Notice in the time-phased record of K that in week 1, K's gross requirements are 120. This is the sum of the planned order releases from week 1 of G and Y, 30 plus 90.

Another point to note in the time-phased record is the relationship between V and its parent, Y. According to the product structure (Figure 14.15), 2 Vs are required for each Y. Planned order releases from Y must, therefore, be multiplied by 2 to provide the correct gross requirements for V. Notice, also, that no orders have been released, so the scheduled receipts row shows all zeroes.

Example 14.6 utilizes lot-for-lot ordering for each component. If a fixed lot size were used, planned order releases would be in increments of the lot size. If, for example, the lot size policy stipulated lots of 100 and a net requirement was 110, the planned order release would be for 200. Ordering in other than a lot-for-lot policy would result in increased inventory levels.

As mentioned earlier in this chapter, it is possible for a component item to have both independent and dependent demand. If this situation exists, two changes must be made in the MRP logic. First, the gross requirements would come from the item's dependent demand parents and from the forecast for the independent demand. Gross requirements will simply be the sum of all sources of demand. Second, because the forecast will not be perfectly accurate, management may wish to consider adding a safety stock. Safety stock could be included in MRP by adding the amount of the safety stock to the net requirements. In this manner, the material requirements plan would show the projected ending inventory for the period to be equal to the safety stock, rather than equal to zero.

MRP has been used, primarily in the manufacturing sector, since the mid-1960s. It has also been applied in the service sector, particularly in health-care environments such as managing inventories of pharmaceutical products. Over time, it has become clear that it functions better in some environments than in others. High-volume, repetitive producers of discrete products tend to use MRP to generate purchase orders, but they are less likely to use it to plan manufacturing orders. MRP is of little use because of the fixed routings and high-volume production, which makes planning simple and the lead times short. Very little WIP inventory exists in these environments, so MRP isn't as necessary.

Nondiscrete manufacturers often have difficulty using MRP because of the yield variability in their processes. There is less of a direct relationship between inputs and outputs in many of the nondiscrete processes, particularly those of basic producers. When yield fluctuates, it is difficult to determine the gross requirements of components. If yield loss in a process is stable, the loss can be factored into the MRP calculations. For example, if there is a 10 percent loss during a process, gross requirements can be inflated by 10 percent. However, if the yield loss fluctuates between 5 percent and 20 percent, planning becomes very difficult. A larger-than-expected yield loss results in a shortage and is resolved by generating another order to make up the difference. A smaller-than-expected yield loss results in excess inventory.

Over the years, many firms have attempted to use MRP as a scheduling tool. They have assumed that if planned order releases were given to the production managers and entered into the processes as they are provided by MRP, no further scheduling would be needed. MRP is not a scheduling tool, however. It is a planning tool. Scheduling must still take place to determine how various orders can be accomplished within each week in a way that uses resources productively and completes orders on time.

DATA ACCURACY

The accuracy of the informational inputs to the MRP logic is critical for the success of this approach. Accuracy problems typically arise in the bill of material and in the inventory record. BOM accuracy is particularly a problem in industries that are in a constant state of change because of technology improvements, such as the aerospace and defense industries. Frequent technological improvements result in frequent changes in the product structure. Extraordinary effort is required to maintain up-to-date and accurate bills of material.

Bill of material accuracy is also difficult to maintain in food and beverage industries. Because many recipes utilize ingredients that vary in intensity and taste, producers must adjust the recipes to maintain taste consistency. Different sources for sugar, for example, will result in a different taste in the finished product unless the proportions of ingredients are adjusted. Soft drinks, candy, and other products that utilize a significant amount of sugar face this kind of problem when they vary the source of sugar as prices change. Similarly, fruit of different quality levels may cause inconsistencies in the taste of jams and jellies, so recipes must be adjusted to compensate for bill of material changes.

The consequences of an inaccurate bill of material can be quite serious. In food production, an inaccurate bill of material or recipe may result in inconsistent taste or appearance and resulting quality problems. In industries that must cope with consistent technological change and BOM variation, the problem can result in missed orders. MRP logic

TABLE 14.2	Time-Phased Records for Example 14.6

Week →	1	2	3	4	5	6	7	8
X Gross Requirements	**100**	**130**	**50**	**80**	**40**	**60**	**110**	**90**
Beginning Inventory	200	100	0	0	0	0	0	0
Ending Inventory	100	0	0	0	0	0	0	0
Net Requirements	0	30	50	80	40	60	110	90
Planned Order Receipts	0	30	50	80	40	60	110	90
Planned Order Releases	30	50	80	40	60	110	90	0
Y Gross Requirements	**210**	**80**	**79**	**90**	**60**	**85**	**90**	**130**
Beginning Inventory	200	−10	0	0	0	0	0	0
Ending Inventory	−10	0	0	0	0	0	0	0
Net Requirements	10	90	79	90	60	85	90	130
Planned Order Receipts	0	90	79	90	60	85	90	130
Planned Order Releases	90	79	90	60	85	90	130	0
G Gross Requirements	**30**	**50**	**80**	**40**	**60**	**110**	**90**	**0**
Beginning Inventory	50	20	0	0	0	0	0	0
Ending Inventory	20	0	0	0	0	0	0	0
Net Requirements	0	30	80	40	60	110	90	0
Planned Order Receipts	0	30	80	40	60	110	90	0
Planned Order Releases	30	80	40	60	110	90	0	0
H Gross Requirements	**30**	**50**	**80**	**40**	**60**	**110**	**90**	**0**
Beginning Inventory	80	50	0	0	0	0	0	0
Ending Inventory	50	0	0	0	0	0	0	0
Net Requirements	0	0	80	40	60	110	90	0
Planned Order Receipts	0	0	80	40	60	110	90	0
Planned Order Releases	80	40	60	110	90	0	0	0
L Gross Requirements	**90**	**79**	**90**	**60**	**85**	**90**	**130**	**0**
Beginning Inventory	170	80	1	0	0	0	0	0
Ending Inventory	80	1	0	0	0	0	0	0
Net Requirements	0	0	89	60	85	90	130	0
Planned Order Receipts	0	0	89	60	85	90	130	0
Planned Order Releases	89	60	85	90	130	0	0	0

Week →	1	2	3	4	5	6	7	8
V Gross Requirements	**180**	**158**	**180**	**120**	**170**	**180**	**260**	**0**
Beginning Inventory	410	230	72	0	0	0	0	0
Ending Inventory	230	72	0	0	0	0	0	0
Net Requirements	0	0	108	120	170	180	260	0
Planned Order Receipts	0	0	108	120	170	180	260	0
Planned Order Releases	108	120	170	180	260	0	0	0
J Gross Requirements	**138**	**200**	**210**	**240**	**370**	**90**	**0**	**0**
Beginning Inventory	400	262	62	0	0	0	0	0
Ending Inventory	262	62	0	0	0	0	0	0
Net Requirements	0	0	148	240	370	90	0	0
Planned Order Receipts	0	0	148	240	370	90	0	0
Planned Order Releases	148	240	370	90	0	0	0	0
K Gross Requirements	**120**	**159**	**130**	**120**	**195**	**180**	**130**	**0**
Beginning Inventory	200	80	0	0	0	0	0	0
Ending Inventory	80	0	0	0	0	0	0	0
Scheduled Receipts	0	0	0	0	0	0	0	0
Net Requirements	0	79	130	120	195	180	130	0
Planned Order Receipts	0	79	130	120	195	180	130	0
Planned Order Releases	79	130	120	195	180	130	0	0
R Gross Requirements	**108**	**120**	**170**	**180**	**260**	**0**	**0**	**0**
Beginning Inventory	355	247	127	0	0	0	0	0
Ending Inventory	247	127	0	0	0	0	0	0
Scheduled Receipts	0	0	0	0	0	0	0	0
Net Requirements	0	0	43	180	260	0	0	0
Planned Order Receipts	0	0	43	180	260	0	0	0
Planned Order Releases	0	43	180	260	0	0	0	0

checks the level of inventory of the items listed in the bill of material and computes the net requirements. If the bill of material is wrong, netting will be done on the wrong component and planned order releases will be generated for the wrong component. When the planned order release for the end product matures, the necessary components will not be present and the end product will not be completed on time.

The inventory record is probably the most difficult informational input to keep accurate. A high level of discipline is required to maintain accurate inventory records. Invariably, a particular item is needed in a hurry and appropriate documentation is skipped, resulting in actual inventory levels being less than the inventory record shows. One approach to maintaining inventory accuracy is **cycle counting,** which is a continuous physical counting of inventory. Whenever the physical count differs from the record, the variance must be resolved and the cause eliminated. Cycle counting has several advantages over the traditional periodic physical counts many companies use. When physical counts are taken infrequently, the individuals doing the counting are not experts and frequently make mistakes. Also, when variances are identified, there is usually no way to find out why the variance exists because too much time has elapsed since the last count. Typically, the physical counts show less in inventory than the record, and the variance is merely written off as "shrinkage." The cause is never solved because it cannot be identified. With cycle counting, the physical counts are done frequently enough to enable the cycle counter to track down the causes of variances and eliminate them. Cycle counting could be considered an application of TQM to maintaining inventory accuracy because it goes beyond accurate counting to identify and eliminate the causes of inaccurate records.

CYCLE COUNTING
An approach to maintaining inventory accuracy by frequent physical counts and resolving any detected variances.

THE EVOLUTION OF MRP

Since the early 1960s, material requirements planning has undergone a process of adaptation that has taken it far beyond a simple tool for the management of dependent demand inventory. The direct relationship between the planned order releases for manufactured items and the capacity requirements for work centers resulted in the linkage and inclusion of capacity planning in what became known as MRP systems. In these systems, the master production schedule, which provided gross requirements for the end items, was checked for capacity feasibility before the MRP logic was begun. After the planned order releases were determined by MRP, they provided an input for a second capacity check that was much more detailed than the first and provided an important input for the scheduling of work centers. These systems evolved into **closed-loop MRP systems** that were closely tied to manufacturing control functions, such as delay reporting and supplier scheduling. The "closed-loop" description implies that feedback is provided by the execution functions so that planning can be updated according to actual results.[14]

CLOSED-LOOP MRP SYSTEMS
Material requirements planning systems with feedback from execution functions.

As the popularity of closed-loop MRP systems increased, the logic was extended to assist in planning for all manufacturing resources, including personnel, cash flow, and facilities. These systems were renamed **Manufacturing Resources Planning (MRPII)** systems. They include the master scheduling, capacity requirements planning, material requirements planning, and execution support systems of the closed-loop MRP system as well as business planning and linkages to financial reporting and the ability to answer "what if?" questions through simulation.[15]

MANUFACTURING RESOURCES PLANNING (MRPII)
An extension of closed-loop MRP systems to include all aspects of business planning, financial reporting, and simulation.

---

[14]J. F. Cox, J. H. Blackstone, and M. S. Spencer, eds., *APICS Dictionary* 7th ed. (Falls Church, Va.: American Production and Inventory Control Society, 1992), 8.

[15]Cox, Blackstone, and Spencer, 8.

The linkages between MRP and capacity planning, within these systems, will be discussed in greater detail in the next chapter.

INVENTORY REDUCTION STRATEGIES

Manufacturers and services have undergone significant pressure to reduce inventories. Inventory reduction provides many competitive advantages, but it also exposes the unwary company to potential problems. Unfortunately, it is difficult for businesses, particularly retailers, to reduce inventory levels without adversely affecting customer service. This problem is most acute if demands are unstable or difficult to predict, as with a new product, a demand that is highly seasonal, or demand that spikes because of a promotion. (See Box 14.2.)

For products with more predictable demands, more frequent deliveries from suppliers have, for many firms, resulted in improved levels of customer service and, at the same time, reduced levels of inventory and related improvements in flexibility. (See Box 14.3.)

High levels of inventory accuracy are a prerequisite to any inventory reduction efforts. The less inventory that there is, the higher the level of accuracy is needed. High levels of inventory hide problems that will result from poor accuracy. Before reducing inventory levels, a successful cycle counting program is imperative.

When reducing inventories, companies frequently create customer service problems by eliminating the wrong products. Targeting items with high-dollar values, a frequent mistake, often leads to customer service problems. Dollar-days is an excellent measure of

OPERATIONS OUTLOOK

BOX 14.2

Toy Retailers and JIT

The inventory reduction strategies brought about by JIT have had numerous positive effects on costs, flexibility, and quality. Unfortunately, when implemented in the wrong environment or when demands are unstable, the result can be detrimental to dependability of delivery and response time.

The toy industry provides some excellent examples. Toy dealers risk being stuck with large inventories of "losers" if they order large quantities before they can predict a toy's success in the marketplace. Many retailers avoid this problem by holding back on orders until they are certain. This hesitancy may cause an individual retailer to be short of a product while its competitors meet demand. If all retailers follow suit, it may also result in the manufacturer not producing enough to meet the demand.

In August 1993, Target Stores noticed that the sales curve for the new Mighty Morphin Power Rangers was rising steeply for a new toy. It was even steeper than the curve had been for Teenage Mutant Ninja Turtles. Target Stores knew a TV show that would provide a tie-in to the Power Ranger was about to air, so the management decided to wait and see how that affected demand.

By the time Target placed its second order for the product, the toy was difficult to acquire. Most U.S. retailers ordered late and were unable to meet the Christmas demand. Only 600,000 units were shipped before the holidays. The demand was estimated to be about 12 million.

Retailers and manufacturers have been realizing that the low inventory levels of JIT may not provide enough of a buffer to deal with unexpected successes.

Because of the short supply of Power Rangers and the high Christmas demand, manufacturers were operating factories round-the-clock in December 1993, paying overtime salaries and premiums for overnight delivery to retailers. Increased costs cut into profits.

Source J. Pereira, "Toy Industry Finds It's Harder and Harder to Pick the Winners," *The Wall Street Journal,* December 21, 1993, sec. A, 1, 5.

OPERATIONS
OUTLOOK

BOX 14.3

Are Music Stores Behind the Beat?

At the 1992 convention of the National Association of Recording Merchandisers (NARM), Robert Morgado, chairman of Warner Music Group, put the music store owners on notice. He threatened them with direct marketing, including 800 numbers and computer networks for mail-ordering tapes and CDs.

Morgado's reaction to what he perceived as retailers' sluggishness in keeping up with changing times was supported by others in the recording business as well. According to Al Teller, chairman of MCA Music Entertainment Group, "The average record store is still in the Stone Age when it comes to creating an exciting environment." Rick Dobbis, president and CEO of PolyGram, complained: "The atmosphere, the selection, and the knowledge of clerks often isn't competitive with the Gap, Benetton, Waldenbooks, and other places we're up against for consumers' disposable incomes. . . . Clerks are uniformly poorly informed and very often have a lousy attitude about their work." Ed Rosenblatt, president of Geffen Records, said: "In many cases, employees don't know the specials offered by their stores and can't even answer simple questions."

The response from retailers was cynical at best. Tower Records president Russ Solomon responded to Morgado's comments by saying: "He doesn't have a clue." Despite the lack of concern on the part of retailers, the home shopping threat to retail music sales is real. Bose Express Music, a mail-order album business, has seen its sales double annually since 1989. Capital recently tried direct sales through TV advertisements on ESPN, MTV, and the Nashville Network.

Some stores have seen an opportunity to differentiate themselves from their competition by providing a "different" environment and better service quality. HMV and Virgin, the two largest album retailers in England, are likely to force U.S. retailers to catch up. Peter Luckhurst, president of HMV's three U.S. stores, claims that his company's philosophy is different from that of U.S. retailers. He says that many U.S. retail chains purchase large quantities of albums infrequently to take advantage of discounts offered by record companies. HMV purchases small quantities frequently so that stocks are maintained better. As HMV expands to new geographic markets, U.S. retailers are being forced to follow suit.

Source "You Can't Always Get What You Want," *Rolling Stone,* September 3, 1992, 13–14, 80.

inventory reduction. The dollar-days of a particular inventory item are determined by multiplying the dollar value of the inventory by the number of days until it will be sold. The number of days until it will be sold can be determined by using the demand forecast or actual customer orders. Dollar-days acknowledges that it isn't merely the dollar value of the inventory that results in carrying costs, but it is also the amount of time the items are kept in inventory. Companies that use dollar-days to reduce inventory levels on the items that have a low dollar value but are slow movers find that they reduce carrying costs more than if they reduced the inventory of high-value items that have a short-time supply. Reducing the inventory of items that have a long-time supply can reduce dollar-days substantially, but does not adversely impact service level.

INVENTORY MANAGEMENT CROSS-LINKS

For service firms and manufacturers, inventory management has a profound impact on other business functions. Perhaps the business function that is impacted the most by the presence or lack of good inventory management practice is marketing, particularly customer service. The availability of what the customer desires has an immediate impact on marketing's ability to accomplish its designated tasks. Lost sales result in short-term revenue losses but also provide competitors with enormous opportunities by giving customers

The TJX Companies, Inc., substantially improved the financial performance of its Hit or Miss stores by overhauling its management information system. TJX was able to lower inventory levels and reduce markdowns by installing a new, integrated database system, which gives Hit or Miss managers information and analysis capabilities in merchandising, administrative, and financial functions. With improved inventory management, Hit or Miss stores are better stocked with fresh merchandise that received high customer acceptance.

Source Courtesy of the TJX Companies, Inc.

a reason to defect. The stockout is like an engraved invitation for the customer to try out the competition. The last thing any manager should want is to give a customer an excuse to go to the competitor.

On the other hand, too much inventory hampers flexibility and response to such an extent that new products can't get to the market quickly enough to capture it or obsolete products have to be scrapped at a financial loss. From a marketing strategy perspective, inventory management is truly a balancing act.

Inventory has a financial impact on firms because it ties up assets in inventory investments. Investments in excess inventory can have serious implications because they involve large amounts of cash invested at a low, or even negative, rate of return. Inventory investments also lack liquidity and have tax implications. Many firms have found that their cash flow could be substantially bolstered if excess inventory were eliminated.

Although not often recognized as financial issues, decreased levels of flexibility, slow quality feedback, and long lead times have long-term implications for revenues because of the negative impact on competitiveness. Every functional area of a business should seek to find a balance between quick response to customer demands and low levels of inventory.

Various business functions also can have implications for inventory management. Pressure to reduce the cost per unit, for example, frequently results in longer production runs, large batches, and utilization of equipment above and beyond what is supported by demand. All of these practices result in increased levels of inventory and the associated financial and competitive costs. A cost per unit emphasis results in departmental measures that stress equipment utilization and serves as an incentive to carry higher-than-necessary levels of inventory.

Many firms have tried to reduce inventory levels only to find that traditional short-term financial performance measures prevented them from doing so. As inventory is reduced through smaller production batch sizes, utilization rates drop, resulting in an apparent increase in cost per unit. Total costs actually decrease, however. Because utilization has historically been used to measure productivity, pressure to increase utilization results in fewer changeovers, resulting in larger batches and higher levels of inventory. This cycle is common among manufacturers that have not recognized the need to adapt measures of productivity to the new objectives of the firm. It is a classic example of the conflict between short-term performance measures and long-term strategic objectives.

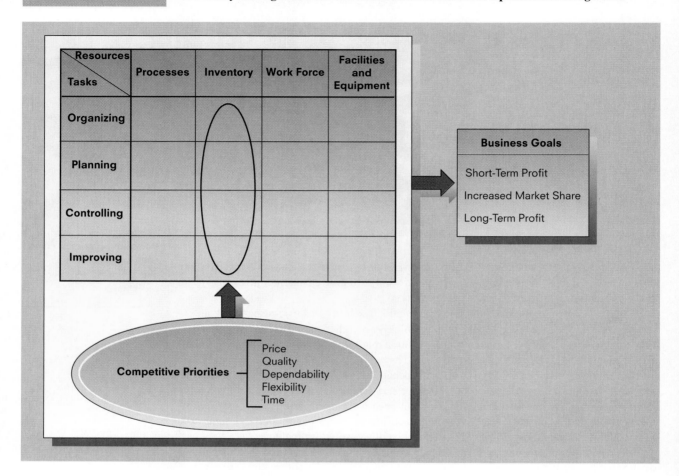

FIGURE 14.16   **Inventory Management and the Task/Resource Model of Operations Management**

The long-term and short-term importance of inventory management decisions are apparent when inventory management is viewed from the context of the task/resource model of operations management, as is illustrated in Figure 14.16. Inventory management systems have significant long-term implications. Day-to-day decisions related to inventory control and improvement practices have significant short-term implications as well. The tradeoffs between long- and short-term decisions are frequent and challenging.

SUMMARY

The management of inventory has emerged as one of the most important challenges for manufacturers and is becoming recognized as more important in the service sector than traditionally viewed. Inventory management presents a difficult task of balancing tradeoffs among competitive capabilities. Increasing inventory may benefit reliability of delivery, but it can adversely affect price, quality, flexibility, and time. Inventory management also presents a tradeoff between short- and long-term goals. Responding to an immediate customer demand is urgent and tends to get placed on a high priority. The reaction to a recent stockout may be to order in much larger quantities next time. This reaction may do far more harm globally than the one instance of stockout.

The greatest challenge in inventory management and inventory reduction is probably in eliminating the causes and reasons for carrying high levels of inventory. This requires that disruptions be eliminated, unreliable sources be replaced, and scheduling approaches be improved. After eliminating the need for all inventory that is used for coping with problems, minimal inventory can be maintained where it is strategically beneficial, improving the firm's competitive position.

WATERPROOF OUTDOORS REVISITED

 Waterproof Outdoors has made a fundamental error in managing inventories. What do you think is the fundamental problem at Waterproof?

Why are forecasts becoming less accurate as product variety increases?

If you were hired as the consultant, what type of inventory management system would you suggest for each type of inventory? Design dependent and independent inventory management systems for Waterproof that are properly linked to each other and that will solve their problems.

QUESTIONS FOR REVIEW

1. Describe the four uses of inventory.
2. What are the financial costs of inventory?
3. What nonfinancial costs result from excess inventory?
4. What is the relationship between order quantity and carrying costs?
5. Compare independent and dependent demand inventory characteristics.
6. How are buffers used to control inventory levels?
7. Why is safety stock required in ROP systems?
8. How can safety stock be calculated to provide a specified level of confidence in satisfying demand during the replenishment lead time?
9. What is the objective of the EOQ formula?
10. What are the primary weaknesses of the EOQ formula?
11. Why does a fixed interval, variable quantity model require more safety stock than an ROP model?
12. How can ABC analysis be used to help select an inventory management technique?
13. What are the informational inputs to MRP logic?
14. How are gross requirements for components determined in MRP logic?
15. What is the difference between a planned order receipt and a scheduled receipt?
16. What is the significance of the low level code in MRP logic?
17. What are the potential effects of inaccurate bills of material or inventory records?
18. Why are dollar-days a particularly useful measure of inventory?

QUESTIONS FOR THOUGHT AND DISCUSSION

1. Why might the selection of inventory management techniques for dependent demand inventory, based on an ABC analysis, not be a wise thing to do?
2. A new purchasing agent in your company is convinced that quantity discounts are the best way to cut costs. How do you convince her that this may not be true?
3. What is the relationship between cost per unit as a performance measure and high levels of work-in-process inventory?

INTEGRATIVE QUESTIONS

1. What would be the impact on competitive priorities of reducing inventory too quickly?
2. What is the effect of appropriate (not too much, not too little) inventory levels on value, as perceived by the customer?
3. How does the use of inventory vary among different types of services?
4. How does the use of work-in-process inventory vary among make-to-stock, make-to-order, and make-to-stock/assemble-to-order manufacturers?
5. How could project planning techniques be applied to an inventory reduction effort?
6. What constraints to inventory management are established by the aggregate plan?
7. How does facility location and transportation affect inventory levels in manufacturing?

PROBLEMS

1. For men's size 10 of a particular cross-training shoe at Happy Feet Shoes, the average weekly demand is nine pairs with a standard deviation of 3. Replenishment lead time is 1 week. What should the reorder point be to maintain a 99 percent confidence of satisfying demand during the lead time?
2. Octagon Frames is a do-it-yourself picture-frame shop. Karen Wilkerson, the owner, maintains an inventory of brushed stainless steel frame stock for customer use. A length of that particular frame stock is 42 inches long. Her supplier can provide 24-hour delivery for a premium price if absolutely necessary, but the normal replenishment lead time for the stock is 4 days. Assuming an annual demand of 630 lengths, and a standard deviation of demand during lead time of 2.66, determine the necessary reorder point to maintain a 97 percent service level during replenishment lead times. The shop is open 315 days per year.
3. Custom Glass manufactures various fiberglass fixtures for the recreational vehicle industry. A standard item, which is produced for stock in a finished goods warehouse, is a fiberglass cover for air-conditioning units that are mounted on the tops of recreational vehicles. Twelve different manufacturers of RVs use the covers. The average weekly demand for the covers is 237 units. The manufacturing lead time for replenishing the inventory is 2 weeks. The standard deviation of demand during the lead time is 54 units. What is the necessary ROP to maintain a lead time service level of 99 percent?
4. From Problem 1, assuming an annual demand of 468 pairs of shoes, an annual carrying cost of $7.80 per pair, and an order cost of $4.00 per order, what is the EOQ for Happy Feet? How many times per year, on the average, will Happy Feet order these shoes?
5. Determine the EOQ for the following case:

   Annual demand = 595 units
   Carrying cost = $3.30 per unit per year
   Order cost = $11.00 per order

6. Determine the EOQ for the following situation. Assume 52 weeks per year.

   Weekly demand = 111 units
   Purchase price = $6.00
   Annual carrying cost = 30 percent of the value
   Order cost = $16.00 per order

7. Basement PCs, a small assembler of PC clones, has a thriving business near a large university campus. It competes on the basis of price, on-site service, and technical assistance. Meg and Chip Abott, the owners, purchase components from a number of different computer component warehouses. Because of the number of students who prefer to have access to university mainframes and student networks from their apartments and residence hall rooms, over half of the computers sold contain internal modems. A nearby supplier of modem cards offers same day delivery and the following quantity discounts for the popular 9600 baud modems:

   Less than 20 units, $32 each
   20–50 units, $31 each
   51 or more units, $29 each

   The annual demand for the 9600 baud modem is 240 units. Carrying costs are $5 per unit per year. The order cost is $2.50. Determine the optimal order quantity.

8. Pet Munchies, a large pet and pet supply store, purchases marine aquarium filtration systems from the manufacturer. Prices are as follows:

   Less than 12 units, $35.95 per unit
   13–100 units, $33.95 per unit
   More than 100 units, $29.95 per unit

   Average annual demand is 210 units. Carrying costs are $13 per unit per year. Order cost is $7. Determine the optimal order quantity.

9. Prism tissue company maintains an MRO inventory of parts for several paper machines. One particular part is replaced frequently. The unbiased forecast usage rate for the part is 4 units per week. The MAD is 1.37 units. Determine the reorder point if a 99 percent confidence of meeting the demand during the lead time is desired.

10. CD's College Supply stocks chemistry lab goggles and is known for its "lowest price" guarantee. Forecast demand is 180 goggles per week. The MAD is 14 units. The forecast is not biased. Replenishment lead time is 1 week. Determine the reorder point if a lead time service level of 97 percent is desired.

11. You have been approached by the manager of a local sporting goods store to establish a reorder point system for basketballs. Annual demand is 260 units. Carrying costs are $8 per ball per year. Order cost is $3.50. The replenishment lead time is 1 week. Assuming 52 weeks per year, the standard deviation of the demand during lead time is 1.6. Determine the EOQ and reorder point with a 95 percent lead time service level.

12. The inventory manager for a make-to-stock upholster-to-order manufacturer of contemporary furniture wishes to establish a reorder point system for finished beachwood chair frames that can be upholstered to meet customer orders with lead time of only 1 week. The aggregate forecast for all upholstery coverings of this particular model of chair frame is 135 units every 10 working days. The forecast is unbiased with a MAD of 20 units. Annual demand is 3,240 units. Replenishment lead time is 10 days. The order cost is $140 per order. Carrying cost is $35 per unit per year. Determine the EOQ and reorder point with a 95 percent lead time service level.

13. Uptown Sporting Goods is a large sporting goods retailer. To reduce order costs, the purchasing manager orders all balls (volleyballs, soccer balls, basketballs, and the like) from the same distributor every other Monday. The average daily demand for a particular basketball is 5.4 with a standard deviation of 1.4. The replenishment lead time is 5 days. There are currently eight basketballs in inventory. The purchasing manager is to place an order today. How many should she order to maintain a service level of 97 percent?

14. The manager of CD's College Supply (from Problem 10 above) is now ordering several items from the goggle distributor and wishes to place orders weekly. The replenishment lead time is 1 week. Forecast demand is 26 units per day with a standard deviation of 9 units. Determine the reorder point if a lead time service level of 97 percent is desired. There are currently 68 goggles on hand.

15. Consider end product X, shown at the top of the next column. The Master Production Schedule (MPS) for X is

Week:	1	2	3	4	5	6	7	8
Quantity:	110	210	230	40	90	210	160	170

There are 224 units of X, 300 units of Y, and 240 units of Z in inventory. Lead time is 1 week for all items. Using MRP logic and time-phased records for X, Y, and Z, determine planned order releases.

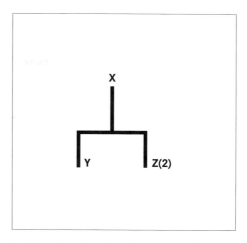

16. Determine planned order releases for end product A and components B, C, D, and E shown in the product structure below:

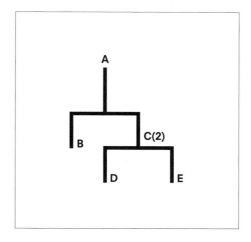

The MPS for A is

Week:	1	2	3	4	5	6	7	8
Quantity:	300	630	710	475	890	860	780	520

Lead times for all items are 1 week. Current inventory levels for the items are as follows:

A	B	C	D	E
580	460	800	1,425	1,350

17. Determine the planned order releases for end product A and its components.

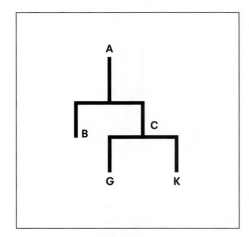

The MPS for A is

Week:	1	2	3	4	5	6	7	8
A:	240	345	243	356	523	245	198	234

Lead times for all items are 1 week. Current inventory levels for the items are as follows:

A	B	C	G	K
315	326	315	520	534

18. Determine the planned order releases for end products A and G and their components.

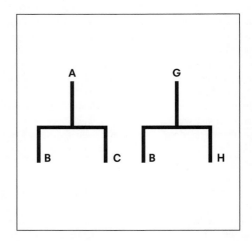

The MPSs are

Week:	1	2	3	4	5	6	7	8
A:	240	345	243	356	523	245	198	234
G:	315	631	534	723	497	862	768	423

Lead time for all items is 1 week. Beginning inventory levels are as follows:

A	G	B	C	H
246	412	945	423	651

19. Determine the planned order releases for end products P and Q and their components.

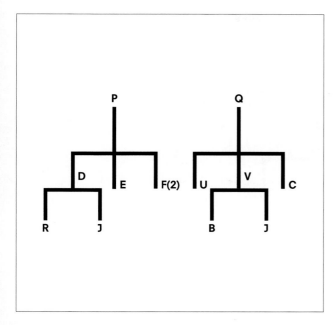

The MPSs are

Week:	1	2	3	4	5	6	7	8
P:	324	534	675	642	285	453	856	453
Q:	473	351	255	564	773	564	196	326

Lead times and beginning inventory levels are given below:

Part	Lead Time	Beginning Inventory
P	1 week	330
Q	1	760
D	2	1,205
E	2	564
F	1	1,345
U	2	423
V	1	651
C	2	423
R	1	673
J	2	1,189
B	2	651

20. Determine the planned order releases for end products X and Z and their components shown on page 446. The MPSs are

Week:	1	2	3	4	5	6	7	8
X:	245	643	423	132	168	150	325	280
Z:	280	452	480	365	285	420	245	535

Lead times and on-hand inventories are given below:

Part	Lead Time	On-Hand Inventory
X	1	330
Z	1	560
Q	2	1,100
R	2	1,714
O	1	490
V	2	210
S	1	462
M	1	346
T	1	872
W	1	468
L	1	210

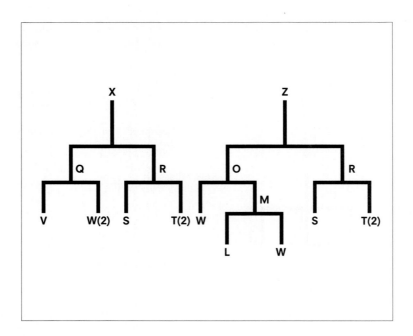

SUGGESTED READINGS

Dillon, Robert E. "Some Simple Steps to Inventory Reduction." *Production and Inventory Management Journal* 31 (1st Quarter 1990): 62–65.

Finch, Byron J., and James F. Cox. "Strategic Use of WIP Inventory: The Impact of Bill of Material Shape and Plant Type." *Production and Inventory Management Journal* 30 (1st Quarter 1989): 63–66.

Meyer, H. "Inventory Accuracy—Is It Worth It? A Case Study." *Production and Inventory Management Journal* 31 (2nd Quarter 1990): 15–17.

Toelle, R. A., and Richard J. Tersine. "Excess Inventory: Financial Asset or Operational Liability?" *Production and Inventory Management Journal* 30 (4th Quarter 1989): 32–35.

MATERIAL REQUIREMENTS PLANNING IN A SPREADSHEET ENVIRONMENT

Although most manufacturing firms use dedicated MRP software for the computations required to determine planned order releases for components and raw materials, many small manufacturers and some not-so-small ones use sophisticated spreadsheets to perform this function. The logic is not complex and the top-to-bottom, left-to-right recalculation protocol used by spreadsheets is consistent with the manual approach used in Chapter 14.

LOGIC

Exhibit 14S.1 presents the structure of a straightforward product. Notice that two components of Z are required to produce one X. The lead times for X and Y are 1 week, and the lead time for component Z is 2 weeks.

The MRP spreadsheet shown in Exhibit 14S.2 utilizes the logic described in Chapter 14. The only difference between the logic of the time-phased record of X and the time-phased record of Y is the source of the gross requirements. The gross requirements of X come from the master production schedule of X. The gross requirements of Y come from the planned order releases of X. The differences between the time-phased records of Y and Z are the logic used to derive gross requirements, the planned releases, and the planned receipts. Gross requirements differ because 2 Zs are required per X. The planned order release and receipt logic differ slightly because of the difference in lead times. The lead time

---

EXHIBIT 14S.1   **Product Structure**

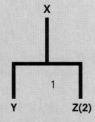

EXHIBIT 14S.2   **MRP Spreadsheet***

	A	B	C	D	E	F	G	H	I
1					MPS				
2		1	2	3	4	5	6	7	8
3	X	100	130	50	80	40	60	110	90
4									
5					MRP				
6	X	1	2	3	4	5	6	7	8
7	Gross Requirements	100	130	50	80	40	60	110	90
8	Beginning Inventory	200	100	0	0	0	0	0	0
9	Ending Inventory	100	0	0	0	0	0	0	0
10	Scheduled Receipts	0	0	0	0	0	0	0	0
11	Net Requirements	0	30	50	80	40	60	110	90
12	Planned Receipts	0	30	50	80	40	60	110	90
13	Planned Releases	30	50	80	40	60	110	90	0
Formulas for Row 7		+b3	+c3	+d3	+e3	+f3	+g3	+h3	+i3
Formulas for Row 8		200	+b9	+c9	+d9	+e9	+f9	+g9	+h9
Formulas for Row 9		b8+b12+ b10−b7	c8+c12+ c10−c7	d8+d12+ d10−d7	e8+e12+ e10−e7	f8+f12+ f10−f7	g8+g12+ g10−g7	h8+h12+ h10−h7	i8+i12+ i10−i7
Formulas for Row 10		0	0	0	0	0	0	0	0
Formulas for Row 11		@IF(+b7−b8< 0,0,b7−b8)	@IF(+c7−c8< 0,0,c7−c8)	@IF(+d7−d8< 0,0,d7−d8)	@IF(+e7−e8< 0,0,e7−e8)	@IF(+f7−f8< 0,0,f7−f8)	@IF(+g7−g8< 0,0,g7−g8)	@IF(+h7−h8< 0,0,h7−h8)	@IF(+i7−i8< 0,0,i7−i8)
Formulas for Row 12		0	+b13	+c13	+d13	+e13	+f13	+g13	+h13
Formulas for Row 13		+c11	+d11	+e11	+f11	+g11	+h11	+i11	0

*Calculated data are shaded in yellow, data entered manually are shaded in gray, and comments are shaded in brown.

for Z is 2 weeks, but the lead time for Y is 1 week. Zeroes have been entered for all scheduled receipts because no orders will be released in this example. The net requirements are computed using the function @IF(CONDITION,X,Y) to make sure that the value will not be negative. This function gives a value *X* if the condition is true and *Y* if the condition is false. The entry for cell B11 would be computed using the expression @IF(+b7 −b8<0,0,b7−b8). Because the condition b7 − b8 < 0 is true, the value for this cell is 0.

	A	B	C	D	E	F	G	H	I
14	Y	1	2	3	4	5	6	7	8
15	Gross Requirements	30	50	80	40	60	110	90	0
16	Beginning Inventory	200	170	120	40	0	0	0	0
17	Ending Inventory	170	120	40	0	0	0	0	0
18	Scheduled Receipts	0	0	0	0	0	0	0	0
19	Net Requirements	0	0	0	0	60	110	90	0
20	Planned Receipts	0	0	0	0	60	110	90	0
21	Planned Releases	0	0	0	60	110	90	0	0
	Formulas for Row 15	+b13	+c13	+d13	+e13	+f13	+g13	+h13	+i13
22	Z	1	2	3	4	5	6	7	8
23	Gross Requirements	60	100	160	80	120	220	180	0
24	Beginning Inventory	200	140	40	0	0	0	0	0
25	Ending Inventory	140	40	0	0	0	0	0	0
26	Scheduled Receipts	0	0	0	0	0	0	0	0
27	Net Requirements	0	0	120	80	120	220	180	0
28	Planned Receipts	0	0	120	80	120	220	180	0
29	Planned Releases	120	80	120	220	180	0	0	0
Formulas for Row 23		b13*2	c13*2	d13*2	e13*2	f13*2	g13*2	h13*2	i13*2
Formulas for Row 28		0	0	+b29	+c29	+d29	+e29	+f29	+g29
Formulas for Row 29		+d27	+e27	+f27	+g27	+h27	+i27	0	0

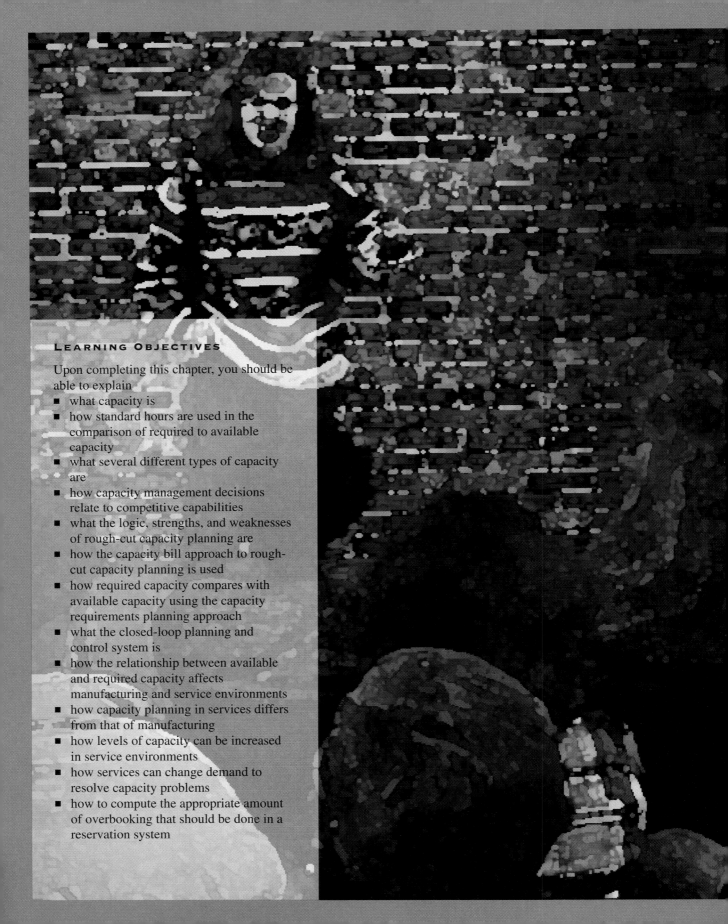

CHAPTER **15**

MANAGING CAPACITY

CROSS-LINKS **Ski for Free at Eagle Mountain**

Eagle Mountain is a medium-sized ski resort in northwestern Wyoming. The Eagle Point community consists of the ski resort itself, a small group of condominiums, a number of villas, eight restaurants, and a small pedestrian mall with shops. The resort has its own pro shop, but there are three independent ski shops as well. Eagle Mountain has ski lift capacity to handle 5,000 skiers, but it restricts ticket sales to 3,500 skiers. Lift lines for 3,500 skiers average 12 minutes. Eagle Mountain management prides itself on being the only ski resort willing to restrict sales of lift tickets to this degree, thereby ensuring that its patrons get in a good day of skiing rather than a day of waiting in line. ■ Pam and Ron Lightfoot bought Eagle Mountain 4 years ago. The resort was barely surviving, serving a local population but almost no out-of-town skiers. Although the Lightfoots knew they could never compete with the large resorts, they were determined to turn the resort into a place that attracted out-of-town and out-of-state skiers as well as people from a nearby large resort for a day of skiing in a different setting. The first 3 years had been tough, but creative marketing efforts had paid off. Close contact with a travel agency chain led to an increase in out-of-state skiers. ■ The resort advertised a discount program for first-timer skiers, which attracted a number of people from other nearby resorts. Pam and Ron also offered free lift tickets to groups of these skiers who were willing to take part in a focus group aimed at generating ideas for improvements. The biggest problem the Lightfoots faced now was cash flow. The resort was solidly in the black from the second week of December through the end of February. However,

the two weeks following Thanksgiving were dismal. ■ Not only was this period rough for Pam and Ron, but it was also bleak for the restaurant and hospitality industry that depended on the resort's ability to attract skiers. Pam and Ron were receiving massive amounts of unsolicited advice from owners of many local businesses. All of it was well-intentioned, but none of it seemed to offer likely solutions to the problem. Finally, it occurred to Pam that maybe they shouldn't be dealing with this by themselves, maybe they should look at the system as a whole. ■ At the next Eagle Mountain Business Owners meeting, Pam presented a plan that she thought would work. She said, "As I see it, all of you depend on our ability to attract skiers. If we can't get skiers to the resort, you don't sell rooms or meals. If your businesses die, even excellent skiing conditions will not bring skiers here. After all, they ski for only about 10 hours per day. The rest of the time they're in your businesses. We would be willing to provide free skiing to out-of-town and out-of-state skiers to get them here in the slow period after Thanksgiving, if we could work out an agreement that would give us a percentage of your revenues." After she spoke, there was silence and then a low level murmer in the crowd. ■ Kelly Hendricks, owner of one of the most successful businesses, was the first to speak. "Why should we pay you out of our revenues? We can't pay our November bills as it is!" ■ Pam responded with a question: "Are your revenues covering your fixed costs right now, Kelly?" ■ "Of course not." Kelly replied. ■ "Well, if our willingness to let skiers in free results in an increase in your revenues, even if you have to give us a share, wouldn't you be better off?" ■

CAPACITY
The capability of a system to perform its expected function and the capability of a worker, machine, work center, plant, or organization to produce output per time period.

In manufacturing systems, **capacity** is often defined as the output per unit time. Services, however, may define capacity differently. A warehousing business, for example, may define capacity in terms of available square feet of warehouse space. A grocery store may define capacity as inches of shelf space. A theater or airline may define it as seats. The term *capacity* may have different meanings for different types of businesses. In service environments like hospitals or restaurants, capacity is measured by the capability to take on a specified number of inputs (patients and customers) rather than the capability to produce outputs, as is often the case in manufacturing. Capacity is more easily understood when it is explained using a word that is similar—*capability.* The *APICS Dictionary* defines capacity as follows:

1. The capability of a system to perform its expected function
2. The capability of a worker, machine, work center, plant, or organization to produce output per time period[1]

COMPETITIVE IMPORTANCE OF EFFECTIVE CAPACITY MANAGEMENT

For the effective organization, planning and control of capacity is a critical management function. Many capacity decisions, like layout and facility location, tend to be long term and are not easily changed. Capacity planning is crucial because it ensures that the business can meet customer demand.

There are countless examples of businesses that under- or overestimate capacity needs. Toyota Motor Corporation's completion of a $1.4 billion dollar plant in Kyushu, for instance, coincided with a slump in demand for economy cars. As a result, the company had total excess capacity of 1 million units. And Toyota is not alone. Analysts estimate that in 1994 Japanese automakers had the capacity to produce about 4 million cars per year above market demand. In contrast, Motorola had to struggle to keep up with demand for its microcontrollers after experiencing a marked increase in orders in late 1992. It opted to boost capacity by spending $115 million for another production facility.

The effects of underestimating capacity needs are that orders must be turned away and revenues are lost. Customers may defect to a more reliable competitor. The effect of overestimating capacity needs can be equally devastating. Early decisions related to facility layout may commit the firm to a product-oriented focus, but high volumes of standardized products may not materialize. Low volumes and high levels of customization may better fit the market. In that case, a process-oriented focus is needed to satisfy this demand effectively. Investments in capacity to meet a demand that never materializes can tie up such a large amount of capital that the firm is drained of its ability to develop and promote new products, keep up with technological developments, and devote the necessary dollars to training and educating its work force.

Capacity decisions also affect other resources. For example, because capacity is used to create inventory, its availability has implications for inventory-related management tasks such as the choice of an inventory control system and the use of safety stocks. The influence that capacity decisions have on processes, work force, and facilities and equipment are direct because elements of these three resource groups are frequently combined to yield capacity.

---

[1] J. F. Cox, J. H. Blackstone, and M. S. Spencer, eds., *APICS Dictionary* 7th ed. (Falls Church, Va.: American Production and Inventory Control Society, 1992), 7.

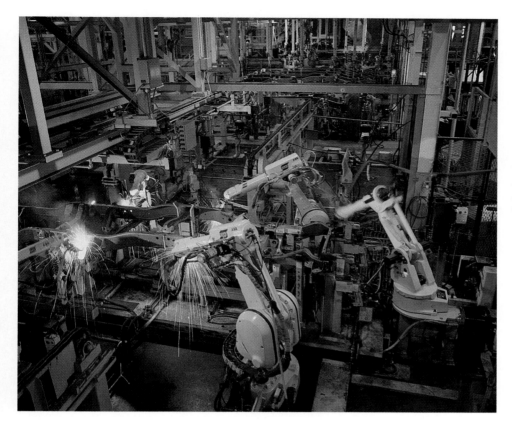

Capacity decisions affect equipment resources. In order to add this new production line to manufacture full frame assemblies for the Dodge Ram pick-up, A.O. Smith's Automotive Products Company was required to make investments in automation and robotics equipment.

Source   Courtesy of A.O. Smith Corporation.

Capacity decisions have many far-reaching effects on a firm's competitive capabilities. Product or service cost is significantly influenced by capacity decisions. Product or process layout decisions, for example, are usually made with the expectation of a certain volume of demand and are based on the objective of reducing production costs per unit produced. Companies often strive to produce at their optimal capacity, or best operating level. Economies of scale are present with all types of capacity decisions, but "more" doesn't necessarily mean "better," so businesses use the term *optimal level of production.* Businesses aim to design their service or manufacturing facilities in such a way that each one closely matches capacity with demand. Excess capacity, however, beyond that needed for protection, can result in substantially higher costs that must either be passed on to the customer (inhibiting the competitive position of the firm) or be absorbed, reducing profit margins. Being forced to run the business at a level above its optimal capacity also has other negative effects. Additional stress on the physical systems results in more frequent breakdowns, work force dissatisfaction, quality defects, and all of the financial costs associated with these undesirable conditions. These costs, too, must be passed on to the customer or absorbed. In some cases, the costs associated with overcapacity can be so high that they lead to serious financial problems. Prestolite Electric Inc., a manufacturer of electrical products, filed for Chapter 11 bankruptcy in 1991 largely because of the inefficiencies that resulted from having some plants that were duplicating the work of other factories.

For manufacturers and services, quality also is greatly influenced by capacity decisions. Because of the long-term nature of these decisions, capacity investments are often a commitment to specific types of processes. Equipment purchased to fulfill a capacity need has certain processing capabilities that are not easily changed. These capabilities frequently define what the business can and can't do for the customer. The firm may attempt to stretch the capabilities of equipment to win an order or persuade a customer, but these attempts frequently result in less-than-satisfactory quality. For example, Ace Clearwater Enterprises ran into problems after winning a series of long-term contracts from Boeing Co. Within about eight months, the small, family-owned business was 71 percent past due with its Boeing orders and had a reject rate of 10 percent on Boeing parts. Ace Management restructured the company and launched a total quality management program in order to avoid losing the lucrative contracts. But being able to meet customer specifications is not just a matter of quality management techniques. It also requires that the equipment have the necessary capabilities. For services, capacity decisions have a more critical impact on quality because capacity shortages, even if only temporary, result in reduced levels of customer contact and poor service quality.

Dependability of delivery is another competitive capability that is directly linked to capacity. A small amount of excess capacity, called **protective capacity,** or safety capacity, provides a function similar to that of safety stock held in inventory. Protective capacity allows manufacturers and services to absorb fluctuations in demand or output to maintain delivery performance. The theory of constraints says protective capacity is crucial and maintains that the balanced plant, a plant in which capacity is balanced with demand, cannot survive because of statistical fluctuations. JIT systems also rely on significant amounts of protective capacity, rather than excess inventory, to cope with unexpected events. U.S. businesses have traditionally strived to trim excess capacity in order to minimize cost per unit. Businesses often go through cycles in which they identify departments or work centers that have low utilizations, an indication of excess capacity, and they reduce capacity at those points, typically through layoffs. Unfortunately, as available capacity comes close to required capacity, the fabled Murphy steps in and any breakdowns, late material deliveries, and quality or other problems become very difficult to absorb. Due date performance is threatened. Management often reacts by bringing capacity back on line in order to meet due date obligations and stabilize cash flows. This change is acceptable for a while because due date performance is usually more important than equipment utilization rates. However, as soon as someone needs a place to cut costs, utilization rates are again examined and capacity is trimmed. This cycle repeats itself in many companies that refuse to acknowledge the importance of protective capacity.

Capacity management has three implications for flexibility. First, the type of equipment chosen to fulfill capacity needs sets limits on the level of flexibility. For example, dedicated special-purpose equipment might be purchased for the manufacturer of a high-volume product that is produced-to-stock in a product-oriented layout. This selection of equipment and layout, however, leaves little room for flexibility. The business would have a difficult time responding to a customer order that required that the product undergo a lot of modification. On the other hand, some companies like Kawasaki Heany Industries make flexibility a priority in capacity planning. Kawasaki ensured it could produce a broad range of motorcycles by trading dedicated production lines for those flexible enough to make various models in small quantities. Process selection and design also contribute significantly to flexibility. The differences between the physical system and layout decisions result in varying degrees of flexibility in the service sector as well. As an experiment, order a Big Mac with ketchup and mustard. McDonald's system cannot accommodate nearly as much demand if it must provide this type of customization with every order. The amount of capacity also influences flexibility. Protective capacity translates into flexibility. The more capacity that there is, the more capable the firm is of adapting to last-minute orders or order changes without seriously affecting the completion date of other orders. A third implication

PROTECTIVE CAPACITY
Capacity above what is required to allow for the operation to cope with disruptions.

surfaces when management compares the advantages and disadvantages of a few large-scale pieces of equipment to a larger number of smaller-scale pieces of equipment. JIT-oriented companies prefer smaller scale equipment because of the added flexibility.

For manufacturers and services, capacity decisions have the potential to influence response time. Manufacturers can handle large orders in short time periods only if they have sufficient capacity. Additional capacity gives manufacturers the luxury of producing smaller batches of products with more frequent setups, thereby reducing inventory levels and lead times. In job shop environments, higher levels of capacity reduce queue lengths, thereby reducing the amount of time that orders spend waiting in line. This capacity reduces the total lead time and results in quicker response to the customer. For services, particularly those with high levels of customer contact, queues are also a serious concern. Long lines may result in *balking*—the tendency for customers not to join a line if it is too long. In the short term, balking results in lost business. It also gives potential customers a reason for trying out the competition, which is a threat to long-term market share.

For services and manufacturers, the ability to manage capacity effectively has short-, medium-, and long-term implications for all competitive priorities across a wide range of resources. Figure 15.1 illustrates the broad scope of implications for capacity management.

| FIGURE 15.1 | **Task/Resource Model of Capacity Management** |

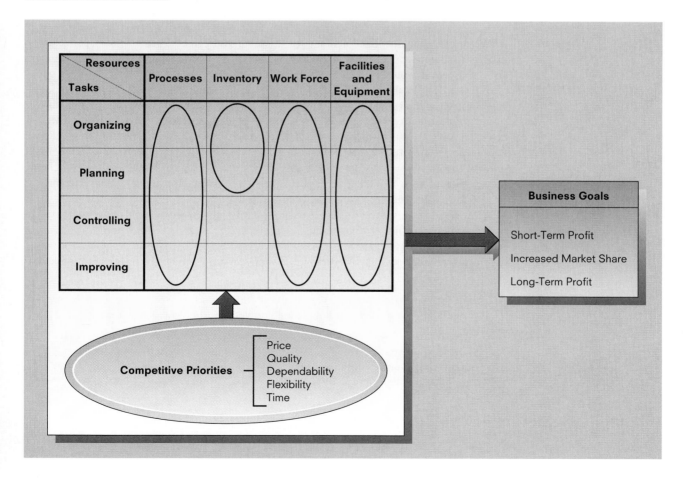

MEASURING CAPACITY

One of the most important aspects of capacity management is that of capacity planning. Capacity planning is the comparison of required capacity with available capacity in order to predict shortages. To be useful, any comparison must be done with like units. Useful information cannot be gained from comparing units per hour to cases per shift, for example, but cases per shift could be converted to units per hour to facilitate a useful comparison. Many capacity requirements come directly from projections of product or service demand, which is in the form of units or customers. But capacity availability is frequently expressed in the form of hours of equipment or worker time, particularly for manufacturers. The number of products required cannot be directly compared with hours of capacity available without a common unit. Product and service demand and equipment and worker time must be translated into a common unit of capacity in order to make a useful comparison. The unit used is standard time.

STANDARD TIME
The length of time that should be required to run one unit through an operation.

The **standard time** is the length of time that should be required to run one product, such as a part, assembly, batch, or end product, through an operation.[2] For example, suppose the standard time for assembling a particular item is 2.5 minutes. If a customer order for 192 units arrived, it could be readily translated into requirements for the assembly department. At 2.5 minutes per unit, 24 units could be completed in a standard hour. Eight standard hours would be required to complete the 192-unit order.

Not only must requirements be converted to standard time, but available capacity must also be converted into the same units. The fact that a department is available for use 8 hours per day does not necessarily mean that one can expect 8 standard hours of output from it. If the department is utilized at a rate of less than 100 percent, because of necessary preventive maintenance, frequent breakdowns, worker rest periods, and the like, the standard hours of output would be reduced to fewer than 8. Furthermore, if the work center or department does not always produce 24 units of the end product per hour of operation, its **efficiency,** or actual output divided by standard output, would be less than 100 percent. To compare the requirements to a realistic expectation of available capacity, utilization and efficiency must be taken into account. Available capacity, stated in terms of standard time available, is often referred to as rated capacity. **Rated capacity** is defined as the demonstrated capability of a system. Rated capacity is equal to hours available times efficiency times utilization. Rated capacity is also known as nominal capacity, calculated capacity, standing capacity, or effective capacity.

EFFICIENCY
Actual output divided by standard output.

RATED CAPACITY
The demonstrated capacity of a system. Also known as nominal capacity.

Most businesses have the ability to temporarily increase their rated capacity above the normal level in response to increases in demand or uneven demand patterns. Because organizations can adjust capacity levels, there are a number of specific types of capacity in addition to those discussed above. The *APICS Dictionary* defines the following types of capacity:

Theoretical capacity: The maximum output capability, allowing no adjustments for preventive maintenance, unplanned downtime, shutdown, and the like.[3]

Demonstrated capacity: Proven capacity calculated from actual output performance data, usually expressed as the average number of items produced multiplied by the standard hours per item.[4]

---

[2]Cox, Blackstone, and Spencer, 48.
[3]Cox, Blackstone, and Spencer, 50.
[4]Cox, Blackstone, and Spencer, 13.

Protective capacity: A given amount of extra capacity at nonconstraints used to protect against breakdowns, late receipts of materials, quality problems, and the like. It provides nonconstraints with the ability to recover from disruptions in order to maintain due date performance.[5]

Productive capacity: The additional output capabilities of a resource when operated at 100 percent utilization.[6]

Budgeted capacity: The volume and mix of throughput upon which financial budgets were set and overhead absorption rates established.[7]

Other types of capacity include:

Design capacity: The normal output that the firm would like to maintain and for which the facilities and equipment were designed.

Maximum capacity: The maximum output possible under the best possible circumstances and maximum use of resources. Maximum capacity is not typically possible for long-term use.

Optimal capacity: The operating level at which the average cost per unit is at its lowest. Management hopes that optimal capacity is equivalent to the design capacity, but this is not necessarily the case. It is sometimes referred to as the best operating level.

The effective management of capacity, that is, organizing, planning, controlling, and improving the use of capacity, is a prerequisite to business success because a firm's capacity is the means by which its product or service is created. A firm's ability to group resources to form capabilities results in competitive advantage. Capacity, the capability to perform the expected function, also results from the grouping of resources. The primary resources pulled together to provide capacity are the facilities, equipment, processes, and work force. These resources make up what is often referred to as the **physical system** for services and manufacturers.

When capacity management is examined from the perspective of the management functions (organizing, planning, controlling, and improving), the physical systems that are in place for producing the goods or services that are sold provide the structure and organization of capacity. The general layout choices of product-oriented, process-oriented, and cellular provide options with which managers organize capacity-related resources.

PHYSICAL SYSTEM
A system composed of the equipment, facilities, inventory, and work force used to produce a product or service.

PLANNING FOR CAPACITY NEEDS

Capacity requirements not only depend on the amount of demand expected but also on the type and timing of that demand. Manufacturers have the advantage of being able to accommodate irregular demands through a combination of capacity and inventory adjustments. Services, on the other hand, are dependent on capacity to meet immediate demand.

The importance and frequency of capacity planning vary depending on the company's characteristics. Companies with excess capacity will not devote as much effort to short-term capacity planning. However, the same company may not have the flexibility to increase capacity easily and may need to devote significant effort and attention to long-term

---

[5]Cox, Blackstone, and Spencer, 40.
[6]Cox, Blackstone, and Spencer, 39.
[7]Cox, Blackstone, and Spencer, 6.

capacity planning. Short-, medium-, and long-term capacity planning is typically done periodically. Its frequency depends on the stability of capacity requirements. For example, if demand for products varies from week to week, capacity planning will need to be done at least weekly. If, on the other hand, production schedules are locked in for a 60-day period, short-term capacity planning within the 60-day period will not be as necessary. Because capacity planning involves a comparison of required to available capacity, there is no need to repeat the comparison unless there is a change.

The following sections provide detailed explanations of the capacity planning processes for manufacturing and services.

CAPACITY PLANNING FOR MANUFACTURING

Managers must use demand forecasts as a primary source of information for capacity planning. Unfortunately, for some types of capacity increases (building a new plant, for example) the necessary lead time may require forecasts so far into the future that accuracy is low. Nevertheless, long-term forecasts must be used for some types of capacity planning. For example, Texas Instruments decided to build a new semiconductor production facility at a cost of more than $750 million based on its long-term forecasts of worldwide demand for semiconductors. For other types of capacity decisions, such as determining work force requirements, the planning horizon is in the medium term because the lead time is not as great. Florida Power and Light, for instance, cut 1,700 jobs from its payroll as part of its 1994 budget planning based on a one-year projection of capacity requirements. Still other capacity decisions, like whether or not an overtime shift is needed, are short term in nature.

Long-Term Capacity Planning   Sources of information for projecting long-term demand for products can include an analysis of product life cycles, a prediction of technological changes expected in the marketplace, and other long-term, often qualitative, forecasts. In order to increase the accuracy of these forecasts, aggregate forecasts are used. The forecast of aggregate demand, in the form of a pseudo-, or all-encompassing product, results in a higher level of accuracy. Manufacturers' objectives are to select generic units that can represent all products. Examples of pseudo-products are generic automobiles for automobile manufacturers or a ton of steel for a steel producer. Some firms use dollars of sales as an aggregate unit of demand, but dollars of sales is often difficult to disaggregate into its end products because changes in prices cause the relationship to change.

The forecast of the aggregate demand for products, combined with strategic directives, industry trends, growth expectations, and limitations of the firm, is frequently called a **production plan.** Manufacturers develop production plans for several years into the future and update them periodically.

For most companies, the primary purpose of the production plan is to provide information for developing a long-term capacity plan that is known as a **resource requirements plan.** Resource requirements planning is the comparison of aggregate capacity requirements (based on the production plan) to projections of available capacity. As mentioned previously, requirements and availability must be expressed in like units. In the case of resource requirements planning, the unit of comparison is the aggregate unit or pseudo-product. One outcome of the resource requirements plan could be that a major increase in capacity would be needed several years in the future. This may lead to a facility location decision-making process, major equipment purchases, an increase in the number of shifts, or inventory buildup in advance.

PRODUCTION PLAN
The aggregate demand forecast, combined with strategic directions, industry trends, growth expectations, and limitations of the firm.

RESOURCE REQUIREMENTS PLAN
The comparison of aggregate capacity requirements, as dictated by the production plan, with available resources.

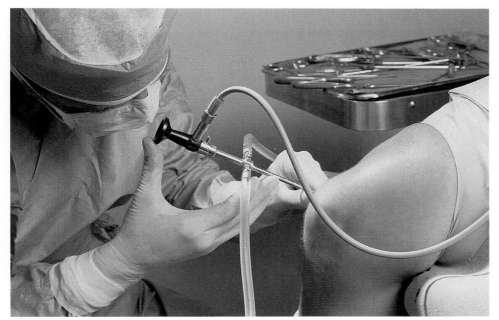

Industry trends help project long-term demand. Relatively inexpensive and convenient outpatient procedures, such as arthroscopy shown here, account for more than half of surgeries currently performed in the United States. Universal Health Services plans to increase its capacity to offer outpatient procedures by expanding the number of its free-standing ambulatory surgery centers. Free-standing ambulatory surgery centers account for 25 percent of outpatient surgeries, and surgery at these centers has been growing 11 percent a year.

Medium-Term Capacity Planning　　Medium-term capacity issues, such as the capacity requirements from one month to the next and the demand on particular departments and work centers, are dependent on the end product mix, which is not available from aggregate demand forecasts. Different end products result in different proportions of demand on the various departments and work centers. For medium-term capacity planning, the demand for particular end products must be translated into standard hours in specific departments and work centers and then compared to capacity available on the same departments and work centers. Although there are a number of ways to translate end product demand into standard hours required on a work center, the most common approach is through the use of a bill of capacity or capacity bill. A **capacity bill** is a description of the capacity required, by any affected work center or department, to produce a unit of a particular end product.

　　The master production schedule (MPS) provides the gross requirements of end products to material requirements planning (MRP). Before the validity of the MPS is accepted, its feasibility should be checked. The capacity required of key work centers to complete the MPS is compared to the capacity available, week by week, for the planning horizon. If the required capacity is less than or equal to the available capacity, the MPS is considered valid and is then used as an input to MRP. If the required capacity is greater than the available capacity, the MPS must be rebuilt until it is valid. The process of validating the MPS through capacity planning is known as **rough-cut capacity planning.** The most commonly used approach to rough-cut capacity planning is the capacity bill approach.

　　When the capacity bill approach is used, the production quantity for each end product, taken from the MPS, is multiplied by the time it takes to produce each end product on each work center. This total provides a rough estimate of the capacity required on each work center. In Example 15.1 we see a demonstration of the capacity bill approach to rough-cut capacity planning.

CAPACITY BILL
A description of capacity required, by any affected work center, to produce a unit of end product.

ROUGH-CUT CAPACITY PLANNING
The process of validating the master production schedule by comparing the available capacity with the capacity needed to fulfill the requirements of the master production schedule.

EXAMPLE 15.1

Rough-Cut Capacity Planning Using the Capacity Bill Approach

Logicworks is a small manufacturer of molded computer accessories that are sold to several large computer retail firms. It produces monitor and printer stands, disk boxes, mouse holsters, and its most successful and complex product, a standard personal computer mouse, the Model 421. The current master production schedule (MPS) for the Model 421 is shown in Table 15.1.

Logicworks' production operation consists of 4 departments. The molding department has 2 injection molding units for plastic components. The cleaning department has 2 cleaning stations, where marks and excess plastic are removed from molded parts. The assembly department has 3 assembly stations used for assembling components and end products. Packaging consists of 3 boxing stations and a shrink-wrap unit.

Figure 15.2 shows the product structure for the Model 421 mouse. Part numbers beginning with M are manufactured in-house, and part numbers beginning with P are purchased from outside vendors.

TABLE 15.1 **MPS for Model 421 Mouse**

Week	1	2	3	4	5	6	7	8
Quantity	4,200	4,800	5,850	5,400	5,900	5,450	4,900	6,000

FIGURE 15.2 **Product Structure for Model 421 Mouse**

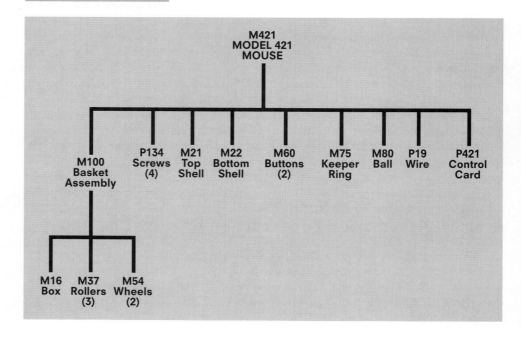

Prior to using MRP to determine planned order release timing and quantities for components, Logicworks validates its MPS with a rough-cut capacity plan using the capacity bill approach, in which required capacity is compared to available capacity. Required capacity is calculated from the MPS and capacity bill data, while the available capacity is determined from **work center masters,** which contain data that describe each work center. The work center master data for each work center are shown in Table 15.2, where the rated capacities, or the standard hours available per week, are calculated by multiplying the number of work centers (a) by the number of hours per day (b) by days per week (c) by utilization % (d) by efficiency % (e). The percentage of utilization is obtained from the historical records of each department, and the percentage of efficiency is calculated by dividing actual input by standard input. Standard input is obtained from the routing, or processing steps, of each manufactured component. Routings are presented in Table 15.3 (page 462).

By extracting information from the product structure and product routings, a capacity bill can be created for the M421. (Recall that a capacity bill is a description of the capacity required by any affected work center or department to produce a unit of a particular end product.) A matrix is used to assist in summing the length of time required in each department for each component. If more than one of a component is required, as is the case with components M60, M37, and M54, this must be taken into account. Table 15.4 (page 463) shows the matrix used to create the capacity bill, and the completed capacity bill is presented in Table 15.5 (page 463).

Required capacity, in standard hours, for each department, for each week, is calculated by multiplying the quantity to be produced that week by the standard hours per unit, for each work center. For example, the capacity required on the molding department for week 1 would be 0.0072833 × 4,200, or 30.6 standard hours, because it takes 0.0072833 standard hours per unit and 4,200 units are to be produced during that week.

The rough-cut capacity plan, for each of the four departments, is presented on page 464 in Table 15.6, which also presents a calculation of the required utilization of each department based on rated capacity. This calculation makes it easy to spot capacity shortages. Any department requiring greater than 100 percent utilization has a capacity shortage. There is a capacity shortage during week 8 in the assembly department. This capacity shortage would need to be resolved before the MPS could be considered feasible. In this situation, a small amount of work could be done the week before to off load the assembly department during week 8. Keep in mind that the rough-cut capacity plan presented here is

WORK CENTER MASTER
A detailed description of a work center, including such information as rated capacity, hours of operation, and historical utilization and efficiency.

TABLE 15.2	**Work Center Masters for Logicworks**

Department	Number of Work Centers a	Hours per Day b	Days per Week c	Utilization % d	Efficiency % e	Rated Capacity per Week $abcde$
Molding	2	8	5	94	95	71.44
Cleaning	2	8	5	91	97	70.62
Assembly	3	8	5	95	93	106.06
Packaging	1	8	5	96	94	36.10

TABLE 15.3	Routings for M421 Components		

Part Number	Description	Department Required	Time per Unit
M421	Completed mouse	Assembly	0.420 minutes
		Packaging	0.200 minutes
M21	Top shell	Molding	0.033 minutes
		Cleaning	0.070 minutes
M22	Bottom shell	Molding	0.033 minutes
		Cleaning	0.050 minutes
M60(2)	Button	Molding	0.025 minutes
		Cleaning	0.010 minutes
M75	Keeper ring	Molding	0.025 minutes
		Cleaning	0.010 minutes
M80	Ball	Molding	0.036 minutes
		Cleaning	0.070 minutes
M100	Basket assembly	Assembly	0.650 minutes
M16	Box	Molding	0.060 minutes
		Cleaning	0.040 minutes
M37(3)	Roller	Molding	0.040 minutes
		Cleaning	0.030 minutes
M54(2)	Wheel	Molding	0.040 minutes
		Cleaning	0.030 minutes

based only on the M421 mouse. If other products were being manufactured using the same equipment, their capacity requirements would have to be included in the calculations of total requirements.

The capacity plan used to validate the MPS is called "rough-cut" because it does not provide a high degree of accuracy. The technique has two major shortcomings that result in inaccuracies. First, because MRP has not been completed prior to the rough-cut capacity plan, on-hand inventory quantities are not considered in the calculation of required capacity. As has been mentioned previously, inventory is equivalent to stored capacity. On-hand inventory reduces the capacity required to complete an order that uses that component. In the calculations made in Table 15.6, any inventory of manufactured components currently

TABLE 15.4   **Matrix for Constructing Capacity Bill of the M421 Mouse (Example 15.1)**

Part Number	Quantity Required	Time in Each Department (minutes)			
		Molding	Cleaning	Assembly	Packaging
M421	1	0	0	0.42	0.2
M21	1	0.033	0.07	0	0
M22	1	0.033	0.05	0	0
M60	2	0.05	0.02	0	0
M75	1	0.025	0.01	0	0
M80	1	0.036	0.07	0	0
M100	1	0	0	0.65	0
M16	1	0.06	0.04	0	0
M37	3	0.12	0.09	0	0
M54	2	0.08	0.06	0	0
Totals		0.437	0.41	1.07	0.2

TABLE 15.5   **Capacity Bill for M421 Mouse (Example 15.1)**

Work Center	Time Required (minutes) a	Time Required (standard hours) $a/60$
Molding	0.437	0.0072833
Cleaning	0.410	0.0068333
Assembly	1.070	0.0178333
Packaging	0.200	0.0033333

on hand would have reduced the capacity required of the departments that helped produce those components. Because it ignores on-hand inventory quantities, rough-cut capacity planning sometimes overestimates total capacity required for the time horizon.

Rough-cut capacity planning is also inaccurate from the standpoint of the timing of capacity requirements. Inherent in the process used to calculate capacity requirements, that of

TABLE 15.6	Rough-Cut Capacity Plan (Example 15.1)

Week	1	2	3	4	5	6	7	8
Molding								
Required	30.6	35.0	42.6	39.3	43.0	39.7	35.7	43.7
Available	71.4	71.4	71.4	71.4	71.4	71.4	71.4	71.4
Required Utilization	42.9%	49.0%	59.7%	55.0%	60.2%	55.6%	50.0%	61.2%
Cleaning								
Required	28.7	32.8	40.0	36.9	40.3	37.2	33.5	41.0
Available	70.6	70.6	70.6	70.6	70.6	70.6	70.6	70.6
Required Utilization	40.6%	46.5%	56.7%	52.3%	57.1%	52.7%	47.5%	58.1%
Assembly								
Required	74.9	85.6	104.3	96.3	105.2	97.2	87.4	107.0
Available	106.0	106.0	106.0	106.0	106.0	106.0	106.0	106.0
Required Utilization	70.7%	80.8%	98.4%	90.8%	99.2%	91.7%	82.4%	100.9%
Packaging								
Required	14.0	16.0	19.5	18.0	19.7	18.2	16.3	20.0
Available	36.1	36.1	36.1	36.1	36.1	36.1	36.1	36.1
Required Utilization	38.8%	44.3%	54.0%	49.9%	54.6%	50.4%	45.2%	55.4%

multiplying the time per unit (from the capacity bill) by the quantity to be produced (from the MPS), is the assumption that all capacity requirements related to a particular MPS quantity will occur during the week the item will be completed. This is a faulty assumption. The backward scheduling process used by MRP demonstrates how lower level components can be required many weeks before the week in which the end product will be finished. The timing inaccuracies can have a variety of effects on the accuracy of rough-cut capacity planning. At times, it results in capacity requirements that are overestimated for one time period and underestimated for the other. The more irregular the demand for the end product, the more inaccurate the timing of the capacity requirements.

Despite the two deficiencies, the rough-cut capacity plan generally does a satisfactory job of validating the MPS. To include on-hand inventory and appropriate timing in the feasibility check of the MPS would require that the capacity plan not be done until after MRP.

It is often more important to have a quick check of the MPS, which can be redone several times if necessary, than it is to have precision. Most manufacturers construct a valid MPS in an iterative process and require a capacity check that can be done in less than an hour. MRP calculations often take 8 hours or more and would not allow for an iterative development of the MPS.

Capacity shortages identified by rough-cut capacity planning must be resolved before the MPS can be considered feasible. Discrepancies between required and available capacity are resolved by reducing capacity requirements or increasing available capacity. For a particular time period with a capacity shortage, requirements may be reduced in several ways. The MPS may be adjusted to move some production to earlier weeks if excess capacity is available. Available capacity may be increased by scheduling overtime or adding a shift to increase to maximum capacity. Subcontracting work outside the firm may also be considered. As a last resort, negotiations may take place with customers to reschedule the order. Under no circumstances should an unfeasible MPS be accepted, however.

Short-Term Capacity Planning　After the MPS has been validated by rough-cut capacity planning, MRP can be used to generate planned order releases for all purchased and manufactured components. MRP will provide more detailed information to complete the third and final capacity plan, known as capacity requirements planning. **Capacity requirements planning (CRP)** is a detailed comparison of required capacity with available capacity on labor and machine resources. The information inputs and results of capacity requirements planning differ significantly from those of rough-cut capacity planning, but the logic used to compute required capacity is somewhat similar.

Recall that MRP provides planned order releases for all manufactured and purchased components and raw materials. The order releases are scheduled to meet the needs established by the quantities and timing of the end products, as stated by the MPS. The process used to compute required capacity for each department or work center with capacity requirements planning is similar to the one used in rough-cut capacity planning. It is necessary to multiply the number of items to be manufactured by the time required to manufacture each one. Rather than use a capacity bill for each end product, however, CRP uses the routing times for each manufactured component. The planned order releases from MRP, rather than the MPS, provide the necessary information on quantities that will be produced. Because of the gross to net calculations of MRP, capacity requirements planning takes into account the effect that on-hand inventory has on capacity requirements. In addition, as will be evident in Example 15.2, capacity requirements planning also creates capacity requirements whose timing is much more accurate than it was in rough-cut capacity planning.

The detailed comparison of required to available capacity is crucial for effective scheduling of resources.

CAPACITY REQUIREMENTS PLANNING (CRP)
A detailed comparison of required capacity, based on the master production schedule, to the labor and machine capabilities of a production department.

EXAMPLE 15.2

After using MRP to determine planned order releases, Logicworks develops a detailed comparison of required and available capacity using CRP. Table 15.7 presents the current inventory levels for the finished products and components.

The lead time for all items is 1 week. Lot-for-lot ordering is the policy for all items. The MRP run for the items yielded the planned order releases presented in Table 15.8.

To compute required capacity for each department, CRP multiplies the quantity to be produced (from the planned order releases) by the time to produce the item (from the routing). For a specific department, total capacity required will be the sum of this product for

Capacity Requirements Planning at Logicworks

TABLE 15.7   Inventory Levels for Logicworks

Part Number	Quantity on Hand
M421	5,000
M100	6,430
P134	23,580
M21	4,150
M22	6,100
M60	8,430
M75	4,560
M80	4,110
P19	6,725
P421	4,100
M16	3,580
M37	12,590
M54	7,300

TABLE 15.8   Planned Order Releases for Logicworks MRP

Part Number	Planned Order Releases							
	1	2	3	4	5	6	7	8
M421	4,000	5,850	5,400	5,900	5,450	4,900	6,000	0
M100	3,420	5,400	5,900	5,450	4,900	6,000	0	0
P134	15,820	21,600	23,600	21,800	19,600	24,000	0	0
M21	5,700	5,400	5,900	5,450	4,900	6,000	0	0
M22	3,750	5,400	5,900	5,450	4,900	6,000	0	0
M60	11,270	10,800	11,800	10,900	9,800	12,000	0	0
M75	5,290	5,400	5,900	5,450	4,900	6,000	0	0
M80	5,740	5,400	5,900	5,450	4,900	6,000	0	0
P19	3,125	5,400	5,900	5,450	4,900	6,000	0	0
P421	5,750	5,400	5,900	5,450	4,900	6,000	0	0
M16	5,240	5,900	5,450	4,900	6,000	0	0	0
M37	13,870	17,700	16,350	14,700	18,000	0	0	0
M54	10,340	11,800	10,900	9,800	12,000	0	0	0

| TABLE 15.9 | | Planned Order Releases for M Items | | | | | | |

| Part Number | Planned Order Releases | | | | | | | |
	1	2	3	4	5	6	7	8
M421	4,000	5,850	5,400	5,900	5,450	4,900	6,000	0
M100	3,420	5,400	5,900	5,450	4,900	6,000	0	0
M21	5,700	5,400	5,900	5,450	4,900	6,000	0	0
M22	3,750	5,400	5,900	5,450	4,900	6,000	0	0
M60	11,270	10,800	11,800	10,900	9,800	12,000	0	0
M75	5,290	5,400	5,900	5,450	4,900	6,000	0	0
M80	5,740	5,400	5,900	5,450	4,900	6,000	0	0
M16	5,240	5,900	5,450	4,900	6,000	0	0	0
M37	13,870	17,700	16,350	14,700	18,000	0	0	0
M54	10,340	11,800	10,900	9,800	12,000	0	0	0

all parts that utilize that department. Because purchased items do not affect capacity requirements, only the M items are of interest to the CRP logic. The planned order releases for M items only are presented in Table 15.9.

Table 15.10 (page 468) presents, for convenience, the routing information first presented in Table 15.3. From Table 15.10 it is evident that eight components require both the molding and cleaning departments. Two components use the assembly department, and one uses the packaging department. The four departments, and the components that require time in each, are presented in Table 15.11 (page 469).

To compute the total capacity required for each week on the molding department, the quantity of M21 to be produced must be multiplied by the time per unit, the quantity of M22 to be produced must be multiplied by the time per unit, and so on, and the capacities required for each component being processed by the molding department must be summed for each week. This is accomplished in Table 15.12 (page 470) for week 1 on all four departments.

Because the MRP output specifies the precise order quantities, as dictated by net requirements and within the boundaries set by order policies, batch sizes, and therefore set-up requirements, are known. If set-up times exist for a department, they would be included in the calculation for required capacity. This would be accomplished by adding the set-up time to the capacity required for each batch of parts. However, in this example there are no set-up times. After capacity requirements are calculated, they are compared to capacity available. Available capacity is calculated just as it was for the rough-cut capacity planning step. Table 15.13 (page 471) presents the completed CRP for each department, for each week.

TABLE 15.10		Routings for M421 Components (Example 15.2)	
Part Number	**Description**	**Department Required**	**Time per Unit (minutes)**
M421	Completed mouse	Assembly	0.420
		Packaging	0.200
M21	Top shell	Molding	0.033
		Cleaning	0.070
M22	Bottom shell	Molding	0.033
		Cleaning	0.050
M60	Button	Molding	0.025
		Cleaning	0.010
M75	Keeper ring	Molding	0.025
		Cleaning	0.010
M80	Ball	Molding	0.036
		Cleaning	0.070
M100	Basket assembly	Assembly	0.650
M16	Box	Molding	0.060
		Cleaning	0.040
M37	Roller	Molding	0.040
		Cleaning	0.030
M54	Wheel	Molding	0.040
		Cleaning	0.030

Rough-Cut versus CRP: A Comparison   Like the rough-cut capacity plan presented earlier, CRP assumes that only the M421 mouse is being manufactured. If other products were being produced, they would also influence capacity requirements. Table 15.14 (page 472) shows the differences between the capacity requirements calculated in the rough-cut capacity plan and those calculated in the capacity requirements plan. The effects of MRP's time phasing of components' requirements, combined with the impact of inventory, result in substantial differences. Keep in mind, however, that aside from the effects of inventory, the timing differences influence requirements from week to week, but not the total requirements over the time horizon.

The comparison of required versus available capacity from CRP is an important component of the scheduling process, and its accuracy has a significant impact on the firm's ability to maintain the degree of flexibility needed to meet due dates and maintain low in-

TABLE 15.11	**Components Requiring Each Department at Logicworks (Example 15.2)**	

Department	Components	Time/Unit
Molding	M21	0.033
	M22	0.033
	M60	0.025
	M75	0.025
	M80	0.036
	M16	0.060
	M37	0.040
	M54	0.040
Cleaning	M21	0.070
	M22	0.050
	M60	0.010
	M75	0.010
	M80	0.070
	M16	0.040
	M37	0.030
	M54	0.030
Assembly	M421	0.420
	M100	0.650
Packaging	M421	0.200

ventory levels. Accurate data from CRP allow departmental management to get a detailed indication of potential capacity shortages. This information allows them to make arrangements for capacity adjustments. Such adjustments might include overtime, combining batches to reduce setups, preventive maintenance schedule changes, the use of temporary employees, or other short-term measures.

The use of temporary employees, through temporary agencies, has become increasingly popular as a means of increasing flexibility. Unfortunately, it can have negative effects as well. (See Box 15.1, page 473.)

Many manufacturers have integrated capacity, materials planning, and feedback from execution activities into systems known as closed-loop MRP systems. A generic example of such a system is shown in Figure 15.3 (page 474). Notice that there are three levels of material, or product, planning (production planning, master production scheduling, and material requirements planning) and three corresponding levels of capacity planning (resource requirements planning, rough-cut capacity planning, and capacity requirements planning).

Because capacity planning involves a comparison of required and available capacity, it is valuable to examine the implications of various relationships between capacity required and capacity available. Figure 15.4 (page 475) provides an example profile of required and available capacity.

TABLE 15.12			CRP for Week 1 at Logicworks (Example 15.2)

Component	Quantity	Time/Unit (minutes)	Total Time (minutes)
Molding			
M21	5,700	0.033	188.10
M22	3,750	0.033	123.75
M60	11,270	0.025	281.75
M75	5,290	0.025	132.25
M80	5,740	0.036	206.64
M16	5,240	0.060	314.40
M37	13,870	0.040	554.80
M54	10,340	0.040	413.60
		Total	2,215.29 (36.92 hours)
Cleaning			
M21	5,700	0.070	399.00
M22	3,750	0.050	187.50
M60	11,270	0.010	112.70
M75	5,290	0.010	52.90
M80	5,740	0.070	401.80
M16	5,240	0.040	209.60
M37	13,870	0.030	416.10
M54	10,340	0.030	310.20
		Total	2,089.80 (34.83 hours)
Assembly			
M421	4,000	0.420	1680.00
M100	3,420	0.650	2223.00
		Total	3903.00 (65.05 hours)
Packaging			
M421	4,000	0.200	800.00
		Total	800.00 (13.33 hours)

Notice the designated intervals in the figure. Interval A, for example, designates a period of time when capacity required is nearly optimal. This will result in production that probably has the lowest per unit cost. During interval B, demand increases up to the point of interval C, which is the maximum capacity. At the maximum level of capacity, overtime is probably being used, equipment is not likely to receive appropriate preventive maintenance, and per unit costs are high. If the time frame of Figure 15.4 were a day, meaning that interval C lasted only a couple of hours, this condition could be tolerated. If the time frame were such that interval C lasted a number of days, serious problems could arise. Interval E shows a period with low demand on capacity. Labor and machine resources are not stressed during this period. Slack periods like E present an opportunity to perform preventive maintenance and to increase inventory to cope with the high demand exhibited by interval G.

Capacity planning is useful not only for equipment use, but also for many other aspects of a manufacturing business. For example, the capacity of the customer service department is important to consider if customers are to be satisfied with their interactions

TABLE 15.13   **Completed CRP for Logicworks**

Week	1	2	3	4	5	6	7	8
Molding								
Required Hours	36.92	41.50	41.02	37.31	40.46	17.70	0.00	0.00
Available Hours	71.40	71.40	71.40	71.40	71.40	71.40	71.40	71.40
Required Utilization	51.71%	58.12%	57.45%	52.26%	56.66%	24.79%	0.00%	0.00%
Cleaning								
Required Hours	34.83	38.48	38.89	35.50	36.97	22.00	0.00	0.00
Available Hours	70.60	70.60	70.60	70.60	70.60	70.60	70.60	70.60
Required Utilization	49.33%	54.51%	55.09%	50.28%	52.36%	31.16%	0.00%	0.00%
Assembly								
Required Hours	65.05	99.45	101.72	100.34	91.23	99.30	42.00	0.00
Available Hours	106.00	106.00	106.00	106.00	106.00	106.00	106.00	106.00
Required Utilization	61.37%	93.82%	95.96%	94.66%	86.07%	93.68%	39.62%	0.00%
Packaging								
Required Hours	13.33	19.50	18.00	19.67	18.17	16.33	20.00	0.00
Available Hours	36.10	36.10	36.10	36.10	36.10	36.10	36.10	36.10
Required Utilization	36.93%	54.02%	49.86%	54.48%	50.32%	45.24%	55.40%	0.00%

TABLE 15.14		Comparison of Rough-Cut and Capacity Requirements Plans						
Week	1	2	3	4	5	6	7	8
Molding Required Hours								
CRP	36.92	41.50	41.02	37.31	40.46	17.70	0.00	0.00
Rough-Cut	30.6	35.0	42.6	39.3	43.0	39.7	35.7	43.7
Cleaning Required Hours								
CRP	34.83	38.48	38.89	35.50	36.97	22.00	0.00	0.00
Rough-Cut	28.7	32.8	40.0	36.9	40.3	37.2	33.5	41.0
Assembly Required Hours								
CRP	65.05	99.45	101.72	100.34	91.23	99.30	42.00	0.00
Rough-Cut	74.9	85.6	104.3	96.3	105.2	97.2	87.4	107.0
Packaging Required Hours								
CRP	13.33	19.50	18.00	19.67	18.17	16.33	20.00	0.00
Rough-Cut	14.0	16.0	19.5	18.0	19.7	18.2	16.3	20.0

with the company. The capacity of warehousing functions are also important. (See Box 15.2, page 475.)

CAPACITY PLANNING FOR SERVICES

Capacity's Influence on Business Success   As with manufacturing, capacity decisions in services are often long-term commitments that greatly affect what the business can do and how successful it will be. The decisions may be directly related to the goals of the business (short- and long-term profit and market share). The factors that determine capacity needs are related to the demand for the service and include such issues as the following:

Average demand

Amount of change of demand

Speed at which changes in demand take place

Predictability of changes in demand

Customer loyalty[8]

The average demand establishes a target for the optimum capacity, which the service hopes is the level of capacity it is designed to have. The amount of change of demand establishes the need for flexibility in personnel scheduling and the need for protective capacity to meet higher-than-usual demands. The speed at which demand changes, combined with the predictability of these changes, provides an indication of how much short-term flexibility in capacity is needed. The level of customer loyalty determines the likelihood of a capacity shortage resulting in a lost sale. The less loyalty there is, the more likely it is that there will be a defection.

In service environments, capacity requirements on some resources are the direct result of the market demand. Other resource capacity requirements, however, are dependent on the requirements for other capacities. For example, the required number of meals to be

---

[8]J. L. Heskett, W. E. Sasser, Jr., and C. W. L. Hart, *Service Breakthroughs* (New York: Free Press, 1990), 136.

OPERATIONS OUTLOOK

BOX 15.1

Temps: The Other Side of the Coin

Many workers are sitting at the same desk doing the same job they've done for years, but they're getting less pay and fewer or no benefits than they'd recently received. This change has occurred as businesses eliminate positions by transplanting workers to temporary employment agencies or by allowing these employees to continue only as independent contractors.

Employment of temporary help grew at a rate 10 times faster than over-all employment between 1982 and 1990. Temporary, contract, and part-time workers now make up about 25 percent of the work force. Employers have increased their hiring of these workers because they cost employers less in benefits and provide them with increased flexibility. Many critics of the excessive use of temps and contracted labor feel that other approaches such as job sharing, phased-in retirement, and retraining may cost more in the short term but would ultimately result in long-term benefits such as lower absentee rates, reduced turnover, better morale, and increased productivity levels. Stanley Nollen, a professor at Georgetown University agrees. In a study of the use of contingent workers at a Fortune 500 company, he found that output of these workers was 8 percent less but compensation was only 6 percent less.

Contract employees frequently end up in a kind of no-man's-land. For example, when employees of ARA Services Inc., a food-service contractor at the Citadel (a state-owned military school), voted to unionize, ARA refused to bargain because it maintained that wages were controlled by the Citadel, even though the Citadel was not the workers' employer. The National Labor Relations Board (NLRB) agreed. The ARA employees are neither government workers with benefits and regular wage increases, as are other employees at the Citadel, nor are they private-sector workers with the right to organize. Laws passed to protect employees from age and sex discrimination are protecting fewer workers, particularly independent contractors.

The use of temporaries is expanding into such positions as data processors, bank tellers, nurses, engineers, and assembly-line workers. Temporaries are not only being used by large firms to add flexibility without increasing the costs of hiring and firing, small firms are using them to grow without having to take on the added expense of staffing increases before they've reaped the benefits of growth.

Some workers, however, prefer temporary employment. It offers flexibility, and for those working for large temporary agencies, it offers a 1 in 3 chance of landing a permanent job. In addition, some temporary agencies offer training and benefits.

While contingent work forces offer advantages to employers, they can also bring problems. Information security has been a problem for some companies using temporary clerical workers. Quality also can be a concern. Beverly Garner started doing quality control work in 1991 as a temporary employee for Schmid Laboratories, a maker of condoms. She became frustrated when, after 10 months of making $3 per hour less than permanent workers, she had not landed a full-time slot. She was fired for coming to work late and calling in sick more than 3 days. She did not deny the tardiness or absenteeism and said that she got to the point that she hated the job because she wasn't being treated fairly. She also said that quality suffered because of the constant turnover of temporaries. In her job in quality control, she said every time a new group of people came to work, there would be more holes in condoms. The personnel manager for Schmid agrees that new workers go through a learning curve, but says quality-control measures prevent defective condoms from reaching the customers. Temporary workers, who make up 30 percent of Schmid's work force, allow the company to avoid large inventory buildups.

The quality problems resulting from the use of temporary workers can have devastating results, and attempts to avoid liabilities can result in lawsuits against both the supplier and user of the temporaries. Du Pont Co.'s Consolidated Coal unit (Consol) told its employees in an internal memo not to interfere if they saw a contract employee doing something dangerous or illegal, unless property or employees were endangered. The memo doesn't encourage employees to look the other way, but reinforces that the contractor is obligated to ensure the safety of its employees. That, however, is not always the case. In the spring of 1992, three contractors and a Consol employee were killed in a coal mine explosion that resulted from contractors welding in an area known to be heavily exposed to methane gas. Consol was cited by federal and state authorities for failing to ventilate and examine for methane. Consol plans to appeal.

The average work week for a temp is 22 hours, but for the 12 months ending November 1993, temporary jobs accounted for a full 15 percent of new jobs. By early 1994, the use of temps had fallen off slightly to 9.6 percent of total employment growth. One reason has been that unions are forcing employers to set limits on the use of temps.

Sources "Hired Out: Workers Are Forced to Take More Jobs with Few Benefits," *The Wall Street Journal*, March 11, 1993, sec. A, 1, 4. "Firms Find Ways to Grow without Expanding Staffs," *The Wall Street Journal*, March 18, 1993, sec. B, 1, 2. "Labor Letter," *The Wall Street Journal*, January 25, 1994, sec. A, 1. "Labor Letter," *Wall Street Journal*, February 22, 1994, sec. A, 1.

FIGURE 15.3	**Closed-Loop MRP System**

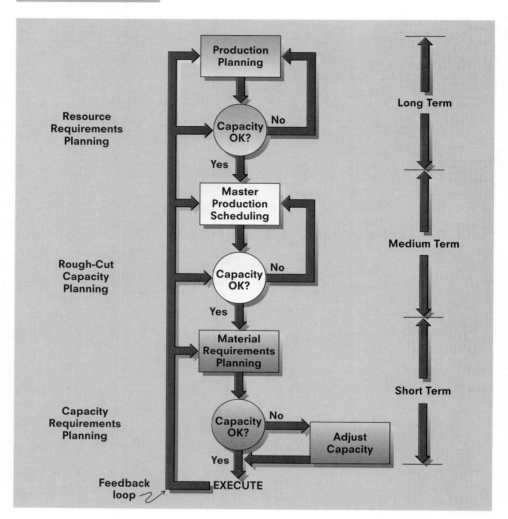

served in a restaurant can be determined directly from demand forecasts. The number of seats needed, however, can be derived from the total number of meals forecast for a given period of time, divided by the number of times the tables will turn over during that period. The number of servers required depends on the number of parties, or tables to be served. The capacity of the kitchen, in terms of meals per hour, depends not just on the number of meals served but also on how quickly the meals should be served (that is, how long customers should wait for a meal). The amount of time customers should wait for a meal is somewhat related to the turnover rate required to be able to satisfy the total demand, but it is also a function of the type of atmosphere desired. Because some resource capacity requirements are directly dependent on the market demand and others can be calculated from those data, capacity requirements in the service sector can be viewed as being of two types—independent demand and dependent demand. These two types of capacity are parallel to the independent and dependent demand inventories discussed in Chapter 14. Safety capacity, used in services just as safety stock is used in manufacturing, should be based on the variability of independent demand capacity requirements.

| FIGURE 15.4 | **Various Conditions of Capacity and Demand for a Manufacturer** |

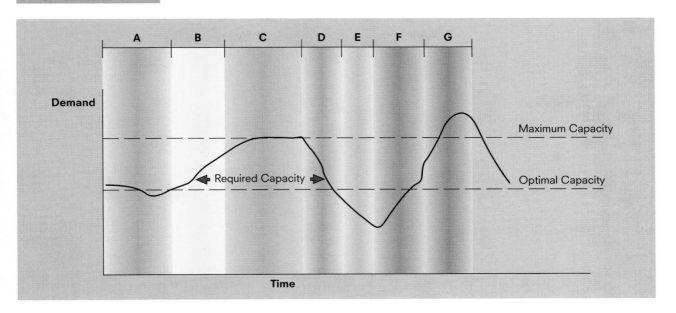

The factors that dictate capacity needs affect short- and long-term profit through their influence on the following significant costs related to capacity:

Fixed costs resulting from capacity investments

Cost of holding excess capacity

Cost of necessary protective capacity

Variable cost per unit

Cost of lost sale

Cost of poor service

OPERATIONS OUTLOOK

BOX 15.2

Capacity Planning in Warehouses

Warehouses can often use the same capacity planning approaches used by their manufacturing counterparts. The critical work center for a finished product warehouse might be handling the paperwork or operating forklifts used for filling orders. In fact, when a large influx of orders appears, product may actually have to be stored elsewhere because it can take up too much space on a shipping dock and prevent other orders from moving. Backlogs can exist in warehouses just as they can exist in manufacturing systems. Orders coming in at a rate greater than they can be processed can result in a backlog that can jeopardize prompt customer service. Backward scheduling, often used in planning for manufacturing start dates, can be applied in the warehousing environment as well. The warehousing manager can work backward from the order due date, taking into account the order-picking lead time, and identify the necessary start time.

Source G. J. Surdell, "Capacity Planning Applies to Warehouses Too!" *P&IM Review with APICS News* (February 1991): 42–47.

CUTTING-EDGE COMPANIES

BOX 15.3

Manufacturers Increase Utilization of Store Floor Space

Phar-Mor Inc., a large discount drug retailer, has developed much closer relationships with suppliers. To a great degree, suppliers dictate how much of their merchandise is carried in Phar-Mor stores and how it is displayed. The benefits to the suppliers are obvious. They mean potentially higher sales. Rubbermaid Inc., for example, has created "Everything Rubbermaid" departments in Phar-Mor stores, increasing the number of Rubbermaid products from 310 to 560. Gibson Greetings Inc. has an expanded greeting card section. Charles Levy Co., a primary supplier of books, tapes, and CDs, is building small bookstores inside Phar-Mor stores and improving music and book selections.

Phar-Mor, which has been in trouble since it was the victim of alleged fraud and embezzlement by several former top executives, is making these changes while in Chapter 11 bankruptcy proceedings. When Phar-Mor filed for bankruptcy protection in August 1992, it owed Rubbermaid $1.6 million, Gibson Greetings $6 million, and Charles Levy more than $9 million.

After the indictment of the former president, it was evident that the earnings potential of the once-fastest-growing discount chain in the United States was far less than previously thought. New management believed that the stores were originally designed too large and wanted to shrink the average 65,000-square-foot store by a third. The managers eliminated the luggage, office supply, and team sportswear departments because those departments had not provided as good a return on the space investment. Finding uses for this excess capacity was problematic because landlords were not thrilled at the prospect of trying to lease partitioned-off sections of the stores to other businesses. The alternative was to widen aisles and increase the display sections of core products like those of Rubbermaid, Gibson, and Charles Levy.

Frank Newman, president and CEO of F&M Distributors Inc., a rival of Phar-Mor, thinks the chain has too much space and is trying to find something to do with it. He does not believe, however, that merely giving suppliers unlimited space is necessarily the answer.

Source   "Phar-Mor Forges Stronger Ties with Manufacturers," *The Wall Street Journal,* March 8, 1993, sec. B, 4.

Investments in capacity result in fixed costs. Investment in capacity that is not supported by demand (excess capacity) places an added burden on the business in the form of excessive fixed costs. (See Box 15.3.) This ties up money that could otherwise be invested in ways that would enhance the firm's capabilities. Capacity levels that are compatible with demand levels result in efficiencies and minimize total costs per unit. Shortages of capacity often result in lost sales, poor service, or both, and the accompanying costs.

Several factors determine capacity needs. The interrelationship between costs and capacity dictate two important guidelines for services. First, they influence the percent of capacity utilization required to break even. This is the point at which revenues obtained from selling the capacity will equal the costs. The greater the investment in capacity, the greater the demand needed to break even. Second, after the capacity is established, these factors interact to determine the profit on investment when the firm operates at its highest sustainable level of capacity utilization.[9]

Capacity management in the service sector, like that of manufacturing, has a significant impact on the firm's market share through its effect on competitive capabilities. To some extent, these effects are similar to those in manufacturing, but there are some substantial differences. Capacity decisions in services have a much greater and more direct effect on quality than do capacity decisions in manufacturing. Because manufactured goods

---

[9]Heskett, Sasser, and Hart, 136.

can be inventoried, the adverse effects of capacity shortages can usually be minimized through effective use of inventory. Capacity shortages in the service sector often result in a lost sale or in operating at less-than-optimal capacity for the prevailing demand. This shortage typically results in service taking longer or not meeting the desired level of quality. Excess capacity can also reduce quality levels. Because of the physical and psychological benefits that a customer expects when purchasing a service, a service that has so much excess capacity that it appears to be in low demand may detract from its quality. Imagine the restaurant or bar that is so large it looks nearly empty even when a significant number of people are present. The customer does not perceive that the business is one of high quality and may, in fact, not be able to experience the social interaction and ambience that is expected as part of the service package. Because of the lack of a finished goods inventory, capacity shortages result in a more direct and immediate impact on dependability of delivery, flexibility, and time. In all cases, the absence of inventory, which decouples manufacturing processes from the customer, results in more immediate and more severe consequences of capacity shortages in a service.

Figure 15.5 provides a profile of how demand and capacity can interact for a service. The relationship of demand and capacity is identical to the profile presented in the figure, but it has implications that are distinctly different from those in manufacturing. It is useful to examine each of these intervals and identify the effect that each demand/capacity relationship has on such factors as cost and quality in a service.

Interval A shows demand to be equal to the optimal capacity level. During this interval, the business will be at or near the lowest cost per unit and at the highest level of service quality. Customers will be getting the amount of attention desired when the system was designed, and management can be confident that the service will look busy enough to attract customers but not too busy to drive them away. Interval B is a period of increasing demand. Employees will probably be stressed during this period and unable to provide the quality of service desired. Customers may not be pleased with the quality and timeliness of

FIGURE 15.5 **Various Conditions of Capacity and Demand for a Service**

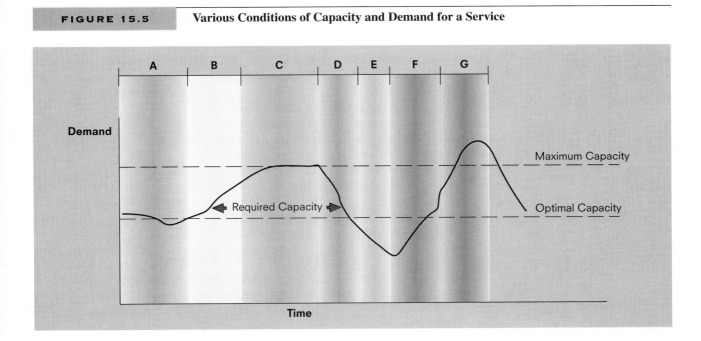

service at this demand level, and depending on their loyalty, they may try the service of a competitor. Interval C presents a serious problem for management. The costs of maintaining this level of output are very high, and the business cannot maintain it for a long period of time. All aspects of the system are likely to be stretched to the limit. Service will likely be poor and will get worse the longer demand remains at this level. The number of defectors will probably increase the longer this situation lasts. Interval D is essentially the same as B, except for the fact that the system has probably not yet recovered from the serious overdemand that occurred earlier. Quality of service will continue to be poor during this interval, but costs will begin to approach the desired level. Interval E designates a period of time with very low demand. The dangers in this interval include the escalation of costs per unit as volume drops but fixed costs remain stable. Depending on their expectations, customers may react negatively to the appearance of a business that's been deserted. Quality may suffer if employees become bored or inattentive, busying themselves with other tasks. Interval F presents an increasing demand, creating a need for a rapid adjustment in capacity. Demand becomes so high in interval G that service quality suffers, and, in fact, business is lost because demand far exceeds capacity. The poor quality of service may give poorly served customers an excuse to give the competition a try next time, and those customers who were not served an immediate reason to go elsewhere.

The time frame of Figure 15.5 has a significant impact on the ramifications of the options available to management. For example, if the time frame extends for only a day, various approaches might be used to temporarily shift demand or capacity. If the time frame is extended to several days or several weeks, however, alternatives available to management would require significant change in either available capacity or the demand. Specific approaches and alternatives to making these types of adjustments are addressed in the following sections.

Adjusting Available Levels of Capacity   One approach to dealing with capacity problems is to increase the level of capacity. Most services can deal with substantial long-term capacity shortages only by increasing capacity. This type of increase may require an expansion or an additional facility. Short-term capacity shortages can be addressed using a number of other capacity-increasing strategies.

Excessive load on capacity that results from irregular arrival of customers and exists for short time intervals is often dealt with by letting queues build up in front of the service. The risks have already been described, but, in short, long lines will drive away customers. Much research has been devoted to the study of waiting lines and the behavior of people in such lines. Various approaches can be taken to make the waiting time more pleasant and seemingly shorter. For example, some Nationsbank branches have digital displays that enable customers to catch up on the latest news while waiting in front of the teller windows. Many service establishments serve free coffee and pastries in their waiting areas, while others provide magazines to help customers pass the time.

For many services, improved effort in demand forecasting will result in a better projection of capacity requirements and less frequent capacity shortages. Even when forecasting is improved, however, some safety or protective capacity is required to absorb unanticipated demand. A supermarket might schedule a few extra checkers for a particular shift or a movie theater could show a film on two screens if there is reason to believe it will be especially popular.

Many services have found that capacity requirements on various resources within the business are not level. Cross-training workers to do a variety of tasks allows those from areas with excess capacity to help out those that may be having a temporary capacity shortage. When cross-training is not a feasible way to deal with demand peaks on certain aspects of the service, there may be other measures that can be taken to improve efficiency. For

Nationwide Insurance has developed a pilot program to improve its capability to speed service. Electronic imaging allows policyholders to bypass drive-in claims station appointments or adjuster visits and go directly to a repair shop that is part of Nationwide's repair service network. The body shop manager (top) records car damage on a camcorder and transmits it in three seconds via a phone line to the computer of a special claims representative (below).

Source Courtesy of Nationwide Insurance; photo by Tom Brunk.

example, if peak demand in a restaurant results in a lack of capacity to bus tables, it might be advantageous to let dishes stack up in the washroom and have a dishwasher bus tables. Emergency efficiency measures that would not be acceptable as standard practice may be used to improve service quality during demand peaks.

For some services, part-time employees or personnel hired through a temporary employment agency provide the most appropriate way to deal with demand peaks. This extra help may result in temporary needs for equipment as well, which in some cases, can be rented for short-term use.

Adjusting Demand on Capacity   The alternative to adjusting available capacity to deal with demand peaks is to change demand patterns so that the demand on capacity is leveled. In some cases, an actual reduction in demand would be preferable to having customers served poorly.

One approach to adjusting demand on capacity is through smoothing. Fitzsimmons and Sullivan present the following several strategies for smoothing demand: partitioning, price differentials, complimentary services, and reservation systems.[10] Partitioning of demand takes advantage of the fact that most services experience several types of demands. For example, customers who walk in without an appointment, or walk-ins, may provide a significant portion of a bank's demand, but daily commercial account transactions may also make up a large part of the business. For a hair stylist, walk-ins may provide a greater source of demand on some days than others. Appointments make up another portion of the demand for hair stylists. Assuming that walk-in demand is consistent from day to day, a business may schedule appointments accordingly to result in a consistent daily demand. On days of high walk-in demand, however, the service would operate at higher-than-optimal levels, reducing service quality and turning away some customers. Increasing the number of appointments during days that traditionally have lower walk-in demand and decreasing the number of appointments on days of high walk-in demand would increase the total number of customers the business can serve and would be likely to improve customer satisfaction. Price differentials are widely used as a demand leveling tool to shift demand from peak periods by offering lower prices during low demand periods. Hotels, airlines, resorts, golf courses, telephone companies, theaters, restaurants, and bars all use price differentials to level demand. This approach has become increasingly popular and has included a technique known as yield management. Yield management is an attempt to maximize revenue by adjusting prices to influence customer demand.

Some businesses have developed complimentary services to increase the use of existing resources during low demand. Convenience stores, for example, have become more like fast-food restaurants. Large grocery stores have added restaurants, video rental, and banking services.

Reservation systems allow the service to sell the "product" before the customer arrives. This service makes it possible to divert the arrival of some customers to other times and avoid random arrivals and long lines. Many businesses have combined the use of reservations and price differentials. For example, most airlines offer lower fares to customers who reserve their seats well in advance of their departure and stay over a Saturday night.

Businesses that use reservation systems to smooth demand often find it necessary to overbook to utilize their capacity at the optimal level because there are often no-shows. There are two costs associated with overbooking. Of primary importance is the opportunity

---

[10]J. A. Fitzsimmons and R. S. Sullivan, *Service Operations Management* (New York: McGraw-Hill Book Company, 1982), 287–293.

cost of the capacity that goes unused because of a no-show. The greater the amount of over-booking, the lower this cost is. The second important cost is the penalty cost of turning away, or bumping, a customer who has a reservation. This cost would include the cost of finding the customer a replacement service and the loss of customer goodwill. The greater the amount of overbooking that there is, the greater this cost is. The appropriate amount of overbooking can be determined by identifying the expected cost of the various options available and selecting the least-cost alternative. Example 15.3 provides an example of how to determine the number of customers to overbook.

EXAMPLE 15.3

Management at the River View Hotel has recognized that no-shows are costing the hotel a significant amount of money. The hotel averages 1.24 no-shows per day. It has collected no-show data from occupancy records for the past 3 years and has organized the data into the table shown in Table 15.15. Because of its proximity to several tourist attractions, the River View Hotel is able to maintain a very high occupancy rate. Management has calculated that the average cost of a no-show is $65. The cost of turning away a customer with a reservation because of overbooking is a serious concern for River View management. It has made arrangements with another hotel to take any customers that are bumped. River View estimates the total cost of bumping and lost goodwill, plus the cost of alternative lodging, is $80.

Overbooking for the River View Hotel

With an average no-show rate of 1.24 per day and a cost of $65 per no-show, no-shows are costing River View $80.60 per day and $29,419 per year. River View can overbook as much as it chooses. But an expected cost of overbooking should be calculated.

SOLUTION

The appropriate solution is reached by seeking a balance between the opportunity cost of the no-show and the cost of bumping a customer. For example, the expected cost of over-booking one reservation per day would be found by computing the expected cost of this alternative, as shown in Table 15.16.

An expected daily no-show cost of $70.70, provided by a one-reservation overbooking policy, would be preferable to the $80.60 daily cost under the status quo. It would result in an expected daily savings of $9.90 (expected annual savings of $3,613.50). To

TABLE 15.15 **No-Show Data from River View Hotel**

Number of No-Shows	Average Frequency of Occurrence per Year	Probability (average frequency/365)
0	140	0.38
1	97	0.27
2	64	0.18
3	34	0.09
4	21	0.06
5	9	0.02

TABLE 15.16		Overbooking by One Reservation at River View	
Number of No-Shows	Probability	Expected Opportunity Cost [a]	Expected Cost of Bumping[b]
0	0.38	0.38(0) = 0	0.38(80) = 30.40
1	0.27	0.27(0) = 0	0.27(0) = 0
2	0.18	0.18(65) = 11.70	0.18(0) = 0
3	0.09	0.09(130) = 11.70	0.09(0) = 0
4	0.06	0.06(195) = 11.70	0.06(0) = 0
5	0.02	0.02(260) = 5.20	0.02(0) = 0
Sum		**$40.30**	**$30.40**
Total expected cost			**$70.70 per day**

[a]Probability times cost of no-shows.
[b]Probability times cost of bumping.

TABLE 15.17		Overbooking by Two Reservations at River View	
Number of No-Shows	Probability	Expected Opportunity Cost	Expected Cost of Bumping
0	0.38	0.38(0) = 0	0.38(160) = 60.80
1	0.27	0.27(0) = 0	0.27(80) = 21.60
2	0.18	0.18(0) = 0	0.18(0) = 0
3	0.09	0.09(65) = 5.85	0.09(0) = 0
4	0.06	0.06(130) = 7.80	0.06(0) = 0
5	0.02	0.02(195) = 3.90	0.02(0) = 0
Sum		**$17.55**	**$82.40**
Total expected cost			**$99.95 per day**

determine if the hotel could gain additional savings by overbooking by two reservations, the same process must be followed, as shown in Table 15.17. Overbooking by two results in higher expected costs than no overbooking or overbooking by one. Overbooking of greater numbers would increase expected costs. The low-cost alternative is to overbook by one.

CAPACITY MANAGEMENT CROSS-LINKS

Capacity management decisions are a key concern of all aspects of the business because they greatly affect competitive capabilities. However, some business functions are more immediately affected than others when capacity problems arise. Those business functions most immediately and directly influenced by capacity decisions are marketing, finance, and human resources.

For some manufacturers, particularly those that produce to stock, inventory decouples the marketing function from direct dependence on short-term capacity. However, for make-to-order manufacturers as well as for services, the marketing function is selling capacity quite directly. Capacity shortages can quickly result in an inability to produce an item or service. If the sales staff is aware of the capacity problem, customers can be steered toward substitute products or services. If the sales force is not aware of the problem, however, promises may be made that are impossible to keep. As companies strive to reduce inventory levels, marketing's direct dependence on capacity rather than inventory will increase, as will its need to be closely attuned to capacity levels and capabilities.

Many capacity decisions have a significant impact on the financial aspects of the firm. Capacity expansions, whether a new facility or a new piece of equipment, require significant investment and careful decision making. Financial experts must help in making these decisions. Unanticipated capacity shortages also affect the firm's financial condition. A firm that is unable to accept new orders or fails to meet an order promise because of capacity shortages can experience unanticipated reductions in revenues.

The human resource management function must also be acutely aware of capacity decisions. Increases in capacity lead to hiring and training of new employees and put increased demand on all personnel functions. Many of the approaches used to gain short-term capacity increases (such as overtime and cross-training) have implications for personnel functions, particularly training efforts, labor/management relations, and union work rules.

SUMMARY

For manufacturers and services alike, capacity will continue to be a management priority because it establishes the firm's capabilities and also accounts for much of its fixed costs. As businesses strive to become more flexible and to respond more quickly, investing in the right type of capacity will become increasingly important. When firms make large capacity investments, they typically pay close attention to utilization. But this often leads to excess production and inventory, which negates any benefit gained by the investment. Variable demand on capacity will continue to be the most difficult aspect to manage, but as managers improve their ability to level demand on capacity through product mix changes and improved relationships with customers, low inventory levels and high utilizations will be possible.

EAGLE MOUNTAIN REVISITED

CROSS-LINKS Will Kelly Hendricks be better off if she adopts Pam's ski-for-free suggestion? Does the revenue-sharing approach Pam recommended seem to be a reasonable application for yield management? Is it beneficial for all owners of restaurants and hotels?

How might the businesses determine the percentage of revenues to be turned over to the ski resort? How might the same concept be used to attract tourists in the summer to bring business to local artists, hotels, and restaurants?

QUESTIONS FOR REVIEW

1. Describe how time available is converted to standard hours.
2. Define the following:
   a. Rated capacity
   b. Theoretical capacity
   c. Demonstrated capacity
   d. Protective capacity
   e. Productive capacity
   f. Budgeted capacity
   g. Design capacity
   h. Maximum capacity
   i. Optimal capacity
3. How do capacity decisions influence the competitive capabilities of price, quality, dependability, flexibility, and response time?
4. Why are the production plan and resource requirements plan developed in aggregate?
5. What is a capacity bill?
6. What is the purpose of rough-cut capacity planning?
7. How are utilization and efficiency data used in determining available capacity?
8. Why is rough-cut capacity planning inaccurate?
9. How are the inaccuracies of rough-cut capacity planning overcome by capacity requirements planning?
10. In services, how does producing at maximum capacity affect quality?
11. Compare the uses of partitioning demand, price differentials, and reservation systems as ways to change demand in services.

QUESTIONS FOR THOUGHT AND DISCUSSION

1. How do universities change levels of demand and capacity? What are the effects of these practices?
2. Identify familiar service firms that struggle with seasonal peaks in demand. How do they cope with the need for flexible capacity?
3. Is yield management a potential tool that universities may wish to look at during periods of low enrollment?
4. What could the impact of inventory record inaccuracy be on capacity planning for a manufacturer?

INTEGRATIVE QUESTIONS

1. How does the misuse of temporary help damage a firm's long-term competitiveness?
2. What limits to future capacity availability are set by the aggregate plan?
3. What could the impact of demand forecast error be on capacity planning?
4. For a manufacturer, what are the relationships among excess capacity, inventory level, and competitive priorities?

PROBLEMS

1. A small manufacturer produces lawn and patio furniture from PVC plastic pipe. The master production schedule, capacity bill, and work center masters are shown here. Validate the MPS using rough-cut capacity planning. Is the MPS feasible?

Week	1	2	3	4	5	6	7	8
Quantity	260	340	310	280	210	240	320	360

Capacity Bill

Work Center	Time Required
Pipe cutting	3.5 minutes
Frame assembly	5.0 minutes
Webbing	7.4 minutes

Work Center Masters

Work Center	Number of Machines	Hours per Day	Days per Week	Utilization %	Efficiency %
Pipe cutting	1	8	5	90	95
Frame assembly	1	8	5	95	92
Webbing	2	8	5	93	96

2. A custom furniture maker promises delivery within 6 weeks of receiving an order. Furniture frames are assembled to stock. Frames are finished and upholstered to order. Management uses a final assembly schedule for checking capacity of the finishing and upholstering departments. The assembly schedule is presented below. Using the data provided in the assembly schedule, work center masters, and capacity bill, compare required capacity to available capacity on each work center, for each week. Is the assembly schedule feasible?

Week	1	2	3	4	5	6	7	8
Quantity	17	19	16	21	17	25	22	23

Capacity Bill

Work Center	Time Required
Finishing	42 minutes
Upholstering	65 minutes

Work Center Masters

Work Center	Number of Machines	Hours per Day	Days per Week	Utilization %	Efficiency %
Finishing	1	8	5.5	80	90
Upholstering	1	8	5	85	85

3. Two products, X and Y, are manufactured. Using the MPS information, the capacity bills, and the work center masters provided in the tables below, create a rough-cut capacity plan.

MPS

Week	1	2	3	4	5	6	7	8
Product X	250	240	254	320	468	310	246	321
Product Y	124	158	163	168	120	135	145	134

Capacity Bills

Product X		Product Y	
Work Center	Time (min.)	Work Center	Time (min.)
a	5.6	a	0
b	4.8	b	5.7
c	3.9	c	4.3
d	0	d	7.8

Work Center Masters

Work Center	Number of Machines	Hours per Day	Days per Week	Utilization %	Efficiency %
a	1	8	6	88	95
b	1	8	6	94	95
c	1	8	5	90	94
d	1	8	5	88	96

4. Products P and Q are manufactured in a small factory. Develop a rough-cut capacity plan to compare required capacity with available capacity using the MPS, capacity bills, and work center masters presented on page 486.

MPS

Week	1	2	3	4	5	6	7	8
P	6,000	6,700	4,530	5,480	4,560	5,400	6,530	5,630
Q	3,755	3,890	5,210	5,955	4,570	2,390	4,310	8,000

Capacity Bills

Product P		Product Q	
Work Center	Time (min.)	Work Center	Time (min.)
a	1.20	a	0.80
b	0.50	b	0.60
c	0.40	c	0.15
d	1.30	d	0.24

Work Center Masters

Work Center	Number of Machines	Hours per Day	Days per Week	Utilization %	Efficiency %
a	2	16	5	92	96
b	2	16	5	95	95
c	2	16	5	95	97
d	2	16	6	94	96

5. A shoe manufacturer is interested in the capacity requirements that result from the planned order releases (from MRP) for one size of its most popular training shoe, the A22. The planned order releases for the A22 are in pairs. The planned order releases for uppers and soles are shown in single units below, even though there must be matching pairs of rights and lefts. Develop the capacity requirements plan for all six work centers using the data presented below. Which work center has the biggest capacity problem?

Planned Order Releases

	1	2	3	4	5	6	7	8
A22 Size 10 (pr)	1,460	1,460	1,460	1,460	1,680	1,680	1,680	1,680
A2210u upper	2,000	2,920	2,920	2,920	2,920	2,920	2,920	0
A2210s air sole	1,600	2,920	2,920	2,920	2,920	2,920	2,920	0

Routings

A22 Shoe		A22 Upper		A22 Sole	
Work Center	Time (min.)	Work Center	Time (min.)	Work Center	Time (min.)
Assembly	1.40	Cutting	1.40	Molding	1.20
Sewing	0.65	Sewing	1.20	Trimming	1.10
Inspection	0.25				

Work Center Masters

Work Center	Number of Machines	Hours per Day	Days per Week	Utilization %	Efficiency %
Assembly	2	8	5	88	95
Sewing	2	8	5	90	94
Inspection	1	4	5	80	88
Cutting	2	8	5	96	94
Molding	2	8	5	85	90
Trimming	2	8	5	80	92

6. A manufacturer produces end product P, which is an assembly of components Q and R. P, Q, and R are produced using four work centers. Using the planned order releases from the MRP, the routings, and the work center masters, create a CRP. Which work center has a capacity problem?

Planned Order Releases

Item	1	2	3	4	5	6	7	8
P	127	134	153	138	132	143	136	143
Q	402	459	414	396	429	408	429	0
R	268	306	276	264	286	272	286	0

Routings

P		Q		R	
Work Center	**Time**	**Work Center**	**Time**	**Work Center**	**Time**
1	4.25	2	4.10	3	5.60
		1	3.40	4	5.75

Work Center Masters

Work Center	Number of Machines	Hours per Day	Days per Week	Utilization %	Efficiency %
1	1	8	5	85	97
2	1	8	5	89	95
3	1	8	5	86	92
4	1	8	5	92	94

7. A small charter air service has recently begun to consider overbooking flights as a way to reduce costs associated with no-shows. Based on the history of no-shows, the following probabilities have been derived:

No-Shows	0	1	2	3	4
Probability	0.19	0.27	0.33	0.14	0.07

This air service has averaged 1.63 no-shows per day at a calculated cost of $110 per no-show. Thus, daily opportunity cost resulting from no-shows is $179.30. The cost to bump an overbooked passenger is expected to be $65. What is the optimal number of passengers to overbook?

SUGGESTED READINGS

Blackstone, J. H. *Capacity Management*. Cincinnati: South-Western Publishing Co., 1989.

Heskett, J. L., W. E. Sasser, Jr., and C. W. L. Hart. *Service Breakthroughs*. New York: Free Press, 1990.

South, J. B., and R. Hixson. "Excess Capacity Versus Finished Goods Safety Stock." *Production and Inventory Management Journal* 29 (3rd Quarter 1988): 36–40.

LEARNING OBJECTIVES

Upon completing this chapter, you should be able to explain

- where scheduling fits in terms of other operations activities
- how Gantt charts are used in conjunction with scheduling
- what the constraint management system of scheduling is
- what the terms *drum, buffer,* and *rope* mean
- what a kanban system is and how it works
- how the drum-buffer-rope system differs from the kanban system
- how local and global priority rules differ
- what techniques can be used to aid the scheduling process in services

CHAPTER 16

SCHEDULING RESOURCES

Pushing Paper at GM&P

Grover, McHugh, and Penn Tax Service (GM&P) provides federal income tax services to business and individual clients. The firm's demand is seasonal, requiring it to hire several temporary employees during the first 4 months of each year. Because the temporary workers lack sophisticated tax knowledge, the firm processes each client through four functional departments. The first function is the Information Sort department. Information Sort is handled by two temporary workers who have worked for GM&P on a seasonal basis for several years. Their task is to segregate the information brought in by clients into appropriate categories, such as income, deductions, and expenses. Following the information sort, the client's file is sent to the Classification department, which is also staffed by temporary employees. There the file is categorized by the type of supporting forms that will be required. For example, if the client has supplemental rent income, the Classification department would note that the appropriate supporting forms are needed. The last step in this department is to include all blank forms in the file. The file then goes to the Forms department where all supporting forms are completed. The last department, known as "1040," is where all support forms are used to complete the 1040 form. The tax is computed and all forms are checked for accuracy. Both Forms and 1040 are staffed by permanent employees. ■ Harlan Fishmeyer, operations manager for GM&P Tax Service, has been monitoring the amount of time it takes to complete tax files. In doing so, he has also paid close attention to the differences between various files and how they have affected processing time. Currently, each department processes files using a first-in/first-out (FIFO) method,

based on when they arrive in the department. But sometimes files do not leave the 1040 department in the same sequence in which they were brought into the Sort department. Harlan is not really concerned about this, but he does wonder if it would make sense to use a different scheduling technique than FIFO. ■ In a meeting with the four department directors, Harlan made this announcement: "During my investigation of our operations, I noticed a number of interesting things. First, it shouldn't be surprising that the amount of time each file spends in a department depends on the number of support forms required to complete it. In fact, we can accurately predict the amount of time in each of the last two departments based on the number of forms identified in the Classification department. I know our customers prefer FIFO, but I wonder if we couldn't improve productivity and average processing time if we use other approaches to sequencing files in each department. My initial reaction to the data I've collected is to continue to use FIFO for sorting and classification. But based on the result of the classification, we should project how long it will take to process each file in Forms and 1040. ■ Based on the projected processing times, we could handle files in a number of ways. We could handle them in order of processing time, short to long. We could also take into account the April 15th deadline and use a process called 'slack.' We would compute slack by figuring out the time remaining until the due date and then subtracting the projected processing time. Files with the least amount of slack would be done first. These are pretty traditional sequencing methods, but I've also heard about some new approaches that we might want to look into. What are your reactions?" ■

The scheduling function plays several important roles in an organization's ability to compete. First, schedules determine when something is to be done, dictating the timing of all events and activities related to the production of goods and services. This function is important in determining an organization's ability to compete on the bases of dependability and time, as well as on the basis of quality in the case of services. Second, scheduling is a means by which organizations can increase the productive use of resources. An ability to utilize existing capacity effectively enhances a firm's capacity to compete on the basis of price because efficient scheduling increases output without increasing fixed costs. (See Box 16.1.)

For manufacturing, scheduling is the means by which companies meet due dates that have been promised to customers. Firms that make promises for delivery, but do not fulfill them because of poor scheduling practices, are perceived as undependable. Automatic Feed Company, maker of coil processing systems, learned that lesson the hard way. Having promised a major order to its largest client on a specific date, it found itself in danger of losing that client—and its reputation—because a shipment of a key component was late arriving from Germany. Fortunately, Automatic Feed was able to implement a program for speedy production and meet its commitment.[1] The ability to create schedules and modify them quickly when changes are needed allows manufacturers to be responsive to customers' demands, reducing customers' lead time and giving them greater flexibility.

Services, too, must schedule their production. But since services cannot store their finished products, they must create schedules that match production to the availability of cus-

At Unocal's Los Angeles Terminal, a cross-functional employee team tackled a costly scheduling problem that occurred when service stations weren't ready to receive a shipment of gasoline. Team members, shown here in a delivery truck at the terminal, improved communications between dealers, drivers, and the terminal, saving the company from $8,000 to $12,000 per month.

Source © Jeff Corwin.

[1]Nathan Weaks, "The Accountant as Production Scheduler," *Management Accounting* (March 1993): 250.

CUTTING-EDGE COMPANIES

BOX 16.1

New Scheduling System at Campbell Soup

Campbell's products are well-known to anyone who shops for food. But most shoppers could not even imagine the intricacies of the company's operation. For example, Campbell's Canadian division produces 250 different varieties and sizes of soups. The Toronto plant runs two 10-hour shifts, 5 or 6 days per week. Like many firms, Campbell's recently developed a plan to reduce inventory levels and simultaneously improve customer service. The project team determined that one of the key ways to reach those goals would be to improve production scheduling.

Before the plant acquired a new computerized scheduling system, all scheduling was done manually. The complexities were enormous. Campbell's has five production stages: blending, filling cans, processing, labeling, and palletizing. Different machines handle each step. Vegetables and meats must be prepared before blending can occur. And capacity constraints prevent everything from being done at once. The product must flow smoothly through the system, and the processes must be synchronized to prevent ingredients from spoiling. The scheduling is further complicated by a mixture of old and new cooking equipment. Changeovers vary in length depending on the machine.

The new scheduling system has improved Campbell's use of resources, ensuring adequate cost margins. It has also enhanced the company's ability to make long-term planning decisions. Now the company can more accurately translate product demand trends into demands on equipment, making it easier to predict the need for additional resources.

Source "Scheduling Software Helps Campbell of Canada Cook," *Production and Inventory Management Journal* (January 1992): 29–30.

tomers. Consider, for example, the scheduling problems airlines must face. A single organization like United Airlines schedules an average of 2,000 flights a day to accommodate thousands of passengers who want to travel on particular routes.[2] Clearly, the scheduling function plays a major role in satisfying the customer in services. Services that are scheduled properly ensure that the customer always has assistance when needed and is not trapped in long lines waiting to be served.

Good scheduling also increases the flexibility of manufacturing and service firms. By using capacity more effectively, organizations often find that they have greater capacity than they expected. This additional capacity provides added flexibility for last-minute adjustments to meet customers' requests. (See Box 16.2.)

The importance of understanding scheduling concepts has been addressed in several of the earlier chapters of this book. For example, the concepts related to assembly line balancing are associated with scheduling in a repetitive environment. The techniques used to plan projects are also directly related to scheduling. The time-phasing, or backward scheduling, logic of MRP is another example of an application of scheduling concepts.

SCHEDULING TECHNIQUES

The scheduling process is influenced by a number of factors: the type of product or service produced; the volume of production of the product or service; the number of different products or services produced (variety); and to some extent, the industry in which the organization competes. Techniques that may be useful in a high-volume repetitive manufacturing environment may not be appropriate for a job shop environment. Strategic capacity, layout and design, and planning and control system decisions also constrain the scheduling

---

[2]Glenn W. Graves et al., "Flight Crew Scheduling," *Management Science* (June 1993): 736.

CUTTING-EDGE COMPANIES

BOX 16.2

The Benefits of Good Scheduling

SMC Pneumatics, whose North American headquarters was established in Indianapolis in 1977, is the world's largest manufacturer of pneumatic components. It services automotive, electronic, and other industrial customers including such well-known companies as Anheuser-Busch, Eli Lilly, Panasonic, Toyota, Honda, and Sony. SMC credits its success to its superior customer service. It offers a product line of more than 6,000 different pneumatic components with over 50,000 variations. Naturally, stocking every variation would result in huge inventory quantities, so SMC operates in what is predominantly a make-to-order environment. It receives a very large volume of orders, but they are usually for small quantities of a wide variety of items. Customers want very short lead times even though they typically order items of varying sizes and configurations that require different routings.

By 1991, production volumes were growing at a rate of 30 percent per year, but scheduling the plant was growing increasingly difficult. The scheduling system required manual data input, which consumed a significant amount of staff time. It also did not take production loads or available capacity into account. Schedulers developed highly arbitrary machine schedules that frequently went unmet—a situation that did not help SMC find a balance between machine efficiency and high-quality customer service.

In 1991, SMC began implementing a computer-based scheduling system that utilized finite capacity scheduling, meaning that the schedules were developed based on capacity loads and available capacity. SMC found that it benefited in the following ways from the improved scheduling:

1. Staff time required to develop schedules has been reduced by 50 percent. (This paid for the software in 1 year.)
2. Demand on machines has been smoothed out.
3. The plant has increased its ability to spot potential problems.
4. Management has been able to plan overtime better and get an increased return for overtime dollars.
5. Supervisory staff has been able to better organize the shop floor.
6. The software has highlighted which machines are chronically overloaded, allowing staff to better assign production to machines.
7. The software has identified instances where a small investment can convert underused machines to take on loads previously assigned to overused machines.

Source R. Jung, C. Mulherin, and T. Riggles, "Finite Capacity Scheduling Helps SMC Improve Delivery, Control Costs," *APICS— The Performance Advantage* (February 1993): 24–27.

process. For example, organizations with excess capacity typically have fewer problems scheduling than organizations with no additional capacity.

A schedule may describe such issues as when a service will be provided, when a product will start and finish production, what orders a particular work center will work on during particular hours of the day, and when a machine will be set up for a new product. For a product, the schedule normally identifies a timetable for performing activities required for production as well as the specific sequence of machines, or routing. It also specifies which machines should work on the product and when. For a machine, the schedule specifies which products to work on, what to do to them, and when.

THE GANTT CHART

One of the early devices still in use for sequencing work activities is the *Gantt chart,* which is a visual model of what resources, such as equipment or employees, are to be doing for a particular period of time. Gantt charts are used for a variety of purposes, including the assigning of jobs to machines and the scheduling of jobs in services and manufacturing. They are most appropriate for use with jobs that are done at relatively few work centers because in those cases lead times are more predictable.

Figure 16.1 shows a Gantt chart that describes the schedules for work centers A1, A2, and A3 as they relate to jobs 100, 101, and 102. On December 6, for example, work center

| FIGURE 16.1 | **Job Sequencing at Work Centers A3, A2, and A1** |

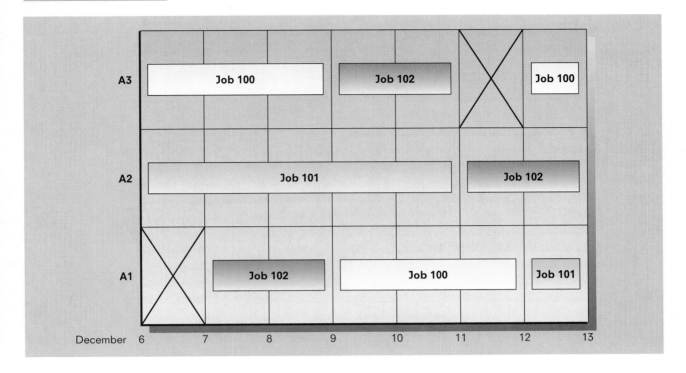

A1 is idle. A1 then has 2 days to complete job 102, and 3 days for job 100, followed by 1 day for job 101. A Gantt chart may also be used to represent what each job is doing, rather than what each work center is doing. For example, instead of listing work centers on the *Y* axis, the jobs could be listed there. For job 100, the first 3 days would be allocated to work center A3, the next 3 days to A1, and then back to A3 again. All of the specific work centers required to complete job 100, for example, would be displayed, as well as the time required to complete each part and the total job.

Gantt charts are useful, but they are somewhat limited in their capacity to display large complex processes. Although the Gantt chart assists in visualizing a schedule, it does not provide direction about how best to schedule. Specific approaches to scheduling manufacturing and service resources are considered in the following sections.

SCHEDULING IN MANUFACTURING OPERATIONS

THE JIT ENVIRONMENT

From a scheduling perspective, the concept of developing a physical flow of materials, which is fostered by a product-oriented layout, is important in a JIT environment. Activities such as setup-time reduction, workplace organization, and reduction of work-in-process inventory are at the heart of the smooth flow of materials desired in JIT environments.

Another concept important to the scheduling function in JIT systems is mixed model production and level loading. For example, at Toyota, where JIT began, the scheduling

Dana Corporation, a manufacturer of vehicle parts and systems, plans schedules to meet the just-in-time needs of its customers. Several times a day, Dana divisions serving Ford Motor Company dial into Ford's mainframe computer to determine how many Dana parts Ford needs and when to ship them. When more parts are needed, Dana schedules the material. This keeps Ford's just-in-time processes running smoothly.

Source   Courtesy of Dana Corporation.

process begins with the demands of the market. The master schedule is based on extensive market research and provides a ballpark sales figure. Normally the company provides these numbers to the plant and suppliers with a 2-month lead time, and gives them more firm numbers a month later. These numbers serve as the basis for daily schedules, which are used to level the production schedule.[3]

To illustrate this process, suppose that Toyota needs 10,000 pickup trucks per month. This demand is translated into a daily need of (10,000 units/20 days per month) = 500 units. The cycle time is then determined. If 500 units must be produced in 8 hours, or 480 minutes, a cycle time of 480/500 = 0.96 minutes is required. The cycle time and number of units needed per day are inputs to determining the required capacity for each process.[4]

The daily production schedule consists of the product mix of design alternatives including body style, color, engine type, and the like. For example, if the product mix of four different vehicle alternatives called P, Q, R, and S, was 20 percent P, 40 percent Q, 30 percent R, and 10 percent S, then there would be 100 Ps, 200 Qs, 150 Rs, and 50 Ss produced daily. The final work center is given the specific requirements in terms of the number of Ps, Qs, Rs, and Ss. These vehicles would be produced in the same sequence and in the same quantity every day.

[3]S. Shingeo, *A Study of the Toyota Production System from an Industrial Engineering Standpoint* (Cambridge, Mass.: Productivity Press, 1989), 97–102.

[4]K. Suzaki, *The New Manufacturing Challenge* (New York: Free Press, 1987), 178–180.

JIT manufacturing is based on a pull system which requires that materials be pulled through the production system based on need. The kanban system presented in Chapter 7, and first developed by Toyota, is one of the communication processes used to let upstream work centers know that inventory is needed.

The basis for kanban systems is the use of inventory buffers between work centers. Each buffer has a maximum size. A **kanban** is a visual signal or card that is used to indicate when an item should be produced and the quantity required to replenish a buffer to the desired level. The purpose of the kanban is to signal the supplier of a particular inventory item (a previous work center, department, or other factory) that more is needed. A single kanban authorizes the production of one container of inventory. Thus, management can control the maximum number of containers of inventory in the system by increasing or reducing the number of kanbans.

There are many types of kanbans in use. They include such adaptations as flashing lights that signal when production is falling behind and colored golf balls that roll through pipes to a machine operator and describe what part to produce next. Verbal requests are another common form of communicating the need for more material.

Special containers can also be used as the kanban for each inventory item. An empty container provides a signal to produce more. Management can control the amount of work-in-process inventory by adjusting the number of empty containers in the system. Another popular modification is the use of colored squares as kanbans, popularized by Hewlett-Packard. The use of colored squares as kanbans is one of the simplest forms of the single card system. Consider two adjacent work centers in which work center A feeds work center B. A colored square is painted or taped on a table between the two work centers. The colored square is the same size and shape as the container used to store the inventory. Work center A places a completed container of material on the colored kanban square designated for that particular item. For example, a red square may designate part X and a green square part Y. Work center B uses inventory produced by work center A to produce its output. Work center A is authorized to produce part X or Y only if its designated square is visible, that is, the square is not covered by a container of inventory. If management feels additional inventory is needed between work centers A and B, more squares may be added. The kanban square is a visual signal of when to produce and when not to produce.

Figure 16.2 provides an illustration of a kanban system using colored squares. In the exhibit, four work centers are shown. Work centers 1 and 3 each have one kanban square.

KANBAN
A visual signal or card used to indicate when an item should be produced and the quantity required to replenish a buffer to the desired level.

FIGURE 16.2   **Example Kanban Using Painted Squares**

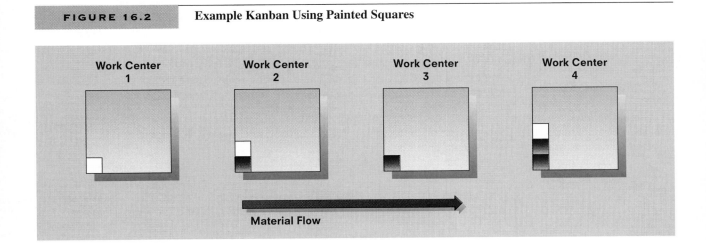

Work Center 1   Work Center 2   Work Center 3   Work Center 4

Material Flow

Work center 2 has two kanban squares and work center 4 has three squares. Two of the squares in work center 4 are filled; one of the two in work center 2 is filled, and the only square in work center 3 is filled. Work center 1 can produce to cover the exposed square at work center 2, and work center 3 is authorized to produce one container of inventory to cover the exposed square at work center 4. Work center 2 cannot produce.

In the typical single card kanban system, a special card is attached to each container when it is filled with inventory. When the container is empty, the attached card is removed and posted, signaling the need for the supplying work center to produce another container of inventory. The supplying work center picks up the posted card and refills the container with the card attached. When any work center demands more material, the preceding work center produces it. In this way, work is triggered at each individual work center throughout the plant. The amount of material a work center produces is based on the amount needed to replenish the buffer to its designated maximum level. No production can occur until there is a card or signal that initiates the process.

Toyota uses a two-card kanban system. One of the cards authorizes the transfer of materials out of a stocking point located midway between work centers. The second card authorizes production when inventory levels at the stocking point need to be replenished.

Kanban systems also provide an effective way of controlling production for both internal and external suppliers. Since the kanban system requires that work centers produce just what is needed, the amount of work-in-process inventory is kept to a minimum. Perhaps more importantly, however, materials are used at a downstream work center soon after they are available from the previous work center. This improvement in quality feedback time means that errors made at the previous work center can be detected more easily, resulting in an overall higher quality product.

THE CONSTRAINT MANAGEMENT APPROACH

Recall that constraint management focuses on the system's constraint. Constraint management-oriented scheduling activities focus on proper utilization of the constraint. The goal is to maximize throughout, or the cash flow generated by the sale of products, while reducing inventory and operating expenses. This is achieved by maximizing the pace of the constraint since it establishes the pace of all other operations in the system. The pace of the constraint is also referred to as the drum, or beat, of the system. It is the first component of what is called the **drum-buffer-rope (DBR)** approach to scheduling.[5] DBR is an approach to control the flow of orders through a production system. The drum dictates the pace at which orders or materials can be brought into the system. Materials brought in at a faster pace will create excess inventory, which increases costs and eventually decreases the throughput of the system. Materials brought in at a slower pace than that of the constraint will mean lost sales because the constraint will not be fully exploited.

Buffers are often used to decouple, or eliminate, direct dependencies between resources. The drum-buffer-rope approach uses a **time buffer** which is defined as

> A quantity of stock created by the offset of lead time to protect against uncertainty in the production process. A time buffer creates a physical amount of stock by the offset of an order's due date.[6]

DRUM-BUFFER-ROPE (DBR)
An approach to controlling the flow of orders through a production system: The drum dictates the pace at which orders/materials can be brought to the system; buffers are used to decouple direct dependencies, and the rope links all the pieces together.

TIME BUFFERS
A quantity of stock created by the offset of lead time to protect against uncertainty.

---

[5]E. Schragenheim and B. Ronen, "Drum-Buffer-Rope Shop Floor Control," *Production and Inventory Management Journal* 31 (Third Quarter 1990): 18–22.

[6]J. F. Cox, J. H. Blackstone, and M. S. Spencer, eds., *APICS Dictionary,* 7th ed. (Falls Church, Va.: American Production and Inventory Control Society, 1992), 50.

The DBR approach utilizes several different time buffers. A **constraint buffer** consists of a time buffer just before the system's constraint. Its purpose is to protect the constraint from disruptions that could reduce the input rate to the constraint and cause it to be idle. The constraint should never be idle because of the system throughput that would be lost. **Assembly buffers** are used to ensure that once a product has been processed by the constraint, it does not have to wait for other components at converging points in the production process. A **shipping buffer** is stock just prior to shipping that essentially builds up a level of finished product to protect customer lead times. Figure 16.3 provides an illustration of the placement of the constraint, assembly, and shipping buffers.

The size or time of each buffer varies with the situation, but generally they provide protection from most of the delays, breakdowns, or difficulties that may occur. If the worst likely delay possible between the first step in the process and work center X (WCX) was 10 hours, a 10-hour time buffer would be sufficient to protect WCX from being shut down for lack of material. This buffer would consist of an amount of stock or orders capable of occupying WCX for a 10-hour time period.

The rope concept forces all the pieces in the system to be linked together. This means, for example, that the rate at which materials are brought to the gating, or first, operation should be tied to the drum, and the timing of material releases should be tied to the rate inventory leaves the time buffers. Conceptually, the rope is the information link between the constraint and the rest of the system.

To demonstrate how the DBR scheduling process works, consider Figure 16.4. Two products, A and B, are produced. Product A has a $30 raw material cost, and requires 15

CONSTRAINT BUFFER
A type of buffer placed immediately prior to the constraint to ensure that it will be supplied with material.

ASSEMBLY BUFFER
A buffer of nonconstraint parts placed prior to an assembly with constraint parts.

SHIPPING BUFFER
A buffer placed immediately prior to shipping to absorb disruptions that could delay shipment.

| FIGURE 16.3 | **Placement of Time Buffers in DBR Scheduling** |

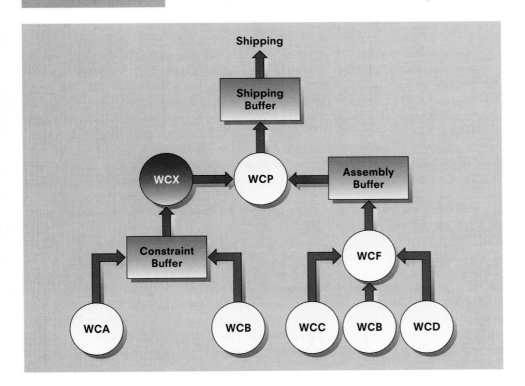

| FIGURE 16.4 | Requirements for Products A and B |

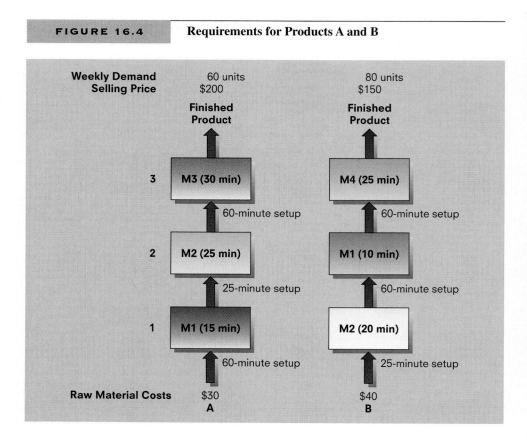

minutes of processing time on machine M1, 25 minutes on M2, and 30 minutes on M3. Product A sells for $200. There is a weekly demand for 60 units of A. Product B has a $40 raw material cost, and requires 20 minutes of processing time on machine M2, 10 minutes on M1, followed by 25 minutes on M4. There is a weekly demand for 80 units of product B. Its selling price is $150. Machines M1, M3, and M4 require 60 minutes of setup time prior to any operation. Machine M2 requires 25 minutes for setup. Weekly fixed expenses are $12,000.

Table 16.1 provides a comparison of required and available capacity for each of the work centers. This capacity check is essential for identifying the constraint. M2 is identified as the constraint for this system because the 3,100 minutes required to process the load exceeds the 2,400 minutes of available capacity by 29 percent. Note that machines M1, M3, and M4 are utilized less than 85 percent of the time.

Table 16.2 provides the information necessary to exploit the constraint and, in fact, determine the pace, or the drum, for the system. Using the exploitation approach presented in Chapter 8, the return per constraint minute is $6.80 for product A and $5.50 for product B. These figures are calculated by subtracting the raw material cost from the selling price to obtain the contribution. The contribution is then divided by the constraint time, which is the amount of time the constraint works on the product. Product A, for example, sells for $200. Raw materials cost $30, leaving a contribution of $170. The contribution is divided by the constraint time of 25 minutes to obtain a return per constraint minute of $6.80. Since the return per constraint minute of product B is $5.50, product A is preferred. Thus, all 60 units

TABLE 16.1   **Required Capacity versus Available Capacity**

Resource	Minutes per Product A	B	Total Required	Total Available	Required Utilization
M1	900	800	1,700	2,400	0.71
M2	1,500	1,600	3,100	2,400	1.29
M3	1,800		1,800	2,400	0.75
M4		2,000	2,000	2,400	0.83

of A are produced, requiring 1,500 minutes of time on machine M2. The remaining time, 2,400 − 1,500, leaves 900 minutes to produce 45 units of product B.

The actual production of product B will be reduced, however, because of the set-up times on the constraint. Assume a decision has been made to produce product A in two production runs of 30 units each and to use two production runs to produce product B. A total of four setups would be required, taking 100 minutes away from production time for product B. Thus, only 800 minutes are available on M2, enough to produce 40 units of product B.

The constraint has been exploited through the decision to meet all of the demand for product A but only part of the demand (40 units) for product B. The next step in the process is to schedule the constraint. As mentioned earlier, producing each product in two batches results in a constraint schedule (the schedule for M2), which is presented in Table 16.3. This is not the only possible constraint schedule. However, it is desirable to work on product A first and product B last because if some of the demand is not met because of a disruption, the last product produced would be the one not completed. Because B is less profitable, it would make sense for it to be processed last. The constraint begins work on product A. After 775 minutes, the 30 units are completed, and 20 units for product B are

TABLE 16.2   **Product Mix and Net Profit**

Product	A	B	Totals
Selling price	$200	$150	
Raw material costs	$30	$40	
Contribution	$170	$110	
Constraint time (minutes)	25	20	
Return per constraint minute	$6.80	$5.50	
Units Produced	60	40	
Revenues	$10,200	$4,400	$14,600
Weekly fixed expenses			($12,000)
Weekly net profit			$2,600

				TABLE 16.3			The Constraint Schedule for M2

Product	Setup Time (minutes)	Quantity Produced (units)	Minutes per Product	Total Time (minutes)	Start Time (minutes)	Finish Time (minutes)
A	25	30	750	775	0	775
B	25	20	400	425	775	1,200
A	25	30	750	775	1,200	1,975
B	25	20	400	425	1,975	2,400

begun. After 1,200 minutes, these 20 units are completed. The process continues until 60 units of A and 40 units of B have been completed.

The constraint schedule provided in Table 16.3 identifies what the constraint must accomplish if 60 units of product A and 40 units of product B are to be produced in two batch sizes each. Of particular concern, however, are the start times for the first batch of B, the second batch of A, and the second batch of B. If any disruption takes place, the materials would not be available to start production at these times. M2 would be idle waiting for their arrival, and the goal of producing 60 A's and 40 Bs would not be met. The constraint buffer is used to prevent this situation from arising. As suggested earlier, the process of determining the most effective buffer size depends on the specific situation, and it is usually done over time, in a trial and error approach. As a starting point, the size of the constraint buffer that will be used here is 240 minutes.

It is helpful to examine the effect that the time buffer has on processing just one unit of product A rather than an entire batch. If a 240-minute buffer is placed in front of M2, as shown in Figure 16.5, the amount of time required for a product to move through the system is increased by 240 minutes. This means that after a necessary completion date has been determined, backward scheduling to determine the necessary start date must include the time the product will spend moving through the 240-minute buffer.

Figure 16.5 shows how the size of the time buffer affects the timing of products that will require M2. By examining the figure closely, the real effect of the time buffer becomes apparent. Suppose product A were released to the system 310 minutes before it was due to be completed. If the processing at M1 went as planned, it arrives at M2 240 minutes before it must start at M2. The result of planning for a 240-minute buffer is that orders are released into the system 240 minutes earlier than they would have been had there not been a buffer.

FIGURE 16.5	Effect of Buffer on Timing of Product A

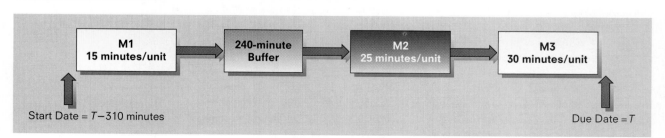

With the buffer in place, a disruption on M1, which delays product A from being completed after the expected 15 minutes, does not result in the constraint's being idle for lack of work to do. Since product A only takes 25 minutes to process on M2 and the total buffer size is 240 minutes, even if the product had arrived on time, there still would have been 215 minutes' worth of work in front of it. The constraint has work to do despite product A being late. In fact, product A is not late. It is just not as early arriving at M2 as planned. It was released so that it would arrive at M2 240 minutes early. As long as the disruption is for less than 240 minutes, it is not late getting processed.

Shipping buffers and assembly buffers are used in a similar fashion in the DBR approach. Using a shipping buffer of 240 minutes, for example, in addition to the 240-minute constraint buffer, would mean that product A would be released to the system at $(T-310) - 240$, or $T - 550$ (read "T minus 550") minutes. If there was no disruption prior to the constraint buffer, it would arrive at the constraint buffer 240 minutes before it needed to start, spend 240 minutes moving through the buffer, and then spend 25 minutes being processed by M2. If the processing at M2 went as planned, it would go directly from there to M3 and begin processing immediately. If the 30-minute process at M3 went well, it would arrive at shipping 240 minutes before it was to be shipped, contributing, along with other products, to the formation of the 240-minute shipping buffer.

Another aspect of DBR scheduling that differentiates it from other approaches is that DBR distinguishes between the production batch size and the transfer batch size. The production batch is the quantity of items produced before the equipment is set up to produce something else. The larger the production batch, the less frequent the setups. The transfer batch is the number of units produced before the units are transferred to the next step in the process. The smaller the transfer batch, the steadier the flow of materials through the system. Wherever appropriate, the preference is that the transfer size be one. That is, when a part has been completed at one work center, it is moved directly to the next work center. This has a significant impact on reducing throughput time and is one of several differences between DBR and kanban.

CONSTRAINT MANAGEMENT VERSUS JIT ENVIRONMENTS

While the kanban system of JIT and the drum-buffer-rope system have similar objectives, they differ in application. Both systems utilize inventory to decouple work centers from one another. JIT uses small buffers to decouple each work center from its predecessor. DBR uses one buffer at the constraint, one at shipping and in converging product flows, and assembly buffers to decouple those entities from the rest of the system. DBR does not attempt to decouple nonconstraints from each other, however.

In the DBR approach, if there are no internal constraints, the market is said to be the constraint. If this is the case, there would be no constraint buffer or assembly buffers, only a shipping buffer. In fact, the shipping buffer becomes the constraint buffer because it is the buffer immediately in front of the market constraint. In this scenario, the system is much more like kanban; it is a pull system from the market demand back to all work centers. It differs in placement of inventory, however. DBR would decouple the entire system from the demand with one buffer, but JIT would decouple each work center from the others. The constraint management logic maintains that because the other work centers have excess capacity, there is no reason to protect them from disruptions. The effect of a disruption could be absorbed by the excess capacity. Figure 16.6 compares a kanban system with a DBR system. Notice that the flow of information in the kanban system goes from one work center to the previous one, but in the DBR system the rope is the direct communication link between the constraint and the release of work into the system.

| FIGURE 16.6 | **Comparison of Buffer Use in Kanban and Drum-Buffer-Rope** |

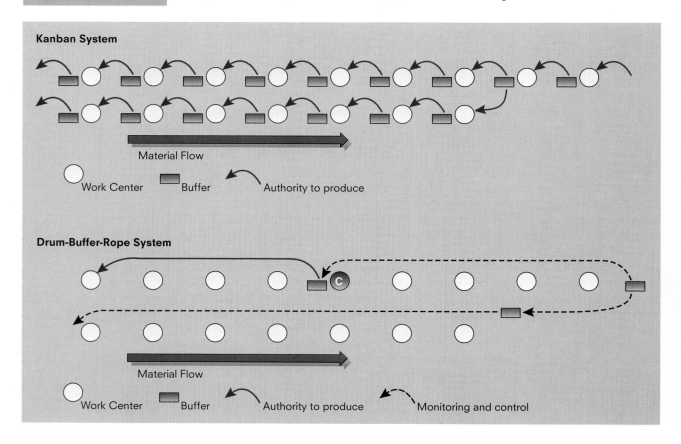

From a more global perspective, both are pull systems linked to the rate of demand, and both focus on continuous improvement. Their approaches vary, however. The JIT system, of which the kanban system is part, minimizes set-up times everywhere, whereas the constraint management system, which incorporates the drum-buffer-rope system, focuses on reducing set-up times only at the constraint. The JIT system has the same size process batch as transfer batch, where constraint management varies the process batch and typically transfers items one at a time to the next work center. Constraint management seeks to improve operations by focusing on the constraint, whereas JIT seeks to eliminate waste and eliminate activities that do not add value everywhere in the organization.

TRADITIONAL SCHEDULING IN JOB SHOP ENVIRONMENTS

Recall from Chapter 7 that the environment of a job shop or process-oriented layout is characterized by product customization. Equipment is grouped together in a functional layout to accommodate the variability from product to product. Because of the routing variability, it is not possible to organize in a product-oriented or flowshop layout. Each product could require a different sequence through the functional departments or work centers. The problem of sequencing jobs or orders at each work center becomes a significant and important task in this environment.

The sequencing decisions are often made with the help of rules that determine the order in which jobs must be completed. If several jobs are waiting to be processed at a work center, as is often the case, the question as to which job should be done next could be answered in a number of ways. Table 16.4 provides some examples of how these decisions are made. The **first-come/first-served (FCFS)** rule is perhaps the most familiar because it is the method used in dealing with customers in most service environments. Individuals get in line as they arrive and wait their turn. In some service environments people take a number to preserve the FCFS sequence.

Another commonly used rule is the **shortest processing time (SPT)** rule. In SPT the job with the shortest processing time is given priority. This rule typically deals effectively with jobs requiring limited amounts of processing but postpones very long jobs indefinitely, often resulting in those jobs being late. In some cases, this rule is used in conjunction with other rules to ensure that long jobs are completed.

The **due date (DD)** rule sequences jobs based on when the jobs must be completed. The job with the earliest due date is given priority. This rule generally performs well in terms of reducing the proportion of jobs that are late. FCFS, SPT, and DD are examples of rules that attempt to determine the sequence at only one operation and are called local priority rules. Although they can be used to schedule any number of workstations, the data that are considered are only relevant to the current work center.

Table 16.4 lists, in addition to these rules, two other rules that include data about other work centers. Critical ratio (CR) and slack per remaining operation (S/RO) acknowledge that the sequence to be done at the current work center should consider other work centers as well. Because they include data about other operations, they are referred to as **global priority rules** and will be addressed in detail following the discussion of local rules.

The priority sequencing rules listed in the table are just a few of the many rules that have been devised. Perhaps one of the reasons there are so many rules is that there does not appear to be one specific rule that is universally accepted as the best for every situation. The example that follows demonstrates how these rules can be used and compared.

FIRST-COME/FIRST-SERVED (FCFS)
A sequencing rule in which orders are processed in the same sequence as they arrived.

SHORTEST PROCESSING TIME (SPT)
A sequencing rule in which orders are processed according to their expected processing times, with shorter times first.

DUE DATE (DD)
A sequencing rule in which orders are processed according to the due dates, with earliest due dates first.

GLOBAL PRIORITY RULES
Sequencing rules that consider information beyond that relating to the operation being sequenced.

TABLE 16.4	**Priority Sequencing Rules**

FCFS	(First-Come/First-Served): Jobs are sequenced based on the time they arrive at a work center, with those arriving first being completed first.
SPT	(Shortest Processing Time): Jobs are sequenced based on the amount of processing time required, with jobs that take the least amount of time being done first.
DD	(Due Date): Jobs are sequenced based on the due date of each job, with the jobs having the earliest due date completed first.
S/RO	(Slack per Remaining Operation): Slack is equal to due date minus remaining processing time. S/RO is the average slack time per remaining operation. Jobs are sequenced based on the S/RO, with the job having the smallest S/RO done first.
CR	(Critical Ratio): Jobs are sequenced based on the ratio of the time remaining until job is due to the time needed to complete the job, with the job having the smallest ratio done first.

EXAMPLE 16.1

Comparison of Local Sequence Rules

The following list of six jobs is presented at a work center for processing. Schedule these jobs using the SPT rule and the DD rule. Which of these approaches is the more effective?

Job Number	Processing Time (a)	Due Date (b)
1	9	15
2	14	32
3	7	29
4	6	16
5	4	12
6	5	36

SOLUTION

The criteria used to compare scheduling rules are based on how late the jobs are, what the average completion time is, and the amount of work-in-process, as measured by the average number of jobs at the work center. In Table 16.5, two additional columns of data have been added to the original data and the jobs have been rearranged by the amount of processing time they require, from shortest to longest. The **Flow Time** column (c) gives the cumulative sum of the processing times. The Days Late column (d) lists zero if the job is early or on time. Otherwise, it is the number of days late as measured by the flow time minus the due date; that is, $d = 0$ if $c \leq b$ and $d = c - b$ if $c > b$. The following definitions permit comparisons of the results of the two approaches:

FLOW TIME
The sum of all processing times of an order.

$$\text{Average completion time} = \frac{\text{flow time}}{\text{number of jobs}}$$

$$\text{Average job lateness} = \frac{\text{days late}}{\text{number of jobs}}$$

$$\text{Average work-in-progress (WIP)} = \frac{\text{flow time}}{\text{processing time}}$$

For the six jobs under consideration, the jobs are first arranged in order based on the processing time (from low to high), as shown in Table 16.5.

The due date schedule is set up in the same way, but the jobs are assigned according to when they are due. Thus, the Due Date column is arranged in ascending order of due dates. Table 16.6 provides the assignments in the due date sequence. As with the SPT, job 5 is done first, followed by jobs 1, 4, 3, 2, and 6.

Note in Example 16.1 that the total processing time is the same for both approaches because the same amount of processing must be done, no matter what the sequence. The average completion time of 21 minutes and the amount of work-in-process of 2.8 for SPT are less than for the DD approach, which has average completion time of 24.5 and work-in-process of 3.27. In general, it can be shown that the SPT rule minimizes the throughput time of the system. The DD rule addresses the due date and generally minimizes lateness, as is true in this case. The DD approach in this example results in an average job lateness of 3.33 days, compared to 4.83 days using the SPT approach. Thus, the rule selected for use

| TABLE 16.5 | | Shortest Processing Time Performance Measures | | |

Job Number	Processing Time a	Due Date b	Flow Time c	Days Late $d*$
5	4	12	4	0
6	5	36	9	0
4	6	16	15	0
3	7	29	22	0
1	9	15	31	16
2	14	32	45	13
Totals	45	140	126	29

Average completion time	$126/6 = 21.00$
Average job lateness	$29/6 = 4.83$
Average number of jobs at work center	$126/45 = 2.80$

$*d = c - b$ if $c > b$; otherwise, the job is not late and $d = 0$.

| TABLE 16.6 | | Due Date Schedule | | |

Job Number	Processing Time	Due Date	Flow Time	Days Late
5	4	12	4	0
1	9	15	13	0
4	6	16	19	3
3	7	29	26	0
2	14	32	40	8
6	5	36	45	9
Totals	45	140	147	20

Average completion time	$147/6 = 24.50$
Average job lateness	$20/6 = 3.33$
Average number of jobs at work center	$147/45 = 3.27$

would depend on whether minimizing throughput time or minimizing lateness is more important.

Because the SPT generally has less work-in-process, it tends to reduce congestion and downstream idle time at the work centers. SPT does not deal effectively with the occasional order that takes an unusually long time to process, however. These orders may never get out of the work center unless a modified rule is used to intervene and move them ahead.

The three local priority rules vary significantly in terms of their performance. Although people generally view the FCFS rule as fair, it usually performs poorly according to all of the performances measures. The DD rule minimizes job lateness but does not perform well according to the other performance measures. The SPT rule performs better than the other two in terms of the amount of WIP and the average completion time, but these advantages become less significant as the overall amount of work in the shop increases.

The global priority rules of slack per remaining operation and critical ratio do not restrict their attention to just one work center but consider other factors that are important to the overall completion of the job. For example, it is important to compare the amount of work to be done at other work centers to the available time until the job's due date. In addition, the number of tasks that remain to be performed should also be taken into consideration.

The two global priority rules presented in Table 16.7 and Table 16.8 should not be compared to local rules because the goals of these approaches are different. Also, after the first job has been completed, the sequence of the remaining jobs may change because all of the remaining jobs have less time until the due date, with no additional processing being done. Because of this, it is necessary to recompute the sequence after the work on each job at each work center has been completed. The use of the rules is illustrated in Example 16.2.

EXAMPLE 16.2

Comparison of Global Sequencing Rules

Five different jobs are currently waiting to be processed at a work center. The processing time at this work center, the remaining processing time left for this job, the number of remaining operations, and the due date are all provided below. Sequence these jobs using the S/RO and the CR rules. An 8-hour workday is assumed.

Job Number	Remaining Processing Time (days)	Time Required for This Operation (days)	Days until Due Date	Remaining Operations
1	18.2	2	24	5
2	17.4	1	30	7
3	11.8	2	28	9
4	9.4	1	20	4
5	30	3	45	6

SOLUTION

Using the slack per remaining operation rule, the amount of slack is computed for each operation and is provided in Table 16.7 along with the S/RO ratios. Job 1 is completed first, followed by jobs 3, 2, 5, and 4. If these jobs are scheduled using the CR rule, computation will show the ratio of the time remaining until the job is due to the total processing time remaining. A number smaller than 1 suggests the job is going to be late. If the ratio is 1, the job will be on time if no delays or idle time occurs. If the ratio is greater than 1, there is some slack time.

In Table 16.8 the ratios have been computed and sequenced from the smallest value to the largest value. Based upon the CR rule, job 1 is completed first, followed by jobs 5, 2, 4, and 3. The two sequencing approaches arrive at the same first job and the same third job, but the other values are different.

TABLE 16.7   **Job Sequencing Using the S/RO Rule**

Job Number	Remaining Processing Time (days) *a*	Time Required for This Operation (days) *b*	Days until Due Date *c*	Remaining Operations *d*	Slack *e* (c − a)	S/RO e/d
1	18.2	2	24	5	5.8	1.16
3	11.8	2	28	9	16.2	1.80
2	17.4	1	30	7	12.6	1.80
5	30.0	3	45	6	15	2.50
4	9.4	1	20	4	10.6	2.65

TABLE 16.8   **Job Sequencing Using the CR Rule**

Job Number	Remaining Processing Time (days)	Time Required for This Operation (days)	Days until Due Date	CR
1	18.2	2	24	1.32
5	28.6	3	45	1.57
2	17.4	1	30	1.72
4	9.4	1	20	2.13
3	11.8	2	28	2.37

SCHEDULING IN SERVICES

Because of the greater degree of customer interaction, services must pay closer attention to customer impressions when sequencing them. When servicing individual customers, most service establishments follow a simple first-come-first-served approach. To improve throughput, however, particularly where the jobs require different amounts of time to complete, such as a supermarket, special express lines have been established for small orders requiring little waiting by the customer. This is actually a special adaptation of the SPT rule. Short jobs are separated from long jobs and given higher priority to reduce their throughput times. In some locations, freeways and interstate highways are designed with express lanes that also allow increased throughput by giving priority to certain "jobs."

In services, scheduling often involves determining when the service is provided because that time has a substantial impact on capacity requirements. If the customer determines when the service must be provided, ways to adjust short-term capacity must be developed. For example, if the demand for tellers at a bank suddenly increases, bank management must have a procedure for dealing with the increase. The solution might be to have loan officers and other managers trained to be tellers. The cross-training of the work force provides short-term help by temporarily rescheduling the work force to adjust to the

To improve the efficiency, speed, and responsiveness of customer service, Long Island Lighting Company developed a mobile communications system. This system facilitates the scheduling of more than 800,000 gas and electric service requests Long Island Lighting receives each year. The new technology enables field workers like the gas customer service specialist shown here to work more efficiently with repair crews and to provide automatic job-status feedback. It also allows customers to schedule routine work at their convenience.

Source Courtesy of Long Island Lighting Company.

variability in demand. For some services, the productive use of expensive equipment is critical to the firm's success. In these instances, the techniques that manufacturers use can often be applied, as Box 16.3 suggests.

If a firm is able to determine when the service is provided, techniques such as reservations and appointments are useful. In appointment systems, the customer is assigned a time when the service will be performed. These approaches are used by many professionals such as doctors, lawyers, and dentists. In each case, the availability of the professional's time is the system's constraint. The rate at which the professional can provide the service must approximate the appointment schedule. When appointments are used and where the rate at which customers are scheduled exceeds the rate at which the service is provided, the customer will have to wait longer than necessary. Quite often professionals maintain a buffer of clients so that if one client is served very quickly or if one doesn't show up, the professional would not be idle. Doctors' offices do this quite frequently, often giving patients an appointment time that is actually an hour before the service will be performed. This ensures that the doctor is able to process as many patients as possible and is never idle. Too large a time buffer, especially in highly competitive services, however, may result in lost customers. A buffer is usually necessary in order to deal with late arrivals and no-shows, but determining the best size for that time buffer is not easy.

Another option for scheduling services is the use of reservations to link each unit of demand to a specific resource. The resources may be rental cars, seats on an airline, hotel rooms, or seats in a restaurant. Reservations can help more fully utilize resources and can also assist in determining the work force demands by providing management with advance knowledge of demand.

Some organizations use a backlog when scheduling services. Rather than use reservations, some restaurants have customers sign in when they arrive, and provide the service

OPERATIONS OUTLOOK

BOX 16.3

JIT Scheduling for Airline Turnarounds

As any frequent flier knows, airlines have difficulties scheduling plane flights. Baggage must be stowed, cabins must be cleaned, supplies must be loaded, planes must be refueled, and passengers laden with carry-on luggage must be accommodated. All of this means that, even on a good day, customers sometimes have to wait. In the summer of 1994, some U.S. airlines—including USAir, United Airlines, and Continental—began to address this problem with an approach called "quick-turn."

Employing setup time reduction techniques common to JIT systems, the quick-turn approach calls for some turnaround tasks to be accomplished before a plane lands. For example, instead of waiting for the plane to empty so catering can determine what supplies and what kind of cleaning will be required, flight attendants are asked to report this information to the pilot. The pilot calls ahead to catering, who can then perform the necessary tasks quickly once the plane has landed and the passengers are off. In addition, some turnaround tasks are simplified or eliminated altogether. Quick-turn flights are often stripped of pillows and blankets,

for example, to reduce the amount of straightening that needs to be done after passengers deplane. And because oversize luggage impedes the boarding process, carry-on luggage on USAir flights must fit in a "sizer box" to determine in advance if it can go into the overhead compartment.

The quick-turn system has shown some early success. At USAir, for example, the daily average of flights has risen from 6 to 7, which means that USAir is able to sell 12,000 more seats a day. But the system is not without disadvantages. If weather or mechanical difficulties cause takeoff or landing delays, it can be hard to get quick-turn schedules back on track. And if several quick-turns are going on at the same time, equipment shortages can develop. Both USAir and Continental have run into problems keeping quick-turn schedules in fog-prone cities—and no airline has tested the system in winter.

Source "New Airline Fad: Faster Airport Turnarounds," *The Wall Street Journal*, August 4, 1994, sec. B, 1,7.

---

when the first opportunity presents itself. This system also provides the restaurant an opportunity to increase drink sales in the bar while customers are waiting for a table. A variation of this system, used by auto repair shops, dry cleaners, film processors, and the like, occurs when an item is brought for service, and the service is promised at some point later in time. Some services, such as 1-day and 2-day mail services and photo development centers, charge more for rapid service.

SUMMARY

The role that scheduling plays in an organization is very important. In a manufacturing environment, effective scheduling enhances the firm's ability to provide consistent on-time delivery of products and do it faster than competitors. This ability provides the company with competitive advantages related to dependability of delivery and response time.

In services, because of the interaction with the customer, scheduling plays a significant role in determining the quality of service a customer receives. Most customers are not interested in a quality service in the future; they want quality service now. By enabling a company to provide its services when customers want them, effective scheduling can provide an advantage that may differentiate one service organization from another.

The scheduling function has been enhanced during the last decade with the introduction of JIT and constraint management techniques. As quality and time become more important for manufacturers and services, scheduling effectiveness has become and will continue to be even more important.

GM&P REVISITED

CROSS-LINKS   Would the quantity of files in the system be a concern for GM&P? What would be the effect of a large quantity of files in process?

Could a pull system like kanban be utilized effectively in this environment? Would it make sense to develop an appointment system that forced clients to hold onto their own files until the system needed them?

What role would the constraining department play? How might it be protected from disruptions? Might drum-buffer-rope be implemented effectively in this environment?

QUESTIONS FOR REVIEW

1. How is a Gantt chart used?
2. What is kanban? How is it used?
3. How is the schedule leveled in a JIT environment?
4. Describe how the drum-buffer-rope scheduling process works.
5. In what ways are drum-buffer-rope and kanban scheduling alike? In what ways are they different?
6. Describe how the due date and shortest processing time rules work.
7. What is the difference between a local and a global sequencing rule?
8. How do the critical ratio and slack per remaining operation take into consideration other work or other work centers?
9. What is the difference between scheduling using an appointment or using a reservation?

QUESTIONS FOR THOUGHT AND DISCUSSION

1. Discuss how the drum-buffer-rope process would work as a scheduling approach at a doctor's office.
2. Discuss the role that scheduling plays in developing a competitive advantage in services.
3. Discuss the effects of changing the number of kanbans in a system.

INTEGRATIVE QUESTIONS

1. How can scheduling be used to develop a competitive advantage?
2. Describe the linkage between capacity management and scheduling.
3. For a manufacturer to meet customer due dates, what must be the connection between scheduling and inventory management?

PROBLEMS

1. Six jobs, their processing times, and due dates are given below (stated in days).
   a. Using the SPT and DD rules, schedule the six jobs.
   b. Compute the average completion times, tardiness, and WIP for each rule and discuss the results.

Job Number	Processing Time	Due Date
1	9	13
2	14	19
3	7	27
4	12	16
5	5	8
6	8	33

2. Work center 101 has six jobs in queue ready to be scheduled. The processing times and due dates in days are also provided.
   a. Using the SPT and DD rules, schedule the six jobs.
   b. Compute the average completion times, tardiness, and WIP for each rule and discuss the results.

Job Number	Processing Time	Due Date
1	4	12
2	15	32
3	5	14
4	10	34
5	11	41
6	12	36

3. Consider the following six jobs, their due dates, and processing times in days.
   a. Schedule these jobs using the first-come-first-served rule, the shortest processing time rule, and the due date rule.

b. Compute the average completion time, average job lateness, and average WIP for each and discuss the results.

Job Number	Processing Time	Due Date
1	12	15
2	7	22
3	11	31
4	10	18
5	8	10
6	4	30

4. Consider the following six jobs (stated in hours). Schedule them using the slack per remaining operation. Assume that the first job has been completed and then reschedule the remaining operations. Does the sequence change? How?

Job Number	1	2	3	4	5	6
Work hours remaining	15	10	8	6	10	7
Hours required for this operation	2	2	3	2	3	6
Due date	25	19	20	17	28	15
Remaining operations	5	4	6	5	7	5

5. Use the critical ratio approach and schedule the jobs at this work center.

Job Number	Total Time	Total Time until Due Date
1	18	35
2	14	26
3	16	24
4	10	20
5	21	24

6. Use the critical ratio method and the slack per remaining operation method to schedule the following jobs. Discuss the results.

Job Number	1	2	3	4	5	6
Work hours remaining	15	17	21	7	8	10
Hours required for this operation	2	1	3	1	4	2
Due date	14	32	45	20	10	21
Remaining operations	3	4	5	3	1	3

SUGGESTED READINGS

Johnson, S. M. "Optimal Two Stage and Three Stage Production Scheduling with Setup Times Included." *Naval Logistics Quarterly* (March 1954): 61–68.

Reimer, G. "Material Requirements Planning and Theory of Constraints: Can They Coexist? A Case Study." *Production and Inventory Management Journal* 32 (Fourth Quarter 1991): 48–52.

Schragenheim, E., and B. Ronen. "Buffer Management: A Diagnostic Tool for Production Control." *Production and Inventory Management Journal* 32 (Fourth Quarter 1991): 74–79.

Taylor, S. G., and S. F. Bolander. "Process Flow Scheduling: Basic Cases." *Production and Inventory Management Journal* 31 (Third Quarter 1990): 1–4.

Umble, M., and M. L. Srikanth. *Synchronous Manufacturing: Principles of World Class Excellence*. Cincinnati, Ohio: South Western, 1990.

MANAGEMENT OF BUFFERS IN DRUM-BUFFER-ROPE

This supplement is intended to provide a more detailed and extended discussion of drum-buffer-rope. The problem presented in Chapter 16, as well as several exhibits, is presented here again for convenience and continuity.

Two products, A and B, are produced. Product A has a $30 raw material cost, and requires 15 minutes of processing on machine M1, 25 minutes on M2, and 30 minutes on M3. Product A sells for $200. There is a weekly demand for 60 units of A. Product B has a $40 raw material cost, and requires 20 minutes of processing time on machine M2, 10 minutes on M1, followed by 25 minutes on M4. There is a weekly demand for 80 units of product B. Product B's selling price is $150. Machines M1, M3, and M4 require 60 minutes of setup time prior to any operation. Machine M2 requires 25 minutes for setup. Weekly fixed expenses of $12,000 exist. See Figure 16.S1 for this scenario.

Table 16.S1 provides the constraint schedule, and Figure 16.S2 demonstrates how a 240-minute constraint buffer affects the start time for product A.

If a 240-minute shipping buffer is used in addition to the 240-minute constraint buffer shown in Figure 16.S2, the start time for product A is further changed. Product A would be released to the system 550 minutes prior ($T - 550$) to its due date. The effect that both of these buffers has on timing is presented in Figure 16.S3.

Suppose M1 broke down for 80 minutes while processing product A. What would be the effect? The immediate effect would be that product A would not arrive at the constraint buffer prior to M2 at $T - 535$ as planned. If there were an 80-minute delay, it would arrive at the buffer at $T - 455$.

Because it doesn't need to begin processing on M2 until $T - 295$, it is not late. In fact, it is still 160 minutes early. It will start on M2 on time because there is no threat to meeting its due date. All orders released to the system are released using similar logic, so the buffer in front of M2 consists of 240 minutes of work *if no disruptions are occurring*. However, if disruptions occur, such as the 80-minute delay of product A, a hole or an absence or inventory will be created in the buffer.

If product A arrives at the buffer at $T - 535$, it will enter the buffer, and 25 minutes later, at $T - 510$, it will be in the position as shown in the closeup view of the 240-minute buffer in Figure 16.S4.

Sixty minutes later, at $T - 450$, product A will have moved in the buffer to the position shown in Figure 16.S5. Keep in mind that there are other products in front of A waiting to be processed at M2 and others coming into the buffer behind A.

Requirements for Products A and B

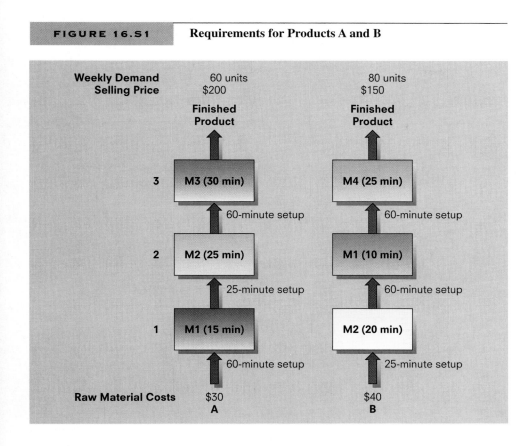

		60 units	80 units
Weekly Demand		60 units	80 units
Selling Price		$200	$150

Finished Product / Finished Product

Raw Material Costs $30 $40
A   B

Product A will leave the buffer to begin processing on M2 at $T - 295$. If a disruption delays the arrival of product A to the buffer, the void created by product A's absence will move through the buffer just as product A would have. The farther this hole penetrates the buffer, the closer product A is to actually starting late on M2. If the hole penetrates completely through the buffer, product A will not begin processing on M2 at $T - 295$. M2 will not be idle, however, because it can begin processing the products that have come into the buffer behind the hole.

When A does arrive, it will be processed. Starting late on M2 will not mean that product A will be completed late and miss its due date, however. Keep in mind that there is also

The Constraint Schedule for M2

Product	Setup	Quantity Produced	Total Time	Start Time	Finish Time
A	25	30	775	0	775
B	25	20	425	775	1,200
A	25	30	775	1,200	1,975
B	25	20	425	1,975	2,400

| **FIGURE 16.S2** | **Effect of Buffer on Timing of Product A** |

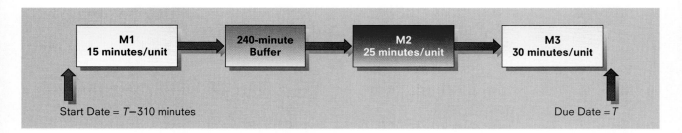

| **FIGURE 16.S3** | **Timing Effects of Time Buffers** |

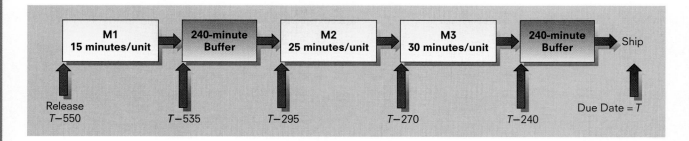

| **FIGURE 16.S4** | **Closeup View of Constraint Buffer** |

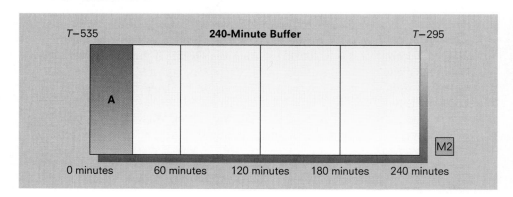

a 240-minute shipping buffer. Late completion on M2 merely means that product A will not arrive at the shipping buffer at $T - 240$. In other words, it will not arrive at shipping as early as had been planned. Failure to arrive at the shipping buffer at $T - 240$ will create a hole in the shipping buffer just as was the case when it arrived late to the constraint buffer. If the hole completely penetrates the shipping buffer, product A will, in fact, miss its due date.

Management monitors the holes in time buffers to provide an early warning of potential problems. Because buffers are established to protect constraints and due date perfor-

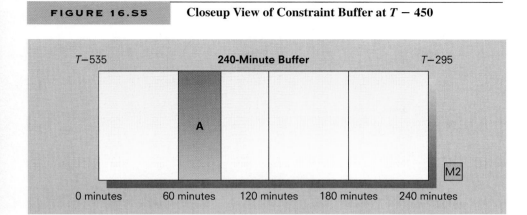

FIGURE 16.S5   **Closeup View of Constraint Buffer at $T - 450$**

mance against disruption, it is expected that there will be holes in the buffer. In fact, if a buffer never has holes in it, there are no disruptions, and therefore, there is no need for the buffer.

PROBLEMS

1. (Refer to Figures 16S.4 and 16S.5) Suppose product A has a due date of T and the constraint and shipping buffers are each 6 hours. When would the raw materials need to be released in order to satisfy the due date requirements?

2. (Refer to Exhibits 16S.4 and 16S.5) Suppose the shipping buffer for product B is 8 hours. If the due date is T, what is the start date? Note, because the constraint is the first operation, there is no need to protect the constraint.

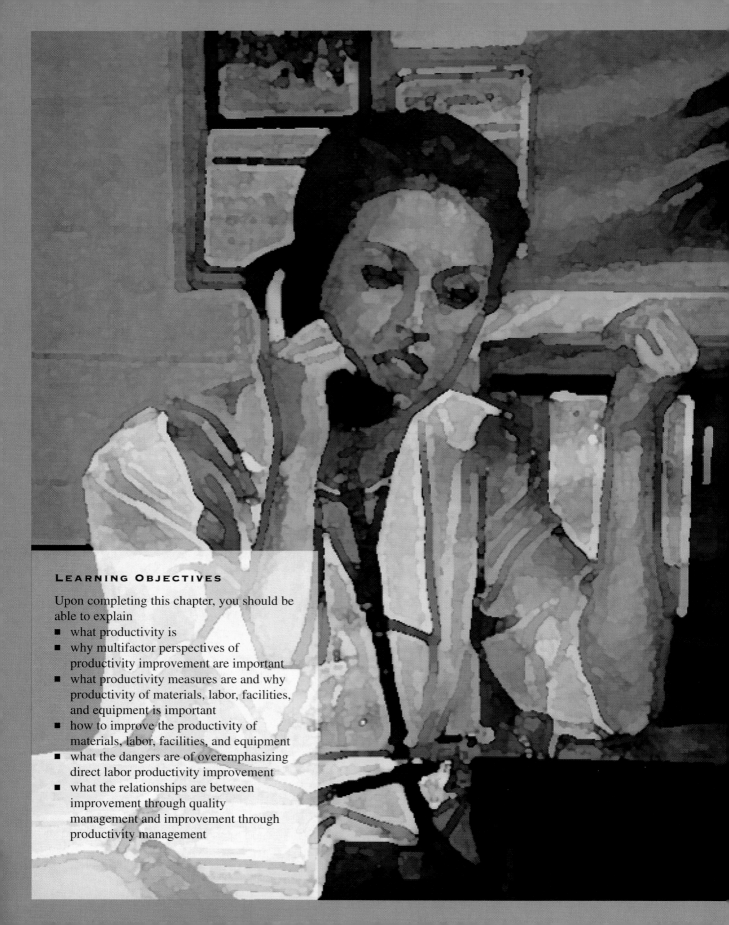

CHAPTER 17

SYSTEM IMPROVEMENT THROUGH PRODUCTIVITY MANAGEMENT

CROSS-LINKS **Accumold's Cost Accountant Goes on the Job Market**

Accumold is a supplier of original equipment plastic parts to the auto industry. Its products include such items as interior trim molding for doors and seats, dashboard components, door handles, window cranks, and steering wheels. Accumold has 11 production facilities. ■ A loud click was the final sound Monica heard before the phone went dead. Monica Seitz was the manager of cost accounting for Accumold's Dayton plant. Her truncated conversation was with Angela Hill, corporate controller. As manager of cost accounting, Angela was in charge of monitoring various performance measures and comparing them to corporate standards. For example, she tracked cost per unit for each product, broken down into direct labor, indirect labor, materials, and overhead. Whenever there was a significant variance from the standard, Angela would call for an explanation. She had to ensure this information was relayed to other managers in the plant to reduce variances. Although Monica did not have supervisory responsibility over the other managers, she often conveyed information to them from Angela's office, so they usually responded to her differently than they did to others. ■ Monica was beginning to think she was dealing with a Jekyll-and-Hyde controller, who vacillated between high praise and severe criticism. Two weeks ago Angela praised the Dayton facility for its ability to reduce inventory levels. It was the only plant of all 11 that had met the corporate goals to reduce inventory by 30 percent. Although Monica felt good about the accomplishment, she also knew that the plant had met inventory reduction goals before, only to see inventory climb back up to previous

levels. ■ It didn't surprise Monica that Angela reacted sternly to this month's cost variances. Indirect labor was up for all manufactured items. There was no denying the fact that increased use of overtime had increased labor costs. In fact, the Dayton plant was Accumold's biggest user of overtime. ■ "This is the same pattern we went through last time," Monica recalled as she thought about the last failed effort to reduce inventory levels. "As we reduced production batch quantities, our quality started to improve, we began to respond more quickly to our customer orders, and we could actually see products flow through the plant." ■ That was history, though, because customers were now complaining about their delivery times. She dreaded the next call from Angela. It would be about her monthly scrap report that had been sent to corporate headquarters that morning. Angela would have it by late afternoon. It contained the largest write-off she had ever made for discarded products. A 3-months' supply of steering wheels, over 6,000 units, had been scrapped because the auto manufacturer changed designs. ■ The ringing of her phone interrupted her thoughts. It was Stan Schaeffer, manager of manufacturing, responding to a message she had left earlier. ■ "What's this about production runs on the steering wheel line?" Stan asked. ■ "I just got chewed out by Angela Hill for this month's labor variances," Monica said. "Our overtime is killing our numbers and, as I see it, the overtime is due to the increased number of setups we're doing. We need to double the batch size on all steering wheel runs to cut down on setups and eliminate overtime." ■ Stan was surprised at the about-face but responded with a cheerful, "Whatever you say!" ■ As Monica drove home from work that night, she couldn't help thinking about the problems at work. "I wish I could get a thorough enough understanding of the link between inventory levels and these variances," she thought to herself. "This is the second time we've cycled through this, and unless it's resolved, we'll probably do it again. Why can our competitors reduce inventory levels, but whenever we try it, our costs go through the roof?" ■ At work the next morning, she spent an hour reviewing the costs and inventory levels from the monthly reports during the plant's previous inventory reduction push. She left her office to get a cup of coffee, and on the way, was chastised by Ron Larch, the plant manager. He was fuming and wanted to know why she had doubled the batch size on the steering wheel line. "Don't you know that the only way we can reduce work-in-process inventory is by reducing the batch quantity? Didn't you learn anything from scrapping all of those excess steering wheels? We'll get chewed out if our inventory levels rise! Especially after we were so successful at reducing them!" ■ When she returned to her office, her secretary buzzed her, "Angela Hill is on line 3. She's been on hold for 5 minutes." ■ "It's time to update my resumé," Monica thought as she picked up the phone. ■

From the outset, this text has emphasized the importance of the strategic priorities of the firm and the role of operations in meeting these priorities. The popular philosophies of TQM, JIT, and constraint management were presented early in the text to enable aspects of these approaches to be better integrated into other discussions. Various chapters also stressed the importance of planning and decision making in ensuring the availability and timeliness of capacity, facilities, and materials. This text began and will end with an emphasis on improvement. This chapter, devoted to productivity improvement, presents several concepts, all related to improving the conversion processes managed by the operations function.

Just as improved quality translates into increased value for the customer and, when applied to every aspect of the business, enhances the firm's ability to compete on all competitive priorities, productivity improvement can also enhance all competitive priorities. It often goes hand-in-hand with TQM, JIT, and constraint management. It should not be surprising that as a firm increases the accuracy and quality level of all business functions, it also increases productivity. In fact, many firms implementing TQM are interested in the productivity improvements as well as quality improvements. It is often impossible to separate quality from productivity. JIT and constraint management implementations are also contributing to productivity improvements for many firms, and as will be discussed later in the chapter, they provide many useful tools.

To best understand the concept of productivity improvement, it is useful to recall from the beginning of this text, that the operations function is responsible for the value-adding conversion of inputs to outputs, as shown in Figure 17.1.

It is also useful to reexamine the concept of productivity. Recall the following productivity equation:

$$\text{Productivity} = \frac{\text{outputs}}{\text{inputs}} \tag{17.1}$$

The effectiveness of the conversion process can be described in terms of productivity because productivity describes how well inputs are used in obtaining outputs. Improving the

FIGURE 17.1   **Traditional View of Value-Adding Conversion Process**

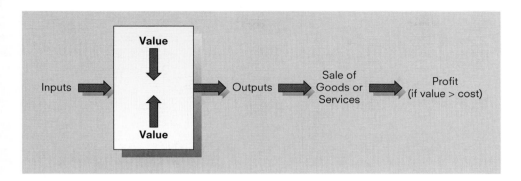

effectiveness of this process, through productivity improvement, can have dramatic effects on the competitive priorities of price, quality, dependability, flexibility, and time. The productivity equation shows that productivity can be improved by increasing the size of the numerator (outputs) or by decreasing the size of the denominator (inputs). Many productivity improvement efforts strive to do both.

Competitive capabilities result from a firm's ability to group resources together, not from merely possessing resources. Productivity improvement frequently results not from increasing the resources, but from improving the way groups of resources interact.

By examining the operations function from a broader perspective the concept of productivity improvement is broadened as well. Notice in Figure 17.1 that value must be added during the conversion process for the outputs to generate revenues. Productivity improvement also occurs, from the customer's perspective, when the value of outputs is increased. From the customer's perspective, the increase in the output's value is a more productive use of input resources.

Many organizations have committed themselves to an environment of continuous improvement of quality and productivity through the implementation of TQM, JIT, or constraint management efforts. When making this commitment for an organization, managers must recognize that continuous improvement requires continuous change. Change is always difficult to manage. Continuous change requires exceptional levels of skill at both the management and employee levels.

MEASURING PRODUCTIVITY

As a prerequisite to productivity improvement, just as in quality improvement, the organization must recognize its current position and be able to identify changes through measurement. There are literally hundreds of productivity measures in use in business today. Many have their roots in Frederick Taylor's research. They range from the most global measures of business productivity, such as return on investment (ROI), to the most specific, such as the efficiency of one machine. Although certain precautions must be taken when using measures of productivity, measurement is an extremely important part of the

TABLE 17.1		Two-Year Productivity Trends for a Tire Company		
Year	**Product**	**Units Produced**	**Price**	**Sales**
1986	A	2,000	$10	$20,000
1986	B	2,000	$20	$40,000
1987	A	1,000	$25	$25,000
1987	B	3,000	$20	$60,000

Source   Adapted from W. B. Chew, "No-Nonsense Guide to Measuring Productivity," *Harvard Business Review* (January-February 1988): 110–118.

improvement process. A firm can only recognize productivity improvement through the improvement of productivity measures. In order to gain a thorough understanding of the opportunities available and the approaches used for productivity improvement, managers must first understand the types of inputs and outputs that are of concern.

Because businesses monitoring productivity measures are often involved in continuous improvement efforts, they must monitor trends in the measures. Interpreting trends is not always easy, however, particularly from ambiguous measures. The data presented in Table 17.1 provide an excellent example of the problem of interpreting ambiguous data. The source of the data is a tire manufacturer.

Table 17.1 shows that it is impossible to determine if productivity has improved from 1986 to 1987. For example, the change in output of total units is 0% (4,000 units each year). Using actual prices, sales increased from $60,000 to $85,000, a change of +41.7% (an increase of $25,000). But if 1987 sales are viewed in terms of 1986 prices, total sales only increased to $70,000, a charge of 16.7%. If instead 1986 sales are considered in terms of 1987 prices, sales totals actually decline from $90,000 in 1986 to $85,000 the following year, a change of −5.6%. This example demonstrates the importance of appropriate measures if a company is to monitor useful and accurate measures of productivity.

MANAGING INPUTS AND OUTPUTS

REDUCTION IN INPUTS

For most businesses, inputs to conversion processes are not free. Inputs include such resources as materials, labor, facilities, energy, and equipment. A firm that can reap the same quantity and value of outputs, but through the consumption of fewer inputs, reduces costs and increases productivity. Increasing productivity by eliminating those inputs that do not add value and minimizing others is known as **lean production.**

LEAN PRODUCTION
Eliminating nonvalue-adding inputs as a way to increase productivity.

Depending on the nature of the inputs reduced, fixed or variable costs will be affected. Variable costs are frequently (and sometimes unfortunately) targeted for short-term gains because the impact is more immediate. Thus firms frequently try to reduce direct labor in an effort to improve productivity. Chew provides an excellent example of this tendency and its potential result in the description of a large New York bank.[1] After expressing concern about labor costs, the bank implemented a productivity measurement system called *transactions per employee* to measure productivity. The program was given a significant amount of attention. The results were even used to determine bonuses for line managers.

The program resulted in an increase in productivity in every department except data processing. Even though staff shrunk elsewhere, data processing came under greater pressure because many operations had been computerized in the effort to boost productivity. The data processing department was forced to increase its staff and add more software and hardware. In this situation, management focused its attention on direct labor and ignored overhead. As a result, the bank merely traded reduced direct labor costs for increased overhead costs. This example supports Chew's emphasis on the simultaneous use of several measures of productivity, known as a **multifactor perspective.** This reduces the likelihood that increases in productivity by one measure will come at the expense of another. Any net reduction in either fixed or variable inputs, however, will result in an increase in productivity if outputs remain stable.

Increasing productivity by reducing inputs can be effective, but using this approach as the only means of improving productivity is dangerous. In the United States, businesses have traditionally focused on this approach to productivity improvement and have neglected efforts to increase outputs, such as those that would result from investments in training and innovation.[2]

MULTIFACTOR PERSPECTIVE
Measuring productivity using several measures simultaneously.

INCREASING OUTPUTS

The alternative to reducing the cost, or input, side of the productivity ratio is to increase the output side. This approach does not result in total cost reduction but may result in a reduction in the cost per unit. For example, if through reduced waste, a restaurant can produce 14 rather than 12 pizzas from a box of dough mix, productivity of inputs increases, total costs stay the same, but costs per unit drop.

If the market can consume the additional outputs, revenues increase, and because costs stayed the same, profits and ROI improve. Unfortunately, day-to-day actions aren't always motivated by profit and ROI. They are frequently motivated by a measure that is much easier to monitor—cost. Because costs are much easier than profit or ROI to measure locally, they are often used in individual departments. The basic assumption is that if costs are reduced, ROI and profits must be improved. But this is not necessarily the case. Because of the tendency to use cost reduction as a measure of productivity improvement, cost-cutting efforts are common. Managers must be very careful, however, when their objective is to reduce costs, particularly cost per unit, because cost per unit is most easily decreased by increasing the volume of output. But by now it should be clear that if the market cannot consume the additional products, increasing the volume of output will increase inventory levels. The result is that the cost per unit drops, but the total direct costs remain the same. Because of the increase in inventory, overhead costs actually increase, and as total costs increase, profit and ROI will actually drop.

The following sections provide specific approaches for measuring and improving productivity. In each case, the common productivity measures specific to the input being

---

[1]W. B. Chew, "No-Nonsense Guide to Measuring Productivity," *Harvard Business Review* 66 (January-February 1988): 110–118.

[2]Thomas A. Stewart, "U.S. Productivity: First but Fading," *Fortune,* October 19, 1992, 55.

discussed are provided. Notice that the productivity measures are of the form presented in equation 17.1, the ratio of outputs to inputs. Cautions concerning various productivity measures are also presented, when appropriate.

PRODUCTIVITY OF MATERIALS

INVENTORY TURNS
A commonly used measure to evaluate the productivity of materials or inventory: the number of times that inventory cycles in a year.

A commonly used measure for the productivity of materials or inventory is inventory turnover, commonly known as **inventory turns**. Inventory turns measure the number of times that inventory cycles in a year, and it is computed by the following formula:

$$\frac{\text{Sales dollars}}{\text{Average inventory level in dollars}} \qquad \textbf{(17.2)}$$

Firms frequently divide their inventory investment into three groups: raw materials, work-in-process, and finished goods. Firms that want to increase the productivity of material inputs would try to increase the overall turns as well as the turns of each inventory category. The basic logic behind this objective is to maximize the return on the investment in inventory. This can be accomplished in two ways. First, by reducing the total amount of inventory through effective independent and dependent demand inventory management, the dollar investment is reduced. If the return is the same, the inventory ROI increases. Second, by reducing the amount of time the money is tied up in the inventory, the return on investment is increased. This is because the return on any investment is improved if the same yield can be obtained in a shorter amount of time. Reducing batch sizes at all levels accomplishes both objectives. Inventory levels drop, and remaining inventory moves through the system faster. The JIT approaches to reducing inventory levels and speeding up material flow are useful in improving the productivity of materials. Accurate record-keeping, made possible through cycle counting, makes lower levels of inventory and faster inventory cycles more feasible.

The productivity of material is also affected by wasted material. Waste comes in many forms, but it is frequently manifested in services and manufacturing in the form of defects. Both defects and yield loss mean that material inputs to the conversion process never made it to the finished product state. Thus, the amount of inputs required for the desired amount of outputs is higher than it should be. Defects and yield loss not only reduce productivity of material inputs, but they also waste the labor, energy, and equipment time that went into their production. Reduction of defects and yield loss can contribute significantly to reducing the denominator of the productivity equation. Statistical process control techniques are excellent methods for improving productivity by eliminating defects and yield loss.

Many firms have increased the rate of material flow through the productive system by using automated materials handling systems. Automated materials handling systems range from automated conveyors to driverless forklifts, known as automatic guided vehicles (AGVs). For example, Acxiom Mailing Services, a direct-mail services provider, uses an automatic guided vehicle system to transport raw materials from its warehouse to its production plant. The system, which can carry up to 8,000 pounds, has increased output and cut costs considerably. Such systems require a significant up-front investment to increase the rate and constancy of the flow of materials in manufacturing operations or, in the case of services, to automate the movement of such items as forms, documents, packages, or luggage. For many manufacturers, the use of automated materials handling systems has enabled them to maintain extremely small transfer batches, smoothing flows, leveling demand on work centers, making scheduling easier and more effective, and reducing quality feedback time.

Intel Corporation uses monorail systems to transfer loads of wafers between production stations, speeding production and increasing efficiency and yields. Improved output at its factories helps Intel respond quickly to faster-than-anticipated growth for its new generation of silicon chips.

Source   Courtesy of Intel Corporation.

PRODUCTIVITY OF LABOR

Businesses measure the productivity of workers in a number of ways. A common measure of the productivity of an individual worker or work center is *efficiency,* which is the ratio of actual output to the standard output, or

$$\frac{\text{Actual output}}{\text{Standard output}} \qquad \textbf{(17.3)}$$

A more global measure of the productivity of the entire work force is simply the sales output divided by the number of workers:

$$\frac{\text{Sales output}}{\text{Number of workers}} \qquad \textbf{(17.4)}$$

This value provides an indicator of overall worker productivity, particularly when compared to industry averages, and it is also frequently used to compare the productivity of one country to another. It is often as much a measure of white-collar productivity, however, because for many industries, the cost of direct labor is small compared to indirect labor and overhead costs, which include many of the white-collar support staff. Despite the fact that direct labor accounts for a relatively small proportion of the cost for most products, direct labor productivity is frequently given the most attention when improvements are needed because direct labor costs are assumed to be variable.

A focus on the direct labor productivity for a particular product might use labor dollars per unit:

$$\frac{\text{Labor dollars}}{\text{Unit}}$$

(17.5)

Productivity problems related to direct labor are typically blamed on the laborers themselves. But two points must be recognized. First, for many businesses, particularly manufacturers, direct labor costs as a percentage of total costs are quite small, frequently less than 10 percent. The potential for cost savings is not nearly as great as in other areas. In addition, for most companies, direct labor costs are not truly variable in the sense of being directly proportional to the volume of products. Because workers are guaranteed pay for 40 hours per week and the pay is not directly related to the number of products produced but rather to the hours worked, labor costs are essentially fixed for many firms. Second, management is responsible for grouping resources together to form competitive priorities. Management decides how to use resources. Productivity problems related to labor are often the result of these management decisions.

Some industries, particularly those that produce large, labor-intensive items such as automobiles, monitor the number of labor hours that go into an average product. These measures are also useful when comparing different businesses in the same industry. For example, in 1992, Ford required one-third fewer labor hours than General Motors to produce an automobile. This labor difference translated into an average cost advantage of $795 per vehicle. Ford used 7.25 hours to produce the stampings for the average vehicle, down 50 percent from 1980. During the same year, however, Japanese auto manufacturers needed only 3.5 hours to accomplish the same stampings.[3]

As has been mentioned previously, productivity must be measured if it is to be improved. For many repetitive jobs, the measurement is efficiency. Most jobs directly related to the production of a good or service, particularly those that are repetitive in nature, have been designed and monitored to the point that a standard for output has been created. For example, a standard for serving customers at a fast-food restaurant might be 35 customers per hour. If, on the average, an employee was able to service only 28 customers per hour, the employee would be operating at only 80% efficiency. Efficiencies are not only used to help determine appropriate projections of available capacity in capacity planning, but they are also useful in measuring the productivity of workers. Suboptimal worker efficiencies however are not the problem, they are symptoms of problems. Their cause might lie in poor quality materials, bad process design, failure to maintain equipment, ineffective training, conflicting instructions, or a number of other management responsibilities as well as motivational or attitudinal difficulties with employees.

The use of efficiency as a measure of labor productivity at the work center level requires that actual output be compared to a standard. A standard is the amount of work a trained worker of average ability is able to do for an 8-hour period. Standards can be created in a number of ways. Two common approaches are using stopwatch time studies or predetermined motion times. Both of these approaches are appropriate for repetitive tasks.

STOPWATCH TIME STUDIES

Stopwatch time studies require that a worker be observed for a long enough time to ensure that a representative sample of repetitions has been observed and timed. The observations must also extend over a long enough period to include aspects of the job that are not per-

---

[3]"A Decisive Response to Crisis Brought Ford Enhanced Productivity," *The Wall Street Journal,* December 15, 1992, sec. A, 1, 13.

formed frequently, such as adjusting equipment or replenishing raw materials. The average task time is calculated and is known as the **observed time.**

The observed time must be adjusted for the worker's pace. Keep in mind that the standard should be appropriate for the average individual. The observed worker may not be average. A **performance rating** is used to increase or decrease the observed time so that it is more representative of the average worker, based on the observer's perceptions of the worker and what an average worker would accomplish.

As is shown in equation 17.6, the observed time multiplied by the performance rating is known as the **normal time.** The normal time is the time it should take a typical qualified worker to complete the task.

$$\text{Normal time} = (\text{observed time})(\text{performance rating}) \qquad \textbf{(17.6)}$$

Normal time is adjusted by another set of factors, known as allowances, to yield the standard time, as shown in equation 17.7. An **allowance** is added as a percentage of the standard time to allow for personal time and rest periods.

$$\text{Standard time} = (\text{normal time})(\text{allowance}) \qquad \textbf{(17.7)}$$

PREDETERMINED MOTION TIMES

Predetermined motion times take advantage of the fact that almost any job can be broken down into a number of basic worker motions. By using a database of basic motions and related times, a standard for a particular job can be developed. Because of the thousands of observations used in the development of the motion times, the job time developed from their use does not need to be normalized. Jobs must be precisely defined in order to use this approach. The use of predetermined motion times has several advantages over stopwatch time studies. First, workers often consider it intrusive and offensive when people observe and time them for long periods. Second, standards for jobs not yet in existence can be developed using predetermined motion times. Third, the standards created by predetermined motion times are more accurate and will be more consistent than those created by stopwatch time studies. One of the best known systems for predetermined motion times is Methods–Time Measurement (MTM). Under this system, the predetermined time values are contained in basic motion tables. Researchers developed the tables by using film analysis to calculate the time required for basic motions such as reach, move, and turn.

Unfortunately, the measurement of productivity for white-collar workers is not as easy or as developed as that of repetitive labor. As has been mentioned earlier, productivity measurement is a prerequisite to productivity improvement. The failure of businesses to measure white-collar productivity effectively has lead to the poor white-collar productivity that currently exists and the tendency for many businesses to make massive cuts in midmanagement staff.

JOB ANALYSIS

Various approaches to job design and job analysis are used to identify ways to improve worker productivity. The use of flowcharts to model the activities performed in a job and provide a way to analyze and improve the activities is quite common. This type of analysis is often needed when workers particularly dislike or complain about a job, turnover is high, or there has been an injury on the job.

Another commonly used approach to increasing worker productivity is known as **work sampling.** Work sampling involves random observation of an employee so that the

---

OBSERVED TIME
Average task time based on observation during a time study.

PERFORMANCE RATING
Observed time adjusted to be representative of the average worker (based on the observer's perceptions).

NORMAL TIME
The time that it takes for a typical qualified worker to complete a given task.

ALLOWANCE
Normal time adjusted to yield a standard time; allowances take into account personal time and rest periods.

WORK SAMPLING
A work measurement technique involving random observations of employees to determine how they spend their time.

At Bank of Boston, quality improvement teams are reshaping the way customers are served by changing the way work gets done. To improve customer service, teams are eliminating unproductive tasks that take time away from satisfying customer needs.

Source Photographer, Len Rubenstein for Bank of Boston.

type of work being done can be recorded. Especially appropriate for nonrepetitive or white-collar work, work sampling studies often provide insight into how workers are spending their time. The objective is not to find out if workers are goofing off but to determine if they are spending a significant percentage of their time doing tasks that might better be done by someone else or eliminated entirely. A large number of random observations, when categorized, provide an accurate assessment of the employees' proportionate expenditure of time.

Many managers have recognized that the key to improving labor productivity is through working smarter not harder. Working smarter requires the elimination of tasks that do not add value or contribute to the production of the service or product. In repetitive jobs, these types of unproductive actions are known as **ineffective worker movements.** The elimination of these types of efforts results in an overall decrease in required inputs and thus increases productivity. Effective managers have also recognized that the true experts on jobs in services and manufacturing are often the workers themselves. Many companies have significantly improved worker productivity by involving workers in the design and analysis of their jobs.

INEFFECTIVE WORKER MOVEMENTS
Unproductive actions in repetitive jobs.

The increased involvement of workers in decision making has become known as empowerment. Unfortunately, many firms have tried to use empowerment as a way to improve worker productivity, but they have not provided workers with the necessary prerequisites. Empowerment will not increase productivity unless the workers have the skills and knowledge to make decisions. Worker empowerment, if approached correctly, requires a significant investment in training. Unfortunately, like many other productivity improvement programs, some companies assume that empowerment is a cure-all. Employees are sometimes given increased responsibility without necessary training and find the experience stressful, frustrating, and, ultimately, a failure. Management blames the empowered labor force for the failure, and everybody loses.

AUTOMATION AND IMPROVED USE OF TECHNOLOGY

In addition to the enhancement of the productivity of materials, various applications of automation have also increased worker productivity. Automated materials handling systems, for example, have eliminated many of these responsibilities from jobs, allowing workers to concentrate more on quality. Automated production equipment, particularly for repetitive tasks, has enabled human resources to be used to monitor and make decisions, rather than repeat the same tasks over and over. At the Mercedes-Benz plant in Sindelfinger, Germany, for instance, an automated platform moves workers along with the cars on the assembly line, enabling them to perform a number of different jobs instead of being limited to just one task. Automation can also eliminate the need to have workers engaged in dangerous tasks or tasks that have no margin for error.

The replacement of workers by automation has increased productivity in many firms. For example, automation helped double productivity at Monsanto's Pensacola, Florida, plant. The decision to replace a worker with automation is typically based on a preference for the higher initial cost of the automated equipment over the ongoing labor costs. But caution must be used in making these decisions. Changes in demand may have significant impact on the payback period for expensive equipment. If the need for capacity declines, workers can be trained to do other necessary jobs, but machines cannot. Investments in automation often restrict a company's ability to improve processes. The functions of machines and robots are limited and cannot easily adapt to improvements that may be made in production processes.

Although there has been an increasing use of automation in both the service and manufacturing sectors, some firms have gone against this trend. Japanese firms in particular have rediscovered the value of worker flexibility and adaptability. They have recognized that human beings are able to provide a level of adaptation and quick decision making that cannot be matched by a robot or automated piece of equipment. Many firms have reacted by replacing robots with humans. Toyota, for example, reduced the number of assembly robots at its new Kyushu automobile plant. But even though the plant's automation rate is almost half that of the company's Tahara facility, productivity has been high. The Kyushu plant has kept the automation rate down to promote quality and encourage teamwork.

The use of computers has also had a dramatic impact on worker productivity in services and manufacturing. For many services, so-called paper-pushing has become a thing of the past. The effect that personal computers have had on individual productivity and information processing has been significant. Computer-aided design (CAD) has revolutionized the product design process and has drastically reduced the product development lead time, resulting in products reaching the market sooner. CAD has greatly increased the productivity of engineers by freeing them from tedious and time-consuming drawing. Computer-aided manufacturing (CAM) involves the linkage of computers to processing equipment or materials handling equipment. Complete CAM processes start with CAD. The design of the product is stored in the form of a mathematical model. The database containing the model can be accessed to generate instructions for the actual manufacture of the product. CAM has changed manufacturing in four important ways.

- CAM allows equipment to operate faster, creating more consistent product quality.
- CAM enables a production line to shift quickly from one product to another, eliminating long changeovers and providing high-volume economical production and customization.
- CAM enables production to adapt product design and product mix to market changes that take place over time, increasing the firm's flexibility.

■ CAM provides a means for integrating all stages of operations, from product design through production and testing.[4]

Computers control the actual processing steps, increasing levels of quality, consistency, and flexibility as well as providing specific instructions to the machines. The linkage of CAD and CAM, commonly known as CAD/CAM, has enabled the manufacturing process to be directly linked to the design process. Computer-controlled machines get their instructions directly from the product design. Design engineers can immediately see results as machines produce to their instructions. For example, Westport Precision Inc. uses a CAD/CAM system to design 3-D models of sheet metal parts. The system is also used to check customer specifications before production begins.

The linkages between design and manufacturing and the increased use of computer controlled equipment have given many manufacturers what was previously unimagined—flexible automation making high-volume customization possible. Not only can automated machines, when controlled by computers, perform difficult operations, but they can also adjust themselves to provide a degree of flexibility from one product or part to another. The result is the capability to produce in high volumes and, at the same time, customize individual products.

The grouping of computer-controlled machines, linked together by automated materials handling systems, has led to the development of flexible manufacturing systems (FMS's). An FMS is analogous to the cellular manufacturing approach in that products requiring similar processing steps are produced in a cell. However, all processing and materials handling aspects of the cell are automated. Currently, FMS's are used primarily in machining operations, where metal parts are produced through grinding, shaping, and lathe operations. FMS's have provided many firms with significant competitive advantage through flexibility and response time, but they are expensive and complex systems.

The future of manufacturing and some services may lie in a level of computer integration that goes beyond the current CAD/CAM and FMS technology. Computer-integrated manufacturing (CIM) is a linkage of all aspects of the firm, including purchasing, marketing, accounting, production, design, planning and control through an integrated information network. CIM is based on a common data and information base, accessed by all functions of the business, making it possible for decisions to be made and executed in a truly integrated fashion.

In addition to productivity gains through the use of CAD/CAM and CIM, manufacturers have also benefited from the implementation of advanced technology information systems. These systems offer better linkages between functions and plants and provide companies with readily available information, which has resulted in productivity gains for many firms. Hewlett-Packard, for example, has been able to maintain decentralized materials purchasing functions, while simultaneously negotiating volume discounts at the corporate level through a system used by all plants and linked to corporate procurement.[5] Many manufacturers no longer send purchase orders to suppliers of components. Suppliers have access to their customers' production schedules and merely deliver the components needed to meet the schedule. Manufacturers have incorporated new information technologies into many processes other than scheduling and supplier networks.

---

[4]Bella Gold, "Computerization in Domestic and International Manufacturing," *California Management Review* 31 (Winter 1989): 129–143.

[5]M. Hammer and J. Champy, *Re-engineering the Corporation* (New York: HarperBusiness, 1993), 94–95.

Services have also increased productivity through the use of high technology. Many retailers, following Wal-Mart's technological lead, have created computerized inventory tracking systems. Levi Strauss, for example, has created its own system used by half of its large accounts.[6] Sales shot up an average of 24% in 1992 for stores using the system. The average sales increase at stores not using the system was 3.6%.

CHANGES IN WORK FORCE TRAINING AND SCHEDULING

Many industries have increased work force productivity by providing means by which workers can better satisfy family and job responsibilities. As skill requirements have become more sophisticated, many firms have developed skill-based pay systems. As employees learn new skills, pay increases. There are a number of advantages to this technique. For the employee, jobs are expanded, often leading to greater job satisfaction. For the employer, the advantages of these systems are increased flexibility and an enhanced ability to utilize employees. Vacation scheduling is also possible with less impact on productivity. Japanese firms have rewarded employees with pay increases according to their skills for years. In a survey of 27 U.S. firms with such systems, 70% to 88% reported higher job satisfaction, product quality, or productivity. Lower operating costs and reduced employee turnover were cited by 70% to 75% of the firms surveyed. Twenty-two Corning plants are on skill-based pay systems. At one Corning plant, workers can increase pay from $9.50 per hour to $13.50 per hour (an annual increase of $8,000) by increasing skills.[7]

Other approaches include such innovations as **job sharing,** where two individuals fulfill the responsibilities and share the pay of one full-time job. Flexible scheduling, or flextime, also allows workers to have greater input in scheduling their hours to meet their job and personal responsibilities.

JOB SHARING
A flexible scheduling option in which two individuals fulfill the responsibilities and share the pay for a position normally staffed by one full-time employee.

IMPROVING PRODUCTIVITY

IMPROVING PRODUCTIVITY OF FACILITIES

The large investment in facilities adds to the high overhead costs of many businesses and puts significant pressure on businesses to use facilities effectively. Many manufacturers assess the productivity of facilities with the following productivity measure:

$$\frac{\text{Sales dollars}}{\text{Square foot}} \qquad \textbf{(17.8)}$$

Costs associated with facilities go far beyond the initial cost of construction. Utility costs, property taxes, lease agreements, and security are all directly related to the square footage of a facility. These costs are significant enough to motivate managers to use space effectively.

Many manufacturers have found that inventory reduction has improved facility productivity by greatly reducing the amount of floor spaced needed. In fact, reduced amounts of floor space are often required after JIT has been introduced. Space previously used as an inventory warehouse now sits empty in many manufacturing operations. Many firms have

---

[6]"The Technology Payoff," *Business Week,* June 14, 1993, 57–68.
[7]"Skill-Based Pay Boosts Worker Productivity and Morale," *The Wall Street Journal,* June 23, 1992, sec. A, 1.

been able to lease this space to other businesses, while others have found ways to use it for their own operations. For example, John Crane Belfab in Daytona Beach, Florida, used to devote about one-quarter of an 8,000-square-foot building to inventory. But since implementing JIT, the firm has reduced inventory levels by 51%. Now business units that generate nearly half of the company's revenues occupy former stockrooms.

Facilities utilized for actual production of goods and services can be made more productive through effective layout planning and effective capacity planning, as discussed in Chapters 12 and 15, respectively.

IMPROVING ENERGY PRODUCTIVITY

The improvement of energy productivity has become a global concern as well as a national objective. The conservation of energy through more energy efficient equipment and facilities is often enhanced by dual sources of energy. For example, many manufacturers have the ability to use natural gas, electricity, and liquid propane for heating purposes and can switch from one to another, depending on the availability and cost. This capability is common in colder climates, where regulations establish priorities for home use of natural gas when temperatures drop below zero. Other companies look for innovative ways to conserve energy. For example, Pedico Products Inc.'s new manufacturing facility has an energy-efficient lighting system that is expected to result in an annual savings of $2,605 in electricity costs.

Firms often measure the productivity of energy use by monitoring sales dollars per dollar of energy expenditure. This measure can be monitored to identify trends and also can be compared to industry averages.

The productive use of energy has implications beyond those of input costs. Many, if not all, firms produce unwanted outputs in the form of by-products, waste, and pollution. Unproductive use of energy results in higher levels of these outputs, which carries a heavy price tag for the company, and ultimately everyone else.

IMPROVING EQUIPMENT PRODUCTIVITY

Because both manufacturing and services require large investments in equipment, its productivity is a concern for most businesses. As mentioned previously, utilization is a commonly used measure of equipment productivity, but it shouldn't be the only measure because that would encourage the running of equipment at rates above what the rest of the system could handle. This could result in a buildup of inventory. Many firms, particularly those that use JIT, monitor on-time delivery from one work center to the next. Quite often, early delivery is considered just as bad as late delivery. Although the use of equipment is one means to accomplish a goal, it should not be the ultimate end.

Companies can improve equipment productivity by decreasing set-up time, improving preventive maintenance, and implementing process improvements. Improved processes, brought about by such techniques as statistical process control, can stabilize processes and prevent defects, thus increasing the number of usable outputs from the same amount time on resources.

Just as automation has increased labor productivity, it has also increased equipment productivity, particularly when it replaces nonautomated equipment. But the large investments required to introduce automation often encourage higher utilizations than are needed to meet demand. Caution must be used so that an increase in equipment productivity does not come at the expense of a decrease in the productivity of inventory.

A reengineered creative process is boosting productivity at American Greetings Corporation. Replacing an outdated pass-it-down-the-line approach, American Greetings' new team approach uses desktop publishing and digital imaging technology so that artists, writers, planners, and photographers can work on products concurrently. It also empowers them to make decisions during all phases of card development, eliminating time-intensive steps.

Source ©1993 American Greetings Corporation. Used with permission.

TRENDS IN PRODUCTIVITY IMPROVEMENT

STARTING OVER: REENGINEERING

Many manufacturing and service firms have determined that the most effective way to improve productivity is to **reengineer,** or redesign, all aspects of the business in an effort to streamline all processes. Under this approach, information processing and form processing are just as important as production processes. Reengineering differs from continuous improvement efforts because rather than seeking incremental improvement, reengineering seeks breakthroughs. Services and manufacturers have begun to dismantle and rebuild with an objective of applying JIT-like leanness to all aspects of the business. The results have been phenomenal for some companies but bleak for some workers who are left without jobs. Productivity-related worker reductions are expected to be particularly heavy in the service sector because much greater potential exists for eliminating nonvalue-adding jobs. In the service sector, some entire industries have adapted reengineering as a way to revamp processes and customer relations. (See Box 17.1.)

Reengineering efforts at many firms, manufacturers and services alike, have led to the recognition of the need to downsize, particularly middle management positions.

Improved processes also have resulted in significant reductions in necessary inputs. The U.S. auto industry has provided an abundance of evidence that demonstrates the power of these types of improvements. (See Boxes 17.2 and 17.3.)

REENGINEERING
Streamlining all processes of a business by redesigning all aspects (with emphasis on breakthroughs versus incremental improvements).

OPERATIONS OUTLOOK

BOX 17.1

Reengineering in the Insurance Industry

A reengineering effort in the insurance industry has had a dramatic impact on the flow of paper in an industry dominated by paper processing. Cigna, for example, is in the process of replacing an estimated 35,000 different corporate forms with electronic forms. The project is expected to be paid for from reduced paper costs in just 1 year.

Other improvements at Cigna have had dramatic effects. For example, following improvements to information systems, customer service representatives were able to process 35% more customer inquiries. This change is extremely important to a company that receives over 30,000 inquiries per month. Customer service representatives have been retrained as generalists who can handle a variety of customer problems, including billing and claims questions, which used to be referred to other departments. After completing just over 1 year of a 4-year reengineering project in customer service, Cigna has seen a 35% increase in productivity and a 65% reduction in costs. When all improvements are made, it is expected that customer service will be able to triple productivity.

Connecticut Mutual Life Insurance has also redesigned work flow across departments. The effort has resulted in productivity gains of between 20% and 60% across all departments. In addition, the $5-million investment in the project was recouped in only 18 months.

Sources "PCs Start Sweeping Away Business Forms," *The Wall Street Journal,* April 26, 1993, sec. B, 8. "Re-engineering Pays off at Cigna," *Computer World,* August 9, 1993, 70. "Re-engineering Repercussions," *Computer World,* June 28, 1993, 149–150.

Reengineering often results in a drastic reduction in inputs to increase a company's productivity. It is important to understand the effect this has on both the firm's productivity and U.S. productivity and the standard of living. Elimination of a job that does not add value increases the firm's productivity, because fewer inputs create an equal level of outputs. The productivity of the United States is also increased because fewer inputs create an equal level of output. Until the person who held the job finds work, however, the standard of living, as defined by gross domestic product per capita, is not changed.

CUTTING-EDGE COMPANIES

BOX 17.2

Improving Productivity in the U.S. Auto Industry

In mid-1993 no goal was more important to General Motors than to close the "productivity gap" between it and Ford Motor Company and Chrysler Corporation. President John F. Smith Jr.'s objective to make domestic operations profitable was expected to result in the elimination of 70,000 to 90,000 blue-collar jobs. Many GM plants were trying to survive through leaner manufacturing methods.

The Saginaw Division, a production line that assembles steering columns for the Grand Am, provides an example of what GM wanted to happen. A new line, designed with the help of UAW production workers, combined with a new steering column design that has 30% fewer parts, resulted in a threefold productivity increase over an old line in the same plant. The equipment for the new line cost more than 30% less than that of the old line, but the quality of the steering column was nearly 7 times greater because of the new design and improved processes.

Source "GM Drive to Step Up Efficiency Is Colliding with UAW Job Fears," *The Wall Street Journal,* June 23, 1993, sec. A, 1.

CUTTING-EDGE COMPANIES

BOX 17.3

Productivity Improvements at Ford

Ford has started to gain a competitive advantage through a combination of engineering advances, increased levels of cooperation between employees and management, and the elimination of nonvalue-adding processes and workers. For example, Ford takes one-third fewer worker hours to build a car, creating a $795 cost advantage over General Motors.

Ford credits an increased level of cooperation with most of the improvement. Like many companies, Ford's im-

provements came about only when the company was in a crisis situation. It had no choice but to improve. One of the more significant changes has been the elimination of rules that prevented workers from doing many tasks and contributed to the lack of productivity. Several process improvements have been the result of employee suggestions.

Source "A Decisive Response to Crisis Brought Ford Enhanced Productivity," *The Wall Street Journal,* December 15, 1992, sec. A, 1, 13.

The firms that seem to be the most effective at increasing productivity try to address both the input and output sides of the productivity equation. Increasing outputs through more effective use of resources and technology as well as eliminating nonvalue-adding steps in processes has resulted in significant productivity gains for some firms.

BUSINESS PROCESS ANALYSIS

Business Process Analysis (BPA) is an approach to improvement that focuses on the processes involved in meeting a customer's needs. BPA is used to define how work is accomplished and identify how customer service could be improved by simplifying steps and eliminating those that do not add value.

The BPA process begins with what the customer wants and ends with what the customer gets. The emphasis is on the complete process used to provide the desired outcome rather than on the responsibilities of individual departments. The goal is to optimize the entire process rather than individual steps within it. The BPA perspective, as illustrated in Figure 17.2, virtually ignores the departmental structure shown in Figure 17.3, but its presence is acknowledged when searching for problems. Since the departmental structure is the source of many problems, BPA devotes a significant amount of attention to those activities that cross departmental boundaries. These activities usually offer opportunities to simplify and eliminate nonvalue-added activities because departments often are not structured in ways to facilitate inter-departmental activity. However, the emphasis is on the process, not on the employee or department. Individuals learn how their jobs fit into the total process rather than viewing their job as separate entities. The performance of the process is more important than the performance of an individual. When errors are identified, the focus is on what part of the process allowed the error to occur, rather than on who made the error.

The choice as to whether BPA or reengineering should be used depends on several issues. Reengineering is probably a more likely choice if there has been a radical change in customer requirements, if tools or technologies are obsolete or inappropriate, or if key capacities or competencies no longer exist within the organization. These are large-scale changes that frequently take several years to change. BPA activities are usually smaller scale and are completed in six months or less.

FIGURE 17.2   **Process View**

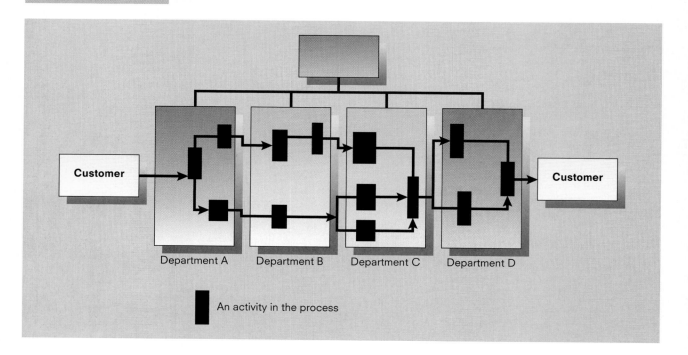

An activity in the process

FIGURE 17.3   **Traditional Departmental Structure**

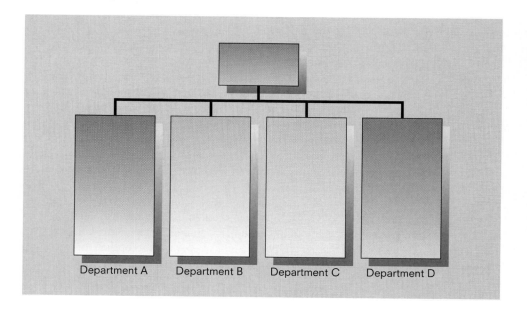

WORK FLOW

As overhead costs have come to dominate the total cost picture for many firms, traditional management focus on inputs, processes, and outputs has shown itself to be less effective. **Work flow**[8] management approaches are becoming increasingly popular as tools to manage these environments. The work flow concept is based on the premise that all employees of a company act in both performer and customer roles. Every task done in a business serves an internal customer. Depending on the particular transaction, and the role in that transaction, one person is the performer and the other the customer. The work flow approach divides the interaction into the four steps described below.

> **Step 1:** Preparation. A request from a "customer" or an offer from a "performer."
>
> **Step 2:** Negotiation. The two parties agree on how the work is to be done and what constitutes success.
>
> **Step 3:** Performance. Work is done and completion is reported to the "customer."
>
> **Step 4:** Acceptance: Customer agrees that work is done satisfactorily.

The "customer" has the final say as to whether the work is done. What might be thought of as a simple management task may consist of a number of work flow loops. Large tasks become such a maize of loops that powerful computer programs have evolved to keep track of processes.

PRODUCTIVITY CROSS-LINKS

Early in this text it was stressed that managers must make the best decisions for the entire business, not for a particular department. This objective impacts productivity improvement as much as any other management area. Businesses frequently improve productivity in one area only to reduce it in others. As mentioned previously, direct labor is the one area that seems to get the most attention when it comes to productivity improvement efforts.

Table 17.2 demonstrates the disproportionate investments a typical company might make in labor productivity improvements. Notice the percentage of total investment in the productivity of direct labor and overhead compared to the percentage of total costs consumed by direct labor and overhead.

When a company invests in productivity improvement, it should recognize the potential for improvement when determining the order in which to target various areas. For example, in the company portrayed in Table 17.2, the potential for reducing direct labor is small. The maximum reduction that could take place would be to reduce the direct labor costs to zero. Although this is clearly impossible, it demonstrates that at the very best, a 10% reduction in total cost through reduction of direct labor would be the absolute maximum. Halving the cost of labor, a significant and probably unfeasible productivity improvement, would result in only a 5% reduction in total production costs. Overhead, on the other hand, presents far greater potential. A 17% reduction in overhead costs, significant, but not impossible for many businesses, results in as great a reduction in total costs as would a 50% reduction in labor costs.

---

[8]"The Wonders of Workflow," *The Economist*, December 11, 1993, 80.

TABLE 17.2	**Costs and Productivity Improvement Expenditures**

	Total Production Costs (%)	Total Productivity Improvement Expenditures (%)
Direct labor	10	39
Materials	36	37
Indirect labor	15	19
Overhead (facilities, equipment, energy, maintenance)	30	5
Depreciation and other	9	<1

Source   Adapted from W. B. Chew, "No-Nonsense Guide to Measuring Productivity," *Harvard Business Review* (January-February 1988): 110–118.

CONSTRAINT MANAGEMENT AND PRODUCTIVITY

Just as JIT and TQM provide useful techniques for improving productivity, constraint management provides an interesting and useful perspective. The global, rather than local, perspective of constraint management provides an emphasis on increasing the productivity of the system rather than individual work centers. Recall that constraint management is based on the premise that the constraint determines the output of any system. Increasing the *system* outputs, while maintaining a stable level of inputs, increases productivity. But investing to increase the outputs of individual work centers in ways that do not increase the system outputs, will not improve system productivity and can actually reduce it. Care should be taken when using any local productivity measure to ensure that an improvement in that measure will also result in a real improvement in total system productivity.

NATIONAL PRODUCTIVITY TRENDS

Rarely a week goes by that the popular press does not refer to the productivity of the United States compared to that in other countries of the world. It is important to understand the issues related to productivity as they are debated by politicians and reported in the press because U.S. productivity is closely related to the standard of living. Just as with a business, national and global productivity measures can be difficult to interpret and can be misleading. As the saying goes, "Statistics don't lie, but liars use statistics."

As a general statement, one can claim that U.S. workers are still the most productive workers in the world. Their rate of improvement, however, is slower than that of workers in some other countries, such as Germany or Japan. In 1990, the average American worker produced $45,100 of goods and services. This compares to $37,850 for the average German worker and $34,500 for the average Japanese worker.[9]

Although it is true that the service sector in the United States has become the largest in the economy, it is not as productive as the manufacturing sector. Service-sector productiv-

[9]T. A. Stewart, "U.S. Productivity: First but Fading," *Fortune,* October 19, 1992, 54.

ity also is not improving as rapidly as that of the manufacturing sector. The private-sector service outputs per hour grew at an average annual rate of 0.7 percent during the 1980s. Manufacturing grew at an average annual rate of 3.8 percent during the same time period.[10] The auto industry provides an example of this trend. Although productivity in auto manufacturing improved 43 percent in the 1980s, productivity in dealerships and repair shops increased only 18 percent and 7.5 percent respectively.[11] The service sector has recognized that it can and must trim excess. Many service businesses, including banking and retailing, have done this by cutting staff.

Despite the sluggish productivity growth in the service sector, its contribution to exports has been increasing but is largely overlooked. The U.S. Commerce Department's monthly trade deficit figures track merchandise only, not services. While there was a $96 billion merchandise trade deficit in 1992 (meaning $96 billion more was imported than exported), U.S. services racked up a $59 billion trade surplus. Imagine the impact if U.S. service-sector productivity improved substantially.

SUMMARY

The productivity of U.S. businesses determines, to a great extent, the standard of living and quality of life in the United States. But increases in a narrow measure of productivity can be obtained at the expense of others. One has to measure a number of factors to get a true picture of the change in productivity.

If a high standard of living and good quality of life are important reasons for productivity improvement, one must look at all aspects of each to avoid trading one improvement for another. A global, long-term view of costs and benefits must be used. It doesn't make sense to trade one aspect of quality of life for another. For example, trading environmental quality for lower priced material goods is ignoring the fact that the cost to clean up the environment may come later, but it will surely come. The system in which each business functions not only includes the industry in which it competes but also the community from which it draws employees, the Earth from which it draws resources, and the atmosphere in which it emits pollutants. As the end of the millennium draws near, the Earth seems to have become smaller and smaller. This is largely because of the capability of one company, one manufacturing plant, or one oil tanker to profoundly affect the planet. Relative to the influence people have on it, the Earth has been reduced in size by the expanding technology of its stewards.

The long-term futures of business and quality of life both lie in the ability of business management to recognize that the system in which it makes decisions is far more expansive that the walls of their building, and the time frame in which they make decisions is far longer than the current accounting period or fiscal year. Decisions must be made from a truly global perspective. This requires an analysis of the effects on the entire global system and a time horizon that takes into account future generations.

---

[10]Stewart, 56.
[11]Stewart, 56.

ACCUMOLD REVISITED

CROSS-LINKS Monica appears to be in a no-win situation. What appears to be the cause of the paradox Monica must deal with? How can she convince Angela Hill that a conflict exists? What other staff members would you try to recruit to help prepare a case that would defend smaller batch sizes?

What steps would you take to try to satisfy inventory goals and labor cost goals? Is this likely to happen in the short term?

QUESTIONS FOR REVIEW

1. What is the relationship between the value-added conversion process and productivity improvement?
2. How does a customer's perspective of value relate to productivity?
3. What is lean production?
4. Compare the effects on productivity of reducing total costs and reducing cost per unit.
5. How can inventory productivity be measured and improved?
6. How is labor productivity measured?
7. What are the dangers of overemphasizing direct labor productivity improvement?
8. Compare the creation of standards using stopwatch time studies to the use of predetermined motion times.
9. How have technological advancements such as automation, robotics, FMSs, CAD/CAM, and CIM influenced productivity?
10. What is reengineering?

QUESTIONS FOR THOUGHT AND DISCUSSION

1. How could TQM, JIT, and constraint management be used to guide productivity improvement efforts?
2. How can productivity be measured in ways that include global costs and long-term time frames?

INTEGRATIVE QUESTIONS

1. What are possible linkages between facility layout and productivity?
2. How do inventory management, capacity management, and scheduling effectiveness affect productivity?
3. What is the relationship between productivity, as viewed by management, and value, as viewed by a customer?
4. How can increased levels of productivity enhance each of the competitive priorities?

SUGGESTED READINGS

Chew, W. B. "No-Nonsense Guide to Measuring Productivity." *Harvard Business Review* 66 (January-February 1988): 110–118.

Meredith, J. R., and M. M. Hill. "Justifying New Manufacturing Systems: A Managerial Approach." *Sloan Management Review* (Summer 1987): 49–58.

Redford, R. "Search for Common Ground." *Harvard Business Review* 65 (May-June 1987): 107–112.

Schonberger, R. J. "Frugal Manufacturing." *Harvard Business Review* 65 (September-October 1987): 95–100.

Skinner, Wickham. "The Productivity Paradox." *Harvard Business Review* 64 (July-August 1986): 55–59.

THE STANDARD NORMAL DISTRIBUTION

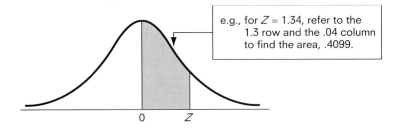

e.g., for $Z = 1.34$, refer to the 1.3 row and the .04 column to find the area, .4099.

Z	.00	.01	.02	.03	.04	.05	.06	.07	.08	.09
0.0	.0000	.0040	.0080	.0120	.0160	.0199	.0239	.0279	.0319	.0359
0.1	.0398	.0438	.0478	.0517	.0557	.0596	.0636	.0675	.0714	.0753
0.2	.0793	.0832	.0871	.0910	.0948	.0987	.1026	.1064	.1103	.1141
0.3	.1179	.1217	.1255	.1293	.1331	.1368	.1406	.1443	.1480	.1517
0.4	.1554	.1591	.1628	.1664	.1700	.1736	.1772	.1808	.1844	.1879
0.5	.1915	.1950	.1985	.2019	.2054	.2088	.2123	.2157	.2190	.2224
0.6	.2257	.2291	.2324	.2357	.2389	.2422	.2454	.2486	.2517	.2549
0.7	.2580	.2611	.2642	.2673	.2704	.2734	.2764	.2794	.2823	.2852
0.8	.2881	.2910	.2939	.2967	.2995	.3023	.3051	.3078	.3106	.3133
0.9	.3159	.3186	.3212	.3238	.3264	.3289	.3315	.3340	.3365	.3389
1.0	.3413	.3438	.3461	.3485	.3508	.3531	.3554	.3577	.3599	.3621
1.1	.3643	.3665	.3686	.3708	.3729	.3749	.3770	.3790	.3810	.3830
1.2	.3849	.3869	.3888	.3907	.3925	.3944	.3962	.3980	.3997	.4015
1.3	.4032	.4049	.4066	.4082	.4099	.4115	.4131	.4147	.4162	.4177
1.4	.4192	.4207	.4222	.4236	.4251	.4265	.4279	.4292	.4306	.4319
1.5	.4332	.4345	.4357	.4370	.4382	.4394	.4406	.4418	.4429	.4441
1.6	.4452	.4463	.4474	.4484	.4495	.4505	.4515	.4525	.4535	.4545
1.7	.4554	.4564	.4573	.4582	.4591	.4599	.4608	.4616	.4625	.4633
1.8	.4641	.4649	.4656	.4664	.4671	.4678	.4686	.4693	.4699	.4706
1.9	.4713	.4719	.4726	.4732	.4738	.4744	.4750	.4756	.4761	.4767
2.0	.4772	.4778	.4783	.4788	.4793	.4798	.4803	.4808	.4812	.4817
2.1	.4821	.4826	.4830	.4834	.4838	.4842	.4846	.4850	.4854	.4857
2.2	.4861	.4864	.4868	.4871	.4875	.4878	.4881	.4884	.4887	.4890
2.3	.4893	.4896	.4898	.4901	.4904	.4906	.4909	.4911	.4913	.4916
2.4	.4918	.4920	.4922	.4925	.4927	.4929	.4931	.4932	.4934	.4936
2.5	.4938	.4940	.4941	.4943	.4945	.4946	.4948	.4949	.4951	.4952
2.6	.4953	.4955	.4956	.4957	.4959	.4960	.4961	.4962	.4963	.4964
2.7	.4965	.4966	.4967	.4968	.4969	.4970	.4971	.4972	.4973	.4974
2.8	.4974	.4975	.4976	.4977	.4977	.4978	.4979	.4979	.4980	.4981
2.9	.4981	.4982	.4982	.4983	.4984	.4984	.4985	.4985	.4986	.4986
3.0	.4987	.4987	.4987	.4988	.4988	.4989	.4989	.4989	.4990	.4990

Source Cumulative standard normal probabilities from $z = 0.00$ to $z = 3.09$, generated by MINITAB, then rounded to four decimal places. From Ronald M. Weiers, *Introduction to Business Statistics*, 2d ed. (Fort Worth: The Dryden Press, 1984).

LEARNING CURVE COEFFICIENTS

Unit Number	85 percent		90 percent	
	Unit Time	Total Time	Unit Time	Total Time
1	1.0000	1.0000	1.0000	1.0000
2	0.8500	1.8500	0.9000	1.9000
3	0.7729	2.6229	0.8462	2.7462
4	0.7225	3.3454	0.8100	3.5562
5	0.6857	4.0311	0.7830	4.3392
6	0.6570	4.6881	0.7616	5.1008
7	0.6337	5.3217	0.7439	5.8447
8	0.6141	5.9358	0.7290	6.5737
9	0.5974	6.5332	0.7161	7.2898
10	0.5828	7.1161	0.7047	7.9945
11	0.5699	7.6860	0.6946	8.6890
12	0.5584	8.2444	0.6854	9.3745
13	0.5480	8.7925	0.6771	10.0516
14	0.5386	9.3311	0.6696	10.7211
15	0.5300	9.8611	0.6626	11.3837
16	0.5220	10.3831	0.6561	12.0398
17	0.5146	10.8977	0.6501	12.6899
18	0.5078	11.4055	0.6445	13.3344
19	0.5014	11.9069	0.6392	13.9735
20	0.4954	12.4023	0.6342	14.6078
21	0.4898	12.8920	0.6295	15.2373
22	0.4844	13.3765	0.6251	15.8624
23	0.4794	13.8559	0.6209	16.4833
24	0.4747	14.3306	0.6169	17.1002
25	0.4701	14.8007	0.6131	17.7132

	85 percent		90 percent	
Unit Number	Unit Time	Total Time	Unit Time	Total Time
26	0.4658	15.2666	0.6094	18.3227
27	0.4617	15.7283	0.6059	18.9286
28	0.4578	16.1861	0.6026	19.5312
29	0.4541	16.6402	0.5994	20.1306
30	0.4505	17.0907	0.5963	20.7269
31	0.4470	17.5377	0.5933	21.3202
32	0.4437	17.9814	0.5905	21.9107
33	0.4405	18.4219	0.5877	22.4985
34	0.4374	18.8593	0.5851	23.0835
35	0.4345	19.2938	0.5825	23.6660
36	0.4316	19.7254	0.5800	24.2461
37	0.4289	20.1543	0.5776	24.8237
38	0.4262	20.5805	0.5753	25.3989
39	0.4236	21.0041	0.5730	25.9719
40	0.4211	21.4252	0.5708	26.5427
41	0.4187	21.8438	0.5687	27.1114
42	0.4163	22.2601	0.5666	27.6780
43	0.4140	22.6741	0.5646	28.2425
44	0.4118	23.0859	0.5626	28.8051
45	0.4096	23.4955	0.5607	29.3658
46	0.4075	23.9030	0.5588	29.9246
47	0.4055	24.3085	0.5570	30.4815
48	0.4035	24.7120	0.5552	31.0367
49	0.4015	25.1135	0.5535	31.5902
50	0.3996	25.5131	0.5518	32.1420

GLOSSARY

ABC ANALYSIS

An approach to classifying inventory based on three classes of importance.

ACCEPTABLE QUALITY LEVEL (AQL)

The percentage level of defects specified by the producer but acceptable to the consumer.

ACCEPTANCE SAMPLING

A type of inspection that manufacturers use to infer a level of quality for a population based on the level of quality of a sample.

ACTIVATION

Production that does not contribute to throughput.

ACTIVITY-ON-ARROW

A project network convention that identifies project activities with arrows. Events are represented with nodes or circles.

ACTIVITY-ON-NODE

A project network convention that identifies project activities with a node or circle. Sequencing is represented with arrows.

AGGREGATE PLANNING

A plan devised to determine how resources will be used to satisfy the demand for goods and services.

ALLOWANCE

Normal time adjusted to yield a standard time; allowances take into account personal time and rest periods.

A-PLANT

A manufacturing process dominated by converging material flows.

APPRAISAL COSTS

Costs associated with item inspection, testing, and system auditing.

ASSEMBLERS

Manufacturers that receive inputs from fabricators and provide finished products for consumers.

ASSEMBLY BUFFER

A buffer of nonconstraint parts placed prior to an assembly with constraint parts.

ATTRIBUTE CHART

A control chart based on data that are counted.

BACKORDER COSTS

Costs associated with not satisfying a customer order.

BACKWARD SCHEDULING

A technique for determining when to order dependent demand inventory that starts at the due date and schedules back to determine the start date.

BASIC PRODUCERS

Manufacturers that transform natural resources into inputs for converters.

BILL OF MATERIAL (BOM)

A listing of quantities of all raw materials, parts, and assemblies that go into an end item.

BRAINSTORMING

A technique for generating a large number of ideas from a group of people in a relatively short period of time.

BREAKEVEN ANALYSIS

Technique for evaluating several alternatives by determining the total cost of each and deciding on the basis of cost.

BUSINESS STRATEGY

Strategy that specifies the boundaries of a business and the basis on which it will compete.

CAPABILITY

The ability of a group of resources to perform a task or activity.

CAPACITY

The capability of a system to perform its expected function and the capability of a worker, machine, work center, plant, or organization to produce output per time period.

CAPACITY BILL

A description of capacity required, by any affected work center, to produce a unit of end product.

CAPACITY REQUIREMENTS PLANNING (CRP)

A detailed comparison of required capacity, based on the master production schedule, to the labor and machine capabilities of a production department.

CARRYING COSTS

Costs associated with holding inventory, including such costs as insurance, storage, damage, and opportunity cost of the dollars invested.

CAUSAL FORECASTING

Using the relationship to an external variable to predict demand.

CAUSE-AND-EFFECT DIAGRAMS

A tool for analyzing data by organizing all the known causes of a problem into a direct cause-and-effect relationship.

CELLULAR MANUFACTURING

A layout in which machinery is grouped into numerous small cells that can process a family of products

CHASE STRATEGY

Aggregate planning strategy that strives to produce exactly what is needed each period to meet the demand of that period.

CHECK SHEETS

A statistical tool (often a predesigned form) that facilitates the collection of data that will be used in detecting possible causes of quality problems.

CLOSED-LOOP MRP SYSTEMS

Material requirements planning systems with feedback from execution functions.

COMPETITIVE ADVANTAGE

Superior value to that of the competition, which results in consumer preference.

COMPETITIVE BENCHMARKING

The process of judging a company's processes or products by comparing them to the world's best, including those in other industries.

COMPETITIVE PRIORITIES

Price, quality, dependability, flexibility, and time.

COMPUTER-AIDED DESIGN (CAD)

Computer programs that speed up the engineering tasks that used to require drawing.

COMPUTER-AIDED DESIGN/COMPUTER-AIDED MANUFACTURING (CAD/CAM)

The linkage of computer-aided design and numerically controlled machines so that engineering designs are communicated directly to manufacturing.

CONCURRENT ENGINEERING

The linking of product and process engineering to create products that better match manufacturing capabilities.

CONSTRAINT

Anything that inhibits a system's performance toward its goals.

CONSTRAINT BUFFER

A buffer placed immediately prior to the constraint to ensure that it will be supplied with material.

CONSTRAINT MANAGEMENT

A management philosophy based on two premises: that the goal of a business is to make more money now and in the future and that a system's constraints determine its outputs.

CONSUMER'S RISK

The probability of accepting a "bad" lot, that is, a lot that is at the LTPD or worse.

CONTROL CHARTS

Charts that monitor production operations by plotting data.

CONTROLLING

Comparing what is actually happening to what was planned and taking appropriate actions to correct the variance.

CONVERTERS

Manufacturers that receive inputs from basic producers and provide inputs for fabricators.

CORPORATE STRATEGY

Strategy that focuses on what businesses a corporation should be in and how resources should be committed to those businesses.

COST OF QUALITY (COQ)

All costs associated with maintaining the quality of goods and services.

CRASHING

A process used to identify the best ways to reduce project duration.

CRITICAL PATH

The path through a project network that takes the longest amount of time.

CRITICAL PATH METHOD (CPM)

An approach to planning and coordinating large projects by directing managerial focus to the project's most critical aspects and providing an estimate of its duration.

CROSS-FUNCTIONAL INTEGRATION

The ability to pull together resources from different business functions to create differentiating capabilities.

CUT-AND-TRY METHOD

A trial-and-error approach to identifying a feasible aggregate plan.

CYCLE COUNTING

An approach to maintaining inventory accuracy by frequent physical counts and resolving any detected variances.

CYCLE TIME

The time (usually maximum time) allowed at each work center to complete its set of tasks on a unit.

CYCLICAL PATTERNS

Repetitive variations that occur less frequently than once every year.

DECISION SUPPORT SYSTEMS

Systems that assemble and make available valuable information to be used in decision making.

DECISION TREE

Diagram that provides a structured approach to decision making that incorporates uncertainty of outcome and expected revenues.

DECLINE

The final stage of the product life cycle, characterized by low demand.

DECOUPLING

Reducing the direct dependency a process has on those that supply it with material.

DEFECTION

A dissatisfied customer who, rather than return, does business with competitors.

DELPHI METHOD

A qualitative forecasting method which uses a panel of experts.

DEMAND FORECASTING

The process of predicting future demand for products or services as a means to schedule production.

DEMAND INFORMATION SOURCE

The point from which demand information is provided to production. The demand source can be the customer or a warehouse.

DEMAND MANAGEMENT

The function of recognizing and managing all of the demands for products to ensure the master scheduler is aware of them.

DEPENDABILITY

The reliability of a product or service in terms of function and the reliability of the producer in meeting promises.

DEPENDENT DEMAND INVENTORY

Inventory whose demand is determined by the demand for other items.

DETERMINISTIC ENVIRONMENT

An environment in which events can be described with certainty.

DIFFERENTIATING CAPABILITY

A capability that results in a firm's differentiation and competitive advantage.

DISCRETE MANUFACTURING

The manufacture of products that can be produced and sold in identifiable units.

DOUBLE EXPONENTIAL SMOOTHING

An exponential smoothing method that includes a trend component.

DRUM-BUFFER-ROPE (DBR)

An approach to controlling the flow of orders through a production system: The drum dictates the pace at which orders/materials can be brought to the system, buffers are used to decouple direct dependencies, and the rope links all the pieces together.

DUE DATE (DD)

A sequencing rule in which orders are processed according to the due dates, with earliest due dates first.

ECONOMIC ORDER QUANTITY (EOQ)

The point at which holding costs and order costs are equal and total inventory costs are minimized.

EFFICIENCY

Actual output divided by standard output.

END-OF-THE-MONTH SYNDROME

The tendency for businesses to increase output near the end of an accounting period in order to maximize sales for that period, rather than concentrating on long-term profits.

ENGINEER-TO-ORDER (ETO)

A manufacturer that designs a product

specifically to meet customer requests.

EXTERNAL FAILURE COSTS

The costs associated with failure of a product or service in the field.

FABRICATORS

Manufacturers that receive inputs from converters and provide inputs to assemblers.

FACILITIES AND EQUIPMENT

Machinery and tools (and the buildings in which they are housed) used in various processes to produce a product or service.

FACTOR RATING

An approach to evaluating location decisions that includes both qualitative and quantitative inputs.

FINISHED GOODS (FG) INVENTORIES

Finished products that have not yet been sold.

FIRST-COME/FIRST-SERVED (FCFS)

A sequencing rule in which orders are processed in the same sequence as they arrived.

FIXED-POSITION LAYOUT

An arrangement of equipment in which resources are brought to the product.

FLEXIBILITY

The ability of a business to adapt to change.

FLEXIBLE MANUFACTURING SYSTEM (FMS)

Automated machines and materials-handling systems that can adjust to meet the specifications of a variety of products.

FLOWCHART

A pictorial representation of the various operations of a process that documents all procedures used.

FLOW TIME

The sum of all processing times of an order.

FOCUS FORECASTING

Employing several forecasting techniques simultaneously and selecting the one that performs best.

FORECAST ERROR

Actual demand minus forecast demand.

FORWARD SCHEDULING

A technique for determining when to order dependent demand inventory that begins with the start date and schedules forward to the due date using expected lead times.

FUNCTIONAL STRATEGY

Strategy that specifies how each functional area of a business carries out the business strategy.

GLOBAL OPTIMIZATION

Maximizing the performance of the system toward its goals.

GLOBAL PRIORITY RULES

Sequencing rules that consider information beyond that relating to the operation being sequenced.

GROUP TECHNOLOGY

The process of grouping products with similar processing requirements into manufacturing cells.

GROWTH

The second stage in the product life cycle, characterized by increased demand as consumers become aware of the product.

HIRING COSTS

Costs associated with identifying, selecting, and training the work force.

HOSHIN KANRI

A form of strategic planning that focuses on a few clearly defined customer breakthroughs to be accomplished in the next three to five years.

HOUSE OF QUALITY

A system of related matrices used in quality function deployment that aids in transforming customer requirements into engineering and design decisions.

INDEPENDENT DEMAND INVENTORY

Inventory whose demand is determined by the market.

INEFFECTIVE WORKER MOVEMENTS

Unproductive actions in repetitive jobs.

INFORMATION EXCHANGE

The passage of information from one business function to another.

INFORMATION SYSTEMS

Systems that provide consistent information used in decision making and aid in the processes of planning and control.

INFRASTRUCTURAL DECISIONS

Decisions that include determinations of work force, quality, production and inventory control, and organizational structure.

INTERNAL FAILURE COSTS

The costs associated with correcting a defect before the customer receives the product or service.

INTRODUCTION

The first stage of the product life cycle, characterized by low volume and low demand.

INVENTORY (CONSTRAINT MANAGEMENT DEFINITION)

The money invested in purchasing things the system intends to sell.

INVENTORY (TRADITIONAL DEFINITION)

Stocked material used to support the production of a good or service.

INVENTORY COSTS

All costs of holding items in inventory.

INVENTORY DOLLAR-DAYS

The dollar value of the inventory (raw materials costs) multiplied by the number of days until it will be sold.

INVENTORY RECORD

A computer file containing information on each item inventoried, including lead time, quantity on hand, supplier, and the like.

INVENTORY TURNOVER

The number of times a firm's inventory cycles (or moves through the system), computed by dividing annual cost of sales by the average inventory level (dollars).

INVENTORY TURNS

A commonly used measure to evaluate the productivity of materials or inventory: the number of times that inventory cycles in a year.

I-PLANT

A manufacturing process dominated by linear material flows.

JIDOKA

A form of worker empowerment that gives workers the power to stop production processing if they believe something is not as it should be.

JOB SHARING

A flexible scheduling option in which two individuals fulfill the responsibilities and share the pay for a position normally staffed by one full-time employee.

JUST-IN-TIME (JIT)

A management philosophy, which originated in Japan, that focuses on the elimination of waste.

KANBAN

A visual signal or card used to indicate when an item should be produced and the quantity required to replenish a buffer to the desired level.

KANBAN SYSTEM

In just-in-time, a system used to link production of each item to the market demand.

LAYOFF COSTS

Costs associated with exit interviews and severance pay.

LAYOUT

The physical arrangement of equipment or departments required in producing a product or service.

LEADING INDICATOR

An external variable that is a good predictor of demand.

LEAN PRODUCTION

Eliminating nonvalue-adding inputs as a way to increase productivity.

LEARNING CURVE THEORY

Theory based on the idea that the time required to produce an item decreases successively.

LEARNING RATE

The rate of improvement from producing the first item, to the second, to the third, and so on.

LEAST SQUARES REGRESSION

A forecasting method that incorporates trend by identifying a linear relationship between data and time.

LEVEL LOADING

In JIT, the practice of stabilizing the load on the production processes for long periods of time.

LEVEL STRATEGY

Aggregate planning strategy that strives to produce the same quantity each period.

LINE BALANCING

The process of assigning tasks to work centers in such a way as to balance the processing times and minimize delay.

LOCAL OPERATING EXPENSE

The operating expense over which a department or managerial unit has full control.

LOCAL OPTIMIZATION

Maximizing part of the system in terms of a local measure of performance.

LOGISTICS FUNCTION

The business function responsible for bringing inputs to the location of the product or service delivery (*inbound logistics*) and transporting outputs to the customer (*outbound logistics*).

LOT-FOR-LOT ORDERING

In material requirements planning, ordering in quantities equal to the net requirements.

LOT TOLERANCE PERCENT DEFECTIVE (LTPD)

The threshold (or upper limit) of percentage defects that the consumer is willing to accept.

LOW LEVEL CODE

Restructuring the bill of materials so that all occurrences of an item are made to coincide with the lowest level of the structure in which the item appears.

LUMPY DEMAND

A demand pattern characterized by time periods of little or no demand followed by time periods of very high demand.

MAKE-TO-ORDER (MTO)

A manufacturer that produces specifically what a customer requests.

MAKE-TO-STOCK (MTS)

A manufacturer that produces goods to replenish a finished goods stock.

MAKE-TO-STOCK/ASSEMBLE-TO-ORDER (MTS/ATO)

A manufacturer that produces product components that are stored for later use; the components are pulled from stock and assembled as orders are received.

MANUFACTURER-BASED QUALITY

Quality as defined by a product's or service's conformance to specifications.

MANUFACTURERS

Businesses that produce a tangible or material product.

MANUFACTURING RESOURCES PLANNING (MRPII)

An extension of closed-loop MRP systems to include all aspects of business planning, financial reporting, and simulation.

MASS SERVICES

Services having low levels of customer interaction and high levels of labor intensity.

MASTER PRODUCTION SCHEDULE (MPS)

A statement of the quantity and timing of requirements for finished products.

MATERIAL REQUIREMENTS PLANNING (MRP)

An approach used to determine the timing and size of orders for dependent demand inventory.

MATURATION

The third stage of the product life cycle, characterized by stable demand and a leveling of growth.

MAXIMUM BUFFER SIZE

In a just-in-time kanban system, the maximum quantity allowed in an inventory buffer.

MEAN ABSOLUTE DEVIATION (MAD)

The average of the absolute values of the differences between actual demand and forecast demand.

MEAN ABSOLUTE PERCENT ERROR (MAPE)

The mean, over time, of the percent errors.

MEAN FORECAST ERROR (MFE)

The mean of the difference between actual demand and forecast demand.

MIXED MODEL PRODUCTION

In JIT, the practice of alternating models in production to match the rate of consumption as closely as possible.

MIXED STRATEGY

In aggregate planning, a combination of chase and level strategies.

MOMENT OF TRUTH

The point in a service encounter in which the customer can judge the quality of the service provided.

MULTIFACTOR PERSPECTIVE

Measuring productivity using several measures simultaneously.

NET REQUIREMENT

The amount of material and the timing of the needed materials that must be provided by either production or purchasing, calculated by subtracting on-hand inventory from gross requirements.

NETTING

The process of determining net requirements (actual amount needed in each time period) of materials by subtracting beginning on-hand inventory from gross requirements (the total expected demand during a time period).

NONDISCRETE MANUFACTURING

The manufacture of products that are in a liquid or powder form for much of the manufacturing process and which are not in discrete units until packaged.

NORMAL TIME

The time that it takes for a typical qualified worker to complete a given task.

NUMERICALLY CONTROLLED (NC) MACHINE

A machine that can be programmed (via mathematical processing instructions) to perform a variety of tasks or produce several variations of a product.

OBSERVED TIME

Average task time based on observation during a time study.

OPEN ORDER

In material requirements planning, an order that has been placed, but not yet filled.

OPERATING EXPENSE

The cost of turning inventory into throughput.

OPERATIONS FUNCTION

The business function that manages the resources required to produce a product or service. These resources include people, facilities, inventories, processes, and systems.

ORDER COSTS

Cost, usually administrative, associated with placing an order for more inventory.

ORGANIZING

Designing and implementing systems to provide structure and consistency.

OVERTIME COSTS

Additional costs associated with working longer hours than normal.

PARETO ANALYSIS

A technique that classifies problem areas according to the degree of importance of the detected defect.

PART DEPLOYMENT

Phase II of QFD, which transforms technical design parameters into parts characteristics and target values.

P CHART

A control chart for attributes used to monitor the proportion of defectives in a process.

P-D-C-A CYCLE

The circular "plan, do, check, act" improvement cycle that is at the core of many TQM efforts.

PERCENT ERROR

For each time period, the absolute error divided by the actual demand.

PERFORMANCE RATING

Observed time adjusted to be representative of the average worker (based on the observer's perceptions).

PHYSICAL SYSTEM

A system composed of the equipment, facilities, inventory, and work force used to produce a product or service.

PLANNED ORDER RECEIPT

The quantity of each material that is to be received in each time period.

PLANNED ORDER RELEASE

The quantity to order in each period to satisfy net requirements.

PLANNING

Arranging in advance for all prerequisites for accomplishing an objective.

PLANNING HORIZON

The number of periods of time for which an organization will schedule its production.

POKA-YOKE

Characterization of a system whose design prevents mistakes or defects.

POSITIONING STRATEGY

A strategy that links the corporate and business strategy to the operations function.

PRECEDENCE DIAGRAM

A diagram showing a sequence of tasks.

PREVENTION COSTS

Costs related to preventing errors or defects from occurring.

PRICE

The amount a customer pays for a product or service.

PRICING STRATEGY

An approach to demand smoothing that uses increases or reductions in prices to level the demand for goods or services.

PROBABILISTIC ENVIRONMENT

An uncertain environment in which events can be determined as probabilities.

PROCESS BATCH

The quantity of items produced before equipment is set up to produce something else.

PROCESS CAPABILITY

The ability of a process to meet, with normal random variability, a customer's specifications.

PROCESSES

Specific procedures comprising actions taken to convert inputs into outputs.

PROCESS FOCUS

A positioning strategy that concentrates on processes as a means of competing.

PROCESS-ORIENTED LAYOUT

A layout in which equipment that performs similar functions is grouped together to facilitate varied processing requirements.

PROCESS PLANNING

Phase III of QFD, which transforms target values into process requirements for manufacturing.

PROCESS YIELD VARIABILITY

Fluctuation of the output of a process caused by inconsistent quality or concentration of inputs.

PRODUCER'S RISK

The probability of rejecting a "good" lot, that is, a lot that meets or exceeds the acceptable quality level.

PRODUCT-BASED QUALITY

Quality as defined by a characteristic or attribute of a product or service.

PRODUCTION LEAD TIME

The total amount of time a unit spends in a production system.

PRODUCTION PLAN

The aggregate demand forecast, combined with strategic directions, industry trends, growth expectations, and limitations of the firm.

PRODUCTION PLANNING

Phase IV of QFD, which links all previous phases to online quality control.

PRODUCTIVITY

The ratio of outputs per unit of input.

PRODUCT LIFE CYCLE

A series of stages characterized by demand levels for the product. The stages include introduction, growth, maturation, saturation, and decline.

PRODUCT/MARKET FOCUS

A positioning strategy in which the resources of the business are organized around the products or services produced.

PRODUCT-ORIENTED LAYOUT

A flow shop in which equipment is arranged in the sequence it is used to produce a specific product.

PRODUCT PLANNING

Phase I of QFD, which translates customer desires into technical design parameters.

PROFESSIONAL SERVICES

Services having high levels of customer interaction and high levels of labor intensity.

PROGRAM EVALUATION AND REVIEW TECHNIQUE (PERT)

An approach to planning and coordinating large projects in which time estimates for activities are uncertain.

Three time estimates are required: optimistic, pessimistic, and most likely.

PROJECT

A set of activities, directed toward a specific purpose, whose completion time extends over several months or more.

PROTECTIVE CAPACITY

Capacity above what is required to allow for the operation to cope with disruptions.

PURCHASING FUNCTION

The business function that supplies the conversion process with necessary material inputs.

PURE SERVICE

A service business whose services do not accompany and are not linked to a tangible product.

QI STORY

A seven-step process for continuous improvement in which the causes of problems are investigated and cause-and-effect relationships are analyzed.

QUALITY

The degree to which a product or service conforms to requirements, as defined by the consumer.

QUALITY AT THE SOURCE

A concept of JIT making each employee responsible for the quality of his or her work.

QUALITY FEEDBACK TIME

The time between producing a defect and finding out that a defect has been produced.

QUALITY FUNCTION DEPLOYMENT (QFD)

A four-phase process that links customer needs and desires to product or service characteristics in the design phase.

QUANTITY DISCOUNTS

Price reductions for buying large volumes.

QUEUE TIME

Time that an order spends waiting between processing steps.

RANDOM PATTERNS

Variations that do not follow an identifiable pattern.

RATED CAPACITY

The demonstrated capacity of a system. Also known as nominal capacity.

RAW MATERIALS (RM) INVENTORY

Material inputs to the transformation process, prior to any processing.

R CHART

A type of variables chart used to monitor process variability within a sample group.

REENGINEERING

A radical improvement process in which all aspects of a business are redesigned to gain a more productive organization.

REGULAR-TIME COSTS

Costs of wages and benefits that workers receive for working normal hours.

REORDER POINT

A predetermined level to which inventory drops and a replenishment order is placed.

RESOURCE REQUIREMENTS PLAN

The comparison of aggregate capacity requirements, as dictated by the production plan, with available resources.

RESOURCES

Direct inputs to the production process for services and manufacturers.

ROUGH-CUT CAPACITY PLANNING

The process of validating the master production schedule by comparing the available capacity with the capacity needed to fulfill the requirements of the master production schedule.

ROUTING

A description of the steps required to produce a product or part.

RUNNING SUM OF FORECAST ERROR (RSFE)

The sum of the differences between actual demand and forecast demand.

SAFETY STOCK

Stock that is held in excess of expected demand to protect against unexpectedly high demand.

SATURATION

The fourth stage of the product life cycle, characterized by subsiding demand.

SCHEDULED RECEIPT

In material requirements planning, the receipt that corresponds to an open order.

SEASONAL INDEX

A seasonal factor found by computing the average demand over a given time horizon and then dividing the actual demand for each period by that average demand.

SEASONALITY

Repetitive short-term variations in demand.

SERVICE ENCOUNTER

The point at which the customer comes into contact with the component of the organization that provides a service.

SERVICE FACTORY

A service having low levels of customer interaction and low levels of labor intensity.

SERVICE LEVEL

The percentage of orders satisfied from stock.

SERVICES

Businesses whose primary objectives are met through the sale of services.

SERVICE SHOPS

Services having high levels of customer interaction and low levels of labor intensity.

SETUP COSTS

The costs associated with changing equipment from producing one product to producing another.

SHIPPING BUFFER

A buffer placed immediately prior to shipping to absorb disruptions that could delay shipment.

SHORTEST PROCESSING TIME (SPT)

A sequencing rule in which orders are processed according to their expected processing times, with shorter times first.

SIMPLE EXPONENTIAL SMOOTHING

A forecasting method based on the previous forecast plus some fraction of forecast error.

SIMPLE MOVING AVERAGE

Average of data with equal weight.

SIMPLIFIED SYSTEMATIC LAYOUT PLANNING (SSLP)

A structured approach to identifying satisfactory facility layouts by using ratings of desired closeness.

SLACK

The amount of time a project activity can be delayed without affecting the completion time of the project.

STANDARD TIME

The length of time that should be required to run one unit through an operation.

STATISTICAL PROCESS CONTROL (SPC)

A procedure used to distinguish between random variability and variability that has an assignable cause.

STRATEGY

The pattern of decision making an organization chooses in order to link resources to goals.

STRUCTURAL DECISIONS

Decisions that include determinations of capacity, facilities, technology, and vertical integration.

THEORETICAL UTILIZATION

Traditionally, in line balancing, the sum of the task times divided by the production lead time.

3-SIGMA

Denotes three standard deviations (the square root of the variance) on each side of the mean.

THROUGHPUT

The rate at which the system generates money through sales.

THROUGHPUT DOLLAR-DAYS

A measure of due date performance that is the dollar value of an order (sales price) multiplied by the number of days the order is late.

TIME

The speed at which a business can respond to customers.

TIME BUFFERS

A quantity of stock created by the offset of lead time to protect against uncertainty.

TIME SERIES

A historical record of demand at fixed time intervals.

T-PLANT

A manufacturing process that has a V-, A-, or I-type of material flow but expands in the last few stages to provide a large number of end products.

TRACKING SIGNAL

A statistical calculation used to monitor the accuracy of a forecast.

TRANSCENDENT QUALITY

Quality as defined by an ideal or condition of excellence.

TRANSFER BATCH

The quantity of items produced before the items are moved to the next processing stage.

TREND

A gradual, long-term movement in data that indicates an increasing, decreasing, or flat pattern of demand.

TURNOVER ADVANTAGE

The financial advantage gained from rapid turnover of inventory.

USER-BASED QUALITY

Quality as defined by a product's or service's fitness for use.

UTILIZATION (CONSTRAINT MANAGEMENT DEFINITION)

The use of resources for production that contributes to throughput.

VALUE ACTIVITIES

The means by which a company can differentiate itself from its competitors.

VALUE-BASED QUALITY

Quality as defined by the degree of excellence at an acceptable price.

VARIABLES CHART

A control chart based on data that are measured along a continuum.

VERTICAL INTEGRATION

A form of business operation in which one firm performs more than one of the stages in the production cycle.

VERTICAL INTEGRATION DECISIONS

Choices an organization makes about the portion of a product or service it will produce itself as opposed to what it will purchase.

V-PLANT

A manufacturing process dominated by diverging material flows.

WEIGHTED MOVING AVERAGE

Average of data with unequal weight.

WORK CENTER MASTER

A detailed description of a work center, including such information as rated capacity, hours of operation, and historical utilization and efficiency.

WORK FLOW

A productivity improvement tool based on the premise that all business interactions can be viewed from a performer/customer perspective.

WORK FORCE

Human resources required to produce a good or service.

WORK-IN-PROCESS INVENTORY (WIP)

Inventory within the production system, no longer raw material, but not yet a finished product.

WORK SAMPLING

A work measurement technique involving random observations of employees to determine how they spend their time.

X-BAR CHART

A type of variables chart used in monitoring the means of a sample group of items.

YIELD MANAGEMENT

Increasing revenues to the greatest amount possible by segmenting the market in such a way as to sell a service for different prices to different segments.

NAME INDEX

COMPANY INDEX

SUBJECT INDEX